学术教科书

Private International Law
国际私法

徐冬根 著

图书在版编目(CIP)数据

国际私法/徐冬根著.—2版.—北京:北京大学出版社,2013.1
(学术教科书)
ISBN 978-7-301-21991-1

Ⅰ.①国… Ⅱ.①徐… Ⅲ.①国际私法-高等学校-教材 Ⅳ.①D997

中国版本图书馆 CIP 数据核字(2013)第 015521 号

| 书　　　名：国际私法(第二版)
| 著作责任者：徐冬根　著
| 责 任 编 辑：郭瑞洁
| 标 准 书 号：ISBN 978-7-301-21991-1/D·3259
| 出 版 发 行：北京大学出版社
| 地　　　址：北京市海淀区成府路 205 号　100871
| 网　　　址：http://www.pup.cn
| 新 浪 微 博：@北京大学出版社
| 电 子 信 箱：law@pup.pku.edu.cn
| 电　　　话：邮购部 62752015　发行部 62750672　编辑部 62752027
|　　　　　　　出版部 62754962
| 印　刷　者：北京宏伟双华印刷有限公司
| 经　销　者：新华书店
|　　　　　　　730 毫米×1020 毫米　16 开本　36 印张　681 千字
|　　　　　　　2009 年 2 月第 1 版
|　　　　　　　2013 年 1 月第 2 版　2015 年 4 月第 3 次印刷
| 定　　价：59.00 元

未经许可,不得以任何方式复制或抄袭本书之部分或全部内容。
版权所有,侵权必究
举报电话:010-62752024　电子信箱:fd@pup.pku.edu.cn

作者简介

徐冬根 1961年12月出生,上海市人,瑞士弗里堡大学法学博士,现任上海交通大学法学院教授、博士研究生导师、国际法研究所所长、国际法学科带头人,中国国际私法学会副会长、《中国国际私法与比较法年刊》编委、国家教育部新世纪优秀人才支持计划入选者、上海市十大优秀中青年法学家、曙光学者、上海市凌云永然律师事务所律师。

曾任瑞士比较法研究所访问学者、美国旧金山大学访问教授、美国天普大学访问教授、加拿大蒙特利尔大学访问教授。曾在美国旧金山大学主讲《中国商法》课程(英语授课),在法国鲁昂大学主讲《中国金融法》(法语授课)、以色列特拉维夫大学和香港城市大学主讲《中国与比较金融法》(英语授课),被海牙国际法学院(Hague Academy of International Law)聘为夏季班课程主讲教授,讲授《比较国际私法》课程(法语授课)。

主持多项全国哲学社会科学研究项目和省部级研究项目。专长国际私法、国际金融法和国际商法的教学、研究和实务工作。在国内外出版专著和合著20本,发表学术论文一百多篇。代表著作有《国际私法趋势论》、《中国国际私法完善研究》、《上海国际金融中心法制环境研究》、《浮动担保比较研究》、《国际金融法》、《信用证法律与实务研究》、《国际金融法律与实务研究》、《美国证券法律与实务研究》、《国际信贷的法律保障》、《国际经济法论》、《WTO规则解析》等著作,在瑞士出版法文著作 Le droit international privé de la responsabilité délictuelle: Evolution récent et la loi chinoise,在荷兰《海牙国际法演讲集》第270卷发表十多万字的法文论文 Le droit international privé en Chine: Une perspective comparative,在法国 Journal du Droit International 发表法文论文 Chonique de jurisprudence en Chine 等。多项科研成果分别获得教育部、司法部、上海市哲学社会科学研究优秀成果奖,多篇学术论文被中国人民大学报刊复印资料《国际法学》和《中国国际法法学精粹》等全文转载。

曾获上海市劳动模范、宝钢优秀教师奖、上海市优秀青年教师奖和上海市育才奖等荣誉。

内 容 简 介

本教材系为配合国际私法"双语"课程的教学而撰写和出版的学术性教科书。教材每章正文内容之前均设有"本章主题词"和"本章导读",对该章的核心内容作出提出和概括。本教材对相关专业术语均加注了对应的英语术语,对基础性的和重要的专业术语导入了英语的定义、解释或释义,对基本理论和原理导入了英语解说,对重要案例导入了英语的事实陈述与英语的法官判决意见和判决理由。在各章正文内容之后,安排有"思考题"、"重要术语提示与中英语对照"、"推荐阅读文献"和英语的"扩展阅读资料",以起到贯通国际私法课程中文教材和英语教材的桥梁作用。

本教材内容包括国际私法的基本原理、国际私法的基本制度、国际私法的立法发展、国际私法的理论学说、国际私法的法律选择方法、国际私法法律关系的主体、国际婚姻家庭关系的法律适用、国际财产关系的法律适用、国际知识产权的法律适用、国际侵权行为的法律适用、国际合同关系的法律适用、国际商事关系的法律适用、国际支付关系的法律适用、国际金融关系的法律适用、国际民商事司法管辖权概论、国际互联网纠纷的管辖权、外国法院民商事判决的承认与执行等十七章。附录部分包括三项内容:国际私法文献与资料扩展网络资源、新世纪中国出版的国际私法著作与教材和最新英文国际私法学术文献。

本教材可以作为高校国际私法课程的教材,尤其适合作为国际私法"双语"教学的教材,也可以作为法学专业本科生和研究生学习和学术研究的重要参考文献。

序　言

本教材《国际私法》是中华人民共和国教育部新世纪优秀人才支持计划项目的立项教材、北京大学出版社法学学术教科书和上海交通大学国际私法双语课程教材。作为上海交通大学法学院国际法学科的带头人，本教材作者从2003年起即开始在上海交通大学法学院积极推动国际法学科的"双语"教学。目前，上海交通大学法学院已经规划和开出了《国际金融法》、《国际经济法》、《国际公法》、《国际私法》等多门课程的"双语"教学。本教材《国际私法》系专为"双语"课程教学的需要而撰写和出版的学术性教科书。《国际私法》（第二版）在首版的基础上，吸收了近年来国际私法在立法、司法实践和学术研究领域的最新成果。

本教材具有以下特点：

第一，专业英语文献丰富。作者在本教材中，从"双语"教学的特点出发，对国际私法课程中所涉及的专业术语，均加注了对应的外文术语，通过超链接的方式，对国际私法课程中基础的和重要的专业术语导入了英语的定义、解释或释义，对国际私法的基本理论和原理导入了英语解说，对国际私法的重要案例导入了英语的事实陈述与英语的法官判决意见和判决理由。

作为为"双语"教学需要而撰写和出版的教材，本教材专门设计了"扩展阅读资料"栏目。每章都为学生精选了与该章内容密切相关的英语扩展阅读文献，使学生在学习完该章的基本知识、基本原理和相关英语术语之后，通过阅读"扩展阅读资料"栏目的英语文献，巩固该章所学到的知识，同时检测自己的专业英语掌握的程度；使学生通过课堂教学和课外阅读的结合，逐步提升专业英语水平，逐渐过渡到阅读全英语的外国教科书和学术文献。

本教材在各章正文内容之后，设置了"重要术语提示与中英语对照"，对本教材中出现的英语的国际私法专业术语，所涉及的相关外国国家的法律法规、案例、国外著名学者的姓名等，通过表格对比的方式，将中文表述与英语原文进行对照，以便学生查找和使用。

第二，文献来源权威性强。本教材所涉及的英语定义、解释和释义，外国相关法律法规条款，国际条约的条款，外国司法判决的案例，英语文献扩展阅读文献资料，均取材自原汁原味的英语权威词典、外国立法汇编、国际条约汇编、法院判例汇编，以及外国社会科学引文索引（SSCI）学术期刊中的重要学术论文和评论以及官方网站,资料的出处和来源具有相当强的权威性。

第三,教材撰写注重学术性。本教材通过脚注(footnote)的方式,在相关页面对所涉及的中文和英语文献、资料和数据的来源均标明出处,本教材广征博引,所涉及的注释总计达到近千个之多。这些注释提供了资料的来源出处和可以深入学习和研究的线索,使学生可以非常方便地按照注释的指引,进行更深入的学习和研究。

第四,专业扩展文献信息量大、资料性强。对于英语文献,在教材的附录部分,作者对国外近几年来(2005—2012年)发表的国际私法英语学术文献(含著作和论文)进行了梳理,选择了一百多篇著作和论文,并列出了清单,注明了作者的姓名,书名和出版年月,论文标题和刊载论文的学术文献及其出版年月;对于中文文献,在本书附录部分,作者精选了新世纪以来出版的在中国具有代表性的国际私法著作与教材,并列出清单。通过本教材所提供英语文献和中文著作教材清单,学生可以非常方便地对自己感兴趣的专题,直接查找相关的学术著作和文献,进行深入学习和研究,同时也便于学生了解和把握国内外国际私法的学术研究和司法实践的最新发展趋势。

总之,这是一部面向法学专业本科生,兼顾国际法专业研究生,全面阐释国际私法基本原理和基本知识,并以进行"双语"教学为特点的教材。本教材突出中英语的双语安排,提供关键概念的重点解释,穿插大量中英语案例及其学理解说,附录部分提供进一步深入阅读的导读文献清单,提供学生扩展阅读的英语专业文本,注重理论与实践的结合,强调相关司法考试的知识点和法规准备,能够满足"双语"教学以及学生掌握知识和准备司法考试的双重要求。

徐冬根

2012年12月21日于上海

目录

第一章 国际私法的基本原理 /1
第一节 国际私法概述 /3
第二节 冲突规范 /7
第三节 连接因素 /10
第四节 准据法 /12
第五节 国际私法的渊源 /14

第二章 国际私法的基本制度 /26
第一节 识别 /28
第二节 反致 /30
第三节 法律规避 /37
第四节 外国法查明 /39
第五节 公共秩序保留 /49

第三章 国际私法的立法发展 /56
第一节 萌芽期间的欧洲国际私法立法 /58
第二节 近代国际私法立法 /60
第三节 当代国际私法立法 /65
第四节 美国的两部冲突法重述 /79
第五节 国际私法法典化及其法哲学思想 /83
第六节 国际私法统一化运动 /89

第四章 国际私法的理论学说 /102
第一节 法则说 /104

第二节 意思自治理论 /108

第三节 近代国际私法学说 /109

第四节 当代国际私法学说 /117

第五章 国际私法的法律选择方法 /136

第一节 传统国际私法的法律选择方法 /138

第二节 最密切联系法律选择方法 /139

第三节 特征性履行法律选择方法及其法哲学思想 /148

第四节 国际私法法律选择方法的发展趋势 /160

第六章 国际私法法律关系的主体 /168

第一节 自然人的法律适用 /170

第二节 法人的法律适用 /177

第三节 国家及其财产豁免权 /184

第四节 作为国际私法主体的国际组织 /194

第七章 国际婚姻家庭关系的法律适用 /202

第一节 结婚的法律适用 /204

第二节 离婚的法律适用 /208

第三节 夫妻关系的法律适用 /211

第四节 亲子关系的法律适用 /213

第五节 收养的法律适用 /215

第六节 监护的法律适用 /217

第七节 扶养的法律适用 /220

第八章 国际财产关系的法律适用 /229

第一节 物之所在地法原则 /231

第二节 国际财产的法律适用 /236

第三节 国际财产继承的法律适用 /239

第九章 国际知识产权的法律适用 /252

第一节 知识产权法律冲突概述 /254

第二节 专利权的法律适用 /259

第三节　商标权的法律适用 /266

　　第四节　著作权的法律适用 /271

　　第五节　国际技术转让法律适用问题 /277

第十章　国际侵权行为的法律适用 /286

　　第一节　侵权行为地法及其演变 /288

　　第二节　侵权行为法律适用的多元化 /296

　　第三节　特殊侵权行为的法律适用 /301

　　第四节　互联网侵权行为的法律适用 /307

第十一章　国际合同关系的法律适用 /317

　　第一节　国际合同法律适用概述 /319

　　第二节　合同自体法 /321

　　第三节　合同法律适用的范围 /334

　　第四节　我国有关涉外合同法律适用的规定 /335

第十二章　国际商事关系的法律适用 /345

　　第一节　商人法及其适用 /347

　　第二节　电子商务的法律适用 /352

　　第三节　国际破产关系的法律适用 /360

第十三章　国际支付关系的法律适用 /377

　　第一节　国际票据的法律适用 /379

　　第二节　信用证的法律适用 /386

　　第三节　国际托收的法律适用 /401

第十四章　国际金融关系的法律适用 /412

　　第一节　国际贷款的法律适用 /414

　　第二节　国际担保的法律适用 /419

　　第三节　国际信托的法律适用 /427

　　第四节　国际保险的法律适用 /436

第十五章　国际民商事司法管辖权概论 /445

　　第一节　国际民商事管辖权概述 /447

第二节　属地管辖权 /448
　　第三节　最低限度联系与长臂管辖权 /451
　　第四节　其他管辖权 /457
　　第五节　挑选法院与不方便法院 /460
　　第六节　我国涉外民商事司法管辖权 /475

第十六章　国际互联网纠纷的管辖权 /484
　　第一节　互联网的特点及其对传统管辖权的冲击 /486
　　第二节　互联网管辖权理论 /496
　　第三节　互联网的管辖依据 /500
　　第四节　国外互联网管辖权的实践 /505
　　第五节　网络侵权的管辖权 /509

第十七章　外国法院民商事判决的承认与执行 /517
　　第一节　外国法院民商事判决承认与执行概述 /519
　　第二节　外国法院民商事判决承认与执行的理论依据 /522
　　第三节　外国法院民商事判决承认与执行的条件 /529
　　第四节　外国法院民商事判决承认与执行的程序与方式 /532
　　第五节　我国关于判决域外承认执行的规定 /535
　　第六节　内地与香港法院民商事判决的相互承认与执行 /537

附录一　国际私法文献与资料扩展网络资源 /545

附录二　新世纪中国出版的国际私法著作与教材 /547

附录三　最新英文国际私法学术文献 /553

第一章

国际私法的基本原理

本章导读

※ 国际私法的基本原理是国际私法学的理论基础。

※ 国际私法,通常有两层含义,即作为部门法的国际私法和作为研究该部门法产生、发展及其规律性以及与邻近部门法关系等问题的国际私法学。前者是特定种类法律规范的总称,是整个法律体系中的一个独立部门;后者是指一种法学理论,是法学中的一门独立学科。

※ 国际私法作为一门独立的学科,有一个逐渐完善的过程。国际私法的名称随着国际私法的发展而呈现出多样化就是一个最好的例证:从法则说开始发展到法律冲突法、法律选择论、法律域外效力论、外国法适用论、法律适用法、涉外私法、国际民法、民法施行法、法例等。这种现象从某一个侧面反映了国际私法的发达和国际私法学术的繁荣。

※ 欧洲大陆各国普遍所称的"国际私法",在英、美等国多称为"冲突法"。

※ 国际私法是有关国际民商事纠纷确定法院管辖权,国际民商事法律关系选择法律,以及法院判决承认和执行的法律规范和制度的总和。

※ 冲突规范,是指由国内法或国际条约规定的,指明某一国际民商事法律关系应适用何种法律的规范,因此又称法律适用规范或法律选择规范。

※ 连接因素,又称连接点,它起一种桥梁的作用,通过它把某一国际民商事法律关系与调整该民商事法律关系的特定国家的法律规范联系起来。

※ 作为国际私法的特有概念,准据法是指冲突规范所指向的、被用来调整当事人权利与义务关系的特定国家的国内实体法或国际统一实体法。

※ 国际私法的渊源是指国际私法的表现形式。国际私法的国内法渊源主要包括国内立法、国内判例和司法解释;国际法渊源主要包括国际条约和国际惯例。

※ 随着社会的发展,国际私法的范围不断扩大,渊源不断充实,国际私法的性质也在慢慢发生变化。根据经典国际私法理论,国际私法最初是国内法,国际私法越发达,其国际性因素就越强。到目前为止,国际私法虽然已完成了由国内法向兼有国内法和国际法性质的转变,但要变成完全意义上的国际法,尚需时日。因而国际私法在可预见的将来并不会完全脱离国内法制度。但随着人类社会的进步,随着国际私法趋同化进一步加强,国际私法的国际法性质将会进一步加强,其最终的性质将会是国际法。

【本章主题词】 国际私法、冲突法、冲突规范、连接因素、准据法

第一节　国际私法概述

一、国际私法的概念

国际私法(**private international law**)一词,通常有两层含义,即作为部门法的国际私法和作为研究该部门法产生、发展及其规律性以及与邻近部门法关系等问题的国际私法学。前者是特定种类法律规范的总称,是整个法律体系中的一个独立部门;后者是指一种法学理论,是法学中的一门独立学科。本书对国际私法的阐述,既包括作为部门法的国际私法,也包括以研究国际私法规范为主并在学术层面上展开研究的国际私法学意义上的国际私法。

【释义】　　　　　　　　private international law

Private international law in general tends to organise social relationships between private citizens or non-State organisations. Private international law is made up of mechanisms that facilitate the settlement of international disputes between the same. It answers three questions:

1. Which country's courts have jurisdiction in a dispute (i.e. conflicts of jurisdiction)?

2. Which country's substantive law is to be applied by the court hearing the case (i.e. conflict of laws)?

3. Can the decision given by the court which declared that it had jurisdiction be recognised and, if necessary, enforced in another Member State (i.e. mutual recognition and enforcement of foreign judgments)?

All these rules aim at a better coordination between legal systems and do not generally seek a particular result in a legal dispute. Private international law thus plays the part of a legal marshalling yard. Practically speaking, in an international dispute, for example, between a French tourist and an Italian hotel manager in Florence, the first question the Italian plaintiff must answer is which country's courts have international jurisdiction. It is likely that in this case the courts of Florence would have jurisdiction. Once this has been determined, this court will decide which law is applicable to the dispute. Here again it is likely that Italian law will apply. It is only when this court has passed judgment that the problem of enforcement abroad will arise. In other words, enforcement rules show how the Italian hotel manager can enforce the judgement in France where the French tourist has assets. Up to recently, each Member State had its own national rules of private international law that its courts applied without taking into consideration the fact that their decision could contradict a court decision already rendered by a foreign court. It was therefore possible in an international dispute, depending on which country's court was chosen, that the solution to a case differed considerably. Technically such divergences were the result of classical bilateral conflicts of law rules. ①

(一) 国际私法的名称

国际私法的名称繁多,欧洲大陆各国较普遍地称之为"国际私法",而美国等国则更多地称之为"冲突法"(**law of conflict of laws**)。

【释义】　　　　　　　law of conflict of laws

The question to be asked by one concerned with conflict of laws is: "what law should be applied to the case at hand?" The process by which a court determines what law to apply is sometimes referred to as "characterization", or "classification." This determination must be made in accordance with the law of the forum. A federal court in a case before it based on diversity of citizenship, for example, determines the conflict of law issue as if it were the highest court in the state in which it is sitting.

Courts faced with a choice of law issue generally have two choices: A court can apply the law of the forum (*lex fori*)—which is usually the result when the question of what law to apply is *procedural*, or the court can apply the law of the site of the transaction, or occurrence that gave rise to the litigation in the first place (*lex loci*)—this is usually the controlling law selected when the matter is substantive.

Federal courts play by different rules than state courts because federal jurisdiction is limited to what has been enumerated in the Constitution. The rules that federal courts must obey regarding which laws to apply are extremely complex and are embodied in the Federal Rules of Civil Procedure.

美国将国际私法称为冲突法(**American conflict of laws**),是有特殊原因的。因为美国是一个联邦国家,其国内各州之间的法律冲突现象远远大于国际法律冲突。因此,美国学者通常将调整州际之间法律冲突的州际私法和调整国际之间法律冲突的国际私法统称为冲突法。

---

① Eleanor Cashin Ritaine, Harmonising European Private International Law: A Replay of Hannibal's Crossing of the Ales? 34 *Int'l J. Legal Info.* 419, 420 (2006).

【释义】　　　　　　American conflict of laws

　　American conflict of laws deals primarily with interstate conflicts. Unlike England which has a single common law, here there are fifty possible variations of state law, to which may be added possible conflicts between state and federal law. Thus the term Private International Law, which prevails on the continent and has currency in England, seem inapposite for the conflict of laws in this Country.①

　　根据学者对国际私法的不同理解,国际私法还有许多名称。主要有"法则说"(theory of statutes)、"法律冲突法"(law of the conflict of laws)、"法律选择法"(choice of laws)、"外国私法"(foreign private law)、"国际民法"(international civil law)等。②此外,旧中国把冲突法法规称为"法律适用条例",原联邦德国称其为"民法施行法",日本称其为"法例"。这些不同的称谓,从不同的角度和层面反映了国际私法的某些属性和特点,或强调它所调整的法律关系仍属涉外民法性质,或强调它着重解决的是法律的冲突问题,或强调它要解决的是本国及外国的民商事法律适用问题。

　　目前我国比较通用的名称,无论作为部门法还是作为一个学科,均采用"国际私法"一词,而相应的英文则普遍采用 Private International Law。

　　(二) 国际私法的定义

　　定义是揭示概念所反映的事物的本质属性,而根据事物的本质属性就可以把某一类事物与其他事物区别开来。给国际私法下定义,就应该揭示国际私法的本质属性。国际私法作为一个独立的法律部门,与其他法律部门的不同之处就在于国际私法调整的对象并不是涉外民商事主体间的权利和义务,国际私法是有关国际民商事纠纷确定法院管辖权、国际民商事法律关系选择法律,以及法院判决承认和执行的法律规范和制度的总和。

二、国际私法定义中"涉外"因素与"私法"的含义

　　(一) 国际私法定义中的"涉外"因素

　　国际私法所涉及的内容往往牵涉到与多个主权国家有关的问题或者纠纷(**problems and disputes having contacts with more than one sovereign**)。

---

①　Luther L. McDougal III, Robert L. Felix, Ralph U. Whitten, *American Conflicts Law: Cases and Materials*, 4th ed., LexisNexis, 2004, p.4.

②　参见余先予主编:《冲突法》,上海财经大学出版社1999年版,第36—38页。

【释义】 problems and disputes having contacts with more than one sovereign

The private international law deals with problems and disputes having contacts with more than one sovereign. One of the parites may be a nonresident of the forum; out-of-country property may be in dispute; or the underlying events may have occurred outside the forum. Since international matter involves contacts with at least two different States and their respective legal systems, it is intuitive that they raise issues of conflicts of laws.

国际私法的对象是在国际交往中产生的涉外或者国际(**international**)民商事法律关系。涉外因素就是指本国法以外的某种法律体系的一种联系。英国著名国际私法学者莫里斯(J. H. C. Morris)就曾指出:所谓涉外因素,是指与英国法以外的某种法律体系的一种联系。这种联系可能由于下述种种情况而出现,如在外国签订或履行合同、在外国发生侵权行为、财产位于国外或当事人不是英国人。在冲突法中,涉外因素是指非英国因素,外国国家是指英国以外的国家。①我国学者也有持这种观点的。② 我国最高人民法院《关于贯彻执行〈中华人民共和国民法通则〉若干问题的意见(试行)》第178条规定:"凡民事关系的一方或者双方当事人是外国人、无国籍人、外国法人的;民事关系的标的物在外国领域内的;产生、变更或者消灭民事权利义务关系的法律事实发生在外国的,均为涉外民事关系……"

【释义】 international

A business is international as opposed to purely domestic when it has contacts with more than one State. These contacts typically result from the fact that some of the parties involved are nationals of, or have their domicile or place of business in, different countries, but they may result from any other element, foremost amongst which the currency in which the payment is to be made.③

(二)国际私法中"私法"的特殊含义

在讨论国际私法的定义时,还要解决的一个问题就是为什么要把它叫做"私法"?这一法律部门之所以被称为"私法",是因为它所调整的是民商事关系,而调

---

① 参见〔英〕莫里斯:《法律冲突法》,李东来等译,中国对外翻译出版公司1990年版,第1页。
② 国际私法中的"涉外因素"的含义,是指与本国法以外的某种法律体系的一种联系。参见胡家强:《对国际私法调整对象和范围的重新认识》,载《中国海洋大学学报》(社会科学版)2003年第1期。
③ See Luca G. Radicati Di Brozolo, International Payments and Conflicts of Laws, 48 Am. J. Comp. L. 307, 308 (2000).

整民商事关系的民商法自罗马时代起就被认为属于"私法"的范畴。根据上述原因,我们认为今天沿用"国际私法"这个名称,只指上述特定含义①,是一种约定俗成的用法。

三、国际私法的性质

对于国际私法的性质,有的学者认为国际私法是国际法②,有的学者认为是国内法,也有的学者认为国际私法是介于国际法与国内法之间的一种独立的法律。③

值得一提的是,有学者从辩证法的角度,以发展的观点来分析国际私法的性质,认为国际私法的整个发展过程是一个从国内法向国际法转变的过程。在这个漫长的过程中,由最初的国内法成分不断增多(量变)到出现国际法成分(质变),再到国际法成分的不断增多(量变)及至最终过渡到国际法(质变)。④这样的观点颇具新意。

第二节 冲突规范

冲突规范是国际私法特有的法律规范,是为完成国际私法解决法律冲突、确立法律适用这一使命而形成的特殊的规律规范。

一、冲突规范的概念

(一)冲突规范的定义

所谓冲突规范(conflict rules),是指由国内法或国际条约规定的,指明某一涉外民商事法律关系应适用何种法律的规范,因此它又称法律适用规范(rules of ap-

---

① 李双元:《国际私法的名称、性质、定义和范围问题》,载《武汉大学学报》1983年第1期。
② 参见宋春林:《论国际私法是国际法的分支》,载《烟台大学学报》(哲学社会科学版)1997年第4期。
③ 参见李双元、金彭年、张茂、欧福勇:《中国国际私法通论》,法律出版社2003年版,第29页。
④ 参见黄世席:《国际私法性质的哲学分析》,载《中国青年政治学院学报》2001年第5期。

plication of law），或法律选择规范（choice of law rules）。①在过去，它曾是国际私法唯一的一种规范形式，因此它又被称为国际私法规范（rules of private international law）。

（二）冲突规范的属性

传统冲突规范表现为具有固定空间连接点的各种冲突规范，是一种"空间定向规则"或"管辖选择规则"（**jurisdiction-selecting rule**）。②

【解说】　　　　　　　　jurisdiction-selecting rule

The approach of jurisdiction-selecting picks between competing states (jurisdiction), rather than between competing rules. Thus, the court does not consider the scope, content, or policy of the substantive rule of law until after choosing the state whose rule will control. In make the initial choice, the jurisdiction-selecting rules are not concerned with which substantive rule is "better", or the parties' intentions, or policy; rather, they are concerned only with identifying a particular event and the jurisdiction (state) in which that event occurred.③

传统冲突规范具有以下几个属性：

第一，系统性。传统国际私法往往以专门法规或法典专章形式制定，并使用统一、准确、可靠的术语。

第二，连续性。传统国际私法一经立法，通常少有修改，即使有修改，幅度一般也不大。

第三，简便性。依靠固定的空间连接因素决定法律适用，法院在运用过程中，较为简便。

二、冲突规范的特点

冲突规范是一种特殊的法律规范，同一般的法律规范相比，它具有以下几个特点：

第一，冲突规范不同于一般的实体法规范，它是法律适用规范。冲突规范仅指明某种涉外民商事法律关系应适用何种法律，它并不直接规定涉外民商事法律关系当事人的权利与义务。

---

① 屈广清主编：《国际私法导论》，法律出版社 2003 年版，第 233 页。值得注意的是，有学者从更广泛的视角给冲突规范下定义，认为凡在处理涉外民事关系及因涉外民事关系而发生争讼时，指定实体问题和程序问题应适用的法律及划分涉外（或国际）民事管辖权的规范，均属冲突规范。参见李双元：《国际私法（冲突法篇）》，武汉大学出版社 2001 年版，第 156 页。

② 参见韩德培主编：《中国冲突法研究》，武汉大学出版社 1993 年版，第 130 页。

③ David H. Vernon, Louis Weinberg, William Reynolds, William Richman, *Conflicts of Law: Case, Materials and Problems*, 2d ed., LexisNexis, 2002, p.249.

第二,冲突规范不同于一般的诉讼法规范,它是法律选择规范。冲突规范并不直接规定当事人的权利和义务,而是在相冲突的法律中指定某一调整涉外民商事关系的法律,它主要是指导一国法院如何选择和适用法律的规范。

第三,冲突规范是一种间接规范,它只起"援用"某一实体法的作用,不能直接构成当事人作为或不作为的准则,因而缺乏一般法律规范所具有的明确性和预见性,当事人也很难据之预见到法律关系的后果。冲突规范虽然不同于实体法规范,但它仍然是调整涉外民商事法律关系的一种手段,只不过它需要与其所指引的某国实体规范相结合,才能最终确定当事人的权利与义务。[1]因此,冲突规范是一种间接规范。

三、冲突规范的类型

(一) 单边冲突规范

所谓单边冲突规范(unilateral conflict rules),是指直接规定某国法律的冲突规范。它既可以明确规定适用内国法,也可以明确规定适用外国法。[2]例如《中华人民共和国中外合资经营企业法实施细则》第 15 条规定:"合营企业合同的订立、效力、解释、执行及其争议的解决,均应适用中国的法律。"就是一条单边冲突规范。

单边冲突规范具有以下特点:第一,稳定性。即各种法律关系通过固定的空间连接点的指引,找到的都是特定的准据法,即法律选择的结果比较确定。第二,可预见性。由于是通过固定的空间连接点进行指引,增大了当事人的合理预期。第三,明确性。单边冲突规范所指向的法律明确、具体,它指向内国法时,就不再指向特定外国法;反之,一旦它指向特定外国法时,就不再指向内国法。

(二) 双边冲突规范

所谓双边冲突规范(bilateral conflict rules),是指并不直接规定适用内国法或者外国法,而只是规定一个可以推定的标准,根据这个标准再结合涉外民商事法律关系的具体情况去推定适用某一国法的冲突规范。例如我国《民法通则》第 147 条规定:"中华人民共和国公民与外国人结婚适用婚姻缔结地法律……"这就是一条双边冲突规范。其中,"婚姻缔结地法律"是一个标准,如果当事人的婚姻缔结地在中国,就适用中国法律,如果当事人的婚姻缔结地在美国,就适用美国法律。目前,双边冲突规范是国际私法中数量最多且最常用的冲突规范。

双边冲突规范的主要特点是内外国法的平等适用性。依传统的双边冲突规

---

[1] 参见肖永平:《肖永平论冲突法》,武汉大学出版社 2002 年版,第 14 页。
[2] 黄进主编:《国际私法》(第二版),法律出版社 2005 年版,第 175 页。

范,内外国法的选择一般取决于空间连接点的指向。双边冲突规范所援引的法律既可能是内国法,也可能是外国法,这在相当程度上保证了内外国法律的平等适用。在法律上,它体现了对内国法和外国法的平等对待。

(三) 重叠性冲突规范

所谓重叠性冲突规范(double rules for regulating the conflict of laws),就是其系属指向两个和两个以上的连接点的法律必须同时适用于某种涉外民商事法律关系的冲突规范。例如1902年在海牙订立的《关于离婚与别居的法律冲突与管辖权冲突公约》第2条规定:"离婚之请求,若非依夫妇之本国法及法院地法均有离婚之原因者,不得为之。"这表明,离婚必须同时适用夫妇之本国法和法院地法,只有两者均认为有离婚原因时,才允许当事人离婚。重叠性冲突规范虽然能够同时满足相关国家利益需要,但是从法律适用角度而言,同时要满足两个条件,这样的适用要求难度过大,实践中无论对于当事人还是对于法院来说,都将造成极大的困难。①因此,该类冲突规范的存在数量不多,发挥作用的领域也十分有限。

(四) 选择性冲突规范

所谓选择性冲突规范(choice rules for regulating the conflict of laws),是指其系属有两个或者两个以上,但是只选择其中之一来调整有关民商事法律关系的冲突规范。根据选择的方式不同,选择性冲突规范可以分为两种,一种为无条件的选择性冲突规范,另一种为有条件的选择性冲突规范。无条件的选择性冲突规范,是指其系属有两个或者两个以上,但是适用法律的人可以任意选择或者无条件地选择其中之一来调整有关民商事法律关系的冲突规范。有条件的选择性冲突规范,是指其系属有两个或者两个以上,但是适用法律的人只能按照顺序或者有条件地选择其中之一来调整有关民商事法律关系的冲突规范。

第三节 连接因素

一、连接因素的概念

连接因素(connection factor)又称连接点(point of contact),它起一种桥梁的作

---

① 屈广清主编:《国际私法导论》,法律出版社2003年版,第244页。

用,通过它把冲突规范中的法律法系与某一特定国家的实体法规范联系起来。常见的连接因素主要有国籍、住所、行为地、物之所在地、法院地等客观标志。当事人之间选择合同准据法的"合意"也可以视为连接点的主观标志。

二、连接因素的特点

连接因素具有以下特点：

第一,连接因素的外在表现形式是一定的客观标志。这些客观标志必须是清晰可辨、易于确认的。在实践中,经常被选择作为连接因素使用的客观标志有国籍、住所、居所、物之所在地、行为地、法院地等。

第二,连接因素发挥着将特定的民商事关系和某国法律连接在一起的媒介或纽带作用。这种作用表现在,根据不同的连接因素连接与其有内在联系的法律关系,同时根据所选择的不同连接因素,确定适用与其特点联系的法律,从而构成不同冲突规范,解决实际法律的冲突问题。

第三,一个冲突规范不限于一个连接因素。规范某种涉外民商事法律关系中当事人行为的法律,特定情况下可以是两个或两个以上的连接因素所指示适用的两个或两个以上国家的法律。①

三、连接因素的分类

根据不同的标准,连接因素可以作不同的分类。

（一）客观连接因素与主观连接因素

客观连接因素主要有国籍、住所、居所、营业所、物之所在地、法院地等,这种连接点是一种客观实在的标志。而相比之下,主观连接因素是一种意定的连接因素,主要指当事人的合意。主观连接因素主要作为确定适用于合同关系的准据法的根据。

（二）静态连接因素与动态连接因素

静态连接因素(constant connecting factor)就是固定不变的连接因素,它主要指不动产所在地以及涉及过去的行为或事件的连接因素,如婚姻举行地、合同缔结地、法人登记地、侵权行为地等。由于静态连接因素是不变的,故便于据此确定涉外民商事法律关系应适用的法律。动态连接因素(variable connecting factor)就是可变的连接点,如国籍、住所、居所等。动态连接因素的存在,一方面加强了冲突规范的灵活性,另一方面也为当事人进行法律规避提供了可能性。

---

① 参见屈广清主编：《国际私法》,法律出版社2003年版,第238页。

第四节 准据法

一、准据法概述

（一）准据法的含义

作为国际私法的特有概念，准据法（**lex causae**）是指冲突规范所指向的、被用来调整当事人权利与义务关系的特定国家的国内实体法或国际统一实体法。[①]对于国际民商事法律关系确定应该适用的法律（即准据法）是国际私法这门学科的主要任务，也是冲突规范的基本目的。实际上，每一条冲突规范就是一条确定准据法的原则。

【解说】　　　　　　　　　　　　lex causae

In the conflict of laws, lex causae is the law or laws chosen by the forum court from among the relevant legal systems to arrive at its judgement of an international or interjurisdictional case. The term refers to the usage of particular local laws as the basis or "cause" for the ruling, which would itself become part of referenced legal canon.[②]

准据法是经冲突规范援用的实体法律，它本身并不属于冲突规范范畴。可以成为准据法的法律分为国内实体法和国际统一实体法。国内实体法包括内国法和外国法。国际统一实体法包括国际条约和国际惯例。

（二）准据法的特点

准据法作为国际私法上的一个特殊范畴，具有如下特点：

其一，准据法必须是经过冲突规范所指定的法律。从国际私法的角度来说，不经冲突规范的指定或援用，直接适用于国际民商事法律关系的法律，无论是国际统

---

① 韩德培主编：《国际私法》，武汉大学出版社1989年版，第56—57页。
② Lex causae, available at http://en.wikipedia.org/wiki/Lex_causae.

一实体规范还是国内法中的实体规范,都不能被称为准据法,只能叫做"直接适用的法律"。①

其二,准据法是能够具体确定国际民商事法律关系当事人权利与义务的实体法。冲突规范之所以指定或援用准据法,是因为准据法作为实体法可以用来调整国际民商事法律关系、解决国际民商事法律冲突。

(三)准据法的类型

根据某一特定涉外民商事法律关系适用准据法的数量和种类,可以把实际适用的准据法分为单一准据法和复合准据法两种形态。②

1. 单一准据法

某一具体的涉外民商事关系完全由冲突规范援引的某一个特定国家的实体法来支配,这个特定国家的实体法就是单一准据法。

2. 复合准据法

如果法院在实际处理某个具体的涉外民商事关系时,根据冲突规范的指定或者案件审理上的需要将两种或两种以上的准据法结合起来,按照一定方法合并适用或从中选择其一适用,这种形态的准据法就是复合准据法。③

二、准据法的适用

在具体的涉外民商事案件中,并非所有的案件都像"人之行为能力,依当事人本国法"那样简单,只要适用一个准据法原则就可以解决的。事实上,准据法的适用是一个很复杂的问题,其主要的适用方式有:

(一)准据法的并行适用

准据法的并行适用指的是,在特定的涉外民商事法律关系中,同时适用几种准据法,只有所有的准据法都得到适用,该涉外的民商事纠纷才能得到解决。

并行适用数种准据法的,一种是由于不同的法律关系依类分层适用数种不同的法律,其适用方式可叫做纵面的并行适用。例如,多数国家的国际私法规定:"因合同而产生的债,依合同缔结地法。"在处理该涉外合同纠纷案件时一方面就合同的本身效力要适用合同缔结地国家的法律;另一方面,这个案件还涉及缔约人的能力问题,根据人的行为依其本国法(大陆法系)或住所地法(英美法系)的原则,还

---

① 有关"直接适用的法",参见徐冬根:《论"直接适用的法"及其与冲突规范的关系》,载《中国法学》1990年第3期。

② 我国有的学者将复合准据法表述为"混合准据法"。参见周海荣:《国际侵权行为法》,广东高等教育出版社1991年版,第158页。

③ 参见王瀚:《论冲突法中复合准据法的适用问题》,载《比较法研究》1997年第3期。

需要同时适用缔约当事人的本国法或住所地法。只有既满足了缔约地国对合同缔结地的法律规定,也满足了当事人本国或住所地国关于缔约人能力方面的法律规定,该合同关系才能成立。准据法并行适用的另一种方法是横面的并行适用,即决定准据法虽然只有一种法律关系,但只要使该法律关系获得成立,则要对各该当事人适用不同的法律。例如,《日本法例》第13(1)条规定:"婚姻成立的要件,依各当事人本国法。"涉及婚姻成立的法律关系,如果当事人是不同国家的青年男女,要使该法律关系获得成立,不能只满足一方国家关于婚姻成立的要件的法律规定,而是必须分别满足各该当事人本国法关于婚姻成立要件的规定。

(二) 准据法的重叠适用

这是指对同一个涉外民商事法律关系重叠适用数种准据法。准据法的重叠适用方式多适用于与国内公益有重大关系的涉外民商事法律关系中。

(三) 准据法的选择适用

这是指在一个涉外的民商事法律纠纷中,同时有几个准据法可以适用,在可适用的数个准据法中,选择其中的一种准据法,若该准据法一经选择适用,其余的准据法就不能被适用。

选择适用的准据法在冲突规范中是一种比较常用的准据法选择方式,其根本目的是要在数个准据法中,选择适用一个准据法,以更有利于法律关系的有效成立。一般地说,它多适用于同法院地国无多大利害关系的领域,如关于法律行为的一般方式、外国人的行为能力、夫妻关系和父子关系等方面。

第五节 国际私法的渊源

法的渊源就是法的表现形式。法在这种意义上的渊源是多种多样的,并且随着社会经济、文化的发展而不断演变,不同的国家在这方面也有所不同。国际私法的渊源是指国际私法的表现形式,它主要包括国内法渊源和国际法渊源两个方面。[①]

[①] 关于国际私法的国内法渊源和国际法渊源,参见毕武卿:《国际私法性质二元论》,载《中国国际法与比较法年刊》(第四卷),法律出版社2001年版,第110页。

一、国内法渊源

任何国家都在不同程度上把调整涉外民商事法律关系的规范规定在国内法中,因此,国内法成为国际私法的一个主要渊源。国际私法的国内法渊源主要包括国内立法、国内判例等。

(一) 国内立法

在成文法国家,国际私法规范大都规定在国内立法中。即使在普通法系国家,国际私法规范在其国内立法中也多有反映。

从国际私法国内立法的发展历程来观察,我们不难发现,国际私法国内立法的发展经历了一个从分散立法到集中立法的过程。在这个过程中,各国由于国情不同,其具体发展程度也有很大的差异。有的国家在经历了相当长时间发展后,从分散立法步入集中立法的阶段,而另外一些国家至今仍然没有系统的国际私法立法,国际私法条文仍然处于分散的状态。

(二) 国内判例

判例法是在社会实践中逐渐形成并发展起来的法律文化和法律传统。

1. 判例法是国际私法的重要渊源

第一,判例是国际私法规则制度产生的源泉。在理论上,法官并不创制法律,而只是发现、宣布和适用既有的法律原则。英国著名学者,如科克(Coke)、黑尔(Hale)、培根(Bacon)等都确信,法官的职责乃是宣告和解释法律,而不是制定法律。[①]但英国的曼斯菲尔德(Mansfield)法官却认为,判决的理由和精神可以成为法律。英国萨尔蒙德法官也主张说,法官造法是毋庸置疑的,而且人们应当承认"法官们被赋予了一种独特的立法权,并且他们是在公开地合法地行使这一权利"[②]。在实践中,在无先例可循时,法官可以创制判例;在有先例的场合,法官也可以通过细分的技术手段,对先例进行扩大或限制性解释,从而间接发展或者改变先例中的原则。这实质上就是创制和发展法律的过程。[③]

第二,判例是国际私法规范的重要补充。英美普通法的习惯(**common law habits**)在于不采取预见一切、包罗万象的立法方式,而是根据法律自身对社会生活变化的反应机制,实现法律的生长和发展。法官在审理案件的过程中,注重将规则

---

① 〔美〕博登海默:《法理学、法律哲学与法律方法》,邓正来译,中国政法大学出版社1999年版,第554页。
② 同上书,第430、432页。
③ 何勤华、李秀清主编:《外国法制史》,复旦大学出版社2002年版,第215页。

因素与人的因素结合起来,使其判决兼顾确定性与灵活性,使法律在一般条件下保持着循序渐进的发展,以维持法律规则与社会生活之间的协调。

【释义】 **common law habits**

In the United States, the authority of a court to choose or fashion a rule of law to determine a controversy before it is, unless controlled by constitution or statute, a matter of judicial reasoning. In our legal system, this involves common law habits of thought and the practice of building doctrine through precedent and the principle of standing upon decided casese, all the adjusting to change. Thus the law of Conflict of Laws largely involves the development of common law doctrine for choice of law in multistate cases, whether they present issues of tort, or contract, or property or some other subject.①

在崇尚判例法的英美法系国家,法官在法律原则和制度的形成、适用和发展中起着重要的作用。法官所享有的特别的法律解释权,为国际私法在英国发展奠定了法律基础。国际私法的调整对象是涉外民商事法律关系,而且其调整仍处于不断发展之中,所以对国际私法而言,无论怎样强调成文法,判例对国际私法的重要补充和完善作用都不容小觑。判例是国际私法法规的重要补充。②

第三,实行判例有助于推进国际私法的统一。要求法官在遇到各种新情况时,通过判例形成新的判例法,创造新的法律原则,事实上就是承认法官的法律创制权(理论上称为法律发现权和宣布权),而且还赋予判例法以适应社会发展需要的能力。在实践中,每当遇到新的情况,法官不但有权利,而且有义务对适用于该新问题的法律原则进行解释和阐述。

2. 两大法系国际私法判例制度之比较分析

在普通法系国家,法院可以通过判例确立法律规范,通常,权威的法院判决作为先例,对下级法院以后处理同类案件具有拘束力,起着法律的作用。因此,国内判例是其国际私法的一种重要渊源。在不少大陆法系国家,判例也是国际私法的一种渊源,即使在有系统成文国际私法立法的国家亦然。例如在法国,除了关于国籍的规定外,其他国际私法规定非常零散,数量也很少。在这种情况下,法国最高法院及其下属法院的判例成为法国国际私法的主要渊源。③在许多大陆法系国

---

① Luther L. McDougal III, Robert L. Felix, Ralph U. Whitten, *American Conflicts Law: Cases and Materials*, 4th ed., LexisNexis, 2004, p.2.
② 韩德培主编:《国际私法新论》,武汉大学出版社1997年版,第35页。
③ 参见〔法〕亨利·巴蒂福尔、保罗·拉加德:《国际私法总论》,陈洪武等译,中国对外翻译出版公司1989年版,第22—23页。

家,其成文国际私法立法对国际私法问题的规定并不是很充分,故法院判例在调整涉外民商事法律关系方面发挥着重要作用。

(1) 英美法系

判例在英美法系国家是国际私法的主要渊源,但是由于判例浩如烟海,而且随着时间的推移会越积越多,这给法官适用判例带来了困难,于是就需要对判例进行汇编,构成判例法。在国际私法方面,主要是由一些著名的国际私法学者或民间机构对判例进行系统的汇编和整理工作。其中影响最大的要数英国著名国际私法学者戴赛(A. V. Dicey)于1896年发表的《冲突法》(The Conflict of Laws)。它全面系统地归纳整理了英国判例中所适用的冲突规范,并逐条加以解释,成为英国法院处理国际私法问题的重要依据,推动了英国冲突法的发展。其后由英国著名学者莫里斯等人相继修订,至今仍被视为经典之作。

美国的判例汇编一开始由私人编撰,官方编撰于1790年才开始,当时的联邦各法院的判决分别刊载于《联邦最高法院判例汇编》(The United States Reports)等三个判例汇编之中。[1]美国法学会作为一个非官方的学术机构,在判例汇编之中也起了很重要的作用。

(2) 大陆法系

第二次世界大战以来,大陆法也加强了法官在创造法律方面的作用。在一些国家,法院的判决,尤其是终审法院的判决所具有的事实上的权威性,得到下级法院的遵守,而且这些先例的重要性也会随着不断重复而重新肯定,这些先例中所阐述的原则也会随着判例数量的增多而增加。

由此可见,判例仍然是英美国际私法的重要渊源,由于历史原因,英美法系国家对判例的先天宠爱仍然蕴藏在人们深层次的法律观念中。[2]他们固守判例法是法的第一渊源的观念。大陆法系国家在重视制定法的同时,对判例的热情也日益增长。两大法系对判例的共同偏爱,主要归因于判例的灵活、包容、开放、具体等优点,它使法官能够从容不迫地应对各种复杂的急剧变化的纠纷,及时协调和解决各种矛盾和冲突。[3]

中国不是判例法国家,判例在中国不是法律渊源,当然也不是中国国际私法的渊源。不过,《最高人民法院公报》上刊载的国际私法案例是了解中国的国际私法实践的一个重要途径。另外,由于我们在国际民商事交往中经常要同判例法国家

---

[1] 参见白红平、康彦荣:《判例在国际私法渊源中价值分析》,载《山西大学学报》(哲学社会科学版)2001年第3期。
[2] 刘想树:《国际私法基本问题研究》,法律出版社2001年版,第98页。
[3] 参见乔雄兵:《国际私法判例制度之我见》,载《2002年中国国际私法年会论文集》,华东政法学院国际法系2002年编印。

打交道,所以,我们也要认真研究这些国家的司法判例,以便知己知彼,并利用它们为中国对外开放服务。

(三) 司法解释

所谓司法解释,是指司法机关在适用法律过程中对具体应用法律问题所作的诠释。在不同的国家,司法解释的具体定义和运作有所不同。不过,在许多国家,司法解释是自成一类的法律渊源。因此,司法解释也成为这些国家的国际私法的渊源。

在中国,司法解释是指国家最高司法机关根据法律的授权,就司法实践中具体应用法律的问题所作的解释。[①]作为针对应用法律问题并对中国司法实践加以总结和升华的最高人民法院的司法解释,由于其对法院的审判活动具有约束力,实际上已成为中国法律的一种渊源。[②]这一点在1997年最高人民法院印发的《关于司法解释工作的若干规定》中得到肯定。该《规定》明确规定:最高人民法院发布的司法解释必须经审判委员会讨论通过;经发布的最高人民法院司法解释具有法律效力;制定和发布司法解释须经过立项、备案、起草、对草案的论证和修改、通过和公告发布等程序;司法解释以公开发布的日期为生效时间,在颁布了新的法律,或者在原法律修改、废止,或者在制定了新的司法解释后,不再具有法律效力。

(四) 国内习惯法

在有的国家,习惯法是一种间接的法律渊源。这里所讲的习惯法是指国家认可并由国家强制力保证实施的习惯。一般来说,这种习惯应确实存在并惯行,人人确信其为法律并愿受其约束;它仅适用于法律未规定事项,且不得违背公共秩序或善良风俗。[③]例如,1966年《葡萄牙民法典》第3条规定,法律有规定时,不违背善意原则之习惯可视为法律。而葡萄牙的冲突规范主要规定在该法典中,故习惯法也是葡萄牙国际私法的渊源。当然,在国际私法的渊源中,习惯法并不具有重要地位。在中国法律中,习惯法没有被明确规定为法律的渊源,当然也不应该被视为中国国际私法的渊源。

二、国际法渊源

国际私法的国际法渊源主要包括国际条约和国际惯例两方面。

(一) 国际条约

通常,一个国家不仅通过制定国内法,而且通过缔结或参加国际条约(**interna-**

---

① 参见江平主编:《中国司法大辞典》,吉林人民出版社1991年版,第6页。
② 参见王景荣:《论中国最高人民法院的司法解释》,载《中国法律》1995年第3期。
③ 参见郑玉波:《法学绪论》,台湾三民书局1992年版,第20—22页。

tional treaty)来处理涉及本国的涉外民商事法律关系。国际条约是国际私法的一种重要渊源。所谓国际条约,系指国家间所缔结并受国际法支配的国际书面协定,不论其载于一项单独文书或两项以上相互有关的文书内,也不论其特定的名称是什么。①

【释义】　　　　　　　　international treaty

An international treaty is an agreement under international law entered into by actors in international law, namely states and international organizations. An international treaty may also be known as international protocol, covenant, convention, exchange of letters, exchange of notes, accord, memorandum of understanding, etc. Regardless of the terminology, all of these international agreements under international law are equally treaties and the rules are the same.②

国际条约有多边国际条约和双边国际条约之分。国际条约,尤其是多边国际公约在国际私法的统一化过程中发挥着日益重要的作用。在世界各国以及有关国际组织的共同努力下,大量的私法领域的国际条约被制定,私法的国际统一正在迅速发展,一个被称为"国际统一私法"或"私法国际统一法"的法律分支正在形成。一些重要的多边国际公约不仅对缔约国有约束力,而且对非缔约国也会产生一定的影响。

(二) 国际惯例

国际惯例(international customs),又称为国际习惯(international usage),它也是一种国际行为规范。在国际私法范围内,有两种不同的国际惯例:一种是当事人必须遵守的国际惯例,即强制性的国际惯例。例如,通过长期国际实践形成的"国家及其财产豁免"原则就属于这种惯例。另外一种是只有经过当事人选择,才对其有约束力的国际惯例,即任意性的国际惯例。

在国际私法中,国际惯例大量存在。在外国人的民商事法律地位方面,如"国民待遇"原则等,在冲突法方面,如"不动产物权依物之所在地法"原则、"公共秩序"原则、"意思自治"原则、"既得权的尊重与保护"原则以及"场所支配行为"原则等,均属于国际惯例。

中国在调整涉外民商事法律关系,解决涉外民商事法律冲突,处理涉外民商事法律争议时,也依法适用国际惯例。1986年《中华人民共和国民法通则》第142条第3款规定:"中华人民共和国法律和中华人民共和国缔结或者参加的国际条约没

---

① 参见1969年5月23日订立的《维也纳条约法公约》第2条。
② http://en.wikipedia.org/wiki/Treaty.

有规定的,可以适用国际惯例。"这表明,中国法院在处理涉外民商事案件时,可以适用国际惯例来处理案件。

根据我国法律适用国际惯例,要注意处理好国际惯例和国内法的关系。首先,按照《民法通则》第142条第3款,适用国际惯例有一个条件,即对有关民商事项,中华人民共和国法律和中华人民共和国缔结或参加的国际条约没有规定。这表明,中国主张在法律适用方面,现有的成文国内法和中国缔结或参加的国际条约的规定优于不成文的国际惯例的规定。其次,针对国内民事活动,《民法通则》第6条规定:"民事活动必须遵守法律,法律没有规定的,应当遵守国家政策。"但针对涉外民商事活动,《民法通则》第142条第3款则规定,当中国法律没有规定时,就不是适用没有法律效力的国家政策了,而是适用国际惯例。进而结合《民法通则》第150条关于适用外国法律或国际惯例不得违背中国的社会公共利益的规定来看,在法律效力方面,国际惯例处于同外国法同等、并列的地位,与根据冲突规范所援引的外国法的效力相同。国际惯例的效力低于国际条约,但高于国家政策。国际惯例同国际条约、国内法和外国法一样,可以作为冲突规范的直接或间接指引对象。再次,按照中国法律规定的合同当事人意思自治原则,当事人可以选择适用实体规范性质的国际商业惯例。在通常情况下,只有当事人选择适用的国际商业惯例,才对该当事人有约束力。而在当事人未选择适用国际商业惯例时,适用国际商业惯例只发生于中国法律和中国缔结或参加的国际条约对有关事项未加规定的情况。最后,根据《民法通则》第150条的规定,适用国际惯例不得违背中华人民共和国的社会公共利益。

(三) 国际判例

国际判例是指国际法院的判例。对于国际法院的判例是否可以成为国际私法的渊源,在理论上有不同的主张。有人主张,国际法院1955年对"诺特包姆案"(Nottebohm Case)的判决[1],1958年对"玛丽·保尔案"(Boll Case)的判决[2],1970年对于"巴塞罗那公司案"(Barcelona Traction Case)的判决[3],在国际私法上具有渊源作用。但也有人对此持不同意见。因为在国际公法上,按照《国际法院规约》第38条,司法判例只能作为确定法律原则的辅助资料。该《规约》第59条也规定,

---

[1] Nottebohm (Liech. v. Guat.), 1955 *I. C. J. Rep.* 4 (Apr. 6); see Ian Brownlie, *Principles of Public International Law*, 6th ed., 2003, pp.395—406.

[2] Boll Case (Neth. v. Swed.), I. C. J. 55 (Nov. 28, 1958), involving interpretation of the 1902 Hague Convention on the Guardianship of Minors. see Adair Dyer, The Internationalization of Family Law, 30 *U. C. Davis L. Rev.* 625, 639—640 (1997).

[3] Barcelona Traction, Light & Power Co. (Belg. v. Spain), Second Phase, 1970 *I. C. J. Rep.* 5 (Feb. 5).

国际法院的裁判除对于当事国及本案外,无拘束力。不过,1958年国际法院对玛丽·保尔案的判决以及该判决所反映的法律意见,的确在国际私法界引起了广泛的讨论,对国际私法的理论和实践有极大的影响。

三、一般法律原则和法律学说

（一）一般法律原则

一般法律原则作为法律(包括国内法和国际法)的渊源已得到普遍的认同。一般法律原则也应该是国际私法的渊源。尽管一般法律原则在国内和国际法律实践中被广泛适用,但法学界对这一概念却没有统一的理解。在我们看来,一般法律原则应为各国国内法律体系和国际法中所包含的共同原则或法律理念。一般法律原则应为各国所承认,它决不着眼于只是偶然一致的一切法律规定,而是着眼于那些以一般的法律理念为基础并可以移用于国际往来的法律原则。[①]一般法律原则到底包括一些什么原则呢？对这个问题,没有统一的答案。被常设国际法院、国际法院及其法官、一些仲裁庭和学者引用过的一般法律原则有:条约必须遵守原则、诚实与信用原则、特别法优于普通法原则、不可抗力免责原则等。在中国国内立法中,一般法律原则是否为法律的渊源尚无明确的规定。

（二）法律学说

法律学说(jurisprudence),有时称为法律科学(science of the law),是指关于全部法律或某一部门法律的学理。在各国实践中,一般不将学说作为法律的直接渊源。按照《国际法院规约》第38条的规定,国际法院也只可以援用各国权威最高的公法学家学说作为确定法律原则的辅助资料。

在中国,法律学说不是法律的渊源,当然也不是国际私法的渊源。但是,权威国际私法学家的学说不仅在实践中对法官和仲裁员的思维、判断有重要影响,而且可以作为确定国际私法原则或规则的辅助资料。

【思考题】

- 请描述你所知道的国际私法是一门怎样的部门法和/或一个怎样的学科。
- 国际民商事案件为什么要进行法律选择？法院能否直接适用法院所在地国家的法律？
- 什么是冲突规范？常见的冲突规范有哪些类别？

---

① 参见王铁崖主编：《国际法》,法律出版社1981年版,第31—32页。

* 什么是连接因素?
* 为什么说准据法是国际私法所特有的概念?
* 如何根据冲突规则的特性在国际私法立法中体现出法律适用的确定性和灵活性?

【重要术语提示与中英文对照】

中文术语	英文对照
国际私法	private international law
法律冲突法	law of conflict of laws
法律选择法	choice of laws
冲突规范	conflict rules
法律适用规范	rules of application of law
法律选择规范	choice-of-law rules
国际私法规范	rules of private international law
管辖选择规则	jurisdiction-selecting rule
单边冲突规范	unilateral conflict rules
双边冲突规范	bilateral conflict rules
连接因素	connection factor
连接点	point of contact
准据法	lex causae
普通法的习惯	common law habits
联邦最高法院判例汇编	The United States Reports
国际条约	international treaty
国际惯例	international customs
国际习惯	international usage
诺特包姆案	Nottebohm Case
玛丽·保尔案	Boll Case
巴塞罗那公司案	Barcelona Traction Case
法律学说	jurisprudence
法律科学	science of the law

【推荐阅读文献】

* 徐冬根:《论当代国际私法发展的四大趋势》,载《华东政法学院学术文集》,浙江人民出版社2002年版。
* 赵相林、邢钢:《全球化视野下的国际私法》,载《河南省政法管理干部学院学报》2003年第2期。
* 杜焕芳:《试论全球化视野中的冲突法:影响与发展》,载《政法论丛》2003年第

5期。

- 赵秀文主编:《国际私法学原理与案例教程》(第一章),中国人民大学出版社2006年版。
- 吕岩峰:《和谐世界中的国际私法观照——以现代国际私法体系的构建为焦点》,载《法学》2007年第8期。
- 霍政欣:《冲突法之谜的经济分析》,载《中国国际私法与比较法年刊》(第十二卷),北京大学出版社2009年版,第531页。
- 陈隆修:《由欧盟经验论中国式国际私法》,载《中国国际私法与比较法年刊》(第十三卷),北京大学出版社2010年版,第3页。
- 周江:《"综合文本"意识下的冲突法研究进路》,载《江苏大学学报(社会科学版)》2012年第2期。
- Lea Brilmayer, Jack Goldsmith, *Conflict of Law, Cases and Materials*,中信出版社2003年版。
- Eleanor Cashin Ritaine, Harmonising European Private International Law: A Replay of Hannibal's Crossing of the Ales? 34 *Int'l J. Legal Info.* 420 (2006).
- Symeon C. Symeonides, Choice of Law in the American Courts in 2006: Twentieth Annual Survey, 54 *Am. J. Comp. L.* 697 (2006).
- James P. George and Anna K. Teller, Conflict of Laws, 60 *SMU L. Rev.* 817 (2007).
- Hay, Weintraub & Borchers, Conflict of Laws, Cases and Materials (13th ed. 2009).
- Basedow, Theory of Choice of Law, 75 *RabelsZ* 32 (2011).

【扩展阅读资料】

1. Choice of Law[①]

A choice of law issue is presented to a court only when three prerequisites are met. First, the case must exhibit multi-jurisdictional connections through the domicile or residence of the parties or the various acts, events or transactions that gave rise to the suit. Choice of law issues cases often arise in suits brought or removed to federal courts on the basis of diversity jurisdiction because the very fact that the parties are domiciled in different states increases the likelihood that conflicts of potentially applicable laws will arise. Second, the party seeking to have the court apply the law of another jurisdiction has the burden of pleading that law and, as a

---

[①] Patricia Youngblood Reyhan, 2005—2006 Survey of New York Law: Conflict of Laws, 57 *Syracuse L. Rev.* 881, 896—897 (2007).

result, parties to a dispute with multi-state or multi-national connections may "localize" the dispute by either failing to recognize or choosing to minimize the multi-jurisdictional connections. Third, the laws of the multiple jurisdictions must be in conflict not only on their face but also when applied to facts of the case. Differences in law without litigational consequences are not "conflicts" with which choice of law rules are concerned. These differences do not have to be outcome determinative, however. In Financial One Public Company, Ltd. v. Lehman Bros. Special Financing, the Second Circuit Court of Appeals, rejecting defendant's argument that, in order to present a choice of law, the differing laws had to be outcome determinative, stated, all that is necessary is that "the differences must be 'relevant' to the issue at hand, and must have a 'significant possible effect on the outcome of the trial.'"

2. Choosing the Applicable Substantive Law[①]

Choosing the applicable substantive law is a question, like personal jurisdiction and judgment enforcement, involving both forum law and constitutional issues. Understanding these issues requires a clear focus on basic principles. First, choice of law is a question of state law, both in state and federal courts. Second, it is a question of forum state law. Renvoi—the practice of using another state's choice-of-law rule—is almost never employed unless the forum state directs it, and, even then, the forum state remains in control. Third, the forum state has broad power to make choice-of-law decisions, either legislatively or judicially, subject only to limited constitutional requirements.

Within the forum state's control of choice of law is a hierarchy of choice-of-law rules. At the top are legislative choice-of-law rules, that is, statutes directing the application of certain states' laws, based on events or people important to the operation of that specific law. Second in the choice-of-law hierarchy is party-controlled choice of law, that is, choice-of-law clauses in contracts that control unless public policy dictates otherwise. Third in the hierarchy is the common law, now controlled in Texas by the most significant relationship test of the Restatement (Second) of Conflict of Laws. This Survey article is organized according to the hierarchy in statutory choice-of-law, followed by choice of law clauses, and concluding with choice of law under the most significant relationship test. Special issues such as constitutional limitations are discussed in the following section. This grouping results in a discussion that mixes Texas Supreme Court opinions with those of Texas intermediate appellate courts, federal district courts, and the Fifth Circuit. In spite of this mix, readers should of course note that because choice of law is a state-law issue, the only binding opinions are those of the Texas Supreme Court.

---

① James P. George and Anna K. Teller, Conflict of Laws, 60 *SMU L. Rev.* 817, 821 (2007).

3. Statutory Choice-of-law Rules①

The Survey period offered five cases involving choice-of-law statutes, all from federal district courts, with the first three applying the Texas codification of the "internal affairs doctrine." Kira, Inc. v. All Star Maintenance is instructive on several issues of choice-of-law advocacy, which the federal district court found necessary in spite of the parties' agreement, both in their contract and their less-than-adequate trial briefs, that Nevada law governed. Kira was an action between LLC owners for several claims arising from two owners' alleged misappropriation of funds and misuse of the trade name. The parties had formed the company under Nevada law to provide maintenance services at Fort Hood, Texas. Two company members then used the company's name and money to form a similar company in Delaware. The operating agreement designated Nevada law, but the court, being precise, pointed out that Texas had a statutory choice-of-law rule designating the law of the state of incorporation to determine the rights, powers, and duties of entity members. This also leads to Nevada law, but the court asked for additional briefs to clarify any conflicts between Nevada and Texas, both as to internal affairs and contractual claims that would be controlled by the parties' choice-of-law clause. The parties' response failed to highlight specific conflicts and alternatively cited Nevada and Texas cases, leading the court to hold that Nevada law would govern, which it apparently determined on judicial notice.

The same statute controlled in Enigma Holdings, Inc. v. Gemplus International S. A., ruling that Luxembourg law governed the corporate governance claims in an action for fraud and corporate internal misdealing, and again in In re Dodgin, an Amarillo bankruptcy case where the court ruled that the laws of the jurisdiction of incorporation of a foreign corporation govern the shareholders' liabilities for the corporation's debts, leading to the application of New Mexico law.

In Webber v. Federal Bureau of Prisons, the Fifth Circuit Court of Appeals upheld the district court's application of Texas law to the prisoner's claims of malpractice against the prison. In Kimberly-Clark Corp. v. Continental Casualty Co., a Dallas federal court, conducting a forum non-conveniens analysis, held that the Texas statute requiring that Texas law govern certain locally insured interests did not apply because the company, despite its primary location in Texas, was a Delaware corporation.

---

① James P. George and Anna K. Teller, Conflict of Laws, 60 *SMU L. Rev.* 817, 822—823 (2007).

第二章

国际私法的基本制度

第二章 国际私法的基本制度

本章导读

※ 国际私法基本制度是国际私法中具有普遍适用意义的内容。国际私法基本制度的主要组成部分是冲突规范,即法律选择适用规范。当国际私法调整某一涉外民事法律关系时,就要涉及适用外国法,但适用外国法往往又会给内国带来不利或不便,于是各国就从各方面限制冲突规范的效力,从而在国际私法中形成了一系列的制度,包括识别、反致、转致、公共秩序保留等。

※ 国际私法中的识别,又称定类、定质或定性,是指法院对国际民商事关系中的某一事实构成或事实情况进行定性分类,并将其归入一定法律范畴的行为和程序。

※ 反致,是指对某一国际民商事关系,甲国根据其冲突规范应适用乙国的法律,而乙国的冲突规范又规定此种关系应适用甲国法,如果甲国法院最后适用甲国法律处理此种民商事关系,即为反致。

※ 反致制度存在的价值意义是能在涉外民商事法律关系中更好地维护内国的利益,不但有利于实现判决结果的个案的确定性,体现形式公正价值;而且有利于实现个案的合理公正,体现实质正义价值。反致制度存在的技术意义是有利于扩大内国法适用范围,给法官保护本国利益创造条件,对传统规则的机械性起到例外的调节作用,在法律适用技术上增加法官选法的机会和空间。

※ 国际私法上的法律规避,又称"诈欺规避",是指国际民商事法律关系当事人,通过有计划地制造构成法院地冲突规范中连接因素的具体事实,以避开本应适用的对其不利的准据法,从而使对其有利的法律得以适用的一种行为。

※ 外国法的查明,又称为外国法内容的确定,在英、美法系国家则称为外国法的证明,是指一国法院根据本国冲突规范指定应适用外国法时,对该外国法的存在和内容的查明。

※ 公共秩序,是指一国国家或社会的重大利益,或法律和道德的基本原则。根据各国普遍实践和许多国际私法公约的规定,在一国依内国冲突规范的指定本应对某一国际民商事关系适用外国法时,如其适用将与内国的公共秩序相抵触,法院即可排除该外国法的适用。各国在排除适用外国法之后,通常都代之以法院地法。

【本章主题词】 识别、反致、法律规避、外国法的查明、公共秩序保留

第一节 识别

一、识别的法律含义

国际私法中的识别(**characterization**)是指法院对国际民商事关系中的某一事实构成或事实情况进行定性分类,并将其归入一定法律范畴的行为和程序。①

【释义】　　　　　　　　**characterization**

In a conflict-of-law situation, a court must determine at the outset whether the problem presented to it for solution relates to torts, contracts, property, or some other field, or to a matter of substance or procedure, in order to refer to the appropriate law. In other words, the court must initially, whether consciously or not, go through the process of determining the nature of the problem; otherwise, the court will not know which choice-of-law rule to apply to the case. This process is generally called "characterization", and sometimes "classification", "qualification", or "interpretation".②

"识别"又可以称作定类(classification)、定质(qualification)或定性。国际私法中的识别过程(**process of characterization**),是指在需要适用某一冲突规范去确定调整有关国际民商事关系的准据法,而又在到底应该适用哪一条冲突规范去确定准据法的问题上发生疑问时,依据一定的法律意识和法制观念对冲突规范所要调整的对象或范围所涉及的有关事实构成或事实情况进行定性分类,进而对冲突规范所要调整的该有关对象或范围本身的法律性质加以认定,并在此基础上确定到底应该适用哪一条冲突规范去确定准据法的过程。③

---

① 参见李双元、金彭年、张茂、欧福勇:《中国国际私法通论》(第二版),法律出版社2003年版,第142页。
② Black's Law Dictionary 226—227 (1999).
③ 参见谢石松:《国际私法中的识别问题新论》,载中国国际私法学会主办:《中国国际私法和比较法年刊》(第二卷),法律出版社1999年版,第93页。

【释义】　　　　　　　　**process of characterization**

Characterization is fancy term for the process of putting labels on problems. Under territorial-oriented choice-of-law rules, every conflicts case requires three levels of characterization: (1) determination of the nature of the substantive problem; (2) interpretation of the choice-of-law rule chosen; and (3) a decision as to which issues are substantive, therefore determined under the law designated by the choice-of-law rule, and which issued are procedural, therefore determined by the forum law.①

二、对法律关系性质的识别

由于不同国家的法律及法律观念不同,对同一涉外法律关系性质的理解会存在差异,这将导致适用不同的冲突规范。因此,识别的第一步就是要给具体的实体问题贴上一个标签:是合同行为还是侵权行为？如果是侵权行为,则适用侵权行为地法;如果是合同,则适用合同的缔结地法或者合同的履行地法,或者适用与合同有最密切联系地法。如在 **Travelers Indemnity Co. v. Lake** 案中,保险公司主张将案件识别为侵权关系,受害人主张适用侵权行为地方,而原告主张双方之间的法律关系是合同关系,应适用合同缔结地法。法院最后将其识别为合同关系,适用合同缔结地法,即特拉华州法。

【案例】　　　　　　**Travelers Indemnity Co. v. Lake**

Lake, a Delaware resident was involved in an accident in Quebec Canada which was caused by an unidentified motorist whose truck hit the truck Lake was driving causing it to crash into a concrete barrier. His employer owned the truck he was driving. The driver of the other truck that caused the accident did not stop and was never found. Lake had an insurance policy with Travelers on his own automobiles that provided $300000 uninsured motorist coverage for damages Lake was "legally entitled to recover." Under Quebec law, Lake's recovery would be limited to $29000. If Delaware law is applicable, Lake could recover up to $300000 from his insurance company. Travelers claimed that *lex loci delicti* required the application of Quebec. The trial court held that the issue of insurance coverage was a contract issued and applied the Restatement (Second) to the case and decided the Lake was "legally entitled" to recover under Delaware law.②

---

① Russell J Weintraub, *Commentary on the Conflict of Laws*, 4th ed, New York Foundation Press, 2001, p.53.

② Luther McDougal II, Robert Felix, Ralph Whitten, *American Conflicts Law: Cases, and Materials*, LexisNexis, 2004, p.20.

由此可见，由于对同一法律关系性质的识别不一致，不但会导致适用不同的冲突规范，还会最终导致适用不同的准据法，直接影响到当事人切身利益。

三、对冲突规则的识别

在确定了法律关系的性质（如合同关系）之后，可以确定合同所适用的法律，如合同适用合同缔结地法。但是，各国的法律对于同一冲突规范中的连接点可能会作不同的解释。例如对于异地订立的合同来说，何为"合同缔结地"？大陆法系理解为"承诺接受地"，英美法系则理解为"承诺发出地"。由于承诺发出地与承诺接受地分处异地，对合同缔结地这一连接点的识别不同，势必导致适用不同的准据法。因此，通过对不同连接点的解释，起到最终确定所适用法律的目的。

四、我国有关识别的规定

我国自2011年4月1日起施行的《涉外民事关系法律适用法》正式将识别称为"定性"，并作出具体的规定。该法第8条规定："涉外民事关系的定性，适用法院地法律。"

第二节 反致

一、反致的概念

反致（**renvoi**）是指对某一国际民商事关系，甲国根据其冲突规范应适用乙国的法律，而乙国的冲突规范又规定此种关系应适用甲国法，如果甲国法院最后适用甲国法律处理此种民商事关系，即为反致。①

【释义】　　　　　　　　　　　renvoi

Renvoi, meaning refer back or refer away, occurs when the forum applies a foreign

---

① 参见李双元、金彭年、张茂、欧福勇：《中国国际私法通论》（第二版），法律出版社2003年版，第159页。

choice-of-law rule that selects law different from that chosen by the forum's rule. If the foreign rules points back to the forum, there is the intriguing possibility that the court will be caught in a circle of references, from forum to foreign law to forum law, without end.①

If a forum court is directed to consult a foreign law, the first question it must address is whether this is a reference solely to the relevant substantive provisions, or to the state's system of law as a whole which would include its choice of law rules. Forums that do not have renvoi provision, refer only to the specific provisions of relevant law. In this way, the same outcome is achieved no matter where the case is litigated so long as the second state would also have applied its own laws. But if that second country actually has choice of law rules requiring it to apply the forum law, a difference in outcome might arise depending on where the plaintiff invokes jurisdiction. Whether a difference actually emerges depends on whether the other state operates a Single Renvoi system. A single renvoi forum always refers to the other law's choice of law rules. If those rules would send the issue back to the forum court, the forum court will accept the first remission and applies its own laws. Thus, equality of outcome is always achieved so long as the competing laws operate different systems.

反致有广义和狭义之分,广义的反致包括狭义的反致(remission)、转致(transmission)、间接反致(indirect remission)和双重反致或外国法院说(**double renvoi or foreign courts theory**)。②

【释义】　　double renvoi or foreign courts theory

There is another system called the double renvoi or foreign courts theory which will also ensure parity of result so long as no other relevant law is using it. In this scenario, the forum court considers that it is sitting as the foreign court and will decide the matter in exactly the same way that the foreign court would. In this system, there can never be more than two remissions, e.g. English forum refers to French law (a single renvoi system) so English law is applied (1st remission) and France accepts the remission (2nd and final). At present, only English law uses this approach.

二、反致制度的产生及其存在的意义

(一) 反致制度产生于实践

尽管欧洲各国法院早在 17 世纪已经开始采用反致制度③,并且有学者认为英

---

① Russell J Weintraub, *Commentary on the Conflict of Laws*, 4th ed, New York Foundation Press, 2001, p. 88.
② 参见韩德培主编:《国际私法新论》,武汉大学出版社 1997 年版,第 181—183 页。
③ 早在 17 世纪中叶荷兰、瑞士在审判实践中就运用了反致,在 19 世纪英国法院分别在 1841 年、1847 年、1877 年运用反致对科尔讼利瓦兹案、佛伦里诉佛伦里案、拉克罗克斯货物案作出判决。

国在 1841 年的法院判决中已经有对反致的讨论(Renvoi was first discussed in an 1841 English decision)①,但在国际私法上对反致进行广泛探讨和争论的典型案例是法国最高法院 1882 年作出判决的 **福果案**(Forgo's Case)。

【案例】　　　　　　　　　　　福 果 案

　　福果是一个非婚生子,具有巴伐利亚国籍,5 岁时随母移居到法国,至 1869 年死亡。福果无子女,死亡时也未立遗嘱,他留有动产在法国。此案对法国来说,是一涉外法定继承案件。根据法国国际私法的规定,继承依被继承人的本国法,本案应适用巴伐利亚法。而根据巴伐利亚继承法的规定,非婚生子女的旁系亲属可以继承非婚生子女的遗产。但巴伐利亚的冲突法规定,动产的继承依死者住所地法。这样,反过来把适用的法律指向了法国法。法国继承的实体法规定,非婚生子的旁系亲属无继承权。法国最高法院在审理该案时,接受了巴伐利亚国际私法对法国法的反致,按法国实体法作出判决,其遗产认定为无人继承财产,判归法国国库。

　　由此,反致制度便在法国判例中宣告确立,并逐渐为各国所关注。②

　　(二) 各国对反致制度的不同态度

　　反致制度一直是国际私法领域争论最为广泛和激烈的问题。理论上,有两种尖锐对立的不同意见,一派赞同反致,一派反对反致。

　　实践中,从国内层面看,有的国家全面拒绝接受反致,其中立法上全面拒绝反致的国家有希腊、伊拉克、秘鲁、埃及、叙利亚、伊朗、摩洛哥等国。从国际层面看,有的国际条约拒绝反致,如 1985 年海牙《国际货物销售合同法律适用公约》。

　　(三) 反致制度存在的价值意义

　　第一,反致制度能在涉外民事法律关系中更好地维护内国的利益。如果我们

---

① William A. Reppy, The Framework of Full Faith and Credit and Interstate Recognition of Same-Sex Marriages, 3 *Ave Maria L. Rev.* 393, 442 (2005).

② According to Ernest G. Lorenzen, The Renvoi Theory and the Application of Foreign Law, 10 *Colum. L. Rev.* 190, 191 (1910), although the English case of 1841 was the first to mention renvoi, "it was not until the adoption of the renvoi doctrine by the French Court of Cassation in the Forgo case, decided in 1882, that the problem attracted the serious attention of the jurists." John Delatre Falconbridge, Renvoi in New York and Elsewhere, in *Essays on the Conflict of Laws* 233, 249 (2d ed. 1954) (1947) cites Dupuy v. Wurtz, 53 N.Y. 556 (1873), as the American case to discuss the possible use of renvoi in choice of law. Erwin N. Griswold, Renvoi Revisited, 51 *Harv. L. Rev.* 1165, 1165 n.1 (1938), says the word "renvoi" was first used in legal writing in English in 1898.

从理论和实践关系的角度看问题,就可以发现理论和实践是一个循环往复的系统。任何理论问题的提出,都是在一定的实践活动中产生的,而实践提出的问题经过人们的思维、判断而抽象出来成为一种带有普遍意义的理论,它又反过来指导实践活动。从反致制度的产生及发展过程来看,反致一经产生便遭到各方面的非难,就是对反致持肯定态度的国家,他们赞成的程度也不一样,但尽管如此,多数国家的判例或立法还是逐渐承认了反致,这说明反致是维护内国利益的有力工具,反致制度符合各国最高管理层的意志,能在涉外民事法律关系中更好地维护内国的利益。因此,反致不论在理论上还是在实践中都是应该得到普遍承认的。

第二,反致制度能够体现形式公正价值,使判决结果具有确定性、可预见性和一致性,案件的审理不因诉讼地不同而产生不同的结果。①努力寻求判决的一致性是国际私法的主要目的所在②,反致制度可以保护涉外民事法律关系的稳定,可以避免当事人挑选法院,如在 **Haumschild v. Continental Casualty Company** 案中,原告对一起发生在美国加州的交通事故,以家庭关系为基础,在美国威斯康星州起诉。威斯康星州最高法院针对原告挑选法院的行为,运用反致,驳回了原告的请求,作出了公正的判决。

【案例】　　　　**Haumschild v. Continental Casualty Company**③

Facts: Wisconsin spouses were riding in California in a truck driven by the husband, when, because of the husband's alleged negligence, there was an accident and the wife was injured. The wife sued her husband in Wisconsin, joining the liability insurer and two owners of the truck. The defendants' motion for summary judgment was granted on the ground that under California law a husband could not be sued in tort by his wife. In a landmark opinion departing from the place-of-wrong rule, the Wisconsin Supreme Court reversed the applied Wisconsin law, which permitted wife-husband suits. The majority rejected the plaintiff's suggestion that Wisconsin law, as that of the marital domicile, be applied because California, the place of the accident, would have done so had it been the forum.④

第三,反致制度有利于实现个案的合理公正,体现实质正义价值。涉外民事法律关系错综复杂,适用不同的法律往往会导致不同的判决结果,影响当事人的利

---

① 参见刘炼:《关于国际私法中反致制度的几点思考》,载《当代法学》2003 年第 10 期。
② 参见刘铁铮:《国际私法论丛》,台湾三民书局 1986 年版,第 23 页。
③ 7 Wis. 2d 130, 95 N. W. 2d 814 (1959).
④ Russell J Weintraub, *Commentary on the Conflict of Laws*, 4th ed, New York Foundation Press, 2001, pp. 88—89.

益,法院运用反致制度选择应该适用的法律,是基于法律的规定,并非法官随心所欲。当一国法院依其冲突规范应适用外国法时,若考虑外国冲突规范就至少有三种选择的可能,即依该外国的冲突规范适用其本国实体法或法院地法或第三国法,从而扩大了法律选择的范围,增加了法律选择的灵活性,克服了法院依本国冲突规范适用外国实体法的盲目性、机械性和可能适用该外国在同样场合下也不愿或不能适用其本国法的非科学性,有利于法官选择适用与案件最密切联系地的法律,选择适用对案件或当事人有更大利益的国家的法律。

因而,采用反致不仅能够满足传统国际私法的要求,也符合现代国际私法的价值观念。

(四) 反致制度存在的技术意义

第一,反致制度有利于扩大内国法适用范围,给法官保护本国利益创造了条件。反致支持限制了冲突规范的效力,扩大了内国法适用范围,这无疑给内国法官适用内国法保护本国利益创造了条件。当然,当适用内国法对内国不利时,法官可采用转致和其他制度进行司法补救。

第二,反致制度对传统规则的机械性起着例外的调节作用[①],有利于达到某种特定目的。1965 年《关于解决国家与他国国民间投资争端的公约》第 42 条规定:"仲裁法庭应依照双方可能统一的法律规则判定一项争端。如无此种协议,法庭适用争端一方缔约国的法律(包括其关于冲突法的规则)以及可适用的国际法规则。"这表明,在当事人没有就仲裁适用的法律进行选择时,应适用争端一方的缔约国的冲突规范所指定的法律。这是因为,关于解决国家与他国国民间投资争端的法律适用,发展中国家与发达国家的观点是对立的,前者主张适用东道国法律,但考虑到某些发展中国家的法制不完备,单纯适用东道国法律,可能不足以正确处理争议,公约允许采用反致这一灵活的做法,使解决争端的准据法变为投资者母国的法律或第三国的法律,从而也排除了东道国法律的适用。[②] 20 世纪 70 年代后的一些海牙公约接受了反致。[③]国内立法中,《葡萄牙民法典》允许用反致作为取得国际法律协调的重要手段,允许用反致来取得某种实际的结果,特别是使某种交易合法化。[④]

第三,反致制度在法律适用技术上增加了法官选法的机会和空间,法院可以在

---

① 参见李双元、徐国建主编:《国际民商新秩序的理论重构》,武汉大学出版社 1998 年版,第 234 页。
② 曾华群主编:《国际投资法学》,北京大学出版社 1999 年版,第 606 页。
③ 如 1978 年第十三届海牙会议制定的《关于夫妻财产法律适用公约》。
④ 韩德培主编:《中国冲突法研究》,武汉大学出版社 1993 年版,第 436 页。

几个相关的法律之间进行选择,有利于达到更合理的判决结果。①反致产生于两个以固定连接点为基础成立的冲突规范之间的消极冲突,实质上是可裁量制度,由法官来决定在具体案件中是否进行反致,因而反致的本质仍然是增加法官选法的机会和空间,克服传统冲突规范单一、僵固的局限,增强传统冲突规范运用过程中的灵活性。至于法官最终是否采纳反致,取决于法官对所涉相关国家实体法内容的考查与权衡。②因此,反致制度本质上是对传统冲突规范单点连接缺乏灵活性、不问法律实质内容的一种补救。但是伴随着现代冲突规则的兴起与发展,与传统冲突规范相适应的反致制度的生存空间和作用将不断受到限制。③

三、反致制度与我国国际私法

作为我国国际私法基本法的《民法通则》第八章和其他有关国际私法规范的立法对于反致和转致问题并没有作出明确的规定。我国早期立法既没有表示接受反致和转致,也没有表示明显拒绝。④但最高人民法院1988年发布的《关于贯彻执行〈中华人民共和国民法通则〉若干问题的意见(试行)》曾涉及反致。该《意见》第178条第2款规定:"人民法院在审理涉外民事关系的案件时,应当按照民法通则第八章的规定来确定应适用的实体法。"这一规定隐含着不采用反致。我国自2011年4月1日起施行的《涉外民事关系法律适用法》也同样不采纳反致制度。该法第9条规定:"涉外民事关系适用的外国法律,不包括该国的法律适用法。"

但是,我国在司法实践中,也有采用转致的案例的,如**"卡帕玛丽"轮抵押合同纠纷案**。

【案例】   "卡帕玛丽"轮抵押合同纠纷案

1990年9月27日,申请人和柏林人银行(共同称为银行方)与被申请人(作为借款方)签订贷款合同,约定:由银行方贷款给被申请人总额为310万美元的款项,用于经营被申请人所属的塞浦路斯籍"卡帕玛丽"(Kappa Mary)轮(该轮于1992年10月16日更名为"帕玛"(Pamar)轮,仍为塞浦路斯籍);柏林人银行委托申请人为其代理人,负责处理上述贷款本金和利息的偿还以及贷款的日常管理事务;被申请人应分6次,以等量连

---

① 吴晓红:《国际私法中的反致制度》,载《新乡教育学院学报》2003年第3期。
② 参见韩汉卿、刘萍:《现代冲突规则解析》,载《2002年中国国际私法年会论文集》,华东政法学院国际法系2002年编印。
③ 参见李双元、徐国建主编:《国际民商新秩序的理论构建》,武汉大学出版社1998年版,第341页。
④ 徐冬根、薛凡:《中国国际私法完善研究》,上海社会科学院出版社1998年版,第193页。

续分期付款的形式向代理人偿还贷款,每隔6个月偿还285000美元。同日,申请人作为抵押权人,被申请人作为船主,双方签订了船舶抵押合同,约定抵押权人和柏林人银行联合向船主提供310万美元的贷款,被申请人将其所有的"帕玛"轮设置抵押。1990年9月27日14时30分,申请人作为抵押权受益人在塞浦路斯利马索尔由当地登记官作了抵押登记。因其他海事请求权人申请扣押并拍卖"帕玛"轮,申请人于1994年7月27日向海事法院提出债权登记申请,请求法院确认至1995年3月31日止,申请人对被申请人抵押债权本息共3663920.10美元。审理过程中,被申请人对申请人的债权请求全部予以承认。双方选择适用中国法律。申请人还向法院提供了《塞浦路斯共和国海商法(暂行)》。

海事法院认为,当事人双方选择适用中国法律,根据《中华人民共和国海商法》第271条的规定:"船舶抵押权适用船旗国法律。""帕玛"轮悬挂塞浦路斯共和国国旗,故处理本案的实体争议应适用塞浦路斯共和国的法律。①

本案当事人分别是英国和希腊人,设置抵押权的船舶国籍为塞浦路斯,法院地为中国。我国的《民法通则》将意思自治原则作为涉外合同法律适用的首要原则。我国《海商法》第269条也规定,合同当事人可以选择合同适用的法律。本案当事人签订的船舶抵押贷款合同没有选择适用法律,但法院在审理本案时作出了适用中国法律处理本案的选择,符合我国法律规定,应予以确认。法院在处理本案时,根据《海商法》第271条"船舶抵押权适用船旗国法律"的规定,鉴于"帕玛"轮悬挂塞浦路斯共和国国旗,故处理本案的实体争议应适用塞浦路斯共和国的法律。根据当事人的选择,本应适用中国法,但是法院根据中国的冲突规范适用船旗国(塞浦路斯)法律,最后法院适用塞浦路斯法律处理本案。因此,该案的法律适用属于国际私法上"转致"。

反致作为国际私法中的一项重要制度,"它不仅能够满足国际私法的传统要求,也符合现代国际私法的价值观念。它是一种十分有用的制度,有其存在的价值和巨大生命力。"②反致作为一种国际私法制度,与其他制度一样,来源于实践,并需要随着实践的发展而发展和完善。

---

① 资料来源:中国法制新闻网,网址:http://www.chinalnn.com/JCArticle_show.asp? ArticleID = 90084。

② 肖永平:《肖永平论冲突法》,武汉大学出版社2002年版,第303页。

第三节 法律规避

一、法律规避的概念

国际私法上的法律规避(evasion of law),又称"诈欺规避"(fraudulent evasion of law),是指国际民商事法律关系当事人,通过有计划地制造构成法院地冲突规范中连接因素的具体事实,以避开本应适用的对其不利的准据法,从而使对其有利的法律得以适用的一种行为。[1]在美国冲突法上,这个问题被表述为"对选法自由的限制"。我国有学者认为,国际私法中的法律规避之界定可作如下表述:在涉外民商事领域,当事人恶意地利用法院地国冲突规范连接点所涵盖的具体事实的立法变化或变更连接点所涵盖的具体事实,并以此为媒介而取得对另一国法律的适用,避开原本应适用的准据法的一种规范层面的选法行为或逃法行为。[2]

国际私法中的法律规避源自法国 1878 年最高法院对鲍富莱蒙王妃离婚案(Bauffremont's Divorce Case)的判决[3],这也是最早确立法律规避的典型案例。其后,国际私法学界便开始了对其广泛的注意和较为深入的研究。传统的法律规避主要在婚姻法等方面,如 **Wilkins v. Zelichowski** 案。

【案例】　　　　　　　　Wilkins v. Zelichowski[4]

Facts: The bride and groom were domiciled in New Jersey. They ran away to Indiana to be married, returning "immediately" to New Jersey. The bride later sought to annual the marriage because she was not 18 when she married, that being the minimum age for marriages in New Jersey. Indiana, however, permitted girls to marry at 16.

---

[1] 参见李双元、金彭年、张茂、欧福勇:《中国国际私法通论》(第二版),法律出版社 2003 年版,第 189 页。对于何谓法律规避,目前教材书中大抵有以下三种观点,具体可参见韩德培主编:《国际私法新论》,武汉大学出版社 1997 年版,第 194 页;余先予主编:《冲突法》,法律出版社 1989 年版,第 112 页;张仲伯主编:《国际私法》,中国政法大学出版社 1995 年版,第 106 页。
[2] 吴德昌:《论国际私法中法律规避的方式》,载《甘肃政法成人教育学院学报》2003 年第 3 期。
[3] 参见李双元、金彭年、张茂、欧福勇:《中国国际私法通论》(第二版),法律出版社 2003 年版,第 189 页。
[4] 26 N. J. 370,140 A 2d 65 (1958).

Held: The marriage was invalid: "New Jersey was the only state having the interest and the purpose in having the ceremony take place in Indiana was to evade New Jersey's marriage policy."[①]

随着现代国际民商事交往的日益增多,法律规避已经渗透到国际民商法的其他各个领域:当事人为了规避对其不利的某些禁止性规定,而改变国籍或住所;当事人为了逃避遗嘱的繁复手续和高昂费用,到一个手续简单且花费较小的国家去成立遗嘱;当事人把一国法律规定不准买卖的物品转移到无此种限制的国家;当事人为了规避在本国成立公司的苛刻条件及繁重税赋而到别国成立公司,然后在其他国家从事经营活动,以及国际海上运输中普遍存在的船舶悬挂"方便旗"的现象等。

二、法律规避的对象

在禁止或者限制法律规避的国家中,对于法律规避的对象是否包括外国强行法的问题,也有不同主张。

(一) 本国强行法

一种主张认为规避法律仅指规避本国(亦即法院地国)强行法。例如1972年《塞内加尔家庭法》第851条规定:"当事人利用冲突规则故意使塞内加尔法不适用时,塞内加尔法取代应适用的外国法。"法国法院早年的判例也持这种立场,认为规避法国法才为法律规避,而规避外国法则不属此类问题,例如,1922年法国最高法院关于**佛莱案**(Ferrai Case)的判决就是这样。

【案例】　　　　　　　　　　佛　莱　案

佛莱及其妻子均为意大利人。由于当时意大利的法律只准"分居",而不准离婚,佛莱之妻为了逃避意大利法律关于离婚的限制,达到离婚的目的,便归化为法国人。随后,佛莱之妻在法国法院诉请离婚,法院依法国法的有关规定作了准予离婚的判决。[②]

在这个案件中,法国法院并没有因佛莱之妻规避意大利关于限制离婚的法律而否定其行为的有效性。

---

① David H. Vernon, Louis Weinberg, William Reynolds, William Richman, *Conflicts of Law: Case, Materials and Problems*, 2d ed., LexisNexis, 2002, p.797.
② 参见韩德培主编:《国际私法》,武汉大学出版社1989年版,第87页。

（二）内、外国强行法

另一种主张认为，规避法律既包括规避本国强行法，也包括外国强行法。① 例如《阿根廷民法典》第1207、1208条规定："在国外缔结的以规避阿根廷的法律为目的的合同是无效的，虽然该合同依缔约地法是有效的。""在阿根廷缔结的以规避外国法为目的的合同是无效的。"又如，1929年英国法院曾认为目的在于逃避美国禁止输入酒类的法律的合同是无效的。② 1979年《匈牙利国际私法》第8条第1款规定："当事人虚假地或欺诈地制造涉外因素时，有关外国法不得适用。"这一规定只笼统规定了法律规避无效，但显然可以理解为规避匈牙利法和外国法都是无效的。

三、法律规避的构成要件

法律规避需要符合一定的构成要件：

第一，当事人主观上有规避法律的故意。法律规避行为都是当事人主观上存在故意的积极行为。过失情形下的法律规避行为是不存在的。而当事人进行法律规避是为了逃避对其不利的本应适用的准据法，而使对其有利的法律得以适用，即其目的是趋利避害。③

第二，当事人的法律规避行为方式，通常都是利用冲突规范来实现的，即都是通过制造构成法院地国冲突规范中"连接因素"的具体事实予以实施的。

第三，客观结果的既遂性。这指的是当事人的行为在客观上已经形成了法律规避的事实，其所希望的某个实体法已得到适用，对其不利的准据法得以排除。因此，只有既遂的法律规避，而不存在未遂的法律规避。

第四节 外国法查明

在国际民商事诉讼中，若一国法院根据内国的冲突规范确定以外国法作为准

---

① 参见李双元主编：《国际私法学》，北京大学出版社2000年版，第238页。
② 参见李双元、金彭年、张茂、欧福勇：《中国国际私法通论》（第二版），法律出版社2003年版，第191页。
③ 参见田曼莉：《国际私法上法律规避效力新诠释》，载《同济大学学报》（社会科学版）2001年第6期。

据法后,接下来所要涉及的便是外国法内容的查明问题。

一、外国法的查明的概念

(一) 外国法的查明的定义

所谓外国法的查明,又称为外国法内容的确定,在英美法系国家则称为外国法的证明(proof of foreign law),是指一国法院根据本国冲突规范指定应适用外国法时,如何查明该外国法的存在和内容。①世界上各国法律纷繁复杂,千差万别,任何法官都很难通晓一切国家的各种法律。因此,当根据冲突法的指引需要适用外国法时,就要对该法的内容进行查明。

(二) 外国法是"事实"还是"法律"

西方普通法系国家的诉讼法把"法律"和"事实"截然分开,按照他们的法律观点,法官只知道其本国法律,而且仅限于知道本国法律;至于事实,则应由当事人举证,法院只根据当事人所证明的事实加以认定,并适用法律来作出判决。各国对外国法究竟属于"事实"还是"法律"有不同的主张。因此,在依冲突规范适用外国法时,就提出这样一个问题,即究竟把外国法视为"法律"还是视为"事实"?

1. 传统英美普通法的观点

英美普通法系的许多国家持"事实说",将外国法查明视为是事实问题(**proof of foreign law as question of fact**),而非法律问题。坚持这种做法的有英国、美国、澳大利亚、比利时、巴西、智利等国。

【说理】　　　　　　proof of foreign law as a question of fact

At common law, the proof of foreign law was a question of fact, a rule that dates back to the time of Lord Mansfield and Chief Justice Marshall, and survived well into 20th century. The content of foreign law was a jury question (at least sometimes), and the jury's decision was reviewed (at least in some courts) under the clearly erroneous rule usually applied to the question of fact.②

英美普通法系的国家大多将外国法视为"事实",其中一个重要原因可以通过美国学者比尔的观点(**position stated by Joseph Beale**)来佐证。

---

① 黄进:《论国际私法中外国法的查明》,载《河北法学》1990年第6期。
② David H. Vernon, Louis Weinberg, William Reynolds, William Richman, *Conflicts of Law: Case, Materials and Problems*, 2d ed., LexisNexis, 2002, p.242.

第二章 国际私法的基本制度

【说理】　　　　　　　　**position stated by Joseph Beale**

One theoretical rationale for the position that foreign law is a question of fact, not of law, is that stated by Joseph Beale: since the only law that can be applicable in a state is the law of that state, no law of a foreign state can have there the force of law.... The terms of the foreign law constitute a fact to be considered in the determination of the case.... The law of the forum is the only law that prevails as such. The foreign law is a fact in the transaction.[①]

2. 现代美国的观点

虽然在英国国际私法的司法实践中,外国法被视为"事实",但是著名国际私法学者马丁·沃尔夫却对此提出异议(**opinion of Martin Wolff**),认为不能单纯地将外国法视为事实。

【说理】　　　　　　　　**opinion of Martin Wolff**

Martin Wolff was able to say that: What the court applies to the facts laid before it is "law", not mere fact. It is meaningless to say that a judge applies a "fact" to facts. Every judicial decision constitutes a syllogism; its major premise is a legal rule and cannot be anything else, its minor is a set of facts.[②]

对此,美国的立法予以回应。20世纪50年代以来,美国冲突法发生革命,对许多传统的规则进行反思和修订,美国1966制定的《联邦证据规则》(Federal Rule of Evidence)改变了普通法系的传统观点,将外国法的证明视为是一个法律问题(**proof of foreign law as a question of law**)。

【说理】　　　　　　　　**proof of foreign law as a question of law**

Various reforms in recent years have changed all of this. Federal Rule of Evidence 44.1, adopted in 1966, provides that the proof of foreign law was a question of law and a court "may consider any relevant material or source." Federal Rule 44.1 provides: A party who intends to raise an issue concerning the law of foreign country shall give notice by pleadings or other reasonable written notice. The court, in determining foreign law, may consider any relevant material or source, including testimony, whether or not submitted by a party or admissible

---

① Joseph H. Beale, *A Treatise on the Conflict of Laws*, vol. 1, 1935, p. 53.
② Martin Wolff, *Private International Law*, 2nd ed., 1950, p. 217.

under the Federal Rule of Evidence. The court's determination shall be treated as a ruling on a question of law.①

二、外国法内容查明的方法

被冲突规范所援引的那个外国法的内容,应当由谁来提供证明? 是由诉讼双方当事人提供呢,还是由法官来提供? 这是一个程序性问题,国际上主要有下列几种做法。

(一) 当事人举证证明

持"事实说"的国家认为外国法查明是事实问题,而非法律问题,主张由当事人举证证明,当然地要求争讼当事人承担外国法内容查明的责任,法官仅仅从法律事实的角度审查当事人的举证,并且当事人举证外国法如同当事人举证一般民事证据,承担一般民事举证的责任后果。

在英国,法院对外国法的立场可归纳为四点:第一,外国法是事实而非法律,所以,它们超出了法官应知晓的范围;第二,作为事实,外国法必须通过规范的方式(通常是专家证言)予以证明;第三,对外国法的证明应遵循适用于证明案件其他事实的有关证据规则;第四,如果外国法未被明确主张或当事人未能充分证明外国法,那么法院就会以英国法取而代之②,如拉查兄弟公司诉米德兰银行案(**Lazard Brothers & Co. v. Midland Bank Ltd.**)。

【案例】　　　**Lazard Brothers & Co. v. Midland Bank Ltd.** ③

Facts: Since before the Russian revolution in 1917, Lazard Brothers were owed money by the *Banque Industrielle de Moscow* (the Moscow Bank), a Russian Bank. In 1930, Lazard Brothers obtained a default judgment against the bank. They could not enforce this judgment in Russia so they sought to attach the debts owed by the Midland Bank to the Moscow Bank. However, various decrees made by the Government of Russia between 1917 and 1921 purported to nationalize and liquidate all banks in Russia; and the question was whether the Moscow Bank had been liquidated at the time the default judgment was obtained. If it did not exist at that time, the default judgment was mull and void and has to be set aside.

Held: Whether the Moscow Bank existed as a juristic person or not was a matter for Soviet law; and that was a question of fact to be proved by qualified experts in the foreign law.

---

① David H. Vernon, Louis Weinberg, William Reynolds, William Richman, *Conflicts of Law: Case, Materials and Problems*, 2d ed., LexisNexis, 2002, p.243.
② Richard Fentiman, *Foreign Law In English Courts*, Oxford University Press, 1998, pp.3—4.
③ [1933] AC 289 House of Lords (Lords Buckmaster, Blanesburgh, Warrington, Russell and Wright).

在英国的司法实践中,英国法院依照英国证据法的规定来评定当事人的引证或专家证言,但法院可以不受这些证据的约束。如果法官已经知道外国法,法官也可以直接认定。根据英国《1972年民事证据法》(Civil Evidence Act 1972)第4条第2款之规定,在高等法院、皇家法院、某些其他法院及其上诉法院或枢密院司法委员会的民事或刑事诉讼中得到确认的载有外国法内容的裁定或判决,可以在以后的民事诉讼中作为证明外国法内容的证据。根据《1981年最高法院法》(Supreme Court Act 1981)第69条第5款的规定,外国法这种"事实"问题,不再由陪审团认定,而是由法官直接认定。

在澳大利亚,外国法需要当事人举证,但是法律对举证的要求规定得比较合情合理,外国法无须专家意见即可被作为证据提交给法院(**foreign statutes proved without expert evidence**)。

【说理】　**foreign statutes proved without expert evidence**

In Australia it is up to the parties to provide their own proof of foreign law, as Australian judges have no obligation to apply or ascertain foreign law ex officio. The rules governing proof of foreign law in Australia are more liberal than many would assume. In all Australian jurisdictions except Victoria, foreign statutes can be proved without the necessity for expert evidence.①

在英、美等普通法系国家,当事人可以提出刊载有关法律内容的权威文件(如官方公报、法院判决书中所引证的条款等),也可请专家证明。如果双方当事人对所应适用的外国法有一致理解,双方可向法院提出一项协议声明,法官就据此肯定该外国法的内容,不必再用其他方式证明。如果当事人对外国法的理解不一致,则应各自提出证据证明自己的观点,最后由法官确定。②

(二)法官依职权去查明

持"法律说"的一些欧洲大陆国家认为,外国法是具有与内国法同等效力的法律,如奥地利、意大利、荷兰、苏联及一些东欧国家,还有拉丁美洲的乌拉圭、秘鲁等国。依"法官知法"原则,在这些国家,外国法的查明责任由法官或法院承担,当事人无举证责任。如荷兰的《民事诉讼法》规定,对外国法的内容,法官依职权查明,

---

① James McComish, Pleading and Proving Foreign Law in Australia, 31 *Melbourne U. L. R.* 423 (2007).
② 余先予主编:《冲突法》,上海财经大学出版社1999年版,第138页。

无须当事人举证。①

（三）法院负责查明，也要求当事人予以协助

持"折中说"的国家，如瑞士、德国、南斯拉夫等国认为，外国法是一种性质不同于内国法的法律，主张由法官主导证明，当事人配合法官查证。②

（四）主要由当事人查明，法院必要时予以协助

采取这些做法的国家认为，外国法是一种不同于其他案件事实的事实，主要由当事人证明。法国以及仿效法国法的一些国家同样认为外国法应该被视为事实，但其与单纯的事实不同，是一种具有附属性的事实。③在这些国家里，查明外国法的责任主要在当事人，但如果法院了解有关的外国法，即使当事人未确切地提供该外国法的内容，法院也可以适用该外国法，而且可以依职权采取措施以确定有关外国法的内容。

三、无法查明外国法的解决办法

在一国法院依本国的冲突规范的指定应适用外国法的情况下，如法官无法查明该外国法，当事人也不能举证该外国法时，应当怎么办？各国的理论和实践基本上采取如下解决办法：

（一）直接适用本国法

这是大多数国家所采取的办法。如《波兰国际私法》第7条规定："无法认定外国法的内容或外国法的系属时，适用波兰法。"英国在司法实践中也采取这种做法。

美国法院也采取类似的做法，当事人不能证明外国法时，推定外国法与美国法相同，但这种被推定的法律仅限于普通法系国家的法律（如英国、加拿大和澳大利亚等国家的法律）。④

（二）类推适用法律

"类推"适用同本应适用的外国法相近似或类似的法律。德国曾有案例采取

---

① 参见袁泉：《荷兰国际私法研究》，法律出版社2000年版，第146页。
② 许贝宁：《外国法内容查明的一般理论再思考》，载《2002年中国国际私法年会论文集》，华东政法学院国际法系2002年编印。
③ 参见李双元、谢石松：《国际民事诉讼法概论》，武汉大学出版社2001年版，第153页。
④ 参见黄进：《论国际私法中外国法的查明》，载《河北法学》1990年第6期。

这种做法①,日本也有判例采取这种做法。②但是,从立法上明确规定外国法无法查明时采取"类推"适用的法律规定并不多见。

(三) 驳回诉讼请求

在美国的司法实践中,当外国法为普通法系国家的法律且不能被当事人证明时,法院推定外国法与美国法相同并适用美国法。但是,当外国法为非普通法系国家的法律且不能被当事人证明时,法院就会认为其诉讼请求或抗辩无根据而予以驳回或不加采纳③,如沃尔顿诉阿拉伯美国石油公司案④(<u>Walton v. Arabian American Oil Company</u>)。

【案例】 **Walton v. Arabian American Oil Company**⑤

Facts: An Arkansas citizen, while temporarily Saudi Arabia, was injured when an automobile he was driving collided with a truck owned by defendant and driven by one of defendant's employees. The defendant, incorporated in Delaware, was licensed to do business in New York, the forum, and was doing much business in Saudi Arabia. Because Saudi Arabia law has to be applied as the law the place of plaintiff's injury, failure of the plaintiff to plead and prove that law resulted in a dismissal of his case on the merits. Under a functional system of choice-of-law, however, no law could be chosen as the necessarily applicable law until the content of that law was known.⑥

---

① 在该案例中,一个厄瓜多尔人依其父亲的遗嘱被剥夺了他对其父亲遗产的保留份额的权利,为此而发生争议。当时,第一次世界大战刚刚结束,无法得到《厄瓜多尔民法典》。但是,法院知道,《厄瓜多尔民法典》是以《智利民法典》为模本的,认为适用同《厄瓜多尔民法典》相似的《智利民法典》比适用法院地法(即德国法)似乎更接近于正确的解决方法。参见〔德〕马丁·沃尔夫:《国际私法》,李浩培、汤宗舜译,法律出版社 1988 年版,第 323—324 页。

② 参见〔日〕北胁敏一:《国际私法——国际关系法Ⅱ》,姚梅镇译,法律出版社 1989 年版,第 63—64 页。

③ 参见李双元、金彭年、张茂、欧福勇:《中国国际私法通论》(第二版),法律出版社 2003 年版,第 193 页。

④ 原告是美国阿肯色州的居民。当他在沙特阿拉伯短暂停留时,他驾驶的汽车与被告拥有的、由被告雇员驾驶的卡车相撞,造成原告的重伤。被告是一家在特拉华州成立、在纽约州获得营业执照、在沙特阿拉伯从事经营活动的公司。事故发生后,原告在美国第二巡回区的一个联邦地区法院起诉。原告在诉讼过程中没有就相关的沙特阿拉伯法律的内容提出主张和进行举证,被告在答辩中也没有就该法律提出主张和提供证据。上诉法院认为:根据联邦的一般规则,外国法是一种待当事人证明的事实,如果当事人提供的证明可以作为证据,则法院必须接受。原告没有提供沙特阿拉伯法,因而法院不愿意也不可能接受原告的主张。结果,上诉法院维持原判,驳回原告上诉。

⑤ 233 F2d 541 (2d Cir.), cert. denied, 352 U. S. 872, 77 S. Ct. 97, 1 L. ED. 2d 77 (1956).

⑥ Russell J Weintraub, *Commentary on the Conflict of Laws*, 4th ed., New York Foundation Press, 2001, pp. 111—112.

（四）默示推定

在当事人无法提供外国法的时候,可以将当事人自愿将案件提交法院处理,作为当事人的默示意思表示,表明当事人同时也愿意将法院地法适用于其案件,如美国新泽西州最高法院在<u>利亚雷案</u>中的做法就是一个典型的例子。

【案例】　　　　　　　　利 亚 雷 案

本案原被告均为美国人,双方曾在法国签订一个借款合同,约定适用法国法,因合同争议诉于美国新泽西州法院。根据有关的冲突规则,应该适用法国法。但原告未能提供或证明有关的法国法律,被告主张应因此驳回原告的诉讼请求。初审法院支持了这一主张。

原告不服,提起上诉,上诉法院维持原判。原告又上诉到新泽西州最高法院。新泽西州最高法院在承认依普通法原则外国法以及美国其他州的法律由当事人作为事实加以证明后始得适用的同时,认为如果不能证明外国法,法院就像对待不能证明诉因或抗辩的事实一样而驳回诉讼,这样做不公正,为解决这一问题,法院推定当事人默许适用法院地法即新泽西州法,依据该法推翻了原判。

在 <u>Erie Railroad Co. v. Tompkins</u> 一案中,美国法院也采取了默示推定的方式来确定案件的准据法。

【案例】　　　Erie Railroad Co. v. Tompkins①

Tompkins was struck by an object projecting from one of the defendants's trains while walking along a railroad right of way in Pennsylvania. He sued the defendant for damages in a federal diversity action in the Southern District of New York. The district court and the court of appeals applied general tort law and allowed recovery, despite the defendant's argument that the issue of liability was one of local law and that Pennsylvania precedent has settled that Tompkins was a trespasser to whom the railroad was not liable for ordinary negligence.

又如在 **Lee v. M/V Gem of Madras** 一案中,美国德州法院在当事人未提供外国法的情况下,适用了法院地法作为本案的准据法。

---

① 304 U. S. 64, 58 S. Ct. 817, 82 L. Ed. 1188, 11 O. O. 246 (1938).

【案例】　　　　　　　Lee v. M/V Gem of Madras①

　　Lee v. M/V Gem of Madras is a claim by a Hong Kong based oil company for fuel delivered in Korea to a ship, the Gem of Madras, registered in India. After defendant ignored plaintiff's $233550 invoice for 1125 metric tons of fuel, plaintiff had the ship seized in Houston and then filed an admiralty claim for breach of contract. Admiralty claims filed in the United States are governed by federal law, which includes a choice-of-law rule based on federal common law requiring the court to consider the place of the wrongful act, the law of the ship's flag, the parties' allegiance or domicile, the place of contracting, the inaccessibility of a foreign forum, and the law of the forum. The court was puzzled why neither party demonstrated the applicability of United States admiralty law to an event having nothing to do with the United States other than the site of seizure but nonetheless applied local law because of the parties' failure to object or plead anything else.

　　美国法院认为,当事人未能就相关的准据法提出任何证明(**If the parties fail to raise the issue of choice of law**),法院应适用法院地法。

【说理】　　　　**If the parties fail to raise the issue of choice of law**

　　If the parties fail to raise the issue of choice of law, the court is not obligated to do so on its own. There is no evidence that either side has argued for application of foreign law. The failure of the parties to alert the court in pleading or otherwise constitutes a waiver of this issue. When both parties have been silent on the issues of which law to apply, it can be said that they have acquiesced in the application of the forum law. This view agrees with that of the Restatement (Second) of the Conflict of Laws which calls for the application of forum law where no or little information regarding the foreign law has been supplied.②

四、我国关于外国法查明的有关规定

（一）关于外国法内容查明的方法

　　对于外国法内容的查明方法,我国早期立法并没有明文规定③,但在最高人民法院《关于贯彻执行〈中华人民共和国民法通则〉若干问题的意见(试行)》(以下简称《意见》)以及我国与其他国家所签订的司法协助条约中,对外国法的查明方法

---

① No. Civ. A. H-05-0631, 2006 WL 568545 at 1 (S. D. Tex. 2006).
② David H. Vernon, Louis Weinberg, William Reynolds, William Richmonan, *Conflicts of Law: Case, Materials and Problems*, 2nd ed., LexisNexis, 2002, p.27.
③ 参见黄进:《论国际私法中外国法的查明》,载《河北法学》1990年第6期。

有着具体的规定。《意见》第193条规定：对于应当适用的外国法律，可通过下列途径查明：(1) 由当事人提供；(2) 由与我国订立司法协助协定的缔约对方的中央机关提供；(3) 由我国驻该国使领馆提供；(4) 由该国驻我国使领馆提供；(5) 由中外法律专家提供。而1988年的《中华人民共和国和法兰西共和国关于民事、商事司法协助的协定》第28条规定：有关缔约一方的法律、法规、习惯法和司法实践的证明，可以由本国的外交代表或领事代表机关或者其他有资格的机关或个人以出具证明书的方式提交给缔约另一方法院。

1988年2月8日生效的《中华人民共和国关于民事、商事司法协助协定》第28条规定："有关缔约一方的法律、法规、习惯法和司法实践的证明，可以由本国的外交和领事代表机关或者其他的有资格机关或个人以出具证明书的方式提交给另一方法院。"该协定了表明了当事人对外国法查明的责任。

我国自2011年4月1日起施行的《涉外民事关系法律适用法》第10条规定："涉外民事关系适用的外国法律，由人民法院、仲裁机构或者行政机关查明。当事人选择适用外国法律的，应当提供该国法律。"

从以上规定可以看出，在我国，法院、仲裁机构或者行政机关承担着查明外国法的责任，对涉外民商事诉讼中所应当适用的外国法，法院、仲裁机构或者行政机关有义务予以查明。在确定外国法的内容时，既尊重当事人提供的有关资料，也重视通过其他途径由法院进行调查，而不是把查明外国法内容的责任完全归置于当事人。当然，法院查明外国法的方法是多种多样的，可以通过外交、司法协助途径，也可以通过法律专家证言的方式，同时，当事人在提供外国法内容方面也起着重要作用。

（二）外国法无法查明时的处理

在我国，当外国法无法查明时，依最高人民法院的《意见》，法院应当适用中国法。我国自2011年4月1日起施行的《涉外民事关系法律适用法》也确认了这一做法。该法第10条规定："不能查明外国法律或者该国法律没有规定的，适用中华人民共和国法律。"这是世界上许多国家所采取的普遍做法。在**渣打（亚洲）有限公司诉广西壮族自治区华建公司案**中，南宁市中级人民法院即在无法查明香港法的情况下，适用了中国法。

【案例】 渣打（亚洲）有限公司诉广西壮族自治区华建公司案

被告广西壮族自治区华建公司在广西南宁市与香港东方城市有限公司签订了《桂林华侨饭店合营企业公司合同》。合同约定，由双方合资兴建并经营桂林华侨饭店。合同签订后,东方城市有限公司与原告渣打(亚洲)有限公司(Standard Chartered Asia Ltd.)签订了一份《贷款协议》。协议约定,东方城市有限公司为中国的合营公司桂林华侨饭店的营造向原告借款2877万港元,并约定此笔贷款由被告担保。同日,应东方城市有限公司与原告的要求,被告向原告出具了一份不可撤销的、无条件的、凭要求即付的《担保书》,并约定该担保书受香港法律管辖,按照香港法律解释。同日,该担保书经广州市公证处公证。后借款人未全额清偿借款,原告向南宁市中级人民法院起诉,要求法院判令被告作为担保人立即偿还贷款本金和利息。

南宁市中级人民法院经审理认为:本案合同约定适用香港法律,原告只提供香港律师出具的法律意见书,证实香港商业贷款的可强制执行性,但此种证明方法所证明的内容是否确实,原告不能举证证实,法院通过其他途径也未能查明香港有关法律的规定,故本案应当适用中华人民共和国法律。①

根据最高人民法院的《意见》第193条的规定,通过法定的几条途径都不能查明应适用的外国法律的,适用中华人民共和国法律。本案中,合同约定适用香港法律,但是未能查明香港有关法律的规定。本案在法院根据上述规定无法查证香港法律的情况下,适用中华人民共和国法律作为处理本案的依据,是正确的。

第五节 公共秩序保留

在国际私法中,公共秩序是一个传统且广为接受的概念,它是一项拒绝适用外国法律的法定理由。②

一、公共秩序概说

所谓公共秩序(**public order**),是指国家或社会的重大利益或法律和道德的基本原则。根据各国的普遍实践和许多国际私法公约的规定,在一国依内国冲突规范的指定本应对某一国际民商事关系适用外国法时,如其适用将与内国的公共秩

---

① http://china.findlaw.cn/info/case/jjal/3911.html.
② David McClean, Morris: *The Conflict of Laws*, 5th ed., Sweet & Maxwell, 2000, p.47.

序相抵触,法院即可排除该外国法的适用。①

【释义】   public order

Public order or *ordre public* is the body of fundamental principles that underpin the operation of legal systems in each state. This addresses the social, moral and economic values that tie a society together: values that vary in different cultures and change over time.

公共秩序,各国的称谓颇不一致,在法语国家中称 ordre public;在西班牙语中称 orden publico;而在英、美学者中又称"公共政策"(public policy);德国学者多喜欢称之为"保留条款"或"排除条款"(vorbenhaltsklausel, ausschie bungsklausel)。② 在我国国际私法学界,目前多称"公共秩序保留"或直接称"公共秩序"。在各国立法中,对公共秩序的表述也各不相同。③

二、适用公共秩序的情况

一般认为,公共秩序适用于以下四种情况：

第一,按内国冲突规范原应适用的外国法,如果予以适用将与内国关于道德、社会、经济、文化或意识形态的基本准则相抵触,或者与内国的公平、正义观念或根本的法律制度相抵触,因而拒绝适用外国法。在这种情况下,公共秩序对法律适用起着一种安全阀的作用,其作用是消极的,即不适用原应适用的外国法。

第二,一国民商法中的一部分法律规则,由于其属于公共秩序法的范畴,在该国有绝对效力,从而不适用与之相抵触的外国法。这里,公共秩序保留肯定内国法的绝对效力,其作用是积极的。

第三,按照内国冲突规则应适用的外国法,如果予以适用,将违反国际法的强行规则、内国所负担的条约义务或国际社会所一般承认的正义要求时,适用外国法将违反国际公共秩序,法院可以不予适用外国法。

---

① 黄进:《国际私法上的公共秩序问题》,载《武汉大学学报》(社会科学版)1991 年第 6 期。
② 参见李双元、金彭年、张茂、欧福勇:《中国国际私法通论》(第二版),法律出版社 2003 年版,第 169 页。
③ 1986 年《联邦德国民法施行法》称为"德国法律的基本原则";《日本法例》称为"公共秩序或善良风俗";1984 年《秘鲁民法典》第 2049 条则称为"国际公共政策或善良风俗";我国《民法通则》则把公共秩序表述为"中华人民共和国的社会公共利益"。参见金彭年:《论国际私法上的公共秩序》,载《杭州大学学报》(哲社版)1989 年第 1 期。

三、我国的公共秩序保留制度

我国在立法上已有关于公共秩序制度的规定。我国《民法通则》第八章第 150 条作为一条通则性的公共秩序条款，没有使用"公共秩序"这样的措辞，而是规定："依照本章规定适用外国法律或者国际惯例的，不能违背中华人民共和国的社会公共利益。"显然，在解释上，"社会公共利益"应与通用的"公共秩序"同义。应注意的是，较之于其他国家的同类法律条文，《民法通则》中这一公共秩序条款的矛头所向，不仅是依我国冲突规范本应适用但却违背我国社会公共利益的外国法律，而且还包括那些违背我国社会公共利益的国际惯例。①这可以说是我国公共秩序条款的独特之处。

我国自 2011 年 4 月 1 日起施行的《涉外民事关系法律适用法》再次确认了"社会公共利益"至上的原则。该法第 5 条规定："外国法律的适用将损害中华人民共和国社会公共利益的，适用中华人民共和国法律。"

公共秩序制度具有很大的灵活性，究竟在何种情况和什么条件下才能适用，在法律上不可能也没有必要作出具体的硬性规定。从目前我国的国情来看，我们认为，我国的公共秩序至少应包括以下几方面的内容：(1) 适用外国法有损于我国国家主权和安全或者有害于我们国家的统一和民族的团结的；(2) 适用外国法违反我国宪法的基本精神，包括四项基本原则的；(3) 适用外国法违反我国主要法律的基本原则的，如婚姻法关于禁止重婚的原则；(4) 适用外国法违背我国根据所参加的或者缔结的条约所承担的义务的；(5) 如果外国法院无理拒绝承认我国法律的效力的，根据对等原则，我们也可以拒绝适用该国的法律。②

【思考题】

- 什么是国际私法中的识别？为什么要进行识别？
- 什么是反致？反致有什么利弊？
- 法律规避的构成条件和效力如何界定？
- 外国法无法查明时，法院如何处理已经受理的涉外案件？
- 什么是公共秩序保留？公共秩序保留在国际私法中起着怎样的作用？

---

① 参见李双元、金彭年、张茂、欧福勇：《中国国际私法通论》（第二版），法律出版社 2003 年版，第 185 页。
② 徐冬根、薛凡：《中国国际私法完善研究》，上海社会科学院出版社 1998 年版，第 195—196 页。

【重要术语提示与中英文对照】

中文术语	英文对照
识别、定性	characterization
定类	classification
定质	qualification
反致	renvoi, remission
转致	transmission
间接反致	indirect remission
双重反致	double renvoi
外国法院说	foreign courts theory
连接点	point of contact
福果案	Forgo's Case
法律规避	evasion of law
诈欺规避	fraudulent evasion of law
鲍富莱蒙王妃离婚案	Bauffremont's Divorce Case
佛莱案	Ferrai Case
外国法的查明	proof of foreign law
拉查兄弟公司诉米德兰银行案	Lazard Brothers & Co v. Midland Bank Ltd.
1972年民事证据法	Civil Evidence Act 1972
1981年最高法院法	Supreme Court Act 1981
沃尔顿诉阿拉伯美国石油公司案	Walton v. Arabian American Oil Company
公共秩序	ordre public
公共政策	public policy

【推荐阅读文献】

- 时琴:《对国际私法中法律规避问题的思考》,载《云南大学学报法学版》2004 年第 1 期。
- 刘萍、马慧珠:《公共秩序保留制度及其在我国的运用》,载《理论导刊》2003 年 7 月。
- 郭玉军:《近年中国外国法查明与适用的理论与实践》,载《武大国际法评论》(第七期),武汉大学出版社 2007 年版。
- 徐冬根:《国际私法趋势论》,北京大学出版社 2007 年版。
- 屈广清:《英国识别问题研究——兼论中国国际私法识别制度之完善》,载《福建法学》2008 年第 1 期。

- 闫卫军:《论冲突法上的识别与识别冲突——兼及冲突法制度本身的不足》,载《政治与法律》2009 年第 4 期。
- 黄梓东、冯霞:《冲突法域反致制度的价值考量及实现》,载《求索》2012 年第 7 期。
- Eric Engle, European Law in American Courts: Foreign Law as Evidence of Domestic Law, 33 *Ohio N. U. L. Rev.* 99 (2007).
- Austen L. Parrish, Storm in a Teacup: The U. S. Supreme Court's Use of Foreign Law, 2007 *U. Ill. L. Rev.* 637 (2007).
- Yeo, Common Law Innovations in Proving Foreign Law, 12 *Ybk. Priv. Int'l L.* 493 (2010).
- Forsyth, Certainty Versus Uniformity: Renvoi in the Context of Movable Property, 6 *J. Priv. Int'l L.* 637 (2010).
- Esplugues, Luis Iglesias & Palao (eds.), Application of Foreign Law (2011).
- Pitel, The Canadian Codification of Forum Non Conveniens, 7 *J. Priv. Int'l L.* 251 (2011).
- Whytoc, The Evolving Forum Shopping System, 96 *Cornell L. Rev.* 481 (2011).
- Susanne L. Goessl, Preliminary Questions in EU Private International Law, 8 *J. Priv. Int. L.* 63 (2012).

【扩展阅读资料】

The status of foreign law[①]

> Generally, when the court is to apply a foreign law, it must be proved by foreign law experts. It cannot merely be pleaded, as the court has no expertise in the laws of foreign countries nor in how they might be applied in a foreign court. Such foreign law may be considered no more than evidence, rather than law because of the issue of sovereignty. If the local court is actually giving extraterritorial effect to a foreign law, it is less than sovereign and so acting in a way that is potentially unconstitutional. The theoretical responses to this issue are:
>
> • (a) that each court has an inherent jurisdiction to apply the laws of another country where it is necessary to achieving a just outcome; or
>
> • (b) that the local court creates a right in its own laws to match that available under the foreign law. This explanation is sustainable because, even in states

---

① http://en.wikipedia.org/wiki/Conflict_of_laws.

which apply a system of binding legal precedents, any precedent emerging from a conflicts case can only apply to future conflicts cases. There will be no ratio decidendi that binds future litigants in entirely local cases.

- (c) that the notional court, when applying a foreign law, doesn't give an extraterritorial effect but recognize, through its own "conflict of laws rule", that the situation at hand falls under the scope of application of the foreign rule. In order to understand this argument one must first define the notion of extraterritorial application of a rule. This notion is susceptible to two distinct meanings:

On the one hand, this notion is used to describe the situation where a local court applies a rule other than the *Lex fori* (local law).

On the other hand, it could mean that the rule is being applied to a factual situation that occurred beyond the territory of its state of origin. As an example of this situation, one can think of an American court applying British tort statutes and case law to a car accident that took place in London where both the driver and the victim are British citizens but the lawsuit was brought in before the American courts because the driver's insurer is American. One can then argue that since the factual situation is within the British territory, where an American judge applies the English Law, he does not give an extraterritorial application to the foreign rule. In fact, one can also argue that the American judge, had he applied American Law, would be doing so in an extraterritorial fashion.

Once the *lex causae* has been selected, it will be respected except when it appears to contravene an overriding mandatory rule of the *lex fori*. Each judge is the guardian of his own principles of *ordre public* (public order) and the parties cannot, by their own act, oust the fundamental principles of the local municipal law which generally underpin areas such as labour law, insurance, competition regulation, agency rules, embargoes, import-export regulations, and securities exchange regulations. Furthermore, the *lex fori* will prevail in cases where an application of the *lex causae* would otherwise result in a fundamentally immoral outcome, or give extraterritorial effect to confiscatory or other territorially limited laws.

In some countries, there is occasional evidence of parochialism when courts have determined that if the foreign law cannot be proved to a "satisfactory standard", then local law may be applied. In the United Kingdom, in the absence of evidence being led, the foreign law is presumed to be the same as the *lex fori*. Similarly, judges might assume in default of express evidence to the contrary that the place where the cause of action arose would provide certain basic protections, e.g. that the foreign court would provide a remedy to someone who was injured due to the negligence of another.

Finally, some American courts have held that local law will be applied if the injury occurred in an "uncivilized place that has no law or legal system."

> If the case has been submitted to arbitration rather than a national court, say because of a forum selection clause, an arbitrator may decide not to apply local mandatory policies in the face of a choice of law by the parties if this would defeat their commercial objectives. However, the arbitral award may be challenged in the country where it was made or where enforcement is sought by one of the parties on the ground that the relevant *ordre public* should have been applied. If the *lex loci arbitri* has been ignored, but there was no real and substantial connection between the place of arbitration and the agreement made by the parties, a court in which enforcement is sought may well accept the tribunal's decision. But if the appeal is to the courts in the state where the arbitration was held, the judge cannot ignore the mandatory provisions of the *lex fori*.

第三章

国际私法的立法发展

第三章 国际私法的立法发展

本章导读

※ 万民法是罗马时期"各民族共有"的法律,是通过罗马外事裁判官的司法活动制定,并被罗马国家用强制力保证实行的适用于罗马公民与非罗马公民之间的法律。

※ 1804年《法国民法典》对世界国际私法的发展产生了深远的影响。其中最重要的影响在属人法方面,它用当事人的本国法代替了住所地法。

※ 英美普通法系国家国际私法的历史显示了英美普通法系国家国际私法的两大特点:固守法律属地原则及追求法律管辖和适用的有效性。

※ 《冲突法重述》是美国国际私法法典化过程中的重要产物。由哈佛大学法学院比尔教授任报告员编纂的美国1934年《第一次冲突法重述》体现了既得权学说的主要观点并有所发展。1971年以里斯教授为主报告人发表的《第二次冲突法重述》,取代了《第一次冲突法重述》,确立了更加灵活更富有弹性的法律选择判断标准。

※ 法典化,不仅仅限于国家权力机关对法律规范的编纂活动和系统化工作,也包括学者、专家或由其组成的社会团体、学术团体草拟系统化法律文件和对法律文件的编纂工作。

※ 国际私法的法典化主要通过两种进路:一种是国际私法的专门化立法,另一种是国际私法法律适用规范的重述。前者以欧洲大陆法系奥地利和瑞士国际私法立法为代表,后者以美国的两次《冲突法重述》为代表。

※ 海牙国际私法会议在国际私法条约化运动中发挥了极为重要的作用。从1893年9月12日第一届海牙国际私法会议在荷兰的海牙举行开始,至今已持续一百多年。

※ 国际统一私法协会是一个专门从事私法统一的政府间国际组织,成立于1926年,总部设在意大利的罗马。中国于1986年1月1日起已正式成为其会员国。

※ 欧盟通过制定条约、颁布"指令"和制定"规则"的方式来进行国际私法的统一活动。其"指令"对所有成员国具有约束力,但是成员国有权选择贯彻和实施这种指令的形式和方法。其"规则"一般具有完全的约束力,并可以在成员国直接适用。

【**本章主题词**】 万民法、法国民法典、冲突法重述、法典化、统一化运动、海牙国际私法会议、国际统一私法协会

第一节　萌芽期间的欧洲国际私法立法

一、罗马万民法与自然法精神

第一个在国际私法历史中显示其对国际私法价值有着重要贡献的当数罗马的万民法(*jus gentium*)。在古罗马，随着商业的发展和罗马征服地区的扩大，罗马公民与异邦人以及被征服地区的居民之间关于适用法律的矛盾越来越突出。异邦人和被征服地区的居民不能享有罗马公民权，不受市民法(*jus civile*)保护。为了调整其内部以及他们与罗马公民相互之间的权利义务关系，公元3世纪产生了万民法。

【释义】　　　　　　　　　　　*jus gentium*

　　Jus gentium means law of nations. In legal theory, that law which natural reason establishes for all men, as distinguished from *jus civile*, or the civil law peculiar to one state or people. Roman lawyers and magistrates originally devised *jus gentium* as a system of equity applying to cases between foreigners and Roman citizens. *Jus gentium* was the part of Roman law that the Roman Empire applied to its dealings with foreigners, especially provincial subjects. Today the Latin term applies the body of laws that makes up international law.

所谓万民法，意思是"各民族共有"的法律，是通过罗马外事裁判官的司法活动制定，并被罗马国家用强制力保证实行的适用于罗马公民与非罗马公民之间的法律。该法绝大部分是调整财产关系，特别是有关所有权和债权关系的实体规范，也有确定外邦人民事法律地位的规范。

万民法作为解决法律冲突的最初形式，是属地性质的国内法，但其内容却是罗马当时势力范围所及的所有国家的共同规则。并且，万民法的适用范围已超出罗马，"最初它适用于意大利半岛各民族，后来则被推广于东方希腊、马其顿等民族"[①]。

[①] 法学教材编辑部罗马法编写组：《罗马法》，群众出版社1983年版，第62页。

万民法自创立之初即体现了自然法的精神。自然法表示一种对公正或正义秩序的信念,这种正义适用于所有为宇宙间最高控制力量支配的人,它不同于实在法。一切自然法学说的出发点是"理性"和"人性"。自然法思想的基础由古希腊哲学家所创设①,法学家们直接而深刻地接受了这一思想,将自然法理论贯注于罗马法,特别是万民法,力图使万民法成为"适于各种人、代表了善良愿望的法和习惯"。古罗马法学家盖尤斯甚至认为万民法就是自然法。②

二、欧洲属人主义时期

属人法(**personal law**)萌芽于罗马时期。

【释义】　　　　　　　　　personal law

Early Romans developed the idea of "personal law," or the idea that "questions concerning an individual's personal status, such as family relationships, were governed by the law of the person's place of residence or citizenship."③

公元476年西罗马帝国灭亡后,欧洲大陆进入一个属人主义的发展阶段。现代国际私法上的"属人法"同这个时期的属人主义不无联系。④这个时期的属人主义是绝对的和极端的属人主义,因为它所奉行的是,一个人无论在什么地方都只受其所属民族的法律支配。这同现代国际私法中建立在法律选择基础上的"属人法"的意义有很大的不同,尽管现代国际私法上的"属人法"是在早期属人主义基础上逐渐嬗变而来的。不过,在这个时期,有时当事人可以指定并非其本民族的法律,而是他们所愿意服从的法律。这是最早的背离属人的民族法原则的例子。而且,在当时的法兰克帝国,国王所颁布的敕令适用于其帝国的全部领土,这些敕令已经是属地性的而不是属人性的了。

10世纪以后,至少在法兰西和德意志,各民族的古老的"属人法"逐渐被属地性的法律代替。封建主对属地范围内的臣民具有绝对的属地管辖权(**feudal lord governed anyone who came under his control**)。

---

① 参见〔英〕D.M.沃克:《牛津法律大辞典》,邓正来等译,光明日报出版社1988年版,第629页。
② 参见沈娟:《冲突法及其价值导向》(修订本),中国政法大学出版社2002年版,第71页。
③ Susan L. Stevens, Commanding International Judicial Respect: Reciprocity and the Recognition and Enforcement of Foreign Judgments, 26 *Hastings Int'l & Comp. L. Rev.* 115, 118 (2002).
④ 参见〔德〕马丁·沃尔夫:《国际私法》,李浩培等译,法律出版社1988年版,第43—44页。

【释义】 feudal lord governed anyone who came under his control

A flaw further exposed by the development of feudalism between the 10th and 12th centuries. The feudal development of defined territories, where "the word of the feudal lord governed anyone who came under his control," introduced the idea of sovereignty, defined as "supreme dominion, authority or rule... of an independent state."①

三、基辅俄罗斯王国的规定

公元911年,基辅俄罗斯王国与希腊人订立了一个条约,其中第13条涉及俄罗斯人在希腊死亡后的遗产处理问题。这条规定的大意是:如在希腊的俄罗斯人死亡,其财产未经遗嘱处置,且在希腊无亲人的,则其财产应发回俄罗斯,交其幼辈近亲属;如其财产已经遗嘱处置,则其财产由其指定的继承其产业的人接受。隆茨认为,这是一条古老的国际私法法则,虽然该法则还不是内容完整的冲突规范,但它确实是解决涉外民事法律冲突的一条规则,可以说是国际私法的萌芽。②

四、英国的习惯法

在英国国际私法发展史上,英国人始终保存了习惯法的悠久传统。这种传统证明英国人是轻视理想、注重实效的民族。他们习惯于从已在过去的案件里取得了实际效果的判决中寻找现在或将来案件判决的可循之章。③他们感到成文法会使他们在实践中因看不到针对性和无法预见后果而不知所措。法律理论和成文法在英美法中因缺乏必要性而发育不良,英国国际私法的力量在于法律管辖和适用的有效性。

第二节 近代国际私法立法

受早期罗马法的影响,近代国际私法在欧洲大陆得到了发展(**development in**

---

① Joel R. Paul, Comity in International Law, 32 *Harv. Int'l L. J.* 1, 13—14 (1991).
② 参见〔苏联〕隆茨:《苏联国际私法教程》,顾世荣译,台湾大东书局1951年版,第48页。
③ 参见沈娟:《冲突法及其价值导向》(修订本),中国政法大学出版社2002年版,第80页。

Continental)。欧洲大陆一大批国际私法学者致力于法律冲突的解决,提出各种学术观点和理论,起草了相关冲突规范,用于解决法律冲突。

【释义】　　　　　development in Continental

During the rise of Universities in the Middle Ages, scholars in Italy rediscovered Romand Law and begain to develop doctrines for the resolution of conflicting laws and customs that abounded in northern Italy and southern Franch. The study of Roman law as a universal common law and the need to reconcile local laws (statuta) gererated the law of conflicts of laws. The interplay between the power of a sovereign to govern persons, property, and transaction within its territory and the claim of individuals abroad to the protection of the laws of their own country had to be resolved. The Italian statutists attempted to devide the statutes into categories real and personal to sort out this inteply.[①]

一、《巴伐利亚法典》和《普鲁士法典》

18 世纪中叶以后,欧洲大陆的立法者开始将国际私法规则订入民法典中。在这些法典中,第一个法典是 1756 年《巴伐利亚法典》。该法典采取了法则说所主张的几个原则,但没有采取动产随人的规则,而是规定无论不动产还是动产,均适用财产所在地法。

1794 年《普鲁士法典》也采取了法则说所主张的一些原则,但对有关合同成立要件和效力等问题的法律适用,未作规定。值得一提的是,该法典在国际私法规则中采取了"维持法律行为效力"的原则。它规定,如果一个人有两个住所,其中一个住所地的法律认为他的合同行为或其他行为有效,而另一个住所地的法律认为无效,那么以前一个法律为准。

二、《法国民法典》和受其影响的其他民法典

在 1804 年《法国民法典》(**French Civil Code**)中,国际私法条文并不多,且其规定并不是很明确和无可挑剔,但该法典对后世国际私法的发展产生了深远的影响。其中最重要的影响就是,在属人法方面,它用当事人的本国法代替了住所地法。

---

① Luther L. McDougal III, Robert L. Felix, Ralph U. Whitten, *American Conflicts Law: Cases and Materials*, 4th ed., LexisNexis, 2004, p.5.

【释义】　　　　　　　　**French Civil Code**

The French Civil Code, originally called the *Code civil des Français*, or *Code Napoléon*, established under Napoléon I. It was drafted rapidly by a commission of four eminent jurists and entered into force on March 21, 1804. Even though the Napoleonic code was not the first legal code to be established in a European country with a civil legal system. it is considered the first successful codification and strongly influenced the law of many other countries. The Code, with its stress on clearly written and accessible law, was a major step in establishing the rule of law. Historians have called it "one of the few documents which have influenced the whole world."

受《法国民法典》影响的民法典主要有《奥地利民法典》(1811 年)、《塞尔维亚民法典》(1844 年)、《智利民法典》(1851 年)、《希腊民法典》(1851 年)、《罗马尼亚民法典》(1865 年)、《意大利民法典》(1865 年)、《魁北克民法典》(1866 年)、《葡萄牙民法典》(1867 年)、《阿根廷民法典》(1871 年)和《西班牙民法典》(1888 年)等,这些法典对国际私法的法律适用规范作出了规定。

值得一提的是,1829 年荷兰制定了一个《国王立法之总则》,单独对国际私法规范作出规定,这是将国际私法规范同民法典相分离之始。①

三、苏黎世国际私法立法和萨克森王国国际私法立法

在 20 世纪之前欧洲的国际私法立法中,1854 年的苏黎世国际私法立法和 1863 年的萨克森王国国际私法立法是两个重要的国际私法立法。②

1854 年苏黎世国际私法立法吸收了当时国际私法领域中的重要理论和学说,并结合瑞士苏黎世州的涉外民事司法实践加以规定,是理论与实践相结合的典范。该立法是在瑞士著名的法学家布伦茨基(Bluntschi)的直接主持下制定的。③该立法的前部包含了 7 条国际私法的法律适用规范。这些规范以"法律适用"为标题,对自然人的能力、家庭关系、物权、债权以及行为方式的法律适用作出了相应的规定。④ 这在当时来说,是一项最为系统、完整的国际私法立法。

---

① 参见梅仲协:《国际私法新论》,台湾三民书局 1984 年版,第 52 页。
② 参见徐冬根:《19 世纪国际私法立法拾遗》,载《法学杂志》1994 年第 4 期。
③ 布伦茨基 1808 年出生于瑞士苏黎世州,他在柏林求学期间曾与国际私法大师萨维尼相识,在波恩获得法学博士后,布伦茨基于 1830 年回到苏黎世州,被聘任为罗马法教授,1836 年又被聘为德国法、瑞士法教授。以后,布伦茨基开始步入政界,1837 年至 1848 年起担任苏黎世州大执政官,并奉命起草苏黎世私法典。
④ 由于受萨维尼的影响,苏黎世国际私法立法在处理涉外家庭关系和涉外继承关系时,以当事人的国籍作为主要连接因素,而摒弃了"住所"这一连接因素;该立法还肯定了反致制度。

萨克森王国国际私法立法见诸于 1863 年的《民法典》第 6 条至第 19 条。萨克森王国国际私法规范和法律适用制度的基本原则是"适用法院地国法",外国法只在例外的情况下才予以适用。①萨克森王国国际私法立法以国籍作为连接因素,这是因为当时在萨克森王国国籍比住所更为确定。

四、1865 年《意大利民法典》

1865 年《意大利民法典》中的国际私法规范是在著名国际私法学家孟西尼主持下制定的。根据 1865 年 4 月 2 日的一项法令,孟西尼成为专家委员会的成员,负责对意大利的民法典进行修订。1865 年《意大利民法典》中的国际私法立法的一个显著特点是,法律适用规范皆采用双边冲突规范的方式。在民事权利方面,它抛弃了歧视外国人的做法,不再提"意大利人"、"本国人"或"外国人",而是统称为"自然人"。此外,该法典的另一个特点是以国籍作为属人法的连接因素。

五、1896 年《德国民法施行法》

1896 年《德国民法施行法》是 19 世纪国内国际私法立法的最高成就的代表,该法第 7 至 31 条为国际私法规范。《德国民法施行法》涉及 7 个方面的问题:涉外民事法律关系中当事人法律地位的确定、法律行为的方式、侵权行为、婚姻家庭关系、继承关系、反致制度和公共秩序保留制度。《德国民法施行法》作为人类历史上首次系统规定民事法律冲突问题的成文法,把国际私法的立法工作大大向前推进了一步。这部法律中的国际私法规定在德国适用了 90 年,直到 1986 年才为新的国际私法法规所代替。当然,它作为近现代第一部系统的国际私法,不可避免地具有它的不成熟性,这主要表现在两方面:第一,它采用的冲突规范主要是单边冲突规范;第二,它局限于与人身有关的民事关系,而物权、债权的法律冲突的解决并没有囊括在内。第三,其冲突规范大多以当事人的本国法为属人法。

六、1898 年《日本法例》

1898 年《日本法例》是国际私法发展史上第一部单行的国际私法法规,共 31 条,经过 1942 年、1947 年、1964 年、1989 年几次修改,现在仍在适用。《日本法例》在内容上受到 1896 年《德国民法施行法》的影响,其中有些规定甚至是后者的复制。但是,其规定在形式上同 1896 年《德国民法施行法》有极大的不同,即没有采用单边冲突规范的形式,而采用了双边冲突规范的形式。《日本法例》主要规定了

---

① See F. K. Juenger, *Choice of Law and Multistate Justice*, Martinus Nijhoff, 1993, pp. 32—34.

下列问题:冲突法总的原则、涉外民事法律关系当事人的法律地位、法律行为的成立效力及方式、物权及其他应登记的权利、法定债权的成立效力及债权的让与、涉外婚姻家庭关系、涉外继承关系等。《日本法例》是19世纪最完善的国际私法立法,但它对合同之债的法律适用未作出明确的规定。

七、普通法系国家的国际私法立法

英美普通法系国家国际私法的历史显示了英美普通法系国家国际私法的两大特点:固守法律属地原则及追求法律管辖和适用的有效性。①英国普通法的这些原因导致英国国际私法(**English private international law**)在18世纪中叶以前发展缓慢。

【释义】　　　　　English private international law

The English law on the conflict of laws actually originated only in the middle of the eighteenth century, when other countries of Europe already had a developed system of rules governing conflicts of laws. The late birth of this branch of the law in England was due, it is submitted, to the special features of the English common law and of the English system of administration of justice...as they prevailed in the course of the previous centuries. These special features of the law and of the administration of justice left their imprint upon the course of development of the English law on conflicts of laws in nineteenth century.②

19世纪,英、美的国际私法主要寓于判例法中③,但在一些单行的立法中也有国际私法的规定。例如,英国1837年《遗嘱法》、1861年《遗嘱法》、1868年《判决延伸法》、1882年《汇票法》、1892年《涉外婚姻法》和1894年《商船法》均含有国际私法规范。19世纪中叶开始,英国国际私法逐步进入勃兴时期,并迅速得到发展。④

---

① 沈娟:《冲突法及其价值导向》(修订本),中国政法大学出版社2002年版,第83页。
② See Luther L. McDougal III, Robert L. Felix, Ralph U. Whitten, *American Conflicts Law: Cases and Materials*, 4th ed., LexisNexis, 2004, p.7.
③ 19世纪的英、美的判例国际私法有如下的共同点:第一,形成了在国际私法上的英美体系(Anglo-American System)。第二,否定外国法的域外效力,把内国法院适用外国法问题,看做是出于礼让或对外国既得权的尊重。第三,重视对判例实践的研究。第四,在实践中对国际法律冲突和区际法律冲突基本上不加区分。第五,坚持以住所地法为属人法。第六,在处理具体涉外案件和制定冲突法规范时,注意追求简单、方便与判决的一致性。
④ 参见陈小云、屈广清:《英国国际私法勃兴之时代背景探析及启示》,载《东南学术》2010年第2期。

第三节　当代国际私法立法

第二次世界大战以来,各国国际私法立法得到迅速发展。当代国际私法立法表现出如下发展趋势:首先,对国际私法规范以国际私法法典或单行法规的形式加以规定。其次,国际私法的调整范围有所扩大。再次,法律选择的灵活性增强。复次,法律选择的适当性加强。最后,"直接适用的法律"的适用范围不断扩大以及实体法解决法律冲突的方法日益受到重视。①

一、欧洲国家国际私法立法

（一）欧洲国家国际私法立法概况

1926 年 8 月 2 日,波兰颁布了两个法典,其中一个是国际私法典,另一个是区际私法典。制定这样完备的国际私法典在当时的欧洲尚属首次。而区际私法典的制定更是开世界区际私法立法之先河。

1942 年《意大利民法典》和 1946 年《希腊民法典》都对国际私法作了规定。前者同 1865 年《意大利民法典》比较起来,只在某些细节上有所不同,毫无新意。后者的第 4 至 33 条为国际私法规定,较为系统和全面,制定水准也比较高。②

英国则颁布了一些涉及国际私法的法规,如 1906 年《与外国人结婚法》、1920 年《司法行政法》和 1933 年《外国判决（互惠执行）法》等。

（二）俄罗斯等国国际私法立法

1. 东欧国际私法立法

1948 年捷克斯洛伐克制定了一个关于国际私法和区际私法以及外国人地位的法律。1949 年保加利亚颁布的《涉外民事法和家庭法》也含有国际私法规定。1964 年捷克斯洛伐克《国际私法及国际民事诉讼法》得以施行。同年,阿尔巴尼亚则颁布了《关于外国人民事权利及适用外国法的法律》。随后颁布和施行的国际

---

① 参见徐冬根:《论国际私法规范的柔性化与刚性化》,载《法制与社会发展》2003 年第 3 期。
② Cf. G. S. Maridakis, Les principaux traits de la récente codification Hellènique touchant le droit international privé, *Recueil des Cours de l'Académie de Droit International de la Haye*, 1954 I, p. 111 ss.

私法立法有:1966年《波兰国际私法》、1975年《德意志民主共和国关于民事、家庭和劳动法律关系以及国际经济合同适用法律的条例》、1979年《匈牙利国际私法》和1982年《南斯拉夫法律冲突法》。这些国际私法立法大都采取单行立法或法典的形式制定,体系和内容较为完备,如1979年《匈牙利国际私法》有75条,而1982年《南斯拉夫法律冲突法》更多达109条。此外,不少立法不仅包含冲突规范,还对外国人的民事法律地位、管辖权和外国法院判决及仲裁裁决的承认与执行等问题作了规定。

2. 俄罗斯国际私法立法

苏联解体后,俄罗斯根据对外民事交往的形势和需求,构建了新的国际私法体系。

俄罗斯新的国际私法从2002年3月1日开始实施,主要条款在《俄罗斯联邦民法典》(第三部分)第四编之中,共计3章(第66至68章),39条(第1186至1224条)其中第66章为一般规定,第67章为人的法律地位的准据法,第68章为财产关系和人身非财产关系的准据法。[①] 1964年《苏俄民法典》第八编的法律适用规范从新的国际私法开始实施之日同时废止。

与前苏联相比,俄罗斯国际私法在立法形式上并没有重大突破,但在立法内容上,调整范围大为拓宽、意思自治原则应用的领域也更为广阔、最密切联系原则成为准据法确定的基本原则、诸多冲突规范均有实质性的改变。[②] 尽管俄罗斯的国际私法立法与以往先比,有了比较大的发展,但是,没有能够制定统一的国际私法法典,则是俄罗斯国际私法立法的最大不足。

3. 白俄罗斯国际私法立法

白俄罗斯共和国(Repblic of Belarus)新的《民法典》于1999年7月1日起生效,其中第7编是关于国际私法的规定。该编共分两章,即第74章(一般规定)和第75章(冲突规范),共42条。内容涉及国际私法的一般原则,人、法律行为、物权、合同和非合同债权、精神财产权以及继承等。但有关婚姻家庭和劳动关系的规定不包括在内。[③]

4. 哈萨克斯坦共和国国际私法立法

哈萨克斯坦共和国的《民法典》于1999年7月1日开始生效,其中第七编包括

---

① 张洪波、姚晓南译,刘慧珊校:《俄罗斯联邦民法典》(第三部分)第四编《国际私法》。具体条款参见中国国际私法学会主办:《中国国际私法与比较法年刊》(第五卷),法律出版社2002年版,第614—626页。

② 参见顾海波:《俄罗斯国际私法立法评析及启示》,载《中国国际私法与比较年刊》(第十一卷),北京大学出版社2008年版,第285页。

③ Oleg Mosgo, Das neue internationale Privaterecht Weissrusslands, *IPRax*, 2000, Heft 2, S.148.

了冲突法的内容。新的立法在内容上大大增加,除了对于先决问题的法律适用没有作出规定外,几乎所有的有关法律适用问题的一般性问题都有了规定。新立法大量采用双边冲突规范。

哈萨克斯坦共和国《民事诉讼法典》也于 1999 年 7 月 1 日开始生效,其中第五编是关于国际民事诉讼法的规定,内容包括外国人的民事诉讼权利、哈萨克斯坦共和国法院的国际管辖权、哈萨克斯坦共和国法院与外国法院之间的民事司法协助以及外国法院判决和仲裁庭裁决在哈萨克斯坦共和国的承认和执行问题。

5. 马其顿国际私法立法

马其顿共和国在 2007 年 7 月 4 日颁布了有关国际私法的立法,制定了一部比较完整的国际私法立法。① 马其顿国际私法共 124 条,分为六章,内容包括第一章基本规定(包括适用范围、避让条款、法律遗漏的填补、公共秩序、反致和指引、法律行为的形式、时效、法国法的适用、多国籍人、无国籍人、外国法的查明、可直接适用的规范);第二章准据法(包括自然人的权利能力和行为能力、法人的权利能力和行为能力、监护和临时保护措施、对失踪者的死亡宣告、自然人的姓名、合同的一般规则、未选择法律时合同的准据法、不动产合同、劳务合同、消费者合同等);第三章国际管辖权与诉讼程序;第四章外国法院判决的承认与执行;第五章特别条款和第六章过渡条款与最后条款。

(三) 英国国际私法立法

英国在一系列法律中对相关的国际私法问题作了规定,主要有:1949 年《婚姻法》、1950 年《仲裁法》、1963 年《遗嘱法》、1968 年《遗嘱法》、1970 年《法律改革(杂项规定)法》、1972 年《扶养令(互惠执行)法》、1972 年《民事证据法》、1973 年《婚姻诉因法》、1973 年《住所与婚姻诉讼法》、1975 年《仲裁法》、1975 年《证据(在其他管辖区)法》、1976 年《收养法》、1976 年《准正法》、1977 年《不公平合同条件法》、1978 年《国家豁免法》、1978 年《国内诉讼与地方法院法》、1979 年《仲裁法》、1980 年《时效法》、1980 年《保护贸易利益法》、1982 年《保险公司法》、1982 年《民事管辖权与判决法》、1984 年《涉外时效期间法》、1984 年《婚姻与家庭诉讼法》、1985 年《儿童诱拐与保护法》、1985 年《公司法》、1986 年《家庭法》、1986 年《潜在损害法》、1986 年《婚姻(禁止关系的亲等)法》、1987 年《婚姻法改革法》、1987 年《信托承认法》、1989 年《儿童法》、1990 年《合同(准据法)法》、1991 年《外国公司法》、1995 年《国际私法(杂项规定)法》、1996 年《仲裁法》、1996 年《家庭法》和《最

---

① 参见《马其顿共和国关于国际私法的法律》,邹国勇译,载《中国国际私法与比较年刊》(第十二卷),北京大学出版社 2009 年版,第 538 页。

高法院规则》等①,它们都规定了一些冲突规范。正因为如此,英国著名国际私法学者莫里斯在其名著《法律冲突法》(第三版)(1984年)中将成文法规列为英国国际私法的首要渊源,而该书的第一版(1971年)将其放在第二位。②不过英国的制定法有其特点,即不论民事、刑事的实体法和诉讼法都没有统一的法典,对某些特定问题虽然制定了单行法,但往往民、刑不分,实体法、诉讼法与国际私法兼及,且修改频繁,同名法令很多,在援用时必须注明法令颁布的年代,而且法令绝大部分是归纳判例而成。③不论概念或原则多来自司法习惯,因而解释和适用时往往需要借助判例。

(四)法国和德国国际私法

法国曾先后在1955年、1959年和1967年提出过三个国际私法草案,尝试修改《法国民法典》中的国际私法规定,但均未得正果。《法国民法典》中国际私法规定的最新修订文本是1998年文本。④

德国1896年颁布了新的国际私法法规,但是该新法规有人身权、婚姻家庭关系和合同之债关系的法律适用问题,却没有包括非合同之债和物权的法律适用问题。1993年联邦司法部起草了一部关于非合同之债和物权的法律适用的国际私法草案,该草案经过修订后,已经于1999年6月1日起正式生效。经过此次修订,德国国际私法法规已经由原来的38条增加到46条。⑤

(五)荷兰国际私法立法

荷兰在20世纪60年代以前是一个以判例法为主的国家⑥,但是在海牙国际私法会议进行国际私法统一化的过程中,荷兰先后批准和签署了大量的国际私法公约。⑦到目前为止,荷兰的国际私法虽然还处于继续编纂之中,但已取得了显著的阶段性成果。⑧荷兰司法部于1992年直接公布了《荷兰国际私法一般制定法草

---

① See Jason Chuah, *Statutes and Conventions on Private International Law*, Cavendish, London, 2nd Edition, 2005.
② See Morris, *The Conflict of Laws*, 3rd. ed. London 1984, pp.7—8.
③ 参见中国大百科全书出版社编辑部编:《中国大百科全书》(法学卷),中国大百科全书出版社1984年版,第712页。
④ 参见李双元、欧福永、熊之才编:《国际私法教学参考资料选编》(上册),北京大学出版社2002年版,第314—317页。
⑤ 韩德培、杜涛:《晚近国际私法立法的新发展》,载中国国际私法学会主办:《中国国际私法与比较法年刊》(第三卷),法律出版社2000年版,第11页。
⑥ Th. M. de Boer, The Hague Conference and Dutch Choice of Law: Some Criticism and a Suggestion, *Netherlands International Law Review* (1993 No.1), pp.1—14.
⑦ Maurice V. Polak, Towards Codified Dutch Private International Law, *Netherlands International Law Review* (1991 No.3), pp.312—345.
⑧ 参见袁泉:《荷兰国际私法研究》,法律出版社2000年版,第51—64页。

案》,该草案的大部分内容是法律选择规范,除此之外还包括管辖权规范和外国判决的承认与执行规范,它不仅反映了荷兰近年来国际私法立法的大部分成果,也在个别之处增加了一些冲突规范。尽管该草案不是正式的荷兰国际私法法典,但是它对有关亲属法领域的司法实践具有指导作用。[1]从荷兰国内先后颁布国际私法单行法的立法活动来看,这充分表明了荷兰政府有着坚定不移地编纂国际私法法典的立法决心。

(六)意大利和列支敦士登国际私法立法

1995年5月31日,意大利公布了单行的《关于改革意大利国际私法制度的法律》。该法有5章,共74条。第1章为总则,第2章为意大利的管辖权,第3章为法律适用(含一般规定、自然人的法律资格、法人、家庭关系、收养、无行为能力人的保护与扶养义务、继承、物权、赠与、合同之债、非合同之债等11节),第4章为外国判决与文书的效力,第5章为过渡条款和最后条款。该法已于1995年9月1日生效。意大利新的国际私法立法在立法内容和立法技术上均具有鲜明的时代特征,代表了当今国际私法立法发展的新趋势。

列支敦士登1996年9月19日颁布了一部新的国际私法法规,该法规于1997年1月1日起生效。[2]新颁布的国际私法立法共56条。第1—11条为总则部分,包括最强联系原则、公共秩序保留、反致、当事人意思自治、规则变更等。第12—28条为国际人法的内容,包括人的身份、能力、婚姻、家庭等问题的法律适用。第29—30条为国际继承法。第31—37条为国际物权法,包括动产物权和不动产物权的法律适用。第38—53条为国际债权法,基本上参照了奥地利国际私法法规的规定。

二、亚洲其他国家国际私法立法

(一)日本国际私法立法

1957年,日本为修改1898年颁行的《法例》,在内阁法制审查委员会下设立了国际私法部。[3]之后日本先后于1964年、1977年、1980年和1989年对《法例》进行数次修订。每次都是因为日本加入相关海牙国际私法公约而作出修订。2006年,日本通过了《法律适用通则法》,取代了百年前的《法例》,并于2007年1月1日开

---

[1] Maurice V. Polak, Michiel J. de Rooij and Lilian F. A. Steffens, *Private International Law in the Netherlands*, Kluwer Law International, 1995, pp.3—5.
[2] Aleander Appel, Reform und Kodifikation des Liechtensteinischen IPR, *Rabels Z* 61 (1997), 512f.
[3] 刘慧珊:《略论国际私法概念的发展》,载中国国际私法学会主办:《中国社会科学院研究生院学报》1985年第4期,第25—34页。

始施行。

《法律适用通则法》分3章43条,关于国际私法的内容集中在第3章。第3章又分为7节40条。① 除了第5条和第6条涉及监护以及失踪宣告的管辖权规则以外,其内容主要是法律选择规则,这基本上和《法例》一脉相承。关于国际裁判管辖权、外国判决的承认和执行、域外送达以及域外取证等制度仍设置在《日本民事诉讼法》、《日本民事执行法》以及相关条约中。第3章第1节是关于自然人的规定,包括自然人的行为能力以及监护、失踪宣告;第2节是关于法律行为的规定,主要是针对合同的规定;第3节是关于物权的规定;第4节是关于法定债权的规定,主要包括无因管理、不当得利以及侵权行为。第5节是关于婚姻家庭的规定,主要包括婚姻的成立及方式、婚姻的效力、夫妻财产关系、离婚、婚生子的父母子女关系的成立、非婚生关系的成立及认领、准正、收养、身份法律行为的方式、监护等。第6节是关于继承的法律制度,包括法定继承和遗嘱继承;第7节是补则,包括本国法的确定、经常居所地法的确定、人际法、反致、公共秩序保留等。最后是附则,包括新法的实施日期、过渡期的法的溯及力、其他法律相应的文字修改等。

(二) 阿拉伯国家国际私法立法

亚洲阿拉伯国家的国际私法立法中,科威特的国际私法立法颇引人注目。1961年科威特制定了《涉外法律关系规范》,内容包括国际民商事关系的管辖权、外国法院判决的效力以及法律适用问题。该法共有74条,其中有43条涉及法律适用问题,对之规定得较为详细、清楚。1980年6月4日,科威特又对1961年立法作出修订,其中包括取消司法管辖权的规定,而将司法管辖权部分移入到新的民事诉讼法典之中。

1976年《约旦民法典》对国际私法中的人的身份及能力、婚姻的成立及效力、扶养、继承、物权和债权等问题作了具体的规定。

20世纪70年代后,阿拉伯也门共和国(北也门)、也门人民民主共和国(南也门)和阿拉伯联合酋长国也分别在其民法典中对国际私法规范作了规定。

这些阿拉伯国家的国际私法立法内容十分相近,都具有以下一些特点:首先,在立法的方式上,阿拉伯国家的国际私法立法都不是以专门化的法典或法规方式出现的,而通常是以民法典的一个组成部分出现的。其次,在阿拉伯国家的国际私法中,属人法通常是本国法,而在这些国家常常也就是宗教法。最后,国际私法立法条款简明,这使法官在适用和解释法律方面存在着很大的随意性。

---

① 参见李旺:《立法研究关于日本新国际私法的立法——日本〈法律适用通则法〉介评》,载《环球法律评论》2007年第5期;齐湘泉:《日本2007年〈法律适用通则法〉评介》,载《中国国际私法与比较法年刊》(第十一卷),北京大学出版社2008年版,第315页。

三、北美洲国家国际私法立法

（一）美国路易斯安那州国际私法立法的改革

美国路易斯安那州曾是法国的殖民地，其法律受法国法的影响较大。当路易斯安那州在 1803 年从法国买来时，曾规定该州必须保持其在西班牙和法国统治下所实施的法律制度。该州原来的冲突规范与《法国民法典》类似，散见于 1808 年制定的民法典中。以后，该州又分别在《保险法典》、《商法典》、《私人信贷和消费者保护法》和《动产租赁法》等法律中订立相应的冲突规范。该州于 1991 年底颁布了第 923 号法案，即《冲突法法案》。该法案共 36 条，作为《民法典》的组成部分，编入《民法典》新增设的第 4 编之中。这些冲突规范共分 8 节。第 1 节为总则，第 2 节为当事人的民事法律地位，第 3 节为夫妻财产关系，第 4 节为继承关系，第 5 节为物权，第 6 节为合同之债，第 7 节为侵权行为之债，第 8 节为应废除的法律条款。该法案吸收了罗马法中"特殊法优于普通法"的原则，规定以往颁布的那些适用于特殊领域的冲突规范与该法案的冲突规范相抵触时，优先适用各特殊领域中的冲突规范。①该法案在规定法律选择总则方面有一个很大的特点，即充分考虑有关国家的利益和立法宗旨。因此，可以说该法案深受"最密切联系说"和"政府利益分析说"等当代美国冲突法理论的影响。②总之，美国路易斯安那州的新冲突法立法虽不及瑞士等欧洲国家的立法那么具体和详细，但在崇尚判例法的美国，路易斯安那州的这项冲突法法案的颁布却极具开拓意义。

（二）美国俄勒冈州合同法律冲突法与侵权冲突法

美国俄勒冈州（Oregon）法律委员会从 2000 年起开始起草涉外合同和侵权领域的冲突规范。新的合同法律冲突法（**codification for contract conflicts**）是俄勒冈州法律委员会制定全面的冲突法典工程中首先被落实并于 2001 年颁布的冲突法律规范。

【释义】　　　　　　**codification for contract conflicts** ③

The Act's structure reflects its judicial orientation, which is particularly apparent in the sequence of the Act's sections. They are arranged in a sequence that charts a roadmap judges

---

① 参见徐冬根：《美国路易斯安那州新冲突法法案述评》，载《法学杂志》1994 年第 3 期。
② See M. A. Moreau Bourles, *Structure du rattachement et conflits de lois en matiere de responsabilite civil delictuelle*, Thèse Paris II, 1985.
③ Symeon C. Symeonides, Oregon's Choice-Of-Law Codification For Contract Conflicts: An Exegesis, 44 *Willamette L. Rev.* 205, 211—212 (2007).

can easily follow. The operative part of the Act begins with section 81.105, which provides that certain contracts that have the specified Oregon contacts are governed by Oregon law, regardless of any other factors. Thus, when a judge encounters a contract with multistate elements, the judge should first look at section 81.105. If the contract fits the specifications of this section, the judge should apply Oregon substantive law, without having to look at the other sections of the Act, and without having to perform a choice-of-law analysis.

If the contract does not fall within the scope of section 81.105, then the judge should inquire on whether the contract is valid as to form (§81.110), capacity (§81.112), and consent (§81.115). If the contract is valid, the judge should inquire on whether the contract contains a choice-of-law clause. If so, the judge should examine the validity and effectiveness of the clause under sections 81.120 and 81.125.

If the contract does not contain a choice-of-law clause, or contains one that is ineffective, the judge should proceed to sections 81.130 and 81.135. If the contract is one of those for which section 81.135 provides presumptive rules, the judge should apply the law designated by the applicable presumptive rule, unless the opposing party invokes the escape contained in that section and demonstrates that another law should apply under section 81.130. If section 81.135 does not provide a presumptive rule for the particular contract, the judge will resort to the general rule of section 81.130 and perform the choice-of-law analysis that section prescribes.

该法强调法院地法的适用。该法第3条是一个单边冲突规范。该条规定，无论合同中的法律选择条款是否有相反规定，或者存在其他因素，此类与俄勒冈州有特定联系的合同应适用俄勒冈州法。这些合同包括：(1) 在俄勒冈州履行服务的合同，或者从俄勒冈州将货物运出的合同，且合同的一方当事人为俄勒冈州或其机构、分支机构；(2) 主要在俄勒冈州履行的建筑合同；(3) 由俄勒冈州居民主要在俄勒冈州境内履行劳务的雇佣合同；(4) 消费合同，如果在订立合同时，消费者是俄勒冈州的居民，且该消费者的缔约意愿是在俄勒冈州内取得的或者是出于在俄勒冈州作出的要约或者发布的广告的影响。[1] 此外，该法还对当事人的意思自治、合同的形式、缔约和能力等法律适用问题作出规定。

《涉外侵权和其他非合同请求法律适用法》(Choice of Law for Torts and Other Non-Contractual Claims)法案共14条，分为四个部分。第一部分(第1至5条)定义法案术语，界定适用范围，并对定性、场所化和其他事实认定以及住所问题作出特别规定；第二部分(第6至7条)规定直接适用俄勒冈州相关立法的情形；第三部分(第8至11条)是法案核心内容，规定侵权和其他非合同请求的法律选择规则；

---

[1] 〔美〕西蒙尼德斯：《2001年美国冲突法司法实践述评》，孔令杰、王莉译，载中国国际私法学会主办：《中国国际私法与比较法年刊》(第六卷)，法律出版社2003年版，第513页。

第四部分(第 12 至 14 条)是其他方面的规定,包括官方评释、法案施行时间和对法案条款编号的说明。①《该法律适用法》适用于侵权和其他非合同请求的法律选择。所谓"非合同请求"是指由"侵权行为或其他任何造成或可能造成损害的行为"引起的诉求。这里的"行为"既包括疏忽导致损害的行为,也包括将来可能发生的行为;"损害"是指对人身和财产的损害,包括可能发生的损害,但前提是损害必须具有可补偿性(即使权利人没有提出赔偿请求)。

(三)加拿大魁北克省国际私法立法

加拿大的魁北克省也曾是法国的殖民地,其民法深受《法国民法典》的影响。②因此,1866 年《魁北克民法典》有一些源于《法国民法典》的冲突规范。③1991 年 12 月 18 日,魁北克议会通过了新的第 10 章为国际私法规范的《魁北克民法典》(**Quebec Civil Code Book X on Private International Law**)。该法典已于 1994 年生效。

【释义】　　Quebec Civil Code Book X on Private International Law④

　　On December 18, 1990, the Minister of Justice deposited Bill 125, the new Civil Code including the Book X on Private International Law. The bill made some minor modifications to the 1988 draft and, after debate in the Quebec Parliament, became law on December 18, 1991. The civilian character and style remains as predominannt in the new legislation as it did in the 1988 draft. Civil law sources are increased.

　　Book X, *Droit International Privé*, covers the whole branch of private international law: jurisdiction, foreign judgments, and choice of law. Furthermore, the draft courageously legislates the generally accepted methodology of solving private international law problems, and takes a realistic, modern, and quasi-revolutionary approach in many ways. Retaining the classical Savigny method as its base, it legitimizes the complementary method of laws of immediate application, innovates with an escape clause, settles some controversial problems—renvoi, characterization, and public order—while deliberately leaving others, such as the incidental question and

---

① 有关《涉外侵权和其他非合同请求法律适用法》的详细评述,参见王晓媛:《美国涉外侵权冲突法的最新发展——俄勒冈州〈侵权与其他非合同请求的法律选择法〉评介》,载《环球法律评论》2011 年第 4 期;许庆坤:《美国侵权冲突法立法的最新进展及其对我国的启示》,载《法学评论》2011 年第 4 期。

② Quebec private international law constitutes a particular system of the conflict of laws. It possesses an origin and tradition of its own and is linked to the French Statutist's School of the eighteenth century. See Paul-Andre Crepeau, De la Responsabilité Civile Extra-Contractuelle en Droit International Privé Quebecois, 39 Can. B. Rev. 9—10 (1961).

③ 以前,魁北克国际私法的渊源集中在 1866 年民法典(尤其是第 6—8 条及第 135 条)以及 1965 年民事诉讼法典(第 68-7073-75 条及第 136—137 条)之中。

④ Jeffrey A. Talpis, The Civil Law In North America: The Civil Law Heritage In The Transformation Of Quebec Private International Law, 84 *Law Libr. J.* 177, 184—188 (1992).

dynamic conflicts, for future development. It is not a simple code but a cadre juridique, wherein un ensemble logique is created.

《魁北克民法典》改变了过去将冲突规范散订于民法典中的做法,用一编即第10编,专门规定国际私法规范。

《魁北克民法典》许多冲突规范受到晚近国际私法立法的影响(**inspired by recent codifications of private international law**),包括海牙国际私法公约、1987年《瑞士联邦国际私法》和1980年《关于合同义务法律适用的公约》的影响。

【释义】 **inspired by recent codifications of private international law**[①]
Aside from the indirect civil law influence of these conventions, some of the articles of the Quebec draft are inspired by recent codifications of private international law in European civil law countries. The influence of the Swiss Code is particularly strong.[②] Wisely, the drafters did not ignore the particular situation of Quebec in North America. Thus, the common law is also the source of some rules, as in the 1977 draft. For example, the *Uniform Commercial Code* is substantially the source of the rules on security interests (arts. 3464 & 3470). As well, the common law method of *forum non convenience* is integrated (art. 3499). Prescription or limitation of actions is governed by the lex fori, as in the common law (art. 3496). Finally, to ensure an *international courtoisie*, the review of foreign decisions is eliminated as a defense against their judicial recognition in Quebec (art. 3520). The presence of two nonunified legal systems (the United States and Canada) also explains the inclusion of specific rules for nonunified systems, although their application is not limited to North America (art. 3440).

《魁北克民法典》第10编共93条,分为四篇。第一篇为总则,共7条,内容包括识别、反致、区际法律冲突与人际法律冲突、公共秩序保留、强制规则、例外条款等。总则规定赋予了整部法律以很大的灵活性。[③]第二篇为国际私法,共11条,内容非常广泛,包括人法、物法、债法三大部分。魁北克此前立法中的许多内容都得到了保留,如属人法上的住所地主义、物之所在地法、继承上的分割制等,同时新法

---

① Jeffrey A. Talpis, The Civil Law In North America: The Civil Law Heritage In The Transformation Of Quebec Private International Law, 84 *Law Libr. J.* 177, 184.

② The escape clause (art. 3445), the rule allowing the court to take into account foreign mandatory rules (art. 3442), the conflict rules on torts (art. 3493) and contracts (art. 3480) and the choice of law in successions (art. 3463) are directly inspired from the new Swiss Code of Private International Law, in force since January 1990.

③ H. Patrick Glenn, Codification of Private International Law in Quebec, *IPRax*, 1994.

典也借鉴了普通法上的一些新的制度,如关于动产担保、信托等的规定。在合同法律适用上,也受到了《罗马公约》的影响。第三篇共21条,它试图为魁北克法院建立一套有关省际和国际私法案件管辖权的完整制度。第四篇共14条,它对在魁北克承认和执行外国判决赋予了较大自由,并废除了对判决的实质审查。①总的来看,由于加拿大魁北克是一个深受法国传统影响的地区,而且它十分有效地抵挡住了英美法的侵蚀,使其国际私法制度既保留了大陆法的传统,又具有英美法的若干特征,具有混合性质。

四、拉丁美洲国家国际私法立法

(一)委内瑞拉国际私法立法

委内瑞拉是拉丁美洲各国最早开始起草国际私法国内立法的国家之一。早在1912年,委内瑞拉开始起草了国际私法草案。1963年委内瑞拉决定重新起草国际私法草案。但委内瑞拉国际私法最终是在1999年4月6日开始生效实施。②该法分为12章,共64条,包括总则、住所、人、家庭、财产、债务、继承、行为形式与证明、管辖权与裁判权、外国判决的效力、诉讼程序以及最后条款等部分。

(二)1984年《秘鲁民法典》

1984年7月24日,秘鲁颁布了新的民法典,该法典自同年11月14日起生效。该法典的第10编为国际私法,第10编共分为四章,包括总则、司法管辖权、法律适用以及外国判决和仲裁裁决的承认与执行。

五、大洋洲国家国际私法立法

澳大利亚是普通法系国家,普通法是其国际私法的一个重要渊源。但在国际私法领域,澳大利亚联邦也制定了不少成文法。例如,在婚姻家庭方面,有1959年《婚姻诉讼法》和1961年《婚姻法》以及取代两者的1975年《家庭法》;在商事方面,有1909年《汇票法》、1966年《破产法》、1981年《公司法》和1986年《支票和支付法令》;在诉讼程序方面,有1901年《送达与执行程序法》、1992年经修订代替前者的《送达与执行程序法》、1903年《司法法》、1984年《外国诉讼法》和1985年《外国国家豁免法》等。另外,一些州也制定了自己的成文国际私法法规,如维多利亚州的1962年《外国判决法》、新南威尔士州的1973年《外国判决(互惠执行)法》等。

---

① 参见韩德培、杜涛:《晚近国际私法立法的新发展》,载中国国际私法学会主办:《中国国际私法年与比较法刊》(第三卷),法律出版社2000年版,第5页。
② 杜焕芳:《委内瑞拉国际私法及其改革述评及其启示》,载梁慧星主编:《民商法论丛》第27卷,金桥文化出版(香港)有限公司2003年版,第459页。

值得一提的是,澳大利亚法律改革委员会于1992年3月提出了冲突法立法草案,全称为《1992年洲和地区冲突法统一法草案》(Draft Uniform State and Territorial choice of law Bill 1992)。该《草案》共有14个条文,分别规定了关于类似于侵权的请求权、机动车交通事故、工人赔偿、合同、公平贸易法、信托、继承、当事人法律选择、实体问题与程序问题的划分等问题的法律适用。《草案》还涉及公共秩序和强制性规范的适用等问题。该《草案》吸收了国际私法的立法经验,尤其是海牙国际私法会议所取得的很多立法成就。①

六、非洲国家国际私法立法

(一) 埃及国际私法立法

埃及1948年颁布的《民法典》,载有国际私法条款。该法典序编第1章第1节规定了一系列调整国际民商事关系的法律适用规范,同时对国际私法的一般问题如国籍冲突、在法制不统一国家准据法的确定、反致、公共秩序保留等也作出了相应的规定。埃及对国际私法立法采取的方式和方法成为临近的非洲和阿拉伯国家的楷模。

(二) 突尼斯国际私法立法

1998年11月27日,突尼斯颁布了新的《国际私法典》,该法典已经于1999年2月1日生效。突尼斯作为一个伊斯兰国家,其国际私法典也带有伊斯兰法的传统。新法典共分五编,共76条,包括总则、管辖权、外国判决和裁定的执行、豁免权和法律适用五个部分。突尼斯国际私法立法在结构上日趋完善,在内容上日趋丰富。突尼斯国际私法典是一部由传统走向现代立法的典范。②

(三) 阿尔及利亚国际私法立法

阿尔及利亚1975年颁布的民法典,其中有16条冲突规范。

2005年,阿尔及利亚颁布新的民法典,对其中的冲突规范也进行了修订和补充。新的法律适用规范分为时间上的法律冲突和空间上的法律冲突两大部分。新的法律适用规范强化了缔约自由和对弱者的保护,并引入现代法律制度,以促进国际民商事交往的正常发展。③

---

① Nygh, Reform of Private International Law in Australia, *RabelZ* 58 (1994), S. 732.
② Bruno Menhofer, Neues Internationales Privatrecht in Tunesien, *IPRax*, 1999, Helf 4, s.266.
③ 参见《阿尔及利亚民法典》(节译),邹国勇译,载《中国国际私法与比较年刊》(第十二卷),北京大学出版社2009年版,第531页。

(四) 其他非洲国家国际私法立法

除埃及外,非洲的其他一些国家也在其民法典或家庭法典中制定了相应的国际私法规范,它们包括《马达加斯加民法典》(1962年)、《中非民法典》(1965年)、《加蓬民法典》(1972年)、《塞内加尔家庭法典》(1972年)、《布隆迪国际私法》(1980年)以及《多哥家庭法典》(1980年)。由于非洲国家的国际私法规范大多以专章或专节形式存在于民法典或家庭法典之中,故主要为法律适用规范。不过,1972年《加蓬民法典》不仅规定了法律适用问题,而且对外国人的地位和外国判决在加蓬的效力问题也作了规定。

七、中国国际私法立法

改革开放以来,我国的国际私法立法进入了一个蓬勃发展阶段。1985年的《继承法》第36条对继承法律适用规范作出规定。1987年1月1日起施行的《民法通则》(2009年8月27日修正)第8章"涉外民事关系的法律适用"(第142条至第150条)则对法律适用规范作出专章式规定。其他一些法律、法规也含有冲突规则,如1990年由原对外经济贸易部发布的《外资企业法实施细则》(2001年修订,第18条、第48条至第49条、第52条、第56条、第64条、第81条)、1991年的《收养法》(1998年11月4日修正,第21条)、1992年的《海商法》第14章"涉外关系的法律适用"(第268条至第276条)、1995年的《票据法》(2004年8月28日修正)第5章"涉外票据的法律适用"(第94条至第101条)、1995年的《民用航空法》第14章"涉外关系的法律适用"(第184条至第190条)、1999年的《合同法》(第126条)、1999年由民政部发布的《外国人在中华人民共和国收养子女登记办法》(第2条、第3条)以及2005年10月27日修订通过的《公司法》(第218条)等。① 此外,最高人民法院的一些司法解释也含有冲突规则,如1985年9月11日《最高人民法院关于贯彻执行〈中华人民共和国继承法〉若干问题的意见》、1988年1月26日《最高人民法院关于贯彻执行〈中华人民共和国民法通则〉若干问题的意见(试行)》、2007年6月11日《最高人民法院关于审理涉外民事或商事合同纠纷案件法律适用若干问题的规定》等。

尽管如此,我国国际私法立法,无论与欧洲瑞士、德国等国家国际私法立法进行横向比较,还是同中国其他部门法立法进行横向比较,均存在明显差距。我国早期法律适用规范存在的诸多问题乃至弊端也比较明显。早期的法律适用规范的条

---

① 参见陈卫佐:《中国国际私法立法的现代化——兼评〈中华人民共和国涉外民事关系法律适用法〉的得与失》,载《清华法学》2011年第2期。

款和内容不够全面和完整,留下不少立法上的空白与缺陷①;部分法律适用规范已经过时,还有部分法律适用规范相互抵触,法律、法规中的法律适用规范与司法解释中的法律适用规范存在不和谐之处。因此,制定相对系统的法律适用法,是完善我国国际私法规范、进一步推进改革开放和形成有中国特色的社会主义法律体系的必然诉求。

2010年10月28日颁布,2011年4月1日起施行的《涉外民事关系法律适用法》②,在中国国际私法立法史上具有里程碑的意义。从我国的立法进程看,该法在相当程度上完成了中国国际私法立法的系统化和现代化,大大推进了我国国际私法法典化的进程,弥补了原有法律适用规范立法之诸多不足和缺陷,标志着我国国际私法立法理念、结构、内容等日趋合理与完善。

《涉外民事关系法律适用法》共设8章52条,内容包括:一般规定(第一章)、民事主体(第二章)、婚姻家庭(第三章)、继承(第四章)、物权(第五章)、债权(第六章)、知识产权(第七章)和附则(第八章)。《涉外民事关系法律适用法》采用了大量选择性冲突规范,并明显地表现出在立法灵活性与确定性间谋求平衡的价值取向,具有相当的开放性、创新性以及国际化的视野。《涉外民事关系法律适用法》明确确认了强制性规范的直接适用;对最密切联系原则的运用有所深化,最密切联系原则不但成为我国涉外法律规范选择的一般原则,而且还从合同法律适用领域深化到有价证券的法律适用领域。《涉外民事关系法律适用法》中明显体现了保护弱者权益的法律的理念,在父母子女人身、财产关系,扶养关系和监护关系的法律适用规则中,保护弱者权益原则得到广泛体现。

《涉外民事关系法律适用法》在立法理念、立法技术、法律适用规范的数量等方面都朝着法制现代化方向迈进了一大步。但它并不意味着国际私法的法典编纂任务已全部完成,因为真正意义上的国际私法法典编纂应是将迄今为止分散在各种法律、法规和司法解释中的冲突规则进行梳理、总结、归纳和创制,集中制定于同一部立法文件中,完成冲突规则的系统化和逻辑化。③ 作为中国国际私法立法现代化过程的重要阶段性成果的《涉外民事关系法律适用法》,不仅是一部在中国特色法律体系中起支架作用的法律,而且有助于提高涉外民商事案件法律适用的确定性、可预见性和灵活性。

---

① 参见肖永平:《中国国际私法立法的里程碑》,载《法学评论》2011年第2期。
② 有关对《涉外民事关系法律适用法》的评论,参见郭玉军:《中国国际私法的立法反思及其完善——以〈涉外民事关系法律适用法〉为中心》,载《清华法学》2011年第5期;郭玉军、车英:《研讨实施适用法律问题推进国际私法立法工作——中国国际私法学会2011年昆明年会综述》,载《武汉大学学报(哲学社会科学版)》2012年第2期。
③ 参见陈卫佐:《涉外民事法律适用法的立法思考》,载《清华法学》2010年第3期。

中国国际私法立法的逐步发展,对于中国法制现代化和改革开放具有重要意义,它同时也是20世纪60年代以来方兴未艾的世界各国国际私法法典编纂运动的重要组成部分。

第四节 美国的两部冲突法重述

《冲突法重述》(Restatement of Conflict of Laws)是美国国际私法法典化过程中的重要产物,是美国普通法中的国际私法规则的总结。从严格意义上,《冲突法重述》并不是立法,而是属于民间学术机构的示范法。但是,由于美国冲突法重述制定的参与人及其制定机构美国法学会(American Law Institute)具有相当的学术权威性,因此《冲突法重述》对美国国际私法的发展产生了重大的影响,在美国国际私法立法发展中具有重要的地位。

一、《第一次冲突法重述》

《第一次冲突法重述》(Restatement of the law of the Conflict of Laws (1934), **First Restatement**)产生于20世纪30年代。1934年,在美国法学会的主持下,由哈佛大学法学院比尔(Joseph H. Beale)教授任报告员编纂的美国《第一次冲突法重述》得以公布,在美国的国际私法发展史上产生了巨大的影响。

【释义】　　　　　　　　First Restatement[①]
According to the standard account, the theoretical basis for the First Restatement system for choice-of-law was the vested rights theory. Developed in this country by Joseph H. Beale[②] and in England by A.V. Dicey[③], the theory explained the forum's use of foreign legal rules in terms of the creation and enforcement of vested rights. According to the theory, the only law that could operate in a foreign territory was the law of the foreign sovereign. When an event

---

① William M. Richman, David Riley, The First Restatement of Conflict of Laws on the Twenty-Fifth Anniversary of Its Successor: Contemporary Practice In Traditional Courts, 56 *Md. L. Rev.* 1196, 1197 (1997).
② See Joseph H. Beale, *A Treatise on the Conflict of Laws* 1967—1969 (1935).
③ See A. V. Dicey, *A Digest of the Law of England with Reference to the Conflict of Laws* 17—25 (A. Berriedale Keith ed., 5th ed., 1932).

(a tort, for example) occurred in the foreign territory, a right was created; the content of that right, of course, could be determined only by reference to the foreign law. The role of the forum court in the choice-of-law process was merely to enforce the right that had vested in the foreign territory according to the foreign law. Crucial for practice under the vested rights theory was to determine when and where a particular right vested, because the law in place where the right vested would control the content of the right. The theory spawned a series of rules, each governing a major area of the law, such as torts, contracts, and property, that controlled the choice-of-law process by identifying a particular contact as the trigger for the vesting of a right. Thus, courts referred tort choice-of-law issues to the law of the place of injury, contract issues to the law of the place of making, and property matters to the law of the situs of the land.

《第一次冲突法重述》体现了既得权学说的主要观点并有所发展，它一方面试图避免适用外国法与属地主权之间的矛盾，另一方面又比较注重当事人的合法权益之保护。① 因为指导理论的冲突性，所以法院在实际的判例当中很迷茫，有时候甚至是不知所措，在当时美国的司法界出现了相当大的混乱局面。

下面我们着重探讨一下《第一次冲突法重述》中的对于合同冲突和侵权冲突的解决这两方面的内容。

在合同领域，《第一次冲突法重述》把有关合同的事项分为了两大部分来解决：第一，有关合同履行方面的问题适用合同履行地法；第二，有关合同的形式、解释以及效力等问题依照合同缔结地法来解决。这属于一般性规定，适用于整个合同法领域，而没有对合同的种类加以区分，法院在判决此类的案例时必须据以引用而不能由当事人任意选择准据法。这一点也成为最为人诟病的地方，受到了猛烈的批判。

在侵权领域，《第一次冲突法重述》确立了侵权地法，并认为适用侵权行为地法可以更容易确认事实，更好地维护当事人的利益。因此法院在审理侵权案件时，必须适用被告被指控的侵权行为事件的最后发生地的法律。上述对于侵权案件依侵权行为地法的规定，是一种强行性规定，法官只能据以适用而不能有其他选择，也没有对各种不同的侵权行为进行分类，没有区分特殊侵权行为和一般侵权行为。这也为以后的种种弊端埋下了隐患。

正如《第一次冲突法重述》所依据的理论基础自身存在很多弱点一样，该重述自其编纂完成公布之日起就已经存在很多弊端，遭到了很多学者的批判。

---

① 邓正来：《美国现代国际私法流派》，中国政法大学出版社2006年版，第17页。

二、《第二次冲突法重述》

(一)《第二次冲突法重述》的制定

理论上的批评和实践中的冷落,将《第一次冲突法重述》推到了修订的边缘。于是,里斯教授和斯科特教授分别被任命为《第二次冲突法重述》(Restatement (Second) of the law of the Conflict of Laws (1971), **Second Restatement**)正副报告员,开始了《第二次冲突法重述》的起草工作。美国法学会于1971年以里斯教授为主报告人发表了《第二次冲突法重述》,以取代《第一次冲突法重述》。

【释义】 **Second Restatement**[①]

The American Law Institute approved the Second Restatement's final draft in 1969, and it appeared in print in 1971. The Second Restatement is eclectic, combining what its drafters believed to be the best of several choice-of-law methodologies. It functions like a code—that is, for any given problem, several Second Restatement sections are likely to apply. It more closely resembles the Uniform Commercial Code; other Restatements tend to pronounce fairly discrete rules of law.

The Second Restatement works through three related functions, described here in the reverse order of their best use. First is section 6—often identified per se with the most-significant-relationship test—with two components. The second functional component is a set of three general principles for torts, contracts, and property. The third functional component is a number of sections focused on specific claims and issues.

Apart from torts, contracts, and property, the Second Restatement has further specific issues for procedure, trusts, status, agency and partnership, business corporations, and administration of estates. Finally, the Second Restatement also deals with personal jurisdiction and judgments; those sections have no direct bearing on choice of law. Texas state and federal courts have applied or cited twenty-nine of these specific sections since 1979.

《第二次冲突法重述》充分考虑了当时在冲突法问题上司法观念所发生的重大变化,这种变化的本质就是要抛弃传统僵化硬性的规则,通过对长期以来被忽视的冲突法的价值进行理性分析,确立更加灵活的法律选择判断标准。《第二次冲突法重述》的这种变化降低了法律的确定性和可预见性。

(二)《第二次冲突法重述》的特点

《第二次冲突法重述》以"最重要联系说"(the most significant relationship)为

---

① James P. George, Judicial Misuse of Governmental Interests in the Second Restatement of Conflict of Laws, 23 *Rev. Litig.* 489, 519—521 (2004).

理论基础,通过以下几种具体方式将现代的灵活方法与传统的硬性规则结合起来。①

第一,规定完全采用"最重要联系"灵活方法的条款。在一些法律适用领域《第二次冲突法重述》没有规定传统的硬性冲突规则,而是完全听由法官依该重述第6条规定的原则自由裁量,决定与案件有"最重要联系"的法律。这些原则包括:州际和国际体制的需要;法院地的相关政策;有利益的其他州的相关政策和它们在决定问题上的相关利益;对正当期望的保护;特别法律领域的基本政策;结果的稳定性、可预见性和一致性以及认定和适用被适用法律的规则的容易程度。

第二,规制通常规定推定适用传统冲突规则的条款。如果《第二次冲突法重述》起草者有充分的信心认定某类案件与特定州的法律有"最重要联系",那么就会规定"通常"应选择该州的法律,只有在极少数情形下,才会直接适用"最重要联系"方法予以矫正。例如《第二次冲突法重述》第156条第2款规定,侵权关系"通常"应适用损害结果发生地州的法律,但如依第6条规定,其他州与案件有"更重要联系"的,则该其他州法律应予适用。②

第三,规定在"除非"(unless)情形下才启用"最重要联系"方法作为"逃避机制"的条款。如果《第二次冲突法重述》起草者有比较充分的信心确定与某类案件有"最重要联系"的法律为某一特定州的法律,那么就会推定适用该特定州的法律,即采用传统的冲突规则,除非案件与其他州有"更重要的联系",则属例外。例如《第二次冲突法重述》第142条第3款规定,法院应适用本州准予诉讼的时效法规,除非受理该诉讼时法院地没有实际意义,以及依与当事人及案情有更为重要联系的其他州的时效法规,该诉讼不得提起。

第四,规定完全推定适用传统冲突规则的条款。《第二次冲突法重述》规定硬性适用某一州法律的条款多数限于财产和继承法律关系。

从上述四类条款来看,第一类条款完全采用灵活的方法;根据第二、三类条款,灵活的方法仍有用武之地,至于这种灵活的方法在多大程度上可以"裁夺"传统的硬性冲突规则,取决于法官的自由裁量;第四类条款则完全保留了推定的传统冲突规则,但其适用范围有限。可见《第二次冲突法重述》相当重视传统冲突规则的作用,但仍以现代灵活的法律选择方法为主。

(三) 对《第二次冲突法重述》的评价

《第二次冲突法重述》在一定程度上保留传统的冲突规则,有助于实现法律选

---

① Symeon C. Svmeonides, W. C. Perdue & A. T. von Mehren, *Conflict of Laws*, West Croup, 1998, pp.135—139.

② G. R. Shreve, *A Conflict-of-Laws Anthology*, Anderson Publishing Co., 1997, p.253.

择的稳定性、一致性和可预见性等"冲突法上的公正"以及内外国法的平等适用。同时,该重述又不排除在某些场合直接援用灵活的法律选择方法,并规定了现代灵活方法对传统硬性规则的"矫正"功能,从而有利于保证各案的公平解决和各州(国)法律政策的实现。从实际应用来看,这样的机制也不至于给法官选择法律造成过大的负担。①

《第二次冲突法重述》对灵活性的追求虽然表明了其对法解释学方法论的偏离,但里斯并没有完全抛弃传统的方法论,他在《第二次冲突法重述》中保留了许多《第一次冲突法重述》中概念法学的痕迹,在程序、物权、信托、财产的管理等领域,《第二次冲突法重述》均规定了比较刚性的法律选择条款。这种折中主义的做法虽并非里斯本意,但在客观上却彰显了《第二次冲突法重述》方法论的多元化倾向,这与当时法学方法论的要求及现状是同步的。

《第二次冲突法重述》所确立的观点为美国各州的冲突法立法和法院解决法律冲突问题带来了积极的影响②,而且这种影响还在不断扩大。

第五节 国际私法法典化及其法哲学思想

一、国际私法法典化的含义

法典化(**codification**),一般是指将众多杂乱的法律规范,予以分门别类,将同性质的法律规范有系统地编纂于同一法典之中。

【释义】　　　　　　　　　　codification

Codification is the process of collecting and restating the law of a jurisdiction in certain areas, usually by subject, forming a legal code. The codification movement developed out of the philosophy of the Enlightenment and began in several European countries during the late

---

① 徐崇利:《冲突规则的回归》,载《法学评论》2001 年第 2 期。
② As of 2003, twenty-four states use the Second Restatement for choice of law in contract cases, and twenty-one use it for torts. See Symeon C. Symeonides, Choice of Law in the American Courts in 2002: Sixteenth Annual Survey, 52 *Am. J. Comp. L.* 1, 4 (2004).

18th century. However, it only gained significant momentum with the enactment of the French Napoleonic Code in 1804.

  而本教材所谓的法典化,是在更宽泛意义上的法典化,它不仅仅限于国家权力机关对法律规范的编纂活动和系统化工作,也包括学者、专家或由其组成的社会团体、学术团体草拟系统化法律文件和对法律文件的编纂工作。古罗马时期的法典编纂工作(codifications in the ancient Roman Empire)取得了辉煌的成果①,为后人法典化工作起到了样板作用。

【释义】   codifications in the ancient Roman Empire

  Important codifications were developed in the ancient Roman Empire, with the compilations of the *Lex Duodecim Tabularum* (The Law of the Twelve Tables)②, which consisted of Table I (Civil Procedure), Table II (Civil Procedure), Table III (Debt), Table IV (Parents And Children), Table V (Inheritance), Table VI (Property), Table VII (Real Property), Table VIII (Torts), Table IX (Constitutional Principles), Tabvla X (Funeral Regulations), Tabvla XI (Marriage), and much later the *Corpus Iuris Civilis*.③ These codified laws were the exceptions rather than the rule, however, as during much of the ancient Roman laws were left mostly uncodified.

  在国际私法的法典化过程中,比较法的作用(the role of comparative law)十分明显。比较法的发展,对国际私法的法典化起到了积极的促进作用。

【说理】   the role of comparative law

  The role of comparative law in drafting new conflicts rules is particularly important during the process of codification. This is true even when such codifications are internal and not international (in fact, notwithstanding the supranational aspects of the discipline, a great ma-

---

 ① 公元四五世纪,法学家们开始编纂皇帝宪令的尝试,这些首次被编纂成册的宪令汇编是以法典的方式出版的。公元6世纪,优士丁尼完成了三部完整系统的法律汇编,包括《优士丁尼法典》、《优士丁尼学说汇编》、《优士丁尼法学阶梯》。在法学学术与立法权的融合下,法典不再是单一的法律文本,也不是简单的法律汇编,而是科学系统的编纂成果,是对法学与法律的提炼与综合。

 ② *Lex Duodecim Tabularum* (The Law of the Twelve Tables) was the ancient legislation that stood at the foundation of Roman law. The Law of the Twelve Tables formed the centerpiece of the constitution of the Roman Republic and the core of the *mos maiorum*.

 ③ The *Corpus Juris Civilis* (Body of Civil Law) is a collection of fundamental works in jurisprudence, issued from 529 to 534 by order of Justinian I, Byzantine Emperor.

jority of conflicts rules have maintained a national origin). Indeed, due to the inherently technical nature of the discipline, legislators often seek advice from conflicts scholars, who are familiar with the laws of foreign legal systems. This familiarity is a natural consequence of the particularly strong academic tradition that has led to a sharing of ideas and concepts all over Europe. In this respect, conflicts law acknowledges the importance of the primary function of comparative law: knowledge of foreign law, leading to a better understanding of one's own legal system. This strong academic tradition has frequently been enhanced, especially in Bruno Oppetit's remarkable course called "le droit international privé, droit savant." This distinctive feature brings it even closer to comparative law, often considered one of the most academic disciplines.

国际私法法典化是国际私法法律规范的系统化编纂工作。

二、专门化立法与冲突法重述代表了国际私法法典化的不同进路

国际私法的法典化主要通过两种进路：一种是国际私法的专门化立法，另一种是国际私法法律适用规范的重述，前者以欧洲大陆法系奥地利和瑞士国际私法立法为代表，后者以美国的两次《冲突法重述》为代表。[①]

欧洲大陆法系国家的国际私法法典编纂主要有两次，第一次是查士丁尼对罗马法的法典化，第二次是19世纪到20世纪欧陆各国大规模的法典编纂活动。[②]欧洲大陆法系国家的国际私法法律适用规范注重确定性和可预见性。从立法技术的角度来看，欧洲大陆法系国家国际私法的立法和法典化大致可以概括为三种不同的模式。

（1）分散式立法。分散式立法将调整国际民商事关系的法律适用规范，分散于本国民法典的不同篇章之中。这是国际私法立法技术发展的第一阶段。采用这种模式的立法以法国最为典型。分散式立法，虽然具有简明扼要、简单易行的优点，但也有其不足之处。它缺乏系统性，不能形成完整的法律适用体系，它没有国际私法总则中的原则、纲领性的规定，对国际私法中的反致、转致、公共秩序保留、法律规避、外国法的查明、区际法律冲突等问题没有作出具体系统的规定。从立法技术上讲，分散立法的模式还只是法律适用规范立法和法典化的雏形阶段。

（2）专章式立法。这是国际私法立法技术发展的第二阶段。采用这种专章或专篇方式制定国际私法规范，最为典型的是19世纪末、20世纪初的《德国民法施

---

① 徐冬根：《论欧、美国际私法法典化的不同进路及其法哲学思想》，载《河南政法管理干部学院学报》2004年第3期。
② 沈娟：《冲突法及其价值导向》（修订本），中国政法大学出版社2002年版，第83页。

行法》,专章式的法律适用规范的特点是,法律适用规范的数量有限,调整对象的范围狭窄,有关的规定较为笼统,即一类法律关系往往只有一条规定,只用一个连接点。采用专章式立法制定的国际私法规范仍然存在着笼统、抽象的缺点,缺乏明确、详细、完备的规定,很难适应现代社会经济发展的需要,无法满足大量复杂的国际民商事关系的需求。

(3) 法典式立法。新近颁布的一些国际私法立法,大多采取法典方式。这种模式虽为英美所首倡,但真正见于成文法的,乃欧洲若干国家的新近颁布的国际私法,其中最具代表性的为 1987 年《瑞士联邦国际私法》(**loi-modèle of the Swiss codification**)。

【释义】　　　　　　　loi-modèle of the Swiss codification

During the last thirty years, most European legal systems have codified their conflicts rules. Comparison between European legal systems became easier as conflicts rules became black-letter rules, contained in statutes rather than in case law which is often unknown abroad. Some recent codifications of private international law have even played the role of "loi-modèle", in particular the Swiss codification. Among the many similarities that can be found in these recently enacted statutes, the escape clause or the development of parties' autonomy outside the field of contracts are particulary notable. This contradicts the long-standing idea that national codifications prevent foreign models from influencing the development of the law. Still, even within Europe where comparative law is more often consulted than in the United States, it plays too limited a role, especially when the comparison is restricted to a few major European legal systems.

瑞士国际私法的这种立法模式,更符合司法实践的需要。法典式立法设有总则部分和分则部分。许多新的法典还规定了法律适用的总的指导原则。

而相反,美国崇尚法律的灵活性,并在灵活性的基础上强化法律的可预见性和安全性,因此美国不是通过由权力机关制定完整的国际私法立法的方式,而是通过由美国法学会这个学术团体牵头制定《冲突法重述》的方式,来实施国际私法的法典化工作。《冲突法重述》的编纂和多次修订工作就是国际私法的法典化工作。由于美国法学会的特殊地位,以及参与国际私法法典化工作的人员不仅有著名的国际私法教授,还有许多美国的著名律师和法官,尤其是一些大法官参与了国际私法法典化的工作,使得美国的《冲突法重述》在美国国际私法法典化活动中具有重要历史地位和现实意义,《冲突法重述》中的许多条款被美国众多州立法和州法院的法官所接受,成为法官处理法律冲突的重要指导思想和指导性规范。

透过欧洲大陆国家国际私法专门化立法和美国《冲突法重述》的表象,我们来看问题的本质:为什么欧洲大陆的奥地利、瑞士和列支敦士登等国家均分别颁布了国际私法专门化立法,而美国国会不制定国际私法立法呢?出现这种现象与两个不同法系的法律文化、法律制度、法律观念的差异性有关,尤其是其中所体现的法律哲学思想,对两种不同的法典化模式起着至关重要的作用。

三、欧洲大陆国际私法法典化体现的是建构理性和分析主义法哲学观

欧洲国际私法的专门立法,作为国际私法规范系统化的一种立法活动,是以建构理性作为其法哲学基础的。[1]法律建构主义认为,一种理性的国际社会生活秩序的基础,可以通过一种全面的法律规则有目的地予以建立起来。自然法主义者也认为,从一些独立于宗教信条的自然原则可以派生出法律规范,如果这些规范被有目的的以一种条例清晰的方式加以制定,那么一个理性的社会基础即由此而奠定。[2]建构主义理性观把我们引向法律实证主义,认为法律是立法者自上而下地创立的"主权者的命令"或者意志。无论是通过早期的《法国民法典》,以后的《德国民法施行法》所表现出来的欧洲国际私法冲突规范立法,还是晚近的《德国国际私法》、《瑞士联邦国际私法》,都反映了这种建构主义的哲学基础。

欧洲大陆的国际私法典,所体现的是一种分析主义的法哲学观。从认识论的视角看,人类依靠概念认识世界,同时也依靠概念控制世界,前者产生科学,后者产生规范。法律就是一种重要的规范形式。现代法律一般包含三项要素,即价值、事实和逻辑,而逻辑的因素在现代国际私法中的作用是十分重要的。现实中的问题通过法律要件和法律效果的关系被逻辑地表示出来,据此保证了国际民商事关系的当事人对法律适用有预测的可能性,进而保证了法的安定性。

欧洲大陆盛行的理性主义,对国际私法法典化活动有重大的推动力作用,这种哲学思想及其制约的思维方法也渗入了国际私法领域,追求冲突规范的明确性和可预见性,成为欧陆国际私法立法中的重要特色。欧洲国际私法的这种立法方式,无疑具有重大的理论意义和现实意义。从法律价值的实现上看,欧洲国际私法充分保障了法的安全价值。[3]法的安全价值表现在国际私法上,指的是法律的确定

---

[1] 建构理性(constructive rationalism),出自〔英〕哈耶克:《法律、立法与自由》,邓正来译,中国大百科全书出版社2001年版。哈耶克用该术语来界定笛卡儿式的唯理主义的哲学思潮。

[2] 〔德〕茨威格特、克茨:《比较法总论》,潘汉典等译,法律出版社2003年版,第136页。

[3] 所谓法律的安全价值是指"法律应对各种行为的法律后果加以明确预示从而使法律有可预见性,使人们在行为之前即可预料法律对自己行为的态度,不必担心来自法律突如其来的打击,从而起到防范其权力阶层人性的弱点的作用"。参见徐国栋:《民法基本原则解释》,中国政法大学出版社1992年版,第328页。

性、可预见性和一致性，代表了反映在明确、平等、可预见的法律规则中的社会利益。①因此，安全往往与稳定性、普遍性相联系，在欧洲大陆国家国际私法法典化的法律选择方法模式，体现了法律的安全价值。

四、美国的国际私法法典化体现的是演进理性和实用主义法哲学观

以美国为代表的英美法系国家以另一种方式，即《冲突法重述》的方式，来推动其国际私法的法典化工作。美国《冲突法重述》体现了与欧洲国际私法专门化立法不同的价值取向，根植于普通法系的美国的《冲突法重述》，是一种对演进理性的反映，是以实用主义的法哲学为思想基础的。演进理性主义者认为，法律是人类群体自生自发的一种秩序，法律没有作者。②美国现代国际私法中诸多法律选择方法说是以实用主义哲学为基础，是现代社会法学等实用主义法学思潮在国际私法领域的反映。实用主义哲学的精髓在于"存在就是有用"，"有用就是真理"。美国大法官霍尔姆斯(Jr. Oliver Wendell Holmes)是将实用主义哲学运用于法理学和法学实践的杰出代表，他主张在行动中发现和创制法律。霍尔姆斯在其巨著《普通法》中的开篇之语就是"法律的生命不是逻辑，而是经验"(The life of the law has not been logic; it has been experience)。③在霍尔姆斯的巨大影响下，美国的私法研究逐步从分析法学偏向现实主义法学。

实用主义强调法律的不确定性，以及法官在法律适用上的灵活性。因此，实用主义哲学思潮对国际私法的影响是深远的。反映在美国国际私法的法律适用规范法典化方面，不是通过权力机关立法的方式，而是通过美国法学会这样的学术团体以冲突法重述的方式表现出来。在上述法哲学思想的影响下，立法被认为是把支配人类关系的现行法律规则固定成一种容易被接受的形式，或者说规则的汇总。立法模式不能阻止法律与不断演进中的社会生活。那么采用《冲突法重述》而非其他方法来推进法律统一，也就成为受实用主义哲学思潮支配，而体现法律演进主义思想的美国国际私法法典化的特殊方式。《冲突法重述》这种特殊的法典化方式，在追求法律开放性和灵活性的同时，也体现了法律安全性价值。它注重法律规范的表达方式、外在形式与内容组织的有机统一。

《冲突法重述》在国际私法立法和法典化运动中的产生和发展，开辟了一条不同于欧洲大陆法系专门立法的新进路，从而在立法对法律价值的实现上，弥补了欧

---

① 刘丹妮：《美国的"冲突法革命"：公平性与安全性的对抗与平衡》，载《理论月刊》2001年第7期，第62页。

② 参见谢辉：《法律的作者》，载郑永流主编：《法哲学与法社会学论丛》（第4卷），中国政法大学出版社2001年版。

③ Oliver Wendell Holmes, *The Common Law*, 1 (1881).

洲大陆法系专门立法模式的缺失,这正是《冲突法重述》在法律价值实现上的意义所在。因此,可以说,《冲突法重述》是在美国这类实用主义思潮占统治地位的国家中,国际私法进行法典化的一种优化方案,理应引起我国国际私法学者的重视,是我们完善国际私法立法必须认真研究和借鉴的一种法典化方式。

第六节　国际私法统一化运动

一、海牙国际私法会议和海牙国际私法公约

海牙国际私法会议(**The Hague Conference on Private International Law**)在国际私法条约化运动中发挥了极为重要的作用。1892年,在荷兰著名法学家阿塞尔(T. M. C. Asser)的倡导和推动下,荷兰政府向欧洲国家发出了召开制定统一的国际私法规则的国际会议的邀请。从1893年9月12日,第一届海牙国际私法会议在荷兰的海牙举行开始,至今已持续一百多年。

【释义】　　Hague Conference on private international law

The Hague Conference on private international law is an intergovernmental organisation, the purpose of which is "to work for the progressive unification of the rules of private international law" (Statute, Article 1).

The First Session of the Hague Conference on private international law was convened in 1893 by the Netherlands Government on the initiative of T.M.C. Asser (Nobel Peace Prize 1911). Prior to the Second World War, six Sessions were held (1893, 1894, 1900, 1904, 1925 and 1928). The Seventh Session in 1951 marked the beginning of a new era with the preparation of a Statute which made the Conference a permanent intergovernmental organisation. The Statute entered into force on 15 July 1955. Since 1956, regular Plenary Sessions are held every four years, the Twenty-First of which met in 2007.

The principal method used to achieve the purpose of the Conference consists in the negotiation and drafting of multilateral treaties or Conventions in the different fields of private international law (international judicial and administrative co-operation; conflict of laws for contracts, torts, maintenance obligations, status and protection of children, relations between spouses, wills and estates or trusts; recognition of companies; jurisdiction and enforcement of foreign judgments). After preparatory research has been done by the secretariat, preliminary drafts of the Conventions are drawn up by the Special Commissions made up of governmental experts. The drafts are then discussed and adopted at a Plenary Session of the Hague Conference, which is a diplomatic conference.①

海牙国际私法会议的发展可分为两个阶段:

从 1893 年第 1 届会议到 1951 年第 7 届会议为第一阶段。这时的会员国主要是欧洲大陆国家,先后有 21 个;日本于 1904 年成为会员国,是当时唯一的一个非欧洲国家的会员国。海牙会议在该期间没有固定的组织,参加会议凭荷兰政府的邀请。在第一阶段,海牙会议先后召开了 6 届会议,在民事诉讼、结婚、离婚、婚姻效力、监护、禁治产及类似保护措施等方面制定了 7 个国际私法公约。

从 1951 年后为第二阶段。海牙会议第二阶段的最大变化是在第 7 届会议上制定了《海牙国际私法会议章程》(Statute of the Hague Conference on Private International Law)。在该规约于 1955 年 7 月 15 日生效后,海牙会议成为一个以逐渐统一国际私法规范为目的的永久性政府间组织。海牙会议的组织机构有四:即(1) 大会;(2) 荷兰国家委员会;(3) 常设事务局;(4) 特别委员会。常设机构的设立,保证了海牙会议工作的正常进行。

在第二阶段,海牙国际私法会议在制定统一国际私法公约方面取得了巨大的成就,各成员国从 1954 至今已经签署了许多公约(**Conventions signed by member states**)。

【释义】   **Conventions signed by member states**②

1. Statute of the Hague Conference on Private International Law
2. Convention of 1 March 1954 on civil procedure
3. Convention of 15 June 1955 on the law applicable to international sales of goods
4. Convention of 15 April 1958 on the law governing transfer of title in international sales of goods
5. Convention of 15 April 1958 on the jurisdiction of the selected forum in the case of international sales of goods
6. Convention of 15 June 1955 relating to the settlement of the conflicts between the law of nationality and the law of domicile
7. Convention of 1 June 1956 concerning the recognition of the legal personality of foreign companies, associations and institutions

---

① About HCCH, http://www.hcch.net/index_en.php? act = text.display&tid = 4.
② See Official website of HCCH, http://www.hcch.net/index_en.php? act = conventions.listing.

8. Convention of 24 October 1956 on the law applicable to maintenance obligations towards children

9. Convention of 15 April 1958 concerning the recognition and enforcement of decisions relating to maintenance obligations towards children

10. Convention of 5 October 1961 concerning the powers of authorities and the law applicable in respect of the protection of minors

11. Convention of 5 October 1961 on the Conflicts of Laws relating to the Form of Testamentary Dispositions

12. Convention of 5 October 1961 Abolishing the Requirement of Legalisation for Foreign Public Documents

13. Convention of 15 November 1965 on Jurisdiction, Applicable Law and Recognition of Decrees Relating to Adoptions

14. Convention of 15 November 1965 on the Service Abroad of Judicial and Extrajudicial Documents in Civil or Commercial Matters

15. Convention of 25 November 1965 on the Choice of Court

16. Convention of 1 February 1971 on the Recognition and Enforcement of Foreign Judgments in Civil and Commercial Matters

17. Supplementary Protocol of 1 February 1971 to the Convention on the Recognition and Enforcement of Foreign Judgments in Civil and Commercial Matters

18. Convention of 1 June 1970 on the Recognition of Divorces and Legal Separations

19. Convention of 4 May 1971 on the Law Applicable to Traffic Accidents

20. Convention of 18 March 1970 on the Taking of Evidence Abroad in Civil or Commercial Matters

21. Convention of 2 October 1973 concerning the International Administration of the Estates of Deceased Persons

22. Convention of 2 October 1973 on the Law Applicable to Products Liability

23. Convention of 2 October 1973 on the Recognition and Enforcement of Decisions relating to Maintenance Obligations

24. Convention of 2 October 1973 on the Law Applicable to Maintenance Obligations

25. Convention of 14 March 1978 on the Law Applicable to Matrimonial Property Regimes

26. Convention of 14 March 1978 on Celebration and Recognition of the Validity of Marriages

27. Convention of 14 March 1978 on the Law Applicable to Agency

28. Convention of 25 October 1980 on the Civil Aspects of International Child Abduction

29. Convention of 25 October 1980 on International Access to Justice

30. Convention of 1 July 1985 on the Law Applicable to Trusts and on their Recognition

31. Convention of 22 December 1986 on the Law Applicable to Contracts for the International Sale of Goods

32. Convention of 1 August 1989 on the Law Applicable to Succession to the Estates of Deceased Persons

33. Convention of 29 May 1993 on Protection of Children and Co-operation in respect of Intercountry Adoption

34. Convention of 19 October 1996 on Jurisdiction, Applicable Law, Recognition, Enforcement and Co-operation in respect of Parental Responsibility and Measures for the Protection of Children

35. Convention of 13 January 2000 on the International Protection of Adults

36. Convention of 5 July 2006 on the Law Applicable to Certain Rights in respect of Securities held with an Intermediary

37. Convention of 30 June 2005 on Choice of Court Agreements

38. Convention of 23 November 2007 on the International Recovery of Child Support and Other Forms of Family Maintenance

39. Protocol of 23 November 2007 on the Law Applicable to Maintenance Obligations.

到2012年,海牙国际私法会议已先后制定了39个国际私法公约。从内容方面来看,这些公约涉及属人法、公司承认、货物买卖、买卖合同、代理、财产、信托、公文认证、交通事故、产品责任、结婚、婚姻财产、离婚承认、收养、扶养、未成年人保护、儿童诱拐、遗嘱方式、遗产管理、继承、民事诉讼以及司法救助等广泛的领域,已不限于海牙会议第一阶段制定的公约所涉及的婚姻家庭和民事诉讼领域。

海牙国际私法会议和海牙国际私法公约不仅在国际立法方面取得了很大的成绩,也对国际私法的国内立法产生了一定的影响(**references to Hague conventions**)。

【释义】　　　　references to Hague conventions

Legislators also make references to international sources of the law, such as the Hague conventions. Even when such conventions have not been ratified, these can operate as persuasive models: indeed, national legislators do not hesitate to select those provisions that suit their needs, ignoring the rest. This pick-and-choose phenomenon is the result of deficiencies that have weakened the unification process. Difficult negotiations among countries with different legal traditions often lead to compromises and result in a final text filled with concessions that fail to satisfy all the participants who, in turn, refuse to ratify the convention they have been negotiating.

二、国际统一私法协会

国际统一私法协会(**International Institute for the Unification of Private Law**, UNIDROIT)是一个专门从事私法统一的政府间国际组织,成立于1926年,总部设在意大利的罗马,宗旨是统一和协调不同国家和国际区域之间的私法规则,并促进

第三章 国际私法的立法发展

这些私法规则的逐渐采用。国际统一私法协会有 61 个会员国。中国于 1985 年 7 月 23 日正式接受该协会章程,并从 1986 年 1 月 1 日起已正式成为其会员国。

【释义】 **International Institute for the Unification of Private Law**①

The International Institute for the Unification of Private Law, also known as UNIDROIT, is an independent intergovernmental organisation. Its purpose is to study needs and methods for modernising, harmonising, and coordinating private international law and in particular commercial law between states, and to draft international Conventions to address the needs. Set up in 1926 as an auxiliary organ of the League of Nations, the Institute was, following the demise of the League, re-established in 1940 on the basis of a multilateral agreement, the UNIDROIT Statute. Its seat is in Rome, Italy. Membership of UNIDROIT is restricted to States acceding to the UNIDROIT Statute. UNIDROIT's 61 member States are drawn from five continents, and represent a variety of different legal, economic, and political systems as well as different cultural backgrounds.

国际统一私法协会的主要任务为:(1) 为建立统一的私法之目的准备各种法律和公约的草案;(2) 为改进私法领域内的国际关系,准备各种协定草案;(3) 承担比较私法的研究工作;(4) 参与协会认为有必要保持联系的其他组织在该领域已承担的任何项目;(5) 组织会议并出版认为值得广泛发行的著作。其机构有:(1) 大会;(2) 主席;(3) 执行委员会;(4) 常设委员会;(5) 行政法庭;(6) 秘书处。

该协会的工作范围同海牙国际私法会议的工作范围有很大的不同,它从事的是实体私法的国际统一工作。该协会一直致力于可以实现统一的私法领域的实体法规则的统一工作,制定了许多统一法公约草案,其中有的公约在外交会议上获得通过(**Conventions, drawn up by UNIDROIT and adopted by diplomatic Conferences**)。

【释义】 **Conventions, drawn up by UNIDROIT and adopted by diplomatic Conferences**②

UNIDROIT has over the years prepared the following international Conventions, drawn up by UNIDROIT and adopted by diplomatic Conferences convened by member States of UNIDROIT:

——Convention relating to a Uniform Law on the International Sale of Goods (The Hague,

---

① Official website of International Institute For the Unification of Private Law, http://www.unidroit.org/.

② http://www.unidroit.org/english/conventions/c-main.htm.

1964)

—Convention relating to a Uniform Law on the Formation of Contracts for the International Sale of Goods (The Hague, 1964)

—International Convention on Travel Contracts (Brussels, 1970)

—Convention providing a Uniform Law on the Form of an International Will (Washington, D.C., 1973)

—Convention on Agency in the International Sale of Goods (Geneva, 1983)

—UNIDROIT Convention on International Financial Leasing (Ottawa, 1988)

—UNIDROIT Convention on International Factoring (Ottawa, 1988)

—UNIDROIT Convention on Stolen or Illegally Exported Cultural Objects (Rome, 1995)

—Convention on International Interests in Mobile Equipment (Cape Town, 2001)

—Protocol to the Convention on International Interests in Mobile Equipment on Matters Specific to Aircraft Equipment (Cape Town, 2001)

—Luxembourg Protocol to the Convention on International Interests in Mobile Equipment on Matters specific to Railway Rolling Stock (Luxembourg, 2007)

—UNIDROIT Convention on Substantive Rules for Intermediated Securities (Geneva, 2009)

—UNIDROIT Protocol to the Convention on International Interests in Mobile Equipment on Matters Specific to Space Assets (Berlin, 2012)

近年来,国际统一私法协会在国际商法的统一方面作出了极大的努力,起草了若干相关的国际商事公约文本(**other commercial instruments**)并将在国际商事公约统一方面作出更大的努力。

【释义】　　　　　　　　other commercial instruments

Other Commercial Instruments includ: the Guide to International Master Franchise Arrangements (1998) the Model Franchise Disclosure Law (2002); and the Unidroit Principles of International Commercial Contracts, the first edition of which was published in 1994, and the second, enlarged edition of which was published in 2004.

UNIDROIT has as a work in progress a draft convention on Intermediated Securities—the "Unidroit Securities Convention." The negotiation process will culminate in the signing of an international Convention addressing the legal framework of intermediated securities. The Working Group for the preparation of Principles of International Commercial Contracts has also started work on additional chapters.

三、区域性的国际私法统一化运动

(一) 泛美会议和《布斯塔曼特法典》

1928年,第6届泛美会议(Pan-American Conference)在古巴首都哈瓦那举行,有21个美洲国家出席。这次会议的重要成果就是在1928年2月20日签订了《国际私法公约》,该公约附有《国际私法法典》。由于该法典是由古巴法学家布斯塔曼特(A. S. de Bustamante)主持编订的,故又称为《布斯塔曼特法典》(Bustamante Code)。该法典除一般规则外,含有国际民法、国际商法、国际刑法和国际程序法4卷,共437条。该法典于1928年11月25日生效,有15个拉丁美洲国家批准了它。

(二) 北欧国家的国际私法统一活动

瑞典、挪威、丹麦、芬兰和冰岛等五个北欧国家在1931年至1936年间,先后缔结了5个国际私法条约,即1931年《关于婚姻、收养和监护的某些国际私法规定的公约》(Convention Containing Certain Provisions of Private International Law regarding Marriage, Adoption and Guardianship)和《扶养费收取公约》(Convention concerning the Collection of Maintenance Allowances,这两个公约于1932年1月1日生效)、1933年《外国判决的承认和执行公约》(Convention on Recognition and Enforcement of Foreign Judgements,1933年7月1日生效)、1933年《破产公约》(1935年1月1日生效)以及1934年《继承和遗产管理公约》(1936年1月1日生效)。1931年的两个公约在1953年略有修订。

北欧五国除对国际私法采取国际公约的方式进行统一外,还以灵活、机动的所谓"立法合作程序"进行私法的国际统一工作。

(三) 比利时、荷兰、卢森堡三国联盟的国际私法统一活动

比利时、荷兰、卢森堡三国于1951年缔结条约成立三国联盟,于1951年5月11日签订了《荷兰、比利时、卢森堡关于国际私法统一法的公约》(The Benelux Convention on Private International Law)。该条约的附件为《国际私法统一法》,是条约的组成部分,共28条,涉及人的身份和能力、婚姻家庭、继承、物权、合同及债务、法律行为及代理、证据、时际冲突和公共秩序等事项。该公约曾于1968年修订。该公约只有卢森堡批准,其他两国虽签署但未批准,未能生效。

(四) 欧盟的国际私法统一活动

1993年1月11日,欧洲联盟(Europe Union,简称"欧盟")正式成立,从此,掀起了欧盟国际私法统一化浪潮。1995年9月签署《破产程序公约》,1997年5月签署《送达公约》,1998年5月签署《布鲁塞尔公约 II》。①特别是1997年《阿姆斯特丹条约》的生效,使欧盟国际私法统一趋势展现出新的特点:新的统一的国际私法法令不再需要经过各成员国内立法机构的立法程序,各成员国法院可以直接予以适用;新的成员国加入欧盟时自动受欧盟统一国际私法的制约。

欧盟国际私法统一化所取得的成果丰硕,包括《2000年第1346号关于破产程序的规则》,此为欧盟以规则形式进行国际私法统一化运动的最早成果之一;《2000年第1347号关于婚姻事项及夫妻双方子女的亲子责任案件的管辖权与判决承认与执行的规则》,该规则增加了一些亲子关系方面的内容;《2000年第1348号关于域外送达的规则》;《2000年关于建立消费纠纷司法外解决机构网络中心的决议》,要求在欧盟内建立一个中心机构,运用司法外手段解决消费纠纷;《2001年关于司法外机构解决消费纠纷和解程序适用原则的建议》,旨在为上面的机构设置一定的运作原则和程序;《2001年第44号关于民商事案件管辖权与判决承认及执行的规则》,该文件规定消费者住所地法院对电子商务纠纷有绝对管辖权;《2001年第1206号关于民商事案件域外取证协助规则》;《2001年建立欧洲民商事司法协助中心的决定》,该中心主要是为欧盟成员国之间开展民商事司法合作事项作协调。……②

2001年《尼斯条约》生效后欧盟国际私法统一化又出现些新动向。如欧盟统一国际私法的立法在程序上更加公开化、透明化,立法速度、效率也大为加强,立法技术更加发达。

欧盟通过制定条约、颁布"指令"和制定"规则"的方式来进行国际私法的统一活动。此处的"指令"对所有成员国具有约束力,但是成员国有权选择贯彻和实施这种指令的形式和方法。制定"规则"是欧盟实现统一私法活动的另一种方法。规则是欧盟国际私法的一个重要渊源。它一般具有完全的约束力,并可以在成员国直接适用。③

(五) 美洲国家组织的国际私法统一活动

1975年,美洲国家组织在巴拿马召开了第一届国际私法会议,制定了6个国际私法公约,即《美洲国家间关于代理人国外行使代理权法律制度的公约》、《美洲国家间关于汇票、本票和发票法律冲突的公约》、《美洲国家间关于支票法律冲突的公约》、《美洲国家间关于国外取证的公约》、《美洲国家间关于遗托书的公约》和

---

① 韩德培、刘卫翔:《欧洲联盟国际私法的特征和发展前景》,载《武汉大学学报》(哲学社会科学版)1999年第1期,第25—29页。
② 参见肖永平、郭树理:《欧盟统一国际私法的最新发展》,载《法学评论》2001年第2期。
③ 黄进主编:《国际私法》(第二版),法律出版社2005年版,第115页。

《美洲国家间关于国际商事仲裁的公约》。

1979年,美洲国家组织又在蒙得维的亚召开第二届国际私法会议,制定了7个国际私法公约和1个附加议定书,即《美洲国家间关于国际私法通则的公约》、《美洲国家间关于国际私法中自然人住所的公约》、《美洲国家间关于贸易公司法律冲突的公约》、《美洲国家间关于支票法律冲突的公约》、《美洲国家间关于执行预防措施的公约》、《美洲国家间关于外国法证明和查询的公约》、《美洲国家间关于外国判决和仲裁裁决域外效力的公约》和《美洲国家间关于遗托书的公约的附加议定书》。

美洲国家组织的上述条约为美洲地区国际私法的统一提供了一整套规则,使美洲国家组织的统一国际私法自成一体,也极大地推动了世界性的国际私法统一化运动向前发展。

(六)非洲国家参与国际私法统一活动

非洲国家参与国际私法统一活动(**Africa's engagement with international institutions dealing with issues of private international law**)方面发展不均衡,一些经济发展比较快、参与国际经济合作强度比较大的国家,在国际私法统一化方面所取得的成绩比较突出,但是总体来说,与其他地区的国家相比,在程度上远远不足。

【释义】 Africa's engagement with international institutions dealing with issues of private international law

Africa's engagement with international institutions dealing with issues of private international law has been minimal, and often indirect. There are currently only three African members of the Hague Conference on Private International Law, namely, Morocco, Egypt, and South Africa. Compared with membership from other regions, Africa is highly under-represented. Some African countries participate indirectly in the work of the Conference through institutions like the Commonwealth and the Asian-African Legal Consultative Organization (formerly Asian-African Legal Consultative Committee), both of which cooperate with the Conference. As of June 1, 2007, 19 African countries were parties to a total of 12 Hague Conventions. In the area of international commercial arbitration, 29 African countries are members of the United Nations Convention on the Recognition and Enforcement of Foreign Arbitral Awards.[1]

---

[1] Richard Frimpong Oppong, Private International Law in Africa: The Past, Present, and Future, 55 Am. J. Comp. L. 677, 681 (2007).

四、国际私法统一化运动展望

统一国际私法的根本目的在于克服各国法律选择法之间的冲突,提高法律选择法对涉外利益关系的调整能力。由于各国司法解释总是在不断地制造新的冲突(**divergent judicial interpretations create new conflicts**),因此,统一国际私法是一件非常困难的工作。尽管如此,统一国际私法的运动,已经成为一种必不可阻挡的历史趋势。

【释义】　　divergent judicial interpretations create new conflicts

Unification is never complete because divergent judicial interpretations create new conflicts. For all these reasons, the Hague conventions which attempt to unify choice-of-law rules, have been severely criticized; this partly explains a recent change of attitude and the search for a new direction. Although it has been assumed that scholars have a greater interest than judges in comparative conflict of laws, some European judges are looking more carefully at foreign models. In such countries as Great Britain, the Netherlands and Germany, the higher courts do resort to comparative law, especially when there is an unsettled point of law. But there is much more than this——the application of a conflicts rule during the judicial process often requires a comparative approach.

【思考题】

- "万民法"是一种怎样的法律?
- 近代国际私法立法有哪些主要成果?
- 什么是国际私法的法典化? 欧洲和美国在国际私法的法典化方面各有什么特点? 其法哲学思想有哪些不同?
- 20 世纪的国际私法统一化运动取得了哪些成绩?
- 海牙国际私法会议和国际统一私法协会取得了哪些主要的成就?

【重要术语提示与中英文对照】

中文术语	英文对照
万民法	*jus gentium*
法国民法典	French Civil Code, *Code Napoléon*,
俄勒冈州合同法律冲突法	Oregon codification for contract conflicts

魁北克民法典第 10 编——国际私法	Quebec Civil Code Book X on Private International Law
冲突法重述	Restatement of Conflict of Laws
美国法学会	American Law Institute
比尔	Joseph H. Beale
第一次冲突法重述	Restatement of the law of the Conflict of Laws (1934), First Restatement
第二次冲突法重述	Restatement (Second) of the law of the Conflict of Laws (1971) Second Restatement
法典化	codification
古罗马帝国的法典编纂	codifications in the ancient Roman Empire
霍尔姆斯大法官	Jr. Oliver Wendell Holmes
法律的生命不是逻辑,而是经验	The life of the law has not been logic; it has been experience
阿塞尔	T. M. C. Asser
统一化运动	unification
海牙国际私法会议	The Hague Conference on Private International Law
国际统一私法协会	International Institute for the Unification of Private Law, UNIDROIT
泛美会议	Pan-American Conference
布斯塔曼特法典	Bustamante Code
比荷卢关于国际私法统一法的公约	The Benelux Convention on Private International Law

【推荐阅读文献】

- 徐冬根:《论欧、美国际私法典化的不同进路及其法哲学思想》,载《河南政法管理干部学院学报》2004 年第 3 期(全文收录于中国人民大学复印报刊资料《国国际法》2004 年第 4 期)。
- 王承志:《美国冲突法重述之晚近发展》,法律出版社 2007 年版。
- 陈卫佐:《海牙国际私法会议对 21 世纪国际私法新发展的贡献》,载《法学》2007 年第 11 期。
- 徐冬根:《国际私法趋势论》,北京大学出版社 2007 年版。
- 刘宁元:《论我国法律适用法体系及其协调和冲突》,载《东方法学》2011 年第 3 期。
- 王晓媛:《美国涉外侵权冲突法的最新发展——俄勒冈州侵权与其他非合同请

求的法律选择法评介》,载《环球法律评论》2011 年第 4 期。
- 齐湘泉:《中国国际私法探源》,载《中国政法大学学报》2012 年第 1 期。
- Lea Brilmayer, Jack Goldsmith, *Conflict of Law: Cases and Materials*, 中信出版社 2003 年版。
- Luther L. McDougal III, Robert L. Felix, Ralph U. Whitten, *American Conflicts Law: Cases and Materials*, 4th ed., LexisNexis 2004.
- Symeon C. Symeonides, Oregon's Choice-Of-Law Codification For Contract Conflicts: An Exegesis, 44 *Willamette L. Rev.* 211—212 (2007).
- Richard Frimpong Oppong, Private International Law in Africa: The Past, Present, and Future, 55 *Am. J. Comp. L.* 677 (2007).
- Opertti Badán & Fresnedo de Aguirre, The Latest Trends in Latin American Private International Law: The Uruguayan 2009 General Law on Private International Law, 11 *Ybk Priv. Int'l L.* 305 (2009).
- Tu (G.), China's New Conflicts Code: General Issues and Selected Topics, 59 *Am. J. Comp. L.* 563 (2011).
- Miguel Virgos, Francisco Garcimartin, Conditional Conflict of Laws Rules: A Proposal in the Area of Bank Resolution and Netting in Cross-border Scenarios, 9 *Int. C. R.* 91—95(2012).
- Katharina A. Byrne, China's New Conflict of Law Code, 2 *Private Client Business* 38 (2012).

【扩展阅读资料】

History of Private International Law[①]

The first instances of conflict of laws in the Western legal tradition can be traced to Greek law. Ancient Greeks dealt straightforwardly with multistate problems, and did not create choice-of-law rules. Leading solutions varied between the creation of courts for international cases, or application of local law, on the grounds that it was equally available to citizens of all states.

More significant developments can be traced to Roman law. Roman civil law (*jus civile*) being inapplicable to non-citizens, special tribunals had jurisdiction to deal with multistate cases. The officers of these specialized tribunals were known

---

① http://en.wikipedia.org/wiki/Conflict_of_laws.

as the praetor peregrini. The Praetor peregrini did not select a jurisdiction whose rules of law should apply. Instead, they "applied" the "jus gentium." The jus gentium was a flexible and loosely-defined body of law based on international norms. Thus the praetor peregrini essentially created new substantive law for each case. Today, this is called a "substantive" solution to the choice-of-law issue.

An early private international law was established in classical Islamic law and jurisprudence as a result of the vast Muslim conquests and maritime explorations during the early Middle Ages giving rise to various conflicts of laws. A will, for example, was "not enforced even if its provisions accorded with Islamic law if it violated the law of the testator." Islamic jurists also developed elaborate rules for private international law regarding issues such as contracts and property, family relations and child custody, legal procedure and jurisdiction, religious conversion, and the return of aliens to an enemy country from the Muslim world. The religious laws and courts of other religions, including Christianity, Judaism and Hinduism, were also usually accommodated in classical Islamic law, as exemplified in al-Andalus, the Indian subcontinent, and the Ottoman Empire.

The modern conflict of laws is generally considered to have begun in Northern Italy during the late Middle Ages and in particular at trading cities such as Genoa, Piza and Venice. The need to adjudicate issues involving commercial transactions between traders belonging to different cities led to the development of the theory of *statuta*, whereby certain city laws would be considered as *statuta personalia* "following" the person whereby it may act, and other city laws would be considered as *statuta realia*, resulting in application of the law of the city where e. g. the *res* would be located (cf. *lex rei sitae*).

Maritime law was also a great driver of international legal rules; providing for the enforcement of contracts, the protection of shipwrecked sailors and property, and the maintaining of harbours.

The modern field of conflicts emerged in the United States during the 19th century with the publishing of Joseph Story's treatise on the Conflict of Laws in 1834. Story's work had a great influence on the subsequent development of the field in England such as those written by A. V. Dicey. Much of the English law then became the basis for conflict of laws for most commonwealth countries.

第四章

国际私法的理论学说

第四章 国际私法的理论学说

本章导读

※ 纵观国际私法的发展史,国际私法最初的表现形式是学说或者学理的形态。自14世纪国际私法产生的时候起到18世纪上半叶以前,国际私法一直处于法理学与科学的阶段,即仅表现为一种习惯法或学说法形态。国际私法学更多地表现为法学家们形而上学的理论思想,许多学说的提出和传播是纯思想性的理论和理念,没有经过实践的充分检验。

※ 其间,巴托鲁斯的"法则说"提出了从法律的性质入手分析法律适用之后,法国学者杜摩兰提出了"意思自治"原则,荷兰著名学者胡伯提出了具有属地主义色彩的"国际礼让说"。

※ 19世纪中叶,德国历史法学派巨子冯·萨维尼在其鸿篇巨著《现代罗马法体系》中提出了"法律关系本座说"的伟大构想,从而揭开了近代国际私法理论发展的新篇章,其本人被誉为近代国际私法之父。

※ 英国学者戴赛倡导了既得权说,他认为,为了保障涉外法律关系的稳定性,对于根据外国法已设定的权利,除了与内国公共政策、道德原则和国家主权发生抵触者外,都应获得承认与保护。

※ 斯托雷提出了"礼让说",他认为一国适用外国法完全是基于礼让,而不是基于义务。

※ 政府利益分析说是柯里所倡导的一种学说:某个州或国家适用其法律规范的目的在于实现其政府的相应政策,所以该州或该国在适用其法律规范方面就存在着某种利益,而这种利益显然是政府利益。法院在审理某个具体案件时,应适用具有合法的或合理的政府利益的那个州或国家的法律。

※ 法国学者弗朗西斯卡基提出,在调整国际民商事关系时,一系列具有强制力的法律规范可以撇开传统冲突规范的援引而直接适用于国际民商事关系。这种能被直接适用的法律规范,就是"直接适用的法"

※ 凯格尔创立了国际私法"利益论"。他指出,在作出国际私法上的决定时,就要顾及案件中的各种利益及其评价。

※ 后现代主义法哲学观及其对国际私法的影响主要表现在:第一,排斥统一性,强调差异性,这种差异性在国际私法上具体为对弱者的特别保护和对妇女的特别保护;第二,否定普遍性,强调多元性;第三,反对确定性,强调多变性。

【本章主题词】 法则说、意思自治、法律关系本座说、既得权说、国际礼让说、本地法说、政府利益分析说、直接适用的法、利益论、后现代主义

第一节 法则说

纵观国际私法的发展史,国际私法最初的表现形式是学说或者学理的形态,故有"学说法"之称。各国学者对法律冲突的解决,提出了各种各样的理论(**sophisticated theories**)。

【解说】   sophisticated theories
Choice-of-law problems occur whenever relatively advanced economic and legal systems come into contact with each other on a frequent basis. Thus, the ancient Greek city-states, the medieval Italians, the Renaissance Dutch, and the modern Americans have all developed sophisticated theories concerning what laws should be applied to a particular problem.①

在14世纪,意大利的法学家首先创立了"法则说"(**statutist doctrine**)。

【解说】   statutist doctrine
By the 14th century, Italian jurists developed the "statutist doctrine," or a "system of conflicts incorporating elements of both the personal law from the Roman system and territorial rule from feudalism," to address the need for conflicts jurisprudence. The statutist doctrine was based on the idea that a court could determine the applicable law by looking to the nature of the laws themselves. The laws were categorized as real "effective only within the limits of the legislating sovereign's territory", personal "effective wherever the affected person was situated", or mixed "laws that were neither real nor personal".②

从公元13世纪到18世纪,在长达五个世纪左右的时间里,作为"学说法"的法

---

① Friedrich Juenger, A Page of History, 35 *Mercer L. Rev.* 419 (1984).
② Susan L. Stevens, Commanding International Judicial Respect: Reciprocity and the Recognition and Enforcement of Foreign Judgments, 26 *Hastings Int'l & Comp. L. Rev.* 115, 118—119 (2002).

则说一直居统治地位,在国际私法发展史上形成法则说时代。

一般认为,近代的国际私法诞生于巴托鲁斯提出"法则说"之时,这是因为正是这一学说关注了外国法的域外效力问题,并第一次在一定范围内承认了这种效力,使外国法的域外适用成为可能。建立在平等基础上的法律选择规则的提出使国际私法的现实性与重要性凸显出来,国际私法的学说发展自此开始。

法则说时代包括意大利法则说、法国法则说和荷兰法则说等三个时期。

一、意大利法则说

意大利法则说(Italian theory of statutes),又称为法则说的"意大利学派"(Italian school)[1],是以意大利法学家巴托鲁斯(Bartolus,1314—1357年)和巴尔都斯(Baldus,1327—1400)为代表的后期注释学派(post-glossators)创立的一种国际私法学说。

巴托鲁斯是波伦亚大学和比萨大学的法学教授,他肯定了城邦(city state)的法则域外效力及其对于非本城邦的居民的可适用性。巴托鲁斯认为:(1)法律行为的方式依行为地法;(2)合同的成立依场所支配行为原则,适用合同缔结地法;(3)物权依物之所在地法;(4)遗嘱的成立要件依立嘱地法;(5)无遗嘱继承依遗产所在地法;(6)程序问题依法院地法。

以巴托鲁斯为代表的意大利法则说,适应当时意大利城邦之间民商事交往的需要,在总结大量的习惯做法的基础上,形成了自己独特的理论体系;该学说不仅试图圆满回答为什么要适用外国法的问题,而且试图归纳出一些普遍适用的原则,为国际私法进一步发展奠定了理论基础。巴托鲁斯时代的法学家们的贡献,在于对法律适用不采取单一的属人或属地原则,即既不单一依人的籍贯或居住地确定法律适用,也不单一地将所有涉外利益冲突关系作为一个整体,无区别地适用同一法律[2],而是站在一法域之外,各法域之间的基础上来提出调整法律冲突的方法,通过区别法律的性质来判断法律的效力范围并进而决定法律的选择。这是该学说对国际私法的重大贡献。

二、法国法则说

法国法学界在研究、接受意大利法则说的同时,形成了法国法则说(French theory of statutes),或者说法则说的法国学派(the French school),法则说的中心便从意

---

[1] See F. K. Juenger, *Choice of Law and Multistate Justice*, Martinus Nijhoff, 1993, pp. 1—16.
[2] 沈娟:《冲突法及其价值导向》(修订本),中国政法大学出版社2002年版,第77页。

大利转移到法国。①法国法则说的代表人物之一是达让特莱(Bertrand D'Argentr,1519—1590年)。

达让特莱系法国北方布列塔尼省的贵族和法学家,著有《布列塔尼习惯法评述》(Commentaire sur la coutume de Bretagne)和《布列塔尼的历史》(Historire de Bretagne)两本书。他出于封建主把领域内的一切人、物、行为都置于当地习惯控制之下的需要,极力鼓吹属地主义原则,推崇一种具有封建割据性的地方自治,法律也只能而且必须在制定者境内适用,其效力原则上不能及于域外。达让特莱所主张的这条属地主义路线,后来为荷兰法学家所继承,并且通过荷兰学派,使英、美在属人法的适用上强调住所地法,在物权关系的法律适用上强调物之所在地法。

三、荷兰法则说

荷兰法则说(Dutch theory of statutes)起源于16世纪末,形成于17世纪,延续至18世纪。它是以荷兰法学家胡伯(Ulrich Huber,1636—1694年)为代表的荷兰学者继承和发展的一种法则说。胡伯提出了礼让(**comity or courtesy**)学说。

【释义】　　　　　　　　　comity or courtesy

Ulrich Huber, a 17th Century Dutch scholar, created the notion of "comity," or "courtesy among political entities… involving especially mutual recognition of legislative, executive, and judicial acts," to explain how a country's laws or judgments could have force outside their own territory despite strict territorial notions of sovereignty. He stated that the sovereign power of each state was limited to its territory, that the sovereign has power over any individual found within his territory, and that where the sovereign court decides to apply foreign law, it does so based on the doctrine of comity. Huber did not believe that sovereigns were required to apply foreign law, but that they did so as a matter of international courtesy. Indeed, he argued that "recognition and enforcement rests upon comity and that it would be declined when the interests of the forum or of its subjects are impaired thereby."②

胡伯著有《论罗马法与现行法》一书,他在该书中阐述了在国际私法上著名的

---

① See F. K. Juenger, *Choice of Law and Multistate Justice*, Martinus Nijhoff, 1993, p.16.
② Susan L. Stevens, Commanding International Judicial Respect: Reciprocity and the Recognition and Enforcement of Foreign Judgments, 26 *Hastings Int'l & Comp. L. Rev.* 115, 119 (2002).

第四章 国际私法的理论学说

"胡伯三原则"(**three maxims of Ulrich Huber**)。①

【解说】　　　　　**three maxims of Ulrich Huber**

Ulrich Huber was successively a professor of law and a judge in Friesland. He wrote the shortest treatiese ever written on the conflict of laws, but his influence on its development in Englang and the United States has been great than that of any other foreign jurist. Huber laid down thress maxims as follows:

(1) The laws of each State have force within the limits of that government, and bind all subject to it, but not beyond.

(2) All persons within the limits of a government, whether they live there permanently or temporarily, are deemed to be subjects thereof.

(3) Sovereigns will so act by way of comity that rights acquired within the limits of a government retain their force everywhere so far as they do not cause prejudice to the power or rights of such government or of its subjects. ②

胡伯的前两个原则强调了主权和法律的属地性(**territory**),且把达让特莱的属地主义主张发展到极致,即完全否定了法律依本身的性质所具有的域外效力。

【释义】　　　　　**territory**

The raise of nation states gave increased enphasis to sovereign authority and the doctrine of territoriality began to dominate the Conflict of laws, particularly under the influence of the seventeenth century Dutch sholar Ulrich Huber. In the effort to reconcile territorial sovereignty which the necessity and convenience of courts determining matters with foreign contacts Huber drew on international law to explain the willingness of the soverign to permit the application of foreign law with in its courts, namely the comity of nations. ③

胡伯的后一个原则阐明了一国适用外国法律的根据和限制,提出了礼让的原则。礼让(**comity**),由此成为国际私法中的一个重要的理论基础。

---

① 即第一,一国的法律仅在其主权所及的领域内有绝对的效力;第二,在一统治者领域内的所有人,无论是常住还是暂住,都视为其国民,并受其法律约束;第三,但是,根据礼让,各统治者承认,已在其本国内实施的法律应该到处保持其效力,只要这样做不至于损害该统治者的国民。See Cheshire & North, *Private International Law*, 12th ed., Butterworths, London Ltd., 1992, pp.20—21.

② See David MaClean, *Morris: The conflict of Laws*, 5th ed., Sweet & Maxwell, 2000, p.533.

③ Luther L. McDougal III, Robert L. Felix, Ralph U. Whitten, *American Conflicts Law: Cases and Materials*, 4th ed., LexisNexis, 2004, p.6.

【释义】   comity

Comity, refers to legal reciprocity—the principle that one jurisdiction will extend certain courtesies to other nations (or other jurisdictions within the same nation), particularly by recognizing the validity and effect of their executive, legislative, and judicial acts. The term refers to the idea that courts should not act in a way that demeans the jurisdiction, laws, or judicial decisions of another jurisdiction. Part of the presumption of comity is that other jurisdictions will reciprocate the courtesy shown to them. The principle of comity first arose through the work of Ulrich Huber. It was subsequently refined by the American judge Joseph Story.

第二节 意思自治理论

一、意思自治理论的产生

法国学者杜摩兰(Charles Dumoulin,1500—1566年)作为法国巴黎高等法院的律师,顺应客观形势的需要,在《巴黎习惯法评述》(Commentaire sur la coutume de Paris)一书中,表现出一种克服法律的封建性、削减宗教法庭的权力以加强中央王权、统一法律的强烈愿望,并且提出在合同关系中,应该适用当事人自主选择的习惯法。杜摩兰提出的主张在国际私法上被称为"意思自治说"(autonomie de volonté)。

杜摩兰主张"物法"从物,无论对于本国人还是外国人,凡涉及境内之物的应依物之所在地法;而"人法"从人,其效力只及于境内境外自己的属民。不过他极力主张扩大"人法"的适用范围,而缩小"物法"的适用范围。①在他看来,民商事法律关系的当事人双方可以通过共同的意思表示,以合同的形式决定应适用的习惯法;如果当事人双方没有在合同中就此载明,则由法院根据案件的全部情况确定。杜摩兰的意思自治原则,后来逐渐成为选择合同准据法的一项普遍接受的原则。

二、意思自治原则的法哲学思想

意思自治原则是近代国际私法的标志,而自然法理论是其形成和发展的法哲

---

① 吕岩峰:《物权法律适用的历史沿革》,载中国国际私法学会主办:《中国国际私法与比较法年刊》(第六卷),法律出版社2003年版,第115页。

学基础。近代自然法哲学是17世纪和18世纪法学世界观的理论体现,主张自然法是人类最高的法律。自然法学者设想出受自然法统治的"自然状态",并将其与"天赋人权"和"社会契约论"等学说相结合,倡导了资产阶级的民主法制观,为近代资本主义提出了一系列法制的基本原则,并推进了包括国际私法在内的若干重要部门法的发展。

近代自然法哲学是国际私法的价值基础。自然法学说充分肯定人的理性、自由意志、平等和权利,是意思自治原则形成的思想基础。自然法渊源于人类的理性,是近代自然法哲学不可动摇的道德准则。[1]自然法学者关于自由意志的理念,使人从对神的依附中彻底地解放出来,成为具有独立人格和自由意志的人,奠定了契约自由和意思自治的思想基础。近代自然法论所倡导的"一切人生而平等,人们对财产、自由和生存有着不可否认的自然权利,政府的正当职责是承认和保护人们之间的平等"[2],这种注重人的自由、强调人的权利的思想成为"意思自治"原则的先导。杜摩兰的"意思自治说"是直接在自然法影响下形成的。

第三节 近代国际私法学说

一、萨维尼的"法律关系本座说"及其联系分析法

萨维尼(F. C. Savigny,1779—1861年)是德国柏林大学的教授,他在1849年出版的《现代罗马法体系》(System des Heutigen Römischen Rechts)一书第八卷中提出了"法律关系本座说"。

(一)法律关系本座说的基本原理

"法律关系本座说"(Sitz des Rechtsverhältnissese),从普遍主义观点出发,认为应该存在着一个"相互交往的国家的国际法律共同体",并且存在着普遍适用的各种冲突规则。为了使涉外案件无论在什么地方起诉,均能适用同一个法律,得到一致的判决,国际民商事关系应适用的法律只应是依其本身性质确定的其"本座"

---

[1] 参见张宏生主编:《西方法律思想史》,北京大学出版社1983年版,第141页。
[2] 参见〔英〕梅里曼:《大陆法系》,顾培东等译,台湾黎明文化事业公司1978年版,第21页。

(Sitz)所在地的法律。在萨维尼看来,"本座"是国际民商事关系在性质上所归属的地点。他认为,任何法律关系依其性质总是与一定的地域的法律相联系的。萨维尼把法律关系分为人、物、债、继承、家庭、法律行为、诉讼关系等几大类,住所是人的归属之处,所以人的身份及能力应以住所为本座;物是可以感知的,并且必须占据一定的空间,故物的所在地应为物权法律关系的本座;债为无体物,并且不占有空间,因而常常需要借助某种可见的外观来表现其形态,故应借此形态来定其本座,这种外观形态可以有两个,一个是债的发生地,另一个是债的履行地,其中履行地更适合于表现债权的外观形态,故应以履行地为本座,因为它是实现债权的场所;行为方式则不论财产行为和身份行为,均应以行为地为本座;程序问题应以法院地为本座。[1]借助于法律关系"本座"的概念,人们可以通过对各种法律关系性质的分析,方便地制定出各种双边冲突规范去指导法律的选择。"本座"概念的提出丰富和发展了国际私法学的理论体系。

(二)"本座"概念的提出对日后国际私法理论的发展具有重大意义

萨维尼的"法律关系本座说"突破了在欧洲存在几百年的法则说的传统,开创了法律适用思维的新方式,对各国的国际私法立法和司法实践产生了广泛的影响。"法律关系本座说"在"法则说"统治国际私法达数百年后,实现了国际私法方法论的根本变革。[2]在这之前,法律适用的思维模式是从法则到法律关系,先把法则分为不同的种类,再把不同的法则适用于不同的法律关系,完全忽视了法则的不变性和法律关系的灵活多变性。在这之后,法律适用的思维模式转变成从法律关系到法则,先对法律关系予以定性,再把法律关系置于法则的调控之下。[3]萨维尼的"法律关系本座说"无论对大陆法系还是英美法系都产生了决定性的影响,以摧枯拉朽般的气势实现了国际私法方法论上的彻底革新,开辟了整个国际私法领域的新天地。

萨维尼的理论实现了国际私法从"学说法"到"制定法"的变革,对推动国际私法典的建立起了积极作用。不仅如此,各国国际私法的立法内容也是参照了"法律关系本座说"的理论逻辑方法,从而各国制定了一系列传统的冲突规范,即将国际民商事关系根据其性质进行分类,再为各类不同的国际民商事关系确定一个法律适用原则。萨维尼提出的一系列准据法公式,都被各国国际私法立法所采纳。虽然晚近国际私法立法对此提出了新的挑战,但萨维尼之学说所蕴含的科学性,据此

---

[1] 张仲伯:《国际私法学》,中国政法大学出版社1998年版,第40页。
[2] 韩德培:《国际私法新论》,武汉大学出版社1997年版,第63页。
[3] 高兰英、蒋琼:《浅议"法律关系本座说"的扬弃》,载《广西政法管理干部学院学报》2002年第3期。

而制定的冲突规范的明确性、稳定性、易操作性等优点仍显而易见。在国际私法立法相对落后的国家,这类传统冲突规范仍占据着主要地位,甚至在国际私法立法较为先进的国家,他们对传统冲突规范的改革也是对传统冲突规范的一种完善,并且其大多数立法内容仍采取的是传统冲突规范的思维模式。可以说,萨维尼所确定的这些冲突规范一直沿用至今,仍具有强盛的生命力,构成近现代国际私法的基本规范。

近现代国际私法把"法律关系本座说"置于一个基础、核心的地位。在继承的基础上加以发扬,在批驳的基础上予以完善,无怪乎有人将萨维尼的理论喻为国际私法上的"哥白尼革命",把萨维尼尊称为"近代国际私法之父"。萨维尼能在一个世纪以前就提出至今仍有深远影响的"法律关系本座说",实乃功不可没。

二、孟西尼的"国籍国法说"

孟西尼(P. S. Mancini, 1817—1888年)是意大利著名的政治家和国际私法学家。作为一个民族主义者,他发表了《国籍是国际法的基础》(Nationality as the Foundation of Law of Nations)的专题演讲,提出了以国籍主义为核心的国际私法三原则。其一为国籍原则,又称本国法原则,即主张一切法律关系,不论其种类如何,原则上要以国籍作为连接因素,以当事人的国籍国法或本国法作为准据法。一国的国民即使身处国外,原则上也只是与自己本国的法律相联系。作为例外,当事人可以适用他们在合同中所指定的法律。① 其二为主权原则,又称公共秩序原则,即主张涉及国家公共利益的事情,不能适用当事人本国法或当事人自由选择的法律,为保护公共秩序而创立的法规应拘束本国境内的一切人。其三为自由原则,又称意思自治原则,即主张合同关系应按当事人意思来决定应适用的法律,或者说合同当事人有选择适用于合同的法律的自由。②

孟西尼的以国籍主义为核心的属人论,在国际私法立法上和学术界都有很大的影响。在19世纪以前,人们一直认为属人法为当事人的住所地法,但后来在《法国民法典》和孟西尼的国籍主义思想的影响下,属人法逐渐形成有国籍国法和住所地法这两种不同的理解,在实践中,不少国家把当事人的国籍国法或本国法当做属人法,而另一部分国家仍坚持以当事人住所地法为属人法。

---

① 参见余先予主编:《冲突法》,上海财经大学出版社1999年版,第57页。
② 关于孟西尼的学说,参见〔德〕马丁·沃尔夫:《国际私法》,李浩培等译,法律出版社1988年版,第61—64页。

三、戴赛的"既得权说"

在 19 世纪以前,英国没有自己的国际私法学。①当国际私法发展到一定程度时,英国开始有了研究适用外国法的理由的理论。英国牛津大学教授戴赛(A. V. Dicey,1835—1922 年)于 1896 年发表的《关于法律冲突的英格兰法汇纂》(A Digest of the Laws of England with Reference to the Conflict of Laws)一书,阐述了"既得权学说"(**theory of vested rights**)。

【解说】　　　　　　　theory of vested rights
　　The court never applies in strictness foreign law; when they are said to do so, they enforce not foreign law, but rights acquired under foreign law.②

戴赛从法律的严格属地性出发,认为一国法院既不能直接承认和适用外国法,也不能直接执行外国法院的判决,因为法院的任务只是绝对地适用内国法律。但是,为了保障涉外法律关系的稳定性,对于根据外国法已设定的权利,除了与内国公共政策、道德原则和国家主权发生抵触者外,都应获得承认与保护。公共政策、道德原则和国家主权发生抵触者外,都应获得承认与保护。根据戴赛的既得权理论,法官只负有适用内国法的任务,他既不能直接承认或者适用外国法,也不能直接执行外国的判决。因此,法官所做的只不过是保护诉讼人根据外国法或者外国判决已取得的权利。③戴赛学说的核心就是一国法院在利用外国法律处理涉外案件时,它并不是承认和执行外国法,而是承认和执行依外国法取得的权利。④ 所以,域外效力不是给予外国法,而只是给予它所创设的权利。

既得权说是在继承了荷兰法则说和斯托雷的礼让说中的属地主义的基础上发展起来的。该学说虽然产生于 19 世纪下半叶,但在 19 和 20 世纪之交风行于英国

---

① 英国法律史中,理论是走在实践后面的,由于英国实践中不考虑外域法的适用,理论上也就无研究法律选择规则的必要。17 世纪,英格兰法院开始有承认外国法院根据外国法所作的判决,以及在案件中适用英格兰法以外法律的例子。这时,英格兰法已经包含了威尔士法,在英国境内主要是英格兰法和苏格兰法两大法域。18 世纪末,英格兰法与苏格兰法的冲突加剧,引起英国法院的重视。但在 19 世纪中叶以前,"法院判决稀少而且常常是没有生气和模糊不清的"。参见沃尔夫:《国际私法》,李浩培等译,法律出版社 1988 年版,第 54、69 页。

② Dicey, *A Digest of the Laws of England with reference to the Conflict of Laws*, 3rd ed., The Boston Book Co., p.11.

③ 参见鲁世平:《美国国际私法既得权时代之法哲学论析》,载《大连海事大学学报(社会科学版)》2009 年第 3 期。

④ David McClean, *Morris: The Conflict of Laws*, 5th ed., Sweet & Maxwell, 2000, p.535.

和美国,可以说,它在英国和美国的国际私法理论的发展历程中起到了继往开来的作用。

四、美国传统国际私法的理论

美国独立以后,创制了以英国普通法为中心的美国法,在国际私法方面的发展迅速。这主要是因为,美国独立之后未能统一各州法律,大量的州际关系使各州之间的法律冲突明显而剧烈,促使理论上发展了对国际私法的研究。①

美国传统国际私法的主要理论渊源来自于欧陆的"国际礼让说"(18 世纪),与英国的"既得权理论"(19 世纪)②,在此基础上形成了以斯托雷为代表(19 世纪后叶)和比尔为代表(20 世纪前叶)的美国国际私法理论流派。

(一)斯托雷的"国际礼让说"

美国独立后,整个法律体制的模式基本上承袭了英国的一套。但在国际私法方面,它则接受了荷兰的法则说。1834 年,同时任美国最高法院法官和哈佛大学法学教授的斯托雷(**Joseph Story**,1779—1845 年)出版了《法律冲突论》(Commentaries on the Conflict of Laws)一书,该书被誉为自 19 世纪以来最杰出的国际私法著作。

【人物】　　　　　　　　　　**Joseph Story**

American thinking about conflicts problems is usually traced the Justice Joseph Story's magisterial treatise, Commentary on the Conflict of Law, Foreign and Domestic (1934), This Extraordinary work was of great influence ont just in U.S., but in Britain and on the Continent as well. Story emphasized the use of comity, a duty of "mutual interest and unity" owed by one state to another.③ Joseph Story, the first great American conflict theorist, assumed the first approach. He belive that the forum court "applied" the foreign law based on the theory of comity—the customary respect given by one sovereign to another.④

斯托雷提出了自己的"礼让说"(doctrine of comity),其理论论点对美国和英国

---

① 沈娟:《冲突法及其价值导向》(修订本),中国政法大学出版社 2002 年版,第 82 页。
② See Kurt H. Nadelmann, Some History Notes on the Doctrinal Sources of American Conflict Law, in *Conflict of Laws: International and Interstate* (Selected Essays),1972,pp.1—20.
③ David H. Vernon, Louis Weinberg, William Reynolds, William Richman, *Conflicts of Law: Case, Materials and Problems*, 2d ed., LexisNexis, 2002, p.239.
④ Ibid., p.247.

国际私法的法律思想产生了巨大的影响。①斯托雷的"礼让说"包括:第一,一国在其领土范围内享有专属的主权和司法管辖权,其法律管辖该国领土范围内的一切人、财产和行为;第二,一国法律不能直接地影响和约束该国领土范围之外的人和财产;第三,一国法律要在他国取得效力,必须取得他国法律和制度明示或暗示的同意。

斯托雷的学说强调了国家主权和管辖权的排他性(**exclusive sovereignty and jurisdiction**)。根据斯托雷的"礼让说",一国适用外国法完全是基于礼让(ex comitate),而不是基于法律义务(ex jure)。

【解说】　　　　　exclusive sovereignty and jurisdiction

Every nation possesses an exclusive sovereignty and jurisdiction within its own territory. The direct consequence of this rule is, that the laws of every state affect, and bind directly all property, whether real or personal, within its territory; and all person, who are resident within it, whether natural born subjects, or aliens; and also all contracts made and acts one within it. A state may therefore, regulater the manner and circumstances, under which property, whether real or personal, or in action, within it, shall be held, transmitted, bequeathed, transferred, or enforced; the condition, capacity, and state, of all persons within it. ②

斯托雷的"礼让说"同时也强调了互惠性(**reciprocity**):适用外国法是一种互惠互利的要求,一国适用了外国法,公平对待了他国公民,为的是本国的法律在外国得到公正的适用和本国的公民也能够在外国得到平等的待遇。

【解说】　　　　　　　　reciprocity

The true foundation, on which the administration of international law must rest, is, that the rules, which are to govern, are those, which arise from mutual interest and utility, from a sense of the inconveniences, which would result from a contrary doctrine, and from a sort of moral necessity to do justice, in order that justice may be done to us in return.③

---

① Joseph Story, *Commentary on the Conflict of Law, Foreign and Domestic*, 1834, p.34.
② Luther L. McDougal III, Robert L. Felix, Ralph U. Whitten, *American Conflicts Law: Cases and Materials*, 4th ed., LexisNexis, 2004, p.8.
③ David McClean, *Morris: The Conflict of Laws*, 5th ed., Sweet & Maxwell, 2000, p.534.

（二）比尔的"既得权说"

美国的比尔（Joseph H. Beale）借鉴英国戴赛的学说，对斯托雷的理论进行了修正，提出了比尔的"既得权说"（**Vested rights theory of Joseph Beale**）。

【学说】　**Vested rights theory of Joseph Beale**

Beale's vested rights theory is founded on a particular view of the functions and nature of law. He devided law in the abstract into two categories: the particular law of a state and the genereal common law. Particular law varied from state to state; its variation resulted from the different statutes in effect in defferent and from the errors that judges made in interpreting the general common law. In contrast, general common law was a single homogenerous philosophical system. While a state might decline to adopt it, the general common law continued in existence nontheless.①

The vested rights theory provided a view of the choice of law process that was more acceptable to the territorialist and formalist jurisprudence of the early twentieth century. The theory propounded by Joseph H. Beale held that foreign law could never operate outside the territory of the foreign souvergin. Rather, the forum's use of foreign law could be explained in terms of the forum's enforcement of a right that had vested as a result of an occurrence in the foreign jurisdiction.②

The premises were that: (1) law is territorial; (2) an obligation breached in one state creates a transitory claim that may be sued on in other states; and (3) law is territorial not in the sense of enforcing the right, but in the sense of creating the right when the operative events occurred.③

该学说认为，跨国（州）民事纠纷实际上是当事人之间的权利（或义务）之争，而当事人的民事权利并不是与生俱来的，而是法律"赋予"的。倘若如此，法律又是如何赋予当事人权利的呢？对此，比尔解释称，只有当特定事件发生后，当事人始得法律上的权利。于是，这些特定事件发生在哪里，哪里的法律就应成为解决当事人之间纠纷的准据法，即当事人依该特定事件发生地法而产生的既得权利，其他国家应予承认。④由于这些特定事件表现为住所的取得、合同的缔结和履行、侵权行为的发生等，以它们作为连接点而形成的美国传统国际私法与欧洲传统国际私法如出一辙，均为一些固定的冲突规则。

---

① Lea Brilmayer, *Conflict of Laws*, 2d ed., Aspen Law & Business, 1995, pp. 20—21.
② David H. Vernon, Louis Weinberg, William Reynolds, William Richman, *Conflicts of Law: Case, Materials and Problems*, 2nd ed., LexisNexis, 2002, pp. 247—248.
③ See generally Joseph H. Beale, *A Treatise on the Conflict of Law* (1935).
④ G. R. Shreve, Choice of Law and the Foreign Constitution, 71 *Indiana L. J.* 284 (1996).

比尔的学说对于美国冲突法的现代化(**modern content of conflict of laws**)具有重要作用。

【人物】　　　　　　　　**modern content of conflict of laws**

As professor Leflar noted: The suject of conflict of laws was first given its modern content by Professor Joseph Beale of Havard, who developed it as a law school course at the turn of the resent century. His three-volume casebook, published in 1901 (with some later additions), included what are still today its standard topics, ...and in a sense fretold the first Restatement of Conflict of Laws, for which Beale was reporter.①

比尔的思想体现在以其为首编撰的1934年美国《第一次冲突法重述》中,认为跨国(州)民事纠纷实际上是当事人之间的权利之争,内国并不承认外国的法律在内国的效力,内国仅承认根据礼让可以获得承认的外国的权利。②该示范法为了使外国的权利根据礼让可以在美国法院获得承认,建立了一套概念主义国际私法观的国际私法规则体系③,它通过连接点这一抽象概念将某一权利固定在某一地域(该地域必定是该权利得以产生的地方),形成了一种概念化的系属公式以及固定的冲突规则来解决适用何国法律的问题。④比尔的思想影响(**influence of Joseph Beale**)深远。

【人物】　　　　　　　　**influence of Joseph Beale**

Joseph Beale's vested-rights theories dominated the first half of the twentieth century and remain an influence today. His three-volume conflicts treatise paralleled the First Restatement, for which he was Reporter or chief architect. Beale used Holmes's vested-rights notion to take Story's territorial concepts in a new direction.⑤

Under the influence of Joseph Beale, the Reporter for the project, the American Law Institute incorporated the vested rights theory into the First Restatement. This traditional system

---

① Rebert A. Reflar, The nature of Conflict of Laws, 81 Collum. L. Rev. 1080 (1981).
② 参见刘铁铮、陈荣传:《国际私法论》,台湾三民书局1998年版,第50—52页。
③ 所谓概念主义,以法国民法典的冠名者拿破仑的名言最有代表性:"将法律化为简单的几个公式是可能的,任何一个能认字并能将两个思想联系起来的人,就能作出法律上的裁决"。转引自沈宗灵:《现代西方法律哲学》,法律出版社1983年版,第98页。
④ 郭树理、唐燕:《功能主义国际私法与概念主义国际私法之互动——最密切联系原则再认识》,载《2002年国际私法年会论文集》,华东政法学院国际法系编。
⑤ James P. George, False Conflicts and Faulty Analyses: Judicial Misuse of Governmental Interests in the Second Restatement of Conflict of Laws, 23 Rev. Litig. 489, n13 (2004).

prevailed in most American courts until the work of a new generation of judges and scholars, trained in legal realism, began to supplant it in the 1950's and 1960's. Even today, the First Restatement system retains a good deal of vitality. In perhaps a quarter of states, it is alive and well as the dominant general choice-of-law methodology.①

Furthermore, even the states that have abandoned the First Restatement for most choice-of-law problem retain it for issues involving interstsnin land. The vested rights theory or its twin, the territory theory, dominated judicial thinking and decisions in the United States for several decades.②

国际私法自13世纪产生以来,经过法则区别说、法律关系本座说等理论的充实与发展,形成了一系列可供司法实践审理涉外民商事案件的"规则"。冲突法规则明确地将法律适用问题用简洁、清晰的公示表达出来,具有确定性和可预见性。制定一个规则的成本要比制定一个标准的成本高出许多③,但是规则却能节省法官审理案件的成本和当事人服从冲突规范的成本,对于迅速有效解决涉外民商法律冲突起到积极的作用。

第四节 当代国际私法学说

随着人类进入20世纪,国际私法的发展也进入了一个新的纪元。第二次世界大战后,国际私法学说百家争鸣,不断推动着国际私法的理论创新。

一、当代国际私法的变革与创新

萨维尼以抽象人格为前提、以意思自治为内核建构的理论隐含着这样一种缺陷:任何一个涉及法律冲突的案件,都应该适用冲突规范所指引的地域的法律,即准据法解决,至于准据法的内容是什么、案件能否得到公正处理则在所不问。这种

---

① Symeon Symeonides, Choice of Law in the American Courts in 1999: One More Years, 48 *Am. J. Comp. L.* 143, 143 (2000).

② Luther L. McDougal III, Robert L. Felix, Ralph U. Whitten, *American Conflicts Law: Cases and Materials*, 4th ed., LexisNexis, 2004, p.11.

③ 参见田洪鋆:《国际私法中规则和标准之争的经济学分析》,载《法制与社会发展》2011年第1期。

漠视案件具体情况、对当事人麻木不仁的做法,在追求实质正义的20世纪显得不合时宜。

变革与创新是当代国际私法的潮流。在20世纪,国际私法学者直接针对传统的国际私法理论和方法进行了重大的变革。在这场变革中,美国国际私法界无疑起了领头的作用。这股变革的浪潮起源于20世纪30年代。1934年,美国哈佛大学法学院教授比尔根据传统的"既得权说"主持编纂的《冲突法重述》出版。次年,他又接着出版了他的三大卷专著《冲突法论》。但就在他的这些著作出版问世的前后,他的观点受到库克(W. W. Cook)、洛伦森(E. G. Lorenzen)和卡弗斯等人的尖锐批评。他们彻底否定了比尔的"既得权说",代之以库克所提倡的"本地法说"和卡弗斯的"规则选择说"或"结果选择说"。

第二次世界大战后,美国的国际私法学说迅速发展,众多的学者出版了大量的著作和文章,学者们对传统的国际私法,尤其是它那通过冲突规范去选择适用准据法的"呆板的"、"机械的"传统方法,纷纷予以猛烈的抨击,并各自提出了独树一帜的新学说。例如,卡弗斯的"优先原则说"、柯里的"政府利益分析说"、艾伦茨威格的"法院地法说"、莱弗拉尔的"较好法律说"、冯·梅伦和特劳特曼的"功用分析说"或"多州法则说"以及里斯(W. L. M. Reese)的"最重要联系说"等。各个学说虽然内容不同,瑕瑜互见,有的十分激烈,有的较为温和,但都积极主张变革传统的国际私法,以适应在现代条件下日趋复杂的涉外法律关系。这些主张变革的新学说,不但在美国法学界引起广泛的注意和热烈的讨论,而且在其他一些国家也受到关注并产生了不可忽视的影响。[1]英国国际私法学者莫里斯曾经指出:"这种现象在其他任何国家,在这门学科许多世纪以来的漫长历史中的其他任何时期,都没有见过过。"[2]由于当代美国国际私法学说直接把矛头指向传统的国际私法,视其为呆板的理论和机械的方法,包含着极大的错误和偏见,并主张用一些更灵活的实用主义理论和方法来代替之,因此,美国国际私法学者艾伦茨威格等人甚至把这种变革称为"革命"。当然,其他国家尤其是欧洲国家的国际私法学者对当代国际私法的变革和创新也作出了自己的贡献,这一点在最密切联系理论的发展过程中表现得尤为明显。下面,笔者结合国际私法的理论发展,讨论一下当代国际私法的变革与创新。

(一)原苏联及东欧国家的国际私法学说

谈到20世纪的国际私法理论,不能不提到原苏联及东欧国家的国际私法学。

---

[1] 参见韩德培、韩健:《美国国际私法(冲突法)导论》,法律出版社1994年版,第2—3页。
[2] 〔英〕莫里斯:《法律冲突法》,李东来等译,中国对外翻译出版公司1990年版,第508页。

1917年十月社会主义革命以后,原苏联及东欧国家逐渐建立了自己的国际私法学,形成所谓"对外政策学派"。①这个学派的学说的出发点是国家的对外政策,认为一个国家的国际私法的内容取决于该国对外政策的任务。隆茨是原苏联国际私法学的代表人物。他认为,国际私法是国家对外政策的反映,服务于国家对外经济交往的需要。原苏联和东欧国家的国际私法学还有一个很大的特点,这就是在国际私法的范围上,突破了西方国际私法理论的传统观念,认为国际私法除包括冲突规范、外国人的民事法律地位规范、国际民事诉讼程序规范外,还包括国际统一实体规范。原苏联的隆茨、匈牙利的萨瑟、德意志民主共和国的魏曼等都持这种观点。

(二)库克的"本地法说"

20世纪初期,戴赛和比尔的"既得权说"取代了斯托雷的"礼让说"在美国国际私法学界的统治地位。但没过多久,既得权理论的地位就开始受到学界的抨击。库克提出"本地法说"是抨击开始的标志之一。

库克(Walter W., Cook, 1873—1943年)1942年出版了《冲突法的逻辑与法律基础》(The Logical and Legal Base of the Conflict of Laws)一书,全面阐述了他的"本地法说"(**local law theory**)。②

【学说】　　　　　　　　　　local law theory

The forum, when confronted by a case involving foreign elements, always applies its own law to the case, but in doing so adopts and enforces as its own law a rule of decision identical, or at least highly similar though not identical, in scope with a rule of decision found in the system of law in force in another state or country with which some or all of the foreign elements are connected, the rule so selected being in many groups of cases, and subject to the exceptions to be noted later, the rule of decision which the given foreign state or country would apply, not to this very group of facts now before the court of the forum, but to a *similar but purely domestic group of facts involving for the foreign court no foreign element*.... The forum thus enforces not a foreign right but a right created by its own law.③

---

① 参见《中国大百科全书·法学》,中国大百科全书出版社1984年版,第73页。
② Walter W., Cook, *Logical and legal Base of the Conflict of Laws*, Harvard Univ. Press, 1942, pp. 20—21.
③ 即一国法院审理涉外案件时,总是适用它自己的法律,尽管有时固然要考虑外国法中的规则,但法院这样做只是采用了该外国的与自己本地法律相同或相似的法律规则,这样就将外国法规则"合并"到"本地法"之中了,实际上是适用本地法,因而法院执行的权利并不是外国的权利,而是根据它自己的法律所创设的权利。

库克认为，一国法院审理涉外案件时，总是适用它自己的法律，尽管有时固然要考虑外国法中的规则，但法院这样做只是采用了该外国的与自己本地法律相同或相似的法律规则，这样就将外国法规则"合并"到"本地法"之中了，实际上是适用本地法，因而法院执行的权利并不是外国的权利，而是根据它自己的法律所创设的权利。

库克的理论，在摧毁美国传统的国际私法理论方面，确实起了很大的作用，因而是当代美国国际私法学说的先驱。晚近美国有关国际私法的一些新学说，不少是在他的影响下形成的。但是，他对于在处理涉外案件时究竟如何考虑和选择应适用的法律这一问题，未能提供建设性的解决方案。因此，有学者认为，库克的理论是破坏性的，而非建设性的。①

（三）柯里的"政府利益分析说"

美国国际私法学者柯里（Brainerd Currie，1912—1963 年）教授主张彻底抛弃旧的国际私法，取而代之以政府利益分析方法。柯里提出了著名的"政府利益分析说"（Governmental interest analysis theory），他认为"冲突法的核心问题或许可以说是……当两个或两个以上州的利益存在冲突时，确定恰当的实体法规范的问题，换言之，就是确定何州利益让位的问题。"② 柯里教授的方法（**Currie's approach**）具有其独特的学术思想。

【学说】　　　　　　　　　　　　Currie's approach

Currie's approach has several distinct elements. As with other choice of las scholars, one of Currie's goals was to consolidate the critisms of the First Restatement. In his view, the essential problem was that such rules nullify state interests, often without even hererby advancing the interests of some other states. This leas courts to seek ways to evade the rules about vested rights.③

柯里教授于 1963 年出版了《冲突法论文选集》（Selected Essays on the Conflict of Laws）一书，集中反映了其"政府利益分析说"的核心内容。④在该著作中，柯里对传统的冲突法制度进行了猛烈的抨击（**attack**）。

---

① See J. H. C. Morris, *The Conflict of Laws*, 4th ed., Stevens & Sons Ltd., 1993, pp.446—447.
② B. Currie, *Selected Essays on the Conflict of Laws*, Duke University Press, 1963, p.178.
③ Lea Brilmayer, *Conflict of Laws*, 2nd ed., Aspen Law & Business, 1995, p.48.
④ 参见邓正来：《美国现代国际私法流派》，法律出版社 1987 年版，第 126—128 页。

【观点】

attack

We would be better off without choice-of-law rules. We would be better off if Congress were to give some attention to problems of private law, and were to legislate concerning the choice between conflicting state interests in some of the specific areas in which the need for solutions is serious. In the meantime, we would be better off if we would admit the teachings of sociological jurisprudence into the conceptualistic precincts of conflict of laws. This would imply a basic method along the following lines:

1. Normally, even in cases involving foreign elements, the court should be expected, as a matter of course, to apply the rule of decision found in the law of the forum.

2. When it is suggested that the law of a foreign state should furnish the rule of decision, the court should, first of all, determine the governmental policy expressed in the law of the forum. It should then inquire whether the relation of the forum to the case is such as to provide a legitimate basis for the assertion of an interest in the application of that policy. This process is essentially the familiar one of construction or interpretation. Just as we determine by that process how a statute applies in time, and how it applies to marginal domestic situations, so we may determine how it should be applied to cases involving foreign elements in order to effectuate the legislative purpose.

3. If necessary, the court should similarly determine the policy expressed by the foreign law, and whether the foreign state has an interest in the application of its policy.

4. If the court finds that the forum state has no interest in the application of its policy, but that the foreign state has, it should apply the foreign law.

5. If the court finds that the forum state has an interest in the application of its policy, it should apply the law of the forum, even though the foreign state also has an interest in the application of its contrary policy, and, afortiori, it should apply the law of the forum if the foreign state has no such interest.①

柯里的"政府利益分析说"涉及几个既独立又相互关联的问题：

第一，政策问题。柯里认为，任何州或国家的法律规范都是用来体现政府政策的，立法者不是法官，也不是其他人，而是政府政策的制定者。立法者制定某一法律规范的目的，是为了通过适用该法律规范而促使政府的某一特定政策得到实现。

第二，利益问题。柯里认为，由于某个州或国家适用其法律规范的目的在于实现其政府的相应政策，所以该州或该国在适用其法律规范方面就存在着某种利益，而这种利益显然是政府利益。然而，尽管美国各州或各国在适用其自己的法律方面都存在着某种利益，但在具体情况下，各州或各国所主张的利益则并不一定是"合法的"或"合理的"。因此，法院在审理某个具体案件时，只能适用具有合法的

---

① Currie, Notes on Methods and Objectives in the Conflict of Laws, in *Selected Essays on the Conflict of Laws* 177, 183—187 (1963).

或合理的政府利益的那个州或国家的法律。

第三,分析方法问题。法官在确定法律适用问题时,如何判断各有关州或国家在具体案件中是否具有合法的或合理的利益呢？根据柯里的理论,法官应当采取"政府利益分析"方法来解决这个问题。然而,法官在运用这种分析方法时,从方法论上来说应当采取两个具体步骤：即首先,必须确定构成某条实体法规范基础的政府政策是什么样的政策,具有何种目的;其次,必须确定制定这一实体法规范的州或国家在将这一政策适用于具体案件时是否具有利益。

柯里提的"政府利益分析说"所创立的法律选择方式属于功能性法律选择方法(**functional method of choice-of-law analysis**)。

【释义】 functional method of choice-of-law analysis

A "functional method of choice-of-law analysis" describes a process that first focuses on the apparently conflicting domestic rules of weo or more jurisdictions having contacts with the parties and with the transaction. The policies underlying each state's rules are identified. Then the question is asked: "Which states are likely to experience the social consequences of implementing or frustrating those policies?" It is one of the premises of functional choice-of-law analysis that at this point many conflicts problems will be resolved. Only one stae will appear to have any "interest" in having its law applied, and its law, therefore, should be applied. The apparent conflict of laws is a "false" conflict. If, one the other hand, there are two or more states whose policies will be advanced by applying their laws, there is a "real conflict."[①]

在进行政府利益分析时,柯里认为,首先,当法院审理涉外案件时,如果涉及适用不同于法院地法的外州法或外国法,那么,它应该考查有关法律各自所体现的政策,并考查有关国家实施这些政策所主张的利益情况。其次,如果法院发现某州或某国家在实施其法律所体现的政策方面有利益,而另外的州或国家没有利益(这就是柯里所说的"虚伪冲突")(false conflict),那么,它就适用唯一有利益的州或国家的法律。再次,如果法院发现两个州或国家均有合法利益,存在着明显的利益冲突(这就是柯里所说的"真实冲突")(true conflict),而其中之一为法院地,那么,它就应该进一步考虑,对任何一方的政策或利益作出抑制性的解释,以避免冲突。如果双方的合法利益冲突仍不可避免,那么,就适用法院地法。最后,如果法院发现两个外州或外国均有合法利益,冲突不可避免,而法院所属州或国为无利益的第三

---

① Russell J Weintraub, *Commentary on the Conflict of Laws*, 4th ed, New York Foundation Press, 2001, p.52.

者,只要不违背公正原则,法院可以以自己不是适合的法院为理由,通过放弃管辖权来回避这个问题;如果法院不能回避,它则应该适用法院地法。

利用柯里的政府利益分析说处理案件,有四个原因(**four reasons why a court utilizing a functional analysis**)导致法院有时需要进行冲突法的功能分析。

【释义】 four reasons why a court utilizing a functional analysis

There are four reasons why a court utilizing a functional analysis of choice-of-law would refer to the conflicts rules of another jurisdiction. (1) The forum wishes to determine whether the other jurisdiction asserts an "interest" in the application of the other jurisdiction's law. (2) The forum has no significant contacts with the parties or the issues and all states with such contacts agree on the choice of law. (3) The forum wishes to reach the same result as the other jurisdiction because the other state has ultimate control over the outcome. (4) The forum is construing a statutory choice-of-law rule that is in territorial form.①

柯里的学说提出来以后,在美国国际私法学界引起很大的反响,直到现在,美国的一些新的国际私法理论也未能彻底摆脱他的学说的影响。美国的一些学者,如巴德(H. Baade)、汉考克(M. Hancock)、希尔(H. K. Hill)和温特劳布(Russell J Weintraub)等,在他们的著作中都支持并详尽阐述了这一学说。②

许多人曾对这一学说加以评论,大家褒贬不一。一般来说,人们对柯里作出的努力都是加以肯定的,他对传统国际私法理论的抨击和批判,可以说动摇了有几个世纪历史的国际私法理论基础,他的政府利益分析方法也有可取之处。但是,对于他的理论和方法仍有许多非议。柯里的学说中那些太过分追求法院地利益和狭隘的区域保护观念,虚假的立法意图③,以及企图彻底抛弃冲突规范及其制度从而否定国际私法的最基本内容的东西,是不可取的。④

(四)弗朗西斯卡基的"法律直接适用论"

在美国国际私法的"革命"汹涌澎湃之际,欧洲国际私法学界也有一股涌动的

---

① Russell J Weintraub, *Commentary on the Conflict of Laws*, 4th ed, New York Foundation Press, 2001, p.94.

② See D. F. Cavers, Contemporary Conflicts Law in American Perspective, 131 *Collected Courses* (1970-III), p.146.

③ 参见宋连斌、董海洲:《国际私法上的"政府利益分析说"探微》,载《政法论丛》2011年第2期。

④ See M. Hancock, Policy Controlled State Interest Analysis in Choice of Law, 26 *ICLQ*, 799 (1977); H. H. Kay, A Defense of Currie's Governmental Interest Analysis, 215 *Collected Courses* (1989-III) pp.13—204;邓正来:《美国现代国际私法流派》,法律出版社1987年版,第97—141页。

暗流,对传统国际私法冲突规范的作用提出质疑。法国学者福勋·弗朗西斯卡基(Phocion Francescakis)采用经验主义方法,从研究法国的判例中发现了在以往法国司法实践中存在一种运用于法律冲突问题的新的法律规范,于1958年发表的《反致理论和国际私法中的体系冲突》(La théorie du renvoi et les conflits de systèms en droit international privé)的学术论文中,首次将这类新的法律规范称为"直接适用的法"(loi d'application immédiate)。①弗朗西斯卡基指出,随着国家职能的改变及其在经济生活中作用的增加,国家制定了一系列具有强制力的法律规范,用以调整某些特殊的法律关系。这些具有强制力的法律规范在调整国际民商事关系时,可以撇开传统冲突规范的援引,而直接适用于国际民商事关系。这种能被直接适用的法律规范,就是"直接适用的法"。②与美国国际私法革命所倡导的国际私法规范柔性化处理的特点相比较,欧洲大陆的国际私法新理论表现出的是一种国际私法规范刚性化趋向。③

(五)凯格尔的"利益论"

1964年,德国国际私法学者吉哈德·凯格尔(Gerhard Kegel)④在海牙国际法学院作了题为《冲突法的危机》(The Crisis of Conflict of Laws)的著名演讲⑤,揭开了欧洲传统国际私法改良的序曲。凯格尔在《国际私法中的概念法学与利益法学》一文中,创立了国际私法"利益论"。凯格尔将国际私法上的利益归纳为三种:当事人利益(Parteiinteressen)、交往利益(Verkehrsinteressen)、秩序利益(Ordnungsinteressen)。凯格尔指出,在作出国际私法上的决定时,就要顾及案件中的各种利益及其评价。利益法学是在批判概念法学的基础上产生并逐步发展起来的。⑥凯格尔强调,要不断发展国际私法,概念法学和利益法学是两个必要的而且是同等必要的方面。概念法学的作用主要体现在国际私法的总论部分(allgemeiner Teil),而利益法学的功能更多地表现在国际私法的各论部分(besonderer Teil),国际私法就是以这种二元结构为基础的统一体。利益论主张扩大法官的自由裁量

---

① 有关该理论的详细讨论,参见徐冬根:《论法律直接适用说及其与冲突规范的关系》,载《中国法学》1990年第3期;徐冬根:《国际私法趋势论》,北京大学出版社2007年版,第九章(法律直接适用论)。
② See Donggen Xu, Le droit international privé de la responsabilité délictuelle: évolution récente et le droit chinois, Edition universitaire Fribourg, Suisse 1992, p.64.
③ 徐冬根:《论国际私法规范的柔性化与刚性化》,载《法制与社会发展》2003年第3期。
④ 德国当代著名的国际私法学家、科隆大学名誉教授,1912年6月26日生于马格德堡,1950年起担任德国科隆大学法学教授。凯格尔一生著述颇丰,其主要代表作有《国际私法中的概念法学与利益法学》(1953)等。1964年他在海牙国际法学院发表的《冲突法的危机》(The Crisis of Conflict of Laws)的演讲使其著称于世。
⑤ Kegel. G, The Crisis of Conflict of Laws, 112 Collected Courses (1964-Ⅲ), p.91.
⑥ 概念法学把法律制度理解为一种由法律概念构成的封闭体系,并据此要求法学研究"逻辑至上",将法官"局限于依照法律概念将案件进行逻辑归类",这样法官几乎成了一台适用法律的机器。

权,但同时认为,法官并不能随心所欲地去理解法律并进而作出相应的判决。① 利益论通过指导法官在审理案件时领悟法律中蕴含的价值取向,对囿于形式思维、接受过严厉的法律实证主义教育的一代法官来说,起到了解救和促进作用。

二、后现代国际私法理论

(一) 后现代主义与后现代法学

后现代主义(**postmodernism**)是一种新的学术思潮,发端于 20 世纪 60 年代,并很快席卷全球,形成一场声势浩大的后现代文化运动。

【释义】　　　　　　　　postmodernism

"Postmodernism is all the rage." Indeed, the use of the label "postmodern" has grown so in the last ten years that it is difficult to know what authors mean when they describe an event or cultural form as postmodern. Postmodernism is a fashionable description of an array of cultural phenomena ranging from architecture to art to science. Indeed, the scholarship of postmodernism is varied and, by its own admission, contains divergent postmodernisms.②

后现代主义于 20 世纪 90 年代初期传入中国。后现代方法从指称意义上讲不是指时间性、操作程度上可视的手段与方法——现代方法之后的具体有形的方法,而是一种哲学视角的方法论意义上的表征,一种新颖独特的价值观。因为从原初意义上讲,后现代主义本质上就是一种精神,一套价值模式。③ 后现代主义具有三个特征(**three conceptions of postmodernism**)。

【说理】　　　　　three conceptions of postmodernism

Postmodernism refers to at least three distinct but related conceptions.

First, according to David Harvey, the most startling fact about postmodernism is its total acceptance of the ephemerality, fragmentation, discontinuity, and the chaotic... But postmodernism responds to that fact in a very particular way. It does not try to transcend it, counteract it, or even to define the "eternal and immutable" elements that might lie within it. Postmod-

---

① 参见邹国勇:《凯格尔国际私法"利益论"述评》,载《2002 年中国国际私法年会论文集》,华东政法国际法系 2002 编印。
② See Andrew M. Jacobs, God Save This Postmodern Court: The Death of Necessity and The Transformation of the Supreme Court's Overruling Rhetoric, 63 U. Cin. L. Rev. 1119, 1143 (1995).
③ 参见王岳川:《后现代主义文化与美学》,北京大学出版社 1992 年版,第 23 页。

ernism swims, even wallows, in the fragmentary and the chaotic currents of change as if that is all there is.

Second, philosopher Jean Francois Lyotard defines the postmodern simply as "incredulity toward metanarratives." Perhaps the major metanarrative to inspire postmodern incredulity is the Enlightenment and its credo that rational thought, the empirical method, and an ever-growing body of science will lead not only to human progress, but to human good.

Third, rather than abstract ideals, postmodernism is "rooted in daily life," especially the commodification of culture. As J.M. Balkin puts it, postmodernism owes more to the shopping mall than to Lyotard, or, in Fredric Jameson's famous phrase, "postmodernism is the cultural logic of late capitalism." ①

后现代法学(postmodern jurisprudence)发端于20世纪下半叶,是从后现代主义的哲学理念和方法进入法学开始的,此后逐渐渗透到各个法学部门。②在中国法学界,朱苏力教授早在1994年就提及这一概念③,在一篇评论波斯纳的书评中分析了后现代主义一些思想来源和特征。④之后,后现代法学就随着这个术语的引入很快在中国法学领域引起强烈反响,赞同者和反对者的声音同样响亮而有力。⑤"后现代法学"是当前法学领域使用最为频繁的词汇之一。

(二) 后现代主义法哲学观及其对国际私法的影响

20世纪下半叶,后现代法学理论逐渐渗入到国际私法学领域当中,形成了后现代国际私法学思潮,它既包括法学家应用后现代理论进行的国际私法专题性研究,也涵盖后现代思想家在其哲学性作品中有关国际私法问题的一般论述,对国际私法发展所产生的影响进行评估和衡量。西班牙格拉那达(Granada)大学洛伦佐(Sanchez Lorenzo)教授在20世纪90年代初期开始将"后现代主义"理论运用到国际私法研究之中,他在1994年发表的《国际私法中的后现代主义》一文中运用后现代主义的理论和方法对国际私法学进行了深入研究。⑥德国海德堡大学吉姆(Erik Jayme)教授对"后现代国际私法"的研究也很突出。1995年,吉姆教授在海牙国际

---

① Barbara Stark, Women and Globalization: The Failure and Postmodern Possibilities of International Law, 33 *Vand. J. Transnat'l L.* 546 (2000).
② Stephen M. Feldman, The Politics of Postmodern Jurisprudence, *Michigan L. Rev.* 95 (1996).
③ 朱景文主编:《当代西方后现代法学》,法律出版社2002年版,第41页。
④ 朱苏力:《什么是法理学?》,载《中国书评》1995年9月,创刊号。
⑤ 关于中国学者对后现代主义比较全面的评价和批判,参见盛宁:《人文困惑与反思——西方后现代主义思潮批判》,生活·读书·新知三联书店1997年版。
⑥ Sanchez Lorenzo, Postmodernismo y Derecho internacional privado, 46 *Revista espanola de Derecho internacional privado*, 557 (1994).

法学院作了题为《文化一体化：后现代国际私法》的演讲。①此后，他又在多个场合对"后现代国际私法"（postmodern private international law）问题进行了比较深入和全面的研究和探讨。②

后现代主义法哲学观及其对国际私法的影响主要表现在以下几个方面：

（1）排斥统一性，强调差异性。

后现代主义哲学的某些主张和方法进入法学，形成了后现代主义法哲学观，主要表现为对理性主义的否定，反对用统一的、固定不变的逻辑来阐释和评价法律，主张不同法律之间的差异性。后现代主义法哲学观动摇了人们曾经深信不疑的那些作为现代法学基石的理念，如理性、个人权利、社会契约、正当程序等。③后现代主义法哲学观认为，既不存在理性的权利主体，也不存在构造法律的抽象理性；法律不是也不可能是一个独立自主的实体，它纯粹是一个社会、文化、历史和语言的创造物。④后现代主义法哲学观强调差异性，这种差异性在国际私法上具体表现在以下几个方面：

第一，对弱者的特别保护。后现代主义法哲学观认为，人类社会是一个息息相关、互相制约的共同体，其成员之间的关系不仅是竞争关系，而且还需要扶助，所以应对弱者进行保护。当代国际私法体现了保护弱者的思想，并将其作为一项基本原则。如1986年《德国国际私法》第30条规定即体现了保护弱者的精神。1996年《列支敦士登国际私法》第48条、1998年《突尼斯国际私法法规》第67条的规定也都体现了这样的立法精神：即不允许以"当事人选择法律"为由剥夺法律所提供给劳动者（雇员）的特殊保护；在无法律选择情况下，一般适用雇员惯常工作地法，以有利于雇员。⑤随着后现代主义法哲学观影响的日益扩大，对弱者给予特殊保护的原则在国际私法中将得到进一步贯彻。

第二，对妇女的特别保护。作为后现代法学组成部分的激进女权主义法学理

---

① Erik Jayme, Identité culturelle et intégration: Le droit international privé postmoderne, *Recueil des cours* 251 (1995), S. 11 ff.

② See Erik Jayme, Kulturelle Identitaet und Kindeswohl im Internationalen Kindschaftsrecht, *IPRax* 1996, S. 237 ff; Internationales Privatrecht und postmoderne Kultur, *ZfRV* 1997, S. 230 ff; Zum Jahrtausendwechsel: Das Kollisionsrecht zwischen Postmoderne und Futurismus, *IPRax* 2000, S. 166 ff.

③ 这些传统理念互相论证，要证明的核心思想是，法律是现代文明的外壳，它保证人们追求理性的理想和幸福。正是因为如此，自启蒙时代以来，浩如烟海的现代法理学著作几乎都是围绕着一个主线而展开的，那就是论证社会为什么要由规则统治而不是个人统治，社会应该用什么样的规则统治，规则如何才能统治。参见信春鹰：《后现代法学：为法治探索未来》，载《中国社会科学》2000年第5期。

④ 参见孙国华、冯玉军：《后现代主义法学理论评述》，载朱景文主编：《当代西方后现代法学》，法律出版社2002年版，第477页以下。

⑤ PM North, JJ Fawcett, *Cheshire and North's Private International Law*, 13th ed., London: Butterworths, 1999, pp. 855—857.

论认为,男性是规则导向的,女性是感情导向的。后现代主义法哲学观认为,女性与男性是有性别差别(**sex differences**)的,要求重新发掘和确认女性的价值。①

【说理】　　　　　　　　sex differences

What, then, is the postmodern "message" that feminist activists can employ? It concerns the role of language in the construction of sexual difference:

The postmodern position locating human experience as inescapably within language suggests that feminists should not overlook the constructive function of legal language as a critical frontier for feminist reforms. To put this "principle" more bluntly, legal discourse should be recognized as a site of political struggle over sex differences.

If sex differences are given by "nature," the liberating potential of legal reform is narrowed; if legal discourse is integral to the social construction of the very differences that seem most immutable, the scope of reform is broadened.

Since the anatomical distinctions between the sexes seem not only "natural" but fundamental to identity, proposing and describing the role of law in the production of the meaning of the female body seems like the most convincing subject with which to defend my case. Legal discourse then explains and rationalizes these meanings by an appeal to the "natural" differences between the sexes, differences that the rules themselves help to produce. The formal norm of legal neutrality [* 1079] conceals the way in which legal rules participate in the construction of those meanings.②

家庭关系中最能体现这种新的理念。国际私法对女性的特别保护体现了尊重女性的后现代主义法哲学价值观,如 1986 年《德国国际私法》第 3 节、1987 年《瑞士联邦国际私法》第 3—4 编、1995 年《意大利国际私法》第 4 章、1996 年《列支敦士登国际私法》第 3 章、1998 年《突尼斯国际私法法规》第 3 章、1998 年《俄罗斯联邦家庭法典》第 7 编(国际私法)、1999 年《白俄罗斯共和国民法典》第 7 编(国际私法)都规定了应适用有利于女性的法律。

(2)否定普遍性,强调多元性。

后现代国际私法理论反对普遍性,倡导国际私法多元化价值观。首先,在国际私法的价值方面,认为单一的正义观念不再存在,取而代之的是多元的、局部的、以多种方式存在的正义。当代国际私法的发展体现了该后现代主义法哲学观的影响,并在以下几个方面有所表现:其一,国际私法的立法模式呈现多元化趋势,仅晚近内国成文单行法典立法模式就出现了瑞士、意大利、罗马尼亚等多种模式。其

---

① Mary Frug, A Postmodern Feminist Legal Manifesto, 105 *Harv. L. Rev.* 1045, 1045 (1992).
② Barbara Johnson, The Postmodern in Feminism, 105 *Harv. L. Rev.* 1076, 1078 (1992).

二,法律选择方法的多元化,出现了"规则"与"方法"的结合、客观性冲突规范与主观性冲突规范的结合、对客观性冲突规范进行软化处理、有利原则的运用、替代条款的广泛接受、干涉规则与国际私法的实体化现象、在反致制度上的折中实践等现象。① 鉴于单独利用某一种法律选择方法难以解决日益纷繁复杂的国际民商事关系,因而需要突破传统观念的束缚,以多元价值观为指导,包括导入新的法律选择方法、采取多种不同法律选择方法的组合,既考虑法律选择方法的确定性,又考虑法律选择方法的灵活性,以及他们之间的适当平衡性②,大大提高法律选择的多元性。其三,国际民商事争议解决方式呈现多元化趋势,国际民事诉讼费用的昂贵和诉讼迟延,使得人们去寻求其他更为简便、经济、灵活的救济途径,即替代性纠纷解决方式来解决国际民商事法律争议,包括国际商事仲裁、国际民商事和解、国际民商事调解、监察员制度、微型法庭,以及网络虚拟法院等,这些方式以其各自特定的功能和特点,与国际民事诉讼相互协调地共同存在,形成一种互补的、满足社会主体多样需求的程序体系和动态的运作调整系统,构成了多元化的国际民商事争议解决机制。③ 后现代主义法哲学观强调方法论上的多元化,拓展了我们在国际私法方法论上的新视角。

(3) 反对确定性,强调多变性。

从法哲学的层面看,确定性所体现的价值就是秩序。④ 秩序的价值在于维系社会关系和社会的稳定性,从而为人类的生活和活动提供必需的条件。国际私法产生、发展的历史表明,它同所有其他法律部门一样,始终追求着秩序。然而,在不同的发展阶段,由于经济文化等发展程度不同,它所追求的侧重点也有所不同。传统国际私法所追求的价值就是为了使涉外民商事案件无论在何国法院起诉都能适用同一国法律,得到同样的判决,避免当事人挑选法院。在国际私法的发展初期,它较多关注的是判决结果的确定性和可预见性。这是与这一时期国际民商事交往的发展程度相适应的。在这一时期,国际的民商事交往虽然已经较多,但法律关系并不复杂,传统的冲突规范往往能比较完满地解决国际民商事交往中的争议。因此,体现判决结果的确定性和可预见性的冲突规范受到学者们和各国立法的肯定。

后现代法学家认为,法并不具有统一的本质和确定性。法从来都是不确定的

---

① 韩德培、杜涛:《晚近国际私法立法的新发展》,载中国国际私法学会主办:《中国国际私法与比较法年刊》,法律出版社2000年版,第23页。
② 在20世纪初,通常牺牲灵活性来满足确定性的需要。参见赵相林、邢钢:《全球化视野下的国际私法》,载《河南省政法管理干部学院学报》2003年第2期。
③ 屈广清、陈小云:《后现代国际私法理论探微》,载《大连海事大学学报》(社会科学版)2003年第2卷。
④ 秩序的基本特征是确定性和明确性。参见卢云主编:《法学基础理论》,中国政法大学出版社1994年版,第209页。

和相对的,法律上的多元性是生活世界的本来状态。①法律的不确定性是由于法律概念和法律结构的不确定性所造成的。②后现代主义法哲学观反映在国际私法理论上,就是越来越重视法律选择方法的多变性,主张法官根据具体情况,采用具体的法律选择方法:或者依法律性质选择法律,或者依法律关系性质选择法律,或者依最密切联系选择法律,或者依政府利益分析选择法律,或者按规则选择方法、分割方法、当事人意思自治方法、比较损害方法、功能分析方法选择法律,或者依有利于判决在外国的承认与执行方法选择法律。③法律选择方法的多变性,为个案的公正解决提供了便利,也为扩大法官的自由裁量权提供了理论基础。

（三）后现代主义与国际私法发展

认真对待后现代主义思潮及其法哲学思想,就是认真对待新的时代和新的法律思维。后现代主义法哲学观以严厉的态度重新审视了现代法学所信奉的那些基本原则,其本质是批判性的,表达方式是辛辣的。不可否认,后现代主义法哲学观已经对当代国际私法的发展产生了深远的影响。

后现代主义法哲学观排斥统一性,强调差异性,主张对弱者和女性给予特别保护;否定普遍性,强调多元性;反对确定性,强调多变性。后现代主义法哲学观可激发我们对现代国际私法理论的反思,对我们正确审视现代国际私法理论具有启发意义。更为重要的是,后现代主义法哲学观突破了传统的一元化思维模式,强调多维度、多视角、多元化地研究国际私法现象和国际私法学问题,为中国国际私法学界探索中国和全球国际私法的未来提供了新思维、新视野和新范式,有利于促进中国乃至全球国际私法的繁荣与发展,促进人类社会文明的进步。④对后现代主义法哲学观及其对国际私法影响的研究和探讨,对于我们繁荣我国国际私法理论学说、提高我国国际私法的学术研究水平具有重大的促进意义。

【思考题】

- "意思自治说"的基本理论要点和法律哲学思想是什么?
- "法律关系本座说"是谁提出来的?该理论的主要观点有哪些?
- 美国学者比尔的"既得权说"与英国学者戴赛的"既得权说"有什么差异?

---

① 参见杜涛:《后现代主义与国际私法研究的新视角》,载《法学论坛》2003 年第 3 期。
② 沈敏荣:《论法律的不确定性与后现代主义思潮》,载《云南社会科学》1998 年第 2 期。
③ 对于不同法律选择方式的介绍和评析,参见韩德培:《国际私法新论》,武汉大学出版社 1998 年版,第 158 页。
④ 屈广清、陈小云:《后现代国际私法理论探微》,载《大连海事大学学报》(社会科学版)2003 年第 2 卷。

第四章 国际私法的理论学说

- 试评析斯托雷"礼让说"。
- 美国学者柯里是如何对传统国际私法进行批评并建立其"政府利益分析说"的?
- 弗朗西斯卡基的"法律直接适用论"基本内容有哪些?
- 什么后现代主义法哲学观?它对国际私法有哪些影响?

【重要术语提示与中英文对照】

中文术语	英文对照
法则说	theory of statutes
意大利法则说	Italian theory of statutes
后期注释学派	post-glossators
法国法则说	French theory of statutes
荷兰法则说	Dutch theory of statutes
胡伯三原则	three maxims of Ulrich Huber
法律的属地性	territory
《巴黎习惯法评述》	Commentaire sur la coutume de Paris
意思自治说	*autonomie de volonté*
《现代罗马法体系》	System des Heutigen Römischen Rechts
法律关系本座	*sitz des rechtsverh(ltnisses*
《国籍是国际法的基础》	Nationality as the Foundation of Law of Nations
《关于法律冲突的英格兰法汇纂》	A Digest of the Laws of England with reference to the Conflict of Laws
既得权学说	theory of vested rights
《法律冲突论》	Commentaries on the Conflict of Laws
礼让说	doctrine of comity
管辖权的排他性	exclusive sovereignty and jurisdiction
礼让	*ex comitate*
法律义务	*ex jure*
对等性	reciprocity
《第一次冲突法重述》	First Restatement of Conflicts of Laws
《冲突法的逻辑与法律基础》	The Logical and Legal Base of the Conflict of Laws
本地法说	local law theory
政府利益分析说	governmental interest analysis theory
《冲突法论文选集》	Selected Essays on the Conflict of Laws
功能性法律选择方法	functional method of choice-of-law analysis

《反致理论和国际私法中的体系冲突》	La théorie du renvoi et les conflits de systèms en droit international privé
法律直接适用论	loi d'application immédiate
《冲突法的危机》	The Crisis of Conflict of Laws
后现代主义	postmodernism
后现代法学	postmodern jurisprudence
后现代国际私法	postmodern private international law
性别差别	sex differences

【推荐阅读文献】

- 徐冬根:《论法律直接适用说及其与冲突规范的关系》,载《中国法学》1990年第3期。

- 马德才:《论萨维尼的"法律关系本座说"在国际私法发展史上的影响》,载《甘肃政法学院学报》2001年第1期。

- 屈广清、陈小云:《后现代国际私法理论探微》,载《大连海事大学学报》(社会科学版)2003年第2卷。

- 徐冬根:《论国际私法规范的柔性化与刚性化》,载《法制与社会发展》2003年第3期。

- 徐冬根:《法律直接适用论》,载《国际私法趋势论》(第九章),北京大学出版社2007年版。

- 耿勇:《斯托雷和萨维尼国际私法思想之比较》,载《太平洋学报》2008年第1期。

- 田洪鋆:《国际私法中规则和标准之争的经济学分析》,载《法制与社会发展》2011年第1期。

- 宋连斌、董海洲:《国际私法上的"政府利益分析说"探微》,载《政法论丛》2011年第2期。

- Symeon C. Symeonides (ed.), *Private International Law at the End of the 20th Century: Progress or Regress?*, London: Kluwer Law International 1999.

- David H. Vernon, Louis Weinberg, William Reynolds, William Richman, *Conflicts of Law: Case, Materials and Problems*, 2d ed. LexisNexis 2002.

- Levin (H.), What Do We Really Know about the American Choice-of-Law Revolution?, 60 *Stan. L. Rev.* 247 (2007).

- Michaels (R.), After the Revolution B Decline and Return of U. S. Conflict of Laws, 11 *Ybk Priv. Int'l L.* 11 (2009).

- Minow (M.) & Singer (J.), In Favor of Foxes: Pluralism as Fact and Aid to the Pursuit of Justice, 90 *B. U. L. Rev.* 903 (2010).

- Bauer (J. P.), Shedding Light on Shady Grove: Further Reflections on the Erie Doctrine from a Conflicts Perspective, 88 *Notre Dame L. Rev.* 939 (2011).

【扩展阅读资料】

Unilateralism or Multilateralism?①

If economic analysis suggests that courts in solving choice of law issues should be open to apply the law of a foreign state—as opposed to pertinent application of the lex fori and creation of new international substantive law—another question arises: how exactly should the line between forum and foreign law be drawn? When should courts apply foreign law and when should they be allowed to resort to forum law? Since the selectivist method emerged in the 12th century two approaches have dominated the scene: first, the so-called unilateralist method of defining the spatial reach of legal norms according to their wish to be applied, and, second, the so-called multilateralist approach of assigning a legal relationship to a legal order according to objective criteria. Today, multilateralism provides the basis of most contemporary choice of law systems in both the United States and Europe. However, elements of unilateralism can be found on both sides of the Atlantic.

1. The Statutists' Method: Defining the Spatial Reach of Legal Norms

The unilateralist method goes back to the Italian scholars of the 12th century. When they were faced with the question of which city-states' law to apply in a particular case they decided to tackle the problem by defining the intended spatial reach of the conflicting local laws. To this end, they divided the respective provisions into two basic categories—personal and territorial. Rules that were considered personal applied to cases involving the citizens of that city-state no matter where they were, whereas territorial rules claimed application to everybody, whether citizen or foreigner, who stayed within the city boundaries. To decide which local law fell into which category the Italian scholars—and their French and Dutch successors—at first relied on the wording of the particular substantive rule. Later on, they based the classification on the presumed or apparent legislative intent. However, no matter which criteria the statutists applied to discern the spatial reach of local laws they did not manage to develop generally accepted solutions for cross-border cases. Hence, it is not surprising that the statutists' unilateral method was eventually superseded and replaced by the multilateral method.

---

① Giesela Ruhl, Methods and Approaches in Choice of Law: An Economic Perspective, 24 *Berkeley J. Int'l L.* 801, 821—823 (2006).

2. Carl Friedrich von Savigny: Assigning the Seat of the Legal Relationship

The founding father of the multilateral method—and thereby the modern approach to choice of law—is Carl Friedrich von Savigny. In his legendary treatise on the "System of Current Roman Law", published in 1849, he promoted the idea that choice of law rules were meant to guarantee uniform results regardless of the place of litigation. Therefore, he argued, the applicable law had to be determined by looking for the one legal order in which the underlying legal relationship belonged. In his words, the applicable law had to be chosen by looking for the legal order where the relationship had its "seat." This seat, he claimed, had to be identified by classifying legal relationships into broad categories and then linking those categories with a legal order by means of connecting factors such as the domicile of a person or the place of a transaction. As a result, he developed a system of a priori choice of law rules that assigned a legal relationship to one particular legal order regardless of whether that legal order had expressed a wish to be applied. In doing so, he rejected the statutists' unilateral method of defining the spatial reach of legal rules and promoted what became later known as the multilateral method.

Today, Savigny's ideas are still readily identifiable in modern choice of law systems. In Europe, for example, the EC Convention on the Law Applicable to Contractual Obligations (Rome Convention) assigns a contract to the law of the state, with which it is most closely connected. In the United States, the Restatement (Second) of Conflicts generally provides for application of the law of the state which has the most significant relationship to a dispute. As a result, both the Rome Convention and the Restatement (Second) apply the multilateral method of assigning a legal relationship to one particular legal order. Moreover, both the Rome Convention and the Restatement (Second) use objective criteria to determine the applicable law that resemble Savigny's notion of the seat of the legal relationship.

3. Modern Forms of Unilateralism

That the unilateral approach was eventually replaced by Savigny's multilateral method does not mean that it simply vanished from the choice of law scene. To the contrary: it formed the basis for the most influential approach that arose in the course of the American conflicts revolution: Brainerd Currie's governmental interest analysis. He advanced a modern form of the unilateralist choice of law method in that he—just like the statutists—set out to determine the applicable law by defining the spatial reach of substantive laws. However, instead of classifying laws according to their personal or territorial purport, Currie advocated an ad hoc judicial interpretation of the involved substantive laws based on the policies underlying those laws. Such an interpretation, he argued, would determine a state's interest in having its law applied in a certain case—the "governmental interest"—which in turn would define the laws' intended sphere of operation in terms of space and designate the applicable law.

Without exaggeration, Currie's governmental interest analysis can be classified as the most important and most influential modern approach to choice of law. In fact, even though a multilateralist approach has prevailed on a large scale both in the United States and Europe, unilateralists elements are present in virtually all contemporary choice-of-law systems. This becomes obvious when looking at the Restatement (Second), which is followed by most of the jurisdictions in the United States. Although it essentially adopts a multilateralist approach by advocating the application of the law of the state that has the most significant relationship with the case in question, it recognizes the concept of state interests as an important factor for the choice of law. Indeed, the process of identifying the state with the most significant relationship comprises, among others, the examination of the relevant policies of both the forum and other interested states. In Europe, although faithful to multilateralism in general, unilaterlists elements can be found in the form of mandatory laws, that are applied to multistate cases simply because of their wish to be applied. According to Article 7 (1) of the Rome Convention, for example, when applying the law of a country, effect may be given to the mandatory rules of another country, if and in so far as, under the law of the latter country, those rules must be applied whatever the law applicable to the contract.

第五章

国际私法的法律选择方法

第五章 国际私法的法律选择方法

本章导读

※ 在国际私法法律选择方法的价值取向上,历来有两种对立的倾向:其一是传统的追求法律适用的确定性;其二是晚近的强调法律适用的灵活性。

※ 无论是欧洲传统国际私法,还是英美传统国际私法,尽管它们赖以建立的学说基础不尽相同,但有一个共同点,即主要由有固定空间连接因素的各种冲突规范所构成。这种被称为"管辖选择"或者"地域导向"规则所涉及的法律选择方法是一种机械的方法,具有确定性,代表了稳定和秩序的法律价值取向。

※ 传统法律选择方法的特点:一是具有确定性,即各种法律关系通过固定的空间连接因素的指引,找到的都是特定的准据法,即法律选择的结果比较确定;二是具有系统性,传统国际私法往往使用统一、准确和可靠的术语。

※ 到了 20 世纪,几乎所有的国家都倾向于法律的灵活性。国际私法的法律选择方法明显呈现出从确定性走向灵活性的趋势。

※ 最密切联系法律选择方法的基础是最密切联系理论,它是 20 世纪最富有创意、最有价值和最实用的国际私法理论。最密切联系理论的独特之处在于它是数代国际私法学者的学术思想和智慧的集合体。按最密切联系法律选择方法,某一国际民商事关系或某一涉外案件应适用与法律关系或该案件有最密切联系的那个国家的法律。

※ 20 世纪 50 年代后,美国的司法实践进一步发展了最密切联系法律选择方法。1954 年的"奥汀诉奥汀案"和 1963 年的"贝科克诉杰克逊案"是其中最有影响的案例。

※ 特征性履行法律选择方法,是指对于双务合同而言,其应适用的法律是反映该合同特征的义务履行人的住所地或营业地的法律。

※ 特征性履行方法发轫于欧洲,是欧洲法学家注重形式逻辑研究方式的成果体现。特征性履行方法上升为法律规范不但是欧洲国际私法形式理性的表现,同时也是追求法律适用确定性的价值体现和排斥法官司法解释权的法哲学思想和理念的体现。

※ 法律选择的软化处理是指坚持冲突规范连接点的基本模式,改变传统单一、固定、刚性的连接点,代之以多层次、开放、软性的连接因素,给法院一个自由选择法律的空间,从而比较相关法律,选出最合适的准据法,求得个案的公正解决。

【本章主题词】 法律选择方法、管辖选择、地域导向、确定性、灵活性、最密切联系、特征性履行、软化处理、规则选择

第一节 传统国际私法的法律选择方法

传统国际私法占主导地位的学说都主张国际私法主要由各种冲突规则构成，如意大利学派中巴托鲁斯的"法则说"、法国学派中杜摩兰的"意思自治说"以及荷兰学派中胡伯的"国际礼让说"等。近代欧洲和美国传统国际私法完整体系的建立则深受萨维尼、斯托雷和比尔等人学说的影响。[①]

一、传统国际私法法律选择方法的特点

无论是欧洲传统国际私法，还是英美传统国际私法，尽管它们赖以建立学说的基础不尽相同，但有一个共同点，即主要由有固定空间连接因素的各种冲突规范所构成。这种被称为"管辖选择"的规则所涉及的法律选择方法是一种机械的方法，具有确定性，代表了稳定和秩序的法律价值取向。

传统法律选择方法具有以下几个特点：一是具有确定性，即各种法律关系通过固定的空间连接因素的指引，找到的都是特定的准据法，即法律选择的结果比较确定；二是具有系统性，传统国际私法往往使用统一、准确和可靠的术语。此外，依传统的"管辖选择"方法，内、外国法律的选择一般取决于空间连接因素的指向，这就在相当程度上保证了内、外国法律的平等适用。

传统法律选择方法又称为"地域导向"的冲突法规则（**territorially-oriented choice-of-law rules**）。

【解说】　　**territorially-oriented choice-of-law rules**

A territorially-oriented choice-of-law rule is one that points to a geographical location as the source of the applicable law before any inquiry is made into the content of that law. The classic example of such a rule is the one selecting the law of the place of wrong for application

---

① 参见徐崇利：《外国法制冲突规则的回归——美国现代国际私法理论与实践的一大发展趋向》，载《法学评论》2000 年第 5 期。

to torts conflicts problems.①

传统法律选择方法的价值取向在于确定性、稳定性和可预见性,但很少顾及纠纷在实体法上能否得到公平和公正的解决。②

二、传统国际私法法律选择方法的局限性

传统国际私法以解决法律冲突的冲突规范为核心,在实践中逐渐形成了一整套与之相关的法律选择方法。传统国际私法通过冲突规范解决法律选择问题时,所采取的方法是"三部曲":首先解决识别问题,即定性问题,决定争议的问题是属于什么法律范畴,例如,是属于合同行为,还是侵权行为等;其次是选定连接因素,例如,是选定当事人的国籍、住所,还是行为地等;最后是法律的查明和适用。根据所选择的连接因素,寻找所要适用的法律,如本国法、住所地法或行为地法等。这种法律选择方法称为"分配法",即将某一个争议问题分配给某一个国家的法律去处理。在进行这种分配的过程中,在选择某一国家之前,还不知道所要适用的法律内容如何,更不知道适用的结果如何。只有在选择后,如果发现所要适用的法律其适用的结果将会影响到内国的根本利益或基本政策时,才利用公共秩序保留制度拒绝适用。冲突规范指出了所要适用的法律后就完成任务了。可想而知,通过这样的方式来解决国际民商事关系中的法律冲突,具有很大的缺陷。因此,传统国际私法在20世纪受到美国学者的猛烈抨击。

第二节 最密切联系法律选择方法

最密切联系方法(the closest connection),又称最重要联系方法(the most significant contact)、最强联系方法(the strongest connection)或最真实联系方法(the most real connection),它是20世纪最富有创意、最有价值和最实用的国际私法法律选择方法。该方法的独特之处在于它不是某个学者个人的观点和思想,而是数代国际

---

① Russell J Weintraub, *Commentary on the Conflict of Laws*, 4th ed., New York Foundation Press, 2001, p.53.

② G.R. Shreve, Choice of Law and the Foreign Constitution, 71 *Indiana Law Journal*, 284(1996).

私法学者的学术思想和智慧的集合体,是法律选择方法论和司法实践不断融合的结晶。最密切联系方法的基础是最密切联系学说。该学说主张,某一国际民商事关系或某一涉外案件应适用与法律关系或该案件有最密切联系的那个国家的法律。[①]

一、最密切联系方法的产生

对于最密切联系方法的产生,我国国际私法学者一般将其渊源追溯到萨维尼的"法律关系本座说"。[②]因为萨维尼强调某一法律关系和某一法域的联系,其"法律关系本座说"揭示了每一种法律关系都有其"本座",而"本座"就是该法律关系与某一法域的联系所在,该法律关系应受"本座"地法支配。但我国也有学者认为从国际私法产生的历史条件看,最密切联系的思想萌芽于国际私法的更早时期。[③]

后人受萨维尼学说的影响,但又嫌"本座"一词太含糊和难于理解,就采用更加通俗易懂的术语来表述这一法律思想。于是,吉尔克(Gierke)用"重心"或"引力中心"(center of gravity)的表述来代替"本座",强调用法律关系本身的"重心"地的法律来调整该法律关系。显然,吉尔克的思想已在萨维尼"法律关系本座说"基础上前进了一步。到后来,英国国际私法学者韦斯特莱克(J. Westlake)在其著作《国际私法论》中进一步抛弃了地域观念,主张法律关系应受同该法律关系有最密切联系的法律(the law of the most closely connected)的支配。至此,最密切联系的思想已经初步形成。最密切联系方法不是简单地继承萨维尼的学说,而是对它的否定之否定。这是因为萨维尼认为任何法律关系只有一个"本座",一旦依这种学说制定出冲突规范,就是一种硬性的冲突规范,法院只得机械地依这种冲突规范去选择法律。相反,依最密切联系方法制定出来的冲突规范,是一种具有弹性的或者说是一种更加灵活的冲突规范,从而避免了传统的冲突规范的僵硬性和机械性,增加了法律选择的灵活性。

早期美国有关最密切联系方法的案例是 **Jones v. Metropolitan Life Insurance Company**。

[①] 参见肖永平:《最密切联系原则在中国国际私法中的应用》,载《中国社会科学》1992年第3期;郑自文:《最密切联系原则的哲学思考》,载《法学评论》1994年第6期。

[②] 参见肖永平:《冲突法专论》,武汉大学出版社1999年版,第199页;韩德培主编:《中国冲突法研究》,武汉大学出版社1993年版,第141—142页。

[③] 参见彭丁带:《最密切联系原则应确立为国际私法的基本原则》,载《南昌大学学报》(人文社会科学版)2005年第4期。

第五章 国际私法的法律选择方法

【案例】　　　　　Jones v. Metropolitan Life Insurance Company

In Jones v. Metropolitan Life Insurance Company, the insured and his daughter, the beneficiary, were residents of New Jersey; the insurance policies were applied for and the premiums were paid in New Jersey. The defendant was a New York corporation and the policies were issued from the home office in New York. The agent had allegedly waived the "unsound health" clause in the life insurance policies. New Jersey law did not permit such oral waivers to alter the terms of the contract. The New York trial court, however, applied New York law and the jury found for the plaintiff.

This was affirmed on appeal.

作为早期有关最密切联系方法（**origins of the significant contacts approach**）的案例，美国纽约州法院在上述案例中对法律的适用进行分析和阐述，通过对合同签订地、合同履行地，甚至合同当事人所选择法律的比较，认为本案应该适用纽约州的法律，即与合同有最密切联系的法律。

【说理】　　　　**origins of the significant contacts approach**

The court, addressing the question of the applicable law, wrote: The cases in New York take various positions on the question of which law governs the validity of a contract. In some the place where the contract was made is said to be determinative. Other cases maintain that the contract is governed by the law of the place of performance. Still other cases rely on the intention of the parties to determine which law governs the contract. The court accurately described the various choice-of-law approaches in use in 1936. The place-of-making rule was firmly entrenched, supplemented by a place-of-performance rule. Another rule looking to the place intended (expressly or impliedly) by the parties was also available. The New York court then added a less common basis for the choice in contract cases: "The last position that the cases take is the one which assumes that it is the grouping of the various elements which have gone to make up the contract that determines which law governs." The court concluded that under any one of these approaches to choice of law, "the contract must be regarded as governed by New York law." This was an early case looking to a grouping of contacts, or "elements" as the court called them. This was an idea that would gain currency.

值得一提的是较早在立法中吸收了最密切联系方法的 1946 年《希腊民法典》。该《法典》第 31 条第 2 款规定，如果一个人兼有几个外国国籍，适用同他有最密切联系的那个国家的法律。

20 世纪 50 年代后，美国的司法实践进一步发展了这一方法。1954 年的"奥汀诉奥汀案"（**Auten v. Auten**）和 1963 年的"贝科克诉杰克逊"（Babcock v.

Jackson)①便是其中最有影响的案例。

【案例】　　　　　　　　　　**Auten v. Auten**②

　　Facts: Mr. Auten left his wife and two children in England and moved to America, and, soon after, procured a Mexican divorce and remarried. Unable to reach a settlement, Mrs. Auten came to this country, and the parties entered into an agreement in New York. The agreement included a provision that neither party should file any action relating to their separation. Mrs. Auten returned to England and some years later, having received only a few payments under the agreement, filed a suit in England to collect back support. This action was not pursued. Years later, she filed an action in New York. Mr. Auten defended on the ground that she had breached the contract by filing the action in England. Both of the lower courts held that New York law applied, and that her commencement of the English action "constituted a rescission and repudiation of the separation agreement, requiring dismissal of the complaint." It was not so clear that her action was a breach under English law. The New York Court of Appeals began its search for the applicable law with the familiar litany: place of making, place of performance, and intent of the parties. The court continued:

　　And still other decisions, including the most recent one in this court [Rubin], have resorted to a method first employed to rationalize the results achieved by the courts in decided cases which has come to be called the "center of gravity" or the "grouping of contacts" theory of the conflict of laws. Under this theory, the courts, instead of regarding as conclusive the parties' intention or the place of making or performance, lay emphasis rather upon the law of the place "which has the most significant contacts with the matter in dispute." This methodology gives to the place having the most interest in the problem paramount control over the legal issues arising out of a particular factual context. It also enables the court "to reflect the relative interests of the several jurisdictions involved." The court concluded that England "had all the truly significant contacts" and had "the greatest concern in prescribing and governing those obligations" owed to an abandoned wife and children in England. When the Auten court, speaking through Judge Fuld, referred to center of gravity and grouping of contacts it followed the line of cases summarized in sections II and III. But the court ultimately wanted to apply the law of the state which had the greatest interest in the matter. This, clearly drawing upon the professors, introduced something new because obviously interests are something different from contacts, though the court did not elaborate upon this.

　　在这个案件中,法官富尔德(Fuld)依据"引力中心"和"联系聚集"的思想,强调让与案件有重大利益关系的法律对该案件有绝对的控制权,从而允许法院适用

---

　　① 该案参见黄惠康、黄进:《国际公法国际私法成案选》,武汉大学出版社 1987 年版,第 329—331 页。
　　② 124 N.E.2d 99 (N.Y. 1954).

与有最密切联系的地方的法律。①

一些著名国际私法学者对"最重要联系"方法的推崇(**significant contacts and the authors**),对"最重要联系"思想的传播起到了推波助澜的作用。

【说理】   **significant contacts and the authors**

Professor Walter Wheeler Cook advised that instead of looking for a presumed intention, the court would "determine the 'proper law' of the contract as being that of the state with which the transaction as a whole has the most vital or substantial connection."

A few years later, Professor Arthur Nussbaum wrote that "analysis reveals that in the place-of-performance cases this 'place' was the 'center of gravity' of the whole contract." He concluded that the "courts' objective has generally been to discover and apply the law of the place to which the most important contacts of the contract go."

Here are the beginnings of a choice-of-law method, at least for contract cases, that might be called a grouping of contacts or center of gravity approach. Instead of looking only to the place of making, or only to the place of performance, the court will consider all of the spatial or territorial contacts relevant to the particular case. In 1945, this view received a boost, in an important and oft-cited case from the Indiana Supreme Court.

与此同时,美国哥伦比亚大学法学院教授里斯主持的《第二次冲突法重述》根据美国司法判例中的"引力中心"、"关系聚集"等观念,提出了一个"最重要联系"的概念。他主张,法院在处理涉外案件时,应适用与案件的事实和当事人有最重要联系的那个地方的法律。里斯把这一思想贯穿到整个《第二次冲突法重述》之中,具体体现在《第二次冲突法重述》第6节"法律选择原则"(**§6. Choice-of-Law Principles**)中。

【法条】   **§6. Choice-of-Law Principles**

(1) A court, subject to constitutional restrictions, will follow a statutory directive of its own state on choice of law.

---

① 在该案中,富尔德法官认为,法院在确定合同准据法时应从质和量这两个角度着眼,对与合同有关的各种主客观连接因素进行权衡,寻找合同的"重力中心地",这种"重心地"就是合同自然隶属的地方。由于合同具有高度的人为性、技术性,因此,采用最密切联系说通常就是通过对合同的谈判地、订立地、履行地、合同标的物所在地、争议发生地、当事人的国籍所属国、住所地、营业地以及法院地等客观因素和合同中使用的文字、术语、单据格式、当事人约定使用的货币以及共同选择的仲裁地等主观因素进行综合的考察,探求一个与合同有关的法律关系的"聚集地",这种法律关系"聚集地"的法律就是与合同有最密切联系的地方的法律,该法律即为合同的准据法。

(2) When there is no such directive, the factors relevant to the choice of the applicable rule of law include

(a) the needs of the interstate and international systems,

(b) the relevant policies of the forum,

(c) the relevant policies of other interested states and the relative interests of those states in the determination of the particular issue,

(d) the protection of justified expectations,

(e) the basic policies underlying the particular field of law,

(f) certainty, predictability and uniformity of result, and

(g) ease in the determination and application of the law to be applied.

由于《第二次冲突法重述》吸收了最密切联系方法(**significant contacts and the Second Restatement**),故最密切联系方法在众多美国国际私法方法中脱颖而出。

【说理】　　significant contacts and the Second Restatement

It is generally agreed that early drafts of the Second Restatement "incorporated the 'center of gravity' or 'grouping of contacts' approach." In 1968, Professor Leflar wrote that "the 'center of gravity' approach is the central feature of the Second Restatement handling of contracts matters." The goal of the Second Restatement was to apply the law of the state which had the most substantial (not significant) relationship with the issue. There were a number of specific rules and presumptions in the Second Restatement, but the general provisions for torts (section 145) and contracts (section 188) listed factors (not contacts) to be considered in determining the most substantial relationship. The early drafts of the Restatement had no overarching policy considerations. This would be partly rectified with the adoption of the principles of section six. However, this "bizarre mixture of territorial bias and focus on the substance of conflicting laws" has resulted in a largely incoherent product. Partly because of this, the Second Restatement "has proved to be a huge success among the courts, but an object of academic derision."

How did significant contacts become such a part of it for some courts? The term was in use, and the Restatement was aiming at a kind of "grouping of contacts" approach. The Restatement listed the relevant contacts in sections 145 and 188, but called them factors. There would have been no discrepancy in terminology if the drafters had called these territorial matters contacts instead of factors. Apparently courts prefer contacts to factors (or at least they are more accustomed to contacts). If a judge in a Second Restatement state was asked what he or she meant by significant contacts, the likely reply would be those things listed in sections 145 and 188 of the Second Restatement. Thus, one use of significant contacts has been to serve as a means of referring to the Second Restatement's factors. This makes it a synonym, and not an independent choice-of-law methodology. And when a court moves on to the principles of section six, contacts (or factors) are left behind.

尽管最密切联系方法本身还不是尽善尽美的,但是它的产生和发展,无论从方法上还是从实践上来说,都具有十分重要的意义。运用最密切联系方法进行法律选择的方法已成为国际私法的一种新趋势。

最密切联系方法一经产生,便对国际私法的发展产生了重大影响,被各国立法和司法实践广泛接受,并不断地加以完善,究其原因,主要是因为该原则具有灵活性特征,赋予了法官自由裁量权,要求法官不能对众多的与特定法律关系密切相关的联系因素置若罔闻,而是要根据案件的具体情况综合考虑各种相关因素,透过各种连接因素的表层去分析该连接因素与特定民商事关系的关联性,以期找到与该特定民商事关系有着最真实的,即本质的、固有的、稳定联系的法律。[①]最密切联系方法的这一特点适应了目前复杂多变的涉外民商事法律关系。

二、最密切联系方法所体现的价值

最密切联系方法实现了法律适用的确定性和灵活性之间的协调,是在法律秩序(确定性)与公正(灵活性)价值之间的平衡选择。最密切联系作为功能主义对传统规则的变革,其出发点便是在于对旧有封闭国际私法的突破,摆脱简单的静态的公式化模式,以期实现在制度层面的弹性化、体系的开放化、个案的公正化等社会价值目标。任何社会的法律都应该是稳定性和灵活性的统一。一方面法律必须保持稳定,不能朝令夕改,为社会秩序提供基本安全保障;另一方面法律又不是静止不变的,它要根据社会关系的不断变化而作出调整,那么就不得不给予法官在这种调整中的自由裁量权。但这种自由裁量权必须有一定的限度,超出这种限度就会破坏法制的统一性。也即只有规定性和适度的自由裁量权相结合才能达到法律稳定性和变动性的统一。最密切联系方法的确定性与灵活性、一致性和可预见性的矛盾互动关系,是法哲学一直争论不休的关于法律的秩序价值和法律的公正价值的关系问题在国际私法学上的反映和体现。如何处理两者之间的矛盾、维持它们的动态平衡,实现法律对人类应有的价值,千百年来始终是法学界所关心的问题。传统国际私法规则具有僵化、机械、呆板与普遍性的特点,只照顾到大部分情况,对特殊情况缺乏变通的方法,故它不能保证个案的公正性。但它却有代表稳定性、明确性和可预见性的一面。随着社会的发展,以秩序束缚而牺牲个体利益的做法日益为人们所抛弃,相对于概念主义的传统国际私法模式的简单的、静态化的统一,最密切联系方法突出其灵活性,其要求从多个连接因素中,权衡确立决定因素所指引的准据法,即由偏重于秩序、稳定而转向注重具体个案中的正义公平的追

---

① 参见董作春:《最密切联系原则本质初探》,载《学术论坛》2001年第2期。

求,这是时代发展的必然趋势,秩序与公平在大多数情况下是一致的,但在个别情况下也会发生冲突,如何平衡两者利益成为最密切联系方法的追求。最密切联系方法克服了传统冲突规则的机械性,具有很强的灵活性。美国法院在司法审判中大量运用最密切联系(**reference to significant contacts**)方案来灵活处理案件。

【说理】　　　　　reference to significant contacts

many courts made significant contacts part of the lexicon, even though the Restatement speaks of significant relationships and factors. For example, in a 1978 case, the Missouri Court of Appeals clearly used the Second Restatement, which it described as "the 'significant contacts' approach."

A federal district court in Texas implicated the Second Restatement when it said "that the 'most significant contacts test' is the Texas choice of law rule."

A federal district court in Colorado, applying the Second Restatement, held: "When considering the particular interests and policies of the states involved in the negligence controversy, I find that Colorado, not Nebraska, has the most significant contacts." The Colorado court then applied the principles and policies of section six and concluded "that Colorado possesses the most significant contacts." In New Jersey, a federal district court used the Restatement Second because New Jersey "has adopted the Restatement standard (significant contacts) to determine which law governs contract claims." Finally, the Maine Supreme Court described the Second Restatement as the "most significant contacts and relationships" test.

The courts in Illinois have frequently referred to a significant contacts rule, but almost always in the context of the Second Restatement. In a 1970 tort case, the Illinois Supreme Court rejected *lex loci delicti*, discussed policies and interests, seemed to adopt the Second Restatement, and ultimately plumped for a significant contacts rule. What did this mean? Subsequent cases affirmed the significant contacts rule while applying the Restatement. The Seventh Circuit Court of Appeals, for example, said that the "Illinois Supreme Court would apply the Second Restatement's 'most significant contacts' test."

灵活性是最密切联系方法的优点,也是它的缺点,因为灵活性赋予法官自由裁量权,足以应付各种例外情况,使个案公正得到较充分的保证。但是若没有对法官自由裁量权的限制,则法官很容易利用这种权力来适用法院地法,那么就会极大破坏了法律的统一性。①受一定限制的最密切联系方法是在法律确定性与灵活性之间所作的一种选择,企图协调国际私法诸价值,赋予了法官一定限度的自由裁量权,正是现阶段法律所需要的。确定性与灵活性,在两者的矛盾互动关系中应该确

---

① 参见彭丁带:《最密切联系原则应确立为国际私法的基本原则》,载《南昌大学学报》(人文社会科学版)2005年第4期。

立一个动态平衡的标准,这就是法律公正或正义价值的实现。如何认识和处理这一问题,一些国际私法学者提出了充满智慧、富有意义的主张,如韩德培教授主编的《中国国际私法研究》第八章[①]、肖永平教授著的《国际私法专论》第十一专题[②]、郑自文博士的《最密切联系原则的哲学思考》[③]、徐伟功教授的《从自由裁量权角度论国际私法中的最密切联系原则》、[④]沈涓教授的《论发展中的最密切联系原则》[⑤]、Th. M. De Boer 的《选择性冲突法》(Facultative Choice of Law)[⑥]、P. Hay 的《灵活性、可预见性与统一性》(Flexibility versus Predictability and Uniformity,)[⑦]等。最密切联系方法的确立和运用,实现了法律适用的确定性和灵活性之间的适当的协调,以它对合同法的调整为例,它仍以合同的场所为依托,以合同的某种客观标志为依据,因而对准据法的确定在一定程度上仍具有确定性。但是,它并非像客观标志原则那样把合同关系"固定"在某个地域的法律上,而是根据要解决问题的性质和特点,以公正合理为目标来确定合同的准据法。[⑧]这样确定的准据法更符合合同关系的本质和目的,因而具有更强的合理性,能够适应国际合同法律适用的公正性和合理性的主观要求。最密切联系方法最突出的贡献在于以富于弹性的连接点取代单一的连接点。[⑨]

最密切联系方法赖以建立的实用主义法哲学为法官自由裁量和灵活适用法律提供了方法基础。最密切联系方法是以实用主义为哲学背景,以追求具体正义为根本价值取向,是自由裁量主义在国际私法领域中的体现。第一次世界大战后,西方国家出现了反思辨、重经验、重现实为特征的哲学运动,这场哲学运动的主体是实用主义哲学。法律是稳定性与变动性的统一。那么我们必须在运动与静止、保守与变革、经久不变与变化无常这些互相矛盾的力量之间谋求某种和谐。那么这一矛盾在国际私法中又演变成为法律的确定性与自由裁量权的对立统一的体现。法律的确定性与自由裁量权之间关系问题一直是法学领域里有争议的重大价值问

---

① 韩德培:《中国国际私法研究》,武汉大学出版社 1993 年版。
② 肖永平:《国际私法专论》,武汉大学出版社 1999 年版。
③ 郑自文:《最密切联系原则的哲学思考》,载《法学评论》1994 年第 6 期。
④ 郑伟功:《从自由裁量权角度论国际私法中的最密切联系原则》,载《法学评论》2000 年第 4 期。
⑤ 沈涓:《论发展中的最密切联系原则》,载黄进主编:《当代国际私法问题》,武汉大学出版社 1997 年版。
⑥ See Th. M. De Boer, Facultative Choice of Law, *Collected Courses of the Hague Academy of International Law*, Martinus Nijhoff Publishers, 1991, p.226.
⑦ See P. Hay, Flexibility versus Predictability and Uniformity, 47 *The American Journal of Comparative Law* 633-349 (1997).
⑧ 参见徐唐棠:《国际私法法律适用的确定性与灵活性之间的张力关系》,载《当代法学》2002 年第 11 期。
⑨ 吕岩峰:《合同准据法论纲》,载《吉林大学社会科学学报》1999 年第 4 期。

题。20世纪,随着实用主义法哲学的兴起,出现司法个人化要求,法官的自由裁量权得到重视。美国著名法学家、社会学派代表人物罗斯科·庞德(Roscoe Pound)曾指出:"一个法律制度之所以成功,是由于它成功地达到并且维持了极端任意的权力与极端受限制的权力之间的平衡。这种平衡不可能永恒地保持。文明的进步社会不断地使法律制度丧失平衡。通过把理性适用于经验之上,然后又恢复这种平衡,而且也只有凭靠这些方式,政治组织社会才能使自己得以永久地存在下去。"① 当最密切联系方法在美国萌芽之时,正是实用主义哲学思潮风靡全美的时期。所以最密切联系方法受到实用主义哲学的影响,并把它作为自己的理论基础,最密切联系方法的实际运用和实用主义哲学主张是一致的。在最密切联系方法的具体运用和法律选择的过程中,主要依赖于法官的司法判断,这就赋予法官极大的自由裁量权,使得法官能在整个案件的审判过程中充分运用其司法实践积累的经验与法律逻辑思维,本着法律公平正义理念来实现法的社会价值能动追求。在英美法系国家中,注重于司法审判的实践,判例也成为其司法制度的正式渊源,为司法审判所援引。司法审判过程不仅是一种简单的机械法律条文运用操作过程,而且为法官在法律精神指引下运用法律进行再创造性劳动提供可能。正是基于这一观念,最密切联系方法得以在美国最先确立并为司法审判所运用,成为对传统概念主义国际私法理念的突破。

由此可见,最密切联系方法的产生与法律选择方法的灵活性价值密切相关。最密切联系方法正是法律选择灵活性价值观在国际私法中的具体体现。

第三节 特征性履行法律选择方法及其法哲学思想

特征性履行(**characteristic performance**),又称特征性之债(characteristic obligation)或特征性义务(typical performance)。

| 【释义】 | characteristic performance |

In bilateral or reciprocal contracts one of the parties usually merely has to pay money, and

---

① Roscoe Pound, Individualization of Justice, 7 *Fordham L. Rev.* 166 (1938).

the characteristic performance of the contract is not the payment of money, but the performance for which payment is due (eg provision of a service or delivery of goods) usually constitutes the centre of gravity and the socio-economic function of the contractual transaction.

所谓**特征性履行**的法律选择方法,是指对于双务合同而言,其应适用的法律是反映该合同特征的义务履行人的住所地或营业地的法律。由于适用的是反映某类合同特征的义务履行一方的法律,显然该法律与该合同的联系最为密切。所以,特征性履行实际上是最密切联系原则的具体化。①

【释义】　　　　　　　　　　特征性履行

特征性履行是与非特征性履行相对而言的。所谓特征性履行,又称为特征性给付,是指双务合同中代表合同本质特征的当事人履行合同的行为。例如,买卖合同中卖方交付物品的给付行为、雇用合同中受雇人提供劳务的给付行为反映了这两种合同的本质特征,因而属特征性履行。而买方支付货款的行为与雇用人支付劳务费的行为均属金钱给付,这种金钱给付行为反映了双务合同的共性,不能反映买卖合同和雇用合同的本质特征,故属于非特征性履行。按照特征性履行说,合同准据法应为担负特征性给付义务的当事人的住所地法,或惯常居所地法,或营业所所在地法。

该方法是以依照合同特征对合同种类进行划分为适用前提的,通过这种方法,可以针对不同种类合同所具有的不同特征,来分别确定支配它们的法律,因而克服了传统冲突规范"合同订立地法"原则或"合同履行地法"原则的刻板性和单一性。②

一、特征性履行方法的形成是欧洲法学家注重形式逻辑研究方式的成果体现

特征性履行方法产生于欧洲,是一种欧洲国际私法理论。特征性履行方法是欧洲国际私法学术思想的理论结晶和学术研究的重要成果。

我国有学者认为有关特征性履行方法的理论研究起源于 20 世纪二三十年代的欧洲。③也有学者认为,该理论最早由瑞士国际私法学者施尼泽(Adolf F. Schnitzer)所提出。④而事实上,该理论的产生日期还要早一些。20 世纪初期,汉博

---

① 邹志洪:《国际私法上最密切联系原则及其发展》,载《武汉大学学报》1992 年第 6 期;刘仁山:《论最密切联系地法适用的限制》,载《中南政法学院学报》1992 年第 3 期。
② 参见徐国建:《国际合同中特征性履行研究》,载《法学评论》1989 年第 2 期。
③ 参见裴普:《论最密切联系原则在涉外合同中的应用》,载《现代法学》1999 年第 4 期。
④ 徐伟功:《从自由裁量权的角度论国际私法中的最密切联系原则》,载《国际私法学》2001 年第 1 期。

格(Harburger)指出,每个合同都有一个不同于其他合同的特征,在买卖合同中,是卖方而不是买方,其住所地在确定法律适用中起着主导作用。[①]以后罗林(A. Rolin)又发展了这一理论,提出了12种不同类别合同的各自特征及其所应适用的法律。[②]著名学者梅利曼在《大陆法系》一书中指出:"法学研究是依据传统的形式逻辑方式进行的,法学家们运用法律的原始材料,通过所谓'逻辑推理'过程,推论出高水平的具有普遍意义的原理。"[③]梅利曼的这一论断,恰恰形象地揭示了欧洲国际私法学者对特征性履行理论的学术研究状况。瑞士国际私法学者施尼泽以1908年《佛罗伦萨草案》(Florence Project)、1926年《波兰国际私法》和1948年《捷克斯洛伐克国际私法》的立法为例,以形式逻辑为指导,通过梅利曼所说的"逻辑推理",对特征性履行方法进行了进一步的概括和提炼,提出了"特征性履行方法"是一种"现代理论"(modern theory)的研究结论[④],从而使"特征性履行方法"这个国际私法法律选择的个别方法,上升到了具有普遍指导意义的一般方法。瑞士国际私法学者施尼泽的学术研究结论,大大地提升了"特征性履行方法"的理论价值,提高了"特征性履行方法"在当代国际私法法律选择中的地位,丰富了当代国际私法法律选择方法的理论宝库。欧洲国家的"法学家们把丰富的时代思想融入法律概念;并构建一个系统化、概念化的法学架构。直至今天,这个法学架构仍然……为司法实践解释和适用法律、判例、法律行为等提供理论依据"[⑤]。此后,欧洲国家的众多国际私法法学家基于自己的社会责任和法律思想,继续潜心致力于特征性履行方法的研究,并取得了令人注目的学术成果。[⑥]

相比之下,美国国际私法学者或者冲突法学者对特征性履行方法的研究成果寥若晨星。在LexisNexis法学数据库检索中,我们将characteristic Performance、characteristic obligation和typical performance三个主题词分别作为论文标题输入之后,

---

① See Zhang Mingjie, *Conflict of Laws and International Contract for Sale of Goods*, édition Paradigme, 146 (1997).
② Ibid.
③ 〔美〕梅利曼:《大陆法系》(第二版),顾培东等译,法律出版社2004年版,第65页。
④ See A. F. Schnitzer, La loi applicable aux contrats, *Revue critique de droit international privé*, 476 (1955 III).
⑤ 参见〔美〕梅利曼:《大陆法系》(第二版),顾培东等译,法律出版社2004年版,第66页。
⑥ For writings on the concept of characteristic performance, see, among others, Hans-Ulrich Jesserun d'Oliveira, Characteristic Obligation in the Draft EEC Obligation Convention, 25 *Am. J. Comp. L.* 303 (1977); Kurt Lipstein, Characteristic Performance, A New Concept in the Conflict of Law in Matters of Contract for the EEC, 3 *Nw. J. Int'l L. & Bus.* 402 (1981); J. Blaikie, Choice of Law in Contract: Characteristic Performance and the EEC Contracts Convention, *Scots Law Times* 241 (1983); H. Kaufmann-Kohler, La prestation charactéristique en droit international privé des contrats et l'influence de la Suisse, *Schweizer Jahrbuch fur Internationales Recht* 195 (1989); Massimo Magagni, *La Prestazione Caratteristica Nella Convenzione Di Roma Del 19 Giugno 1980* (Milan 1989).

竟然没有查到一篇以该主题词为论文标题组成部分的学术论文和文献。可见,美国学者对在欧洲发展了将近一百年的特征性履行方法的学术问题,置若罔闻,竟然没有一位美国国际私法学者或者冲突法学者以特征性履行方法为题展开过任何研究、探讨或者评论。这充分展现了美国法律文化和法律思想的一个侧面。正如顾培东教授在《大陆法系》译者序中所指出:"美国学者面对异域制度、异域文化通常都保持着一种特有的自豪与优越。"①而正是这种自豪和优越感,使得美国国际私法学者或者冲突法学者对特征性履行方法这个学术问题不屑一顾。而相比之下,欧洲国际私法学者对特征性履行方法的研究,却持续了上百年,至今仍然源源不断地有相关的学术成果问世。②

二、特征性履行方法上升为法律规范是欧洲国际私法形式理性的表现

形式理性(formal rationality)是法律的重要属性之一。③所谓形式理性是指一种纯形式的、客观的,不包含价值判断的理性,它主要表现为形式的合理逻辑。④法律的形式理性是指由理智控制的法律规则的系统化、科学化以及法律制定和适用过程的形式化。⑤欧洲大陆法系的国际私法注重"建立在理性主义基础上,系统地按逻辑联系组织起来的成文法规"⑥的法典化。崇尚国际私法的形式理性一直是欧洲大陆法系国家国际私法学者的基本追求。大陆法系各国把各自的国际私法立法视为法典化的重要组成部分。特征性履行方法通过立法,上升为各国国际私法中的法律选择规范,是欧洲大陆法系国家注重国际私法立法的结果,是欧洲国际私法形式理性的具体表现。特征性履行方法上升为法律规范,主要有两条路径,其一是国际私法的国内立法,其二是合同法律适用的国际统一化立法运动。

在国际私法的国内立法方面,早在1908年,《佛罗伦萨草案》就吸收了特征性履行的思想。1926年《波兰国际私法》(以后更新为1965年《波兰国际私法》)、1948年《捷克斯洛伐克国际私法》(以后更新为1964年《捷克斯洛伐克国际私法与国际民事诉讼法》),以及原民主德国的《国际私法》的立法,均采纳了特征性履行

---

① 〔美〕梅利曼:《大陆法系》(第二版),顾培东等译,法律出版社2004年版,"译者序",第1页。
② see, eg, Nicky Richardson, The Concept of Characteristic Performance and the Proper Law Doctrine, 1 *Bond L. Rev.* 284 (1989); Paolo Michele Patocchi, Characteristic Performance: A New Myth in the Conflict of Laws? Some Comments on a Recent Concept in the Swiss and European Private International Law of Contract, in *Festschrift Für Lalive* 113 (Paris 1993).
③ 一般认为,研究法律理性的真正起点始于德国学者马克斯·韦伯(Max Weber, 1864—1920年)。韦伯对法学理论的重要贡献是详尽阐述了理性问题,参见〔美〕博登海默:《法理学:法哲学与法律方法》,邓正来译,中国政法大学出版社1999年版,第141页。
④ 严存生:《法之合理性问题》,载《法律科学》1995年第4期。
⑤ 黄金荣:《法的形式理论》,载《比较法研究》2000年第3期。
⑥ 何勤华、李秀清主编:《外国法制史》,复旦大学出版社2002年版,第309页。

方法作为确定合同法律适用的方法。此后,欧洲大陆法系其他一些国家,如波兰、奥地利、南斯拉夫等国纷纷效仿,将特征性履行方法纳入其国际私法立法之中。欧洲大陆法系国家的国际私法立法,根据特征性履行法律选择方法的理论,将合同分为不同的种类,进而确定各种不同合同的特征性履行。这种做法不但考虑到了不同类型的合同应有不同的冲突规则,而且还考虑到了合同与有关国家以及当事人之间的联系,可以避免抽象的"适用与合同有最密切联系的国家的法律"这个原则性规定的缺陷,使法院操作简便,不必再对每一合同具体分析其与什么国家有最密切联系。

在国际合同统一化立法运动方面,最早体现特征性履行法律选择方法思想的范例是由欧洲国家所积极倡导和推动的 1955 年海牙《关于国际货物买卖法律适用公约》(<u>The 1955 Hague Convention on the Law Applicable to International Sales of Goods</u>)。

【释义】 The 1955 Hague Convention on the Law Applicable to International Sales of Goods

The 1955 Hague Convention on the Law Applicable to International Sales of Goods was sponsored by the Hague Conference on Private International Law. It was ratified by Belgium, Denmark, Finland, France, Italy, Niger, Norway, Sweden, and Switzerland and came into force in 1964.

Article 3 of the Convention provides that when the parties have not contractually designated the governing law, the sale shall be governed by the domestic law of the country in which the vendor has his habitual residence at the time when he receives the order. If the order is received by an establishment of the vendor, the sale shall be governed by the domestic law of the country in which the establishment is situated.

The next paragraph provides that the sale shall be governed by the domestic law of the country in which the purchaser has his habitual residence, or in which he has the establishment that has given the order, if the order has been received in such country, whether by the vendor or by his representative, agent or commercial traveller.

The law to be applied thus depends on where the buyer's order is received. If the order was received by the seller's subsidiary, branch office, or agent in the buyer's country, the law of buyer's country governs the transaction. In the majority of international sales cases, however, the buyer's order is received in the seller's country, and the law of the seller's country therefore governs the transaction.[1]

---

[1] Henry Mather, Choice of Law for International Sales Issues not Resolved by the CISG, 20 *J. L. & Com.* 155, 183 (2001).

该公约第3条规定,如果买卖合同当事人未指定应适用的法律,依卖方收到订单时惯常居所地国家的国内法。该公约虽然没有明确采用"特征性履行"这一专业术语,但是,该公约所规定的"卖方收到订单时惯常居所地国家的国内法",实质上就是根据特征性履行方法所确定的承担特征性履行义务的当事人的住所地或者惯常居所地的法律。因此,上述1955年海牙公约在合同法律选择的方法上,也是深受特征性履行思想影响的。

大陆法系国际私法中有关特征性履行方法,无论是在其国内立法,还是在国际统一化立法上,其所体现的价值观,是力求使所制定的国际私法法律适用规范在适用于各种不同的事实状态时,清晰而无须任何解释,逻辑严密而不出现任何冲突,从而使国际私法规范的适用成为法院适用法律的一个"自动"的过程。特征性履行方法,由最初的学术思想上升到欧洲大陆法系各国的立法规范,成为国际私法法律选择的规范,是欧洲大陆法系国际私法形式理性的表现,也是欧洲大陆法系各国私法成熟的标志。法国思想家孟德斯鸠(Baron de Montesquieu,1689—1755年)曾经说过:人们遵守法律并不是由于恐惧法律,而是由于热爱法律。①这种法律文化下的国际私法制度的构建,是人类文明和理性的体现。英国学者托兰德认为:"理性是真正的第一法律,是生命的灿烂光华。"②欧洲大陆法系各国通过立法活动,实现了将国际私法的特征性履行理论与实践相融合的目标,并从实践中产生了统一的法律选择适用规则,使特征性履行这种法律选择方法上升为国际私法合同法律选择的普遍准则。

三、特征性履行方法是欧洲大陆法系追求法律适用确定性的价值体现

欧洲大陆法系的传统法律价值观是严格维护法律的"确定性"。法律的"确定性"在大陆法系国家"获得了至高无上的价值",并成为"最重要的法律原则"。③尽管维护法律的"确定性"必然在个案中牺牲公正原则,但是大陆法系国家却不惜这种代价,以个案的不公正来确保整体的公正。

欧洲大陆法系国家的国际私法规则历来注重法律适用的确定性。制定完整、清晰、逻辑严密的国际私法立法,是国际私法立法者对"确定性"法律价值的重要领会和贯彻。特征性履行方法首先萌发于欧洲大陆,是国际私法法律适用追求确定性思想的具体表现。欧洲大陆法系国家有关特征性履行方法的立法,遵循了法律适用"确定性"的法律思想和价值观。

---

① 参见〔法〕孟德斯鸠:《罗马盛衰原因论》,婉玲译,商务印书馆1962年版,第17页。
② 〔英〕约翰·托兰德:《贬神论要义》,陈启伟译,商务印书馆1997年版,第35页。
③ 〔美〕梅利曼著:《大陆法系》(第二版),顾培东等译,法律出版社2004年版,第49—50页。

以1987年《瑞士联邦国际私法》为例,该法在涉及特征性履行方法的部分,结合5种合同,分别规定了各自的特征性履行(**characteristic obligation**)行为,使法院可以非常便利地依照立法规则,为每一种合同找到所对应的应适用的法律。①

【法条】　　　　　　　　　　characteristic obligation

Art. 117

B. Absence of a choice of law

1 In the absence of a choice of law, the contract shall be governed by the law of the State with which it is most closely connected.

2 It is presumed that the closest connection exists with the State in which the party who must perform the characteristic obligation is habitually resident or, if the contract was concluded in the exercise of a professional or commercial activity, where such party has his place of business.

3 In particular, the following shall be considered the characteristic obligation:

a. The obligation of the alienator, in contracts of alienation;

b. The obligation of the party transferring the use of a thing or a right, in the case of contracts concerning the use of a thing or a right;

c. The service provided, in the case of mandates, work and labor contracts, and similar service contracts;

d. The obligation of the custodian, in custodial contracts;

e. The obligation of the guarantor or the surety, in guaranty or surety contracts.②

特征性履行理论强调每一个合同关系都有一个特征,并且只有一个特征,根据该特征就能对号入座,确定该合同关系所适用的法律。按照这种精确定位的方式来确定合同的法律适用,具有很强的确定性。所以,特征性理论的思想首先在大陆法系国家萌发,并为大陆法系国际立法所体现。作为具有"概念明确、条例清晰、逻辑严密"的法典传统的欧洲大陆国家,瑞士国际私法立法在特征性履行方法的立法上蕴涵着国际私法学者们的智慧,使得合同的法律选择体现出了显著的"确定性"。而这种法律的确定性(la sécurité juridique)是瑞士国际私法立法者认为"绝对必要"③的价值追求。

---

① 《瑞士联邦国际私法》第117条规定:"以下履行行为特征性履行:(1)转让所有权合同中转让人的转让。(2)使用某物或某种权利的合同中,给予使用的当事人的履行。(3)委托、承揽或其他劳务合同中,劳务的提供。(4)仓储合同中保管人的履行。(5)担保或保证合同中,担保或保证人的履行。"

② Article 117 of Switzerland's Federal Code on Private International Law (CPIL) of December 18, 1987.

③ 陈卫佐:《瑞士国际私法法典研究》,法律出版社1998年版,第176页。

第五章 国际私法的法律选择方法

根据大陆法系法律"确定性"法律价值的要求,法官不但不得创制法律,而且还应谨慎地遵循已经制定的立法进行司法活动。这是欧洲大陆法系国家在司法制度方面与英美法系国家的重大差异。大陆法系不允许法官的意志渗入法律的创制和解释,而只能根据法律的规则进行司法活动。特征性履行的法律选择方法,除了得到欧洲大陆法系国际私法学者的大力推崇和相关国际私法立法的体现之外,同时也为欧洲大陆法系国家的法院所遵循。欧洲大陆法系国家的许多法院判例体现了特征性履行的法律选择方法,其中包括德国法院的判例①、荷兰法院的判例②、瑞士法院的判例③,以及一些国际商事仲裁案件的裁决。④例如,在 **Chevally c. Genimporter S. A.** 一案中,瑞士联邦法院即根据特征性履行方法来判定案件所应适用的法律。

【案例】 Chevally c. Genimporter S. A.

This case was about a franchise concluded in Geneva with a Belgian supplier. The Tribunal Fédéral held that the sell's law was applicable. The Tribunal Fédéral views the criterion of characteristic performance as almost an absolute principle overriding the principle of closest relationship itself. The Tribunal Fédéral declated: *En l'espece, les parties n'ont pas désigné le droit qu'elles pouvaient voir appliquer à leurs rapports. Elles n'ont pas non plus manifersté a cet égard leur volonté par actes concluants; ... Si le contrat provisoire de concession du 16 décembre 1947 est contract de vente, il sera, sauf indications contraires, soumis dans tous ses effets au droit belge, comme loi du pays de la venderesse dont la prestation caractérisise le repport juridique.* ⑤

本案涉及一份特许权转让合同,合同由瑞士的 Chevally 和比利时供应商 Genimporter 公司于 1947 年 12 月 16 日在瑞士日内瓦签署。瑞士联邦法院认为,本案应适用比利时卖方所在地的法律。瑞士联邦法院在判决中指出:"本案中,当事人没有指定合同所应适用的法律……如果将该特许权转让合同视为是一个买卖合同的话,除非有相反规定,应适用具有特征性履行的卖方所在地的比利时法律。"

欧洲大陆法系国家法官在审理过程中没有英美法系法官的自由裁量权,因而

---

① See OLG Munchen, March 2, 1994, published in *Neue Juristische Wochenschrift Rechtsprechungs Report* 1075, 1076 (1994); KG Berlin, January 24, 1994, published in *Recht Der Internationalen Wirtschaft* 683, 683 (1994); OLG Frankfurt, June 13, 1991, published in *Neue Juristische Wochenschrift* 3102, 3102 (1991).

② See, most recently, Rechtbank Amsterdam, October 5, 1994, reprinted in 13 *Nederlands Internationaal Privaatrecht* 195, 195 (1995).

③ See, e.g., Asbrink Eiker v Rapid Maschinen und Fahrzeuge AG (Tribunal Fédéral, 100 II 450, 451).

④ See, e.g., Arbitral Tribunal ICC, No. 7197, reprinted in *Journal du Droit International* 1028, 1030 (1993).

⑤ See Zhang Mingjie, *Conflict of Laws and International Contract for Sale of Goods*, édition Paradigme, 1997, p.158.

强调立法的明确、清晰和逻辑严密至关重要。法律的确定性是其最基本的价值和目标。特征性履行方法所倡导的适用特征性履行方当事人的住所地或者居所地法律的理论,在司法实践中对于法院确定合同所适用的法律,具有重要的意义。

四、特征性履行方法是欧洲大陆法系国家排斥法官司法解释权的法哲学思想和理念的体现

在大陆法系国家的法哲学理念中,不承认法官有任何的衡平权,无论法官对法律作何种解释,都意味着"法官立法",而特征性履行方法的推广和实施,正是大陆法系国家排斥法官司法解释权这种法哲学思想和理念的具体体现。大陆法系对司法解释权和法官平衡权的否定,决定了对法院司法审判活动的限制和制约。在大陆法系,法官只能谨慎地在立法者所设定的框架内进行司法审判活动,而不能越雷池一步。与欧洲大陆国际私法学者的法哲学理念相反,美国国际私法学者或者冲突法学者更注重法律适用的灵活性。美国国际私法学者或者冲突法学者对特征性履行方法及其相关理论视而不见,而热衷于"最密切联系原则"。由于"法律原则"是不确定的规定,是模糊的规定。这种不确定的规定,采用模糊的概念,授予法官以自由裁量权。①美国国际私法学者或者冲突法学者所积极倡导的最密切联系原则,赋予法官以充分的自由裁量权。权力是一把双刃剑,在立法者们考虑采取最密切联系原则,赋予法官自由裁量的灵活性同时,也在一定程度上放任了自由裁量权力本身,使其有了随意适用的空间,这对法律内在的稳定秩序、追求的确定性目标构成威胁。由于法官自由裁量的扩大而导致法律判决的随意性,是对法律确定性的最大破坏。最密切联系原则与大陆法系国家排斥法官司法解释权的思想是有冲突的。为了克服最密切联系原则的不确定性,使法律制度的运作在具体的实践中不偏离其原有的初衷,有必要对最密切联系原则进行规范化。而特征性履行方法的产生和发展,恰恰顺应了这样的一种需求。特征性履行的主要作用(**main purpose of the presumption**)在于它克服了最密切联系方法过分灵活的缺点,而在法律适用的灵活性与确定性之间达到一种平衡。

【释义】　　　　main purpose of the presumption

The main purpose of the presumption is to provide a compromise—a compromise between those who seek certainty and predictability in the determination of the applicable law and thes who, like Englsih lawyers, see merit in the flexibility of the gerenral rule.

---

① 参见徐国栋:《民法基本原则解释》,中国政法大学出版社 1992 年版,第 21 页。

特征性履行方法限制了法官随时适用和解释法律的司法解释权,增强了法律适用的确定性。所以说,特征性履行方法是为克服法官自由裁量权的滥用而产生和发展起来的一种理论和方法,集中体现了欧洲大陆法系国家排斥法官司法解释权的法律思想。

五、特征性履行方法与最密切联系原则的结合体现了两大法系严格规则主义和自由裁量主义价值观的逐步融合

大陆法系在不断的变革过程中,其极端性的特征渐次消退,与普通法系的差异逐渐缩小,两大法系呈现出相互交融、彼此吸收的历史发展趋势。法律根植于文化之中,它在一定的文化范围内对特定社会的特定时间和地点所出现的特定需求作出回应。从根本上说,法律是人们认为、阐述和解决某些社会问题的方法。如果说,大陆法系与普通法系的传统差异产生于不同国家彼此之间的文化差异,那么,现今两大法系的相容与交汇,也正是基于各国文化在全球化的浪潮中不断趋同。[①]徐国栋先生认为:法律概念的模糊是由于其内涵的不确定性而导致的外延不确定。[②] "最密切联系原则"作为美国冲突法的一个重要原则,从其产生起,就是一个模糊的概念。这是英美法的特征所决定的,这种模糊性可以为法官适用法律提供一个很大的自主空间。如今,通过"特征性履行方法"与"最密切联系原则"相结合这种模式,既克服了最密切联系原则的模糊性,使合同法律适用的选择具有了确定性[③],又保持了一定的灵活性,因此受到英美法系国家和大陆法系国家的普遍赞同。国际私法领域内在20世纪80年代以后制定的一些国内立法与国际条约,呈现了灵活运用特征性履行方法与最密切联系原则结合方式的趋势,使判决结果确定性与法律适用灵活性之间的矛盾得到调和,体现了两大法系严格规则主义和自由裁量主义价值观的逐步融合。特征性履行方法与最密切联系原则的结合主要表现为以下三种方式。

(一) 以特征性履行方法作为确定最密切联系的法律的一般原则

这种方式的特点是根据合同的性质,单纯地按特征性履行方法确定各种合同的法律适用。采用这种方式的主要代表国家是捷克斯洛伐克。捷克斯洛伐克最早将特征性履行方法运用于国际私法立法之中。1964 年《捷克斯洛伐克国际私法与国际民事诉讼法》第 10 条规定:当事人未选择法律时,应适用下列法律:(1) 买卖

---

① 参见〔美〕梅利曼:《大陆法系》(第二版),顾培东等译,法律出版社 2004 年版,"译者序",第 7—8 页。
② 参见徐国栋:《民法基本原则解释》,中国政法大学出版社 1992 年版,第 15 页(内容提要)。
③ 参见李旺:《论国际私法中最密切联系原则的意义及存在的问题》,载《清华大学学报》(哲学社会科学版)2003 年第 5 期。

及物品加工供应合同,依缔结合同时卖方或加工者所在地(或住所地)法;(2)不动产的合同,依不动产所在地法;(3)运送合同(运送合同、发货合同及其他合同),依缔结合同时承运人或发货人所在地(或住所地)法;(4)保险合同,包括不动产的保险合同,依缔结保险合同时,保险人所在地(或住所地)法;(5)批发合同和类似合同,依缔结合同时批发商所在地(或住所地)法;(6)商业代理及经纪合同,依缔结代理合同时代理人或经纪人所在地(或住所地)法;(7)多边商业交易合同,依支配其整个关系最为合理的法律。①

从上述捷克斯洛伐克国际私法关于特征性履行的规定可以看出,该法仅对合同的种类进行划分,进而规定应当分别适用的法律,而未对出现比法律规定更加密切联系国家的法律的情况进行规定,也未明确说明特征性履行是最密切联系原则的一种方法。有学者将这种方式称为"纯粹的特征性履行模式"。②

特征性履行方法与最密切联系原则的这种结合方式,一方面,相对于传统的冲突规范而言,增加了法律选择的宽度;另一方面,相对于英美法系完全交由法官自由裁量的做法而言,在很大程度上又限制了法官的自由裁量权,增加了法律适用的确定性。

(二)以固定规则作为特征性履行应用中最密切联系的具体化

这种方式的特点是规定合同适用与之有最密切联系的法律,然后规定若干主要合同的固定的冲突规则,并明确规定这些固定规则是最密切联系原则的具体化。采用该模式的主要代表国家是奥地利。1978年《奥地利国际私法》第1条规定:"(1)与外国有连接事实,在私法上,应依与该事实有最密切联系的法律裁判。(2)本联邦法规(国际私法)所包括的适用法律的具体规则,应认为体现了这一原则。"该法第35条第2款规定:"凡未作法律的协议选择,或虽作出而不为联邦法规所承认者,概依第36至49条的规定解决。"该法第36条到44条分别对银行合同、保险合同,交易所合同、拍卖合同、消费者合同、使用不动合同、无体财产合同、雇佣合同等应适用的法律作出了规定。同时该法还明文规定了特征性履行方法是推定最密切联系法律的方法,是最密切联系原则的具体化运用,因而被称为"准特征性履行模式"。③该模式一方面在立法上明文规定特征性履行方法是最密切联系原则的具体化,另一方面根据特征性履行方法为相关合同规定了所应适用的法律,体现

---

① 参见徐冬根、刘晓红、单海岭主编:《国际公约与惯例(国际私法卷)》,法律出版社1997年版,第334页。

② 参见谢保军、孙乐鹏:《论国际私法中的特征性履行理论》,载《甘肃政法成人教育学院学报》2003年第2期。

③ 同上。

了较强的确定性。

（三）以"特征性履行方法"作为"最密切联系原则"的具体化，同时又规定例外条款

这种立法思想是确定性原则与灵活性原则的统一。以"特征性履行方法"作为"最密切联系原则"的具体化，是法律适用确定性原则的具体反映，而同时又规定例外条款，则是法律适用灵活性的表现。这种方式综合了特征性履行和最密切联系原则的优点，既在一定程度上限制了法官的自由裁量权，保证了法律和判决的确定性，同时又赋予法官一定限度的自由裁量权，以应对新情况和新形势，从而保证了司法活动的灵活性的要求。如1987年《瑞士联邦国际私法》规定，除采用"特征履行"以外，还可以以"保护一方当事人特殊利益的需要"为依据，而适用"特征履行"以外的法律；即使那些适用"特征履行"规则的合同，在某些特殊场合，如果情况证明它与其他法律有更密切的联系，也可以不适用"特征履行"方所在地法而适用有更密切联系的法律；由于各种法律关系错综复杂，新的法律关系可以随时产生，对法律未作规定的，仍然依最密切联系原则为指导，采用权衡各种连接因素的方法来确定其所应适用的法律。

依照理性主义的看法，世界是可能通过经验认识加以把握的，而且为了社会的安全，应凭借理性的力量制定具有确定性的法律。然而历史主义认为，人的认识受历史条件的制约，因而是相对的、不确定的。为了使法律既有确定性，又能应对社会发展变化的需要，必须将理性主义与历史主义的对立加以调和。反映在立法上，就是对确定性和灵活性的对立加以调和。①而立法中将最密切联系原则与特征性履行方法相融合，就是这种调和的现实化。上述三种特征性履行方法与最密切联系原则相结合的方式，尽管其侧重点有所不同，但其实质都是一致的。特征性履行方法与最密切联系原则的这种完美结合，体现了两大法系严格规则主义和自由裁量主义价值观的逐步融合。特征性履行方法中原则与规则相统一的理念，确定性与灵活性相结合的价值取向，对中国涉外民事法律适用法的立法具有重要的启迪意义。②

---

① 参见徐国栋：《民法基本原则解释》，中国政法大学出版社1992年版，第31页。
② 参见徐冬根：《国际私法上的特征性给付方法：规则还是原则？——为涉外民事法律适用法的立法而作的法理学思考》，载《清华法学》2010年第3期。

第四节 国际私法法律选择方法的发展趋势

国际私法法律选择方法的发展趋势主要表现为从机械规则到弹性处理,从确定性到灵活性的发展。充分认识法律冲突本质是正确选择法律的前提,而法律冲突的本质往往决定法律选择方法。现代国际私法通过采用冲突规范的软化处理,提高法律选择的质量,给予法官适当的自由裁量权,使得传统的机械规则发展成为当代国际私法规范。

一、冲突规范的软化处理

所谓软化处理(softing process)指坚持冲突规范连接点的基本模式,改变传统单一、固定、刚性的连接点,代之以多层次、开放、软性连接因素,给法院一个自由选择法律的空间,从而比较相关法律,选出最合适的准据法,求得个案的公正解决。对国际私法改革持积极态度的学者主张在保留冲突规范的前提下,通过各种途径和手段改进国际私法的法律适用机制。传统的冲突规范所采用的法律选择方法,以法律关系本座说为基本指导理论,强调法律适用的一致性和稳定性。这种一致性和稳定性同时又增加了法律选择的可预见性,在当时受到人们的普遍认同。随着国际私法的进一步发展,对僵固、呆板的传统国际私法进行软化处理被提到了前所未有的高度。冲突规范既然也是一种行为规范,它就要求人们遵守和执行,就不允许离开它而把每一个案件都交由法院依照各自的裁量规则去解决,否则,就不会有冲突规范可言。但是,在指引准据法的连接因素上采取僵化的绝对的立场,则肯定是不能实现这一目的的。国际私法与任何其他理论与方法一样,都必须反映客观世界,反映社会生活的变化和发展。随着科学技术的进步及国际贸易和人员流动空前规模的高涨,传统的法律选择方法也必须有所发展。传统的冲突规则面对新形势所暴露出来的一些缺陷,虽不表明它已到了穷途末路,但是表明这种方法需要改造,需要加工,需要注入更多的灵活性,以适应迅速变化的社会现实。为了实现这个目标,国际上逐渐兴起一种对冲突规范进行软化处理的潮流。①通过用灵活

---

① 参见李双元:《我国国际私法理论研究和立法工作中的几个问题》,载《政法论坛》1996年第3期。

开放型的系属公式代替僵硬封闭型的系属公式;以归纳方式提炼出适合时代要求的法律选择规范,使法律选择更具可操作性,从而可以较好地适应各种新的涉外民商事关系的需要。

(一) 采用灵活的开放型的系属公式对连接因素作软化处理

用灵活的开放型的系属公式代替僵硬的封闭型的系属公式,这首先表现在合同领域,然后再逐步扩展到其他有关领域。当然,这里需要指出的,采用灵活的开放型的系属公式代替传统的僵硬的封闭型的系属公式来对连接因素作软化处理是有限度的,否则整个国际私法都可归结为一句话:"涉外法律关系由与该法律关系具有最密切联系的法律支配",这样就会否定国际私法的存在。事实上,封闭的连接因素和开放性的连接因素代表着两种不同的法律价值观:前者代表确定性和可预见性,而后者代表灵活性和针对性。人们既不能完全抛开固定的连接因素,也不能不规定一些开放性的连接因素,而必须是两者有机的统一。如《奥地利国际私法》一方面将最密切联系作为总的指导原则规定下来;另一方面却又规定:该法所包括的适用法律的具体规定,则应认为体现了这一原则。《瑞士联邦国际私法》也要求首先适用它所规定的各具体冲突规则,只有在案件的事实与规定的准据法有微弱的联系,而与另一个法律明显地更有密切联系的时候,该法所确定的准据法才可以不适用。总的说来,人们对开放型连接因素的需要程度,制约着封闭的连接因素的适用,反过来,封闭的连接因素在它符合案件实际的情况下,又限制了开放型连接因素的作用。[①]

(二) 通过归纳方式提炼出适合时代要求的法律选择规范

众所周知,在思维方法上,大陆法系国家的哲学和法学推崇演绎法,英美法系国家的哲学和法学推崇归纳法。对归纳法的强调,是经验主义哲学的必然结果和重要组成部分。培根认为,归纳法是以科学试验、经验事实为基础的,它是避免和根除假象的适当的补救方法,是唯一正确的科学方法。[②]归纳法开辟了通向真理的另一条道路,它的成立之根本原因,在于承认"科学主要是经验性的,它归根到底不得不诉诸观察和实验"[③]。归纳法的前提是人类行为的差异性,因此它强调自由裁量和司法个别化,以达到每一个案子都获得正义解决的目标。

从理论上说,归纳法是从个别开始然后到达一般的一种思维方法。由于英美判例法是从个案中导出法律规则,再将这些规则适用于个别的案件。判例法的归

---

① See Stoffel, W. A., Le rapport juridique international, *Mélanges von Overberck*, Fribourg, 1990, pp. 421 ss.
② 参见朱德生等:《西方认识论史纲》,江苏人民出版社 1983 年版,第 127—128 页。
③ 〔英〕丹皮尔:《科学史》,李珩译,商务印书馆 1975 年版,第 12 页。

纳方法并不排斥创造性的法律科学,它常常从外界吸收新因素并用类推的方法发展这些新因素,或将这些因素与现存的法律因素相结合,创造出更新颖的复合物。这些新复合物往往不是观念逐渐展现的结果,而是人们为规定某一具体情况而努力的结果,它导向适用一个具体的解决方法。在其背后,其他人也进行尝试性的归纳,甚至设计出一个更为广泛的制度。因此,当我们回顾它的时候,我们说一种观念正在实现,可是观念只有在事件发生之后才能得到整理、安排,并使其明显地发生作用。①可见,归纳法强调,观念产生于事实之后而不是事实之前,而观念的产生是艰苦的尝试性归纳的结果,而不是演绎的结果。美国国际私法学界的改革,以卡弗斯为代表的一些美国学者秉承了英美法中归纳法的传统,通过对具体案例的分析总结,提炼出一系列适应现代社会需要的法律选择方法,并将之上升为一些较为固定的法律选择规则。

二、弹性处理原则与法律选择质量

近几十年来,各国对国际私法的立法和操作又作了很大的改进。最明显的是,法官更注重提高法律选择的质量。对于如何选择法律,各国都认为不能仅仅依靠机械的冲突规范去套各式各样的具体案件,但究竟如何选择法律,则众说纷纭。

就如何提高法律选择的质量而言,国际私法学者们总结出若干可供借鉴的经验。首先,关于法律选择的对象,各方都认为应该抛弃过去那种偏重法律管辖的现象,而转向注意法律内容选择,即由管辖选择转为规则选择。那么,究竟如何选择法律呢?在法律选择问题上完全抛弃冲突规范是有害的,因为如果失去某种较为一致的标准,而由各个法院的各个法官在各个案件中凭自己的直觉、感情、理智及经验去选择法律,这样做尽管可能会使法官得到一时的心安理得,但实际上最终仍是不公平的。尤其是在国际关系中,任何人的理智和感情都带有"地域性",法官也不会例外,此地的法官认为适用甲国法是公正的,而彼地的法官依据他的公平观念可能会认为适用乙国法更合理些。显然,作为一种标准或依据,公平的概念是比较抽象的。公平的概念用来批判不公平的传统冲突规范是可以的、必需的,而且在建立新的冲突规范时也应以公平观念作指导,但仅以公平作标准来决定是非则不可靠。应将公平观念具体化,使其成为可以普遍适用的规则。例如,在侵权行为交通事故的准据法问题上,对于判断一个人是否违反交通规则以及能否据此确立其责任,应依交通事故地的法律,而对于该人因交通事故造成他人伤害的赔偿问题,应

---

① 〔美〕庞德:《法律史解释》,邓正来译,华夏出版社 1989 年版,第 132—133 页。关于庞德的相关法律思想,可参阅其著作:Roscoe Pound, *Introduction of the Philosophy of Law*, New Haven, 1954; *The Task of the Law*, ancaster, Pa. (1944).

适用能使其损失得到较适宜的补偿的法律。①

在美国第七巡回上诉法院对 **In re Air Crash Disaster Near Chicago** 案的判决中,法官巧妙地运用了法律选择方法,对案件的法律适用问题进行了系统的分析。这种对选择方式的综合和灵活的运用手法,可以作为跨州侵权诉讼中确定准据法的典范。②

【案例】 **In re Air Crash Disaster Near Chicago**③

On May 25 1979, a crash of a DC-10 had happen near Chicage, Illionos as it took off from O'hare. One hundred and eighteen actions filed in California, Hawaii, Illinois, Michigan, New York and Puerto Rico, where consolidated in Federal District Court for Illinois. Plaintiffs and their decedents resided in all of the jurisdictions listed above, plus Connecticut, Indiana, Massachusetts, New Jersey, Vermont, Japan, the Netherlands, and Saudi Arabia. The designer and builder of the plane, McDonell Douglas, a Maryland corporation, has its principal place of businesses in Missouri and manufactured the DC-10 in California. Defendant American Airlines, the carrier, a Delaware corporation, has its principal place of businesses in New York until 1979, but moved it to Texas during that year. The court opined for more than 50 pages as it dealt with a single aspect of the case, punitive damages.④

在该案中,被告对惩罚性损害赔偿(punitive damages)提出了异议。地区法院审查后认为,提起诉讼各州的法律选择规则均指向同一结论:麦道公司可以被诉求惩罚性损害赔偿,而美国航空公司则不能被要求。⑤ 上诉法院部分推翻了地区法院的判决,认为麦道公司和美国航空公司均无须承担惩罚性损害赔偿。上诉法院强调,虽然各种选择方法表面上存在差异,但其实质是相同的,在根本上是为了确定最密切利益州,并适用其实体法。

【思考题】

* 传统国际私法法律选择方式有什么特点?
* 最密切联系法律选择方法的产生对当代国际私法发展具有哪些意义?

---

① 参见周海荣:《论当今国际私法的若干新动向》,载《中国法学》1988 年第 4 期。
② 参见王承志:《美国集团诉讼中的法律选择问题》,载《法学评论》2007 年第 2 期。
③ In re Air Crash Disaster Near Chicago, 644 F. 2d 594 (7 th Cir. 1981)。
④ David H. Vernon, Louis Weinberg, William Reynolds, William Richman, *Conflicts of Law: Case, Materials and Problems*, 2d ed., LexisNexis, 2002, p.31.
⑤ In re Air Crash Disaster Near Chicago, Ill. on May 25, 1979, 500 F. Supp. 1044, 1054 (N. D. Ill. 1980)。

- 什么是特征性履行方法?
- 特征性履行与最密切联系的结合方式有几种?
- 什么是国际私法冲突规范的软化处理?

【重要术语提示与中英文对照】

中文术语	英文对照
法律选择方法	law-selecting approach
地域导向的法律选择规则	territorially-oriented choice-of-law rules
管辖选择的规则	jurisdiction-selecting rule
最密切联系理论	theory of the closest connection
最重要联系理论	theory of the most significant contact
最强联系理论	theory of the strongest connection
最真实联系理论	theory of the most real connection
引力中心	center of gravity
有最密切联系的法律	the law of the most closely connected
早期有关最密切联系方法	origins of the significant contacts approach
奥汀诉奥汀案	Auten v. Auten
贝科克诉杰克逊	Babcock v. Jackson
法律选择原则	choice-of-law principles
第二次冲突法重述	Restatement Second of the law of the conflict of laws, Second Restatement
特征性履行	characteristic performance
特征性之债	characteristic obligation
海牙1955年关于国际货物买卖法律适用公约	The 1955 Hague Convention on the Law Applicable to International Sales of Goods
惯常居所	habitual residence
欧洲经济共同体	European Economic Community
关于合同债务的法律适用公约	Convention on the Law Applicable to Contractual Obligations, EEC Convention
1980年罗马公约	The 1980 Rome Convention
纽迈叶诉库纳案	Neumeier v. Kuchner
软化处理	softing process
惩罚性损害赔偿	punitive damages

【推荐阅读文献】

* 徐崇利:《外国法制冲突规则的回归——美国现代国际私法理论与实践的一大发展趋向》,载《法学评论》2000 年第 5 期。
* 徐冬根:《国际私法的柔性化与刚性化》,载《法制与社会发展》2003 年第 3 期(全文收录于《中国国际法学精粹(2004 年卷)》)。
* 彭丁带:《最密切联系原则应确立为国际私法的基本原则》,载《南昌大学学报(人文社会科学版)》2005 年第 4 期。
* 徐冬根:《论国际私法的哲理性》,载《华东政法大学学报》2010 年第 1 期。
* 徐冬根:《国际私法上的特征性给付方法:规则还是原则?——为涉外民事法律适用法的立法而作的法理学思考》,载《清华法学》2010 年第 3 期。
* 〔美〕拉夫·迈克尔:《美国冲突法革命的衰落与回归》,袁发强译,载《华东政法大学学报》2011 年第 6 期。
* 杨利雅:《冲突法视域中的强行法——以〈适用法〉第四条规定为视角》,载《西南民族大学学报(人文社会科学版)》2012 年第 8 期。
* 孙建:《论我国国际私法法律适用的确定性与灵活性》,载《法学评论》2012 年第 2 期。
* Russell J Weintraub, *Commentary on the Conflict of Laws*, 4ed edition, New York Foundation Press, 2001.
* David H. Vernon, Louis Weinberg, William Reynolds, William Richman, *Conflicts of Law: Case, Materials and Problems*, 2d ed. LexisNexis 2002.
* Giesela Ruhl, Methods and Approaches in Choice of Law: An Economic Perspective, 24 *Berkeley J. Int'l L.* 801(2006).
* Mills (A.), Federalism in the European Union and the United States: Subsidiarity, Private Law, and the Conflict of Laws, 32 *U. Pa. J. Int'l L.* 369 (2010).
* Pitel (S.), Reformulating a Real and Substantial Connection, 60 *U. N. Br. L. J.* 177 (2010).
* Borchers (P.), J. McIntyre Machinery, Goodyear, and the Incoherence of the Minimum Contacts Test, 44 *Creighton L. Rev.* 1245 (2011).
* Symeon C. Symeonides, Choice of Law in the American Courts in 2011: Twenty-Fifth Annual Survey, 60 *American Journal of Comparative Law* (2012).

【扩展阅读资料】

The Choice between Approaches: Substantivism or Selectivism?[①]

If from an economic perspective state courts should not always apply the *lex fori* they face the problem of determining the applicable law in cases that touch on different legal orders. In the history of private international law, essentially two methodological approaches have emerged to solve this problem: first, the substantive method of creating new substantive law and, second, the selectivist method of choosing between existing laws. Up until today, the latter has prevailed in both Europe and the United States. However, the former was applied during Roman times and in England up to the 18th century. Additionally, it was advocated by a number of American and European scholars during the 20th century.

1. The Roman *Praetor Peregrinus* and the English Law Merchant

The beginnings of the substantivist approach to choice of law are to be found in Roman times, more specifically in the 3rd century B.C. Back then, Romans were increasingly engaged in international trade and, therefore, had to face more and more legal disputes involving members of foreign countries. But instead of applying their own law in cases that had connections to foreign legal orders—as the Greeks did—the Romans created a new institution empowered to handle litigation involving non-Romans: the praetor *peregrinus*. Drawing on general legal principles, the notion of good faith as well as his own legal imagination, he solved multistate cases by ad hoc crafting new substantive rules especially designed for cross-border transactions. These new substantive rules gradually developed into a separate body of norms, the *ius gentium*, which applied to international disputes only and was distinct from the *ius civile* that regulated disputes between Roman citizens.

The Roman substantivist method invented by the praetor *peregrinus* died out when the *ius gentium* was incorporated into the *ius civile* and codified in the Corpus *Juris Justinianus*. However, it had a revival in the English commercial and maritime courts several centuries later. These courts, which existed next to the forum-oriented common law courts, did not apply the common law, which had been developed to meet the needs of a rural society. Instead they referred to the Roman praetor *peregrinus* and engaged in the ad hoc development of a set of new substantive rules especially designed for commercial and maritime cases. These rules that became later known as law merchant and maritime law drew on different historic and geographic sources and claimed universal application. However, they met the same fate as the ius gentium because they were eventually absorbed by the English common law courts and indistinguishably incorporated into the common law.

[①] Giesela Ruhl, Methods and Approaches in Choice of Law: An Economic Perspective, 24 *Berkeley J. Int'l L.* 801, 815—817 (2006).

2. The Statutists' Method: Choosing Among Existing Laws

The roots of the selectivist method—and thereby the roots of modern choice of law theory—are to be found in the statutists' method developed by Italian scholars in the 12th century. When they had to answer the question how to solve disputes between members of different city-states they did not develop a new set of substantive rules as the Romans did. Instead, they applied the law of one or the other city-state and thus made a choice between existing laws rather than blending them. In practice, this method of choosing the applicable law from existing laws has prevailed up until today. Even Carl Friedrich von Savigny—who criticized the workings of the statutists' method insofar as it amounted to a unilateral choice of law theory—did not question that international disputes had to be solved by applying the laws of one of the states involved. However, the substantivist approach formed the basis for some of the most important American approaches to choice of law in the 20th century.

3. Modern Forms of Substantivism

At the beginning of the 20th century, choice of law in the United States was dominated by the vested rights theory. First formulated by the English scholar Albert V. Dicey and later brought to the United States by Joseph H. Beale, it advanced the idea that courts decided cases according to foreign law if a right had been created abroad. What made the vested rights theory so important, however, was not the theory itself but the reaction it triggered in the academic community when it was eventually incorporated into the Restatement (First) of Conflicts. Today known as the American conflicts revolution, conflicts scholars across the country engaged in a vigorous debate about the foundations of choice of law and advocated countless new methodological approaches. One of the most important and influential approaches that emerged from this debate was Friedrich K. Juenger's best law approach. As a reaction to the perceived arbitrariness of the vested rights theory of the Restatement (First), he suggested that courts should not choose between application of existing laws but strive for the application of the best law. Arguing that national laws were not suited for the resolution of international disputes he granted courts the right to ad hoc construct new substantive rules especially designed for international cases. Juenger's writings were embraced and enhanced by a number of American scholars, notably Luther M. McDougal, Arthur T. von Mehren and Donald T. Trautmann as well as—in Europe—Ernst Steindorff. They all promoted—to different degrees and according to different guidelines—the ad hoc crafting and application of new substantive law rules. However, the response from practice was more than faint. In the United States, a substantivist approach was finally rejected in 1969 when the Restatement (Second) of Conflicts was adopted. In Europe, it was never seriously considered as a relevant approach to choice of law.

第六章

国际私法法律关系的主体

第六章 国际私法法律关系的主体

本章导读

※ 自然人属人法是指关于人的身份和能力所适用的法律,亦即关于人的身份和能力的准据法。国籍和住所作为与人紧密相关的因素,是自然人属人法的两个基本连接点。其中,以自然人国籍所属国为连接点的属人法习惯性地被称为当事人的本国法,以自然人住所为连接点的属人法即当事人住所地法。

※ 国籍是指一个人属于某个国家的国民或公民的法律资格。一个自然人同时具有两个或者两个以上的国籍的情况,称为国籍的积极冲突;一个自然人不具有任何国籍的情况称为国籍的消极冲突。

※ 住所是指一个人以久住的意思而居住的某一处所。

※ 各国对法人住所采取不同的标准,大致可以概括以下几种:以主事务所所在地(管理中心所在地)为法人住所;以营业中心所在地为法人住所;以章程规定的地方为法人住所;以成立地为法人住所;以公司股东的国籍来决定公司的住所。

※ 外国法人的承认,就是指内国根据本国法律对外国法人的资格进行审查,承认并允许其在内国的一定范围内从事民商事活动的过程。

※ 国家及其财产管辖豁免,又称国家豁免或主权豁免,是指国家根据国家主权和国家平等原则不接受他国管辖的特权。

※ 国家及其财产管辖豁免包括三个方面:(1)司法管辖豁免。它是指未经一国同意时,他国不得以该国作为被告起诉,也不得对位于该国境内的他国国家财产提起诉讼。(2)诉讼程序豁免。它是指除非一国明示同意,他国不得以该国在其境内的国家财产作为诉讼担保,加以查封或扣押,也不得强迫该国提供诉讼费用的担保。(3)强制执行豁免。它是指一国在国际民事诉讼中无论是充当原告还是自愿作被告,未得到该国的明示同意,他国法院不得根据其判决对该国的财产予以强制执行。

※ 国家及其财产管辖豁理论包括:绝对豁免论、限制豁免论(又称"职能豁免说")和废除豁免论等几种主张。

※ 我国认为,在坚持国家主权豁免原则的前提下,基于正常经济交往的需要,国家可以在特殊情况下,以协议或其他形式对具体案件或某些事项放弃豁免权。我国主张国家豁免的范围主要是国家行为和国家财产。

※ 国际组织的特权与豁免来自于成员国的授权。

【本章主题词】 自然人属人法、国籍、住所、居所、法人、国家、管辖豁免权

第一节 自然人的法律适用

一、国际私法中的自然人

自然人在国际民商事法律关系中的主体资格取决于其所具有的权利能力和行为能力。一国的自然人只要按照其本国法律规定具有民事权利能力和民事行为能力,就可以在内国作为国际民商事法律关系的主体,从事国际民商事活动。各国对本国自然人在内国作为国际民商事法律关系的主体资格一般都不加限制,或只在某些特殊问题上有所限制。

外国自然人,只有在东道国肯定其具有一定的民商事法律地位时[①],才能在东道国成为国际民商事法律关系的主体。现今,世界各国都已承认外国人在内国具有一定的民商事法律地位,在一些国家还规定外国人与内国人在民商事法律地位上平等,享受国民待遇。但是我们也必须看到,各国对外国人在内国的民商事法律地位的具体规定并不完全一样。[②]本国自然人和外国自然人的主体地位并非理所当然地相同,还是需要视各国具体的规定而定。

二、自然人的属人法

国际私法中与自然人主体资格密切相关的是属人法制度。

所谓自然人属人法(personal law)是指关于人的身份(status)和能力(capacity)所适用的法律,亦即关于人的身份和能力的准据法。国际私法中的身份,是一个人与民事法律规定的权利与义务有直接联系的法律地位,如丈夫、妻子、父母、子女、成年人、未成年人等;国际私法中的能力,则是一个人在民事法律上享受权利、履行义务和承担责任的资格,即民事权利能力与民事行为能力。

国籍和住所(**nationality and domicile**)作为与人紧密相关的因素,是自然人属

---

① 在历史上,曾有外国人在内国毫无法律地位的情形,也曾有外国人在内国处于特权地位的情形,这两种情形都极大地阻碍了国际民商事法律关系的建立和发展。

② 一些国家为了维护本国的利益,并不主张外国人与内国人在民商事法律地位上绝对平等。有时外国人在内国并不能参加某种民事活动,因而也就不能作为这种民商事法律关系的主体。

人法的两个基本连接点。

【释义】 nationality and domicile

The change from domicile to nationality on the continent of Europe stated in France with the promulgation of the *Code Napoéon* in 1804. In matter of personal status these *coutume* applied to persons dominiciled within the province. The change from domicile to nationality on the continent of Europe was accelerated by Mancini's famous lecture delivered at the University of Turin in 1851.①

其中,以自然人国籍所属国为连接点的属人法习惯性地被称为当事人的本国法,以自然人住所为连接点的属人法即当事人住所地法。长期以来,两者共同构成自然人的属人法并作为属人法的两大派别而对峙存在。

后来随着属人法的发展,为了调和两大派别在属人法上的矛盾,还常常用惯常居所地(**habitual residence**)法来代替住所地法或本国法作为属人法。

【释义】 habitual residence

Habitual residence has long been a favourite expression of the Hugue Conference on Privat International Law. It seems that there is no real distinction between the two concepts habitual residence and ordinary residence; or at least, they share a common core of meaning. The habitual residence can not be acquired in a single day as an appreciable period of time. A settled intention are required. To Acquire a habitual residence, a person must take up residentce in the relevant country and live there for a period which shows that the residence has become habitual. The length of that period is not fixed; it must depend on the circumstances.②

三、自然人的国籍

(一) 自然人国籍的概念

国籍(nationality)是指一个人属于某个国家的国民或公民的法律资格。③国籍是区别内国人和外国人或无国籍人的重要标志,是各国国民在国际交往中受本国外交保护的依据,也是国家对某些国际私法案件行使司法管辖权的根据。同时也

---

① David McClean, Morris, *The conflict of laws*, 5th ed., Sweet & Maxwell, 2000, p.44.
② Ibid., p.22.
③ 王进主编:《国际私法》(第二版),法律出版社 2005 年版,第 133 页。

是构成解决自然人亲权、继承关系等方面法律冲突系属公式的重要因素。①国籍还是某一案件可否界定为国际民事案件的标识之一,同时也是许多国家确定本国法院可否受理国际案件的因素之一。为了处理涉外民事法律问题往往需要首先认定当事人的国籍。

对于国籍的法律性质,国内外学者对此形成了几种主张:英国学者认为,国籍是一个人对国家的忠诚义务(allegiance);德国学者认为,国籍是人民对国家的绝对服从(obedience);法国学者认为,国籍是个人与国家之间的合同(contract)关系,国家与个人双方都负有各自的权利和义务,并可像合同一样随时解除这种关系。②

(二) 自然人国籍的冲突

1. 自然人国籍的积极冲突及其解决方法

国籍的积极冲突,是指由于各国关于自然人取得、丧失或者恢复国籍所采取的原则或者所实行的主义不同,使得一个自然人同时具有两个或者两个以上的国籍的情况。

对于自然人国籍的积极冲突,各国在实践中主要采取如下方法加以解决:

第一,在当事人所具有的两个或两个以上的国籍中有一个是内国国籍时,国际上较为通行的做法是以内国国籍为准,这就是把该当事人优先视为内国人,以内国法为该人的本国法。

第二,在当事人具有的两个或两个以上的国籍均为外国国籍时,如何确定其本国法,则各国的实践不一,归纳起来主要有以下几种做法:其一,以当事人最后取得的国籍为准。其二,以当事人的住所或惯常居所所在地国国籍为准。其三,以与当事人有最密切联系的国籍优先,以该国法律为其本国法。1921年海牙常设仲裁院对卡内伐罗(Canavaro)案的裁决③,是采用关系最密切国原则来解决国籍的积极冲突。其四、由受案法院的法官裁定。④

第三,对当事人所具有的两个或两个以上的国籍不作内国国籍和外国国籍的区分,为确定应适用的法律,只以与当事人有最密切联系的国籍为准。⑤

2. 自然人国籍消极冲突及其解决方法

国籍的消极冲突,是指由于各国关于自然人取得、丧失或者恢复国籍所采取的原则或者所实行的主义不同,使得一个自然人不具有任何国籍的情况。国籍的消

---

① 参见丁伟主编:《国际私法学》,上海人民出版社2004年版,第132页。
② 参见董立坤:《国际私法论》,法律出版社1988年版,第114—115页。
③ 参见李浩培:《国籍问题的比较研究》,商务印书馆1979年版,第215—220页。
④ 参见丁伟主编:《国际私法学》,上海人民出版社2004年版,第134页。
⑤ 参见黄进主编:《国际私法》(第二版),法律出版社2005年版,第133—134页。

极冲突,可分为三种情况:生来便无国籍;原来有国籍后来因身份变更或者政治上的原因而变得无国籍;属于何国籍无法查明。①

对于无国籍自然人采取补救,主要有几下几种方法:

第一,根据1954年签订的《关于无国籍人地位的公约》第12条的规定②,将无国籍的当事人住所地国家视为其国籍所属国;如果无国籍的当事人其住所不能确定时,则将其居所所在地国家视为其国籍所属国;如果无国籍的当事人没有居所时,将其现住所视为其住所地,以住所地国家视为其国籍所属国。

第二,根据《关于无国籍人地位的公约》第32条的规定,缔约各国应尽可能便利无国籍人入籍和同化。它们应特别尽力加速办理入籍程序,并尽可能减低此项程序的费用。

第三,根据《关于无国籍人地位的公约》第23条的规定,为解除无国籍自然人无保护状态的不利因素,缔约国对合法居住在其领土内的无国籍人,就公共救济和援助方面,应给以凡本国国民所享有的同样待遇。所谓"合法居住"是指居住国准许其居住。所谓"公共救济"是指全社会所有成员都能享受的救济权利,具有全社会福利性质。

(三) 中国有关自然人国籍的规定

根据我国《国籍法》以及最高人民法院《关于贯彻执行〈中华人民共和国民法通则〉若干问题的意见(试行)》,我国对于自然人国籍的确定有如下规定:

第一,不承认中国人具有双重国籍。《国籍法》第5条规定:"父母双方或一方为中国公民,本人出生在外国,具有中国国籍;但父母双方或一方为中国公民并定居在外国,本人出生时即具有外国国籍的,不具有中国国籍。"该法第9条规定:"定居外国的中国公民,自愿加入或取得外国国籍的,即自动丧失中国国籍。"

第二,最高人民法院《关于贯彻执行〈中华人民共和国民法通则〉若干问题的意见(试行)》第182条规定:"有双重或多重国籍的外国人,以其有住所或者与其有最密切联系的国家的法律为其本国法。"我国《涉外民事关系法律适用法》第19条规定:"依照本法适用国籍国法律,自然人具有两个以上国籍的,适用有经常居所的国籍国法律;在所有国籍国均无经常居所的,适用与其有最密切联系的国籍国法律。"

第三,对于无国籍人,我国《国籍法》第6条规定:"父母无国籍或国籍不明,定居在中国,本人出生在中国,具有中国国籍。"第7条规定:"外国人或无国籍人,愿

---

① 参见李双元主编:《国际私法》,北京大学出版社2006年版,第160页。
② 《关于无国籍人地位的公约》,参见王铁崖、田如萱编:《国际法资料选编》,法律出版社1982年版,第119—132页。

意遵守中国宪法和法律……可以经申请批准加入中国国籍。"我国目前并没有关于解决国籍消极冲突的明文规定,但是最高人民法院《关于贯彻执行〈中华人民共和国民法通则〉若干问题的意见(试行)》第181条规定:"无国籍人的民事行为能力,一般适用其定居国法律;如未定居的,适用其住所地国法律"。《涉外民事关系法律适用法》第19条规定:"自然人无国籍或者国籍不明的,适用其经常居所地法律。"由此可见,我国目前的立法和实践还是较接近于国际上的一般做法的。

四、自然人的住所

(一) 住所的概念

自然人住所(**domicile**)是国际私法中一个重要制度,它是确定涉外民商事案件的管辖权和法律适用的一个重要的连接点。

【释义】　　　　　　　　　　　　Domicile

The domicile is not uniform throughout the world. To a civil lawyer it means habitual residence, but at common law it is regarded as the equivalent of a person's permanent home.①

住所是指一个人以久住的意思而居住的某一处所。②自然人的住所,在普通法系国家通常指的是其家的所在地,即是自然人居住、家庭生活、社会和市民生活的中心地。③在这些国家中住所一般又可分为三类(**three kinds of domiciles**),即原始住所、选择住所和法定住所。

【释义】　　　　　　　　　three kinds of domiciles

These are three kinds of domiciles:

(1) domicile of origin, which is the domicile assigned by law to a child when he was born. (2) domicile of choice, which is the domicile which any independent person can acquire for himself by a combination of residence and intention. (3) domicile of dependency, which means that the domicile of dependent persons is dependent on, and usually changes with, the

---

① P. M. North, *Cheshire and North's Private International Law*, 10th ed., London: Butterworths, 1979, p.157.
② 参见徐冬根、王国华、萧凯:《国际私法》,清华大学出版社2005年版,第65页。
③ 参见单海玲:《论涉外民事关系中住所及惯常居所的法律适用》,载《比较法研究》2006年第2期。

domicile of someone else, e.g. the parent of child. ①

（二）自然人住所的法律冲突

由于各国关于住所的法律规定不同或事实认定各异,因此会产生自然人住所的法律冲突,包括自然人住所的积极冲突和消极冲突。

1. 自然人住所的积极冲突及其解决方法

自然人住所的积极冲突是指一个人同时拥有两个或者两个以上的住所。关于积极冲突的解决,有以下几个主张:第一,以个人的意思选择住所。第二,如果一个人有两个以上的住所,其中一个住所在法院地国,法院地法优先适用,即以法院所在地的住所为准。第三,根据法律关系的性质和该法律关系所适用的法律确定一个住所。第四,内国住所与外国住所发生冲突的,选择适用内国法为住所地法;外国住所地与外国住所发生冲突的,根据住所取得的时间,或以先取得的住所为住所,或以最后取得的住所为住所;如果一个人同时取得两个住所,或以与当事人关系最密切的住所为住所,或以当事人现在居住地的住所为住所。当事人无居所的,则以父或母的最后住所为住所。②以上四种解决方法中,显然第四种是比较合理的。

2. 自然人住所的消极冲突及其解决方法

自然人住所的消极冲突,是指一个人无任何法律意义上的住所。各国实践中主要采取两种解决办法。第一,以当事人的居所或惯常居所代替其住所。第二,以当事人曾有过的最后住所为其住所,如无最后住所,则以其居所或惯常居所代替其住所。在当事人居所或惯常居所也没有的情况下,一般以当事人的现在地作为住所地。

（三）我国有关住所的规定

我国《民法通则》第 15 条规定:公民以他的户籍所在地的居住地为住所,经常居住地与住所不一致的,经常居住地视为住所。1990 年最高人民法院对经常居住地作出了相应司法解释:"公民离开住所最后连续居住 1 年以上的地方,为经常居住地。""当事人的住所不明或者不能确定,以其经常居住地为住所;当事人有几个住所的,以与产生纠纷的民事关系有最密切联系的住所为住所。"我国自 2011 年 4 月 1 日起施行的《涉外民事关系法律适用法》第 20 条规定:"依照本法适用经常居

---

① David McClean, Morris, *The Conflict of Laws*, 5th ed., Sweet & Maxwell, 2000, pp. 24—25.
② 参见韩德培主编:《国际私法新论》,武汉大学出版社 2004 年版,第 71 页。

所地法律,自然人经常居所地不明的,适用其现在居所地法律。"上述这些规定及司法解释构成了我国住所的法律制度。

五、自然人行为能力

（一）自然人行为能力的概念

自然人的行为能力是指法律所确认的自然人通过自己的行为从事民事活动,享有民事权利和承担民事义务的能力。

（二）自然人行为能力的法律适用

各国关于自然人行为能力的法律规定不同导致法律冲突。对自然人行为能力的法律适用,国际上的通行做法是依当事人属人法,但有两个例外或限制,一是处理不动产的行为能力适用物之所在地法;二是有关商务活动的当事人的行为能力可以适用行为地法,即只要其属人法或行为地法认为自然人有行为能力,则应认为有行为能力。

（三）我国关于对自然人民事行为的法律适用

我国《民法通则》第143条中规定:"中华人民共和国公民定居国外的,他的民事行为能力可以适用定居国法律。"最高人民法院《关于贯彻执行〈中华人民共和国民法通则〉若干问题的意见(试行)》作出了进一步的补充,其规定为:定居国外的我国公民的民事行为能力,如其行为是在我国境内所为,适用我国法律,在定居国所为,可以适用其定居国法律。外国人在我国领域内进行民事活动,如依其本国法律为无民事行为能力,而依我国法律为有民事行为能力,应当认定为有民事行为能力。无国籍人的民事行为能力,一般适用其定居国法律,如未定居,适用其住所地国法律。[①] 我国《涉外民事关系法律适用法》第12条规定:自然人的民事行为能力,适用经常居所地法律。自然人从事民事活动,依照经常居所地法律为无民事行为能力,依照行为地法律为有民事行为能力的,适用行为地法律,但涉及婚姻家庭、继承的除外。

---

① 徐冬根、王国华、萧凯:《国际私法》,清华大学出版社2005年版,第71页。

第二节 法人的法律适用

一、法人概述

(一) 法人的概念

法人(legal person)指按照法定程序设立,有一定的组织机构和独立的财产,并能以自己的名义享有民事权利和承担民事义务的社会组织。[①]法人在国际经济交往和合作中发挥着重要作用,国际私法必须解决法人作为国际私法主体的有关法律问题。

自1900年《德国民法典》首先确认了法人的民事主体地位之后,世界各国民事立法都相继确立了法人的民事主体地位,赋予法人以民事权利能力。[②]然而,各国法人的民事权利能力的内容却存在较大的差异。[③]这表明了各国对法人制度的不同理解,因而有必要进行冲突规范的制定。

(二) 法人及其分支机构的国际私法主体地位

法人同自然人一样,是国际私法的基本主体。

法人的分支机构,按照国际上通行的法律原则,不具有独立的法人资格。公司法人的分支机构通常被称为分公司。虽然法人分支机构不具备法人资格,但它通过合法登记,也可以有自己的名称和组织机构,并可以支配其经费。在法人的授权下还可以从事一定的民商事关系,如采购、定约、交易等,银行的分行可以向客户提供贷款,保险公司的分公司可以开展保险业务。法人的分支机构有自己的住所、权利能力、行为能力,有自己的营业执照。法人分支机构或非法人组织在国际民商事交往中,也应具备一定的主体资格。

[①] 韩德培:《国际私法新论》,武汉大学出版社2002年版,第133页。
[②] 王文红:《谈法人的民事权利能力》,载《河南公安学刊》1998年第4期。
[③] 如《日本民法典》第43条规定:法人权于目的范围内享有权利能力;《瑞士民法典》第53条规定:法人的权利能力原则上与自然人相同,但例外为自然人所未有者,法人不得享有之。

二、法人的住所及其冲突解决方法

（一）各国确定法人住所的标准

各国对法人住所采取不同的标准,大致可以概括以下几种:

1. 以主事务所所在地(管理中心所在地)为法人住所

法人的住所地就是法人的主事务所或者法人的管理中心(administration center)所在地。一个法人只有一个主事务所,以之作为确定法人住所的标志,也比较简单明确。日本、德国、意大利、法国等许多大陆法系国家采用这种主张。①采取以主事务所所在地为法人住所的一个著名案例是德国的 **Überseering BV v. Nordic Construction Company Baumanagement GmbH** 案。

【案例】　　**Überseering BV v. Nordic Construction Company Baumanagement GmbH** ②

该案中一家依荷兰法律成立并在荷兰登记有事务所的公司对依德国法律成立的被告提起了诉讼,德国地区法院发现荷兰公司在德国没有登记住所地,但其事实住所地在德国。地区法院驳回了原告的诉讼请求,原因是法院认为原告是一家荷兰公司,没有在德国提起诉讼的能力,紧接着上诉法院也驳回了原告的上诉请求,因为德国法规定,在外国成立的公司要在德国参与民事诉讼必须要在德国重新设立,依该外国法取得的诉讼能力不能在德国自动获得。③

2. 以营业中心所在地为法人住所

以法人营业中心所在地(place of principal business)为法人的住所地,最能反映法人与特定地域的真实联系,法人运用自己的资本进行营业活动的地方,是该法人实现其经营目的的地方,该地与法人的生存有重要的关系,并且,法人的营业所在地相对比较稳定,以法人营业中心所在地作为法人的住所地,还可以防止法人进行法律规避。埃及、叙利亚和韩国等国家即采取这种方法。④有关主营业地标准的著名案例是 1956 年**苏伊士运河公司国有化案**。

---

① 如 1896 年《日本民法典》第 50 条规定:"法人以其主事务所所在地为住所。"
② Case C-208/00, Überseering BV v. Nordic Constr. Co. Baumanagement GmbH (NCC), 2002 E. C. R. I-9919 (2002).
③ Opinion of Advocate General Ruzi-Jarabo Colomer on Überseering BV v Nordic Construction Company Baumanagement GmbH (NCC), (2001).
④ 例如《韩国关于涉外民事法律的法令》第 29 条规定:"商业公司的法律行为能力适用其营业地法。"

【案例】 苏伊士运河公司国有化案

1956年埃及把苏伊士运河收归国有。其理由是:按照国际私法,苏伊士运河的营业中心地在埃及,因此该公司是埃及公司,埃及有权将之收归国有。英、法反对埃及的国有化措施,英、法认为苏伊士运河公司的董事会在英国,其资本属于英法两国的自然人、法人所有,因此该公司是英国公司。埃及不理睬英法的异议。于是,英、法组织联军,向埃及发动了"苏伊士运河战争",结果英、法联军大败,埃及顺利收回苏伊士运河。[①]

苏伊士运河公司国有化案所涉及的法律问题就是,确定公司国籍的标准是主事务所标准还是营业地标准,这也是埃及和英、法的分歧点。

3. 以章程规定的地点为法人住所

法人登记成立时一般都在其章程中规定了自己的住所,因此,法人的住所,应依法人章程的规定。然而,法人章程规定的住所实际上并不一定是法人的经营场所或者管理中心,将其作为适用法人属人法或者涉外民事案件管辖权的依据,可能会导致不公正结果的产生。

4. 以成立地为法人住所

法人的住所类推于自然人的原始住所,即法人的住所在其成立地(**place of incorporation**)。英国、美国和印度等国即采此说。

【案例】 place of incorporation[②]

The place of incorporation rule is the oldest and was once the most widely used approach for determining a corporation's nationality. It was first developed to help resolve conflict of laws problems, specifically to determine which law, as between the law of several jurisdictions with some contact or relation to a corporation, should be applied to resolve issues regarding the corporation's legal status and the conduct of its internal affairs. For these purposes, under the Anglo-American rule, a corporation was deemed to be a national of the country in which it was incorporated and the laws of that country were held to constitute the so-called "personal law" of the corporation which governed its internal operations.[③]

The place of incorporation rule is rooted in the concession or artificial person theory of the corporation that was prevalent in the first part of the nineteenth century, before the adop-

---

[①] 参见赵秀文主编:《国际私法学原理与案例教程》,中国人民大学出版社2006年版,第74页。
[②] Linda A. Mabry, Multinational Corporations and U.S. Technology Policy: Rethinking the Concept of Corporate Nationality, 87 *Geo. L. J.* 563, 584 (1999).
[③] See R.E.L. Vaughn Williams & Matthew Chrussachi, The Nationality of Corporations, 49 *Law Q. Rev.* 334, 334 (1933).

tion of general incorporation statutes. This theory held that the corporation was a legal fiction: an artificial person created by the state that existed only in contemplation of the law. Insofar as the corporation owed its very existence to some national system, jurists reasoned that the corporation logically could be a citizen only of the state whose laws created it.

The use of the place of incorporation to identify the nationality of a corporation also was influenced by practical considerations. A company's place of incorporation is easily ascertainable. As such, it provided a measure of certainty and predictability in choice-of-law matters for both state administrators and the regulated firms.

关于设立地说最著名的案例是 1812—1814 年英美战争时期的案件 The Society for the Propagation of the Gosper v. Wheeler(1814)案①,该案判决认为在英国成立的公司对美国而言是外国人,两国宣战后就自动成为敌国法人。②而英国最早适用该规则的历史可以上溯到 1724 年。③

5. 以公司股东的国籍(nationality of stockholders)来决定公司的住所

该标准以公司股东的国籍来决定公司的住所,公司多数股东为何国人,公司就具有何国住所。有关股东国籍标准的最著名案例是 **巴塞罗那电力公司案**(The Barcelona Traction Case④)。

【案例】　　　　　　　　巴塞罗那电力公司案

案件的双方当事人是比利时政府和西班牙政府,巴塞罗那电力公司是 1911 年在加拿大多伦多成立的一家公司,该公司的股份主要由比利时人持有。1948 年该公司在西班牙经营业务时,因违反西班牙法律,被西班牙法院宣告破产,比利时政府在国际法院对西班牙提起诉讼。国际法院首先要解决的问题是,比利时是否有权对一个在加拿大成立的公司的股东(比利时国民)行使外交保护权。国际法院认为,当涉及某一外资公司的不法行为时,国际法规则只允许公司的母国行使外交保护权。本案中西班牙的破产措施是针对巴塞罗那电力公司本身,而非针对公司股东,因此在本案中巴塞罗那电力公司的国籍是比利时政府能否对该公司行使外交保护权的关键。国际法院认为公司的

---

① See the Society for the Propagation of the Gospel v. Wheeler, 2 Gall. 105, Ded. Cas. 13, 156 (1814).

② It was held that a corporation incorporated in England was an alien in the United States and that the corporation automatically became an alien enemy after the declaration of war. See A. Farnsworth, *The Residence and Domicile of Corporations*, 309 app. III (1939).

③ See Ernst Rabel, *The Conflict of Laws: A Comparative Study*, 31 (2d ed. 1960) (citing Dutch West India Co. v. Henriques Van Moses, 93 *Eng. Rep.* 733 (1724)).

④ 本案的英文资料详见本章扩展阅读资料。

国籍由公司成立地来决定,公司的成立地在加拿大,因此公司的国籍是加拿大国籍,比利时政府无权对该公司行使外交保护权。因此国际法院驳回了比利时政府的请求。①

该案中比利时政府对巴塞罗那电力公司住所的确认标准就是公司股东的国籍,但是比利时政府以股东国籍作为国籍的主张未被国际法院所接受。这一标准的实用性很差,如果是股份公司,股东分属多个不同国家,股东国籍根本就无法确定,因此现代国家几乎不采用这一标准。

6. 我国的做法

我国《民法通则》第 39 条规定:"法人以它的主要办事机构所在地为住所。"我国《公司法》第 10 条规定:"公司以其主要办事机构所在地为住所。"据此可以认为,我国采用的是上述第一种主张,即是以法人的主要办事机构所在地为法人的住所。

(二) 法人住所与营业所的区别

法人的住所和法人的营业所是两个不同的概念。法人的营业所是法人从事经营活动的场所。法人的营业所可能与法人的住所在地理位置上是一致的(如采取营业中心地说国家的法人),也可能不相一致(如采取管理中心地说国家的法人,其营业所与管理中心不在同一地域时)。

为解决法人营业所的冲突,我国最高人民法院《关于贯彻执行〈中华人民共和国民法通则〉若干问题的意见〈试行〉》第 185 条规定:"当事人有两个以上营业所的,应以与产生纠纷的民事关系有最密切联系的营业所为准;当事人没有营业所的,以其住所或者经常居住地为准。"

(三) 法人住所的冲突及其解决方法

各国关于法人住所的不同规定,可能导致法人住所冲突的产生。对于法人住所的冲突,各国一般是依"内国标准"加以解决,即每一个国家都只依本国确定法人住所的标准来判定法人的住所在何处。具体的做法有:第一,任何法人,只要依内国确定法人住所的标准在内国有住所,内国便只确认其在内国的住所,而对该法人在外国依有关外国法取得的住所不予确认。第二,法人在内国无住所,而在两个以上外国有住所时,内国仍然依照自己的标准来判定该法人的住所在哪个国家。

三、法人的民事权利能力和行为能力

法人的权利能力,就是法人所具有的参与民事法律关系并取得民事权利和承

---

① 参见张潇剑:《国际私法论》,北京大学出版社 2004 年版,第 261—262 页。

担民事义务的资格。而法人的行为能力,则是法人通过自身的行为取得民事权利并承担民事义务的资格。法人的权利能力和行为能力同时开始和同时终止,其范围也是一致的。①

由于各国民事立法的规定不尽相同,在国际私法实践中,法人的权利能力、行为能力常常发生法律冲突。②而国际上通行的做法就是依法人属人法的规定,也就是依法人的国籍国或住所地国的法律加以解决。因此,法人的国籍在解决法人的权利能力和行为能力的法律冲突问题上至关重要。法人的国籍是东道国给予其境内法人不同待遇的依据。③

我国对外国法人的确定采取注册登记主义,最高人民法院《关于贯彻〈中华人民共和国民法通则〉若干问题的意见(试行)》第184条规定:"外国法人以其注册登记地国家的法律为其本国法……"我国最高人民法院印发的《关于贯彻执行〈中华人民共和国民法通则〉若干问题的意见(试行)》中作了如下规定:"外国法人以其注册登记地国家的法律为其本国法,法人的民事行为能力依其本国法确定。外国法人在我国领域内进行的民事活动,必须符合我国的法律规定。"我国还有不少法律直接规定了外国法人可以享有的具体权利。

我国自2011年4月1日起施行的《涉外民事关系法律适用法》采取以登记地主义为主,主营业地主义为辅的原则。该法第14条规定:法人及其分支机构的民事权利能力、民事行为能力、组织机构、股东权利义务等事项,适用登记地法律。法人的主营业地与登记地不一致的,可以适用主营业地法律。法人的经常居所地,为其主营业地。

四、外国法人的承认制度

外国法人的承认,就是指内国根据本国法律对外国法人的资格进行审查,承认并允许其在内国的一定范围内从事民商事活动的过程。外国法人欲在内国享受权利,承担义务,作为法人在内国进行活动,原则上必须取得内国法律对其人格的承认。④

(一) 外国法人的承认

对外国法人的承认,主要有以下几种方式:

(1) 从法律上予以承认,这又称作特别承认主义。也就是说,外国法人必须根

---

① 梁慧星:《民法总论》,法律出版社1996年版,第67页。
② 如法国、意大利和葡萄牙等承认合伙为法人,而英国、德国和瑞士等国对此则不予承认;又如德国商法规定登记为公司成立的要件,而日本仅将其作为对抗第三人的要件。
③ 比如"国民待遇"、"最惠国待遇"、"对等待遇"。参见杨占栋:《法人国籍的法律意义及其确定标准》,载《滨州教育学院学报》2000年第4期。
④ 董立坤:《国际私法论》,法律出版社2000年版,第153页。

据国内法的程序,由外国法人向内国申请登记,经国家专门机关审查批准。①

(2)根据条约相互承认,这就是相互承认主义。根据双边条约或者多边条约,凡在缔约国合法成立的法人,其他缔约国也承认其法律人格。

(3)自由承认主义,又称一般承认主义。也就是说,承认外国法人无需经过特别的承认程序,也不需要由条约予以规定,而只需外国法人办理简单的行政手续,外国法人即可取得进行业务活动的权利。

(4)分类承认。这就是指以何种方式承认外国法人,要根据外国法人的具体情况,或者采取特别承认,或者采取条约相互承认,或者采取一般承认,这种方法比较灵活,为许多国家所采用。

(二)我国对外国法人的承认制度

我国《宪法》第18条第2款规定:在中国境内的外国企业和其他外国经济组织以及中外合资经营企业,都必须遵守中华人民共和国的法律。它们的合法权益受中华人民共和国法律的保护。该条规定为我国外国法人承认制度的建立和完善提供了基本法律依据。但是,我国并没有对外国法人承认作出集中的规定,其主要法律依据散见于有关涉外经济法律、法规、条例中。

1. 我国对外国法人的承认方式

外国公司是指中国境外的某个国家或地区依法正式登记注册的并开展经营活动的具有外国法人资格的外国企事业单位在中国境内设立的分支机构。②根据我国《公司法》的规定,外国公司在中国境内设立分支机构,必须向中国主管机关提出申请,并提交其公司章程、所属国的公司登记证书等有关文件,经批准后,向公司登记机关依法办理登记,领取营业执照。在我国,经批准登记的外国法人的在中国的分支机构可以外国法人驻中国常驻代表机构的名义在中国进行生产经营活动。反之,在中国未经登记,不得在中国境内开展经营活动。如**美国立新世纪公司在中国传销被查案**。

【案例】　　　　　美国立新世纪公司在中国传销被查案

"美国立新世纪"未在深圳注册,擅自利用深圳市其他公司的办公场所,销售其生产的保健品和护肤品。一次购买港币2080元的"美国立新世纪"产品,就可以成为公司"会员",享受七折优惠,并在发展一定数量的新"会员"后成为"经销商"。加入"会员",

---

① 〔德〕托马斯·莱塞尔:《德国法人中的民法制度》,张乃根译,载《中外法学》2001年第1期。
② 林承铎:《外国公司法人认许与外国公司法人人格的区分理论》,载《河北科技大学学报》2007年第3期。

可直接与香港立新世纪公司签订协议,并可以发展下线,依据发展下线的数量和下线的销售额,确定自己的"会员"级别,级别越高,收入越多。

深圳市工商执法人员对恒天伟业公司的营业场所进行突击检查,当场查获参与传销人员77人,暂扣免疫宝、强肝宝、活力芦荟等"美国立新世纪"产品一批。在现场还查扣了"美国立新世纪"的宣传材料、独立经营商申请表、协议书及401个已办好的"美国立新世纪"会员卡及有关收据。三名主要涉案人员被移送公安机关处理。

据悉,2002年以来,一些境外企业非法入境从事传销和变相传销活动的情况突出,引起社会的普遍关注。中国工商行政管理机关也先后查处了慕立达、康宝莱、如新、莱克瑟斯、爱博美娜等境外企业入境从事传销和变相传销违法案件。①

2. 我国对外国法人的承认条件

外国法人要在中国取得许可而从事业务、经营活动,须符合下列基本条件②:第一,必须在其内国依法设立并登记注册,取得法人资格。我国《公司法》明确规定了外国公司在中国境内设立分支机构,必须依法办理登记,并且领取营业执照。外国公司必须按照规定向其在中国境内的分支机构拨付经营活动或业务活动所需的资金,国务院规定了营运资金最低限额的,必须达到最低限额的标准。第二,外国法人所经营的业务,必须符合我国社会利益,不能有悖我国法律,有损中国主权。第三,外国法人只能在我国政府允许的范围和指定的地点从事业务活动。内国法律或者条约明确规定外国人不能享受的权利,外国法人不能享受。第四,外国法人的申请手续必须符合我国法律规定的要求和程序。

第三节 国家及其财产豁免权

一、国际私法上的国家

(一) 国家作为国际私法主体的含义

国家(**state**)是国际私法的主体。对国家的范畴,2004年《联合国国家及其财

---

① 资料来源:2004年8月8日中国新闻网,网址:http://finance.sina.com.cn/x/20040808/0954932631.shtml. 2008年7月1日访问。

② 龙卫球:《法人本质及其基本构造研究》,载《法学评论》1998年第3期。

产管辖豁免公约》(United Nations Convention on Jurisdictional Immunities of States and Their Property)作出了具体的界定。

【法条】   **State**

"State" means: (i) the State and its various organs of government; (ii) constituent units of a federal State or political subdivisions of the State, which are entitled to perform acts in the exercise of sovereign authority, and are acting in that capacity; (iii) agencies or instrumentalities of the State or other entities, to the extent that they are entitled to perform and are actually performing acts in the exercise of sovereign authority of the State; (iv) representatives of the State acting in that capacity.①

国家作为国际私法主体是指国家可以依据民商事法律,以国家本身的名义或该国中央政府的名义,或正式委派个人或机构代表国家,与自然人、法人、其他国家或国际组织发生涉外民商事法律关系,国家本身直接在这种关系中享受权利与承担义务,并以国库财产来承担民事上的责任。②

(二) 国家作为国际私法主体的特殊性

国家作为国际私法主体的特殊性主要表现在:

第一,国家作为主权者,根据国际法和国际惯例,享有包括他国法院管辖在内的豁免权(**exemption from the jurisdiction of the courts of another state**)。

【释义】   exempt from the jurisdiction of the courts of another state

States are exempt from the jurisdiction of the courts of another state. Court means any organ of a state which is entitled to exercise judicial functions, notwithstanding its name. The United Nations Convention on Jurisdictional Immunities of States and Their Property does not present a definition of judicial functions as they vary under different legal systems and constitutional structures. However, the International Law Commission Commentary 1991 explains that those functions might be exercised also by administrative organs in connection with a legal proceeding. They comprise adjudication of litigation, dispute settlement, determination of questions of law or fact, orders of provisional or enforcement measures and other functions related to a proceeding, but not functions in the administration of justice like the appointment

---

① Article 2(1)(a) of the United Nations Convention on Jurisdictional Immunities of States and Their Property.
② 张潇剑:《国际私法论》,北京大学出版社2004年版,第274页。

of judges.①

第二,国家作为国际民商事关系的主体也具有民事能力,即具有民事权利能力和行为能力,但与自然人和法人的民事能力有很大不同:首先,国家的权利能力和行为能力往往是国家所独有的,一般自然人或法人不能享有,如发行国债的能力,这种能力只有作为主权者才能够享有。其次,国家的民事权利能力和行为能力的范围与内容是国家通过立法程序来制定的,也就是说,国家自己设定自己的权利能力和行为能力,而自然人与法人则无此权力。②

第三,国家以国库的财产对其民事活动承担责任。凡以国家名义参与的涉外民事活动,所产生的法律后果由国家直接承担,国家以国库的全部财产对其行为承担无限责任。③

第四,国家授权有关机构及个人以国家名义从事民事活动。国家作为国际私法的主体,通常是授权有关机构(如政府各部及其所属机构或驻外商务代表处等)或其负责人以国家名义参与涉外民事活动,被授权的机构或个人必须以国家名义并根据国家的意志参与民事活动。

二、国家及其财产豁免

国家豁免(state immunity),或主权豁免(sovereign immunity),是指国家及其财产根据国家主权和国家平等原则不接受他国管辖的特权。④

国家豁免理论最早产生于两个最基本的国际法原则——主权平等原则(principle of sovereign equality of states)⑤和平等者之间无支配权原则(rule *par in parem non habet imperium*)。⑥ 一般认为,美国最高法院所受理的 **The Schooner Exchange v. McFaddon** 一案是确认国家豁免理论的最早的司法判例。该判例是学者们在讨论国家豁免权学术问题时经常援引的著名案例。

---

① *Yearbook of the International Law Commission* (1991) Vol. II Part Two, p.14.
② 章尚锦、许青森主编:《国际私法》,中国人民大学出版社 2007 年版,第 140 页。
③ 张潇剑:《国际私法论》,北京大学出版社 2004 年版,第 275 页。
④ 王铁崖:《国际法》,法律出版社 1995 年版,第 93 页。
⑤ Applying the test proposed by Professor Schwarzenberger, the principle of sovereign equality is undoubtedly a fundamental principle of international law. Georg Schwarzenberger & E. D. Brown, A Manual of International Law 6th ed., 1976, p.35.
⑥ L. Oppenheim, H. Lauterpacht, *International Law. A Treatise*, Vol. I, London, Longmans, Green and Co., 1947, p.239.

第六章 国际私法法律关系的主体

【案例】　　　　　The Schooner Exchange v. McFaddon①

In 1812, while sailing off the American coast, a commercial schooner, the *Exchange*, owned by two citizens of Maryland, was seized by the French navy. By general order of the emperor Napoléon Bonaparte, the French navy converted the schooner into a ship of war. When bad weather forced the *Exchange* into the port of Philadelphia, the original owners brought an *in rem* libel action against the ship for recovery of their property. The French government resisted the action, arguing that, as a ship of war, the *Exchange* was an arm of the emperor and was thus entitled to the same immunity privileges as the emperor himself.

On appeal to the Supreme Court, Chief Justice John Marshall identified the theoretical dilemma at issue. On the one hand, he observed, international law dictated that "the jurisdiction of the nation within its own territory is necessarily exclusive and absolute." According to this long-established principle, the moment the *Exchange* entered U.S. territorial waters off the eastern seaboard, it became subject exclusively to the national authority of the U.S. government, an authority that encompassed the U.S. district court's initiation of adverse legal proceedings against it. On the other hand, Justice Marshall took notice of another fundamental principle of international law: that the world is composed of distinct nations, each endowed with "equal rights and equal independence." This principle of sovereign equality, he believed, discouraged one sovereign from standing in judgment of another, coequal sovereign's conduct. If the *Exchange* had been converted, as the French government argued, into an arm of the French emperor (and was thus a direct extension of his sovereignty), then the United States, as France's equal under international law, would be remiss in adjudging the ship's ownership through its courts. International law thus appeared simultaneously to grant the United States authority to adjudicate a dispute over property present within its territory and to prohibit the exercise of this jurisdiction because that property now purportedly belonged to a foreign government.②

美国最高法院马歇尔大法官（Justice John Marshall）认为，本案涉及的是"一艘正在执行法国皇帝的任务的国家军舰"，该军舰享有司法管辖豁免权。③

对于国家及其财产豁免的外延（**extention of immunity**），2004 年《联合国国家及其财产管辖豁免公约》作出了具体的界定。

---

① 11 U.S. (7 Cranch) 116 (1812).
② By Lee M. Caplan, State Immunity, Human Rights, and Jus Cogens: A Critique of the Normative Hierarchy Theory, 97 *A. J. I. L.* 741, 746 (2003).
③ Supreme Court of the United States 1812, 11 US (7 Cranch) 116, 3 L. Ed. 287, reprinted in H. Steiner, D. F. Vagts, Transnational Legal Problems, 2nd ed., Mineola, NY, Foundation Press 1976, p.642.

【释义】 extention of immunity

The expression immunity from jurisdiction is not confined to immunity from adjudication, but includes the right of the foreign state to exemption from the execise of all adjudicative, administrative and executive powers in relation to a judicial proceeding. Consequently, the exemption applies to all stages of a judicial process, like the institution of a proceeding, service of process, procedural orders and decisions as well as judgments on the merits in all instances. However, since the core of the proceeding has to be of judicial character, autonomous administrative proceedings are not covered by the Convention. The Convention further governs the immunity of a foreign states property from measures of constraint, such as attachment, arrest, execution or prejudgment conservatory measures.[①]

国家及其财产管辖豁免包括三个方面：

（一）司法管辖豁免

国家及其财产的司法管辖豁免（Jurisdictional immunities of states and their property）是指未经一国同意时，他国不得以该国作为被告起诉，也不得对位于该国境内的他国国家财产提起诉讼。

（二）诉讼程序豁免

国家及其财产的诉讼程序豁免是指除非一国明示同意，他国不得以该国在其境内的国家财产作为诉讼担保，加以查封或扣押，也不得强迫该国提供诉讼费用的担保。

（三）强制执行豁免

国家及其财产的强制执行豁免是指一国在国际民事诉讼中无论是充当原告还是自愿作被告，未得到该国的明示同意，他国法院不得根据其判决对该国的财产予以强制执行。

三、国家豁免理论

在涉外民事诉讼中，国家及其财产能否享有豁免权的问题，在国际私法上有几种不同的理论：

（一）绝对豁免论

绝对豁免论（doctrine of absolute immunity）理论认为，一个国家，不论其行为的

---

① *Yearbook of the International Law Commission* (1991) Vol. II Part Two, p.13.

第六章　国际私法法律关系的主体

性质如何,在他国享有绝对的豁免,除非该国放弃其豁免权。该理论的依据是:国家是主权者,身份及平等主权者之间无管辖权。

（二）限制豁免论

限制豁免论(**restrictive theory of state immunity**),又称"职能豁免说",产生于19世纪末,主张把国家的活动分为主权行为和非主权行为。主权行为享有豁免权,而非主权行为不享有豁免权。

【释义】　　　　restrictive theory of state immunity

In the 20s and 30s of the twentieth century, domestic courts of Belgium and Italy started to apply a restricted concept of immunity, denying the immunity of states for commercial acts. The Brussels Convention for the Unification of Certain Rules Concerning the Immunity of State Ships of 1926 followed this approach restricting immunity to vessels owned by states as well as such cargoes employed exclusively for public and non-commercial purposes.

After the end of the Second World War, the concept of restrictive immunity was increasingly accepted by states; they recognized a certain need in this respect since otherwise they were afraid to be rejected as partners of individual persons or private companies because of the absence of judicial enforcement of the transactions entered by them.①

20世纪50年代之后,普通法系国家纷纷制定法律,主张限制豁免论。②近年来发生在美国的 **Verlinden B. V. v. Central Bank of Nigeria** 案,就是限制豁免论在司法实践中运用的典型案例。

【案例】　　　　Verlinden B. V. v. Central Bank of Nigeria ③

A Dutch corporation brought suit against the Central Bank of Nigeria, an instrumentality of Nigeria, in the United States District Court for the Southern District of New York, alleging that Central Bank breached a letter of credit. The Dutch corporation alleged jurisdiction under 2 of the Foreign Sovereign Immunities Act (28 USCS 1330). Central Bank moved to dismiss

---

①　Gerhard Hafner, Ulrike Khler, The United Nations Convention on Jurisdictional Immunities of States And Their Property, *Netherlands Yearbook of International Law*, Volume XXXV, 2004, p.349.

②　See, e.g., The Foreign Sovereign Immunities Act, 28 U.S.C. § §1330, 1391(f), 1441, 1602—1611 (2000); The (British) State Immunity Act, ch. 33 (1978), reprinted in 10 *Halsbury Stat.* 641 (4th ed. 1985), and in 17 *Int'l Legal Mat'ls* 1123 (1979); The (Canadian) State Immunities Act, ch. 94, 1980—1982 Can. Stat., reprinted in 21 *Int'l Legal Mat'ls* 798 (1982).

③　Supreme Court of the United States: 461 U.S. 480; 103 S. Ct. 1962; 76 L. Ed. 2d 81; 1983 U.S. LEXIS 30; 51 U.S.L.W. 4567. January 11, 1983, Argued; May 23, 1983, Decided.

for, among other reasons, lack of subject matter jurisdiction. The District Court dismissed the complaint, holding that Central Bank was entitled to sovereign immunity. The United States Court of Appeals for the Second Circuit affirmed, holding that the Act exceeded the scope of Article III of the United States Constitution (647 F2d 320).

On certiorari, the United States Supreme Court reversed and remanded. In an opinion by Burger, Ch. J., expressing the unanimous view of the court, it was held that the Foreign Sovereign Immunities Act does not violate Article III by authorizing a foreign plaintiff to sue a foreign state in a United States District Court on a nonfederal cause of action.

(三) 废除豁免论

废除豁免论(doctrine of abolishing immunity)产生于20世纪40年代末50年代初。英国国际法学家劳特派特是该理论的创始人。废除豁免论主张从根本上废除国家豁免原则,并确认国家不享有豁免是一般原则。此学说应用、赞同者甚少。

各国在不同时期,可能会根据本国经济和社会发展以及对外交往需要而持不同理论。如美国对国家豁免的理论,从历史的视角看,经历了一个从基于"优雅"与"礼让"而给予外国国家及其财产以豁免,然后到绝对豁免,再到有限豁免的变化过程(**Evolution of U. S. legal doctrine relating to state immunity**)。

【叙述】 Evolution of U. S. legal doctrine relating to state immunity

It was in 1812 that the Court first recognized a foreign state's claim to immunity from legal process—though not as a matter of right, but of "grace" and "comity," and subject to recognition or withdrawal by the decisions of the executive branch. Until 1952, the executive branch followed the theory of absolute immunity, typically requesting courts to dismiss all claims against friendly sovereigns. In that year, the State Department issued the "Tate Letter," in which it announced that it would "thereafter" follow the theory of restrictive immunity. In other words, the department would continue to request immunity for foreign states in claims based on their public acts, but would discontinue the practice of making requests in claims based on their private acts. In applying these standards, the department periodically succumbed to political considerations, however, and its decisions suffered from a high level of inconsistency. To remedy this problem, Congress enacted the Foreign Sovereign Immunities Act (FSIA) in 1976, which "codified... the restrictive theory of sovereign immunity" and transferred decision-making authority from the executive branch to the judicial branch.①

---

① Charles H. Brower II, International Decision: Republic of Austria v. Altmann, 124 S. Ct. 2240, 99 A. J. I. L. 236, 237 (2005).

四、我国关于国家及其财产管辖豁免的理论与实践

我国法院尚未审理过涉及外国国家及其财产豁免的案件,但自新中国成立以来,我国曾被动地在其他一些国家或地区被诉。

从理论上看,1979 年**湖广铁路债券案**以来,我国国际法学界对国家及其财产豁免问题开始进行研究,并发表了许多具有价值的文章和著述。

【案例】 湖广铁路债券案

美国公民杰克逊等 9 人持有湖广铁路的债券。[①] 1979 年 11 月,他们向美国亚拉巴马州北区地方法院东部分庭对中华人民共和国提起诉讼,要求偿还他们所持有的湖广铁路债券本金 1 亿美元外加利息和诉讼费。法庭受理了他们的诉讼。并于同年 11 月 13 日向中华人民共和国发出传票,指明由中华人民共和国外交部长黄华收,要求被告中华人民共和国于收到传票后的 20 天内提出答辩,否则作缺席判决。中国外交部拒绝接受传票,将其退回。

美国亚拉巴马州北区地方法院东部分庭关于湖广铁路债券案的审理遭中华人民共和国和拒绝后,法庭于 1982 年 9 月 1 日对本案作出了缺席裁判。判决中华人民共和国赔偿原告 41 313 038 美元,另付利息和诉讼费。

中国政府对美国亚拉巴马州北区地方法院东部分庭的判决拒绝接受,认为它是违反国际法的,是无效的。理由是依据国际法,国家享有主权豁免权,一国法院不得强行将外国国家列为被告。所以美国法院对中华人民共和国没有管辖权。另外,中华人民共和国政府调查了湖广铁路债券的渊源,认定它属恶债。

中国政府就此理由与美国国务院进行了多次交涉。经过两国政府官员的几次会谈,美国国务院决定干涉此案。美国国务院乔治·普·舒尔茨和国务院法律顾问戴维斯—鲁宾逊分别于 1983 年 8 月 11 日和 12 日发表了声明。中国接受了美国的建议,聘请了美国律师出庭申辩。律师以中华人民共和国享有绝对主权豁免;本案不属《美

---

① 湖广铁路是指"湖北、湖南两省境内的粤汉铁路"和"湖北省境内的川汉铁路"。因这两线铁路都在湖广总督的辖区范围内,故名。为加快铁路的修建,当时的湖广总督张之洞奉命督办后,便向国际上筹措借贷。1909 年 3 月 7 日,中德草签了借贷合同,决定向德国的德华银行借款。英、法两国得知此事后也认为有利可图,故通过抗议、照会对清政府施加压力,强迫清政府接受它们的借款。这使清政府只好搁置中德的借贷合同,另于 1909 年 6 月 6 日与英、法、德三国草签了借款合同。之后,美国又以"机会均等"挤进了该借贷合同。所以湖广铁路的借贷合同最后是以清政府邮传部大臣(盛宣怀)为一方,以德国的德华、英国的汇丰、法国的东方汇理等银行和"美国资本家"(以下称银行)为另一方在北京签订。合同签订后,德、英、法、美上述银行于 1911 年以清政府的名义发行"湖广铁路五厘利息递还金镑借款债券"(简称"湖广铁路债券")600 万金英镑。该债券利息从 1938 年起停付,本金 1951 年到期未付。

国法典》第 28 卷第 1605 条规定的"商业活动";原告的传票送达不完备;原告未能依《美国法典》第 28 卷第 1608(E)条的规定,证明被告具有责任而使其提出的求偿要求和权利得以成立等理由指出法庭判决无效。要求撤销缺席判决。另外,美国司法部向亚拉巴马州地方法院提出了"美国利益声明书",要求法院考虑舒尔茨和鲁宾逊的声明,考虑美国的利益,支持中国的申辩。在美国政府的干预下,法庭重新审理了此案,作出新的决定,撤销了原来的判决,驳回了原告的诉讼。之后原告又向美国联邦第十一巡回法院提起上诉和要求美国最高法院重新审理,未获成功,致使此案于 1987 年 3 月 9 日告终。

在实践中,我国政府关于国家及其财产管辖豁免问题历来主张和坚持国家主权豁免原则,反对他国恣意破坏国家主权豁免原则的做法,并主张通过当事国之间达成国际协议的方式来消除有关国家间在国家豁免问题上的立场分歧。一方面,主张和坚持中国作为一个主权国家,其行为和财产享有当然的豁免权,非经同意,不受任何外国法院的审判,如在 1949 年两航飞机案、1950 年"永灏号"油轮案、1953 年威尔斯法哥银行存款案、1957 年<u>贝克曼诉中华人民共和国案</u>、1979 年烟火案、1979 年湖广铁路债券案中,我国政府均表明了严正立场。另一方面,中国法院从不受理任何控告外国国家和政府的案件。

【案例】 贝克曼诉中华人民共和国案

[案情] 原告卡赖·贝克曼和阿凯·贝克曼是本奇特·约翰逊·贝克曼的孩子和继承人,他们在瑞典斯德哥尔摩市法院对中华人民共和国提起诉讼,并向法院申请对中华人民共和国送达传票。他们声称:1954 年 10 月 4 日,位于斯德哥尔摩市并属于他们死去的父亲遗产的不动产,未经他们同意,被其父的遗产管理人卖给了中华人民共和国。他们主张,该项不动产的出售并非属于遗产管理人的权限,并且是对他们不利的。据此,请求法院宣告该项不动产买卖无效。经瑞典外交部向中国驻瑞典大使馆询问,中国驻瑞典大使馆认为它享有豁免权,拒绝应诉。

[判决] 斯德哥尔摩市法院裁定,原告申请对中华人民共和国送达传票应予驳回。法院认为,原告在申请中所指争议,涉及中华人民共和国购买的并拟用于该国大使馆的财产所有权问题,中华人民共和国在该案中应享有豁免权。在上诉审中,斯德哥尔摩市法院的裁定得到了上诉法院的肯定。

但是，我国也从不把国家主权豁免问题绝对化。在坚持国家主权原则和国家主权豁免原则的前提下，基于正常经济交往的需要，国家可以在特殊情况下，以协议或其他形式对具体案件或某些事项放弃豁免权。同时，我国主张国家豁免的范围主要是国家行为和国家财产。我们严格区分国家行为和国家财产同具有独立法人资格的国有企业或公司的私法行为和财产，对后者我国不主张也不要求在外国享有司法豁免权。

除外交实践外，我国在立法实践与条约实践方面也同样表现出我国关于国家及其财产管辖豁免的主张。目前，我国尚无专门的有关国家及其财产豁免方面的具体立法，但在有关法的原则性规定中，如《中华人民共和国外交特权与豁免条例》第4条中，已在一定程度上反映了我国的基本立场和主张。

在条约实践方面，我国在坚持国家豁免原则的同时，承认国家可以自愿放弃其豁免权，并认为以国家同意为基础，在条约中对这种放弃予以规定是可取的方式，如1958年中苏《通商航海条约》及附件中就有类似规定。另外，我国签订或参加的国际公约，如1975年参加的1961年《维也纳外交关系公约》、1979年参加的1963年《维也纳领事关系公约》、1980年参加的1969年《国际油污损害民事责任公约》等，其中关于国家及其财产豁免的规定，对我国同样也是适用的。

从国家及其财产豁免的角度分析，我们可以得出以下几点：

第一，我国法律明确规定了外国人（包括国家元首、政府首脑、外交部长等）、外国组织、国际组织以及外国机构（包括国家元首、政府、一国外交部门以及一国在外国的使领馆等）在我国享有管辖豁免和执行豁免。[①]这里的外国组织应指经外国授权代表国家行使主权权力的国家的下属机构或其他有关组织。

第二，对享有外交特权与豁免的外国人提起的诉讼，我国按照自己缔结或参加的有关国家及其财产豁免的国际条约的规定办理。在国际条约没有规定时，我国法律规定可以适用国际惯例。根据《中华人民共和国外交特权与豁免条例》第26条的规定，我国在国际交往中，对外交特权与豁免实行对等原则。由此我们可以将此原则推而广之适用于国家及其财产豁免问题之中，即若外国法院对我国国家及其财产豁免权进行限制，我国也可以对其国家和财产豁免权加以限制。

---

① 黄进：《国家及其财产豁免问题研究》，中国政法大学出版社2003年版，第235页。

第四节 作为国际私法主体的国际组织

一、国际组织概述

国际组织(**international organization**)是指由国家组成的政府间组织。

【释义】   **international organization**

The term "international organization" means a public international organization in which the United States participates pursuant to any treaty or under the authority of any Act of Congress authorizing such participation or making an appropriation for such participation, and which shall have been designated by the President through appropriate Executive Order as being entitled to enjoy the privileges, exemptions, and immunities herein provided. President shall be authorized, in the light of the functions performed by any such international organization, by appropriate Executive order to withhold or withdraw from any such organization or its officers or employees any of the privileges, exemptions, and immunities provided for in this title (including the amendments made by this title) or to condition or limit the enjoyment by any such organization or its officers or employees of any such privilege, exemption, or immunity. The President shall be authorized, in his Judgment such action should be Justified by reason of the abuse by an international organization or its officers and employees of the privileges, exemptions, and immunities herein provided or for any other reason, at any time to revoke the designation of any international organization under this section, whereupon the international organization in question shall cease to be classed as an international organization for the purposes of this title.[①]

作为国际私法主体的国际组织具有自身的特点:第一,国际组织以自身名义参加涉外民事法律关系,具有独立性。第二,政府间国际组织在参与国际民商事法律关系时享有一定的特权和豁免权。第三,国际组织所从事的民事活动都是执行职务及实现其宗旨所必要的。国际组织的权利能力和行为能力受基本法律文件的严

---

① Section 1 of the United States International Organizations Immunities Act, *Public Law* 79—291, 29 December 1945. See http://www.usunnewyork.usmission.gov/hc_docs/hc_law_79_291.html.

格限制,常常是不完整的,国际组织只有在其国际条约和该组织章程范围内才有民事权利能力和行为能力。超出这个范围,便无权利能力和行为能力。

二、国际组织的国际法律人格

所谓国际法律人格,是指独立参加国际关系并直接承受国际法上的权利和义务的集合体,具有国际法律人格的实体才能成为国际法的主体。[1]一个国际组织基于其国际人格所享有的权利和义务范围取决于其特定的宗旨和职能,离开了主权国家的授权,任何国际组织在法律上的行为能力和权利能力都是不存在的。

国际组织的国际法律人格是有限的,只能在一定范围内和一定程度上参与国际法律关系,具有一定限度的权利能力和行为能力。它的法律人格是派生的,是成员国通过基本文件而授予的,或是从基本文件中引申出来的,其权力与活动范围不得超越组织章程的规定,只能在执行其法定职能时才能得到承认,在其组织宗旨所需的范围内才有资格享有权利和承担义务,其职能范围是受其建立之初时的基本文件严格规定的。

三、国际组织特权与豁免的法律依据

国际组织本身不享有主权,因此它的特权与豁免并不是自始享有的。它的特权与豁免最早来源于外交特权和豁免。

国际组织特权与豁免的法律根据是多种多样的,既有国际条约,又有国内立法。通常国际组织的组成条约都包括一个基本条款,规定成员国有义务向组织、其他成员国使团及组织职员提供在其本国境内的特权与豁免。联合国成立后,制定了一系列的以联合国为中心的有关国际组织法律地位、特权和豁免的公约:包括1946年的《联合国特权与豁免公约》(Convention on the Privileges And Immunities of The United Nations)[2]、1947年联合国与美国签订的关于联合国会所的规定等。

国际组织的特权与豁免来自于成员国的授权。成员国之所以授予国际组织以特权和豁免是因为国际组织在一定程度上或某些方面代表着成员国的愿望和利益。[3]

四、国际组织特权与豁免的具体内容

《联合国特权与豁免公约》所规定的特权与豁免已被其他普遍性的国际组织作为模式予以仿效。为贯彻联合国《联合国特权与豁免公约》,美国国会通过了

---

[1] 饶戈平主编:《国际组织法》,北京大学出版社1996年版,第101页。
[2] Adopted by the General Assembly of the United Nations on 13 February 1946.
[3] 如《联合国宪章》第105条和其他国际组织的章程及有关的规定都明确规定国际组织的特权与豁免是执行其职务和实现其宗旨的需要。

《国际组织豁免法》(United States International Organizations Immunities Act),赋予国际组织特权与豁免(**privileges and immunities**),包括司法管辖豁免,判决执行豁免,国际组织的会所、财产和公文档案不受侵犯,国际组织的财产、资产免受征用、调查、没收、侵夺和其他形式的干涉,货币和财政特权,通讯自由。

【法条】　　　　　　　　**Privileges and immunities**

International organizations shall enjoy the status, immunities, exemptions, and privileges set forth in this section, as follows:

(a) International organizations shall, to the extent consistent with the instrument creating them, possess the capacity (i) to contract; (ii) to acquire and dispose of real and personal property; (iii) to institute legal proceedings.

(b) International organizations, their property and their assets, wherever located and by whomsoever held, shall enjoy the same immunity from suit and every form of Judicial process as is enjoyed by foreign governments, except to the extent that such organizations may expressly waive their immunity for the purpose of any proceedings or by the terms of any contract.

(c) Property and assets of international organizations, wherever located and by whomsoever held, shall be immune from search, unless such immunity be expressly waived, and from confiscation. The archives of international organizations shall be inviolable.

(d) In so far as concerns customs duties and internal-revenue taxes imposed upon or by reason of importation, and the procedures in connexion therewith; the registration of foreign agents; and the treatment of official communications, the privileges, exemptions, and immunities to which international organizations shall be entitled shall be those accorded under similar circumstances to foreign governments.①

国际组织正式职员享有特权与豁免权具体表现在以下方面:人身、私人住所和财产不可侵犯;民事、刑事的司法管辖豁免和行政管辖豁免,组织行政首长及其副手、助手通常被赋予完全的司法管辖豁免,而其他官员,只有执行公务行为时才能享有管辖豁免;薪金免纳税捐,通常国际组织的职员免纳薪金所得税;出入境便利。②

随着特权与豁免问题在实践中的逐渐发展和进一步完善,国际组织会在今后的国际生活中发挥更大的作用。

---

① Section 2 of the United States International Organizations Immunities Act, *Public Law* 79—291, 29 December 1945. See http://www.usunnewyork.usmission.gov/hc_docs/hc_law_79_291.html.

② 参见饶戈平主编:《国际组织法》,北京大学出版社1996年版,第228页。

【思考题】

- 什么是自然人属人法？自然人属人法包括说那些内容？
- 如何解决自然人国籍的积极冲突？
- 试述我国的法人承认法律制度。
- 什么是国家豁免权？它包括哪些内容？
- 请分析并评价有限豁免原则。
- 国际组织有哪些豁免权？国际组织豁免权来自哪里？

【重要术语提示与中英文对照】

中文术语	英文对照
自然人属人法	personal law
身份	status
能力	capacity
国籍	nationality
忠诚义务	allegiance
服从	obedience
卡内伐罗案	Canavaro
住所	domicile
法人	legal person
分支机构	branch
注册营业地	registered office
管理中心	administration center
营业中心所在地	place of principal business
股东的国籍	nationality of stockholders
巴塞罗那电力公司案	The Barcelona Traction Case
国家豁免	state immunity
主权豁免	sovereign immunity
法院管辖豁免	exemption from the jurisdiction of the courts
主权平等原则	principle of sovereign equality of states
平等者之间无支配权原则	rule *par in parem non habet imperium*
马歇尔大法官	Justice Marshall
国家及其财产的司法管辖豁免	Jurisdictional immunities of states and their property
联合国国家及其财产管辖豁免公约	United Nations Convention on Jurisdictional Immunities of States and Their Property

绝对豁免论	doctrine of absolute immunity
限制豁免论	restrictive theory of state immunity
废除豁免论	doctrine of abolishing immunity
国际组织	international organization
联合国特权与豁免公约	Convention on the Privileges and Immunities of The United Nations
美国的国际组织豁免法	United States International Organizations Immunities Act
特权与豁免	privileges and immunities

【推荐阅读文献】

- 李浩培:《国籍问题的比较研究》,商务印书馆1979年版。
- 李双元、蒋新苗主编:《现代国籍法》,湖南人民出版社1999年版。
- 陈杰:《公司国籍判断标准之评析——兼论我国公司国籍判断标准的完善》,载《天赋新论》2006年第6期。
- 赵威、张文瑞:《美国外国主权豁免法中商业豁免例外的适用》,载《成都大学学报(社会科学版)》2010年第5期。
- 杜新丽:《从住所、国籍到经常居所地——我国属人法立法变革研究》,载《政法论坛》2011年第3期。
- 练爽:《论主权财富基金的司法豁免——以〈联合国国家及其财产管辖豁免公约〉和〈美国外国主权豁免法〉为例》,载《中国政法大学学报》2011年第4期。
- Lee M. Caplan, State Immunity, Human Rights, and Jus Cogens: A Critique of the Normative Hierarchy Theory, 97 *A. J. I. L.* 741, 746 (2003).
- Andrea K. Bjorklund, Reconciling State Sovereignty and Investor Protection in Denial of Justice Claims, 45 *Va. J. Int'l L.* 809 (2005).
- K. A. D. Camara, Costs of Sovereignty, 107 *W. Va. L. Rev.* 385 (2005).
- Judith Wallace, Corporate Nationality, Investment Protection Agreements, and Challenges to Domestic Natural Resources Law, 17 *Geo. Int'l Envtl. L. Rev.* 365 (2005).
- Ryan Micallef, Liability Laundering and Denial of Justice: Conflicts Between the Alien Tort Statute and the Government Contractor Defense, 71 *Brook. L. Rev.* 1375 (2006).
- Sloane (R.), Breaking the Genuine Link: The Contemporary International Legal Regulation of Nationality, 50 *Harv. Int'l L. J.* 1 (2009).
- Stewart (D. P.), Samantar and the Future of Foreign Official Immunity, 15 *Lewis & Clark L. Rev.* 633 (2011).
- Veerle Van Den Eeckhout, Corporate Human Rights Violations and Private Interna-

tional Law: a Facilitating Role for PIL or PIL as a Complicating Factor? 6 *H. R. & I. L. D.* 192 (2012).

【扩展阅读资料】

Barcelona Traction, Light and Power Company, Ltd. ①

Judgment of 24 July 1964

Proceedings in the case concerning the Barcelona Traction, Light and Power Company, Limited (Belgium *v.* Spain) were instituted by an Application of 19 June 1962 in which the Belgian Government sought reparation for damage claimed to have been caused to Belgian nationals, shareholders in the Canadian Barcelona Traction Company, by the conduct of various organs of the Spanish State. The Spanish Government raised four Preliminary Objections.

The Court rejected the first Preliminary Objection by 12 votes to 4, and the second by 10 votes to 6. It joined the third Objection to the merits by 9 votes to 7 and the fourth by 10 votes to 6.

President Sir Percy Spender and Judges Spiropoulos, Koretsky and Jessup appended Declarations to the Judgment.

Vice-President Wellington Koo and Judges Tanaka and Bustamante y Rivero appended Separate Opinions.

Judge Morelli and Judge *ad hoc* Armand-Ugon appended Dissenting Opinions.

First Preliminary Objection

In its Judgment, the Court recalled that Belgium had on 23 September 1958 filed with the Court an earlier Application against Spain in respect of the same facts, and Spain had then raised three Preliminary Objections. On 23 March 1961 the Applicant, availing itself of the right conferred upon it by Article 69, paragraph 2, of the Rules of Court, had informed the Court that it was not going on with the proceedings; notification having been received from the Respondent that it had no objection, the Court had removed the case from its List (10 April 1961). In its first Preliminary Objection, the Respondent contended that this discontinuance precluded the Applicant from bringing the present proceedings and advanced five arguments in support of its contention.

The Court accepted the first argument, to the effect that discontinuance is a purely procedural act the real significance of which must be sought in the attendant circumstances.

---

① See http://ita.law.uvic.ca/documents/ICJ-BarcelonaPreliminary_001.pdf.

On the other hand, the Court was unable to accept the second argument namely that a discontinuance must always be taken as signifying a renunciation of any further right of action unless the right to start new proceedings is expressly reserved. As the Applicant's notice of discontinuance contained no motivation and was very clearly confined to the proceedings instituted by the first Application, the Court considered that the onus of establishing that the discontinuance meant something more than a decision to terminate those proceedings was placed upon the Respondent.

The Respondent, as its third argument, asserted that there had been an understanding between the Parties; it recalled that the representatives of the private Belgian interests concerned had made an approach with a view to opening negotiations and that the representatives of the Spanish interests had laid down as a prior condition the final withdrawal of the claim.

According to the Respondent what was meant by this was that the discontinuance would put an end to any further right of action, but the Applicant denied that anything more was intended than the termination of the then current proceedings. The Court was unable to find at the governmental level any evidence of any such understanding as was alleged by the Respondent; it seemed that the problem had been deliberately avoided lest the foundation of the interchanges be shattered. Nor had the Respondent, on whom lay the onus of making its position clear, expressed any condition when it indicated that it did not object to the discontinuance.

The Respondent Government then advanced a fourth argument, having the character of a plea of estoppel, to the effect that, independently of the existence of any understanding, the Applicant had by its conduct misled the Respondent about the import of the discontinuance, but for which the Respondent would not have agreed to it, and would not thereby have suffered prejudice. The Court did not consider that the alleged misleading Belgian misrepresentations had been established and could not see what the Respondent stood to lose by agreeing to negotiate on the basis of a simple discontinuance; if it had not agreed to the discontinuance, the previous proceedings would simply have continued, whereas negotiations offered a possibility of finally settling the dispute. Moreover, if the negotiations were not successful and the case started again, it would still be possible once more to put forward the previous Preliminary Objections.

Certainly the Applicant had framed its second Application with a foreknowledge of the probable nature of the Respondent's reply and taking it into account but, if the original proceedings had continued, the Applicant could likewise always have modified its submissions.

The final argument was of a different order. The Respondent alleged that the present proceedings were contrary to the spirit of the Hispano-Belgian Treaty of Conciliation, Judicial Settlement and Arbitration of 19 July 1927 which, according to the Applicant, conferred competence on the Court. The preliminary stages provided for by the Treaty having already been gone through in connection with the original proceedings, the Treaty could not be invoked a second time to seise the Court of the same complaints. The Court considered that the Treaty processes could not be regarded as exhausted so long as the right to bring new proceedings otherwise existed and until the case had been prosecuted to judgment.

For these reasons, the Court rejected the first Preliminary Objection.

第七章

国际婚姻家庭关系的法律适用

第七章 国际婚姻家庭关系的法律适用

本章导读

※ 国际婚姻家庭关系包含跨国结婚、离婚、夫妻关系、父母子女关系、收养、监护和扶养等一系列法律关系。由于各个国家的社会、历史、人文背景均不相同,有关婚姻家庭的法律很难统一。在涉及具体的婚姻家庭关系上,就会产生适用何种法律的冲突。

※ 结婚的法律冲突主要体现在结婚的实质要件和形式要件等方面。其法律适用原则主要有:婚姻举行地法、当事人属人法以及混合适用婚姻举行地法和当事人的属人法。

※ 离婚是当事人解除婚姻关系的一种法律行为。有关离婚的法律冲突不但涉及离婚管辖权的冲突,更涉及离婚的法律适用的冲突。一般而言,法院地法、当事人的属人法以及法院地法和属人法的混合适用成为离婚法律冲突的适用规则。

※ 夫妻关系是一种基于合法有效的婚姻而产生法律关系,包括夫妻的人身关系和夫妻的财产关系。通常,各国采用夫妻属人法、法院地法和行为地法以及意思自治原则来解决夫妻关系的法律适用问题。

※ 亲子关系也称为父母子女关系,是指父母和子女相互之间的一种法律关系,包括父母子女之间的人身关系和财产关系。有关亲子关系的法律适用规则主要有:属人法、支配婚姻效力的法律以及使子女婚生更为有利的法律。

※ 收养是根据法律程序创设的收养人和被收养人之间的拟制的亲子关系。有关收养的法律冲突主要适用法院地法、属人法以及收养关系发生地法。

※ 监护是监护人对未成年人或禁治产人的人身和财产利益依法实施监督和保护的一种法律制度。监护的法律冲突主要适用属人法以及法院地法。

※ 扶养是指特定的亲属之间一方对他方给予生活上的扶助,包括夫妻之间、亲子之间、姻亲之间的相互承担生活供养义务的法律行为。属人法、最密切联系原则以及相关的国际公约中所规定的冲突规则被用来解决收养的法律冲突。

※ 我国《婚姻法》规定的扶养关系包括父母子女之间的相互扶养,夫妻之间的相互扶养,以及在一定条件下,其他家庭成员之间的扶养,并将这三种扶养关系视为一个整体,统一适用同一个法律规定,即适用与被扶养人最密切联系国家的法律。

【本章主题词】 结婚、离婚、婚姻举行地法、收养、监护、扶养

第一节 结婚的法律适用

一、结婚的法律冲突

结婚(marriage)的法律冲突主要体现在结婚的实质要件和形式要件等方面。

结婚的实质要件包括当事人必须具备的条件和当事人必须排除的条件。结婚的实质要件一般是指当事人必须达到法定婚龄、自愿结婚、没有配偶、不在禁止结婚的血亲之内、没有不能结婚的疾病等。

结婚的形式要件是指结婚应该具备的形式,一般包括民事登记、宗教方式等。英国认为,婚姻的实质要件应该是双方同意、一夫一妻,并且是在适宜结婚的时间段。[①]

我国法律规定的婚姻的实质要件是,双方自愿、没有配偶、没有法律禁止结婚的情形等。由于各国关于结婚的实质要件和形式要件规定并不完全相同,因此,法律适用上的冲突在所难免。

二、婚姻举行地法的适用

婚姻的实质要件和形式要件适用婚姻举行地法,是有关结婚的法律适用的一条基本法律适用规则,如欧敦诉欧敦案(**Ogden v. Ogden**)。

【案例】 **Ogden v. Ogden**[②]

Facts: The appellant, an Englishwoman domiciled in England, married in England Léon Philip, a 19-year-old Frenchman domiciled in France. This marriage took place without the consent of Léon Philip's parents as required by the French Civil Code. When his parents found out about the marriage they brought him back to France and had the marriage annulled before the French courts. Thereafter the appellant married William Ogden. This relationship, howev-

---

[①] C P. M. North, *Cheshire and North's Private International Law*, 10th ed., London: Butterworths, 1979, p.297.

[②] [1908] P 46 Court of Appeal (Sir Gorell Barnes P, Cozens Hardy MR and Kennedy L J).

er, also failed; and William Ogden petitioned the English courts for a decree of nullity based on the applicant's prior marriage to Léon Philip. At first instance the court granted the decree of nullity and the appellant now appealed.

The crucial question was whether the marriage to Léon Philip was valid or not; and the only ground (ignoring for the present the French decree of nullity) on which it could be argued that it was invalid was that Léon Philip lacked capacity to marry under his domiciliary law because of the absence of parental consent.

Held: The absence of parental consent was a matter of form which was governed by the *lex loci celebrationis*, viz, English law.... Alter very careful consideration of the present case we have come to the conclusion that the first point must be decided against the appellant, and that the marriage between her and Léon Philip must be declared valid in England.

Comment: Note how unenviable Mrs Odgen's position was. She could not divorce Léon Philip in France (because under French law she was not married to him at all); and she could not divorce him in England since (at that time) the English courts had no jurisdiction to grant a divorce because Philip was domiciled in France. There was really nothing that she could do to get rid of the husband she had married in a fit of youthful indiscretion!

如果按照婚姻举行地法有效缔结的婚姻,则其效力在其他国家也应该得到承认;如果按照婚姻举行地法为无效的婚姻,则在其他国家也不具有效力。

有的国家,视婚姻为一种合同关系或者是一种法律行为,那么,根据场所支配行为的原则,其成立的实质要件和形式要件也应该适用行为地法;婚姻类似一种既得权利,根据既得权保护的理论,在一国有效缔结的婚姻,其效力也应该得到其他国家的承认;此外,婚姻的有效与否,直接关系到一个国家的善良风俗和公共秩序,并且,适用婚姻举行地法也简便易行。在结婚的实质要件方面采用婚姻举行地法规则的主要有拉丁美洲国家以及美国的许多州,比如美国《第一次冲突法重述》第 **§131 and §132** 的规定。

【条文】　　　　　　　　　　**§131 and §132**

In accordance with the clauses of §131 and §132, a marriage is valid everywhere if the requirements of the marriage law of the state where the contract of marriage takes place are complied with; a marriage is invalid everywhere if any mandatory requirement of the marriage law of the state in which the marriage is celebrated is not complied with.

三、当事人属人法的适用

结婚与当事人的身份地位密切相关。因此,有些国家主张有关结婚的实质要件问题适用当事人的属人法。只要当事人的婚姻符合当事人属人法的规定,则其婚姻为有效婚姻。如果当事人的属人法相同,则根据其共同的属人法来确定其婚姻的实质有效性和形式有效性。但是,如果当事人的国籍或者住所不同,则比较麻烦,应区分不同的情况,确定应适用的属人法。有的国家规定分别适用双方各自的属人法,如日本就作如此规定,波兰、奥地利的国家也采用此种做法①;有的国家则采用累及适用双方当事人的属人法的做法,如匈牙利。在英美法系国家,当事人的身份适用其属人法,即住所地法。班戴尔诉班戴尔(**Baindail v. Baindail**)②就是这方面的典型案例。

【案例】 Baindail v. Baindail③

Facts: In 1928 the respondent, a Hindu domiciled in India, married an Indian woman in India according to Hindu rites. This marriage was a polygamous marriage by the customs and laws of the Hindu race and was valid in India. In 1939, while his Indian wife was still living, the respondent went through a ceremony of marriage with the petitioner, an English woman domiciled in England, at a registry office in London. In 1944 the petitioner, having discovered an invitation to the respondent's former Hindu marriage, presented a petition for nullity on the ground of bigamy. Barnard J granted a decree. The respondent appealed.

Held: Appeal dismissed.

这是一个有婚姻关系的法律适用的案例。法院所要解决的问题是:(1) 被告是不是一个已婚的男子?(2) 如果他是一个已婚的男子,他是否具有在英国再次结婚的能力?根据英国的国际私法规则,当事人的婚姻能力适用当事人的住所地法。在本案中,由于被告班戴尔的住所在印度,所以这一原则导致适用印度法律。依据印度法,被告班戴尔已经依据印度教的仪式与一名印度女子结婚,该婚姻是有效的。因此,被告是一名已婚男子。同时,印度的习惯和法律允许一夫多妻,因此,被告有再次结婚的权利。但是,被告的上述权利在英国,却不符合英国实体法的规定,被认为违反"人的常理"和英国的公共政策。④因此,被告在英国的再婚在英国是无效的。为此法院判决,同意原告提出的班戴尔在英国的婚姻无效的诉讼请求,

---

① 黄进主编:《国际私法》(第二版),法律出版社 2005 年版,第 472 页。
② 有关本案详细案情,参见王军主编:《国际私法案例教程》,中国政法大学出版社 1999 年版,第 86 页。
③ [1946] 1 All ER 342 Court of Appeal (Lord Greene MR, Morton and Bucknill L J J).
④ 参见王军主编:《国际私法案例教程》,中国政法大学出版社 1999 年版,第 90 页。

四、混合适用婚姻举行地法和当事人的属人法

由于婚姻既涉及婚姻举行地法又涉及当事人双方的属人法,有些国家在确定婚姻的法律适用规则时采用婚姻举行地法和当事人的属人法并用的情况。或者以婚姻举行地法为主,兼采当事人的属人法;或者以当事人的属人法为主,兼采婚姻举行地法,以此来衡量当事人婚姻的有效性。比如,《瑞士联邦国际私法》第45条规定,在外国有效缔结的婚姻,瑞士也承认其有效。但是,当事人任何一方为瑞士人或双方在瑞士有住所的,其在国外的婚姻予以承认,但规避瑞士法律的除外。《日本法例》第13条第2款和第3款规定,关于婚姻的方式,原则上适用婚姻举行地法,符合当事人一方的本国法规定的方式,也有效。采用混合适用的规定,可以避免跛脚婚姻的现象,为许多国家所接受。

五、我国有关结婚法律适用的规定

我国《民法通则》的规定比较简单,而且不够完善。《民法通则》第147条仅仅规定,中华人民共和国公民和外国人结婚适用婚姻举行地法。

我国《涉外民事关系法律适用法》对结婚的法律适用作出了补充。该法第21条规定:结婚条件,适用当事人共同经常居所地法律;没有共同经常居所地的,适用共同国籍国法律;没有共同国籍,在一方当事人经常居所地或者国籍国缔结婚姻的,适用婚姻缔结地法律。第21条对于结婚条件的规定采用了有条件的选择性法律选择规则,废弃了原来单一适用婚姻缔结地法的做法。但这种改变是否符合中国的具体情况还有待商榷。因为这条规定的使用者不仅有可能是中国法官,还有可能是中国的民政部门的婚姻登记机关。根据该条的规定,从理论上可以推断出在一些情况下应适用的法律很有可能为外国法,那么中国的婚姻登记机关是否有能力运用外国法审查当事人是否符合结婚条件?结婚适用婚姻缔结地法在实践中简便易行,以往的司法实践中亦未出现明显的问题,维护法律的稳定性和连续性,坚持以前的规定也未尝不可。[①] 我国《涉外民事关系法律适用法》第22条进一步规定:结婚手续,符合婚姻缔结地法律、一方当事人经常居所地法律或者国籍国法律的,均为有效。这种选择性法律适用规范的运用,便于当事人办理结婚手续,有助于婚姻在形式上的合法有效。

---

① 参见郭玉军:《涉外民事关系法律适用法中的婚姻家庭法律选择规则》,载《政法论坛》2011年第3期。

第二节 离婚的法律适用

一、离婚的法律冲突

目前,各国关于离婚(divorce)的条件规定不一。有的只是规定离婚的一般原则,比如,德国规定,婚姻破裂时得离婚;如夫妻共同生活关系不复存在,并且已不能期待恢复共同生活关系时,婚姻破裂。① 有的规定离婚的法定条件,比如《法国民法典》规定了三种离婚的情形,包括双方同意、生活破裂和错误等,并列举了详细的内容。② 还有的国家规定离婚必须先别居5年,如意大利。对于离婚的程序,各国的规定也不相同。有的国家规定离婚必须采用法院判决的形式,比如德国规定,离婚仅得由夫妻一方或双方的申请,经由法院判决而为之。③ 有的国家采用协议离婚和判决离婚相结合的方式,允许调解离婚,比如法国规定,诉讼前应进行调解,诉讼期间也可调解,协议离婚的发给协议离婚证书,判决离婚的由法院作出离婚判决。④ 还有一些国家,奉行宗教离婚的方式,只要在教堂、寺院表示离婚即可。⑤ 各国处理离婚事务的机构也不同。有的由民政机关以调解方式解决,有的通过法院办理。

综上,有关离婚的法律冲突不可避免地产生,不但涉及离婚管辖权的冲突,更涉及离婚的法律适用的冲突。

二、离婚财产的法律适用

(一) 法院地法的适用

离婚适用受理案件的法院地法(**forum law**),是英美等国家遵行的法律适用规则。

---

① 《德国民法典》第1565条第1款。
② 参见《法国民法典》第229—246条。
③ 《德国民法典》第1564条。
④ 《法国民法典》第251条。
⑤ 张仲伯主编:《国际私法学》,中国政法大学出版社1999年版,第372页。

第七章 国际婚姻家庭关系的法律适用

【解说】   **forum law**

American courts virtually always apply forum law in divorce. As long as domicile is a jurisdictional prerequisite to divorce, the forum will be an interested jurisdiction.

English court when diciding whether to recogise foreign divorces have never examined the grounds on which the decree was granted in order to see whether they were sufficient by English domiest law. When English courts have themselves assumed jurisdiction, they have never applied any other law than that of England.①

采用这一冲突规则的理由主要是考虑到离婚涉及一国的公共秩序和善良风俗。一旦确定了离婚案件的管辖权,在法院所在地的法律就应该被适用于具体的离婚案件。

法院地法常常就是当事人的住所地或居所地的法律,如英国有关离婚的冲突法规则(**English rules of the conflict of laws relating to divorce**)。

【解说】   **English rules of the conflict of laws relating to divorce**

The question of choice of law has never been prominent in the English rules of the conflict of laws relating to divorce, which has always been treated as primarily a jurisdictional question. On the one hand, English courts when deciding whether to recognize foreign divorces have never examined the grounds on which the degree was granted in order to see whether they were sufficient by English domestic law. On the other hand, when English courts have themselves assumed jurisdiction, they have never applied any other law than that of England.②

(二)属人法的适用

离婚是解除婚姻关系的一种行为,直接关系到人的身份问题。因此,有的欧洲国家主张离婚适用当事人的属人法(**personal law**)。

【解说】   **personal law**

Courts on the continent of Europe have, since the beginning of the twentieth centure, of-

---

① See David McClean, *Morris: The Conflict of Laws*, 5th ed., Sweet & Maxwell, 2000, p.234.
② David H. Vernon, Louis Weinberg, William Reynolds, William Richman, *Conflicts of Law: Case, Materials and Problems*, 2d ed., LexisNexis, 2002, p.834.

tern applied foreign law, usually the law of the parties nationality. This has sometimes involved them in very complicated problems, especially when the parties are of different nationalities.①

瑞士规定,瑞士法院有管辖权的涉外离婚案件,适用瑞士法;如果夫妻双方有共同的外国国籍,而只有一方在瑞士有住所时,适用他们共同的国籍国法;当共同外国法不准离婚时,如果夫妻一方为瑞士人或者在瑞士居住 2 年的,适用瑞士法。②也有的人认为离婚的准据法和结婚的应当一致,如果婚姻成立适用属人法作为准据法,那么,婚姻的解除也应当适用属人法作为准据法。

(三) 法院地法和属人法的混合适用

对于离婚,多数的欧洲大陆国家采用本国法和法院地法相结合的做法。有的规定选择适用属人法或法院地法,比如波兰;有的则规定重叠适用法院地法和属人法,比如德国。③另外,在许多立法中体现了有利于离婚的趋势。④

三、离婚所涉财产的法律适用

离婚是夫妻关系的解除。离婚案件除了涉及人身关系之外,还同时涉及夫妻财产的分割。通常,对于不动产的分割,适用不动产所在地法(situs rule),如 **Kirstein v. Kirstein** 案。

【案例】　　　　　　　　　　Kirstein v. Kirstein⑤

The husband's parents conveyed North Carolina land to the Kentucky-domiciled husband and wife. The Kentucky court granting the divorce awarded the property to the husband, apparently guided by equitable principles established in the state of Kentucky. When the wife attacked the judgment at the situs, the North Carolina court, after declaring the Kentucky decree void for lack of jurisdiction, proceeded to apply North Carolina law to determine the spouses' interests. Under situs law, a conveyance to both husband and wife created a tenancy by the entireties that converted into a tenancy in common upon divorce. Thus, despite the Kentucky decree, the wife retained a one-half interest in the property.⑥

---

① See David McClean, Morris: *The Conflict of Laws*, 5th ed., Sweet & Maxwell, 2000, p.234.
② 《瑞士联邦国际私法》第 60—61 条。
③ 张仲伯主编:《国际私法学》,中国政法大学出版社 1999 年版,第 374 页。
④ 黄进主编:《国际私法》(第二版),法律出版社 2005 年版,第 354 页。
⑤ 64 N. C. App. 191, 306 S. E. 2d 552 (1983).
⑥ Robby Alden, Modernizing the Situs Rule for Real Property Conflicts, 65 *Tex. L. Rev.* 585, 611 (1987).

四、我国有关离婚所涉财产法律适用的规定

我国《民法通则》第147条规定,离婚适用受理案件的法院所在地的法律。由此,我国法院受理的离婚案件,就只适用我国的法律。我国《涉外民事关系法律适用法》对此作出了进一步的细分,将离婚分为协议离婚与诉讼离婚两种情况,分别适用不同的法律。对于协议离婚,该法第26条规定:当事人可以协议选择适用一方当事人经常居所地法律或者国籍国法律。当事人没有选择的,适用共同经常居所地法律;没有共同经常居所地的,适用共同国籍国法律;没有共同国籍的,适用办理离婚手续机构所在地法律。对于诉讼离婚,该法第27条规定适用法院地法律。

我国《涉外民事关系法律适用法》第26、27条在协议离婚的法律适用上允许当事人有限的意思自治,但在诉讼离婚的法律适用上只采用单一的法院地法。其实,在当事人协议离婚的情况下,当事人就有关离婚事宜已达成合意,法律适用不是一个难题,是否允许意思自治意义不大。反倒是在离婚诉讼中,如能借鉴欧洲国家的有关立法经验,允许当事人在一定范围内选择离婚应适用的法律,可以提高法律适用的确定性和可预见性,符合当事人的期望,简化程序,提高诉讼效率。[①]

第三节 夫妻关系的法律适用

一、夫妻关系的法律冲突

夫妻关系是一种基于合法有效的婚姻而产生的法律关系,包括夫妻的人身关系和夫妻的财产关系。

夫妻人身关系,包括同居义务、忠诚及扶助义务、住所决定权、从事职业和社会活动的权利以及子女的教育权等各个方面的关系。

夫妻财产关系(matrimonial property regimes)是夫妻双方对于家庭财产的权利和义务,主要包括婚姻对于夫妻婚前财产的效力,婚姻存续期间财产的归属,也包括夫妻对于共同财产的处分等方面的内容。

---

① 参见郭玉军:《涉外民事关系法律适用法中的婚姻家庭法律选择规则》,载《政法论坛》2011年第3期。

对于这些问题,由于各国的社会、经济、文化等方面的背景不同,在法律规定上也不尽相同。在涉及具体的夫妻关系时,就会产生法律适用上的冲突。

二、夫妻属人法的适用

有的国家主张适用当事人的属人法来调整夫妻人身关系和财产关系的法律冲突。欧洲一些国家主张适用当事人的本国法,拉美一些国家主张适用当事人的住所地法。而在夫妻的属人法不同时,有的国家主张适用夫的本国法。而对于夫妻人身关系,现在多主张适用双方共同的属人法,比如日本。一些排除夫妻财产关系意思自治的国家,规定夫妻财产关系适用当事人的属人法,比如希腊、波兰等国家。

三、法院地法和行为地法的适用

夫妻关系涉及法院地国和行为地国的公共秩序以及善良风俗,因此,对于夫妻人身关系,也有的国家主张适用法院地法或行为地法,比如英国,关于丈夫是否可以对妻子施加强力,以及一方对他方的扶养义务如何等问题,适用法院地法。

四、意思自治原则的适用

夫妻关系在有些国家被看做是一种特殊的合同关系。在涉及夫妻财产关系的法律适用问题时,他们也主张适用意思自治原则。比如,《奥地利联邦国际私法法规》、《日本法例》。

1978 年海牙国际私法会议制定的《夫妻财产制法律适用公约》(Convention on the Law Applicable to Matrimonial Property Regimes)[1]对于夫妻财产关系也采用意思自治原则[2],允许夫妻双方通过选择来确定适用于夫妻财产的法律(**designation of law by spouses**)。

【法条】   designation of law by spouses

The matrimonial property regime is governed by the internal law designated by the spouses before marriage. The spouses may designate only one of the following laws—

(1) the law of any State of which either spouse is a national at the time of designation;

(2) the law of the State in which either spouse has his habitual residence at the time of designation;

(3) the law of the first State where one of the spouses establishes a new habitual resi-

---

[1] Concluded 14 March 1978, entered into force 1 September 1992.

[2] 参见徐冬根、薛凡:《中国国际私法完善研究》,上海社会科学出版社 1998 年版,第 321 页。

dence after marriage.

The law thus designated applies to the whole of their property.

Nonetheless, the spouses, whether or not they have designated a law under the previous paragraphs, may designate with respect to all or some of the immovables, the law of the place where these immovables are situated. They may also provide that any immovables which may subsequently be acquired shall be governed by the law of the place where such immovables are situated.①

五、我国有关夫妻关系法律适用的规定

我国《涉外民事关系法律适用法》对夫妻关系中的人身关系和关系的法律适用作出区分,分别规定了不同的法律适用规范。

对于夫妻人身关系,该法第 23 条规定适用共同经常居所地法律;没有共同经常居所地的,适用共同国籍国法律。

对于夫妻财产关系,该法第 24 条规定:当事人可以协议选择适用一方当事人经常居所地法律、国籍国法律或者主要财产所在地法律。当事人没有选择的,适用共同经常居所地法律;没有共同经常居所地的,适用共同国籍国法律。

第四节 亲子关系的法律适用

一、亲子关系的法律冲突

亲子关系也称为父母子女关系,是指父母和子女相互之间的一种法律关系。包括父母子女之间的人身关系和财产关系。父母子女之间的人身关系包括婚生父母子女和非婚生父母子女的关系。由于各国关于子女是否婚生、非婚生子女的准正以及财产等方面的规定并不相同,甚至,有的国家所采用的概念是其他国家所不使用的,因此,在父母子女关系的法律适用方面就会产生冲突。

---

① Article 3 of the Convention on the Law Applicable to Matrimonial Property Regimes.

二、属人法的适用

父母子女关系,与当事人的身份密切相关。因此,属人法常常得到适用。比如,在确定子女是否婚生的问题上,就会适用当事人的属人法,如摩塔拉等诉总检察长等案(**Motala and Others v. Attorney-General and Others**)。

【案例】　　**Motala and Others v. Attorney-General and Others** ①

Facts: This case concerned whether the children of Mr and Mrs Ismail Motala were citizens of the United Kingdom and Colonies or not. However, it is not necessary for us to enter the maze of nationality law. Suffice it to say that the nationality status of some of the children depended upon whether they were legitimate or not. The circumstances surrounding the marriage of the parents were the following: the marriage took place according to Sunni Muslim rites in 1950 in what is now Zambia but was then Northern Rhodesia. Apparently this would have been an invalid marriage under the *lex loci celebrationis* but under the law of India the marriage would have been valid and the children legitimate. Throughout the parents retained their domicile of origin in India. The crucial question was whether two children, Safiya and Faruq, born in Northern Rhodesia before independence, were legitimate (in which case they were citizens of the United Kingdom and Colonies) or illegitimate (in which case they had no such entitlement?)

The petitioners contended that a person's status is to be determined by the law of his domicile. If that law treats him or her as legitimate then it is submitted English law will recognise that legitimacy for all purposes concerned with status. The authorities show that there is a reservation in cases which concern the succession to real property or to titles. The contention of the petitioners is that since by the law of India which was the law of Ismail's domicile the children are recognised as legitimate pursuant to the marriage of 1950, their status should be so recognised by English law.

有的国家主张适用父母的属人法,具体又可分为适用生母之夫的属人法,比如德国;生父的住所地法,比如英国;适用父母共同的属人法,比如奥地利,或者各自的属人法,比如美国或者父母一方的本国法,比如日本。而有的国家为了保护子女的利益,则会适用子女的属人法,比如波兰。还有的国家主张适用父母和子女的共同属人法,比如南斯拉夫。

三、支配婚姻效力的法律

有的国家,对于子女是否婚生的问题,主张适用支配婚姻效力的法律,比如,《土耳其国际私法和国际诉讼程序法》第15条规定,子女婚生适用子女出生时调整

---

① [1990] 2 FLR 261 Family Division (Sir StephenBrown P).

其父母婚姻效力的法律。

四、使子女婚生更为有利的法律

对于子女是否婚生的问题,有的国家适用对子女更为有利的法律,比如奥地利、匈牙利和秘鲁等。①

五、我国有关亲子关系法律适用的规定

我国《涉外民事关系法律适用法》第25条规定:"父母子女人身、财产关系,适用共同经常居所地法律;没有共同经常居所地的,适用一方当事人经常居所地法律或者国籍国法律中有利于保护弱者权益的法律。"

第五节 收养的法律适用

一、收养的法律冲突

收养(**adoption**),是根据法律程序创设的收养人和被收养人之间的拟制的亲子关系。各国关于收养成立的条件、收养的效力、收养的解除等规定并不完全相同。因此,有关收养方面的法律适用冲突在所难免。

【法条】　　　　　　　　adoption

　　Adoption is one option used to provide care for children who are unable to live with their birth families. It is a legal process where legal rights and responsibilities are transferred from birth parents to adoptive parents. There are two types of adoption: local, from within State, and intercountry, from other countries. The Government shares responsibility for intercountry adoption with the States and Territories. Local adoption is solely the responsibility of the States and Territories.②

---

① 参见黄进主编:《国际私法》(第二版),法律出版社2005年版,第356—357页。
② See website of Australian Government Attorney—General's Departmenthttp: //www. ag. gov. au/www/agd/agd. nsf/Page/IntercountryAdoption_WhatisAdoption.

二、国内法的适用

（一）适用法院地法

有关收养成立的实质要件适用法院地法，比如英国。如果英国法院对于收养案件有管辖权，则在法律适用方面适用英国法而不适用其他国家的法律。美国也持同样主张。

（二）适用属人法

收养关系是拟制的亲子关系，与人的身份密切相关，因此，在有关收养成立、收养的效力等法律适用问题上，有的国家主张适用当事人的属人法。有的主张适用收养人的属人法，比如意大利、奥地利等；有的主张适用被收养人的属人法，比如法国曾有这样的判例；有的国家主张适用他们各自的属人法，比如日本、希腊、秘鲁等国家。

（三）适用收养关系发生地法

收养也是一种法律行为。有的国家主张收养的成立和收养的效力等问题适用收养关系发生地的法律，比如瑞士规定，在瑞士宣告收养的条件，适用瑞士法。①

三、国际公约的适用

国家之间的儿童收养问题，缔约国也可以适用国际公约的规定。1993 年《儿童保护和国家间收养合作公约》(**Hague Convention of May 29, 1993 on Protection of Children and Co-operation in respect of Intercountry Adoption**)就规定了有关儿童收养的问题。

【法条】　　Hague Convention of May 29, 1993 on Protection of Children and Co-operation in respect of Intercountry Adoption②

The main purpose of the Convention was to establish safeguards to ensure that intercountry adoptions take place in the best interests of the child and with respect for the child's fundamental rights as recognised in international law, and to establish a system of co-operation amongst Contracting States to ensure that those safeguards are respected.

---

① 《瑞士联邦国际私法法规》第 77 条第 1 款。
② The final text of the Convention on Protection of Children and Co-operation in Respect of Intercountry Adoption (Hague Adoption Convention), a multilateral treaty, was approved by 66 nations on May 29, 1993 at The Hague. The goal of the Convention is to protect the children, birth parents and adoptive parents involved in intercountry adoptions and to prevent abuses. Currently, 68 countries have joined the Convention.

The Convention shall apply where a child habitually resident in one Contracting State ("the State of origin") has been, is being, or is to be moved to another Contracting State ("the receiving State") either after his or her adoption in the State of origin by spouses or a person habitually resident in the receiving State, or for the purposes of such an adoption in the receiving State or in the State of origin.①

Articles 4 and 5 of the Convention contain detailed requirements for intercountry adoptions, involving consideration of the proposed adoption by the "competent authorities" in each country. The issues to be considered in the State of origin include the fact that the child is adoptable; that an intercountry adoption is in the child's best interests; that all necessary consents have been given; and that, having regard to the age and degree of maturity of the child, its wishes and opinions have been duly considered. In the receiving State, it must be determined that the prospective adoptive parents are eligible and suited to adopt, and have been counselled as may be necessary; and that the child is or will be authorized to enter and reside permanently in that State.

四、我国有关涉外收养法律适用的规定

我国《涉外民事关系法律适用法》第28条规定:"收养的条件和手续,适用收养人和被收养人经常居所地法律。收养的效力,适用收养时收养人经常居所地法律。收养关系的解除,适用收养时被收养人经常居所地法律或者法院地法律。"对于收养,该条以"经常居所地"作为基本连结点,体现了对经常居所地连结点的重视。②

第六节 监护的法律适用

一、监护的法律冲突

监护(guardianship)是监护人对未成年人或禁治产人的人身和财产利益依法实施监督和保护的一种法律制度。承担监护义务的人为监护人,受监护人监督和保

---

① Article 2.
② 参见郭玉军:《涉外民事关系法律适用法中的婚姻家庭法律选择规则》,载《政法论坛》2011年第3期。

护的人为被监护人。监护不是一种权利,而是一种义务。① 有的国家只有监护一种制度,而有的国家于监护之外,尚有"保佐"制度,即前者针对完全无行为能力人,后者针对限制行为能力人。有的国家只允许亲属任监护人;多数国家规定监护人只能是一人;而有的国家却允许数人任监护人。② 当然,虽然各国具体规定有所不同,但监护制度的存在,其作用在于,在自然人具有权利能力而无行为能力的情况下,帮助这种自然人的权利能力得到实现,从而得到生存和发展,使社会成员之间的互助义务得到法律的强制性保障。各国对于监护人的条件及其职责、被监护人的范围等规定不同,由此产生法律适用上的冲突。

二、涉外监护的法律适用

(一) 适用被监护人的属人法

从国际公约和各国国内法的有关立法来看,原则上都是主张适用被监护人的本国法。而一些美洲国家主张适用被监护人的住所地法。这种立法考虑到了在内国的外国人的人身或财产也可能需要设立监护的情况,体现了监护制度保护被监护人利益的宗旨。③

(二) 法院地法的适用

有的国家,对于监护案件,积极主张管辖权。一旦确定本国对于监护案件有管辖权,则只适用自己国家的法律,即法院地法,如英国。英国法中有一条重要原则经常被适用于决定有关监护人问题,即首先和首要考虑子女利益的原则,如英国1971年《监护判例法》即作如此规定,美国 Michael Bast v. Shelley Rae Rossoff 案为这方面比较典型的案例。

【案例】　　　　　**Michael Bast v. Shelley Rae Rossoff**④

The parties, both practicing attorneys in New York City, were married in September 1986. During their marriage, they had one child, a daughter Morton Elizabeth, born on March 15, 1989. They separated in July 1990 and in February 1992, settled the custody and visitation issues by stipulation. They agreed to a "shared time allocation", whereby plaintiff (father) would have the child with him from Wednesday evening to Sunday evening one week, and

---

① 参见黄进主编:《国际私法》(第二版),法律出版社2005年版,第362页。
② 参见李双元主编:《国际私法》,北京大学出版社2006年版,第379页。
③ 参见黄进主编:《国际私法》(第二版),法律出版社2005年版,第363页;李双元主编:《国际私法》,北京大学出版社2006年版,第401页。
④ 91 N.Y.2d 723, 697 N.E.2d 1009, 675 N.Y.S.2d 19 (1998).

Wednesday evening to Thursday morning the following week. In April 1993, Supreme Court held a hearing to resolve the issue of child support. Plaintiff then earned $76876 per year and defendant earned $83118 per year. In November 1995, Supreme Court issued a comprehensive opinion in which the court attempted to reconcile the shared custodial arrangement with the requirements of the CSSA. Nevertheless, the court concluded that the CSSA "applies" to cases of shared custody.

三、有关监护法律适用的国际条约

关于监护的法律适用,早在 20 世纪初,海牙国际私法会议就主持制定了两个公约,即 1902 年的《未成年人监护公约》(Convention of 12 June 1902 relating to the settlement of guardianship of minors)和 1905 年的《禁治产及其类似保护措施公约》(Convention of 17 July 1905 relating to deprivation of civil rights and similar measures of protection),分别对未成年人监护的法律适用作了规定。[1]此后,海牙国际私法会议一直关注这一领域的冲突法问题,分别制定了有关的公约。

(一) 关于未成年人监护的国际公约对法律适用的规定

1.《关于未成年人保护的机关的权限和法律适用公约》

1961 年海牙国际私法会议制定的《关于未成年人保护的机关的权限和法律适用公约》(Convention Concerning the Powers of Authorities and the Law Applicable in Respect of the Protection of Minors)第 1 条就首先规定了未成年人的惯常居所地国的司法机关和行政机关有权采取措施,以保护未成年人的利益,并得采取其国内法规定的措施。该公约采用"惯常居所"这一连接因素而成功地协调了在有关自然人身份问题上长期存在的本国法主义与住所地法主义的对立。[2]

2.《关于父母责任和保护儿童措施的管辖权、法律适用、承认、执行和合作公约》

1996 年海牙国际私法会议通过的《父母责任和保护儿童措施的管辖权、法律适用、承认、执行和合作公约》(Convention on Jurisdiction, Applicable Law, Recognition, Enforcement and Co-operation in respect of Parental Responsibility and Measures for the Protection of Children)明确提出以其取代 1902 年《未成年人监护公约》和 1961 年海牙公约。新公约共 7 章 63 条,确定了儿童惯常居所地国行使采取保护儿童措施的管辖权的基本原则,同时允许离婚法院地国的并存管辖权和其他有最密

---

[1] See http://en.wikipedia.org/wiki/List_of_Hague_Conventions_on_Private_International_Law.
[2] 参见李双元主编:《国际私法》,北京大学出版社 2006 年版,第 401—402 页。

切关系国家的补充管辖权,具有管辖权的机关采取措施时适用本国法。公约第3条对父母责任的准据法作了明文规定,即适用儿童惯常居所地法。

(二) 关于成年人监护的国际公约对法律适用的规定

2000年海牙国际私法会议通过了《关于成年人国际保护公约》(Convention on the International Protection of Adults)。该公约在缔约国间取代了1905年的海牙《禁治产及类似保护措施公约》。

四、我国有关涉外监护法律适用的规定

长期以来,我国冲突法规范中一直没有关于涉外监护法律适用的规定,只是最高人民法院在1988年发布的《关于贯彻执行〈中华人民共和国民法通则〉若干问题的意见(试行)》第190条对涉外监护法律适用问题作了规定:"监护的设立、变更和终止,适用被监护人的本国法律。但是,被监护人在我国境内有住所的,适用我国的法律。"可见,中国法院在司法实践中,适用被监护人本国法作为处理涉外监护问题亦为一般原则,同大陆法系国家的主张一致。但是在被监护人在中国境内有住所的情况下,不论被监护人本国法关于监护的规定如何,中国坚持适用中国法即被监护人住所地法。这一规定比大陆法系国家的规定更进了一步,将被监护人的本国法和住所地法有机结合起来。①

自2011年4月1日起施行的我国《涉外民事关系法律适用法》引入了保护弱者的原则。该法第30条规定:"监护,适用一方当事人经常居所地法律或者国籍国法律中有利于保护被监护人权益的法律。"

第七节 扶养的法律适用

一、国际扶养的概念及其认定

扶养(maintenance),是指根据身份关系在一定的亲属之间,由有经济能力的一方为无能力生活的一方提供扶助,以使其得以维持生活的一种法律制度。在扶养

---

① 参见黄进主编:《国际私法》(第二版),法律出版社2005年版,第363—364页。

关系中,提供扶养的一方为扶养义务人,接受扶养的一方为扶养权利人。扶养关系一般分为三种类型,即夫妻之间的扶养、亲子之间的扶养以及其他亲属间的扶养。①

国际扶养,也即涉外扶养,通常是指特定的亲属间,一方是外国人或者长期居住在国外,另一方为本国人或者长期居住在本国境内,他们之间依法存在的一方必须对另一方承担供养基本生活费责任的法律关系。由于扶养关系是以特定的亲属关系为基础的,因此涉外扶养关系的认定主要取决于扶养主体的国籍或住所与外国有联系的事实。②

二、国际扶养的法律适用制度

不同的国家由于种种原因,适用不同的扶养制度。这些不同的扶养制度总体上可以概括为三种③:

第一种,区分不同性质、不同种类的扶养关系分别确定法律适用。这些国家通常是将夫妻之间的扶养和亲子之间的扶养看做夫妻关系和亲子关系的必备内容,因此规定这两种扶养分别适用调整夫妻关系和亲子关系的法律,而其他亲属间的扶养则单独确定法律适用。

第二种,不加以区分、广义理解扶养关系,统一确定法律适用。比较有代表性的立法有1982年《土耳其国际私法和国际诉讼程序法》、1964年《日本法例》,两者均规定,扶养义务适用义务人本国法。

第三种,只对某一类扶养关系的法律适用作出规定。如1964年《捷克斯洛伐克国际私法及国际民事诉讼法》仅对亲子之间的扶养关系规定了法律适用,该法规定:"(1)父母子女关系,包括扶养和教育,依子女的本国法。子女居住在捷克斯洛伐克社会主义共和国境内,只要对子女有利,就依捷克斯洛伐克法律。(2)父母向子女的扶养请求权,依父母的本国法。"

三、国际扶养的法律适用原则

各国在实践中,对涉外扶养关系的法律适用主要采用以下几种原则:

1. 适用被扶养人属人法

大多数的国家在涉外扶养关系方面都主张这一适用原则,理由是这些国家都认为,扶养制度是为被扶养人的利益而设置的,故应以被扶养人的利益为优先考虑。

---

① 根据我国《婚姻法》的规定,这里所称的扶养,指广义上的扶养,即包括扶养、抚养和赡养。
② 参见杜新丽:《国际私法实务中的法律问题》,中信出版社2005年版,第170页。
③ 参见邓杰:《国际私法分论》,知识产权出版社2005年版,第258—259页。

2. 适用扶养人属人法

采用这一原则的国家认为扶养义务是扶养制度的基础和本体,而且扶养义务因为一定身份关系的存在而产生,因而应当适用扶养义务人的属人法。

3. 适用扶养人和被扶养人的共同属人法

扶养义务在一定亲属之间是双向的、可逆的,即此时的扶养权利人可能成为彼时的扶养义务人,因此在确定涉外扶养关系的法律适用时,应兼顾扶养人和被扶养人的利益而考虑双方的共同属人法,这种观点在近些年的国际私法立法中有一定的影响力。

4. 重叠适用被扶养人属人法和法院地法

也有一些国家从平衡扶养人与被扶养人之间的利益、防止本国扶养人承担过重扶养义务的角度出发,主张涉外扶养关系应重叠适用被扶养人属人法和法院地法。

5. 适用最有利于被扶养人的法律

适用最有利于被扶养人的法律,就是要求从法律适用结果出发,直接适用最有利于被扶养人的实体法律规则,从而真正切实有效地维护被扶养人的利益,这也是贯彻保护弱者利益原则的体现。这种适用原则较之被扶养人属人法适用原则而言,显然是一个立法上的进步,毕竟冲突法层面的保障永远不如实体法层面的保障来得更为直接和有效,因为被扶养人的属人法并不一定就是最有利于被扶养人的法律,某些时候可能恰恰相反。① 近些年来,越来越多的国家在国内法方面采取这一适用原则。

6. 最密切联系适用原则

有的国家将最密切联系原则引入扶养关系的法律适用中来。采取这一原则主要是为了照顾被扶养人的利益,对被扶养人给予更多的保护,该原则有一定的灵活性。

四、海牙《扶养义务法律适用公约》的法律适用规则

1973 年海牙《扶养义务法律适用公约》(**Hague Convention on the Law Applicable to Maintenance Obligations**)第二章规定了有关扶养的法律适用规则。

首先是适用扶养权利人惯常居所地法(**law of the habitual residence**)。

【法条】　　　　　　　law of the habitual residence

The internal law of the habitual residence of the maintenance creditor shall govern the

---

① 参见肖永平:《中国冲突法立法问题研究》,武汉大学出版社 1996 年版,第 312 页。

maintenance obligations referred to in Article 1. In the case of a change in the habitual residence of the creditor, the internal law of the new habitual residence shall apply as from the moment when the change occurs.①

其次是适用扶养权利人和扶养义务人共同本国法(**law of their common nationality**)。

【法条】 **law of their common nationality**

If the creditor is unable, by virtue of the law referred to in Article 4, to obtain maintenance from the debtor, the law of their common nationality shall apply.②

再次是适用受理机关所在地法(**law of the authority**)。

【法条】 **law of the authority**

If the creditor is unable, by virtue of the laws referred to in Articles 4 and 5, to obtain maintenance from the debtor, the internal law of the authority seized shall apply.③

值得一提的是,2007 年 11 月,海牙国际私法会议第 21 届外交大会在荷兰海牙召开。57 个成员国、14 个观察员及多个国际组织派代表与会。中国代表团由外交部、最高人民法院、司法部、驻荷兰使馆、香港和澳门特别行政区政府派人组成。会议按海牙会议惯例选举荷兰私法常设政府委员会主席 Struycken 教授为大会主席,中国代表团团长薛捍勤大使当选大会副主席。经过近二十天的密集谈判,会议以协商一致方式通过了《扶养义务法律适用议定书》(Protocol on the Law Applicable to Maintenance Obligations),包括中国在内的 71 个国家代表团签署了会议最后文件。④

五、我国关于涉外扶养关系的法律适用

我国《婚姻法》规定的扶养关系包括父母子女之间的相互扶养、夫妻之间的相

---

① Article 4.
② Article 5.
③ Article 6.
④ 参见中华人民共和国外交部网站,网址:http://big5.fmprc.gov.cn/gate/big5/www.fmprc.gov.cn/chn/wjb/zzjg/tyfls/wjzdtyflgz/zgyyggjjghgjhy/t422930.htm

互扶养,以及在一定条件下,其他家庭成员之间的扶养。我国将这三种性质不同、种类不同的扶养关系视为一个整体,统一适用同一个法律规定,即适用与被扶养人最密切联系国家的法律。

我国《涉外民事关系法律适用法》采纳了与《婚姻法》中有关扶养关系法律适用规范不同的规范,并体现了国际私法中保护弱者的精神。该法第29条规定:"扶养,适用一方当事人经常居所地法律、国籍国法律或者主要财产所在地法律中有利于保护被扶养人权益的法律。"该条有关扶养的法律适用采用了由法官选择有利于被扶养人利益的法律选择规则。较之《民法通则》采用的最密切联系原则,本条规定进一步明确允许法官在多个法律中选择适用对扶养权利人有利的法律,与国际社会对扶养法律适用的立法趋势基本一致。① 这样,法官可以根据具体的情况,灵活地作出不同的选择:在法律适用的内容上,确认扶养关系的存在,可以选择有利于扶养关系成立的法律;在扶养费的给付方面,则可以选择适用规定扶养费数额较高的法律,使被扶养人的处境更为有利。

【思考题】

- 如何解决涉外结婚的法律冲突问题?
- 解决涉外离婚法律冲突的原则有哪些?
- 我国关于涉外婚姻家庭关系的冲突规范作了哪些规定?
- 收养、监护、扶养法律适用各有什么特点?

【重要术语提示与中英文对照】

中文术语	英文对照
结婚	marriage
结婚举行地法	*lex loci celebrationis*
欧敦诉欧敦案	Ogden v. Ogden
班戴尔诉班戴尔案	Baindail v. Baindail
法院地法	forum law
英国有关离婚的冲突法规则	English rules of the conflict of laws relating to divorce

---

① 参见郭玉军:《涉外民事关系法律适用法中的婚姻家庭法律选择规则》,载《政法论坛》2011年第3期。

摩塔拉等诉总检察长等案	Motala and Others v. Attorney-General and Others
一夫多妻婚姻	polygamous marriage
离婚	divorce
收养	adoption
儿童保护和国家间收养合作公约	Hague Convention on Protection of Children and Co-operation in respect of Intercountry Adoption.
监护	guardianship
扶养	maintenance
认领	recognition of illegitimate child
关于未成年人保护的机关的权限和法律适用公约	Convention concerning the powers of authorities and the law applicable in respect of the protection of minors,
国际性诱拐儿童民事方面公约	Convention on the Civil Aspects of International Child Abduction
父母责任和保护儿童措施的管辖权、法律适用、承认、执行及合作公约	Convention on Jurisdiction, Applicable Law, Recognition, Enforcement and Co-operation in respect of Parental Responsibility and Measures for the Protection of Children
成年人国际保护公约	Convention on the International Protection of Adults
扶养义务法律适用公约	Hague Convention on the Law Applicable to Maintenance Obligations
惯常居所地法	law of the habitual residence
共同本国法	law of the common nationality
受理机关所在地法	law of the authority
扶养义务法律适用议定书	Protocol on the Law Applicable to Maintenance Obligations

【推荐阅读文献】

- 董立坤：《国际私法中的婚姻法律冲突》，载《中国社会科学》1982 年第 4 期。
- 蒋新苗：《国际收养法律制度研究》，法律出版社 1999 年版。

- 徐冬根:《人文关怀与国际私法中弱者利益保护》,载《当代法学》2004 年第 5 期。
- 杜新丽:《国际私法实务中的法律问题》,中信出版社 2005 年版。
- 黄进主编:《国际私法》(第二版),法律出版社 2005 年版。
- 郭玉军:《涉外民事关系法律适用法中的婚姻家庭法律选择规则》,载《政法论坛》2011 年第 3 期。
- 周琳:《中国涉外亲属法之冲突法立法演进》,载《中国外资》2012 年第 8 期。
- Brian H. Bix, State Interests in Marriage, Interstate Recognition, and Choice of Law, 38 *Creighton L. Rev.* 337 (2005).
- Veronica Torrez, Cheryl Coleman and Tina Burleson, The International Abduction of International Children: Conflicts of Laws, Federal Statutes, and Judicial Interpretation of the Hague Convention on the Civil Aspects of International Child Abduction, 5 *Whittier J. Child & Fam. Advoc.* 7 (2005).
- Tobias Barrington Wolff, Interest Analysis in Interjurisdictional Marriage Disputes, 5 *Dukeminier Awards* 49 (2006).
- Barbara Stark, When Globalization Hits Home: International Family Law Comes of Age, 39 *Vand. J. Transnat'l L.* 1551 (2006).
- Mark Strasser, The Future of Marriage, 21 *J. Am. Acad. Matrimonial Law.* 87 (2008).
- Spector (R.), A Guide to United States Case Law under the Hague Convention on the Civil Aspects of International Child Abduction, 12 *Ybk. Priv. Int'l L.* 139 (2010).
- Araya Kebede (A.), *Conflict of Family Laws in Ethiopia: Interstate Conflict of Family Laws under the Federal Democratic Republic of Ethiopia (FDRE): The Choice of Law Aspect*, LAP LAMBERT Academic Publishing, 2011.
- Fausto Pocar, The European Harmonisation of Conflict of Laws Rules on Divorce and Legal Separation: Is Enhanced Co-operation a Correct Approach? *I. F. L.* 24 (2012 Mar).
- Cristiana Cianitto, Mariagrazia Tirabassi, Conflict of Laws: Adoption—Welfare of Child, 1 *O. J. L. R.* 302 (2012).

第七章　国际婚姻家庭关系的法律适用

【扩展阅读资料】

Marriage Rules of Conflict of Laws[①]

A. Principal Connecting Factors

When a legal relationship in matters of family law is connected to more than one country, one must choose which country's laws are to be applied. In family law, this choice of law is critical, because the laws of various jurisdictions differ in family matters much more than in any other legal sphere. Few, if any, areas of the law express cultural and religious mores more clearly than family law.

In an international family, the partners may, for example, be British and Italian subjects, married in Belgium, domiciled in Switzerland, later moving to New York. These links to various jurisdictions are called connecting factors (points de rattachement) or, in the USA, points of contact.

Family law matters are most closely connected to the laws of a person's home state or country (personal law). In some jurisdictions such as Denmark, Norway and the common law countries, personal law is based on the country of domicile, while in others the country of citizenship generally is determinative. However, neither of these connecting factors is considered as absolute; rather, they are seen as principles open to exceptions.

The concept of habitual residence has been introduced as an alternative connecting factor to the principles of nationality and domicile, to avoid conflict between them. It is also an alternative to the differing concepts of domicile in common and civil law jurisdictions. Habitual residence differs from domicile in that the element of intention (animus) is weaker. It requires only a regular physical presence in a country and not the additional subjective element of intention required by the principle of domicile. It has often been said that the domicile system allows a person to change the law governing his or her personal situation at will by changing his or her domicile. It is, in this sense, a more individualistic system. The system of nationality, on the other hand, is based on the idea that a person is bound to his or her state and that the personal law can only be changed by act of state. In contemporary private international law there is a strong trend away from the nationality principle and towards domicile or habitual residence as decisive for the choice of law in personal matters.

---

① Barbara E. Graham-Siegenthaler, Marriage Recognition in Switzerland and Europe, 32 *Creighton L. Rev.* 133—134 (1998).

B. Connecting Factors under Swiss Law for the Contracting of a Marriage

In Switzerland, conflict-of-laws is governed by the Private International Law Statute (PIL Statute), which came into force on January 1, 1989. With the exception of international treaties which take precedence in accordance with Swiss law, this statute now conclusively regulates this area of law. It regulates questions of jurisdiction and applicable law, as well as recognition and enforcement of foreign decisions. In the area of family law, the principal connecting factor is that of habitual residence and domicile (as opposed to citizenship, which plays a relatively minor role).

For a particular legal issue, the applicable law is designated by means of a point de rattachement, or point of contact. Most conflict-of-jurisdictions rules, and all recognition and enforcement rules, state only what Switzerland's courts will or will not do. As in the more recent Hague Conventions, the Swiss conflict rules use non-technical autonomous concepts such as "habitual residence" rather then technical terms appearing in other Swiss statutes. An exception may be the more technical and principal connecting factor of "domicile" as defined in the statute.

In the area of family law, one of the principal connecting factors is to the domicile of the parties, or the party who is considered to be deserving of special protection. For persons without a domicile but with habitual residence in Switzerland, particularly children, many provisions secure jurisdiction at the place of habitual residence.

Swiss authorities consider themselves internationally competent to conclude a marriage if either the bride or groom is domiciled in or is a citizen of Switzerland. Foreigners without a domicile in Switzerland may be permitted by competent authority to marry if the marriage will be recognized in the prospective spouses' countries of domicile or citizenship. The applicable law for marriages in Switzerland is Swiss law or, alternatively, if the parties are non-Swiss, the law of one of their countries of citizenship. The form of the marriage ceremony, however, is always governed by Swiss law (i.e., the marriage must be solemnized by a Swiss registrar of civil status).

第八章

国际财产关系的法律适用

本章导读

※ 物之所在地法,即财产权关系客体所在地的法律。在国际财产权关系中,物之所在地法是最普遍适用的法律。物之所在地法与物的权利间具有最重要的关联。对于有体物而言,其所在地就是它的物理空间的场所,当事人很容易判断和确定特定物的具体所在地,使财产权关系的法律适用具有确定性。

※ 对于物之所在地法原则的适用,存在两种不同的主张与实践。一种是区别主义,认为不动产适用物之所在地法,而动产适用所有人的住所地法;另一种是统一主义,即不论标的物为动产还是不动产,均适用物之所在地法。

※ 相关机构所在地法是物之所在地法的新发展,系海牙国际私法会议在《中介机构所持证券若干权利法律适用公约》中所倡导。

※ 物之所在地法原则的适用范围十分广泛,它几乎包括与财产有关的所有问题:动产与不动产的区分;财产权客体的范围;财产权的种类和内容;财产权的取得、转移、变更和消灭的方式及条件;财产权的保护方法。

※ 物之所在地法适用的例外主要包括:运送中物品;船舶、飞行器等运输工具;外国法人终止或解散时有关财产权;与人身有关的财产等。

※ 不动产适用不动产所在地法是最普遍适用的冲突规范。

※ 传统上,动产适用所有权人的属人法。从19世纪末开始,许多国家逐渐在立法和司法实践中主张动产适用动产交易时所在地的法律。

※ 对于船舶、飞机等交通运输工具,一般主张适用其船旗国法或注册登记国法。

※ 我国不动产的所有权、买卖、租赁、抵押、使用等民商事关系,均适用不动产所在地法律。动产的租赁关系适用出租人营业所所在地法。

※ 遗产继承区别制,是指在国际继承中,将遗产区分为动产和不动产,动产适用被继承人属人法,不动产适用不动产所在地法。遗产继承同一制是指在国际继承中,不区分动产和不动产,统一适用不动产所在地法。

※ 立遗嘱能力的法律适用,英国、美国等采取不动产遗嘱适用不动产所在地法,动产遗嘱适用遗嘱人住所地法。

※ 对于无人继承财产,各国都规定归国家所有。对于无人继承财产归属问题的法律适用规则,有的国家规定适用被继承人的本国法;有的国家规定适用财产所在地法;有的国家适用继承准据法。

【本章主题词】 物之所在地法、法定继承、遗嘱继承、无人继承遗产

第八章　国际财产关系的法律适用

第一节　物之所在地法原则

一、物之所在地法

物之所在地法（situs rule, *lex loci rei sitae*）即财产权关系客体所在地的法律。目前，在国际财产权关系中，物之所在地法是最普遍适用的法律。

【释义】 situs rule

Conflicts law has undergone an immense revolution in the last thirty years. The situs rule for real property, however, is no different today than it was one hundred and fifty years ago when Justice Story first organized conflicts law in the United States. The territorially based doctrine of lex situs requires that the law of the situs of property govern choice-of-law decisions when real property is at stake. Courts continue to reach choice-of-law decisions for real property disputes by mechanically applying the situs rule, giving little consideration to concepts of fairness and justice. Jurisdictional decisions for real property disputes are also decided by reference to the traditional rule of lex situs. The unjust results created by blind application of territorial conflicts rules still obtain in real property disputes while more enlightened legal theories govern practically all other disputes.[①]

一般认为，物之所在地法与物的权利间具有最重要的关联。而且，对于有体物而言，其所在地就是它的物理空间的场所，当事人很容易判断和确定特定物的具体所在地，使财产权关系的法律适用具有确定性，这对所有权人以及第三人的利益以及交易安全，都是最为妥当的保护。

对于物之所在地法的适用，存在两种不同的主张与实践。一种是区别主义，认为不动产适用物之所在地法，而动产则适用所有人的住所地法；另一种是统一主义，即不论标的物为动产还是不动产，均适用物之所在地法。目前，统一主义为大多数国家的国际私法立法所接受。统一主义所倡导的物之所在地法之所以能够盛

---

① Robby Alden, Modernizing the Situs Rule for Real Property Conflicts, 65 *Tex. L. Rev.* 585 (1987).

行主要有两个原因(**reasons for the *situs* rule**)。

【说理】   reasons for the *situs* rule

  The first of these reasons has to do with modern recording systems and the necessity of keeping title research simple by allowing the searcher to apply the law of the situs to all legal problems that the search may uncover. The record will not reveal many of the factors that might favor application of law other than that of the situs, such as the fact that the parties to a transaction have a settled residence elsewhere. Even if such matters were revealed, it would substantially complicate the title search and increase its cost to require the searcher to ferret out the foreign law, gain an understanding of its nuances and apply it to the problem at hand.①

  The second reason for applying the law of the situs is well stated in an early draft of the second Restatement: Land and things attached to the land are within the exclusive control of the state in which they are titled, and the officials of that state are the only ones who can lawfully deal with them physically. Since interests in immovable cannot be affected without the consent of the state of the situs, it is natural that the latter's law should applied by the courts of the states.②

二、物之所在地法的新发展:相关中介机构所在地法

  海牙国际私法会议起草并于 2002 年通过的《中介机构所持证券若干权利法律适用公约》规定,证券物权冲突适用"相关中介机构所在地法"(place of the relevant intermediary approach,简称 PRIMA),这是物之所在地法的新发展。有学者认为:间接持有体制下投资者权益的来源是账户,而不是直接持有体制下的证书。尽管该账户只是一些无形的电子记录,但它毕竟还是交易双方交易期望之所在。该账户对投资者来说,首先是其权益的证明与代表;对交易的受让人来说,它是其期望之标的。受让人与投资者进行交易,就是针对账户的交易,所以,交易势必要在账户之所在地进行。这样,尽管当事人的住所或者国籍也许一时难以确定,或者能够容易确定,当事人的属人法也往往与动产物权之间的联系也不那么密切。③ 证券物权冲突适用"相关中介机构所在地法",顺应了证券无纸化和跨国化条件下间接持有体制的现实需求,有力地推动了传统的物之所在地法的发展。

---

  ① Russell J Weintraub, *Commentary on the Conflict of Laws*, 4th ed, New York Foundation Press, 2001, p.502.
  ② Restatement, Second, Conflicts of Law ch.7, Topic 2, 12—13 (tent. Draft No. 5, 1959.)
  ③ 鲁世平、孙晓珍:《论物权冲突法的新发展:证券"相关中介机构所在地法"》,载《西北大学学报(哲学社会科学版)》2012 年第 1 期。

三、物之所在地法的适用范围

物之所在地法原则的适用范围十分广泛(**broad application of situs rules**),它几乎可以适用与财产有关的任何问题。

【释义】　　　　**broad application of situs rules**

The law of situs governs the requisites of a deed to land, the quantum of the estate conveyed the validity of a will devising land, the determination of the question whether the will has been revoked, whether a trust can be created in real estate, whether a grantor has legal capacity to convey. It would be affectation to multiply instances, for the general principle is well known and thoroughly established. ①

The situs rules is alive and well in the modern choice-of-law practice. It figures prominently in the Second Restatement, and with a few exceptions, contemporary judicial opinions apply it to nearly all questions involving real property. ②

物之所在地法的适用范围包括下列几个方面:

第一,物之所在地法适用于动产与不动产的区分。在通常意义上讲,动产和不动产的区别在于财产是否能从一个地方移动到另一个地方,能移动之财产为动产,不能移动之财产为不动产。不过,在现实中,尽管各国法律对财产之属于动产或不动产一般都有明文规定,但往往并不只做上述这种简单的划分,且不尽相同。例如,1811年《奥地利民法典》规定池塘里的鱼和森林中的野兽为不动产,德国民法将展览用房屋视为动产。英国法视土地权利证书为不动产。在我国,1988年《最高人民法院关于贯彻执行〈中华人民共和国民法通则〉若干问题的意见(试行)》第186条规定:"土地、附着于土地的建筑物及其他定着物、建筑物的固定附属设备为不动产……"这意味着其他财产均为动产。由于各国在动产和不动产的区分上不完全一致,在国际民事交往中,当要决定某财产为动产还是不动产时,国际上一般都主张依物之所在地法来进行识别。

第二,财产权客体的范围由物之所在地法决定。笼统地讲,作为财产权客体的物在范围上是十分广泛的,凡是存在于人身之外,能为人力所支配和控制并能够满足人们的某种需要的财产,都能够成为财产权的客体。因此,财产权客体的范围只

---

① Hebert Goodrich, Two States and Real Estate, 89 *U. Pa. L. Rev.* 417—418 (1941).
② William Richman & William Reynolds, Prologomenon to an Empirical Restatement of Conflicts, 75 *Ind. L. J.* 417, 417 (2000).

能由物之所在地法决定。

第三,财产权的种类和内容由物之所在地法决定。根据财产权法定主义原则,财产权的种类是由法律具体规定的。对于财产权的种类和内容,各国一般都主张依物之所在地法确定。

第四,财产权的取得、转移、变更和消灭的方式及条件,一般由物之所在地法决定。财产权的取得、转移、变更和消灭是基于一定的法律行为或法律事实而发生的,各国法律对其方式及条件都有自己的规定。这些问题在实践中一般根据物之所在地法决定。

第五,财产权的保护方法由物之所在地法决定。当财产权人在其财产权受到侵害时,他可以依法寻求对其财产权的保护。在民法上,财产权的保护方法主要有财产权人请求停止侵害,排除妨碍,恢复、返还原物,消除危险,确认其所有权或其他财产权存在,损害赔偿等。财产权人是否有上述请求权以及如何行使均应依物之所在地法决定。

四、物之所在地法适用的例外

虽然物之所在地法原则在财产权关系的法律适用上运用得非常广泛,但由于某些物的特殊性或处于某种特殊状态之中,使某些财产权关系适用物之所在地法成为不可能或不合理,因而在各国实践中,这一原则并不是解决一切财产权关系的唯一的冲突原则。归结起来,物之所在地法适用的例外主要有如下几个方面。

1. 运送中物品财产权关系的法律适用

运送中的物品处于经常变换所在地的状态之中,难以确定到底以哪一所在地法来调整有关财产权关系。即使能够确定,把偶然与物品发生联系的国家的法律作为支配该物品命运的准据法,也未必合理。而且,运送中的物品有时处于公海或公空,这些地方不受任何国家的法律管辖,并不存在有关的法律制度。因此,运送中物品的财产权关系不便适用物之所在地法。[①]在实践中,运送中的物品的财产权关系的法律适用问题主要有如下解决办法:

(1) 适用送达地法。如1987年《瑞士联邦国际私法》第101条规定:"运输途中的货物,其财产权的取得与丧失适用货物送达地国家的法律。"土耳其和南斯拉夫的国际私法也作了类似规定。

(2) 适用发送地法。如1964年捷克斯洛伐克《国际私法与国际民事诉讼法》第6条规定:"依照合同运送的货物,其权利之得失,适用该标的物发运地法。"

---

① 参见余先予主编:《冲突法》,上海财经大学出版社1999年版,第185页。

(3) 适用所有人本国法。如 1939 年《泰国国际私法》第 16 条第 2 款规定:"把动产运出国外时,适用起运时其所有人本国法。"在理论上,还有学者主张适用交易时物品实际所在地法或转让合同的准据法。

不过,运送中的物品并不是绝对不适用物之所在地法的。在有些情况下,如运送中物品的所有人的债权人申请扣押了运送中的物品,结果运送暂停止,或运送中的物品因其他原因长期滞留于某地,该物品的买卖和抵押应适用该物品的现实所在地法。

2. 船舶、飞行器等运输工具之财产权关系的法律适用

由于船舶、飞行器等运输工具处于运动之中,难以确定其所在地,加上它们有时处于公海或公空,而这些地方无有关法律存在,因此,有关船舶、飞行器等运输工具的财产权关系适用物之所在地法是不恰当的。

关于船舶的准据法,其性质与动产和不动产有很大区别,若以所在地作为准据法则不适当。因为它经常移动,出入于本国水域、公海和外国水域之间,所在地很不固定,如果适用所在地法,准据法就很不稳定,甚至可能一日数变。当船舶航行于公海时,则根本没有所在地法。因此国际上一般主张,有关船舶、飞行器运输工具的财产权关系适用登记注册地法或者其国旗国法或标志国法。如 1978 年《奥地利联邦国际私法法规》第 33 条第 1 款规定,水上或空中运输工具的财产权依注册国的法律,但铁路车辆依在营业中使用该车辆的铁路企业有其主营业所的国家的法律。

我国《海商法》第 270 条和第 271 条也分别规定:"船舶所有权的取得、转让和消灭,适用船旗国法律。""船舶抵押权适用船旗国法律。船舶在光船租赁以前或者光船租赁期间,设立船舶抵押权的,适用原船舶登记国的法律。"第 272 条还规定:"船舶优先权,适用受理案件的法院所在地法律。"

3. 外国法人终止或解散时有关财产权关系的法律适用

外国法人在自选终止或被其所属国解散时,其财产的清理和清理后的归属问题不应适用物之所地法,而应依其属人法解决。不过,外国法人在内国境内因违反内国的法律而被内国取缔时,该外国法人的财产的处理就不一定适用其属人法了。

4. 与人身有关的财产的法律适用

对于与人身有关的财产的法律适用,美国《第一次冲突法重述》采用了"当事人的住所地法"(**law of the parties domicile**)。

【**法条**】　　　　　law of the parties domicile

The most notable exceptions are the rules dealing with the rights of married persons in each other's property; they refer to the law of the parties domicile.①

第二节 国际财产的法律适用

一、不动产的法律适用

不动产(real property)是不能移动或移动就会损失其经济价值的物,其处所是固定的,其所在地的确定自然十分容易。在国际财产权关系中,不动产适用不动产所在地法,即适用物之所在地法,是最普遍适用的冲突规范。②因此,物之所在地法也成为国际私法上用来解决有关国际不动产关系的法律冲突的一项冲突原则。③在立法上,1804年《法国民法典》第3条第2款规定:"不动产,即使属于外国人所有,仍适用法国法律。"不动产财产权依物之所在地法已成为国际私法上的一项得到普遍承认和争执最少的规则。

二、动产的法律适用

动产(movable property)是可以移动的物,其处所常常带有短暂性和偶然性,不易确定。动产的这种特性给其所在地的确定带来了困难。

(一)动产适用所有权人的属人法

早期的国际私法主张动产财产权适用所有权人或者占有人的属人法(住所地法)来解决。

根据中世纪的"动产随人(*Mobilia personam sequuntur*)"的法谚,学者们主张动产的财产权关系适用其所有人的属人法。理由在于,动产所在地易于变动,难以确定固定的所在地,如果适用物之所在地法会导致动产的权利义务关系欠缺确定性,不利于交易的安全和便利。此外,动产在当时的经济条件下,远不及不动产的重要

---

① See Restatement (First) of the Conflict of laws, (§§259—290).
② 参见董立坤:《国际私法论》,法律出版社1988年版,第268页。
③ See Lea Brilmayer, Jack Goldsmith, *Conflict of Laws*, CITIC Publishing House 2003, p.72.

第八章 国际财产关系的法律适用

性,可以作为属地管辖原则的例外。①基于这种考虑,即便是适用物之所在地法,也是推定动产的所在地为其所有人的住所地,从而援用动产所有人的住所地法。19 世纪欧洲大陆国际私法的立法,均受到区别主义的物之所在地法原则的影响。

动产财产权适用所有权人的属人法(住所地法),也遭到了许多的反对意见(**objections**)。

【说理】　　　　　　　　**objections**

Several obviously objections can be made to that rule. First, the parties to a commercial sale may have different domiciles; whose then should control? Further, much modern business is conducted by corporations, and corporate domicile is often a mere legal technicality. Finally, corporations as well as individuals often conduct business far from their domiciles; a party to a sale of property far from home would not naturally expect the validity of the sale to be governed by the law of his domicile.②

(二) 动产适用物之所在地法

从 19 世纪末叶开始,许多国家逐渐在立法和司法实践中抛弃了"动产随人"原则,转而主张动产适用动产交易时所在地的法律。如著名的 **Cammell v. Sewell** 案,该案的判决即适用动产交易时的动产所在地法(挪威法)。

【案例】　　　　　　　　**Cammell v. Sewell**

Facts: Plaintiffs were the English insurers of a cargo of lumber shipped on a Prussian vessel from a Russian port to England. The ship ran aground in Norwegian waters, and the cargo was unloaded and sold at auction pursuant to the request of the ship's master. The purchaser resold the lumber to defendants, English merchants. The plaintiffs brought suit in Norway against the master and the purchaser, Clausen, seeking to have the auction sale invalidated. But the Diocesan Court confirmed it. Plaintiffs brought this action in England. After the lower court held for the defendants, plaintiffs appealed.

Held: Judgment for defendant affirmed. The court first determined that it need not recognize as conclusive the judgment of the Norwegian Diocesan court. On the choice-of-law question, however, the court held that Norwegian law applied: We think that the law on this subject was correctly stated by the Lord Chief Baron in the course of the argument in the Court below, where he says "if personal property is disposed of in a manner binding according

---

① 李双元:《国际私法(冲突法篇)》,武汉大学出版社 2001 年修订版,第 436 页。
② Herbert Goodrich, *Goodrich on Conflict of Laws*, 2d ed., 1938, pp.404—406.

to the law of the country where it is, that disposition is binding everywhere."... On the evidence before us, we cannot treat Clausen otherwise than as an innocent purchaser, and as the law of Norway appears to us, on the evidence, to give a title to an innocent purchaser, we think that the property vested in him, and in the defendants as sub-purchasers from him, and that, having once so vested, it did not become divested by its being subsequently brought to this country and, therefore, that the judgment of the Court of Exchequer should be affirmed.①

美国《第一次冲突法重述》也采用"动产交易时所在地法"(**law of the location of movable at the time of transaction**)的原则,来处理动产交易的法律适用问题。

【法条】　law of the location of movable at the time of transaction

For nearly all *inter vivos* transactions of movables, the First Restatement prescribes the law of the place where the movable was located at the time of the transaction. Thus, the situs rule applies to conveyances (§§255—258), adverse possession (§259), mortgage (§265), conditional sale (§272), liens and pledges (§279), powers of appointment (§283), and trusts (§294).

但是,也有一些国家的立法不分动产和不动产,凡是财产权关系,一律适用物之所在地法。如日本1898年颁布的《法例》第10条规定:"关于动产及不动产的财产权及其他应登记之权利,依其标的物所在地法。"1982年《土耳其国际私法和国际诉讼程序法》第23条规定:"动产和不动产的所有权以及其他财产权适用物之所在地法律。"可以肯定地说,自本世纪以来,物之所在地法也成为解决有关动产财产权法律冲突的基本冲突原则。②

当今在动产财产权关系的法律适用方面,物之所在地法原则已经取代了传统的属人法原则。

三、我国的财产法律适用制度

(一) 不动产的法律适用

我国《民法通则》第144条规定:"不动产的所有权、适用不动产所在地的法

---

① David H. Vernon, Louis Weinberg, William Reynolds, William Richman, *Conflicts of Law: Case, Materials and Problems*, 2d ed., LexisNexis, 2002, pp.273—274.
② 吕岩峰:《财产权法律适用的历史沿革》,载《中国国际私法与比较法年刊》(第六卷),法律出版社2003年版,第114页。

律。"但 1988 年最高人民法院《关于贯彻执行〈中华人民共和国民法通则〉若干问题的意见(试行)》第 186 条却指出:"……不动产的所有权、买卖、租赁、抵押、使用等民事关系,均应适用不动产所在地法律。"

(二) 动产的法律适用

对动产的法律适用问题,我国《民法通则》及最高人民法院的司法解释均未加明确。最高人民法院《关于贯彻执行〈中华人民共和国民法通则〉若干问题的意见(试行)》只规定,动产的租赁关系应适用出租人营业所在地法。

第三节 国际财产继承的法律适用

一、法定继承的法律适用

(一) 法定继承的法律冲突

法定继承(statutory succession),又称无遗嘱继承,是指按照法律规定的继承人的范围、顺序以及继承人应继承的份额的财产继承。①各国有关法定继承的继承人的范围、继承的顺序、继承的份额以及遗产分配的方法等方面的规定并不相同,因而会产生法律适用上的冲突。比如,有关继承人的范围,有的国家规定得很宽泛。德国规定,被继承人的配偶、子女、孙子女、曾孙子女和玄孙子女等直系卑血亲和父母、祖父母、曾祖父母和高祖父母等直系尊血亲等亲属都有继承权。我国继承法规定,继承人包括被继承人的配偶、子女、父母、兄弟姐妹、祖父母、外祖父母以及其他对被继承人尽了扶养义务的人。又比如,有关配偶对遗产继承的份额,各国规定也不相同。②由于各国的法律规定不同,对于国际法定继承适用不同国家的法律,就会导致不同的处理结果。

随着医学等科学技术的发展,关于可以继承财产的子女范围问题(**Who qualifies as a child**),成为国际私法上的新问题。

---

① 参见徐冬根:《中国国际私法完善研究》,上海社会科学院出版社 1998 年版,第 334 页。
② 参见张仲伯主编:《国际私法学》,中国政法大学出版社 1999 年版,第 401 页。

【问题】　　　　　　　Who qualifies as a child?

A number of issues exist under the broad topic of who qualifies as a child for intestacy purposes (e.g., adopted children, stepchildren, and children born outside of marriage). However, the most recent, that of children born of assisted reproduction, is considered here. In recent years, a demographic trend has emerged allowing children born as a result of assisted-reproductive techniques to inherit under state succession laws. Because of new technological reproductive techniques, such as surrogacy, egg donation, and posthumous conception, a new potential exists in which children may be born from mothers who may or may not be genetically linked to the child and even from parents who have died prior to conception. Although techniques of artificial insemination and issues of posthumous birth have existed for some time, technology has placed a new strain on old laws that allow a child to inherit from a decedent only if he exists at the time of his parent's death or is born within 300 days of death of the father.①

（二）法定继承法律适用制度

1. 单一制

单一制(unitary system)也叫同一制,是指在国际继承中,不管遗产是动产还是不动产,一律适用被继承人的属人法。②同一制反映了继承的身份法性质,使得继承关系的法律适用简便易行,但是法院所作出的判决可能得不到不动产所在国的承认与执行。在采用同一制的国家中,有的国家以被继承人的本国法为属人法,比如意大利、日本、奥地利、德国、西班牙、荷兰、伊朗、巴拿马等;而有的国家以住所地法为被继承人的属人法,比如挪威、丹麦、巴西、秘鲁、尼加拉瓜、危地马拉、冰岛等。1928 年《布斯塔曼特法典》也规定,继承依被继承人的属人法。③

1988 年《死者遗产继承法律适用公约》(Convention on the Law Applicable to Succession to the Estates of Deceased Persons)也采用了同一制,该公约第 3 条(**Article 3**)对此作出了具体的规定。

【法条】　　　　　　　　　Article 3

(1) Succession is governed by the law of the State in which the deceased at the time of his death was habitually resident, if he was then a national of that State.

(2) Succession is also governed by the law of the State in which the deceased at the time

---

① Ronald J. Scalise, Civil Law, Procedure, and Private International Law: New Developments in United States Succession Law, 54 *Am. J. Comp. L.* 103, 108 (2006).
② 参见黄进主编:《国际私法》(第二版),法律出版社 2005 年版,第 367 页。
③ 《布斯塔曼特法典》第 7 条。

of his death was habitually resident if he had been resident there for a period of no less than five years immediately preceding his death. However, in exceptional circumstances, if at the time of his death he was manifestly more closely connected with the State of which he was then a national, the law of that State applies.

(3) In other cases succession is governed by the law of the State of which at the time of his death the deceased was a national, unless at that time the deceased was more closely connected with another State, in which case the law of the latter State applies.

2. 分割制

分割制(scission system)也叫区别制,是指在国际继承中,将遗产区分为动产和不动产,动产适用被继承人属人法,不动产适用不动产所在地法。①区别制反映了继承的财产法性质,有利于案件的审理以及判决的执行,但是,如果被继承人的遗产分处不同的国家,则会造成法律适用上的困难。

采用区别制的国家主要有英国、美国、法国、比利时、智利、泰国、保加利亚、卢森堡以及加蓬等。比如,英国即以被继承人的住所地法(**law of the domicile**)为其属人法。

【规则】   **law of the domicile**

The rule has been established for some two hundred years that movable property in the case of intestacy is to be distributed according to the law of the domicile of the intestate at the time of his death. This law determines the class if person to take, the relative proportions to which the distributes are entitled, the right of representation, the rights of a surviving spouse and all analogous questions.②

(三) 被继承人的住所地法

从上面的分析可知,目前大多数国家有关遗产法定继承的问题,均规定动产适用被继承人死亡时住所地法律。被继承人死亡时住所地有时比较容易识别,有时却难以识别。如在美国西弗吉尼亚法院受理的 **White v. Tennant** 一案,对哪里是被继续人的住所地,认定起来颇费周折。

---

① 参见黄进主编:《国际私法》(第二版),法律出版社2005年版,第367页。
② P. M. North, *Cheshire and North's Private International Law*, 10th ed., London: Butterworths, 1979, pp.598—599.

【案例】 White v. Tennant

The White family owned a mansion-house located in West Virginia, and there Michael White grew up. After marriage he lived with his wife Lucinda for several years on a far on Day's Run, fifteen miles away. He still retained an interest in the family farm, and eventually the White family reached an arrangement in which Michael agreed to move to the Pennsylvania part of the farm and live there. He then sold the Day's Run farm to prepare to move to Pennsylvania.

Having sent some goods on ahead, on the morning of April 2, 1885, he left his old house with his wife and remaining furnishings with the declared intent of making the Pennsylvania house his home that evening. He arrived in Pennsylvania about sundown and unloaded their goods. The house being damp and uncomfortable, and Lucinda complaining of feeling unwell, the couple returned to the mansion-house in West Virginia for the evening. Lucinda was sick with typhoid fever, and unable to leave the house. Although Michael returned to the Pennsylvania house several times to take care of the stock and generally to look after it, he was destined never to liver there-for he, too, was attached with typhoid fever and died shortly thereafter, at the mansion-house in West Virginia. His wife survived.

The question before the court was the domicile of Michael at his death. If he was domicile in West Virginia, Lucinda would receive his whole personal estate; if in Pennsylvania, she would be entitled to only half of the estate.

Snyder J: If it is shown, that a person has entirely abandoned his former domicile in one state with the intention of making his home at a fixed place in another state with no intention of returning to his homer domicile and then establishes a residence in the new place for any period of time, however brief, that will be in law a change of domicile, and the latter will remain his domicile until changed in like manner. The facts in this case conclusively prove, that Michael White, the decedent, abandoned his residence in West Virginia with the intention and purpose not only of not returning to it, but for the expressed purpose of making a fixed place in the State of Pennsylvania his home for an indefinite time. When he left his former home without any intention of returning, and in pursuance of that intention did in fact move with his family and effects to his new home with the intention of his residence for an indefinite time.①

二、遗嘱继承的法律适用

(一) 遗嘱继承的法律冲突

遗嘱(wills)是被继承人生前依法对其遗产或其他事务进行预先处分,并于死后发生法律效力的法律行为。遗嘱继承(testate succession)就是按照被继承人的遗

---

① David H. Vernon, Louis Weinberg, William Reynolds, William Richman, *Conflicts of Law: Case, Materials and Problems*, 2d ed., LexisNexis, 2002, pp.14—15.

嘱而进行的继承,即在不违反法律中某些强制性规定的前提下,被继承人变更法定继承中有关继承人的范围、顺序以及继承份额等规定,而按自己的意思处理其遗产的继承。遗嘱继承优先于法定继承。由于各国关于遗嘱能力、遗嘱方式、遗嘱的解释和遗嘱的撤销等问题实质要件和形式要件的规定不同,因此会产生有关遗嘱继承的法律冲突。

近年来,关于遗嘱有效性问题的发展趋势是朝有利于遗嘱有效的方向发展。只要遗嘱的形式要件在实质上符合法律要求,法院即可以认定遗嘱有效,这就是"实质相符说"(**doctrine of substantial compliance**)。

【解说】　　　　　　　doctrine of substantial compliance

A great degree of liberalization has occurred in the formal requirements for an effective will or testament. The trend is decisively toward enforcement of wills that do not comply with the standard form requirements, if the testator's intent can be safely ascertained and no fraudulent activity is suspected. The approaches adopted by courts and legislatures for non-complying wills include employing the idea of harmless error in wills, granting courts a power to "dispense" with noncompliance, and utilizing the doctrine of substantial compliance. ①

(二) 立遗嘱能力的法律适用

有关立遗嘱人能力的法律适用,不同的国家规定也不相同。有的国家规定适用遗嘱人立遗嘱时的属人法,比如日本规定,遗嘱的成立及效力,依立遗嘱时遗嘱人本国法。②有的国家规定适用遗嘱人死亡时的属人法,比如匈牙利。③还有的国家规定适用遗嘱人立遗嘱时或死亡时的本国法。④

而英国、美国等则采取不动产遗嘱适用不动产所在地法,动产遗嘱适用遗嘱人住所地法(**law of the domicile**)。

【解说】　　　　　　　law of the domicile

The capacity of a testator is determined by the law of his domicile; and there is no dis-

---

① Leigh Shipp, Comment, Equitable Remedies for Nonconforming Wills: New Choices for Probate Courts in the United States, 79 *Tul. L. Rev.* 723 (2005). Similarly, many jurisdictions grant judges the power to dispense with harmless errors in the revocation, alteration, or revival of a will.
② 《日本法例》第 26 条。
③ 《匈牙利国际私法》第 36 条。
④ 《奥地利国际私法》第 30 条。

tinction between lack of capacity due to immaturity or status and incapacity arising from ill health. The meaning of this statement is clear enough if he is domiciled in the dame country at the time both of his making the will and of his death. ①

(三) 遗嘱方式的法律适用

有关遗嘱的方式的法律适用原则,各国规定也不相同。采用单一制的国家认为,无论动产和不动产,遗嘱方式只要符合设立遗嘱人的本国法或立遗嘱地的法律,均视为有效。比如泰国规定,遗嘱方式,依遗嘱人本国法或依遗嘱地法。②一些普通法国家采用不同的态度,在法律适用的连接因素上,它们比较重视住所地作用(**role of domicile**)。

【解说】 **role of domicile**

In the view of the common law, domicile is the only connecting factor that determines that law to govern the formal validity of a will of movables. The formal requirements of the law of the country where the testator is domiciled at the time of his death must be satisfied. His nationality, his domicile tempore testament and the place where he executed his will are inadmissible factors. The disadvantages of so rigid a principle were brought to light by the case of Bremer v. Freeman in 1857, where it was held that the will made in the English form of a British subject who died domiciled in France was invalid, since it neglected the formalities prescribed by French law.③

例如在英国,住所是确定动产遗嘱方式有效性的唯一的一个连接点,比较典型的案例有 **Groos v. Groos** 案。

【案例】 **Groos v. Groos**

A Dutch lady made her will in Holland constituting her husband heir of her movable property except for the "legitimate portion to which her descendents were entitled". She died domiciled in England, leaving her husband five children surviving. By Dutch law the "legiti-

---

① P. M. North, *Cheshire and North's Private International Law*, 10th ed., London: Butterworths, 1979, pp.599—600.

② 《泰国国际私法》第40条。

③ P. M. North, *Cheshire and North's Private International Law*, 10th ed., London: Butterworths, 1979, p.601.

mate portion" of the children was three-fourths of the estate, but by English law it was nothing. It was held that, since the will operated under English law, the whole estate passed to the husband.①

（四）遗嘱撤销的法律适用

有关遗嘱撤销的法律适用规则（**rules relating to revocation**），各国的规定也不相同。

【解说】　　　　　　rules relating to revocation

Since the rules relating to revocation vary from country to country, the problem is to ascertain the law that determines what suffices to revoke an existing will. According to English internal law, a will may be voluntarily revoked either by a fresh will or by its destruction *animo revocandi* effected by the testator himself or by some authorized person in his presence. Further, its automatic revocation may result from the later marriage of the testator.②

有的规定适用撤销时遗嘱人的本国法，比如日本。③ 有的规定适用撤销时遗嘱人的住所地法，比如泰国。④有的则根据撤销遗嘱的不同方式适用不同的法律。这方面比较典型的案例为 **Loustalan v. Loustalan** 案。

【案例】　　　　　　Loustalan v. Loustalan

A spinster, after making a will, married a man domiciled in England and subsequently died domiciled in France. By English internal law a will is revoked by marriage, but this is not so under French law. In order to decide whether the will was revoked it was necessary to decide whether this was a matrimonial question governed by English law or a testamentary question governed by French law. Vaughan-Williams L.J., in the Court of Appeal, held that the question was one of the matrimonial law, English law applied and the will was revoked.⑤

---

① P. M. North, *Cheshire and North's Private International Law*, 10th ed., London: Butterworths, 1979, pp.606—607.
② Ibid., p.611.
③ 《日本法例》第 27 条。
④ 《泰国国际私法》第 42 条。
⑤ P. M. North, *Cheshire and North's Private International Law*, 10th ed., London: Butterworths, 1979, p.613.

(五) 关于遗嘱和继承的《海牙公约》的法律适用规则

海牙国际私法会议制定了三个有关遗嘱的法律适用公约,以统一有关遗嘱和继承的冲突法规则。即 1961 年《遗嘱处分方式法律适用公约》、1973 年《遗产国际管理公约》和 1988 年《死者遗产继承的准据法公约》。其中,最有影响的是 1988 年《死者遗产继承的准据法公约》。公约规定,除了遗嘱的方式、遗嘱人的能力、夫妻财产制以及非依继承方式获得财产权益以外,一切遗产继承的法律适用问题,均适用本公约。该公约确立的遗嘱继承的基本制度为:第一,采用了同一制的遗产继承制度;第二,采用了以惯常居所地为主的连接因素与最密切联系相结合的方法确定准据法;第三,引进意思自治原则,允许被继承人选择适用于继承协议的法律;第四,肯定了转致制度;第五,规定了区际与人际法律制度以及公共秩序保留制度。

三、无人继承财产的法律适用

(一) 无人继承遗产的法律冲突

无人继承遗产(estate by escheat),也叫绝产,是指没有法定继承人也没有遗嘱继承人,或者全部继承人都放弃继承权或都被剥夺继承权的遗产。对于无人继承财产,各国都规定归国家所有,但是,国家以什么名义取得无人继承财产,却有不同的主张。有的国家主张继承权理论,即国家以特殊继承人的资格取得无人继承财产,比如德国、意大利、西班牙等国家。德国规定,继承开始时,被继承人既无血亲,又无配偶,以被继承人死亡时所属邦之国库为法定继承人。被继承人如果不属于任何邦的德国公民,则以德国国库为其法定继承人。[①]有的国家主张先占权理论,即国家以先占权取得无人继承财产。比如英国、美国、法国等。法国规定,一切无主物或无人继承的财产,或继承人放弃继承的财产,均归国家所有。[②]对无人继承的财产采用不同的主张,其处理的结果便不相同。由此,法律冲突的产生不可避免。

(二) 无人继承遗产归属问题的法律适用

对于无人继承财产归属问题的法律适用规则,各国的做法并不相同。有的国家规定适用被继承人的本国法,比如德国;有的国家规定适用财产所在地法,比如奥地利。有的国家适用继承准据法,比如英国。我国对于无人继承的财产,规定:无人继承又无人受遗赠的财产,归国家所有;死者生前是集体所有制组织成员的,归所在集体所有制组织所有。[③] 最高人民法院《关于贯彻执行〈中华人民共和国民

---

① 《德国民法典》第 1936 条。
② 《法国民法典》第 539 条。
③ 《中华人民共和国继承法》第 32 条。

法通则〉若干问题的意见(试行)》第 191 条规定,在我国境内死亡的外国人,遗留在我国境内的财产如果无人继承又无人受遗赠的,依照我国法律处理,两国缔结或参加的国际条约另有规定的除外。

四、我国有关遗产继承法律适用的规定

我国《继承法》规定了法定继承的法律适用原则:遗产的法定继承,动产适用被继承人死亡时住所地法律,不动产适用不动产所在地法律。① 但是,《继承法》对遗嘱继承的法律适用规则未作出规定。

我国自 2011 年 4 月 1 日起施行的《涉外民事关系法律适用法》对继承法律适用作出了新的规定。

对于法定继承,该法第 31 条规定适用被继承人死亡时经常居所地法律,但不动产法定继承,适用不动产所在地法律。

对于遗嘱继承,该法第 32 条规定,符合遗嘱人立遗嘱时或者死亡时经常居所地法律、国籍国法律或者遗嘱行为地法律的,遗嘱均为成立。

对于遗嘱效力,该法第 33 条规定适用遗嘱人立遗嘱时或死亡时经常居所地法律或者国籍国法律。

对于遗产管理等事项,该法第 34 条规定适用遗产所在地法律。

对于无人继承遗产的归属,该法第 35 条规定适用被继承人死亡时遗产所在地法律。

当我国《继承法》第 36 条的规定与我国《涉外民事关系法律适用法》上述有关继承法律适用的规定不一致时,应适用《涉外民事关系法律适用法》的有关规定。

我国《涉外民事关系法律适用法》中法定继承的法律适用仍然采用动产继承法律适用与不动产继承法律适用相区别的做法,但具体法律适用规则是有所差别的。我国《涉外民事关系法律适用法》将"经常居所地"这一概念提到了重要的高度,并作为继承法律适用的重要连接因素;单独列出了不动产法定继承法律适用规范;在强调遗产时,相关的法律适用规则采用"遗产所在地"作为连接因素,如第 34 条和 35 条的规定。

【思考题】

- 什么是物之所在地法?物之所在地法可适用于哪些财产关系?不可适用于哪

---

① 《中华人民共和国继承法》第 36 条、《中华人民共和国民法通则》第 149 条。

些财产关系?
- 什么是区别主义?什么是统一主义?
- 动产法律适用和不动产法律适用有什么不同?
- 你知道法定继承的单一制和分割制有什么区别吗?
- 关于遗嘱和继承的《海牙公约》确立了哪些法律适用规则?
- 简述我国有关财产法律适用和遗产继承法律适用的规定。
- 无人继承财产如何处理?
- 我国《涉外民事关系法律适用法》对继承法律适用作出了哪些新的规定?

【重要术语提示与中英文对照】

中文术语	英文对照
物之所在地法	situs rule, *lex loci rei sitae*
当事人的住所地法	law of the parties domicile
不动产	real property
动产	movable
动产随人	*Mobilia personam sequuntur*
动产所在地法	law of the location of movable
法定继承	statutory succession
死者遗产继承法律适用公约	Convention on the Law Applicable to Succession to the Estates of Deceased Persons
动产	movables
不动产	immovables
单一制、同一制	unitary system
分割制、区别制	scission system
立遗嘱能力	capacity of testator
遗嘱	wills
遗嘱继承	testate succession, testamentary succession
实质相符说	doctrine of substantial compliance
遗嘱撤销的规则	rules relating to revocation
被继承人属人法	the deceased's personal law
无人继承财产	estate by escheat

【推荐阅读文献】

- 李双元、周辉斌、黄锦辉:《趋同之中见差异——论进一步丰富我国国际私法物权法律适用问题的研究内容》,载《中国法学》2002年第1期。

- 吕岩峰:《物权法律适用的历史沿革》,载《中国国际私法与比较法年刊》(第六卷),法律出版社2003年版。
- 屈广清、周后春:《论物权法律适用的分割制》,载《大连海事大学学报(社会科学版)》2004年第1期。
- 鲁世平、孙晓珍:《论物权冲突法的新发展:证券"相关中介机构所在地法"》,载《西北大学学报(哲学社会科学版)》2012年第1期。
- 宋晓:《意思自治与物权冲突法》,载《环球法律评论》2012年第1期。
- Susman, Godfrey & McGowan, Modernizing the Situs Rule for Real Property Conflicts, 65 *Tex. L. Rev.* 587—591 (1987).
- Leigh Shipp, Comment, Equitable Remedies for Nonconforming Wills: New Choices for Probate Courts in the United States, 79 *Tul. L. Rev.* 723 (2005).
- Ronald J. Scalise, Civil Law, Procedure, and Private International Law: New Developments in United States Succession Law, 54 *Am. J. Comp. L.* 103 (2006).
- Frigo (M.), Ethical Rules and Codes of Honor Related to Museum Activities: A Complementary Support to the Private International Law Approach Concerning the Circulation of Cultural Property, 2009 *Int'l J. Cult. Prop.* 49 (2009).
- Lein (E.), Further Step Towards a European Code of Private International Law: The Commission Proposal for a Regulation on Succession, 11 *Ybk Priv. Int'l L.* 107 (2009).
- Sanders (A.), Private Autonomy and Marital Property Agreements, 59 *Int'l & Comp. L. Q.* 571 (2010).
- Frantzen (T.), Party Autonomy in Norwegian International Matrimonial Property Law and Succession Law, 12 *Ybk. Priv. Int'l L.* 483 (2010).
- Philip Shepherd, The Lex Situs Rule and How it Continues to Trap the Unwary, 27 *B. J. I. B. & F. L.* 277 (2012).

【扩展阅读资料】

A Brief History of Lex Situs [1]

American conflicts law was first organized into a general, coherent body by Justice Story in his book *Commentaries on the Conflict of Laws*. Justice Story sought

---

[1] Susman, Godfrey & McGowan, Modernizing the Situs Rule for Real Property Conflicts, 65 *Tex. L. Rev.* 585, 587—591(1987).

to collect the previously "loose and scattered" materials into an organized treatise that stated accepted conflicts laws. In preparing this treatise, he relied on European and Roman law as stated by leading European jurists, and especially on English common law. Justice Story's primary reliance on English precedent coincided with American courts' adoption of English common-law principles for deciding choice-of-law issues, including English principles regarding real property.

In matters involving land, English lawyers and courts simply assumed that English law would govern; thus English cases contain little discussion of the situs rule. This assumption was not surprising as England was not divided into sovereign states and its courts refrained from hearing cases requiring the application of foreign law. The historical distribution of power among English common-law courts, which had exclusive jurisdiction over title to English lands, and the ecclesiastical courts, acting in equity, also affected real property laws in England. The jealous manner in which the common-law courts guarded their jurisdiction over real property made them unwilling to apply any law but their own on questions involving land. In addition, because of the division between the common law and equity, common-law courts did not have available the equitable remedies that might have modified the absolute English rule.

Ignoring the fact that the nature of the United States as a federal nation made English precedent less persuasive, Justice Story relied solely on English cases and opinions to develop his choice-of-law formulae for real property. Like his rules for contracts and torts, Justice Story focused on one territorial contact—in this case, the situs of the land. Justice Story insisted that "the laws of the place, where such property is situate, exclusively govern in respect to the rights of the parties, the modes of transfer, and the solemnities, which should accompany them." American courts had unthinkingly adopted the English rule, and Justice Story's exposition reinforced the rule's position.

The *Restatement (First) of Conflict of Laws* solidified the situs rule's absolute position. Following Professor Beale's mechanical and territorially oriented approach, the *Restatement* referred all questions regarding real property to the law of the situs. As with the earlier English cases, the *Restatement* made little attempt to justify the situs rule. In an era when *Pennoyer v. Neff* held sway and legal thinkers were raised on territorial theories, the situs rule must have seemed self-evident.

Unlike the other lex loci choice-of-law rules, such as those for contracts and torts, the situs rule controls both choice of law and jurisdiction. Even though the contract or tort lex loci rules might mandate application of State X's law, courts in State Y could still hear a case so long as the parties were properly before the court. The fact that the contract had been executed or the injury had occurred in another state was irrelevant for jurisdictional purposes. The territorial contact of real property, however, played an important role not only in deciding which state's law to apply, but also in deciding whether a court could maintain jurisdiction over suits purporting to adjudicate interests in land located in a foreign state. As a jurisdictional rule, the situs rule affected not only a court's initial decision on whether to hear a case, it also dictated the narrow limits for a court's decree. Early United States Supreme Court decisions held that courts having jurisdiction over the parties could determine the legal interests of those persons in extrastate land. The court, however, could not issue decrees that acted directly on the extrastate land itself. Deciding whether a court decree acted directly on the person was not always easy.

With the Supreme Court decisions in *Clarke v. Clarke* and *Fall v. Eastin*, Justice Story's choice-of-law formula became a firmly established rule for jurisdiction, leaving little room for nonsitus court decisions. Consistent with the principle developed in *Pennoyer v. Neff*, jurisdiction was based on physical power. Given the predominance of the power theory of jurisdiction, it is perhaps unremarkable that the Supreme Court held in *Clarke* and *Fall* that a nonsitus court lacked jurisdiction in disputes over extraterritorial land. Obviously, only a situs court could exercise the requisite power over land within its borders, thus *Clarke* and *Fall* relieved a situs court of its obligation to accord full faith and credit to a nonsitus decree. Even if a nonsitus court followed Story's choice-of-law rule and applied the law of the situs, a decree affecting title to extrastate land would still be void for want of jurisdiction. Additionally, except for a minor concession in *Durfee v. Duke* that a sister-state's jurisdictional finding must be recognized, the Supreme Court has never directly altered the position it took in *Clarke* and *Fall*. State courts continue to rely on these two cases in refusing to recognize nonsitus decisions "directly affecting" title to real property.

During the last half century, American conflicts laws and principles of jurisdiction have abandoned this territorial approach for issues other than real property. The *Restatement (Second) of Conflict of Laws* abandoned the *First Restatement*'s lex loci rules for contract and tort choice of law, replacing them with a "most significant relationship" test. *International Shoe Co. v. Washington* and *Shaffer v. Heitner* dispensed with *Pennoyer*'s territorial focus for jurisdiction, with the Supreme Court substituting a nexus requirement and shifting the focus to fairness.

Unfortunately, this reevaluation and reformation has not extended to the situs rule. For real property, the *Second Restatement* maintains that it is still "a firmly established principle that questions involving interests in immovables are governed by the law of the situs." Thus, the rule for real property has remained much the same as Justice Story first stated it in 1834. In addition, because neither *Clarke* nor *Fall* has been overruled, the situs rule continues to restrict jurisdiction.

第九章

国际知识产权的法律适用

第九章　国际知识产权的法律适用

本章导读

※ 知识产权,是人们对于自己的智力活动创造的成果和经营管理活动中的标记,信誉依法享有的权利。

※ 知识产权主要包括下列权利:与文学、艺术及科学作品有关的权利,即版权;与表演艺术家的表演活动,与录音制品及广播有关的权利,即邻接权;与人类创造性活动的一切领域内的发明有关的权利,即专利发明、实用新型及非专利发明享有的权利;与科学发现有关的权利;与工业品外观设计有关的权利;与商品商标、服务商标、商号及其他商业标记有关的权利;与防止不正当竞争有关的权利;一切其他来自工业、科学及文学艺术领域的智力创作活动所产生的权利。

※ 保护知识产权的传统国际公约主要有《保护工业产权巴黎公约》(1883年)、《保护文学和艺术作品伯尔尼公约》(1886年)和《国际商标注册马德里协定》(1891年)。

※ 世界贸易组织的《与贸易有关的知识产权协议》是国际知识产权公约中第一个规定了实体和程序事项的国际公约。该协议规定了受保护的知识产权的内容:版权和邻接权,商标权,地理标志权,工业品外观设计权,专利权,集成电路布图设计,以及未披露过的信息专有权。

※ 各国专利法上对专利保护的严格地域性限制,在冲突法上也可以理解为:专利在登记国的保护适用登记地国家的法律。

※ 商标权法律冲突的解决,各国主张不尽相同,但从发展趋势来看,大多数国家适用权利发生地国法。

※ 对于如何解决著作权的法律冲突,各国法律规定和学者的主张各不相同。有适用被请求保护国法、适用侵权行为发生地国法等,各国国际私法立法在这方面的法律适用原则还不一致。

※ Itar-Tass俄罗斯新闻案是美国关于著作权的法律适用规则的重要案例。审理该案的美国联邦第二巡回法院采取分割方法,法院根据最密切联系原则确定了俄罗斯法律为判断著作权归属关系的准据法,根据侵权行为地法原则确定了美国法律为著作权侵权的准据法。

※ 国际技术转让是指一国的技术转让人将一定的技术越过国境、通过某种方式转让给他国的技术受让人的行为。狭义的国际技术转让仅指商业性的国际技术转让。

【本章主题词】　知识产权、地域性、专利权、商标权、著作权、国际技术转让

第一节　知识产权法律冲突概述

一、知识产权的概念

知识产权（**intellectual property**），是人们对于自己的智力活动创造的成果和经营管理活动中的标记，是人们就其智力创造的成果依法享有的专有权利。①

【释义】　　　　　　　　intellectual property

Intellectual property, often known as IP, allows people to own their creativity and innovation in the same way that they can own physical property. The owner of IP can control and be rewarded for its use, and this encourages further innovation and creativity to the benefit of us all. In some cases IP gives rise to protection for ideas but in other areas there will have to be more elaboration of an idea before protection can arise. It will often not be possible to protect IP and gain IP rights (or IPRs) unless they have been applied for and granted, but some IP protection such as copyright arises automatically, without any registration, as soon as there is a record in some form of what has been created.

具体地讲，知识产权主要包括下列的一些权利：与文学、艺术及科学作品有关的权利，即版权；与表演艺术家的表演活动，与录音制品及广播有关的权利，即邻接权；与人类创造性活动的一切领域内的发明有关的权利，即专利发明、实用新型及非专利发明享有的权利；与科学发现有关的权利；与工业品外观设计有关的权利；与商品商标、服务商标、商号及其他商业标记有关的权利；与防止不正当竞争有关的权利；一切其他来自于工业、科学及文学艺术领域的智力创作活动所产生的权利。②

---

① 吴汉东主编：《知识产权法》，中国政法大学出版社1999年版，第1页。
② 《建立世界知识产权组织公约》第2条第8款，转引自郑成思：《知识产权法》，法律出版社1997年版，第4页。

二、知识产权的地域性

（一）知识产权的地域性表现

知识产权作为一种无形的财产权利，其一个重要的特点就是地域性（territoriality）。所谓知识产权地域性，是指根据一国法律产生的知识产权只在该国范围内有效，在其他国家将得不到承认。从另一个角度讲，一国只保护根据本国法律产生的知识产权，而不保护依他国法律产生的知识产权。① 建立在地域性之上的传统规则（**traditional rules**）是知识产权不涉及法律冲突问题。

【释义】　　　　　　　　　traditional rules

Generally speaking, the territoriality of intellectual property rights precludes the conflict of law issues to arise at all, if not the conflicts of interests and policies. This rule applies to the existence of the rights and the defenses, as well as injunctive relief and other remedies.②

Historically, enforcement of patent rights was limited to infringement activity occurring solely within the borders of the United States. Brown v. Duchesne③ stated the patent rights Congress grants are domestic in character and confined to the boundaries of the United States; Dowagiac Mfg. Co. v. Minnesota Moline plow Co., et al.,④ stated patent rights are confined to the United States and its territories and such rights do not extend to acts occurring wholly outside the U.S.⑤

知识产权仅仅依照一定国家的法律产生，只能在其依法产生的地域内有效。⑥一国赋予的知识产权没有域外效力，其他国家对该种权利并无保护的义务。由于各国均对发生在本国境内的知识产权的占有、利用和处分关系独立行使属地立法管辖权。知识产权的国内法保护及其严格的地域性特点，一直继续到19世纪末叶。

---

① 冯术杰、于延晓：《知识产权地域性成因以及发展》，载《法学》2006年第6期。
② Francois Dessemontet, A European Point of View on the ALI Principles-Intellectual Property: Principles Governing Jurisdiction, Choice of Law, and Judgments in Transnational Disputes, 30 Brook. J. Int'l L. 849, 860—863 (2005).
③ 60 U.S. 183, 195 (1856).
④ 235 U.S. 641, 650 (1915).
⑤ Katherine E. White, The Recent Expansion of Extraterritoriality in Patent Infringement Cases, 2007 UCLA J.L. & Tech. 1, 1(2007).
⑥ 在知识产权一体化进程很快的欧洲和非洲法语国家，知识产权在一定程度上已经得到了在该地域内的跨国统一程度的保护。

(二) 知识产权严格地域性的突破

20世纪以后,知识产权严格地域性的国内法保护已满足不了权利人的利益需要,突破对知识产权保护的地域性(**expansion of the territoriality**)限制和各国立法规定不同所带来的障碍,已成为大势所趋。①

【释义】   expansion of the territoriality

  The American Law Institute (ALI) Principles have been premised up to now on the impacted market test, but this may change in the future. There are, however, two areas where the territoriality principle is of no relevance.

  The first area in which the principle of territoriality is not useful involves rights which are not registered because it is too difficult for the right to be ascribed a definite location. Examples of IP rights which often suffer from this problem include: unregistered copyrights, trade secrets, right of publicity, rights or factual situations protected under unfair competition law, and protection of unregistered designs. It might be argued that these areas may still be subject to territoriality, in the sense that claims under those rights will be subject to the law of the country for which protection is sought. From a European viewpoint, although the national traditions may differ in practice, the principle of the country of origin (Cassis de Dijon Principle) might be found applicable.

  The second arena where territoriality has no relevance involves those IP rights in which ownership is better regulated in a centralized manner. Most recent endeavours to determine who is entitled to claim ownership of a copyright or a patent lead to the application of the law of origin of the work (recent Greek law) or the law of the employee relationship. For example, under the Munich Convention on Patents, in employee-employer cases, the law to apply is the law of the place where the employee is mainly employed, or, if it cannot be determined, the law to be applied shall be that of the State in which the employer has its place of business to which the employee is attached. It is along those lines that IP ownership is regulated in the ALI Principles. However, a much-disputed provision on transferability of IP rights refers back to territoriality. In Europe, we think it is a setback to fragment the entitlement to a given IP right under several municipal laws, which is the basis for valid assignments or licenses throughout the world.②

这种地域性以及各国对于知识产权保护的立法差异,使知识产权发生法律冲突成为必然。

---

 ① 参见余先予主编:《冲突法》,法律出版社1989年版,第285页。
 ② Francois Dessemontet, A European Point of View on the ALI Principles-Intellectual Property: Principles Governing Jurisdiction, Choice of Law, and Judgments in Transnational Disputes, 30 *Brook. J. Int'l L.* 849, 861—863 (2005).

我国多数学者认为,知识产权法律冲突的产生与否取决于它的地域性特征。当知识产权的地域性被突破的时候,知识产权法律冲突便会随之产生。而地域性被突破的范围和程度,也就是知识产权法律冲突存在的范围和程度。① 但是,也有学者对这种观点持反对意见,认为知识产权的地域性不是知识产权法律冲突产生的障碍,国际知识产权关系的产生决定了知识产权法律冲突的存在。② 我们认为,国际知识产权关系是建立在地域性基础之上的,权利人在行使权利时所处的不同状态和其所在的法域紧密联系,若没有各国在知识产权立法上的差异也就不存在冲突一说。

(三) 知识产权的法律冲突

知识产权法律冲突产生应具备两个基本条件:一是各国有关知识产权的法律在保护范围、保护期限以及权力取得方式等问题上各不相同;二是内国承认外国法的域外效力。当更多的国家在签订有关保护知识产权的国际公约后,缔约国之间相互承认对方国家知识产权的域外效力时,便使得知识产权的法律冲突从可能性化为现实性。

三、知识产权法律冲突的调整方法

目前,调整涉外知识产权法律关系,在国际法领域,主要有直接调整和间接调整两种方法:

(一) 直接调整——国际统一实体法

直接调整法律冲突的方法是指有关国家间通过双边或者多边国际条约的方式,制定统一的实体法,用以直接支配国际民商事关系当事人权利义务关系的一种方法。

关于知识产权的国际统一实体法适用有如下特点:第一,调整知识产权法律冲突的统一实体法直接规范有关知识产权的实体性问题,例如商标权中关于商标注册标准或商标分类及优先权的规定;第二,这种统一实体法规范以知识产权权利人、义务人为直接规范对象。这也是由于统一实体法主要是调整平等主体间民事法律关系的;第三,统一实体法的适用不需经过冲突法的指引。

知识产权产生于西方国家,两个调整知识产权法律冲突的基本公约(**two basic conventions**)也首先在西方发达国家之间缔结。

---

① 朱榄叶、刘晓红主编:《知识产权法律冲突与解决问题研究》,法律出版社 2004 年版,第 105 页。
② 参见徐祥:《论知识产权的法律冲突》,载《法学评论》2005 年第 6 期。

【释义】 **two basic conventions**

As is well known, intellectual property developed in England, France, the United States, Germany, and Russia in the nineteenth century. Those nations were, however, in commerce with each other resulting in numerous bilateral treaties on copyright or trademarks. As the number of nations involved in global commerce and trade increased in the second half of that century, two basic conventions were concluded, the Paris Convention (1883) and the Berne Convention (1886), after which there was no longer the need to have the national status of an author follow his works to another country. Instead, it sufficed that the author's and the recipient's countries acceded to the Berne Convention and, therefore, the minimal protection applied to this author, as well as the guarantee of non-discrimination or "national treatment." The multilateral treaties were widely considered a great advancement over the bilateral arrangements.①

（二）间接调整——冲突法的适用

间接调整法律冲突的方法是指通过冲突规范指出应当适用某个国家的法律来调整该国际民商事关系当事人间的权利义务的一种方法。②

间接调整的方法是解决法律冲突的传统方法，与直接调整的方法相比较，存在一定程度的复杂性和结果的不可预见性。③由于不能直接规范当事人的权利义务，给当事人预见法律行为的后果带来了一定的困难。

四、我国有关知识产权法律适用的规定

我国自 2011 年 4 月 1 日起施行的《涉外民事关系法律适用法》对知识产权法律冲突的法律适用规范，作出了规定。

该法第 48 条规定："知识产权的归属和内容，适用被请求保护地法律。"这里的"被请求保护地"有学者认为应将其理解为"被请求保护的权利地"。这一理解的理由在于：第一，基于知识产权地域性和独立保护原则，权利人所获得的知识产权是以地域为界的一项权利，各国分别依据各自的法律对知识产权客体赋予权利并提供保护。即使针对同一客体，权利人在各国所获得的仍然是各不相同且各自独立的权利。第二，正确理解"被请求保护地"的含义，需要回归它的语源。"被请

---

① Francois Dessemontet, A European Point of View on the ALI Principles-Intellectual Property: Principles Governing Jurisdiction, Choice of Law, and Judgments in Transnational Disputes, 30 *Brook. J. Int'l L.* 849, 851 (2005).

② 李双元：《国际私法学》，北京大学出版社 2000 年版，第 8 页。

③ 宁敏、宋连斌：《涉外知识产权法律冲突的产生及其特点》，载《法律科学》1991 年第 3 期。

求保护地"一词来源于《伯尔尼公约》第5条第(2)款中的"the laws of the country where protection is claimed"。"the country where protection is claimed"这一短语含义较为模糊,既可能是指提起保护请求的国家(例如法院地),也可能是指被请求给予保护的国家(例如侵权行为地、权利登记地或者注册地)。对此,国际上占有主导地位的观点是将其理解为"country for which protection is claimed"(被请求提供保护的国家),而不是提起保护请求的国家。[①] 我们同意这样的观点和看法。"被请求保护地"不能简单地等同于法院地,也不能简单地将其理解为提起请求的保护地。

对于知识产权转让和许可,我国基本上将其纳入合同法律适用范畴,并采纳了合同法律适用的一般原则和规则。该法第49条规定:当事人可以协议选择知识产权转让和许可使用适用的法律。当事人没有选择的,适用本法对合同的有关规定。

对于知识产权的侵权责任,该法第50条规定适用被请求保护地法律,当事人也可以在侵权行为发生后协议选择适用法院地法律。

第二节 专利权的法律适用

一、专利权的法律冲突

专利(**patents**)是专利权的简称。

【释义】　　　　　　　　　　　patents

Patents grant an inventor the right to exclude others from producing or using the inventor's discovery or invention for a limited period of time.

专利是指一项发明创造,即发明、实用新型和外观设计向国家知识产权局提出专利申请,经依法审查合格后,向专利申请人授予的在规定的时间内对该发明创造享有的专有权。

---

① 吴文灵、朱理:《涉外知识产权关系的法律适用——以涉外民事关系法律适用法第七章为中心》,载《人民司法》2012年第9期。

专利权的法律冲突,是指涉及两个或两个以上不同法域的专利法对专利法律关系的规定各不相同,却又竞相适用于该专利法律关系,从而造成的该专利法律关系在法律适用上冲突的现象。

二、专利法律适用的原则

(一) 国内法的适用

各国专利法对专利保护的严格地域性限制(strict application of the doctrine of territoriality in patent infringement cases),在冲突法上也可以理解为:专利在登记国的保护仅适用登记地国家的法律。既然专利权离开了登记国就失去保护,那么适用登记地国家的法律才能使它获得保护就成了逻辑上的必然结论。如美国早期所受理的 <u>Brown v. Duchesne</u> 案件,法院强调专利保护的严格属地性原则。

【案例】　　　　　　　　　Brown v. Duchesne①

In *Brown*, the patented invention was an improvement in constructing gaff in sailing vessels. The patentee alleged that the defendant used the patented invention in Boston, violating the patentee's rights. The defendant was the captain of a French schooner that was built, owned, and manned by French subjects and docked in Boston Harbor. While in France, the vessel was equipped with the patented invention, which had been "in common use in French merchant vessels for more than twenty years...."

The patentee did not argue that it was infringement for the foreign vessel to be fitted with the patented invention in France, a foreign port. The issue patentee wanted resolved was whether the vessel could use the patented invention "within the jurisdiction of the United States, while she is temporarily there for purposes of commerce, without the consent of the patentee?

The Court recognized that the Patent Clause, which grants Congress the power to "promote the Progress of Science and the useful Arts," is domestic in its character and is "necessarily confined within the limits of the United States." Consequently, the Court found the Patent Clause does not grant Congress the power to regulate a foreign country's commerce or vessel of commerce, where such vessel occasionally visits ports of the United States in pursuit of commercial aims.

The Court interpreted the patent statutes as merely granting patentees means of compensation from those who trespass upon their inventions within the United States. Such patent rights, limited by the boundaries of the United States, "cannot extend beyond the limits to which the law itself is confined." Any use of the patented invention outside the United States was not an infringement of those rights. Concentrating on the patentee's rights, the Court not-

---

① 60 U. S. 183 (1856).

ed that the patentee sustained no damage from the defendant's use and the defendant derived no material benefit from "a single voyage to the United States... in the ordinary pursuits of commerce."

Finally, the Court stated that the patent laws should be "construed in the spirit in which they were made... [and not go] far beyond the object they intended to accomplish." The Court concluded that a foreign vessel, lawfully entering a port of the United States, equipped with patentee's invention, did not infringe the patent if such invention was installed legally in the foreign vessel's home port, authorized by the laws of such country.

In order to find infringement in *Brown*, the Court suggested the patented invention would need to have been manufactured while at the United States port, or have been sold in the United States port. Such activities would have affected the patentee's sales in the United States, thus interfering with the patentee's rights. Since the plaintiff sustained no such damage and defendant received no such advantage, there should be no compensation.

Brown represents a very strict view of territoriality, as the Court would not grant damages for activity that occurred beyond the territorial boundaries of the United States.①

本案中,美国专利人发明的帆船上的一个铁钩专利技术,在法国制造的帆船上得到使用。后来,被告的帆船因为商业运输而进入美国。原告在美国起诉被告侵犯其专利权。但是,受理该案的美国法院认为,本案所适用的美国专利法具有严格的属地性。被告在美国之外使用美国专利,不构成对美国专利的侵权。使用了美国专利技术的法国帆船来美国经商,不能以此判定其侵犯美国专利。只有当外国人在美国境内生产该专利产品或者销售该专利产品,专利权人才能获得赔偿。

Brown v. Duchesne案确立了专利保护的严格地域性原则,专利在登记国的保护仅适用登记地国家的法律的法律适用原则。

有些国家的国际私法已明确规定了解决专利权法律冲突的双边冲突规范。如1979年《匈牙利国际私法法规》将知识产权法律适用列为一个专章,其中关于专利权的规定如下:"对发明者或其利益继承人的保护,适用专利证发出国或专利申请地国法。"

至于有关专利的实体法,值得一提的是美国的专利法(**U. S. patent laws**)。

【释义】 U. S. patent laws

U.S. patent laws were enacted by Congress under its Constitutional grant of authority to protect the discoveries of inventors. The main body of law concerning patents is found in Title

---

① Katherine E. White, The Recent Expansion of Extraterritoriality in Patent Infringement Cases, 2007 *UCLA J. L. & Tech.* 1, pp. 8—12 (2007).

35 of the United States Code. In order to be patented an invention must be novel, useful, and not of an obvious nature. Such "utility" patents are issued for four general types of inventions/discoveries: machines, human made products, compositions of matter, and processing methods. Changing technology has led to an ever expanding understanding of what constitutes a human made product. Specific additions to the Patent Act provide, in addition, for design and plant patents. Prior to a recent amendment prompted by the Agreement on Trade-Related Aspects of Intellectual Property (TRIPS) accompanying the Uruguay Round GATT, patents were normally issued for a non-renewable period of seventeen years, measured from the date of issuance. Under the amended provision (which took effect June 8, 1995) the term will be twenty years measured from the date of application. Patent infringement cases arise under Federal patent law over which the Federal courts have exclusive jurisdiction. The Federal agency charged with administering patent laws is the Patent and Trademark Office. Its regulations, pertaining to Patents, are found in Parts 2—6 of Title 37 of the Code of Federal Regulations. Each patent application for an alleged new invention is reviewed by a examiner to determine if it is entitled to a patent. While historically a model was required as part of a patent application, in most cases today, only a detailed specification is necessary. If an application is rejected, the decision may be appealed to the Patents Office's Board of Appeals, with further or alternative review available from the United States Court of Appeals for the Federal Circuit, or in the United States District Court for the District of Columbia. In 1975 the Patent Cooperation Treaty was incorporated into Title 35.

当外国专利权人到东道国申请专利时,东道国可以直接适用自己的国内法来调整由外国当事人参加的专利关系。

我国《专利法》对专利的国际保护制度作出了明确规定。我国专利法规定的有关涉外专利方面的主要制度是：

(1) 在中国没有经常居所或营业所的外国人、外国企业或者外国其他组织在中国申请专利的,依照其所属国同中国签订的协议或者共同参加的国际条约,或者依照互惠原则,根据中国专利法办理。外国人的一切专利事务应当委托中华人民共和国国务院指定的专利代理机构办理。

(2) 中国单位或者个人将其在国内完成的发明创造向外国申请专利的,应当首先向中国专利局申请专利,并经国务院有关主管部门同意后,委托国务院指定的专利代理机构办理。

(3) 中国境内的外资企业、中外合资企业的工作人员的发明创造,分职务发明和非职务发明。职务发明创造的专利申请权属于企业,非职务发明创造的专利申请权属于发明人或设计人。申请被批准后,专利权归申请的企业或者个人所有。

(4) 外国人申请专利,依条约或互惠原则享受优先权。

可见我国的专利法同世界各国专利法一样,为外国人在中国申请专利和中国人去外国申请专利创造了条件,当事人的涉外专利关系可以直接受我国专利法的保护。

(二) 国际条约的适用

专利权的国际保护除适用国内法的规定外,主要是适用国际条约,其中多边条约更具有重要作用。用国际条约统一专利国际保护的条件,避免了法律冲突,使专利的国际保护简便易行,应该说是一个好方法。所以专利国际保护公约的参加国家比较多,适用范围较为广泛。目前国际上调整专利及其国际保护的国际公约主要有:

1. 调整专利法律关系的基本公约——《保护工业产权巴黎公约》

1883 年签订的《保护工业产权巴黎公约》(Paris Convention for the Protection of Industrial Property)(以下简称《巴黎公约》),属开放性的多边国际公约,对所有参加国的效力都是无期限的。《巴黎公约》是专利法律关系方面最常适用,影响最大,成员国最多的国际公约,最新修订文本是 1979 年文本,目前有 184 个成员国。①

《巴黎公约》的基本目的是保证一个成员国的专利权在所有其他成员国得到保护。但由于各成员国的利益矛盾和立法差别,《巴黎公约》没有制定统一的专利法,而是以各成员国国内立法为基础进行保护。《巴黎公约》在尊重各成员国的国内立法的同时,规定了各成员国必须共同遵守的几个基本原则,如国民待遇原则、优先权原则、强制许可原则、专利独立原则等,以协调各成员国的专利立法。

2. 调整专利法律关系的专门公约——《专利合作条约》

《专利合作条约》(Patent Cooperation Treaty,PCT),由美国、英国、法国、日本、联邦德国等 25 个国家于 1970 年签订于华盛顿。条约已于 1978 年 1 月生效,最新修订文本是 2002 年文本。条约完全属程序性的,其中心内容是统一成员国的专利申请、检索和审查等制度和程序。根据条约规定,一项发明通过一次国际申请,便可以在国际机构初步审查之后同时转给申请人指定的几个缔约国去获得批准,这就减少和避免了专利申请人及各国专利审查机关的重复劳动,简化了专利申请程序,为加快国际科学技术情报的交流,为专利保护的国际化创造了条件。

3.《与贸易有关的知识产权协议》

世界贸易组织(World Trade Organization,WTO)的《与贸易有关的知识产权协议》(Agreement on Trade-Related Aspects of Intellectual Property, TRIPS)是国际知识产权公约中第一个规定了实体和程序事项的国际公约。该协议首先规定了保护的知识产权的内容,他们包括专利权、商标权、版权和邻接权、地理标志权、工业品外观设计计权、集成电路布图设计、未披露过的信息专有权等。

---

① See website of The World Intellectual Property Organization (WIPO), http://www.wipo.int/members/en/.

《与贸易有关的知识产权协议》强化专利保护的要求主要体现在协议的第27、28、31、32、33、34、25、61条等诸条中。《与贸易有关的知识产权协议》的主要内容包括:第一,协议扩大了可授予专利的主题范围。第二,延长了专利保护期限,保护期限(发明专利)应为自申请日起20年。第三,扩大了专利权的权能。第四,对政府强制许可规定了苛刻的条件。第五,确定了对专利授权、无效、撤销等政府行政行为的司法审查制度。第六,就方法专利侵权问题确立了举证责任倒置制度,加强了专利权人在司法审判中的地位。第七,确立了以刑事手段保护专利及其他知识产权的原则。

三、发达国家对专利法律冲突的处理实践

英美等国家的法院主要是通过最低限度联系(minimum contacts)原则和连带原则来挖掘在外国未经许可实施内国专利权的行为与内国的联系的。

所谓"最低限度联系"原则是指只要在外国发生的"侵犯"内国专利权的行为和美国存在某种"联系",美国法院就可以以此联系为据管辖该案。美国联邦巡回法院所受理的 **AT&T v. Microsoft Corp.** 案就是这方面的典型案例。

【案例】　　　　　　　　　　AT&T v. Microsoft Corp. ①

In the course of its foreign software distribution, Microsoft creates master versions of its software in the United States that are then distributed overseas for foreign replication and distribution. These master versions begin as source code, the language humans use to write software. The source code is then compiled into object code, making the product ready to be lasered onto a "golden master" disk or to be transmitted electronically. Microsoft sends these golden master disks and the object code contained therein to foreign computer manufacturers. These foreign manufacturers then replicate the object code contained on the master disks. The foreign-replicated copies are then used to install the software on computers for sale overseas. Thus, foreign manufacturers do not use the single disk Microsoft exports overseas to install Microsoft's software on computers overseas; instead, the manufacturers use the foreign-replicated copies of this disk to install the software. Microsoft's only exports in this process are its master disks and electronically transmitted copies of its software.

Microsoft acknowledges that it intends for the master disks and electronically transmitted copies of its software to be used to install software on computers manufactured and sold overseas. Microsoft also concedes that the exportation of the object code in question is an essential step in the process of foreign manufacture of computers running the Windows operating system.

---

① AT&T v. Microsoft, 414 F.3d 1366.

In 2001, AT&T filed a patent infringement action against Microsoft in the Southern district of New York alleging that Microsoft's Windows operating system employs AT&T's patented speech codecs. AT&T's claims included an allegation that the foreign installation of Microsoft's Windows software triggered §271(f) liability because Microsoft "supplied" the patented speech component to foreign computer manufacturers when it provided the Windows master disks and electronically transmitted copies of Windows to the manufacturers. Microsoft moved for partial summary judgment on AT&T's §271(f) claim arguing that 1) the exported object code is not a "component" as used in §271(f), and 2) the copies of the exported object code are not "supplied from" the United States.[①]

The Federal Circuit, in AT&T v. Microsoft Corp., held that copying in a foreign country of software made in the United States infringed United States patents under United States law. Such a holding "provides extraterritorial expansion to U.S. law by punishing under U.S. law 'copying' that occurs abroad." This decision holds a defendant liable for activity occurring entirely outside of the United States. Perhaps, this case reflects aspects unique to the technological nature of software.

In AT&T, the court looked to the nature of software inventions as an excuse to treat them differently from inventions involving other technological arts. Despite difficulties in separating computer software from its existence as an arrangement of algorithms.[②]

AT&T案开创了突破地域性的先例。此前,美国法院一致遵循专利地域性原则,并严格受地域性限制。

所谓"连带"原则是指如果在外国发生的"侵犯"内国专利权的行为与内国管辖的案件具有连带或者代理上的关系,则内国法院可以依据这种关系对在外国实施的行为进行管辖。[③]**Unilever Plc. v. Gillette(U. K.) Ltd.**案就是一个根据连带原则处理专利法律冲突的著名案例。

【案例】　　　　　　**Unilever Plc. v. Gillette(U. K.) Ltd.**

吉列(Gillette)消费品跨国公司的美国母公司发明了一种除臭剂配方。英国吉列公司根据美国母公司向其提供的程式将新配方应用到了一种新的除臭剂产品中。这种除臭剂产品由英国吉列公司在英国境内出售。英国原告Unilever公司指控该产品侵犯了

---

① Hasan Rashid, AT&T Corp. V. Microsoft Corp. in the Supreme Court, 13 *B. U. J. Sci. & Tech. L.* 281, 282—283 (2007).

② Katherine E. White, The Recent Expansion of Extraterritoriality in Patent Infringement Cases, 2007 *UCLA J. L. & Tech.* 1, 1 (2007).

③ 参见朱榄叶、刘晓红主编:《知识产权法律冲突与解决问题研究》,法律出版社2004年版,第58—59页。

该公司的专利权并试图增加美国吉列公司为被告,以查明只有在美国才能查明的事实。由于英国吉列公司提供的证据表明该公司是自行决定使用新配方进行生产并将产品投入市场的,其行为与美国母公司无关,因此,英国高等法院拒绝向美国吉列公司签发传票,但英国上诉法院否决了这一判决并查明了美国吉列公司与英国吉列公司"协同行为"或"行为一致"的事实。这些事实包括:产品的唯一性;销售必然构成侵权这一事实;美国吉列公司了解 Unilever 的专利;美国吉列公司和英国吉列公司的母子附属关系;英国吉列公司向其美国母公司就应用该配方制成可销售的产品进行咨询的技术秘密协议;世界范围内美国吉列公司因医学原因有权否决其任何海外子公司拥有任何新产品的权利,以及来自美国波士顿对其子公司新产品的合法的出港证等。据此,上诉法院认为可以追加美国吉列公司为当事人并对其行使管辖权。[1]

本案中,美国吉列公司并没有直接在英国境内实施侵犯原告所拥有的英国专利权的活动,因此根据地域性管辖原则,英国法院无权对其行使管辖权。但英国上诉法院通过查明的一系列事实,挖掘出了美国吉列公司与英国吉列公司在英国实施的侵犯原告英国专利权的行为之间的连带关系,从而认定美国吉列公司事实上也以默示的方式参与了这起侵权活动,并实现了对美国吉列公司的管辖。

各国虽然对在外国未经许可实施内国专利权的行为进行了管辖,并认定该行为侵犯了内国的专利权,构成了侵权,但是地域性管辖原则并没有被突破。这是因为,各国行使管辖权的依据并非是内国的专利权在外国也具有法律效力,因此在外国未经许可实施该专利权的行为构成侵权,而是看似是在外国实施的行为实际上与内国发生了某种联系。[2]

第三节 商标权的法律适用

一、商标权及其法律冲突

传统意义上的商标(**trademarks**),作为商品的标记,是工商企业用来标明其商

---

[1] 参见罗艺方:《跨国知识产权侵权管辖原则的新发展对传统地域管辖原则的突破》,载《政法学刊》2003 年第 3 期。

[2] 参见吕岩峰:《知识产权之冲突法评论》,载《法制与社会发展》1996 年第 6 期。

第九章 国际知识产权的法律适用

品,并使该商品与他人制造或销售的商品有所区别的文字、名称、记号、图案或把上述各种因素结合起来的一种标志。

【释义】 trademarks

Trademarks are generally distinctive symbols, pictures, or words that sellers affix to distinguish and identify the origin of their products. Trademark status may also be granted to distinctive and unique packaging, color combinations, building designs, product styles, and overall presentations. It is also possible to receive trademark status for identification that is not on its face distinct or unique but which has developed a secondary meaning over time that identifies it with the product or seller. The owner of a trademark has exclusive right to use it on the product it was intended to identify and often on related products. Service-marks receive the same legal protection as trademarks but are meant to distinguish services rather than products.①

商标权又称商标专用权,是指商标所有人在法律规定的有效期限内,对其经商标主管机关核准注册的商标所享有的独占地、排他地使用和处分的权利。商标权是一种独占权,具有排他性,只有商标所有人才能使用,或转让给别人使用或出售给别人。任何人不得申请注册与受到法律保护的注册商标相同或类似的商标。假冒他人已经注册的商标便构成侵权行为,要承担法律责任。

在知识产权数字化的今天,随着商标新来源的增加(**new indicators of source**),商标权的外延又有了进一步的扩展。

【释义】 new indicators of source

Trademark rights accrue as the mark is used in commerce and consumers identify the mark with a certain source of goods or services. In the context of electronic commerce, such visual or audible signals will continue to serve as indicators of source, much as they have in physical commerce. Additionally, some new indicators of source, such as digital signatures or other cryptographic fingerprints, may begin to serve in the capacity of at least some trademark functions.②

---

① See website of Cornell University, Law school, http://topics.law.cornell.edu/wex/Trademark, visited on 1st August 2008.
② Dan L. Burk, Trademark Doctrines for Global Electronic Commerce, 49 *S. C. L. Rev.* 695, 699 (1998).

随着商品经济国际化的迅猛拓展,成功的商标品牌将成为一国民族经济振兴的标识之一。①因此,商标权也日益成为知识产权家族中重要的一员。各国商标权的保护制度存在着法律冲突,因此必须通过法律的方式解决这些法律冲突。

二、国内法的适用

商标权法律冲突的解决,各国主张不尽相同。商标权法律冲突的解决依权利发生地国法、使用行为地国法、侵权行为地国法、权利人的属人法的主张都有。但从发展趋势来看,大多数国家适用权利发生地国法。

国内实体法的适用方面,各国国内立法对于外国人在各该国注册商标都予以法律保护,外国商标注册申请人可以适用申请国的法律来调整商标注册关系,以维护其合法权益。各国商标法一般都规定赋予外国人(主要指外国企业)在商标权方面以国民待遇。

值得一提的是美国的商标保护制度(**protection of trademarks in the United States**)。

【释义】　　Protection of trademarks in the United States

Trademarks may be protected by both Federal statute under the Lanham Act, and states' statutory and/or common laws. Congress enacted the Lanham Act under its Constitutional grant of authority to regulate interstate and foreign commerce. A trademark registered under the Lanham Act has nationwide protection. Under the Lanham Act, a seller applies to register a trademark with the Patent and Trademark Office. The mark can already be in use or be one that will be used in the future. The Office's regulations pertaining to trademarks are found in Parts 1—7 of Title 37 of the Code of Federal Regulations. If the trademark is initially, approved by an examiner, it is published in the Official Gazette of the Trademark Office to notify other parties of the pending approval so that it may be opposed. An appeals process is available for rejected applications. Under state common law, trademarks are protected as part of the law of unfair competition. Registration is not required. See Unfair Competition. States' statutory provisions on trademarks differ but most have adopted a version of the Model Trademark Bill (MTB) or the Uniform Deceptive Trade Practices Act (UDTPA). The MTB provides for registration of trademarks while the UDTPA does not. Further protection of trademarks is provided by the Tariff Act of 1930.

各国商标法都规定,住所或营业所在国外的外国人申请商标注册,必须委托国

---

① 王雷:《个案中对域外注册商标能否保护的法理研究》,载《政法论坛》2006年第2期。

内代理人办理。

为了使我国的商标注册规定与国际商标注册立法和实践的发展趋势相一致,我国《商标法》第 17 条规定:外国人或者外国企业在中国申请商标注册的,应当按其所属国和中国签订的协议或者共同参加的国际条约办理,或者按对等原则办理。第 18 条规定:外国人或者外国企业在中国申请商标注册和办理其他事宜的,应当委托国家指定的组织办理。外国商标申请人只要按照我国商标法及其实施细则的有关规定,委托我国国家指定的组织向商标主管部门申请商标注册,经审查核准后,即可获得我国法律的保护。这样外国商标注册申请人就可以直接依靠我国的国内立法来确定商标法律关系。

三、国际条约的适用

为了便于一国的商标在国外取得法律上的有效保护,国际社会从 19 世纪末期起先后签订了一系列有关保护商标权的国际公约。

(一)《巴黎公约》

《巴黎公约》除保护专利权外也保护商标权,但这方面的内容比较简单,需要订立专门协定来补充。

(二)《商标国际注册马德里协定》

《商标国际注册马德里协定》(Madrid Agreement concerning the International Registration of Marks)于 1891 年签订于西班牙的马德里。协定经过六次修改,现在使用的是斯德哥尔摩修订文本。缔结《马德里协定》的目的是为了简化商标国际注册的手续。参加这个协定的国家必须是《巴黎公约》的成员国。现在这个协定由世界知识产权组织负责管理,参加协定的有法国、意大利、联邦德国、南斯拉夫等 20 多个国家,英国和美国没有参加。按照《马德里协定》,凡缔约国国民或在缔约国国内有住所或营业机构的人,必须在该国商标主管部门取得注册,然后向该国主管部门提交国际注册申请书(不能直接向世界知识产权组织国际局提交),并交纳注册费。该国主管部门审查核实后,然后转呈世界知识产权组织(World Intellectual Property Organization, WIPO)国际局。国际局经过批准后即予以公布,并通知申请人选定的缔约国。被选定的缔约国接到通知后,如不同意接受应在一年内向国际局提出,并说明拒绝的理由,其理由应同该国关于商标注册的法律规定相符。如在一年内没有表示拒绝,这个商标即被认为在该国获得注册。马德里协定大大简化了商标国际注册的手续。协定规定的保护期限为 20 年,到期可以申请续展。协定还规定有 6 个月的优先权期限。但申请人商标权的取得,仍取决于各成员国的国内法。

(三)《尼斯协定》

1957年,一些国家在法国的尼斯市缔结了《为商标注册目的而使用的商品与服务的国际分类尼斯协定》(Nice Agreement concerning the International Classification of Goods and Services for the purpose of the Registration of Marks),简称《尼斯协定》。目前有法国、联邦德国、英国、美国等30多个国家参加了这一协定。

《尼斯协定》所建立的国际分类法,把所有的商品分为34个类,把所有的服务项目分为8类,在类下面又把具体的商品与服务项目分为1万项,按拉丁字母A、B、C、D的顺序排列。

根据《尼斯协定》规定,各成员国的商标公报、官方商标注册、检索档案等,都应当使用国际分类法。目前除尼斯协定成员国外,还有三十多个国家也使用协定所建立的国际分类法。此外,《马德里协定》、《商标注册条约》、《班吉协定》以及《欧洲共同体统一商标条例》等国际公约也都宣布采用这一国际分类法。

(四)《商标图形要素国际分类协定》

1973年,由法国、联邦德国、南斯拉夫等国发起,在维也纳缔结了《建立商标图形要素国际分类维也纳协定》(Vienna Agreement for Establishing and International Classification of the Figurative Elements of Marks)。这个国际分类法把所有商标的图形分为29个类,300个支。例如,第五类是"植物",下面的支是花支、蔬菜支等。在花支下,又分为玫瑰分支、牡丹分支等。这个协定虽然还没有生效,但世界知识产权组织国际局在管理马德里协定和商标注册协定时,已经在国际注册程序中使用了按照协定建立起的商标图形分类法。

(五)《商标注册条约》

1973年在维也纳召开的外交会议上,奥地利、联邦德国、英国、美国等14个国家缔结了《商标注册条约》(Trade Mark Registration Treaty),少数国家提交了批准书,使该条约在1980年正式生效。按照这个条约,申请人可以直接向世界知识产权组织的国际局申请国际注册,而不需要先在本国注册。该条约规定,被选定国家的批准期限为15个月,允许采用英文和法文申请注册。

《商标注册条约》在简化商标国际注册手续方面又比《马德里协定》前进了一步。

第四节 著作权的法律适用

一、著作权的法律冲突

著作权(**copyright**),英语国家称为版权,法语国家称为作者权,日本和中国等国家称为著作权。

【释义】   copyright

A copyright is a form of intellectual property that grants its holder the legal right to restrict the copying and use of an original, creative expression, such as a literary work, movie, musical work or sound recording, painting, computer program, or industrial design for a defined period of time. The rights enforceable under copyright protection cover the use only of intangible creations—the story told within a book is protected from misuse as opposed to the printed copy itself, or the form of a sculpture as opposed to the actual carved rock. A copyright gives the owner the exclusive right to reproduce, distribute, perform, display, or license his work. The owner also receives the exclusive right to produce or license derivatives of his or her work. Limited exceptions to this exclusivity exist for types of "fair use", such as book reviews. To be covered by copyright a work must be original and in a concrete "medium of expression." Under current law, works are covered whether or not a copyright notice is attached and whether or not the work is registered. In 1989 the U.S. joined the Berne Convention for the Protection of Literary and Artistic Works.

作为一个法律概念,著作权是一种所有权,它通常是指个人或法人对其文学、科学和艺术作品的某种独占权利。

各国调整著作权的立法不尽相同,著作权也会发生法律冲突。

二、国内法的适用

对于如何解决著作权的法律冲突,各国法律规定和学者的主张各不相同。1979年《匈牙利国际私法》规定:"著作权依被请求保护的国家的法律。"同年《奥地利联邦国际私法法规》规定：著作权的创立、内容和消灭，依使用行为或侵权行为发生地国家的法律。有的国家则从著作权利用的合同角度来确定解决法律冲突的原则，如1966年《波兰国际私法》规定：出版合同，依发行人缔约时住所地法。可见，国际私法在这方面的法律适用原则还不一致。

在国内实体法的适用方面，各国有关著作权的国内立法，一般都对外国作者在本国首次发表的作品，依据国际公认的地域原则（也称作品国籍原则），视为本国作品，给以与本国作品相同的保护，而不管作者为何国人、住所在国籍。因此，首次在内国发表的外国作品，在内国所形成的著作权关系应适用发表国的国内立法予以调整。

我国《民法通则》规定：公民、法人享有著作权（版权），依法有署名、发表、出版、获得报酬的权利。在实践中，根据上述立法的精神，结合有关的国际惯例，我们对首次在我国用中文或外文发表的外国作品，采用"作品国籍"原则，给予与我国公民的作品相同的法律保护。同样，我国作者的作品首次在其他国家出版，按照"作品国籍"原则，也可以得到出版商所在国的法律保护。

三、国际条约的适用

有关著作权的国际条约主要有《保护文学和艺术作品伯尔尼公约》和《世界版权公约》，这些国际条约在国内法上的接受主要有两种方法。普通法系的国家如英国、加拿大等国家，它们为了使两公约在国内适用，要求必须通过国内立法机关的立法行为将条约内容制定为国内法，即必须将条约制定为国内法后，才能在国内适用。瑞士、法国等欧洲大陆国家同时也包括日本却将国际条约一般地纳入国内法，承认国际条约是国内法的组成部分，而且国际条约的效力高于国内法。国内法对国际条约的接受在国际实践中形式很多，然而"条约必须遵守原则"却保证了这些形式在实质上的统一。

（一）《保护文学和艺术作品伯尔尼公约》

《保护文学和艺术作品伯尔尼公约》（Berne Convention for the Protection of Literary and Artistic Works）（以下简称《伯尔尼公约》），由英国、法国、德国、比利时等10个国家于1886年在瑞士首都伯尔尼签订，于1887年12月生效。《伯尔尼公约》经过多次修订，现在实行的是1979年的修订本，目前已经有184个国家参加了该公约。[①] 1992年7月1日中国决定加入该公约，10月5日成为该公约的第93个成员国。

[①] See website of The World Intellectual Property Organization (WIPO), http://www.wipo.int/members/en/.

《伯尔尼公约》是世界上第一个保护文学、艺术和科学作品的国际公约,为著作权的国际保护奠定了基础。伯尔尼公约确立了三项原则:

(1) 国民待遇原则。公约第3条规定,如果作者为任何成员国的国民,其作品无论是否出版,或者作者为非本同盟成员国的国民,其作品首次在本同盟的一个成员国内出版,在这两种情况下均享有各成员国给予其本国国民作品同等的保护。此外公约还规定,任何作品如果在首次出版后30天内在两个或两个以上其他国家内出版,则该作品在几个国家内,应同时受到保护。

(2) 自动保护原则。指一成员国的作品不需要办理任何手续,就可以在其他成员国内受到保护。

(3) 独立保护原则。指一成员国的作品,在另一成员国依法受该国法律的保护,不以作品在其本国正受到保护为条件。

(二)《世界版权公约》

《世界版权公约》(Universal Copyright Convention)是美国等50个国家于1952年在日内瓦制定的一项国际版权公约,现在实行的是1971年的巴黎修订本,目前该公约已拥有65个成员国。中国于1992年7月30日递交了加入《世界版权公约》的官方文件,同年10月30日对中国生效。①

《世界版权公约》的内容与《伯尔尼公约》大致相同,所不同的是版权的保护期,世界版权公约为作者有生之年加死后25年,而伯尔尼公约规定为作者有生之年加死后50年。此外,伯尔尼公约规定作品的版权不依赖于任何手续,而世界版权公约则要求作者在作品中须载明作者姓名、出版年月和版权符号。

(三)《班吉协定》

《班吉协定》是1977年、非洲知识产权组织12个法语国家在中非首都班吉通过的一项协定,现在实行的是2002年的修订本。该协定《附件七》是迄今世界上出现的第一部跨国著作权法。它之所以被看做是一部跨国法,而不仅仅是一个地区性的多边公约,主要有两个标志:

第一,它不仅像《伯尔尼公约》等那样,规定了权利人具有哪些权利,而且还对怎么行使这些权利也作了详细具体的规定;

第二,它的实体法中的大多数规则,并不仅仅限于为成员国内国法划一个起始线(即"最低要求"),而是对成员国规定出明确、具体的要求。

《班吉协定》总则第15条明确规定:在任何一个成员国内,依本协定附件所作出的最终司法判决,对成员国具有约束力。

---

① See website of UNESCO, http://erc.unesco.org/cp/convention.asp? KO = 15241&language = E.

协定《附件七》规定,作品创作完成之日即为受著作权保护的起始日,作品标题享受与作品内容同样的保护,无论在什么状态下进行创作(包括受雇佣进行创作),作品的著作权首先归作者本人所有。该文件还规定,法律、司法与行政判决、时事新闻等不享受版权保护。

四、著作权冲突规则的新发展

Itar-Tass 俄罗斯新闻案(**Itar-Tass Russian News Agency v. Russian Kurier, Inc.**)是美国关于著作权的法律适用规则的重要案例。

【案例】　　Itar-Tass Russian News Agency v. Russian Kurier, Inc.①

This case involved a Russian language weekly in New York that copied and published various material from sources in Russia. The issue had to do with the extent to which Russian and American copyright law applied. The result is contrary to the previous presumption that only the law where the infringement occurred would apply. ② In this case it was determined that the ownership of the copyrights were a matter of Russian law because it was "the state with the most significant relationship to the property and the parties". Once the ownership was established United States law applied to determine relief for damages since that is where the violations occurred. The effect of the ruling in these immediate circumstances related to the allocation of damages among several plaintiffs, one of whom was found under Russian law to have only very limited rights. The broader effect is in the need to look at foreign law to determine whether a person owns a copyright, and this presumably involves looking at expiry rules that could either accelerate or postpone expiry dates.

该案在美国联邦第二巡回法院审理时,上诉方为在纽约地区发行的一家俄文周报社,被上诉方有几家主要的俄罗斯报纸和杂志社、俄罗斯塔斯新闻社和俄罗斯记者联合会。该案事实清楚,主要是上诉方未经授权将被上诉方报纸、杂志上的文章摘录在自己的报纸上。在初审中,初审法院裁定禁止该周报社继续从事上述摘录行为并且对侵权行为给予赔偿损失,该州报社不服遂上诉。上诉法院认为该案首先要解决一个在涉及多国的著作权案件中如何确定准据法的问题。法院根据最密切联系原则确定了俄罗斯法律为判断著作权归属关系的准据法,根据侵权行为

---

① Itar-Tass Russian News Agency v. Russian Kurier, Inc,153F. 3d 82. (2d Cir. 1998).
② National treatment under the Berne Convention merely assures that the national law of infringement will be applied uniformly to foreign and domestic authors; it provides no guidance on the question of ownership. Indeed, the Berne Convention Implementation Act specifically provides that the rights eligible for protection "shall not be expanded or reduced" by virtue of the Berne Convention.

地法原则确定了美国法律为著作权侵权的准据法。①

五、互联网著作权纠纷的法律适用

互联网著作权纠纷主要因互联网著作权侵权行为而引起。互联网著作权纠纷主要有以下几种表现形式：第一，擅自将传统媒体上发表的作品移植到网站上。未经作者许可就将其享有完全著作权的文学艺术作品刊登在网站上，侵犯了其信息网络传播权和获取报酬权等。第二，发表在一个网站上的作品被另一个网站擅自使用。如同在书刊上发表的作品一样，不经权利人同意不得随意转载，否则视为侵权。第三，将网上作品擅自下载并发表在传统媒体上。②面对网络著作权侵权案件的日益增多，加强对网络著作权的保护势在必行。

通过互联网侵犯著作权应如何确定准据法？这是国际私法学科所面临的新问题，对传统国际私法著作权法律适用规则提出了新的挑战（**internet will change the paradigm of conflict of laws**）。

【说理】 internet will change the paradigm of conflict of laws

A new concern has emerged that the internet will change the paradigm of conflict of laws. No localization is meaningful when a given content can be downloaded in hundreds of jurisdictions. The answer is not to consider uplink as determinative because that makes it too easy for infringers to go to a copyright or IP heaven. Instead, the infringement happens where the market is impacted. A substantial impact must be the test, not an intentional targeting. There may be several countries where infringement takes place. However, these problems can be alleviated with some preemptive measures such as installation of a filter, or refusal to sell to clients from a given country or countries which would preclude the risk of liability for infringement on the IP rights in these countries. The balance of interests is to be found between e-business and content providers, allowing e-businesses, on the one hand, to target some markets, but making them accountable, on the other hand, for infringement occurring in the markets from which they derive their benefits.③

例如，如果一个人，其惯常居所在 C 国，它未经许可在 A 国上传了一首流行音

---

① 参见孙皓：《版权冲突规则的发展——从 Itar-Tass 俄罗斯新闻案谈起》，载《科技与法律》2003 年第 1 期。
② 参见张觉龙、张志伟：《浅谈网络著作权的法律保护》，载《法制与社会》2007 年第 11 期。
③ Francois Dessemontet, A European Point of View on the ALI Principles-Intellectual Property: Principles Governing Jurisdiction, Choice of Law, and Judgments in Transnational Disputes, 30 Brook. J. Int'l L. 849, 863 (2005).

乐,放在他自己的互联网网页上,因此任何人都可以通过互联网获取该音乐。我们可以假设在 B 国的另一个人下载了该音乐到自己的电脑上。那么,关于该行为是否构成侵权以及如果构成侵权应获得何种救济应以哪一国的法律为准居法呢?该法律问题应当识别为著作权的侵权问题,有关的行为是在 A 国上传音乐,这一行为侵犯了音乐作者向公众公开作品的专有权利。①由于互联网的特点,该侵权行为的结果是,使得该音乐可以被全球的公众所获得,任何人下载并使用该音乐的行为,均会导致上传该音乐的人对作者著作权的侵犯。

美国联邦宾夕法尼西部地区法院在近年来所受理的 **Twentieth Century Fox Film Corp. v. iCrave TV** 一案中,就是这类互联网著作权侵权的典型代表案例。

【案例】　　　　**Twentieth Century Fox Film Corp. v. iCrave TV**②

iCrave TV, a Canadian website, picked up broadcast signals from Canadian programs, and from US television programming received across the border. iCrave then converted those signals into videostreaming format and made them available via its website.

US TV producers brought suit in federal court in the Western District of Pennsylvania, where the president and international sales manager of iCrave TV resided. The court found general personal jurisdiction over the Canadian business entity on the basis of its continuous and systematic contacts with Pennsylvania. iCrave TV claimed that the acquisition, conversion, and redistribution of the US programming was lawful under Canadian law (pertaining to Canadian law regarding secondary transmissions of broadcast performances). In theory, iCrave TV restricted access to its website to Canadian users only; however, identifying and supplying a Canadian telephone area code easily circumvented this restriction.

To determine choice of law, the court found sufficient points of attachment with the US to allow the application of the US Copyright Act to the defendants' activities. The court then concluded that the infringement occurred within the US when US citizens received and viewed the unauthorized streaming of the copyrighted materials, disregarding the fact that the streaming transmission began in Canada.③

本案中,被告 iCrave TV 是一家加拿大的网站,将在加拿大所收到的美国电视台跨境传送到加拿大的信息,经过数据处理后放到其网站上供听众下载使用,美国电视节目制造商 20 世纪福克斯电影公司在美国联邦宾夕法尼西部地区法院对

---

① 如世界知识产权组织《表演和录音制品公约》中第 10 条规定的 Right of Making Available of Phonograms 和第 14 条规定的 Right of Making Available of Phonograms。
② Twentieth Century Fox Film Corp. v. iCrave TV, No 00-121 (W. D. Pa. Jan. 20, 2000).
③ Raquel Xalabarder, Copyright: Choice of Law and Jurisdiction in the Digital Age, 8 *Ann. Surv. Int'l & Comp.* L. 79, 94—96 (2002).

iCrave TV 提起侵权之诉。iCrave TV 抗辩提示,"二次传送"这种行为在加拿大是合法的行为。但是美国法院认为,当美国公众在网站上下载并使用 iCrave TV 网站上放置的未经授权的美国 20 世纪福克斯电影公司节目,即使这种下载的数据来自于加拿大境内,也应被认为与美国有足够的联系,因此,本案应适用美国法律。而根据美国法律,iCrave TV 的这种"二次传送"行为,被视为是构成侵犯著作权的行为。

在上述案例中,由于下载电视节目的人,不限于美国公众,也可能是其他国家的公众,那么法院应适用何国法律呢?显然,每一个国家的法院都会因为下载行为发生在本国而适用本国的法律,那么本案中就可能会因为出现原告在多个不同国家法院提出诉讼而适用多个不同国家的法律的情况。

为了避免出现这种现象,有学者提出了在跨国电子数据传输过程中造成侵权适用"单一法"(single governing law)的概念,即无论跨国电子数据传输过程涉及多少个国家,也无论在多少个国家产生的实际的损害,侵权的损害赔偿问题仅适用一个国家的法律[1],即互联网著作权侵权统一适用作品来源国法律。[2]

另一种可能的选择是适用著作权权利人有最密切联系的法律,包括著作权权利人的住所地法、居所地或营业地法,理由是可以以受到侵权行为损害的权利的所在地法来确定损害。[3]

第五节　国际技术转让法律适用问题

一、国际技术转让的概念

国际技术转让(International Transfer of Technology)是指一国的技术转让人将

---

[1] Graeme W. Austin. Social Policy Choices and Choice of Law For Copyright Infringement in Cyberspace. 79 *Or. L. Rev.* 575, 575 (2000).

[2] 根据《伯尔尼公约》第 3 条规定,"已发表作品"应理解为在其作者同意下出版的著作,不论其复制件的制作方式如何,但考虑到这部著作的性质,复制件的发行在数量和方式上需要满足公众的合理需要。戏剧、音乐戏剧或电影作品的上演,音乐作品的演奏,文学作品的当众朗诵,文学或艺术作品的广播或转播,美术作品的展出及建筑作品的建造不是发表。

[3] André Lucas, Private International Law Aspects of the Protection of Works and of the Subject Matter of Related Rights Transmitted over Digital Networks, *WIPO Forum on Private International Law and Intellectual Property*, WIPO/PIL/01/1 Prov.

一定的技术越过国境、通过某种方式转让给他国的技术受让人的行为。狭义的国际技术转让仅指商业性的国际技术转让。①根据世界知识产权组织出版的《发展中国家许可证贸易指南》，国际技术转让中的"技术"是指：不论某种知识是否体现为发明、外观设计、实用新型或植物新品种，不论它反映在技术情报、技能技巧中，还是反映在专家提供的安装、建立、维持、管理工商企业的服务中，只要它是制造产品或实施工艺流程或提供服务的系统性知识，就被认为是"技术"。②另外，联合国贸易和发展会议（United Nations Conference on Trade and Development）在《国际技术转让行动守则（草案）》（Draft International Code of Conduct on the Transfer of Technology）中亦指出："技术转让是指为制造某种产品、应用某种工艺流程或提供某种服务而转让系统的知识。"

二、国际技术转让中法律适用的特点

由于国际技术转让交易与一般的国际货物买卖或其他经济贸易在合同标的、双方当事人的权利义务等方面有所不同，因而在法律适用方面也形成了一些独有的特点。

第一，从适用法律条款上看，具有复杂性。由于该种合同关系主体除自然人、法人外，往往还包括国家。合同的标的一般也不是一次性交付，涉及的法律关系复杂，因而适用的法律也比较复杂。

第二，从所适用的法律内容上看，其公共政策性较强。这主要表现在各国有关国际技术转让的强制性法规较多，管制也较为严格。一般来说，发展中国家侧重于对技术引进的管理和管制，而多数发达国家则侧重于对技术出口的管理和管制。

第三，从法律冲突以及冲突的可能性上看，这种冲突主要集中在国际技术转让合同关系的法律适用上。一方面，国内对涉外技术转让的强制性法规较多，而这些强制性法规与一国的公共政策及公共秩序密切相关，对与本国有关的涉外技术转让具有强制效力。另一方面，这种强制性法规又具有严格的地域性。各国均从属地主义原则出发，不承认这些法律、法令的域外效力，而仅适用本国的有关法律、法令，从而导致仅适用法院地或仲裁地的公共政策的结果。③

---

① 郭寿康主编：《国际技术转让》，法律出版社1989年版，第155页。
② 龚柏华主编：《国际经济合同》，复旦大学出版社1997年版，第262页。
③ 张丽娜：《论国际技术转让的法律适用》，载《海南大学学报》2003年第3期。

三、国际技术转让的法律适用

(一) 当事人意思自治原则的限制

国际技术转让合同的标的往往涉及重大利益,加之公共政策性强,从而限制了当事人对适用法律的选择,这种限制较之一般的国际货物买卖要严格得多,这也是国际技术转让法律适用中最主要的特点。从合同适用法律的选择上看,对当事人意思自治具有一定限制性。

(二) 适用最密切联系国家的法律

在实践中,当事人可能由于疏忽或各方意见相持不下或有意回避等原因而未能在合同中订立法律适用条款,或者虽订有法律适用条款,但由于某种原因而被确认无效。这时国际技术转让合同通常适用与国际技术转让有最密切联系国家的法律。

(三) 适用技术输入国法律

在国际技术转让中,发展中国家强调适用技术输入国法律的支配。这是因为:(1) 技术输入国是合同主要履行地所在国;(2) 技术输入国是技术受让人的住所地或营业地所在国,或国籍所属国;(3) 在技术转让人将技术合同依约交给技术受让人以后,该项技术事实上是处于技术输入国控制之下的。技术输入国与国际技术转让合同连接因素较多,技术输入国的法律作为国际技术转让合同的准据法具有更大的合理性。

(四) 适用强制性规则

在国际技术转让的法律适用领域中,"强制性规则"的适用具有重要意义。所谓强制性规则即无论当事人选择了哪个国家的法律,也无论在当事人未作出有效法律选择时,国际技术转让合同的准据法是怎样确定的,有关的"强制性规则"均须适用。如按照许多国家关于技术转让审批制度的规定,当事人之间的国际技术转让合同若未经国家的主管机关审批,则根本不能成立。无论是发达国家还是发展中国家,无论是技术输出国还是技术输入国,各国都制定了大量的"强制性规则"。

当国际技术转让合同涉及"限制性商业惯例"的冲突时①,大多数国家主张将

---

① 限制性商业惯例是指滥用或者谋取滥用市场支配地位,损害发展中国家利益的行为。经常被认定的国际技术转让中的限制性商业惯例包括搭售、回授条款、限制技术受方对引进技术改进和发展、权利不争、限制技术受方使用技术的地域或者销售产品的市场,对于国际技术转让中限制性商业惯例的管制,以行为是否损害技术受方利益作为判定依据。

限制性商业惯例作为本国的强制性规则,强制适用于有关的国际技术转让合同,而不管其准据法如何。

【思考题】

- 试述知识产权的地域性。
- 知识产权的传统国际公约有哪几个?
- 专利权、商标权和著作权发生法律冲突时,在国内法的适用上,应分别适用什么法?
- 试分析 Itar-Tass 俄罗斯新闻案所表现出来的著作权法律适用规则发展新趋势。
- 互联网著作权纠纷的法律适用有哪些不同的主张?
- 什么国际技术转让中的强制性规则?

【重要术语提示与中英文对照】

中文术语	英文对照
知识产权	intellectual property
地域性	territoriality
专利权	patent
美国的专利法	U.S. patent laws
专利局	Patents Office
保护工业产权巴黎公约	Paris Convention for the Protection of Industrial Property
专利合作条约	Patent Cooperation Treaty, PCT
世界贸易组织	World Trade Organization, WTO
与贸易有关的知识产权协议	Agreement on Trade-Related Aspects of Intellectual Property, TRIPS
商标权	trademark
美国商标保护制度	protection of trademarks in the United States
商标国际注册马德里协定	Madrid Agreement concerning the International Registration of Marks
保护文学和艺术作品伯尔尼公约	Berne Convention for the Protection of Literary and Artistic Works

世界知识产权组织	World Intellectual Property Organization, WIPO
为商标注册目的而使用的商品与服务的国际分类尼斯协定	Nice Agreement concerning the International Classification of Goods and Services for the purpose of the Registration of Marks
建立商标图形要素国际分类维也纳协定	Vienna Agreement for Establishing and International Classification of the Figurative Elements of Marks
商标注册条约	Trade Mark Registration Treaty
著作权	copyright
世界版权公约	Universal Copyright Convention
Itar-Tass 俄罗斯新闻案	Itar-Tass Russian News Agency v. Russian Kurier, Inc.
国际技术转让	International Transfer of Technology
联合国贸易和发展会议	United Nations Conference on Trade and Development
国际技术转让行动守则（草案）	Draft International Code of Conduct on the Transfer of Technology

【推荐阅读文献】

- 徐冬根：《与贸易有关知识产权规则》，载徐冬根编著：《WTO 规则解析》，西南财经大学出版社 2002 年版。
- 李新庄：《知识产权法律冲突的性质及其对国际私法的影响》，载《中州学刊》2003 年第 3 期。
- 徐冬根、陶立峰：《对网络条件下著作权合理使用的思考》，载《华东政法学院学报》2003 年第 4 期。
- 郑成思：《知识产权法新世纪初的若干研究重点》，法律出版社 2004 年版。
- 蔡兰荣：《网络环境下知识产权的法律适用》，载《商场现代化》2007 年第 21 期。
- 冯晓青主编：《知识产权法》，中国政法大学出版社 2008 年版。
- 吴文灵、朱理：《涉外知识产权关系的法律适用——以涉外民事关系法律适用法第七章为中心》，载《人民司法》2012 年第 9 期。
- Raquel Xalabarder, Copyright: Choice of Law and Jurisdiction in the Digital Age, 8 *Ann. Surv. Int'l & Comp. L.* 79 (2002).
- Joel R. Reidenberg, Technology and Internet Jurisdiction, 153 *U. Pa. L. Rev.* 1951

(2005).
- Graeme B. Dinwoodie, The International Intellectual Property Law System: New Actors, New Institutions, New Sources, 10 *Marq. Intell. Prop. L. Rev.* 205 (2006).
- Christian A. Camarce, Harmonization of International Copyright Protection in the Internet Age, 19 *Pac. McGeorge Bus. & Dev. L. J.* 435 (2007).
- De Miguel Asensio (P.), Applicable Law in the Absence of Choice to Contracts Relating to Intellectual or Industrial Property Right, 10 *Ybk. Priv. Int'l L.* 199 (2008).
- Trimble (M.), When Foreigners Infringe on Patents: An Empirical Look at the Involvement of Foreign Defendants in Patent Litigation in the U.S., 27 *Santa Clara Comp. & High Tech. L. J.* 499 (2011).
- Neumann (S.), Intellectual Property Rights Infringements in European Private International Law: Meeting the Requirements of Territoriality and Private International Law, 7 *J. Priv. Int'l L.* 583 (2011).
- Paul Torremans, Carmen Otero Garcia-Castrillon, Reversionary Copyright: a Ghost of the Past or a Current Trap to Assignments of Copyright? 2 *I. P. Q.* 77 (2012).

【扩展阅读资料】

"The Pirate": Historical and Political Analysis of Intellectual Property in the United States [①]

> Stemming from an English common law background of authors' copyright and Letters of Patent privileges, the U.S. Constitution included a provision for the promotion of the "Science and useful Arts, by securing for limited Times to Authors and Inventors the exclusive Right to their respective Writings and Discoveries." The Intellectual Property Clause, as it is now known, was presented at the 1785 Constitutional Convention in Philadelphia shortly before it adjourned and was unanimously approved, astonishingly, with little to no debate. This lack of discussion carried through the ratification process. Scholar Marci Hamilton suggests that from this "scant debate" and the literal text, "the Framers believed the progress of knowledge was in the national interest," and they were willing to suppress copying and imitation for limited periods so that technology and expression "would progress and the community would benefit."

---

① Jennifer A. Crane, A Comparison of Intellectual Property Rights in the United States and the People's Republic of China, 7 *Chi.-Kent J. Intell. Prop.* 95, 95 (2008).

Interesting to note, this enumerated power of the U.S. Congress to "Promote the Sciences and useful Arts" is contained in the only clause that also articulates a specific mode of effecting that power. As well, the Clause contains limits to this power, namely that the right be granted for a "limited" time, "exclusively" to the author or inventor, and that the innovation must advance "Science and the useful Arts." So ingrained in the American psyche is this desire to encourage a broad range of innovation through capital benefit, the U.S. Supreme Court has never felt compelled to "render an opinion as to the meaning of either 'science' or 'useful arts' as used." The accepted definition of "Science," as understood in the eighteenth century by the framers, is generally "knowledge" or "learning" while the "useful Arts" means simply "helpful or valuable trades." The framers included the Intellectual Property Clause not only to ensure limitation of the incentive-monopolies for invention and creativity, but also to encourage innovation in all aspects of knowledge and industry.

The framers of the U.S. Constitution drew just as heavily from the English common law practice of granting Letters of Patent and copyright protections as from the English repugnance for monopolies when establishing the Intellectual Property Clause. In English practice, Letters of Patents and copyrights were considered privileges from the Crown rather than a right springing from and vested in a creative work. The English practice exempted holders of Letters of Patents and copyrights from the prohibition of monopolies and did not encourage innovation so much as merging of power for the artisans or publishers in the Crown's favor. The U.S. Constitution's Intellectual Property Clause functions to separate monopolist forces, "correspondingly weakening them to the benefit of the people." The existence of the Intellectual Property Clause indicates the importance of intellectual property rights to the framers, who were uncertain if the U.S. Congress would have the power to recognize property rights of inventors and authors without an explicit grant of authority. In order to restrict monopolies and incentivize innovation and creative expression, they not only stated the specific power but the mode in which it was to be effected.

Yet the United States was not always the beacon of intellectual property law honesty that it presents itself as today. The early history of American intellectual property abounds with tales of piracy, theft, imitation, and deceit. In his first State of the Union address, George Washington spoke of his concerns about the future of the U.S. economy and called on Congress to create legislation not only to encourage domestic innovation, but also for "the introduction of new inventions from abroad." During Thomas Jefferson's presidency, then Secretary of State Alexander Hamilton put together a report outlining a plan to become Europe's economic rival. Hamilton wanted to impose stiff tariffs on imported European goods and to use the "tariff wall" protection to foster a robust domestic patent system. Key to Hamilton's plan was the immigration of skilled foreign workers to the young nation. He effectively sent forth the message to immigrants to "bring your nation's industrial secrets to America."

The early U.S. copyright laws and policies actually encouraged piracy of foreign literary works. Domestic copyright protection was greatly valued by the United States, as evidenced by twelve of the thirteen original colonies enacting their own copyright legislation before adopting the federal Constitution. While the Copyright Act of 1790 prohibited copying works by U.S. authors, it supported the piracy of foreign works by not recognizing foreign copyrights and prohibiting non-citizens from registering a U.S. copyright. As the United States attempted to create its own artistic culture, Americans "wanted foreign copyrighted works on the cheap." At one point, Charles Dickens' novel *A Christmas Carol* sold in Great Britain for the equivalent of $2.50, while a copy could be purchased in the United States for about $0.06. The piracy of foreign copyrights continued in the United States until 1891 when the U.S. Congress passed legislation allowing copyright relations with other countries. However, U.S. protection of English-language literary works only extended to works manufactured domestically until 1986 when the amendment to the copyright act lapsed.

U.S. patent legislation chronologically coincided with copyright legislation. The laws enacting the early patent protections enabled infringement of domestic and international inventions alike. The first Patent Act in the United States was enacted in 1790. The original Patent Act required inventors to submit petitions directly to the Secretary of State, Thomas Jefferson. The Secretary of State, together with the Secretary of War and the Attorney General, reviewed all patent petitions, but the number of petitions quickly became burdensome. In three years (1790—1793), 57 U.S. patents were granted, 114 petitions were still pending, and dozens of petitions were denied. The Patent Act of 1793 attempted to correct the system by doing away with a review of each petition. Rather, an inventor simply needed to register his invention with the U.S. Department of State. As could be expected, this led to multiple patenting of the same invention. Some of this duplication was innocent when separate inventors unknowingly registered the same inventions. Other times, this duplication was far more fraudulent. Each patent petition was a matter of public record. A person could view the record at the Department of State's record room, steal whatever idea he thought profitable, and register it again as his own. Another loophole of the 1793 Act lay in the fact that only American citizens were eligible for a U.S. patent, enabling an American businessman to "bring a foreign innovation to the United States and commercialize the idea, all with total legal immunity" and even government support. The U.S. Congress amended the Act in 1800 to allow foreign citizens who resided in the United States for two years to petition for a patent; in 1832, the Act was revised to enable foreigner citizens who lived in the United States for twelve months and who swore an oath of intention for U.S. citizenship to petition. The substance of the Patent Act remained authoritative until 1836 and enabled American entrepreneurs to steal some of Europe's most profitable trade secrets and technologies, becoming "by national policy and legislative act, the world's premier legal sanctuary for industrial pirates."

One famous example of this piracy involves the U.S. citizen Francis Cabot Lowell. In 1810, Lowell set out to steal the Cartwright loom—an invention that allowed England to become the world leader in textiles. So vital was this technology that England "forbade the export of the machinery, the making or selling of drawings of the equipment and the emigration of the skilled workers." Lowell visited England under the guise of traveling for health reasons—the cold damp air could somehow aid his constitution. Those he met were taken with the Harvard graduate's charm and credentials. Eager to show off their innovative devices, which they guarded jealously from each other, British textile producers gave Lowell guided and detailed tours of their factories. Unbeknownst to his hosts, Lowell possessed an almost photographic memory and recorded everything he saw and heard each night in his journals. Despite the fact his belongings were futilely searched twice before he departed for home, Lowell smuggled the plans for the Cartwright loom out of England and recreated them in his own factory. Lowell created the Boston Manufacturing Company with his stolen technology and encouraged politicians to increase import tariffs, thus successfully pushing England's cloth out of the American market. Lowell's story is by no means unique. Not until the U.S. economy achieved a certain robustness and U.S. citizens sought recognition of their intellectual property rights abroad did the United States truly install effective protection of international intellectual property.

The U.S. system of intellectual property rights requires intellectual property owners to maintain watch over their own rights. Copyrights and patents may be granted, and trademarks and trade secrets recognized, but in order for intellectual property to have any value in the United States, individuals and businesses must police the related industry and use the U.S. legal system to enforce their rights. America employs a structure that relies on an individual safeguarding his rights through litigation. The grants of exclusive rights for intellectual property are, therefore, worthless unless an owner remains vigilant in the policing of potential infringers. Adequate protection is only possible with a responsive judicial system and investigative and protective rights-holders.

第十章

国际侵权行为的法律适用

第十章　国际侵权行为的法律适用

本章导读

※ 侵权行为的法律适用问题在传统国际私法中并不占有很重要的地位,然而到了20世纪50年代以后,随着科学技术的迅猛发展和国际交往的日益增多,跨国侵权行为案件日趋增多,侵权行为法律适用问题开始成为当代国际私法最重要的课题之一。

※ 长期以来,侵权行为适用侵权行为地法是传统国际私法的一条重要的冲突规范。

※ 侵权行为地可以识别为加害行为发生地和损害结果发生地。

※ 依英国法,在外国发生的侵权行为,在英国追究法律责任的,必须符合两个基本条件:第一,该行为如果在英国发生,必须是可追诉的;第二,该行为依行为地法必须是不正当的行为。符合了这两个条件,英国法院才予以受理,并适用英国法来处理案件。这一规则称为"双重可起诉原则"。

※ 侵权行为自体法是在批判单一的、机械的法律适用原则的基础上提出来的,因此它是对侵权行为地法、法院地法、当事人本国法、当事人住所地或惯常居所地法的总括。

※ 对传统侵权行为冲突规范进行软化处理的方式主要有:适用与双方当事人具有最密切联系的州的法律、采用多种连接因素指引侵权行为准据法、区分不同种类的侵权行为分别规定不同的冲突规范、采用分割方法适用不同的法律。

※ 公路交通侵权行为的法律适用原则为最密切联系原则、自体法原则等。

※ 涉外产品责任的法律适用原则为最密切联系原则、最有利于原告原则和排除适用被告不可预见法律的原则。

※ 网络侵权行为是指通过网络技术平台,在网络环境下实施的侵害网络权益主体及其他人的人身和财产等民事权益的行为。网络侵权行为的基本特征是:侵权行为实施空间的虚拟性和跨地域性、司法管辖的不易确定性、网络侵权行为的隐秘性。

※ 网络侵权行为的法律适用原则为最密切联系原则、当事人意思自治原则和适用法院地法原则。

【本章主题词】　侵权行为地法、双重可起诉原则、侵权行为自体法、网络侵权

第一节　侵权行为地法及其演变

一、侵权行为适用侵权行为地法

侵权行为(**torts**),是指以作为或者不作为的形式侵害他人人身权利或者财产权利,致使他人遭受损害而应承担民事赔偿责任的行为。①

【释义】　　　　　　　　　　　　**torts**

　　Torts are civil wrongs recognized by law as grounds for a lawsuit. These wrongs result in an injury or harm constituting the basis for a claim by the injured party. While some torts are also crimes punishable with imprisonment, the primary aim of tort law is to provide relief for the damages incurred and deter others from committing the same harms. The injured person may sue for an injunction to prevent the continuation of the tortious conduct or for monetary damages. Among the types of damages the injured party may recover are: loss of earnings capacity, pain and suffering, and reasonable medical expenses. They include both present and future expected losses.

　　There are numerous specific torts including trespass, assault, battery, negligence, products liability, and intentional infliction of emotional distress. Torts fall into three general categories: intentional torts (*e.g.*, intentionally hitting a person); negligent torts (causing an accident by failing to obey traffic rules); and strict liability torts (*e.g.*, liability for making and selling defective products). Intentional torts are those wrongs which the defendant knew or should have known would occur through their actions or inactions. Negligent torts occur when the defendant's actions were unreasonably unsafe. Strict liability wrongs do not depend on the degree of carefulness by the defendant, but are established when a particular action causes damage.

　　侵权行为法的目的在于通过民事法律制度,惩罚加害人,故应由行为地国决定是否应该对加害人课以侵权责任和损害赔偿(**damages**)。

---

　　① 张潇剑:《国际私法学》,北京大学出版社 2000 年版,第 350 页。

第十章 国际侵权行为的法律适用

【释义】 **damages**

In a legal sense, is the sum of money the law imposes for a breach of some duty or violation of some right. Generally, there are two types of damages: compensatory and punitive. (The term "damages" typically includes both categories, but the term, "actual damages" is synonymous with compensatory damages, and excludes punitive damages.)

Compensatory damages, like the name suggests, are intended to compensate the injured party for his loss or injury. Punitive damages are awarded to punish a wrongdoer. There are other modifying terms placed in front of the word damages like "liquidated damages," (contractually established damages) and "nominal damages" (where the court awards a nominal amount such as one dollar). For certain types of injuries statutes provide that successful parties should receive some multiple of their "actual damages"—e.g., treble damages.

There are general principles governing what types of damages are awarded. Itt is generally recognized, for instance, that punitive damages are not available for breaches of contract except when it is proven that the breach was wanton, willful and deliberate.

侵权行为适用侵权行为地法(*lex loci delicti*),是传统国际私法的一般法律适用规则。

美国《第一次冲突法重述》以侵权行为地法(**law of the place of wrong**)作为最基本的准据法。

【条文】 **law of the place of wrong**

The Restatement First contans over fifty sections on torts, but nearly all choose the "law of the place of wrong". Thus, the law of the place of wrong controls the existence of a legal injury (§378), defendant's standard of responsibility (§381), causation (§383), contributory (§387), defenses to liability (§388), survival of actions (§390), and the measure of damages (§412).[①]

然而值得一提的是,澳大利亚只是在 ***Regie Nationale des Usines Renault SA v. Zhang*** 案之后才开始正式确立侵权行为地法在其侵权行为法律适用中的应有地位。澳大利亚在此前的 150 年期间,对于国际侵权行为的法律适用一直遵循英国的其他法律适用规则。

[①] See William Richman & William Reynolds, *Understanding Conflict of Laws*, 3d ed., 2002, §65[a].

【案例】   *Regie Nationale des Usines Renault SA* v. *Zhang*①

Facts: The plaintiff/respondent in this action, Mr Fuzu Zhang, had been living in NSW on a student visa since 1986. In February 1991, after receiving advice from Australian immigration authorities that he would be granted permanent residency if he made an application from outside Australia, he travelled to the French-administered territory of New Caledonia. There he hired a Renault 19 sedan, designed and manufactured in France by the defendants/appellants, the Renault companies. Both of these are French corporations that are not registered in Australia. While Mr Zhang was driving the car an accident occurred resulting in the car somersaulting onto its roof, which was crushed into the passenger compartment. Despite hospital treatment in New Caledonia and further medical attention in NSW, the plaintiff has been left permanently disabled by the severe spinal injuries that he sustained. Mr Zhang now resides in NSW.

Mr Zhang subsequently commenced proceedings against the Renault companies in the Supreme Court of NSW, claiming damages for personal injuries allegedly caused by the defective design and manufacture of the vehicle.

At Trial: At first instance, Smart J agreed to stay the proceedings after "weighing all the factors" in favour of and against hearing the claim in NSW. While "practical considerations" tended to favour a hearing in Sydney, the facts that the accident occurred in New Caledonia and the allegedly defective design and manufacture took place in France meant that French law should be applied in this case. On the basis of this finding, it was held that the case should be remitted to a French or New Caledonian court.

Zhang appealed to the NSW Court of Appeal on the grounds that the primary judge had erroneously ruled that French law would be the lex causae, and thus that his discretion in staying the proceedings had miscarried.

This appeal was upheld. In particular, Stein JA found that the role of the lex loci delicti was to be restricted to the question of justiciability, as determined through the double actionability rule, and that Australian law should be applied in this case. The court accordingly re-exercised the trial judge's discretion, and refused to stay the proceedings.

On Appeal to the High Court: The Renault companies appealed to the High Court. A majority of the High Court of Australia dismissed the appeal.②

国际上,侵权行为适用侵权行为地法是有其理由的:第一,是因为行为人的侵权行为扰乱了当地国家的社会秩序,且使该国因此种行为而蒙受的损失最大。第二,是因为侵权法属于社会保障法,为了加重侵权案件的加害人对行为的危险的预

---

① [2002] HCA 10.
② Matthew Duckworth, Regie Nationale des Usines Renault SA v Zhang Certainty or Justice? Bringing Australian Choice of Law Rules for International Torts into the Modern Era, 24 *Sydney L. Rev.* 569, 570—571 (2002).

测与评价的责任,以侵权行为地法最为恰当。同时此种债的发生,是基于法律的规定,而非债权人之间的合意,为了加强行为人的法律责任,也要求适用行为地法追究侵权行为。

二、对侵权行为地的不同识别

各国对侵权行为地的识别不尽相同。

(一) 将加害行为发生地识别为侵权行为地

一种观点主张,应该以加害行为发生地作为侵权行为地。这种观点认为,规定一般人的行为标准,便于了解何者可为,何者不可为,以及他所期待的正当行为。就这一基础来看,应由行为地国决定当事人的行为及结果是否应负责任。这主要是大陆法系国家如德国、瑞士、意大利等国的观点。①

(二) 将损害结果发生地识别为侵权行为地

另一种观点主张,应该以损害结果发生地作为侵权行为地。这种观点认为,规定一般人应获得的法律保护,以防他人加害,应以损害结果发生地为标准。②以此观点所形成的规则,称为"损害结果发生地规则"(**place-of-impact rule**)。

【释义】　　　　　　　　　place-of-impact rule

The place of the wrong is the place where the last event necessary to make an actor liable for an event take place. In the words of the Restatement First, the forum should apply the law of "the place where the harmful force first take places effect upon the body," or in other words, the law of the place of impact. ③

早期英美各国均持这一观点,尤其是美国《第一次冲突法重述》中,明确指出,侵权行为地就是"最后事件地"(place of last event)或"损害结果发生地"(place-of-impact),这方面的典型案例如 **Glencore Internantional Ag and Others v. Metro Trading International Inc** 案。

---

① See Vischer F., *Droit international privé*, Fribourg, 1974, p.204.
② See Batiffol H., *Aspects philosophiques du droit international privé*, Paris, 1956, n.560.
③ David H. Vernon, Louis Weinberg, William Reynolds, William Richman, *Conflicts of Law: Case, Materials and Problems*, 2d ed., LexisNexis, 2002, p.252.

【案例】 Glencore Internantional Ag and Others v. Metro Trading International Inc[①]

Facts: The defendant Metro Trading International Inc (MTI) was engaged in the buying, blending and selling of fuel oil either to vessels as bunker fuel for their own consumption or to traders on the international oil marker as cargoes or part cargoes of fuel oil. These activities were carried out in Fujairah itself and in the waters of Fujairah. Parcels of oil received by MTI were generally not kept in segregated tanks. The claimants all entered into agreements at one time or another with MTI under which they deliverd oil products to MTI for storage. In February 1998 MTI became insolvent and could not continue its operations. A receiver was appointed. The oil claimants (which included Glencore) all asserted proprietary claims to the oil held by MTI. However, during this time MTI had obtained finance from a number of banks in order to run its business. There banks claimed they were entitled to a first charge over various sums of money due to MTI and over the products remaining in storage.

MTI and the purchasers alleged that questions of the passing of title to oil situated in Fujairah was governed by the law of Fujairah under which property has passed from oil companies to MTI and from MTI to the purchasers. The oil company disputed that, relying on the terms of contracts between themselves and MTI and upon a different understanding of the effect of the law of Fujairah.

Held: The claims being made by the oil claimants against the purchasers were for wrongful interference with goods. By section 11 of Private International Law (Miscellaneous Provisions) Act 1995 the applicable law for determining issues relating to tort was generally the law of the country in which the events constituting the tort occurred. All relevant acts occurred in Fujairah where the goods were situated at the relevant time. The law of Fujairah governed such claims.

采用损害结果发生地法作为侵权行为准据法,具有便利性和法院中立性(**simplicity and forum neutrality**)两个优点。

【评论】 simplicity and forum neutrality

One great virtue of the place-of-injury rule is that it is simple and essy to apply. This may seem trival now, but after an exploration of the complete and confusing array of modern choce-of-law systems, simplicity may acquire the nostalgic allure of the ten-cent coke. The Rule is also forum-reutal; in other words, it produces the same result regardless of where the lawsuit is brought.[②]

---

① (2001) 1 Lloyd's Rep 284 QB.
② David H. Vernon, Louis Weinberg, William Reynolds, William Richman, *Conflicts of Law: Case, Materials and Problems*, 2d ed., LexisNexis, 2002, pp.253—254.

(三) 将加害行为发生地和损害结果发生地均识别为侵权行为地

也有观点主张凡与侵权事件发生地有关的地方,包括侵权行为发生地和损害结果发生地,均可作为侵权行为地,可允许受害人自由选择任何一项发生地为行为地。①

三、对侵权行为地法的批判

但是随着现代科学技术和交通条件的发展,侵权行为地正像合同缔结地一样,往往带有偶然性。用这种因偶然的原因发生在某个地方的法律来定行为人的责任,是不符合案件实际情况的,当事人的权益也无法得到妥善的保护;同时由于各国对侵权行为地的理解不同,也会使侵权行为地不易确定,且依不同的国家来解释会得出不同的结果。在实践中,经常可见一个侵权行为在一国发生,其继续和损害的发生则在其他几个国家的情况,这样也难于判定其中哪一国为加害行为发生地,哪一国为损害结果发生地。因此在一个复杂的侵权案件中,对侵权行为地的确定会遇到困难。因此对侵权行为机械地适用侵权行为地法的做法越来越受到学者的批评。②

四、侵权行为地法与其他法律的复合适用

随着侵权行为领域的扩大,侵权行为准据法的适用也日益出现多样化的趋势。侵权行为地法与其他法律的复合适用情况也越来越多。其中最为典型就是重叠适用和双重可起诉原则。

(一) 重叠适用

即以侵权行为地法为准据法,只有当侵权行为人为内国人时,方受法院地法限制的有条件的折中主义。按照该理论,关于侵权行为的成立及其效力,以侵权行为地法为准据法。当侵权行为人为外国人时,只适用侵权行为地法;当侵权行为人为内国人时,则重叠适用法院地法,其目的在于保护内国人的利益。③

(二) 双重可起诉原则

即以侵权行为地法为准据法,兼顾行为地法的折中主义。英国即采用这种主

---

① 参见金宁:《关于侵权行为地法适用的若干问题》,载《法律科学》1992 年第 2 期。
② See Loussouarn, La Conférence de la Haye sur la loi applicable en matière d'accidents de la circulation routière, *Journal De Droit International* 1969, p. 8.
③ See Kahn-Freund, Delictual Liability and the Conflict of Laws, *Recueil Des Cours De L'Académie De Droit International De La Haye*, 1968 II, p. 12 ss.

张。依英国法,在外国发生的侵权行为,在英国追究法律责任的,必须符合两个基本条件:第一,该行为如果在英国发生,必须是可追诉的;第二,该行为依行为地法必须是不正当的行为。符合了这两个条件,英国法院才予以受理,并适用英国法来处理案件。[①]这方面最为典型的案例是菲利普诉艾尔案(**Phillip v. Eyre**)。

【案例】　　　　　　　　　　Phillip v. Eyre[②]

　　Fact: This was an action complaining of false imprisonment and other injuries to the plaintiff by the defendant in the island of Jamaica. The defendant was governor of the island at the time that a rebellion broke out on the island, which the governor and others acting under his authority suppressed by force of arms. An Act was subsequently passed by the legislature of the island (receiving royal assent) under which the defendant and all officers and other persons who had acted under his authority, were indemnified in respect of all acts, matters, and things done in order to put an end to the rebellion and all such acts were thereby made and declared lawful, and were confirmed. The defendant pleaded that the grievances complained of were measures used in the suppression of the rebellion, and were reasonabley and in good faith considered by the defendant to be proper for the purpose of putting an end to the rebellion, and so were included in the indemnity. A number of objections were leveled at the validity of the Act.

由菲利普诉艾尔案所阐述的"双重可起诉原则"(**double actionability**),成为英国侵权行为法律适用的一条重要准则。

【释义】　　　　　　　　　Double actionability

　　As a general rule, an act done in a foreign country is a tort and actionable as such in England, only if it is both (a) actionable as a tort according to English law, and (b) civilly actionable according to the law of the foreign country where it was done.

这方面的著名案例还有英国上院审理的 **博伊斯诉查普林案**(Boys v. Chaplin)。

---

① See Cheshire, North, *Private International Law*, 11th ed., London, 1987.
② [1870] LR 6 QB 1.

【案例】 博伊斯诉查普林案①

该案的原告和被告都是英格兰的居民,暂时在马耳他的英国军队中服役。一次原告乘坐由被告驾驶的摩托车,由于驾驶人的过错,摩托车与一辆汽车相撞,使原告受了重伤。根据损害结果发生地马耳他的法律,原告可得到英镑的赔偿费;根据英国法律,原告也可得到英镑的赔偿费。最后法院判决原告可得到英镑的赔偿费。此案发生在马耳他,根据马耳他及英国两国的法律,皆认为被告的行为已构成侵权行为,所以英国法院受理了此起侵权案,并按照本国的有关法律规定作出如上判决。

五、我国有关侵权行为法律适用的规定

我国《涉外民事关系法律适用法》第44条规定:"侵权责任,适用侵权行为地法律,但当事人有共同经常居所地的,适用共同经常居所地法律。侵权行为发生后,当事人协议选择适用法律的,按照其协议。"我国《涉外民事关系法律适用法》将当事人意思自治原则作为一般侵权法律适用中的首要原则,即在处理一般侵权关系的法律适用时,应首先考虑当事人意思自治原则,其次是当事人共同经常居所地原则,如果以上原则都不能适用,最后采用侵权行为地法原则。

我国《涉外民事关系法律适用法》第44条在一般侵权行为法律适用中明确赋予当事人选择法律的权利,这体现了充分尊重当事人意愿的立法意图。侵权行为之债是一种法定之债,往往在加害人和受害人之间形成势不两立的局面。② 从这一角度讲,很难理解采用当事人意思自治原则解决其法律适用问题的做法。但是有些国家的立法出于对当事人处分自身权利的尊重、增强法律适用的可预见性、加快案件审结等因素考虑,将意思自治原则引入侵权法领域,如1987年的《瑞士国际私法》第132条规定了侵权行为发生后当事人可随时协商选择适用法院地的法律。我国的上述做法,显然是受到瑞士国际私法立法精神的影响。赋予当事人意思自治原则在侵权法律适用中以首要位置,这种做法不仅体现了中国对当事人私权的尊重,具有一定的开创性,而且,也体现了国际私法的实体取向。当事人意思自治原则把选择法律的权利赋予当事人,既可以克服侵权行为地法原则带来的机械和僵化,又可以避免最密切联系原则因对实体正义理解差异而导致的结果的不确定。在侵权法律冲突规范中,无论是从冲突正义,还是从实体正义的价值取向分析,当

---

① [1971] A.C. 356 (H.L.).
② 参见邹淑环:《侵权行为法律适用的三大变化及我国的立法实践》,载《天津商业大学学报》2011年第6期。

事人意思自治都优于其他规范。①《涉外民事关系法律适用法》将意思自治原则作为首要原则，充分尊重当事人在涉外侵权纠纷处理的地位和作用，不仅可以实现案件结果的可预见性和确定性，而且还可以提高案件审判的效率，减少成本，从而最有效地实现我国涉外侵权关系法律适用中的冲突正义与实体正义。我国《涉外民事关系法律适用法》第44条同时还确立了当事人共同属人法原则。一般侵权的法律适用在坚持适用侵权行为地法的同时，吸纳对当事人有共同经常居所地适用共同经常居所地法的做法，有助于涉外侵权案件的合理解决。

第二节　侵权行为法律适用的多元化

自20世纪50年代以来，美国国际私法革命首先对侵权行为地法发起猛烈抨击，从而导致侵权行为法律适用的繁荣景象。法院在处理侵权行为案件时，开始适用法院地法、最密切联系的法律或最有利于原告的法律，以确保受害人能够得到必需的损害赔偿，充分体现法律的公正性。

一、适用法院地法

德国学者萨维尼认为，侵权行为与法庭的公共秩序、善良风俗关系密切，故侵权行为应适用法院地法。该学说后来得到维希特等其他德国学者的支持，并被苏联、希腊等国际私法采用，但始终未予普遍接受。

二、适用最密切联系的法律

20世纪50年代后期至70年代初的美国冲突法革命，在侵权行为的法律适用方面，开始采用最密切联系原则。在实践中这种转折点标表现在1963年纽约上诉法院审理的著名的贝科克诉杰克逊案（**Babcock v. Jackson**）。

---

① 参见贺琼琼：《论意思自治在侵权冲突法中的现代发展——兼评〈涉外民事关系法律适用法〉之相关规定》，载《武汉大学学报（哲学社会科学版）》2011年第6期。

第十章 国际侵权行为的法律适用

【案例】 **Babcock v. Jackson**[①]

Facts: Miss Georgia Babcock and her friends, Mr and Mrs William Jackson, all residents of Rochester NY left that city in Mr Jackson's automobile, Miss Babcock as guest, for a weekend trip to Canada. Some hours later, as Mr Jackson was driving in the Province of Ontario, he apparently lost control of the car; it went off the highway into an adjacent stone wall, and Miss Babcock was seriously injured.

Upon her return to New York she brought an action against William Jackson alleging negligence on his part in operating his automobile.

At the time of the accident there was in force in Ontario a statute providing that "the owner or driver of a motor vehicle, other than a vehicle operated in the business of carrying passengers for compensation, is not liable for any loss or damage resulting from bodily injury to, or the death of, any person being carried in... the motor vehicle". Even though no such bar is recognised under New York state's substantive law of torts, the defendant moved to dismiss the complaint on the ground that the law of the place where the accident occurred governs and that Ontario's guest statute bars recovery.

审理该案的法官认为：在此案中，安大略省虽然是损害结果发生地，但双方当事人都是纽约居民，旅行从纽约开始，又在纽约结束，汽车是在纽约登记的年保险，如果适用安大略省的法律，一是安大略省只是该案件发生的偶然因素，二是被告不需要赔偿（安大略省的客人条例规定，如果是免费搭载乘客，车主或司机免除责任），这对受害人显然不公平，纽约州作为重力中心（**center of gravity**）与此案具有最重要的联系，所以应适用纽约州法。

【释义】 **center of gravity**[②]

Fuld J: Comparison of the relative "contacts" and "interests" of New York and Ontario in this litigation, vis-à-vis the issue here presented, makes it clear that the concern of New York is unquestionably the greater and more direct and that the interest of Ontario is at best minimal. The present action involves injuries sustained by a New York guest as the result of the negligence of a New York host in the operation of an automobile, garaged licensed and undoubtedly insured in New York, in the course of a weekend journey which began and was to end there.

In sharp contrast, Ontario's sole relationship with the occurrence is the purely adventitious circumstance that the accident occurred there...

---

① [1963] 12 NY 2d 473; 191 NE 2d 279 New York Court of Appeals (Desmond C J, Dye, Burke, Foster, Fuld, Van Hoorhis and Scileppi J J).

② Ibid.

The issue here, however, is not whether the defendant offended against a rule of the road prescribed by Ontario for motorists generally or whether he violated some standard of conduct imposed by that jurisdiction, but rather whether the plaintiff, because she was a guest in the defendant's automobile, is barred from recovering damages for a wrong concededly committed. As to that issue, it is New York, the place where the parties resided, where their guest-host relationship arose and where the trip began and was to end, rather than Ontario, the place of the fortuitous occurrence of the accident, which has the dominant contacts and the superior claim for application of its law. Although the rightness or wrongness of defendant's conduct may depend upon the law of the particular jurisdiction through which the automobile passes, the rights and liabilities of the parties which stem from their guest-host relationship should remain constant and not vary and shift as the automobile proceeds from place to place. Indeed, such a result, we note, accords with "the interests of the host in procuring liability insurance adequate under the applicable law, and the interests of his insurer in reasonable calculation of the premium".

美国《第二次冲突法重述》总结了《第一次冲突法重述》实施以来美国国际私法的理论实践,在侵权行为法律适用原则上,其第7章第145条"总则"(**§145 The General Principle**)以最重要关系原则代替了损害地法原则。

【条文】　　　　　　　　**The General Principle**
§145 The General Principle

(1) The rights and liabilities of the parties with respect to an issue in tort are determined by the local law of that state which, with respect to that issue, has the most significant relationship to the occurrence and the parties under the principles stated in §6.

(2) Contacts to be taken into account in applying the principles of §6 to determine the law applicable to an issue include: (a) the place where the injury occurred, (b) the place where the conduct causing the injury occurred, (c) the domicil, residence, nationality, place of incorporation and place of business of the parties, and (d) the place where the relationship, if any, between the parties is centered.

These contacts are to be evaluated according to their relative importance with respect to the particular issue. ①

---

① 该条款的含义为:第一,当事人对侵权行为某个问题上的权利义务,按照第6条规定的原则,依与该事件及当事人有重要联系的州的本地法。第二,在采用第6条的原则决定某个文体问题时,应当加以考虑的联系包括:(1)损害发生地;(2)加害行为发生地;(3)当事人的住所、居所、国籍、公司成立地和营业地;(4)当事人之间有联系时其最集中的地方。这些联系按其对特定问题的重要程度加以衡量。

现在,英国法院也采纳了最密切联系原则作为确定侵权行为法律适用的原则,奥地利、土耳其、《比荷卢国际私法统一法公约》,以及海牙1968年《关于交通事故法律适用公约》都纷纷采用此说。侵权行为领域开始出现了以"有最密切联系的法律"为代表的一系列新发展。[①]

我国《民法通则》对侵权行为的法律适用也作了明确的规定,侵权行为的损害赔偿,适用侵权行为地法。如果当事人双方国籍相同或者在同一国家有住所的,也可以适用当事人本国法律或者住所地法律。虽然立法上未对侵权行为地作出明确规定,但在司法解释中规定:它包括侵权行为发生地和侵权行为结果发生地,当两者不一致时,由法院从中选择其一加以适用。从而说明,各国立法现在对侵权行为不再单一以损害地或实施地为法律适用的原则,而是综合运用,同时也考虑当事人的国籍、住所、居所等因素,在一定程度上也采用最密切联系原则。

三、适用最有利于原告的法律

一些国家的国际私法立法从保护受害人的角度出发,采用利益分析及结果选择等方法,允许受害人在一定范围内选择一种对其最为有利的法律。[②]《瑞士联邦国际私法》第139条的规定(**Article 139**)赋予当事人的选择余地更大。[③]

【法条】   **Article 139**

Claims founded on an infringement of personality rights by the media, especially by the press, radio, television, or other means of public information, shall be governed at the option of the injured party by:

a. The law of the State in which the injured party has his place of habitual residence of the tortfeasor should have foreseen that the effects would occur in that State;

b. The law of the State in which the tortfeasor has his place of business or place of habitual residence; or

c. The law of the State in which the effects of the infringement have occurred if the tortfeasor should have foreseen that the effects would occur in that State.

---

① See Imhoff-Scheier, Patocchi: *L'acte illicite et l'enrichissement illegitimes dans le nouveaux droit international privé suisse*, Zurich, 1990, p.46 ss.

② See Bucher, *Les actes illicites dans le nouveaux droit international privé suisse*, CEDEDAC 1987, pp. 115—116.

③ 第139条规定:基于传播媒介,特别是报纸、无线电、电视或其他大众传播媒介对个人人格的损害而提出的诉讼请求,经受害人选择,由下列法律支配:(1)受害人习惯居所地国家的法律,如果侵权行为人应当预计到侵权行为会发生在那里;(2)加害人的营业地或习惯居所地国家的法律;(3)损害结果发生地国家的法律,如果加害人应当预计到结果会在该国发生。

四、列序适用

由于侵权行为的牵涉面很广,为此就需要有多样化的连接因素来支持,根据不同领域的侵权行为,适用不同的连接因素。一些国家对侵权行为法律适用的诸多原则进行排序,按照法定的序列进行适用,《瑞士联邦国际私法》第 132 条和第 133 条有关侵权行为法律适用(**applicable law of tort**)的规定就颇具特色。

【法条】　　　　　　　　　applicable law of tort

Art. 132

II. Applicable law

1 In general

a. Choice of law by the parties

The parties may agree any time after the event causing damage has occurred that the law of the forum shall be applicable.

Art. 133

b. Absence of a choice of law

1 If the tortfeasor and injured party have their place of habitual residenc e in the same State, claims founded in tort shall be governed by the law of that State.

2 If the tortfeasor and the injured party do not have their place of habitual residence in the same State, the claims shall be governed by the law of the State in which the tort was committed. If the injury occurs in another State than the State, in which the act that caused injury arose, the law of that State shall be applicable if the tortfeasor should have foreseen that the injury would occur there.

3 Notwithstanding the preceding paragraphs, if a tort violates an existing legal relationship between the tortfeasor and the injured party, claims founded in tort shall be governed by the law applicable to that legal relationship.

可见,《瑞士联邦国际私法》第 132 条允许当事人在侵权行为发生后,随时协商选择所适用的法律,但是该选择以法院地法为限。第 133 条规定,如果加害人和受害人在同一国家具有共同惯常居所的,则应适用该国的法律;如果加害人和受害人的惯常居所不在同一个国家的,则应适用侵权行为实施地的法律。

五、适用侵权行为自体法

在对侵权行为单一适用侵权行为地法进行批判的同时,国际私法学者提出了"侵权行为自体法"(proper law of the torts)的学说。1951 年英国的莫里斯教授在

《哈佛法律评论》发表的《论侵权行为的自体法》一文中,提出了侵权行为自体法理论。莫里斯在批评了侵权行为地法机械化适用方式的基础上,受合同自体法(proper law of the contract)的启发,将最密切联系原则引入侵权领域,创立了侵权行为自体法的理论。莫里斯认为,尽管在大多数情况下仍要适用侵权行为地法,但是,应该有一种足够广泛而且足够灵活的冲突规范,以使其能顾及各种例外情况。这种冲突规范就是,侵权行为问题适用侵权行为自体法。因此,所谓侵权行为自体法,就是与侵权事件及当事人有最密切联系的法律。[①] 1984 年,英国法律委员会和苏格兰法律委员会的联合工作小组就侵权行为的准据法提出联合报告,正式确立侵权行为自体法在英国的法律地位。

侵权行为自体法理论的运用,把单一的冲突规范的形式发展成了多重的冲突规范体系,使国际私法原来的封闭型的规范改变成开放型的规范,适应了现在采用多元化冲突规范的发展趋势,改变了连接因素的单一性的应用方式。但该理论并未抛弃传统冲突规范的形式和内容,而是在其中增加了新的内容,使有关法律原则既能保持长期以来人们所认可的原则,又能符合社会发展的需要。

第三节 特殊侵权行为的法律适用

一、公路交通侵权行为的法律适用

公路交通侵权行为,作为特殊的侵权行为,最早和一般侵权行为一样,主要是单一适用侵权行为地法或者法院地法。后来渐渐发展了最密切联系原则、自体法原则、重叠适用原则等。

(一)英美国家的司法实践

在公路交通侵权行为中,最早采用最密切联系地法作为涉外侵权行为准据法的国家是美国。1963 年美国纽约州法院在审理贝科克诉杰克逊(Babcock v. Jcakson)一案时,没有适用损害结果发生地法而适用了纽约州的法律。[②]

---

① Morris, *The Conflict of Laws*, 3rd. ed., London, 1984, p.310.
② 参见胡迪:《侵权行为法律适用原则的比较研究》,载《当代法学》2003 年第 6 期。

(二) 海牙《公路交通事故法律适用公约》

1971年在海牙订立的《公路交通事故法律适用公约》(Convention on the Law Applicable to Traffic Accidents,下称《海牙公约》)是规范含有涉外因素的公路交通事故法律适用的统一冲突法公约。关于涉外公路交通事故准据法的确定,《海牙公约》第3条规定应适用事故发生地国家的法律,这依然属于传统的"行为地规则"。但《海牙公约》第4条(**Article 4 of the Hague Convention**)又规定了一系列的例外情况作为上述冲突规范的补充。①

【条文】　　　　Article 4 of the Hague Convention

a) Where only one vehicle is involved in the accident and it is registered in a State other than that where the accident occurred, the internal law of the State of registration is applicable to determine liability

—towards the driver, owner or any other person having control of or an interest in the vehicle, irrespective of their habitual residence,

—towards a victim who is a passenger and whose habitual residence is in a State other than that where the accident occurred,

—towards a victim who is outside the vehicle at the place of the accident and whose habitual residence is in the State of registration.

Where there are two or more victims the applicable law is determined separately for each of them.

b) Where two or more vehicles are involved in the accident, the provisions of a) are applicable only if all the vehicles are registered in the same State.

c) Where one or more persons outside the vehicle or vehicles at the place of the accident are involved in the accident and may be liable, the provisions of a) and b) are applicable only if all these persons have their habitual residence in the State of registration.

The same is true even though these persons are also victims of the accident.

《海牙公约》还规定,在应适用车辆的登记国法时,如果车辆未经登记或在几个国家内登记,则以车辆惯常停驻的国家的内国法代替适用。上述两条规定确立了事故准据法的适用规则。

《海牙公约》对涉外交通事故的法律适用规定得比较详细和合理,受到各国和国际私法学者的广泛认可,也对不少国家的相关立法产生了一定的影响。

---

① 该条规定:(1) 只有一辆车涉及事故,且该车又非在事故发生地国内登记,则登记国的国内法可予适用;(2) 在两辆或两辆以上的车涉及事故且所有车辆均于同一国家登记时,适用该登记地国的法律;(3) 如果在事故发生地,车外的一人或数人卷入事故且有可能负有责任,并且他们均于车辆登记国有惯常居所的,适用该登记国的法律,即使这些人同时也是事故受害人时亦同。

二、国际航空运输中侵权行为的法律适用

根据《华沙公约》和《海牙议定书》的规定,国际航空运输是指根据各当事人所订的合同约定,不论在运输中有无间断和转运,其始发地点和目的地点是在两个缔约国的领土内有一个约定的经停地点的任何运输。①

(一) 航空器对地(水)面第三人造成损害赔偿的法律适用

航空器对地(水)面第三人造成损害是指飞行中的航空器或者从航空器上掉下来的任何人或物体可能对地面(或水面)上的人或物造成的损害。

通说认为,航空器对地(水)面第三人造成的损害适用侵权行为地法。我国在坚持这一原则的前提下,把损害分割成对地面第三人的损害与公海上对第三人的损害。根据《中华人民共和国民用航空法》第189条的规定,民用航空器对地面第三人的损害赔偿适用侵权行为地法,民用航空器在公海上对水面第三人的损害赔偿适用受理案件的法院地法。

(二) 航空器之间碰撞责任的法律适用

航空器之间的碰撞是指两个或两个以上的航空器之间发生直接或间接的接触而发生的事故。对于国籍相同的航空器之间的碰撞,一般适用航空器的共同国籍国法。而对于国籍不同的航空器之间的碰撞,情况就复杂了。《意大利航行法典》规定,在其他主权国家内的航空器碰撞适用侵权行为地法,而在公海等无主权地域的地区的碰撞适用意大利法。而1982年《南斯拉夫法律冲突法》第29条规定,引起赔偿责任的事件发生于公海的船舶或飞机上的,其船舶国法或飞机的登记国法应视为引起赔偿责任的行为发生地法。该条规定的是航空器位于公海上时,对于在航空器上发生的侵权行为,应将航空器的登记国法视为侵权行为地法,也就是说,这种情形引起的损害赔偿应适用航空器登记国法。②

三、海上油污损害的法律适用

(一) 国际条约优先适用原则

国际社会为寻求法律的统一作了积极的努力,制定了一些有关海事法律问题的国际公约,包括统一实体法公约和冲突法公约,其中就有许多是有关海上油污损害和赔偿方面的公约。发生海上油污损害,有国际条约的,应优先适用。

---

① 参见沈娟主编:《国际私法》,社会科学文献出版社2006年版,第290页。
② 参见孙玉超:《国际航空运输领域侵权行为法律适用问题研究》,载《河南省政法管理干部学院学报》2006年第1期。

(二) 侵权行为地法原则

各国的实践表明,在处理发生在一国管辖水域内的油污损害赔偿时,主要考虑的就是侵权行为地法。其立法本意是为了使受到水域污染损害的国家获得比较充分合理的赔偿。因为该国的海域受到污染,海洋生物的生存环境就会遭到破坏,渔业、旅游业等行业也会受到不同程度的影响,并且居民的生存环境也会受到威胁。选择适用污染损害结果发生地的法律不仅有利于保障污染损害的受害方的利益,而且能够使其享有的赔偿请求权无论在性质上还是在范围上趋于稳定,从而保证此种法律关系的稳定性。① 美国法院1978年审理的"阿莫科·卡地号"船油污损害赔偿案(**In re Oil Spill by the Amoco Cadiz**)也采用了侵权行为地法这一原则。②

【案例】 **In re Oil Spill by the Amoco Cadiz**③

The supertanker Amoco Cadiz, which had been built in Spain by a Spanish company, Astilleros Espanoles, S.A., broke up off the coast of France in 1978, causing an extensive oil spill. French citizens who allege damage from the oil spill are plaintiffs in a suit in federal district court in Chicago under the admiralty jurisdiction. The principal defendants are Astilleros and various affiliates of Standard Oil Company (Indiana), including Amoco Transport Company, the owner of the Amoco Cadiz. The plaintiffs argue that Amoco (as we shall refer to Standard and its affiliates) is liable for the damage because of negligent operation of the ship and Astilleros because of negligent or defective design and breach of implied warranty. Amoco filed a cross-claim against Astilleros under Rule 13(g) of the Federal Rules of Civil Procedure and a third-party complaint against Astilleros under Rule 14(c)—pleadings that we shall refer to jointly as the "cross-claim"—alleging that Astilleros was primarily responsible for the accident and should therefore be ordered to reimburse Amoco in whole ("indemnity") or substantial part ("contribution") for any damages that Amoco is ordered to pay the plaintiffs.

对于该案的法律适用,主审法官认为,本案中原告方所主张的所有损害都是在法国近海岸产生的,因此如果证明法国法与美国法的规定有不同之处,本案所适用的法律应为法国法。但事实证明二者并无不同之处,索赔人也主张适用美国法,因而本案依据美国法进行审理。

---

① 参见屈广清主编:《海事国际私法新编》,法律出版社2005年版,第123页。
② 1978年3月16日Amoco公司的Cadiz号超级油轮在英吉利海峡距法国西北部布列塔尼(Bretagne)海岸约25km的海上遭遇风暴触礁并很快断裂,使所载22.3万吨石油全部泄入海中,造成了数额巨大的近岸油污损害。
③ 699 F.2d 909; 1983 U.S. App. LEXIS 30801; 37 Fed. R. Serv. 2d (Callaghan) 589; 19 ERC (BNA) 1596.

(三) 法院地法原则

在海事侵权中，法院地法的作用就比较突出，这一原则的适用主要体现在公海上发生的不同国籍船舶之间的侵权行为。在实践上，这一原则也得到了一些国际公约和国家立法的承认。

我国《海商法》第 273 条第 2 款也规定，船舶在公海上发生碰撞的损害赔偿，适用受理案件的法院所在地的法律。一国法院可能会因为其沿岸受到污染、油污受害方在该国扣船或者是肇事船所属国的法院而获得对油污案件的管辖权。如果受污染国没有相应的油污立法，并且又没有参加有关的国际公约，则法院可能会适用法院地法来解决油污损害赔偿问题。

(四) 干预国法原则

根据 1969 年《国际油污损害民事责任公约》(International Convention on Civil Liability for oil Pollution Damage, 1969)，各国政府有权采取行动防止或减少海上事故造成的污染。①由于沿岸国及时采取了干预措施，其领海或是专属经济区虽未受到污染，但却产生了采取预防措施的费用和采取该措施而造成的进一步的损害。采取干预措施的国家是潜在的油污损失国，正因为该国认为公海上的油污会有蔓延到其领海的危险性，所以该国才采取了干预措施以防止污染造成更大损失，所以在法律适用问题上有必要采取干预国法律。

四、涉外产品责任的法律适用

随着经济全球化和现代科技的不断发展与进步，产品的跨国流通日益普及，产品在满足人们生活的便利与舒适的同时，各种涉外产品责任 (**products liability**) 纠纷也不断发生。不同国家的产品责任法适用于同一产品责任案件时，就会导致法律冲突。涉外产品责任的法律适用作为解决法律冲突的重要方法，目前在国际上出现了一些新的法律适用原则。

【释义】　　　　　　　　products liability

Products liability refers to the liability of any or all parties along the chain of manufacture of any product for damage caused by that product. This includes the manufacturer of component parts (at the top of the chain), an assembling manufacturer, the wholesaler, and the retail store owner (at the bottom of the chain). Products containing inherent defects that cause harm to a consumer of the product, or someone to whom the product was loaned, given, etc.,

---

① 参见〔加拿大〕威廉·台特雷：《国际海商法》，张永坚等译，法律出版社 2005 年版，第 368 页。

are the subjects of products liability suits. While products are generally thought of as tangible personal property, products liability has stretched that definition to include intangibles (gas), naturals (pets), real estate (house), and writings (navigational charts).

Products liability claims can be based on negligence, strict liability, or breach of warranty of fitness depending on the jurisdiction within which the claim is based. Many states have enacted comprehensive products liability statutes. These statutory provisions can be very diverse such that the the United States Department of Commerce has promulgated a Model Uniform Products Liability Act for voluntary use by the states. There is no federal products liability law.

In any jurisdiction one must prove that the product is defective. There are three types of product defects that incur liability in manufacturers and suppliers: design defects, manufacturing defects, and defects in marketing. Design defects are inherent; they exist before the product is manufactured. While the item might serve its purpose well, it can be unreasonably dangerous to use due to a design flaw. On the other hand, manufacturing defects occur during the construction or production of the item. Only a few out of many products of the same type are flawed in this case. Defects in marketing deal with improper instructions and failures to warn consumers of latent dangers in the product.

Products Liability is generally considered a strict liability offense. Strict liability wrongs do not depend on the degree of carefulness by the defendant. Translated to products liability terms, a defendant is liable when it is shown that the product is defective. It is irrelevant whether the manufacturer or supplier exercised great care; if there is a defect in the product that causes harm, he or she will be liable for it.

对于产品责任,大多数国家将其视为侵权责任。各国理论和实践上对涉外产品责任已逐步确立了以下几种法律适用规则。

(一) 最密切联系原则

产品责任适用侵权行为发生时与侵权行为以及当事人有最密切联系的国家的法律,是现代各国产品责任法律适用的一个基本规则。

(二) 最有利于原告原则

在产品责任中,消费者在产品侵权案件中是最大的受害者,并且处于弱势地位。因而在涉外产品责任的法律适用上,最大限度地保护消费者利益应作为一项重要的指导原则。为了更好地维护受害人的合法权利,美国的卡弗斯教授提出了"优先选择原则",认为原告有权从所涉国家的法律中选择适用某一法律作为准据法,这种选择的范围包括:(1) 产品生产地法;(2) 原告惯常居所地法;(3) 取得产品地法;(4) 损害结果发生地法。

这种"优先选择原则"的学说对美国法官产生了重大的影响。对于绝大多数的法官来说,处理产品责任较好的法律应该是能保证受害者可以从缺陷产品制造商处获得赔偿的法律规则。美国法官的这种做法直接导致了"最有利于原告"的法律适用原则在美国的盛行。这样,原告在不同连接点法律规定的利益不一致时,可以选择适用其中最有利于他的那个连接点指向的法律,使审理案件的法院能及时、有效地保护其利益。在产品责任法律适用问题上,允许受害人在某些确定范围的法律中选择适用,使他能够选择自己认为最能保护其利益的法律,使得对其救济、补偿在其最大的法律选择空间里得到实现。

(三)排除适用被告不可预见法律的原则

在涉外产品责任法律适用制度上,为了平衡当事人双方的利益,各国在采用最密切联系和最有利于原告原则的同时,以排除被告不可预见的法律的适用作出限制。如《瑞士联邦国际私法》第133条规定了适用损害结果发生地法律须以加害人可以预见到损害将在该国发生为条件。这样的规定一方面排除了产品损害结果发生地及受害人惯常居所地的偶然性使被告承担不公正责任的可能性;另一方面体现了平等对待原、被告双方当事人,显示出法律选择对双方当事人利益的统筹兼顾。

(四)我国有关涉外产品责任法律适用的规定

我国自2011年4月1日起施行的《涉外民事关系法律适用法》第45条规定:"产品责任,适用被侵权人经常居所地法律;被侵权人选择适用侵权人主营业地法律、损害发生地法律的,或者侵权人在被侵权人经常居所地没有从事相关经营活动的,适用侵权人主营业地法律或者损害发生地法律。"该条规定就将产品责任侵权行为法律纠纷解决的法律选择的权利交给被侵权人,因产品责任遭受损害的受害人可以选择一个对自己最为有利的法律,以达到实质上的公平。① 可见,我国《涉外民事关系法律适用法》在法律适用规范的确定方面,采取了让受害人充分选择所适用的法律,体现了对受害人充分、有效的法律保护。

第四节 互联网侵权行为的法律适用

互联网的广泛应用改变了人类的生存、生活与生产方式,但同时网络侵权案件也层出不穷,对传统的国际私法法律适用规则提出了挑战。

---

① 参见邹淑环:《侵权行为法律适用的三大变化及我国的立法实践》,载《天津商业大学学报》2011年第6期。

一、网络侵权行为的概念

网络侵权行为是指通过网络技术平台,在网络环境下实施的侵害网络权益主体及其他人的人身和财产等民事权益,应当承担侵害赔偿等民事责任的行为。网络侵权行为在司法实践中大致表现为侵犯隐私权,侵犯著作权、商标标识、域名、专利权等知识产权,侵犯人格权,侵犯商业秘密等不正当竞争行为。网络作为一种特殊媒介,使得通过其实施的侵权行为具有区别于传统侵权行为的特征:

第一,侵权行为实施空间的虚拟性和跨地域性。网络空间没有国界与地域(**no territorially based boundaries**),网络侵权是发生在网络这个特定的虚拟空间范围内的,离开网络环境,网络侵权无从谈起。由于网络通信线路的跨地域、跨国界的特点,网络侵权突破了传统侵权空间的地域性特点,将侵权空间扩大了。

【释义】　　　　　　　　　no territorially based boundaries

Cyberspace has no territorially based boundaries, because the cost and speed of message transmission on the Net is almost entirely independent of physical location. The system is indifferent to the physical location of those machines, and there is no necessary connection between an Internet address and a physical jurisdiction.①

第二,司法管辖的不易确定性。因特网将全球的计算机及其网络连为一体构成了一个独特的网络空间,同一侵权行为往往同几个地点相联系,物理位置在网络空间中的意义微乎其微,从而使传统管辖权的基础在网络空间中发生了动摇。因此面对纷繁复杂的网络案件,人们不得不寻找新的管辖依据。

第三,网络侵权行为的隐秘性。网络侵权行为主体实施的侵权行为大多是通过对网络数据信息的复制、改变、破坏等操作来完成,信息本身是看不见、摸不着的,侵权行为的发生又十分迅速,转瞬即失、不留痕迹,侵权后果又常常不易被发现,使得网络侵权实施者往往难以被确认。其侵权实施地、损害结果发生地的问题复杂而难以确定,特别是对侵权主体的确认、侵权行为的举证、行为与结果之间的因果关系证明等都更为棘手。

第四,网络侵权类型的多样性。网络侵权行为按照其侵害的对象来分类,主要有以下类型:与知识产权有关的网络侵权行为②,与公民人身权有关的网络侵权行

---

① Lea Brilmayer and Jack Goldsmith, *Conflict of Laws: Cases and Materials*, 5th ed., Citic Publishing House and Aspen Publisher Inc., 2003, p.813.

② 如在网络中传输的信息大部分属于知识产权的范畴,在网络中使用和发行传统的文学作品、艺术作品、科技作品、计算机软件、专利和商标等造成的对知识产权的侵犯无疑成为最主要的类型。

为,与公民财产权有关的网络侵权行为等。①

二、网络侵权行为的法律适用

网络侵权行为的特征,使得这种侵权行为在法律适用上有着新的特点,对传统侵权行为的法律适用原则提出了新的挑战。网络侵权对于传统国际私法最大的挑战在于连接点问题。网络作为一个虚拟的空间,传统的侵权行为地的适用已经失去了原有的意义,就连传统的连接点这一纽带也开始变得飘忽不定。而主观连接点如最密切联系原则和当事人意思自治原则则发挥着越来越重要的作用。

(一) 最密切联系原则

最密切联系原则主张侵权行为适用与侵权案件有最密切联系的法律。②这一理论可以使法院在司法实践中把各种不同情况的侵权诉讼分别进行处理,并能使法院对个案所包括的各种社会因素作出充分的分析和考虑。最密切联系原则适用的这些特点刚好解决了网络侵权连接点难以确定,侵权行为隐秘性、跨地域性,行为实施空间虚拟性等特点而造成的法律适用的困难。在网络侵权的法律适用中,最密切联系原则显示了其强大的生命力。

(二) 当事人意思自治原则

对于网络侵权行为的法律适用,可以考虑采用当事人意思自治原则,允许当事人在他们的交换协议中合意选择支配他们之间可能会产生的侵权责任的法律。③而在缺乏当事人合意选择的情形下,则可以适用最密切联系原则。

(三) 适用法院地法

雅虎公司涉嫌拍卖亲纳粹物品案(**Licra and UEJF v. Yahoo! Inc.**),是一起典型的涉外互联网纠纷案件。

【案例】 **Licra and UEJF v. Yahoo! Inc.**④

Yahoo! Inc. ("Yahoo!"), a U.S. corporation and one of the world's leading web portals, has an Internet auction site that offered for sale Nazi memorabilia such as flags, stamps, and

---

① 参见张铂炎:《网络侵权及其法律适用》,载《法制与社会》2008 年第 5 期。
② 参见金彭年:《中国国际私法典示范法:侵权条款及其法理》,载《中外法学》1995 年第 3 期。
③ 但是也有学者认为,在网络侵权案中应对当事人意思自治原则作出限制。参见贺旭红:《跨国网络侵权的法律适用》,载《甘肃政法学院学报》2008 年第 3 期。
④ Lea Brilmayer and Jack Goldsmith, *Conflict of Laws: Cases and Materials*, 5th ed., Citic Publishing House and Aspen Publisher Inc., 2003, pp. 851—852.

military souvenirs. Persons at computers in France could access this site through links on the French language portal of Yahoo! 's French subsidiary, Yahoo! France, or by accessing Yahoo! 's portal directly from France by typing www.yahoo.com into a computer browser. The international League Against Racism and Anti-Semitism (Licra) and the Union of French Jewish Students (UEJF) sued Yahoo! And Yahoo! France, alleging violations of Article R. 645-2 of the French penal code, a World War II-era law criminalizing the exhibition or sale of racist materials. The plaintiffs asked the Court to force Yahoo! to block French users' access to Nazi objects for sale on Yahoo! 's U.S. auction site.

  Yahoo! Inc. has argued that French court is not territorially competent over the matter, because the alleged fault is committed on the territory of the United States. It further argues for rejection of plaintiffs' claims on the ground that the duties of vigilance and prior censure, which the petitioners would seek to impose upon it are impossible obligation, first in terms of the law and the American constitution, in particular the First Amendment of the Constitution which institutes the liberty of expression and then in view of the technical impossibility of identifying surfers who visit the auction service.

  After having heard all the parties, the Paris Court: (a) order Yahoo! Inc. to take such measures as will dissuade and render impossible any and all consultation on Yahoo.com of the auction service for Nazi objects as well as any other site or service which makes apologies of Nazism or questions of the existence of Nazi crimes; (b) orders a subsequent hearing during which Yahoo! Inc. shall submit the measures, which it intends to implement to end, the harm and the nuisance suffered by the plaintiffs and to prevent any new incidents of nuisance; (c) finds Yahoo! Inc. liable to pay to the Licra an amount of 10000 Francs on the basis of article 700 of the New Code of Civil Procedure.

  Yahoo! Inc. 所设的拍卖网站在其本国(美国)是合法的,但在法国,购买和销售纳粹商品是违法的,是伤害法国人民感情的行为,构成了对法国人民的侵权,所以为法国国内法所禁止。法国居民可以通过互联网在其本国访问该拍卖网站,在法国法院看来,这是 Yahoo! Inc. 在其境内销售纳粹商品的行为。巴黎法院在审理此案时,适用了法院地法,即法国法,并对 Yahoo! Inc. 作出了处罚决定。

  总之,对于网络侵权的法律适用,应该随着实践的发展而发展。在关注网络侵权法律适用实践发展的同时,应更加注重国际私法的核心价值取向。

三、我国有关网络侵权法律适用的规定

  《涉外民事关系法律适用法》第 46 条规定,通过网络或者采用其他方式侵害姓名权、肖像权、名誉权、隐私权等人格权的,适用被侵权人经常居所地法律。可见,"经常居所地"成为我国侵犯人格权法律适用的重要连接因素,体现了属人法趋同

化的倾向。① 一方面,经常居所地具有可操作性,能较好地弥合民法法系国家与普通法法系国家在属人法传统连结因素上的冲突。与住所地和国籍相比较,经常居所地具有显著的优越性。相较于住所而言,经常居所地并不过分强调当事人久居的意思表示,因此法官更容易确定一个当事人的经常居所地。在属人法的连结点上,提高经常居所的地位,对于国际贸易的发展和商业行为的规制是极为有利和必要的。同时,经常居住地对于缓解住所与国籍的冲突、协调住所地主义与国籍原则的分歧颇有裨益。另一方面,经常居所地更能真实地反映出当事人意图使其受控制的法律,从而有利于基于此作出的判决获得承认与执行。

【思考题】

- 传统侵权行为适用什么法律?
- 侵权行为地法,根据不同的识别方式包括哪些不同的法律?
- 侵权行为自体法的具体内容是什么?
- 试比较各国立法对特殊侵权行为法律适用的不同规定。
- 网络侵权行为有什么特点?网络侵权行为对传统侵权行为法律适用规则有哪些挑战?

【重要术语提示与中英文对照】

中文术语	英文对照
侵权行为准据法	applicable law of a tort
损害赔偿	damages
侵权行为地法	*lex loci delicti*, law of the place of wrong
损害结果发生地规则	place-of-impact rule
最后事件地	place of last event
便利性和法院中立性	simplicity and forum neutrality
博伊斯诉查普林案	Boys v. Chaplin
双重可起诉	double actionability
菲利普诉艾尔案	Phillip v. Eyre
贝科克诉杰克逊案	Babcock v. Jackson
重力中心	center of gravity
侵权行为自体法	proper law of the torts

---

① 参见杜新丽:《从住所、国籍到经常居所地——我国属人法立法变革研究》,载《政法论坛》2011年第3期。

软化处理	softening process
公路交通事故法律适用公约	Convention on the Law Applicable to Traffic Accidents,
阿莫科·卡地号案	In re Oil Spill by the Amoco Cadiz
产品责任	products liability
网络空间没有国界与地域	Cyberspace has no territorially based boundaries
雅虎公司涉嫌拍卖亲纳粹物品案	Licra and UEJF v. Yahoo! Inc.

【推荐阅读文献】

- 周海荣:《国际侵权行为法》,广东高等教育出版社 1991 年版。
- 贺旭红:《跨国网络侵权的法律适用》,载《甘肃政法学院学报》2008 年第 3 期。
- 杜新丽、王克玉:《论涉外侵权法律适用法的价值目标及实现路径》,载《法学杂志》2010 年第 2 期。
- 霍政欣:《涉外侵权之债的法律适用——以"7·23 甬温线特别重大铁路交通事故"中外籍伤亡乘客的赔偿为视角》,《法商研究》2011 年第 6 期。
- 贺琼琼:《论意思自治在侵权冲突法中的现代发展——兼评〈涉外民事关系法律适用法〉之相关规定》,载《武汉大学学报(哲学社会科学版)》2011 年第 6 期。
- 邹淑环:《侵权行为法律适用的三大变化及我国的立法实践》,载《天津商业大学学报》2011 年第 6 期。
- Kahn-Freund, Delictual Liability and the Conflict of Laws, *Recueil Des Cours De L'Académie De Droit International De La Haye* (1968 II).
- Donggen Xu, *Le droit international privé de la responsabilité délictuelle: Evolution récent et la loi chinoise*, Editions universitaires Fribourg, 1992.
- Stuart Dutson: Product Liability and Private International Law: Choice of Law in Tort in England, 47 *Am. J. Comp. L.* 141—146 (1999).
- David H. Vernon, Louis Weinberg, William Reynolds, William Richman, *Conflicts of Law: Case, Materials and Problems*, 2d ed., LexisNexis, 2002.
- K. N. Hylton, Torts and Choice of Law: Searching for Principles, 56 *J. Legal Educ.* 551 (2006).
- Jack L. Goldsmith & Alan O. Sykes, Lex Loci Delictus and Global Economic Welfare: Spinozzi v. ITT Sheraton Corp., 120 *Harv. L. Rev.* 1137 (2007).
- Schwartze (A.), A European Regime on International Product Liability: Article 5 Rome II Regulation, 2008 *Nederl. IPR.* 430 (2008).
- He (Q.), Recent Developments with Regards to Choice of Law in Tort in China, 11

- García-Castrillón (O.), International Litigation Trends in Environmental Liability: A European Union-United States Comparative Perspective, 7 *J. Priv. Int'l L.* 551 (2011).
- Jan Oster, Rethinking Shevill, Conceptualising the EU Private International Law of Internet Torts against Personality Rights, 26 *I. R. L. C. T.* 113 (2012).

【扩展阅读资料】

Choice of Law in Tort in England Post-Private International Law Act 1995[①]

A. Choice of law rule

Part III of the Private International Law (Miscellaneous Provisions) Act 1995 (UK) provides for a new choice of law rule in tort or delict. The law on characterization for private international law purposes is unaffected by the Act. The pre-existing common law choice of law rule in tort is abolished in so far as the Act applies. The Act makes it clear that it is only the pre-existing choice of law rule in tort that it abolishes. Therefore, inter alia, the law on mandatory rules of the forum, and the rules of evidence, pleading, practice and procedure are not affected.

Section 11 of the Act provides the general choice of law rule:

"11. (1) The general rule is that the applicable law is the law of the country in which the events constituting the tort or delict in question occur.

(2) Where elements of those events occur in different countries, the applicable law under the general rule is to be taken as being—(a) for a cause of action in respect of personal injury caused to an individual or death resulting from personal injury, the law of the country where the individual was when he sustained the injury; (b) for a cause of action in respect of damage to property, the law of the country where the property was when it was damaged; and (c) in any other case, the law of the country in which the most significant element or elements of those events occurred.

(3) In this section 'personal injury' includes disease or any impairment of physical or mental condition."

The general rule applies, in contrast to the pre-existing common law rule, to all tort cases regardless of where the tort was committed. Section 12 provides an exception to the general rule:

---

① Stuart Dutson, Product Liability and Private International Law: Choice of Law in Tort in England, 47 *Am. J. Comp. L.* 129, 141—146 (1999).

"12.—(1) If it appears, in all the circumstances, from a comparison of — (a) the significance of the factors which connect a tort or delict with the country whose law would be the applicable law under the general rule; and (b) the significance of any factors connecting the tort or delict with another country, that it is substantially more appropriate for the applicable law for determining the issues arising in the case, or any of those issues, to be the law of another country, the general rule is displaced and the applicable law for determining those issues or that issue (as the case may be) is the law of that other country.

(2) The factors that may be taken into account as connecting a tort or delict with a country for the purposes of this section include, in particular, factors relating to the parties, to any of the events which constitute the tort or delict in question or to any of the circumstances or consequences of those events."

All of the cases with which this article is concerned will be cases of personal injury and/or property damage. Accordingly, the general rule will provide that the applicable law will be the law of the country where the injury was sustained and/or the property was damaged. Therefore, in cases in which the product is manufactured outside England and the injury or damage occurs within England the applicable law will generally be that of England. Accordingly, the CPA will be applicable and England's tort law will also be applicable un less the s. 12 exception is relevant.

B. The Section 12 exception

During the Lord Chancellor's Second Reading Speech on the Act his Lordship placed a great deal of emphasis on the inclusion of the word "substantially" in s. 12. He stated that "The exception is not in tended to operate every time another applicable law might be more appropriate but only where it would be substantially so."

Briggs has stated that the position under the s. 12 exception "will differ little from the common law position taken in Boys v. Chaplin and Red Sea Insurance Co. v. Bouygues S. A. In particular it leaves it open to a court to mark an exception in terms of a law being more closely connected to the issue as well as on the footing that the law indicated by the general rule 'has no interest' in its being applied to the particular case." However, the terms of s. 12 do not appear to reflect any aspect of the question whether to apply a law or not would serve any interest which the law was devised to meet—a consideration in Lord Wilberforce's formulation of the exception to the general rule in Boys v. Chaplin. However, despite this and slightly different verbal formulations, it appears that the effect of the pre—and post—Act exceptions will be identical for present purposes. That the exceptions relate to different general rules will not alter the application of the exception for present purposes. Accordingly, in their application to the cases with which this article is concerned, the examples given in relation to the exception to the pre-Act general rule are equally valid here. VI. Application of the Common Law Choice of Law Rule in Tort and Part III of the Private International Law (Miscellaneous Provisions) Act 1995 (UK) to the CPA and the English Common Law Tort of Negligence. It has previously been concluded by the present author that the better view is that in any case in which a person suffers injury or damage that occurs within the UK due to a defective product, wherever it was manufactured, the CPA is applicable to a foreign manufacturer, whatever his residence or domicile, and to the importer into the member States domiciled anywhere within the EC member States. It was also concluded that the CPA is limited in its territorial application to cases in which personal injury or property damage occurs within the UK.

Of the application of the rules of private international law to the CPA to determine its application, the apparent manifestation of Parliament's intention that the CPA apply to all producers wherever they are resident or domiciled, and to importers domiciled within the member States, would appear to override the application of any choice of law rule in the determination of whether the Act applies to importers domiciled within the member States or to producers or production anywhere in the world. However, the relevant choice of law rule may nevertheless be applied to the statute to determine its territorial scope. In pre-Private International Law (Miscellaneous Provisions) Act 1995 cases, if the cause of action can be described as a foreign tort, then the CPA and the English common law tort of negligence will be applicable in the case of a foreign producer or importer domiciled within the member States, if the production of a defective product or the importation of a defective product from outside the member States would be civilly actionable both in England and in the foreign country where it was done, unless another country has the most significant relationship with the occurrence and the parties. If these two conditions cannot be satisfied then the court will not be able to apply any substantive law to the case unless the proviso is applicable. If the proviso applies then the court will apply the law of the country that has the most significant relationship with the occurrence and the parties, to the case. In cases in which the production of a defective product, or the importation of a defective product from outside the member States, takes place within: a State that has enacted legislation based upon the Directive into its own law; a country that has a strict product liability law; or, any country in which the producer of a product can be held liable to compensate a person who suffers personal injury or property damage due to a defective product, and the conditions to establish that liability in that country exist; the first two conditions will always be able to be satisfied, and the only issue that will require consideration will be whether the exception applies. In those country in which fault is required to be proved in order for the producer to be held liable to compensate a person who suffers personal injury or property damage due to a defective product, fault on the part of the producer must be proved before the second limb of the general rule can be satisfied. This will be so despite the fact that the plaintiff is relying on the CPA—a UK statute creating a strict liability cause of action. In post-Private International Law (Miscellaneous Provisions) Act 1995 cases, the CPA and the English common law of tort will be applicable in the case of a foreign producer or importer if the events constituting the tort occur within England, unless it is substantially more appropriate that the law of another country be applied. If the events do not occur within England, or if the proviso applies, then the court will apply the law of another country to the case. In cases of personal injury the relevant events will occur within England if the individual was there when he sustained the injury. In cases of property damage they will occur within England if the property was damaged there. Therefore, the CPA and the English common law of tort will apply to foreign producers and importers domiciled outside England but within the member States in cases in which: the personal injury was sustained, or the property damage occurred, within England, and it is not substantially more appropriate that the law of another country be applied; or, the personal injury was sustained, or the property damage occurred, outside England, but it is substantially more appropriate that the law of England be applied.

第十一章

国际合同关系的法律适用

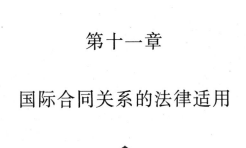

本章导读

※ 合同的法律适用,就是合同的法律选择或合同准据法的确定。

※ "整体法"主张合同准据法适用于合同的所有领域,即合同准据法同时支配与合同有关的所有问题,一个合同原则上只适用一个法律。

※ "分割法"主张对合同进行分割,把合同的诸问题或各个环节分解开来,在法律适用上采取分而治之的办法,即合同的不同问题或环节分别适用各自的准据法。

※ 按照合同自体法理论,合同准据法应当包括三个部分,即:(1)如果当事人明确选择了合同所适用的法律,则应将他们所选择的法律作为合同的准据法;(2)如果当事人未对法律作出选择,但根据合同的条款能够推断出他们对法律适用的意思的话,则应将合同中所默示的适用于合同的法律作为合同的准据法;(3)如果当事人既没有明确选择所适用的法律,也没有在合同中表现出默示的意图,则由法院适用与案件有最密切联系的法律作为合同的准据法。

※ 合同自体法的运用首先涉及意思自治原则,即合同当事人可以通过明示方式选择合同的准据法。但是,合同当事人根据意思自治原则选择合同准据法是有限制的:当事人选择法律的行为应该是善意的,即当事人的明示选择不得违反有关国家强行法的规定和公共秩序;当事人不得选择与合同毫无联系的国家的法律。

※ 通过最密切联系原则确定合同准据法是合同自体法理论的重要组成部分,即在当事人没有通过明示或者默示的方式选择合同准据法时,应适用与合同法律关系有最密切联系的法律。法院在考虑与合同法律关系有最密切联系的因素时,应考虑这些客观标志:合同履行地、合同订立地、当事人住所地、被告所在地、法院地或仲裁地。最密切联系原则的运用需要借助于特征性履行方法。

※ 中国有关涉外合同法律适用的规定是国际条约优先适用、允许当事人自主选择所适用的法律,以最密切联系原则为补充,以国际惯例为补缺。

※ 中外合资经营企业、中外合作经营企业和中外合作开发勘探自然资源合同只能适用中国法。

【本章主题词】 整体法、分割法、合同自体法、明示选择、默示、最密切联系

第十一章　国际合同关系的法律适用

第一节　国际合同法律适用概述

一、合同准据法的概念

合同的法律适用,就是合同的法律选择或合同准据法(applicable law of a contract)的确定。合同准据法一词有广义和狭义之分。从广义上讲,合同准据法是指解决涉及合同的一切法律适用问题的准据法。而狭义上的合同准据法是直接确定合同当事人的权利与义务的法律,主要用于解决合同的成立、合同的内容与效力、合同的履行与解释等问题。一般而言,当事人在合同中选定的合同准据法,多是指狭义的合同准据法。

二、合同法律适用的整体法

有关合同准据法的适用范围,各国的理论、立法和司法实践存在分歧和对立。有的国家主张,合同准据法适用于合同的所有领域,即合同准据法同时支配与合同有关的所有问题,这种方法通常称为"整体法"(unity of contract)。整体法主张一个合同原则上只能适用一个法律(**a single law**)。

【观点】　　　　　　　　　　　a single law

Professor Loussouarn, insisted that the contract shall be submitted to a single law, viewing the contract is a unity from both economic and judicial points of view.[①]

Professor Batiffol confirmed that a contract forms a psychological, commercial and economic unity, and such unity must be submitted to a single law.[②]

三、合同法律适用的分割法

然而,用单一的准据法调整错综复杂的合同关系未免缺乏针对性和合理性。

[①] Y. Loussouarn, La Convention de la Haye d'octobre 1985 sur la loi applicable aux contrats de vente internationale de merchandise, *Revue Critique de droit internaitonal privé.*, 1986, pp.278—279.

[②] H. Batiffol, *Les contracts en droit international privé comparé*, MacGill University, 1981, p.162.

因此,一些学者主张对合同进行分割,把合同的诸问题或各个环节分解开来,分别适用法律(**plurality**)。

【观点】   plurality

Professor Lagarde believed that it is the necessary corollary of rules of the conflict of laws which are characterized by plurality. For example, in a contact for the sale of a movable, no one will be surprised that issues of party capacity are submitted to their personal law, the form of contract to the law of place of making, and the transfer of real tights to the law of the *situs* of the movable. It is always possible that the parties themselves want their contract to be governed by different laws. There is no obstacle for the dépeçage made by the parties of the contract.①

在法律适用上采取分而治之的办法,即合同的不同问题或环节分别适用各自的准据法,这种方法通常称为"分割法"(**dépeçage**)。②

【释义】   dépeçage

Dépeçage has been defined as "applying the rules of different states to determine different issues".③ Dépeçage refers to the concept whereby different issues within a particular case may be governed by the laws of different states. In common law countries dépeçage is usually used to refer to a single contract which provides that different parts of the contract shall be governed by different laws.

The term "dépeçage" is often defined as a choice-of-law method that cuts up a case and applies the law of different legal systems to different issues. Thus, a court employs Dépeçage when it applies the law of State A to one issue and applies the law of State B to another issue.

The leading American choice-of-law approaches encourage extensive dépeçage. The Second Restatement requires that its "most significant relationship" test be applied separately to each contract issue. This can result in the law of State A being applied to one issue while the law of State B is applied to another issue. Similarly, interest analysis approaches permit a court to find that State A has the only (or greater) interest in one issue and that State B has the only (or greater) interest in some other issue. Note, however, that whether the court uses the Re-

---

① P. Lagarde, Le dépeçage dans le droit international privé des contracts, *Rivista di dirtto international rpivatoe* 1975 IV, pp. 649—650.

② 分割一词来源于法文 dépeçage,音译为"德帕沙治",意为"切碎"、"分块"。参见邓正来:《美国现代国际私法流派》,法律出版社 1987 年版,第 132 页。美国冲突法著作常用 picking and chooosing 表达同一语义,英国学者则用 fragmentation。

③ Russell J Weintraub, *Commentary on the Conflict of Laws*, 4th ed, New York Foundation Press, 2001, p.96.

statement or interest analysis, it always applies one approach, one analytical method with one set of factors to consider, to all issues.①

"分割法"理论在国际私法上产生了一定的影响(**influence**),一些国家接受了"分割法"理论,以便针对合同的不同环节的不同特点,恰如其分地适用法律。

【观点】 influence

The concept originated in civil law countries, but has also been adopted in common law countries such as the United Kingdom and Ireland pursuant to the Rome Convention on the Law Applicable to Contractual Obligations.②

第二节 合同自体法

一、合同自体法概述

(一) 自体法的概念

自体法(**proper law**)是对法律适用问题的解决提出一种理论、一个标准、一种方法,其主旨在于告诉人们应该怎样确定合同"准据法",或者说应该依据什么原则和标准来确定合同"准据法"。

【释义】 Proper law

In a Conflicts lawsuit, one or more state laws will be relevant to the decision-making

---

① Henry Mather, Choice of Law for International Sales Issues not Resolved by the CISG, 20 *J. L. & Com.* 186 (2001).

② 《关于合同义务法律适用的公约》第3条第1项规定:"合同依当事人选择的法律。法律选择必须通过合同条款或具体情况相当明确地加以表示或表明。双方当事人可以自行选择适用于合同的全部或部分的法律。"第4条第1项又规定:"凡未依第3条选择适用法律的合同,依与之有最密切联系的国家的法律。但合同的可分割的部分同另一国有较紧密的关系,则该部分得作为例外,依据其他国家的法律的规定。"

process. If the laws are the same, this will cause no problems, but if there are substantive differences, the choice of which law to apply will produce a different judgment. Each state therefore produces a set of rules to guide the choice of law, and one of the most significant rules is that the law to be applied in any given situation will be the *proper law*. This is the law which seems to have the closest and most real connection to the facts of the case, and so has the best claim to be applied.

All laws, to a greater or lesser extent, are reflections of the public policies of the state that enacted them. The more important the policy to the society, the greater the claim of the relevant law to be applied. Thus, if laws exist to protect citizens, the law of the place where loss or damage is sustained might have a strong claim to apply: e.g. in a traffic accident, two cars collide because of faulty maintenance and both drivers are injured—the local laws exist to provide some degree of protection for all those who use the roads in that state, setting minimum standards for the design and maintenance of vehicles, specifying what levels of insurance should be carried, setting the minimum age and qualifications for the right to drive, etc.

But the problem with accepting the claim of any one state to have its law apply is that the result may be somewhat arbitrary. So, in the example given, if neither driver had a residence in the state, and the cars were both maintained outside the state, the laws of other states may have an equal or better claim to apply.①

在我国，对"proper law"（自体法）②这个国际私法特有的术语，有许多不同的译法，如"准据法"③、"本有法"④、"适当法"⑤、"特有法"⑥、"关系法"⑦、"宜用法"⑧、"宜用准据法"⑨等。还有主张翻译为"适当关系法"、"关系密切地法"⑩的。造成这种局面的原因，固然由于英文本身词义的庞杂，但主要还是因为人们对"proper law"这个概念的内涵存在不同的理解。从英文看，proper 一词含义甚广，中

---

① See http://en.wikipedia.org/wiki/Proper_law.
② 参见韩德培：《法律行为方式的准据法》，载中国大百科全书出版社编辑部编：《中国大百科全书（法学卷）》，中国大百科全书出版社 1984 年版，第 473 页。
③ 参见刘慧珊：《Proper Law 问题探析》，载中国国际私法学会主办：《中国国际私法与比较法年刊》（第七卷），法律出版社 2005 年版，第 3—32 页。
④ 同上。
⑤ 参见马汉宝：《国际私法总论》，台湾吉丰印制有限公司 1990 年版，第 141 页。在此作者是将 proper law theory 译为"适当法说"的。还可参见吕岩峰：《英国"适当法理论"之研究》，载《吉林大学社会科学学报》1992 年第 5 期；吕岩峰：《物权法律适用的历史沿革》，载中国国际私法学会主办：《中国国际私法与比较法年刊》（第六卷），法律出版社 2003 年版，第 130 页。
⑥ 参见李双元：《国际私法（冲突法篇）》，武汉大学出版社 1987 年版，第 344 页。
⑦ 参见吕岩峰：《英国"适当法理论"之研究》，载《吉林大学社会科学学报》1992 年第 5 期。
⑧ 参见朱学山：《论合同宜用法》，载《涉外民事经济法律研究》，中山大学出版社 1991 年版，第 231 页。
⑨ 参见董立坤：《国际私法》（修订本），法律出版社 2000 年版，第 57 页。
⑩ 参见黄进、肖永平：《国际私法领域内重要理论问题综述》，载《中国社会科学》1990 年第 6 期。

文译作"自体"只取一种含义,且只代表一种看法。除此之外,英国学者安顿(Anton)将 proper 一词译为适当。我国卢峻教授的观点与安顿相去不远。日本学者折茂丰在其专著《涉外不法行为法论》中把它理解为固有的法。

而将 proper law 译为"自体法",是我国著名国际私法学家韩德培教授在《中国大百科全书(法学卷)》中首先提出来的。[①]

自体法与合同准据法具有相同作用,但是,这二者还是有区别的。"自体法"和"准据法"的最终目的虽然都是为了确定国际民商事关系当事人的实体权利和义务,但"准据法"是指经过冲突规范指引用来确定国际民商事关系的某个国家的民商实体法,它是依据某一冲突规范中的连接因素,结合国际民商事关系的现实情况确定的。自体法是指某一法律关系客观上要求适用的法律。将 proper law 译为自体法,可以使人们明白法律关系与准据法之间的内在一致性,自体法理论的核心就在于揭示这一内在一致性。[②]

自体法与准据法有密切的关系,两者常发生交叉和重叠。自体法表示的是准据法的一种应有或固有状态,即自体法是具体准据法确定前的一种可能状态,当这种可能变成现实时,自体法即是准据法。也就是说,我们可以认为自体法是准据法的前身,准据法则是自体法的一种延伸。[③]

"自体法"理论发端于合同法领域,后来又扩展到侵权行为及其他领域,经历了依当事人意图的"主观论"时期和依最密切联系原则的"客观论"时期,自体法正处于"现代论"时期,主张"主观论"和"客观论"的相互补充和结合。被称为"客观论"与"主观论"的黄金结合的"自体法理论",汲取了法律适用历史发展过程中的全部精华,并且使之有机结合,既具有确定性又具有灵活性

(二)合同自体法的概念

合同自体法(**proper law of the contract**)是用来解决合同法律适用的一种理论和方法,是自体法理论在合同法律适用领域的具体应用。

【释义】　　　　　　　　proper law of the contract

The proper law of the contract is the main system of law applied to decide the validity of most aspects to the contract including its formation, validity, interpretation, and performance. The proper law test today is three-stage:

---

① 肖永平:《中国国际私法立法问题研究》,武汉大学出版社 1993 年版,第 97 页。
② 李广辉、陈孝杰:《试论国际私法中的自体法理论》,载《河南师范大学学报》(哲学社会科学版)2000 年第 5 期。
③ 肖永平:《准据法概念新论》,载《法学杂志》1992 年第 1 期。

It is the law intended by the parties when the contract was made which is usually evidenced by an express choice of law clause; or

It is implied by the court because either the parties incorporated actual legal terminology or provisions specific to one legal system, or because the contract would only be valid under one of the potentially relevant systems; or

If there is no express or implied choice, it is the law which has the closest and most real connection to the bargain made by the parties. ①

合同自体法是英国国际私法上的一个特有的历史范畴②，它的理论和实践有一个发展过程。合同自体法的历史(**history of the proper law of the contract**)，可以溯源到19世纪的英国。

【释义】　　　　　history of the proper law of the contract

In the Conflict of Laws, the validity of a contract with one or more foreign law elements will be decided by reference to the so-called "proper law" of the contract. Until the middle of the 19th century, the courts applied the *lex loci contractus* or the *law of the place where the contract was made* to decide whether the given contract was valid. The apparent advantage of this approach was that the rule was easy to apply with certain and predictable outcomes. Unfortunately, it was also open to abuse, e.g. the place could be selected fraudulently to validate an otherwise invalid contract; it might lead to the application of laws with no real connection with the transaction itself, say, because the parties signed the agreement while on holiday; or it might have been difficult to decide where the contract was made, e.g. because it was negotiated and signed on a railway journey through several states.

To avoid these difficulties, some courts proposed applying the *lex loci solutionis* or the *law of the place of performance of the contract*. This produced difficulties in cases where the contract required each party to perform its obligations in a different country, or where the place of performance was dictated by later circumstances. However, as the public policies driven by the theory of freedom of contract evolved, the Doctrine of Proper Law emerged.

一般认为,合同自体法理论是由意思自治说演变而来的,所以它可以溯源至法国16世纪的杜摩兰(Charles Dumoulin)。在杜摩兰提出意思自治理论后,各国在立法和司法实践中纷纷对意思自治原则予以采纳,其中英国是最早将当事人意思自治(party autonomy)应用于审判中的国家。而在阿尔博特郡诉奥斯特拉雷申保险公司一案(Mount Albert Borough Council v. Australasian etc, Assurance Society Ltd,

---

①　See http://en.wikipedia.org/wiki/Contract_(conflict),2008年8月30日访问。
②　David McClean, *Morris: The Conflict of Laws*, 5th ed., Sweet & Maxwell, 2000, p.321.

1938)中,英国枢密院莱特法官(Lord Wright)最后给合同的自体法进行了理论上的概括:"合同的自体法就是英国法院在确定合同的债权债务时所适用的法律。在确定这些事项时,英国法院拒绝将合同的缔结地法或履行地法作为排他的、机械的或唯一的标准,而是按照当事人的意愿,结合合同的条款、当事人的状况和当时的环境来决定。也许当事人在条款中已经明示地指出他们想要适用于合同的法律,在这种情况下,法院一般地将会同意他们的选择。但有时当事人根本没有考虑到这个问题,此时法院就不得不对当事人的意愿进行推断,或按照一个诚实理性的人在缔约时考虑到这个问题时所必然选择的法律来为当事人作出选择。"①这段话将一个多世纪以来当事人意思自治原则与自体法理论的关系进行了全面、彻底的总结,并使之形成了一个系统的确定自体法的理论。

(三)合同自体法的内容

合同自体法理论包括三个规则(**three rules**)。

【释义】　　　　　　　　　　three rules

In England three rules have been developed to assist the court in determining the proper law of a contract. Thus the traditional English approach is for the judge to enquire first whether there is an express selection of the proper law by the parties (*Rule 1*), secondly, if not, whether there is an implied selection (*Rule 2*), and thirdly, if not, with which system of law did the transaction have its closest and most real connection (*Rule 3*).②

这三个规则是:

(1)合同自体法第一规则:当事人明示选择合同准据法。如果当事人明确选择了合同所适用的法律,则应将他们所选择的法律作为合同的准据法;

(2)合同自体法第二规则:默示推定合同准据法。如果当事人未对法律作出选择,但根据合同条款能够推断出当事人意思的,则应将合同中所默示适用于合同的法律作为合同的准据法;

(3)合同自体法第三规则:如果当事人既没有明确选择所适用的法律,又没有在合同中表现出默示的意图,则由法院适用与案件有最密切联系的法律作为合同的准据法。③

---

① 参见傅静坤:《合同冲突法论》,法律出版社1999年版,第36—37页。
② Nicky Richardson, The Concept of Characteristic Performance and the Proper Law Doctrine, 1 *Bond L. Rev.* 284 (1989).
③ See David McClean, *Morris: The Conflict of Laws*, 5th ed., Sweet & Maxwell, 2000, p.321.

经过这样的概括论述,合同自体法理论就成为一个可以直接运用的、系统的、有具体程序规范和实体内容的原理,这就是自体法法律选择方法的优势(**the advantage of the proper law approach**)。在某种意义上讲,合同自体法实际上是合同法律适用上的意思自治说和最密切联系说的结合,合同自体法只是对支配与合同有关的各种问题的法律的一种概括、简洁和方便的表述。

【释义】　　the advantage of the proper law approach

The advantage of the *proper law* approach is that it builds in flexibility rather than offering a mechanical rule. Suppose that there is a contract between an Italian company and an English partnership for the sale of goods made in Greece to be shipped from Belgium on a ship flying the flag of Panama to a Swedish port. Adopting a rule such as the *lex loci contractus*, i.e. apply the law of the place where the contract was made, might actually select a law having no other connection with the substance of the bargain made by the parties. Similarly, picking the *lex loci solutionis*, i.e. the law of the place where the contract is to be performed, may prove to be equally irrelevant, assuming that there is only one place where performance is to occur: in the example, there is manufacture in Greece, delivery to Belgium, loading in Belgium, carriage on the high seas, and unloading in Sweden. So, if the contract does not make an express selection of the law to apply, the parties are deemed to have chosen to be bound by the law with which the contract has the closest and most real connection.[①]

二、当事人明示选择合同准据法

(一) 当事人可以明示选择合同所适用的法律

合同自体法理论第一规则认为,当事人可以明示选择法律。这也是意思自治说(theory of autonomy of will)的基本主张。如果合同当事人通过明示方式选择了适用于合同的法律,那么该项法律就是合同的准据法。

(二) 当事人选择法律的行为应该是善意的

通常,当事人选择法律的行为应该是善意的,即当事人的明示选择不得违反有关国家强行法的规定和公共秩序。[②]

大陆法系国家及其他众多国家都主张意思自治必须是有限制的。例如,1804

---

① See http://en.wikipedia.org/wiki/Proper_law,2008 年 8 月 30 日访问。
② 如美国 1971 年的《第二次冲突法重述》指出:在美国,当事人自主选择的法律不能与其法律本应作为合同准据法的州的基本政策相抵触,而所谓其法律本应作为合同准据法的州,便是那个对合同当事人具有更大利益的州。

年《法国民法典》第 6 条规定："不得以特别的约定违反有关公共秩序和善良风俗的法律。"1980 年欧洲共同体《关于合同义务法律适用的公约》第 16 条规定："如依照本公约的规定适用任何国家的法律规范明显地与法院地的公共政策不符时,可拒绝适用。"

（三）应禁止当事人选择与合同毫无联系的国家的法律

关于当事人对法律的选择,历来存在两种对立的观点:一种主张意思自治是绝对的、无限制的,当事人甚至可以选择与合同毫不相干的法律;另一种则主张意思自治是相对的、有限制的,当事人必须选择与合同有实际联系的法律。①

传统的英国冲突法理论及判例对限制当事人意思自治持反对意见,主张无限制的意思自治,允许当事人选择与合同毫无关系的法律。其理由是:英国是一个历史悠久的海上贸易大国,其有关国际贸易与海上航运的法律制度最发达、最完善,因而不管合同是否与英国有联系,一旦英国法被当事人选为合同准据法,都应予承认。这一立场在英国枢密院 1939 年审理"维他食品公司诉乌纳斯轮船公司"(**Vita Food Products Inc. v. Unus Shipping Co. Ltd.**)一案中得到了充分的体现。

【案例】　　**Vita Food Products Inc. v. Unus Shipping Co. Ltd.**②

Facts: Unus Shipping, a Nova Scotian company, owned a vessel, the Hurry On, and agreed with Vita Food Products (a New York company) in bills of lading signed in Newfoundland to carry in the Hurry On a cargo of herrings from Middle Arm (a Newfoundland port) to New York. Through the captain's negligence the vessel ran aground and the cargo was damaged. Vita Foods sued Unus Shipping in the Nova Scotian courts and, on appeal, came before the Privy Council. The Newfoundland Sale of Goods Act 1932 provided that the Hague Rules (governing the limitation of liability of shipowners for damage to cargo) should apply to every shipment of goods from a Newfoundland port and that every bill of lading issued in Newfoundland should contain an express statement that the Hague rules applied. The bills of lading issued in respect of the herring contained no such statement, but did contain in addition various clauses limiting liability in an express choice of English law. (Although the Hague rules were part of English law, they only applied to shipments from United Kingdom ports.) Did the Hague rules apply or did the clauses limiting liability m the bills of lading apply? ③

Held: That the parties' choice of English law was effective: and this was so even if the bill of lading were illegal under the law of the place where they were issued (Newfound).

---

① 徐冬根、薛凡:《中国国际私法立法完善研究》,上海社会科学院出版社 1998 年版,第 207 页。
② ［1939］AC 277 Privy Council（The parties may expressly choose the law to govern their contract）.
③ Charles Wild, 150 *Leading Casess: Conflict of Laws*, Old Bailey Press, 2003, p.149.

本案中，原告维他食品公司与被告加拿大乌纳斯轮船公司订立了一份租船合同，由原告租用被告所有的船只从芬兰装运货物去纽约。根据提单规定，合同受英国法支配，并约定被告对于其船员因过失而造成的损害负责。后因船长过失引起了货损，当事人发生纠纷，在英国进行诉讼。该案后来上诉到英国枢密院。审理此案的英国枢密院莱特法官认为该合同虽与英国毫无关系，而当事人却选择了英国法，这并不妨碍对合同适用英国法。他进一步指出：尽管纽芬兰的法律规定当事人的每一提单都应明示受《海牙规则》的调整，而该提单却没有作这样的明示，因而依纽芬兰法，上述免责约定是无效的。但在该合同中，当事人约定适用英国法是符合"善意"、"合法"、"无规避公共政策"三项条件的，应予承认。而英国法是承认这种免责约定的。原告为此败诉。这一案件表明，英国在实践中对合同当事人选择法律的范围是没有什么限制的。

大陆法系国家及其他众多国家都主张意思自治必须是有限制的。日本学者折茂丰在其所著的《国际私法各论》一书中将当事人选择法律的范围限制在三个方面：其一，当事人的选择仅限于特定国家的任意法，不能排除强制性法规的适用；其二，当事人的选择必须是善意的，不能采取法律规避的手段；其三，当事人只能选择与合同有实际联系的法律。折茂丰的上述观点反映了这些国家在立法与实践中所持的共同立场。①

美国《统一商法典》第 1 章第 105 条规定，有关货物买卖合同，当事人可以任意选择另一国、州的法律，但这些国家或州的法律必须与合同有"合理的联系"。

三、以默示的方式推定合同的准据法

合同自体法第二规则认为在当事人没有明示选择法律时，可以默示的方式推定其选择的法律。这意味着在当事人没有明示选择法律，而只作了一种默示选择，即当事人未在合同中明确表示其选择法律的意向时，法院或其他主管机关仍可从合同的条款和性质，或者从案件总的情况中推断出当事人的意向，推断如果合同当事人考虑到这个问题时，他们会选择什么样的法律作为合同的准据法。如管辖权选择条款或仲裁条款可以作为一个标准来推定当事人的默示意图，如果当事人约定某个国家的法院对合同有专属管辖权，或者约定仲裁在某个国家进行，通常可以推论法院地国或者仲裁地国的法律即是解决合同争议的自体法。其他还能帮助法院揭示当事人的默示选择的因素是当事人的国籍、住所，合同标的物的性质及其所在的位置，

---

① 参见余先予主编：《冲突法》，上海财经大学出版社 1999 年版，第 206 页。

合同规定的支付货币等。①在一般情况下,如果合同或其某些条款根据某个法律有效,而根据另外一个法律无效,通常认为当事人打算适用的是使合同有效的那个法律。

这种肯定合同当事人默示选择合同准据法的做法,已得到越来越多的国家的承认和采用。事实上,现在不仅有许多国家,如英国、美国、法国、德国、奥地利和瑞士等国的立法和判例肯定合同当事人默示选择有效,而且许多国际法公约,如1955年海牙《国际有体动产买卖法律适用公约》、1978年海牙《代理法律适用公约》、1980年欧洲共同体《关于合同义务法律适用的公约》和1986年海牙《国际货物买卖合同法律适用公约》,也都对这种默示选择持肯定的态度。这表明,承认合同当事人的默示选择意向也是国际合同法律适用原则发展的一个趋势,是对当事人意思自治原则的进一步贯彻和深化。

四、以最密切联系原则确定合同准据法

(一) 自体法理论第三规则的具体化运用

自体法理论第三规则认为,如果当事人既没有明确选择所适用的法律,又没有在合同中表现出默示的意图,则由法院适用与案件有最密切联系的法律作为合同的准据法。法院通过对与合同在地理位置上具有特殊联系的因素(**facts having specific geographical connections**)的比较,确定合同由与交易有最密切联系和最真实联系的法律支配。

【释义】 facts having specific geographical connections

The general rule is that the proper law is the primary system of law which governs most aspects of the factual situation giving rise to the dispute. This does not imply that all the aspects of the factual circumstances are necessarily governed by the same system of law, but there is a strong presumption that this will be the case. So, the process of legal analysis undertaken by the courts in each case identifies all the facts that have a specific geographical connection, e.g. where the parties reside or their businesses operate, where any agreement was made, where relevant actions were performed, etc. Once all the relevant connecting factors have been identified, the law of the state that has the greatest number of connections will be the proper law. In the event of a tie, the connecting factors which relate to performance will be given a greater weight than the connecting factors affect form. In most cases, this weighting will produce a clear winner.②

---

① 参见索光举:《试析合同自体法理论的完善与发展》,载《信阳师范学院学报》(哲学社会科学版)1997年第2期。

② See http://en.wikipedia.org/wiki/Proper_law,2008年8月30日访问。

(二) 最密切联系原则所依据的客观标志

最密切联系原则主张,合同准据法应为与合同法律关系有最密切联系的法律。基于最密切联系原则,法院应当根据合同中的各种具体情况,找出那个与合同有最实际、最密切联系的法律,作为合同的准据法。法院通过对最密切联系客观标志等因素的分析来确定最密切联系的法律。在各国的立法和司法实践中,最密切联系原则常用的客观标志有以下几种①:

1. 合同履行地

合同履行地(place of performance),又称为债务履行地。合同履行地在实践中通常是合同预定结果的发生地、合同标的物所在地,也是最容易发生争议的地方,许多国家都主张以合同履行地法作为与合同有最密切联系的法律,如 **The Assunzione** 案。②

【案例】　　　　　　　　　**The Assunzione**③

Facts: A charterparty that contained no express choice of law clause had been signed in Paris by the agents of French shipers and Italian shipowners. The charterparty was for the carriage of wheat from France to Italy in the Assunzione, an Italian ship, and the wheat was being shipped as part of an exchange agreement between the French and Italian Governments (although the shipowners were unaware of this latter fact). The charterparty was in English with additional clauses in French. A great porption of the freight and demurrage were payable in lire in Italy. The bills of lading were in French but endorsed by the Italian consignees. Did French law or Italian law govern the contract?④

Held: After weighing the various factors, Italian law was the proper of the contract. Singleton JL: With regard to the circumstances which support the defendants' contention that

---

① 参见余先予主编:《冲突法》,上海财经大学出版社1999年版,第207页。
② 这是一个涉及法国商人租用意大利船舶从法国敦刻尔克装运谷物去意大利威尼斯的租船合同争诉案。在诉讼过程中,租船方提出应以合同缔结地法即法国法作为合同准据法,船则主张应以船旗国国法即意大利法作为合同准据法。这一案件与法国和意大利都有密切的联系。合同与法国的联系表现为:合同是在法国巴黎订立的,法国为缔约地;合同的格式是法国式的,而且合同的补充条款是用法文书写的;作为合同一方当事人的租船人为法国经纪人并代表法国政府。合同与意大利的联系主要表现为:船籍为意大利,即船旗国法为意大利法;交货港为意大利威尼斯,即合同履行地为意大利;运费和船舶滞期费用意大利货币支付,且付款地在意大利那不勒斯;提单已背书给意大利受托人;作为合同一方当事人的船主为意大利人,而且在意大利热那亚与那不勒斯经商。在该案中,仅从连接因素的数量来考察,合同与法国和意大利的联系几乎不差上下,两者势均力敌,法院不得不将与合同有关的各种因素综合起来,放到天平上衡量,看一看究竟哪边的"分量"重一些,以确定合同关系的"重力中心"。结果,法官们一致认为租船人在那不勒斯用意大利货币支付运费和滞期费具有决定性的意义,因此,判定合同与意大利法律的联系最为密切,即以合同履行地法即意大利法作为合同的准据法。
③ [1954] P 150 Court of Appeal.
④ Charles Wild, 150 *Leading Casess*: *Conflict of Laws*, Old Bailey Press, 2003, p.135.

Italian law should be applied, I mention these: the ship was an Italian ship owned by two Italians in partnership, and a ship wearing the Italian flag: the owners were Italians, the master was an Italian; the contract was for carriage From a French port to an Italian port: the cargo was to be delivered at an Italian port. It is right to say that loading was at a French port and discharging at an Italian port, and one may appear to cancel the other, but there are further considerations: tile charterparty provided that freight and demurrage should be paid in Italian currency. I have read clause 16 of the charterparty; I bear in mind that 80 percent of the Freight had to be paid in Italy before the ship arrived at an Italian port, and the balance had to be paid at the discharging port. Clause 7 as to demurrage payable in Italian lire, too, is of importance on this part of the case. The next point is that the bills of lading were indorsed by Italian consignees before the arrival of the ship at Venice.

这一案例表明,从质的角度来分析,在众多的连接因素中,合同履行地的分量最重。法国著名学者巴迪福认为,合同履行地往往在实质上与当事人的利益有较大关联,合同的价值在于合同的履行,在履行合同时,事实上不能完全避免履行地法的干预。有鉴于此,在英美国家的不少判例中,法院常常适用合同履行地法作为合同的准据法。

2. 合同订立地

合同订立地(place-of-making),又称为合同缔结地。合同订立地是目前世界上多数国家采用的标志。由于合同订立地这一客观标志明确易定,以其为依据确定准据法具有预见性和稳定性,因此被各国广泛采用。美国学者比尔通过对合同履行地和合同订立地的比较,支持合同订立地说(**Beale's choice on place-of-making rule**)。

【说理】　　　　　　Beale's choice on place-of-making rule

With the alternative reject, Beale settled on the place-of-making rule: That this rule is theoretically sound there can be no doubt. The rule is based on the necessary of some law to raise an obligation between parties, and of this there can be no question. If two parties agree to do a thing, their agreement does not and cannot create any binding obligation to do it. The obligation created by the promise is merely a moral and social one, with which the law has nothing to do. It is only the law affixes the promise a legal obligation of performance that the parties can be said to have entered into a contract in a true sense. The question whether a contact is valid can on general principles be determined by no other law than that which applies to the acts, that is, by the law of the place of contracting. If the law at that place annexes an obligation to the acts of the parties, the promise has a legal right which no other law has power to take away except as a result of new acts which changes it. If on the other hand the law of the place where agreement is made annexes no legal obligation to it, there is no other law which has power to do so.

  Beale also argued for the law of place-of-making on the ground that it was easier for the parties to ascertain and follow. Parties meeting at the place of making to negotiate their contract can seek legal counsel there to determine that state's governing law. The parties are unlikely to return to their respective domiciles to get legal advice, and they might not be able to find legal counsel expert in the law of the place of performance. This argument obviously contemplates a face-to-face meeting of the parties in the place of making.①

  对于合同订立地来说,最大的问题是,如果合同不是由双方当事人在同一个地点订立的,而是通过通讯方式订立的,则合同的订立地如何确定呢? 为此,美国《第一次冲突法重述》采用信箱规则(**mailbox rule**)。

【规则】   mailbox rule

  Section 236(b) adopts the mailbox rule or dispatch rule of the famous case of *Adams v. Lindsell*: when an offer for bilateral contract is made in one state and an acceptance is sent from another state to the first state in anauthorized manner the place of the contract is the state from which the acceptance is sent.②

  然而,运用这一客观标志确定合同准据法也存在一些弊端:其一,合同的订立地具有一定的偶然性,与合同不一定有密切联系,以合同订立地法作为合同准据法常常缺乏针对性;其二,当事人可以任意选择合同订立地,以合同订立地法作为合同准据法可能鼓励当事人规避本应适用的与合同联系最密切的法律;其三,对于隔地订立的合同,其订立地难以确定,如英美普通法系国家主张合同订立地为承诺发出地,大陆法系国家则认为合同订立地为承诺接受地。

  3. 当事人住所地法,特别是债务人住所地

  债务人住所地通常就是债务履行地或合同标的物所在地。以这一客观标志为依据确定合同准据法有利于保护债务人的利益。因此,有些国家主张以债务人住所地法作为合同准据法。由于在双务合同中当事人互为债务人、债权人,对于应以哪个当事人的住所地法作为合同准据法,同样存在争议。有的国家为了避免这个问题,笼统规定以缔约时双方当事人的住所地法为合同准据法。

---

  ① David H. Vernon, Louis Weinberg, William Reynolds, William Richman, *Conflicts of Law: Case, Materials and Problems*, 2d ed., LexisNexis, 2002, p.259.

  ② Ibid., p.260.

4. 被告所在地

在合同关系中,被告通常是不特定的,谁都不能预见将来哪一方充当被告,以被告所在地作为客观标志确定合同准据法对合同当事人双方来说是公正的,因此,有的国家主张以被告所在地法作为与合同有最密切联系的准据法。然而,自视能严格履行合同义务,不会充当被告的当事人通常不愿意采用这一客观标志。

5. 法院地或仲裁地

一些国家主张以法院地或仲裁地作为与合同有最密切联系的客观标志,其理由主要有两点:一是任何国家的法官或仲裁员都有适用本国法律审理案件的职责;二是当事人虽未约定适用何国法律,但当他们将其合同争议交由法院或仲裁机构审理时,可以推定他们意图适用法院地法或仲裁地法。然而,一味适用法院地法或仲裁地法有可能忽略了与合同有最密切联系的法律,甚至可能导致当事人任意挑选法院地或仲裁地规避法律的结果。

尽管与合同有最密切联系的客观标志有许多,但按照最密切联系说,法院在确定合同准据法时仅仅以其中某一个客观标志为依据。

(三) 以特征性履行方法辅助最密切联系原则的应用

最密切联系原则的运用应结合特征性履行方法。特征性履行方法所依据的单一的具体连接点反映了合同的本质,这一连接点在与合同有关的众多的连接点中无疑"分量"最重,与合同的联系最为密切,因此,这一方法能正确、客观地推定与合同有最密切联系的国家的法律。[1]目前,瑞士、奥地利、荷兰、德国、波兰和匈牙利等国以及1980年欧洲共同体《关于合同义务法律适用的公约》、1985年《国际货物买卖合同法律适用公约》都采纳了这种做法。

以特征性履行方法确定与合同有最密切联系的法律这种做法,使最密切联系原则在理论上更加完整,也使得合同自体法理论形成一个完善的体系,在实践中更易操作,备受学术界和司法界推崇。它的运用展示了最密切联系原则这一合同法律适用原则更加光明的前景。[2]以《瑞士联邦国际私法》为例,该法即采用特征性履行方法具体例举了5种合同的特征性履行。[3]

---

[1] Xu Donggen, Le Droit International Privé en Chine: Une Perspective Comparative, *Collected Courses of the Hague Academy of International Law* (Vol. 270). The Hague, Martinus Nijhoff Publishers, 1999, p. 132.

[2] 徐冬根:《论当代国际私法发展的四大趋势》,载《华东政法学院学术文集》,浙江人民出版社2002年版,第296—297页。

[3] See Knoeofler, Schweizer, *Précis de droit international privé suisse*, Berne, 1990.

第三节 合同法律适用的范围

根据"分割法"的观点,应该对当事人的缔约能力、合同的形式、合同的成立、合同的解释、合同的履行等问题或环节的法律适用,分别予以考虑。

在立法和司法实践中,对于合同的各个方面,在分别予以考虑的基础上,各个方面都适用同一项法律,如美国《第一次冲突法重述》对合同准据法的适用范围(extent of the governing law)作出了规定。

【条文】 extent of the governing law

Section 332 of the Restatement First provided that the law of the place of making governs capacity to make the contract, the necessary form, if any, in which the promise must be made; the mutual assent or consideration, if any, required to make a promise binding,; any other requirements for making a promise binding; fraud, illegality, or any other circumstances which make a promise void or voidable; except as stated in §358, the nature and extent of the duty for the performance of which a party becomes bound; the time when and the place where the promise is by its terms to be performed; the absolute or conditional character of the promise.[①]

当然,法院也可以对当事人的缔约能力、合同的形式、合同的成立、合同的解释、合同的履行等问题或环节的法律适用分别予以考虑,分别适用不同的法律。

一、合同当事人缔约能力的法律适用

解决合同当事人缔约能力的法律冲突通常适用下列法律:

(1)属人法。属人法是支配当事人行为能力的一般原则,也是解决当事人缔约能力方面法律冲突的基本原则。欧洲大陆法系国家普遍采用了这一原则。

(2)缔约地法。鉴于缔约地易于确定,而且缔约者均属于缔约地法律支配下

---

① David H. Vernon, Louis Weinberg, William Reynolds, William Richman, *Conflicts of Law: Case, Materials and Problems*, 2d ed., LexisNexis, 2002, pp. 253—254.

的暂时主体，英美普通法系国家大都主张以缔约地法作为缔约能力的准据法。

（3）兼采属人法与缔约地法。由于属人法与缔约地法各有利弊，许多国家都趋利避弊，在采用属人法的同时，兼采缔约地法，即合同当事人的缔约能力依属人法，但依缔约地法有行为能力者，其合同行为有效。

二、合同形式的法律适用

有关解决合同形式法律冲突的准据法，过去通常是直接援引"场所支配行为"的原则，以合同缔结地法作为唯一的准据法。然而，一概由行为地法支配行为的方式缺乏应有的灵活性，同时也限制了合同当事人的自由选择权。因此，现代不少国家都倾向于把传统的、单一的"场所支配行为"原则演变为一种有多个连接点可供选择的选择性冲突规范。例如，1987年《瑞士联邦国际私法》第124条规定：合同当事人缔结合同时都在场的，合同形式只要符合合同的准据法或合同缔结地法即为有效；合同当事人缔结合同时在不同的国家的，合同的形式只要符合这些国家的法律即可。

三、合同成立的法律适用

各国在实践中解决有关合同成立的法律冲突时，主要采取以下两种做法：

（1）根据"场所支配行为"原则，以合同缔结地法作为准据法。英国在司法实践中主张，隔地合同的成立依合同缔结地法。

（2）适用合同准据法，即以支配合同内容的法律作为合同成立问题的准据法。

四、合同内容与效力的法律适用

根据目前绝大多数国家的立法和司法实践以及国际条约的规定，在合同内容与效力的法律适用问题上，最通行的做法是首先采用意思自治原则，适用当事人合意选择的法律；在当事人没有作出法律选择时，适用与合同有最密切联系的法律。

第四节　我国有关涉外合同法律适用的规定

一、国际条约优先适用

作为一个主权独立的国家，我国一贯恪守条约必须遵守的国际法准则。我国

《民法通则》第142条第2款规定："中华人民共和国缔结或者参加的国际条约同中华人民共和国的民事法律有不同规定的,适用国际条约的规定,但中华人民共和国声明保留的条款除外。"我国《海商法》第268条第1款和《民用航空法》第184条第1款也作了国际条约优先于国内法的相同规定。

二、允许当事人自主选择所适用的法律

合同当事人意思自治原则是我国涉外合同法律适用的基本原则。我国《合同法》第126条规定："涉外合同的当事人可以选择处理合同争议所适用的法律,但法律另有规定的除外。……"《民法通则》第145条第1款规定："涉外合同的当事人可以选择处理合同争议所适用的法律,法律另有规定的除外。"按照最高人民法院的解释,对于"合同争议"应作广义的理解,即凡是双方当事人对合同是否成立、合同成立的时间、合同内容的解释、合同的履行、违约的责任,以及合同的变更、中止、转让、解除、终止等发生的争议,均应包括在内。可见,这里所谓"处理合同争议所适用的法律"就是指"适用于合同的法律",或"合同准据法"。我国《海商法》第269条和《民用航空法》第188条在分别规定海事合同和民用航空运输合同的法律适用时已改为"合同当事人可以选择合同适用的法律"。显然,这样的表述更为科学。自2011年4月1日起施行的《涉外民事关系法律适用法》第41条规定："当事人可以协议选择合同适用的法律。"

三、以最密切联系原则为补充

最密切联系原则是我国立法确立的涉外合同法律适用的补充原则,这一原则是对当事人意思自治原则的必要补充。我国《合同法》第126条第1款、《民法通则》第145条第2款、《海商法》第269条、《民用航空法》第188条和我国最高人民法院2007年发布的《关于审理涉外民事或商事合同纠纷案件法律适用若干问题的规定》,都明确规定:合同当事人没有选择合同适用的法律或处理合同争议所适用的法律的,"适用与合同有最密切联系的国家的法律"。我国《涉外民事关系法律适用法》第41条规定："当事人没有选择的,适用履行义务最能体现该合同特征的一方当事人经常居所地法律或者其他与该合同有最密切联系的法律。"

我国在司法实践中,形成了一套<u>合同法律适用规则</u>。

【条文】 　　　　　　　　　　合同法律适用规则

按照最密切联系原则,各种涉外合同所应适用的法律分别为:

（1）国际货物买卖合同，适用合同订立时卖方营业所所在地的法律。如果合同是在买方营业所所在地谈判订立的，或者合同主要是依买方确定的条件并应买方发出的招标订立的，或者合同明确规定卖方须在买方营业所所在地履行交货义务的，则适用合同订立时买方营业所所在地的法律；

（2）银行贷款或者担保合同，适用贷款银行或担保银行所在地的法律；

（3）保险合同，适用保险人营业所所在地的法律；

（4）加工承揽合同，适用加工承揽人营业所所在地的法律；

（5）技术转让合同，适用受让人营业所所在地的法律；

（6）工程承包合同，适用工程所在地的法律；

（7）科技咨询或设计合同，适用委托人营业所所在地的法律；

（8）劳务合同，适用劳务实施地的法律；

（9）成套设备供应合同，适用设备安装运转地的法律；

（10）代理合同，适用代理人营业所所在地的法律；

（11）关于不动产租赁、买卖或抵押的合同，适用不动产所在地的法律；

（12）动产租赁合同，适用出租人营业所所在地的法律；

（13）仓储保管合同，适用仓储保管人营业所所在地的法律。

以上13种涉外合同的准据法，大多数属于担负特征性给付义务的合同当事人的营业所所在地法律，这说明我国司法实践在确定与合同有最密切联系的法律时与目前世界上盛行的"特征性履行"主张是一致的。

我国自2011年4月1日起施行的《涉外民事关系法律适用法》对"代理"作出专门规定："代理适用代理行为地法律，但被代理人与代理人的民事关系，适用代理关系发生地法律。当事人可以协议选择委托代理适用的法律。"该项法律适用规范与上述最高人民法院司法解释中的"代理合同"的法律适用相比更具体。

值得注意的是，我国将"国际货物买卖合同"作为一类特殊的合同加以处理，规定了若干在不同情况下所应适用的法律。参照1986年海牙《国际货物买卖合同法律适用公约》的规定，我国对国际货物买卖合同的法律适用确定了一组选择性的冲突规范。这些冲突规范是针对经常出现的若干种情况制定的，以便法院能够根据不同的案情，选择采用其中应适用的冲突规范。这比单纯运用特征性履行办法，机械地适用卖方履行地法，更有利于保证法律适用结果的合理性。

四、以国际惯例为补缺

我国《民法通则》第142条第3款规定："中华人民共和国法律和中华人民共和

国缔结或者参加的国际条约没有规定的,可以适用国际惯例。"采用这一原则对于弥补我国现行立法的不足具有积极的意义。但是,根据我国的立法精神,适用国际惯例必须以我国法律以及我国缔结或者参加的国际条约对于合同当事人争议的问题未作规定为条件。同时,适用国际惯例也不得违反我国法律的基本原则和社会公共利益。这反映了我国在涉外合同法律适用问题上所采取的原则性和灵活性高度统一的立场。

五、三类特殊外商投资企业合同必须适用中国法

我国现行立法对于在我国境内履行的外商投资企业合同的法律适用作了专门规定。我国《合同法》第126条第2款明确规定:"在中华人民共和国境内履行的中外合资经营企业合同、中外合作经营企业合同、中外合作勘探开发自然资源合同,适用中华人民共和国法律。"这是一条不容当事人更改的绝对强制性规范。我国《涉外民事关系法律适用法》确认了强制性规范的适用。该法第4条规定:"中华人民共和国法律对涉外民事关系有强制性规定的,直接适用该强制性规定。"我国这一涉外合同法律适用的特殊原则也是对当事人用意思自治方式选择合同准据法的一种限制。

上述三类合同必须适用中国法律是由这些合同的特殊性质所决定的。中外合资经营企业与中外合作经营企业是我国目前利用外国直接投资的两种主要方式,由于两者都是中外资本的结合,理论界倾向于将两类企业通称为"合营企业",把中外合资经营称为"股权式合营"(equity joint ventures),把中外合作经营称为"合同式合营"(contractual joint ventures)。这两类合营企业合同在适用法律时也有相同的特点。按照各国的立法和实践以及通行的国际惯例,一般都把合同缔结地法、合同履行地法或与合同最有密切联系的法律作为合同的准据法。在中国境内设立的中外合资经营企业与中外合作经营企业在中国注册登记,是中国的法人;合营企业合同是依照中国的法律在中国缔结,并经中国政府批准的;合营企业的营业所位于中国;合营企业合同的主要履行地也在中国;合营企业合同的一方当事人又是中国法人。综观各种连接因素,合营企业合同无疑与中国的联系最为密切。因此,两类合营企业合同适用中国法具有充分的法律依据。从整个世界范围来看,在立法中规定合营企业合同适用东道国法律的国家也不乏其例。

鉴于中外合作勘探开发自然资源的方式同中外合资经营与中外合作经营具有许多相似之处,因此,中外合作勘探开发自然资源合同具有合营企业合同的一般特征:合同依照中国法律在中国缔结并经中国政府批准生效,合同履行地在中国,合同一方当事人是中国法人,因而合同与中国的联系最为密切。与此同时,这类合同本身还具有一个不可忽视的重要特征,即合同当事人勘探开发的对象是我国主权管辖下的自然资源。根据1974年《建立新的国际经济秩序宣言》和《建立新的国际经济秩序的行动纲领》以及《各国经济权利和义务宪章》等国际性法律文件的规定,国家对其所属的自然资源享有永久的主权。这种主权当然包括司法管辖权和适用本国法律的权利。除此之外,自然资源还涉及我国境内的不动产,而"不动产物权依物之所在地法"是各国普遍采用的冲突规范。这一切表明,在中国履行的中外合作勘探开发自然资源合同适用中国法完全符合国际私法的一般原理。

六、对消费者合同和劳动合同法律适用的规定

(一)消费者合同法律适用的规定

我国《涉外民事关系法律适用法》对消费者合同和劳动合同单独作出规定。

该法第42条规定:"消费者合同,适用消费者经常居所地法律;消费者选择适用商品、服务提供地法律或者经营者在消费者经常居所地没有从事相关经营活动的,适用商品、服务提供地法律。"

这一规定是中华人民共和国建国以来首次用国家立法的形式明确了国际消费者合同的法律适用问题,体现了对消费者这个弱势群体的特殊保护,具有先进性和开放性。[1] 中国保护模式先进性主要表现在它借鉴了国外立法的做法,基于消费者合同的特殊性,明确规定了消费者合同适用消费者经常居所地法,并允许当事人选择所适用的法律;开放性主要体现在它采用了双边冲突规范的形式,表明了对国内外消费者一视同仁的态度。

(二)劳动合同法律适用的规定

我国首次规定涉外劳动合同的法律是1987年最高人民法院发布的《关于适用〈涉外经济合同法〉若干问题的解答》,其中第6条第8款规定:"劳务合同适用劳务履行地的法律。"后来该《解释》不再适用,我国再没有出台有关涉外劳动合同的法律适用的特别规定。实践中,法院倾向于认为我国《劳动法》和《劳动合同法》是强制性规定,直接予以适用,既不适用当事人选择的外国法律,也不通过最密切联系原则适用外国法。[2] 这种做法忽略了冲突法上对于劳动者作为弱者一方的保护,与国际私法追求公正价值取向不符。

我国《涉外民事关系法律适用法》改变了劳动合同法律适用无规则可依的状

---

[1] 参见许军珂:《论消费者保护的法律选择模式——欧美模式与中国模式之比较、启示与思考》,载《法学家》2011年第5期。
[2] 参见齐彦伟:《论涉外劳动合同的法律适用对弱者的保护——兼评我国〈涉外民事关系法律适用法〉的相关规定》,载《黑龙江省政法管理干部学院学报》2011年第3期。

况,该法第43条规定:"劳动合同,适用劳动者工作地法律;难以确定劳动者工作地的,适用用人单位主营业地法律。劳务派遣,可以适用劳务派出地法律。"

我国《涉外民事关系法律适用法》第43条的这个规定对于我国处理涉外劳动合同争议具有重要意义。涉外劳动合同的法律适用规范的产生,弥补了我国在劳动合同法律适用规范立法上的空白。第43条的法律适用规范,体现了对作为弱势一方的劳动者权利的充分保护。我国立法之所以规定劳动合同适用劳动者工作地法律,是因为劳动者对于其所在工作地的工作环境和相关的法律规定相对较为熟悉,一旦发生劳动争议,更有利于劳动者主张权利。

对于劳务派遣,可以适用劳务派出地法律的规定。这在一定程度上满足了我国在外派劳务实践中劳动合同法律适用的需要。如果劳动者工作地法律对劳动者的保护与我国法律相比力度较弱,根据这一规定,法官可以根据情况选择适用对劳动者权益保护更有利的准据法。这种灵活的安排给劳动者的权利保护提供了空间。

【思考题】

* 什么是合同法律适用的整体法?它与分割法有什么区别?
* 谈谈你对合同自体法理论的理解和认识。
* 合同自体法理论包括哪些内容?
* 根据最密切联系原则,在确定合同准据法时,有哪些客观标准?
* 特征性履行方法在确定合同准据法过程中有什么功能?
* 我国对三类特殊合同的法律适用有什么规定?为什么?
* 我国对消费者合同和劳动合同的法律适用有哪些规定?

【重要术语提示与中英文对照】

中文术语	英文对照
合同准据法	applicable law of a contract
整体法	unity of contract
适用一个法律	a single law
分别适用法律	plurality
分割方法	dépeçage
自体法理论	the doctrine of the proper law
阿尔博特郡诉奥斯特拉雷申保险公司一案	Mount Albert Borough Council v. Australasian etc, Assurance Society Ltd.

确定自体法	determination of a proper law
自体法方法的优势	advantage of the proper law approach
赖特法官	Lord Wright
在地理位置上具有特殊联系的因素	facts having specific geographical connections
自体法	proper law
当事人意思自治	party autonomy, autonomy of will
维他食品公司诉乌纳斯轮船公司	Vita Food Products Inc. v. Unus Shipping Co.
最密切联系	most significant relationship
重力中心规则	center-of-gravity rule
自然场所	natural seat
合同场所化理论	theory of localization of contracts
合同履行地	place of performance
合同订立地	place-of-making
信箱规则	mailbox rule
股权式合营	equity joint ventures
契约式合营	contractual joint ventures

【推荐阅读文献】

- 黄进、肖永平:《国际私法领域内重要理论问题综述》,载《中国社会科学》1990年第6期。
- 吕岩峰:《英国"适当法理论"之研究》,载《吉林大学社会科学学报》1992年第5期。
- 刘晓红:《论国际私法中对涉外合同责任与侵权责任竞合之处理》,载《华东政法学院学报》2001年第2期。
- 王军、陈洪武:《合同冲突法》,对外经济贸易大学出版社2003年版。
- 曾郁:《国际合同的法律适用》,载《广东省社会主义学院学报》2008年第1期。
- 齐彦伟:《论涉外劳动合同的法律适用对弱者的保护——兼评我国〈涉外民事关系法律适用法〉的相关规定》,载《黑龙江省政法管理干部学院学报》2011年第3期。
- 许东珂:《论消费者保护的法律选择模式——欧美模式与中国模式之比较、启示与思考》,载《法学家》2011年第5期。
- Xu Donggen, Le Droit International Privé en Chine: Une Perspective Comparative, *Collected Courses of the Hague Academy of International Law* (Vol. 270), Martinus Nijhoff Publishers 1999.
- Zhang Mo, Choice of Law in Contracts: A Chinese Approach, 26 *Nw. J. Int'l L. & Bus.* 289 (2006).

- Patricia Youngblood Reyhan, 2005—2006 Survey of New York Law: Conflict of Laws, 57 *Syracuse L. Rev.* 943—946 (2007).
- Bonomi (A.), The Rome I Regulation on the Law Applicable to Contractual Obligations: Some General Remarks, 10 *Ybk. Priv. Int'l L.* 165 (2008).
- Albornoz (M.), Choice of Law in International Contracts in Latin American Legal Systems, 6 *J. Priv. Int'l L.* 23 (2010).
- Maultzsch (F.), Choice of Law and Ius Cogens in Conflict of Laws for Contractual Obligations, 75 *RabelsZ* 60 (2011).
- Jieying Laing, Statutory Restrictions on Party Autonomy in China's Private International Law of Contract: How Far Does the 2010 Codification Go? 8 *J. Priv. Int. L.* 77 (2012).
- Louise Merrett, Employment Contracts in Private International Law, 133 *Employment Law Journal* 21(2012).

【扩展阅读资料】

Contracts Choice of Law in the Absence of a Choice of Law Clause①

GlobalNet Financial.com, Inc. v. Frank Crystal & Co., Inc., presented conflicts related to both contracts and torts claims and thus called for a determination of applicable law under both contract and tort choice of law regimes. GlobalNet brought suit alleging that Crystal, its insurance broker, breached its contractual duties as well as its fiduciary duties and was negligent in failing to notify GlobalNet that its directors and officers liability policy (D & O policy) was at risk of cancellation for non-payment of premiums. Both plaintiff and defendant moved for summary judgment on these claims.

Globalnet was a Delaware company with offices in Boca Raton, Florida at the time its relationship with defendant began. Defendant, Crystal, was a commercial insurance broker incorporated and headquartered in New York. It has offices throughout the United States, including two in Florida. Defendant arranged for plaintiff to purchase a D & O policy for the period covering 1999 through 2001. During the fall of 2001, GlobalNet was purchased by a London-based company. Up until this time the premiums on the policy had been paid out of GlobalNet's Florida office. When the company was acquired, responsibility for its financial affairs moved to London.

---

① Patricia Youngblood Reyhan, 2005—2006 Survey of New York Law: Conflict of Laws, 57 *Syracuse L. Rev.* 881, 943—946 (2007).

In August, 2001, AI Credit Corporation (AICCO), the company through which GlobalNet financed the payment of its D & O insurance premiums, sent a financial statement to GlobalNet's Boca Raton address but this communication was returned. In fact, GlobalNet had closed the office to which the statement was sent some two months before. The envelope returned to AICCO contained a new address in Boca Raton for GlobalNet and AICCO changed its records to reflect this fact and re-sent the statement. In early October 2001, AICCO sent a notice to the new address indicating that GlobalNet's D & O coverage would be cancelled for non-payment of premiums at the end of that month. At the end of October, AICCO sent a further notice indicating cancellation of the policy. The address to which AICCO was sending these notices was a company that had been spun-off from GlobalNet sometime before the latter was acquired by the London company. GlobalNet's associate general counsel had expressly authorized the forwarding of GlobalNet's mail to this address. Personnel at that company were directed by GlobalNet to send forwarded mail to London. Although the company forwarded most mail, the AICCO notices were never received in London and GlobalNet was unaware of the cancellation of the policy. Defendant Crystal received telephone calls from AICCO concerning the cancellation and received formal notice of the cancellation.

In spring 2002 GlobalNet made three separate claims under the policy. The carriers refused coverage on the ground that the policies had been cancelled. GlobalNet then brought suit against Crystal.

The court began its analysis by finding an actual conflict between New York and Florida law regarding the nature of the relationship between an insurance broker and the insured. Under Florida law, the broker has a fiduciary duty to the insured and may be held liable under both contract and tort theories for violation of this duty. Under New York law, a broker has no such duty and owes the insured "no more than the common law duty to procure the insurance coverage that the insured requests." Because plaintiff sought recovery under contract and tort theories, this difference in legal rules compelled an examination of both New York's contracts choice rules and its choice rules.

The court turned first to resolution of the choice with respect to the contract claims. Disagreeing with the analysis of the district court, the Second Circuit characterized the issue as solely focused on the contract between the insured and the broker, not the contracts and agreements ultimately secured by the broker for the insured. The cases primarily relied on by the district court involved coverage issues making it appropriate to give attention to the geographic scope of the coverage. In the Second Circuit's opinion, the instant cases required a far simpler choice of law analysis, proceeding under a normal "grouping of contacts" or "center of gravity" test. The court found an adequate grouping of contacts to justify choice of New York law, inasmuch as the policies were brokered in New York by a New York broker and the financial agreements were brokered in the state between the insured and another New York company. Thus, although the Second Circuit disagreed with the route taken by the district court, it nonetheless arrived at the same destination with respect to the contract claims.

As to the tort claims, the Second Circuit characterized those claims as conduct-regulating. Plaintiff had sought to have Florida law chosen on the ground that Florida possessed "a significant interest in regulating the conduct of brokers who knowingly [dealt] with a Florida-based insured to provide coverage for a risk that was primarily located in Florida." The district court had held that New York law governed because the alleged breach by defendant occurred there. The Second Circuit agreed. All of the acts by defendant alleged to be negligent took place in New York and a straightforward application of New York's choice of law rules in tort pointed to the place of the tort as the appropriate source of governing law for a conduct-regulating issue. Applying New York law, the court upheld the grant of summary judgment to the defendant.

第十二章

国际商事关系的法律适用

本章导读

※ 商人法是指产生于西欧中世纪的，由商人们在其商事实践中所创造的，规制商人行为的独立法律规范体系。

※ 商人法作为国际商事实践中产生并逐渐成熟起来的"自治性"法律体系或法律部门，顺应了国际商事关系发展的客观需要，并展现出日渐蓬勃的生命力。

※ 商人法的适用，归纳起来主要有三种做法：第一，允许当事人选择现代商人法而不参照任何国内法。第二，将现代商人法与国内法结合起来适用。第三，限制现代商人法规则的适用。

※ 电子商务是指以互联网为依托，通过计算机与计算机之间信息的交流与互动而发生的商事活动。

※ 联合国国际贸易法委员会《电子商务示范法》是国际上第一个关于电子数据交换的法规。它的出台，向各国立法者提供了一套国际公认的示范法，使有关电子数据交换的一些主要法律问题得以解决。

※ 2005年11月联合国大会上决议通过的《国际合同使用电子通信公约》是有关电子商务的第一个专门性公约。公约的目的是采用统一规则消除对国际合同使用电子通信的障碍，公约确立了媒介和技术选择自由原则。

※ 电子商务的法律适用原则的主流做法是：以意思自治原则作为电子商务法律适用的首要原则，以最密切联系原则作为电子商务适用的辅助原则，确保适用保护电子商务中处于消费者一方的强制性规则。

※ 法院地法在国际破产的法律适用问题上起着重要的作用。破产程序、破产债权、破产财团和破产管理通常均适用法院地法。

※ 根据普遍破产主义原则，在跨国破产中，只应该有一个破产宣告，由一个破产程序来解决世界范围内的针对债务人财产的所有求偿要求。

※ 属地破产主义原则，又称复合破产制，强调每个国家对位于本国境内的财产有固有的管辖权。根据该原则，一国法院所作的破产宣告，其效力仅及于破产人在该国领域内的财产，每个国家的法院根据本国破产法，将债务人位于本国境内的财产分配给债权人，法院任命破产管理人的权限也仅限于搜集破产人在本国的财产。

【本章主题词】 商人法、电子商务、破产、破产域外效力

第十二章　国际商事关系的法律适用

第一节　商人法及其适用

一、商人法的产生及界定

商人法(**law merchant**),有学者译为"商业习惯法"①、"国际贸易习惯法"②、"国际商事法"③或"商法"④。

【释义】　　　　　　　　　　law merchant

The law merchant is spoken of under a number of names, including international, transnational, or supranational commercial law; international customs or usages; general principles of international commercial law; and lex mercatoria.

Regardless of the label, the same phenomenon—a set of rules encompassing the trading practices of the international merchant community—is being described. However, the criterion for determining the ambit of lex mercatoria… does not solely reside in the object of its constituent elements, but also in its origin and its customary, and thus spontaneous, nature.⑤

商人法这一概念可以溯源到中世纪。在词源上,它源自拉丁语"jus mercatorum",有"商人的法律"(**lex mercatoria**)之义。它起源于国际商业、航运、保险、银行等商事机构在从事跨国性贸易活动过程中所逐渐达成的法律共识。这种法律共识反映在这些商事机构所订立的合同条款之中。

---

① 〔英〕施米托夫著,程家瑞编:《国际贸易法文选》,赵秀文译,中国大百科全书出版社1996年版,第2页。
② 柯泽东:《国际贸易习惯法与国际贸易》,载《法治学刊》1996年第1期。
③ 〔法〕米歇尔·维拉利:《国际商事法——第三种法律秩序的理论探讨》,李泽锐译,载《法学译丛》1986年第6期。
④ 韩健:《国际商事仲裁法的理论与实践》,法律出版社1993年版,第247页。
⑤ Michael T. Medwig, The New Law Merchant: Legal Rhetoric and Commercial Reality, 24 *Law & Pol'y Int'l Bus.* 589—590 (1993).

【释义】　　　　　　　　lex mercatoria

Lex mercatoria, was originally a body of rules and principles laid down by merchants themselves to regulate their dealings. It consisted of usages and customs common to merchants and traders in Europe, with slightly local differences. It originated from the problem that civil law was not responsive enough to the growing demands of commerce: there was a need for quick and effective jurisdiction, administered by specialised courts. The guiding spirit of the merchant law was that it ought to evolve from commercial practice, respond to the needs of the merchants, and be comprehensible and acceptable to the merchants who submitted to it. International commercial law today owes some of its fundamental principles to the Law Merchant as it was developed in the medieval ages. This includes choice of arbitration institutions, procedures, applicable law and arbitrators, and the goal to reflect customs, usage and good practice among the parties.①

那么什么是商人法呢？对于商人法的定义，学者们的意见是有分歧的。

英国学者 Schmitthoff 认为，商人法是适用于国际贸易领域的独立于国内法的"自治法"。美国学者 Frederick Pollock 认为，商人法与其说是商人们的特殊规范，不如说是商人之间商业交易的特殊规范。②我国学者徐国建认为商人法通常是指从事国际贸易活动的各国商人在实践中所共同认可并遵守的统一规范国际贸易活动的某些习惯和规则。③上述学者对商人法的定义不外乎是从两个角度来进行概括的，即或者从它所调整的法律关系的主体角度来概括，或从它的内容来概括。我们认为，商人法是指产生于西欧中世纪的、由商人们在其商事实践中所创造的、规制商人行为（**by merchants and for merchants**）的独立法律规范体系。

【释义】　　　　　by merchants and for merchants

The law merchant, was the creation of merchants, by merchants and for merchants. They ran their own courts, and it was their law. So far as the law itself was concerned, there were probably some mercantile customs that made trading possible—some quite local and some of wider extent. These customs did not, however, add up to a mercantile legal system, for wherever we see such a system created it is the work of men who are imbued with a scheme of law that is not the creation of merchants but, in the case of England, of the customary courts of the realm.④

---

① Law Merchant, Wikipedia, http://en.wikipedia.org/wiki/Law Merchant (last visited Dec. 9, 2007).
② Frederick Pollock & Frederic W. Maitland, *The History of English Law*, vol.1, Cambridge, 1978, p.467.
③ 徐建国:《现代商人法论》，载《中国社会科学》1993 年第 2 期。
④ Charles Donahue, The Empirical and Theoretical Underpinnings of the Law Merchant: Medieval and Early Modern Lex mercatoria, 5 *Chi. J. Int'l L.* 21, 36 (2004).

第十二章　国际商事关系的法律适用

之后,经由漫长的国际商贸实践,这种经当事人协商一致所达成的法律共识进而转化为商事习惯做法——也即后来形成的商人法。这种复兴的商人法被称为"现代商人法"(modern lex mercatoria)或"新商人法"(**new law merchant**)。

【释义】　　　　　　　　　new law merchant

The new law merchant is a manifestation of the commercial community's growing disenchantment with national legal systems. Over the last century, merchants have slowly begun to extricate their commercial disputes from the tangled regulatory web of the national legal order. Evidence of merchant hostility towards state institutions is not hard to find. Some of the largest American companies, for example, have such ill feelings about litigation that they have pledged themselves to "negotiate and settle disputes early before litigation takes on a life of its own." On a transnational level, the problem is much worse, especially in the United States, which other nations view as a "horrid land of litigation." In order to escape the labyrinth of conflicting national laws, international merchants submit their disputes to a-national arbitral bodies, and increasingly, arbitrators are resolving disputes by applying an a-national body of private customary law—the law merchant.①

二、商人法在世界各国的适用

现代商人法理论一经提出,即对许多国家的国内立法与司法实践产生了重大影响。对商人法的适用,归纳起来主要有三种做法:

第一,允许当事人选择现代商人法而不参照任何国内法。法国是这一做法的最具代表性的国家。法国 1981 年《民事诉讼法典》第 1496 条规定,仲裁庭适用于合同的法律是当事人选择的法律规范,在无这种选择时,适用它认为适当的法律规则。同时规定,在任何情况下,仲裁庭都应考虑到商业惯例。值得注意的是,法国《民事诉讼法典》中使用的是"法律规则"(rules of law),而不是"法律"(law)一词,其意义在于,"法律规则"不仅包括国内法,还包括商法或其他非国内法渊源。②法国在国际商事仲裁中的实践也确实证明了这一点。1979 年国际商会仲裁庭依现代商人法规则对 Pabalk Ticaret Sirketi v. Norsolor S. A.③案所作的裁决,法国法院予

---

① Michael T. Medwig, The New Law Merchant: Legal Rhetoric and Commercial Reality, 24 *Law & Pol'y Int'l Bus.* 590 (1993).

② Ole Lando, The Lex Mercatoria in International Commercial Arbitration, in *International and Comparative Law Quarterly*, 753—754 (Vol. 3, 1985).

③ See W. Michael Reisman, W. Laurence Craig, William Park, & Jan Paulsson, *International Commercial Arbitration* 203—204 (1997).

以承认。对该案的裁决,奥地利最高法院也予以了确认。这说明现代商人法的适用得到了这两个国家司法实践的承认。此外,允许当事人在国际商事关系合同中选择适用现代商人法规则的还有丹麦、南斯拉夫、瑞士等国。

第二,将现代商人法与国内法结合起来适用。世界上大多数国家都采用这种做法,如美国《统一商法典》第 1-205(3)节、《日本商法典》第 1 条的规定都是将现代商人法规则与其国内法结合起来适用的。

第三,限制现代商人法规则的适用。英国是典型的对现代商人法进行严格限制的国家。其仲裁法中有这样的一项原则,即争议应按照固定的法律原则而不应按照个别仲裁员所坚持的所谓"公正"或"公平"的原则来解决。

三、商人法在我国的法律适用

我国对现代商人法理论的系统研究起步较晚,但有关现代商人法具体问题的研究,却自 1978 年我国实行改革开放政策以来就一直没有间断过。

(一)我国有关现代商人法的国内立法现状

我国在立法上对作为现代商人法的核心和本体内容的"国际惯例"有明确规定。如 1986 年《民法通则》第 142 条第 3 款明确规定:"中华人民共和国法律和中华人民共和国缔结或参加的国际条约没有规定的,可以适用国际惯例。"1992 年《海商法》、1995 年《票据法》和《民用航空法》也重申了这一立场。在理论上,我国学者也对现代商人法的概念、性质、渊源及适用,以及我国现代商人法的理论与实践等问题进行了探讨和研究。①我国学者对现代商人法促进国际贸易发展的积极作用大都持肯定态度,并认识到了国内法的局限性。

(二)我国立法中的现代商人法适用条件

概括起来,现代商人法在我国适用的条件主要有:

第一,该国际商事争议问题的准据法是中国法。这是指现代商人法规则在我国的适用必须以经冲突规范的指引,确定我国的法律为争议问题的准据法为前提。如果该争议问题的准据法为外国法,或者是我国香港、澳门特别行政区的法律,则现代商人法规则能否适用要看该准据法的规定如何。如果该准据法允许适用现代商人法,该现代商人法规则才能得到适用;反之,则不能得到适用。

第二,在中国法律和中国缔结或参加的国际条约对该争议问题没有规定的场合,才能适用现代商人法规则。由此可以看出,现代商人法规则在我国的适用条件

---

① 如徐国建的《现代商人法论》及黄进、胡永庆的《现代商人法论——历史和趋势》等。

第十二章 国际商事关系的法律适用

必须包括我国法律与我国缔结或参加的国际条约对国际商事争议问题没有相应的规定。

第三,在我国适用现代商人法规则须以该现代商人法规则的存在为前提。这就涉及一个对现代商人法规则的识别与查明问题。对于查明的途径问题,参照我国法律规定的查明外国法的途径,即法院在审理涉外民商事案件时遵循"以事实为根据,以法律为准绳"的原则,当依据我国法律的指定,应当适用的法律为现代商人法规则时,人民法院有责任查明该现代商人法规则的内容,当事人也有举证的责任。

第四,按照我国法律的有关规定,现代商人法规则在我国的适用还不得违反我国的社会公共利益,否则,就将排除其适用。**新加坡达斌公司利用假提单欺诈案**是我国司法实践中出现的一个比较典型的因违反我国社会公共利益而排除现代商人法规则适用的案例。

【案例】 新加坡达斌公司利用假提单欺诈案

海南省木材公司与新加坡达斌私人有限公司签订了购买坤甸木的合同,合同规定采用信用证方式付款。后来,达斌私人有限公司利用泰坦船务公司签发的提单及其他单证到新加坡结汇银行结汇,结汇银行要求开汇行中国银行海口分行支付货款183万美元。中国银行海口分行经审查,全部单证符合信用证要求,于是通知海南省木材公司付款赎单。而海南省木材公司通过调查了解到,卖方根本没有装货上船,所提供的提单及其他单证全是伪造的,于是拒不付款赎单,并向广州海事法院起诉,申请冻结该信用证下货款。广州海事法院进行了认真的审查后认为,本案有关证据表明,卖方是利用船务公司签发的假提单进行欺诈。如果用《跟单信用证统一惯例》处理本案,则其欺诈行为就会得逞,海南省木材公司的合法权益就要受到损害。根据国际私法上的公共秩序保留制度,广州海事法院裁决不予适用《跟单信用证统一惯例》,而适用我国《民法通则》和《民事诉讼法》的有关规定,依法冻结了中国银行海口分行的信用证项下的货款。

该案判决后,在我国国际私法学界引起了很大的争论。深入分析一下此案,我们可以发现,此案本应适用商人习惯法——《跟单信用证统一惯例》,但是如果法院予以适用,将会导致我国当事人即海南省木材公司的合法权益受到损害,不仅如此,适用该国际惯例会使欺诈行为得逞,违背民法中的"公序良俗"原则,所以,我们支持该案中法院的判决。

总之，不论在立法实务上，还是在理论探讨上，现代商人法和作为其核心的"国际惯例"在我国受到了越来越多的关注。

第二节　电子商务的法律适用

互联网产生时间不长①，但是发展速度惊人，目前，以互联网为基础的电子商务已经成为全世界的重要商务活动②，中国通过网络进行商业交易的人数与日俱增③，出现了良好的发展趋势，中国政府决心在 2020 年将中国建设成为一个电子商务的创新典范(**intention to make China a global leader in innovation by 2020**)。

【背景】　intention to make China a global leader in innovation by 2020

The government of the People's Republic of China (P.R.C.) has announced its intention to make China a global leader in innovation by 2020. Many Chinese business leaders share this goal. The primary focus of this national strategy is to transform China into an exporter of high-technology products based on Chinese designs rather than merely a low cost, high volume manufacturer of products based on technology developed in other countries. Recently some reforms of P.R.C. commercial law have been made in light of their contributions to this strategy. The first reform focuses on the domestic standard for accounting software issued in 1989 that successfully removed obstacles to the greater use of computerized accounting systems by local businesses and promoted the growth of the domestic accounting software industry. The second reform is the inclusion of general electronic commerce enabling legislation in the 1999 Contract Law which in theory removed impediments to the use of electronic commerce by Chinese businesses but in reality appears to be too abstract and general to provide much certainty to par-

---

①　In 1993, Marc Andreesen developed the first web browser called Mosaic X that allowed for searches on the internet. The combination of HTML, which made graphically-attractive web sites, and an internet browser, which made it easier to access those web sites, made the world wide web more user-friendly to the public. See Cindy Chen, United States and European Union Approaches to Internet Jurisdiction and Their Impact on E-Commerce, 25 *U. Pa. J. Int'l Econ. L.* 426 (2004).

②　2007 年 5 月份，根据研究机构 comScore 公布的报告，全球网民数量达到了 7.72 亿。参见新浪网：http://tech.sina.com.cn/i/2007-07-15/10341616842.shtml, 2008 年 6 月 20 日访问。

③　根据艾瑞公司联合淘宝网发布的《2007 中国网购报告》，2007 年国内参加网购的用户达到了 5500 万左右，参加网购的网友这一年平均每人在网上消费了 1080 元，全国网购市场总量达 594 亿元。参见新华网：http://news.xinhuanet.com/life/2008-01/31/content_7530964.htm, 2008 年 6 月 20 日访问。

ties wishing to form contracts using electronic media. The third reform is the adoption of the 2004 Electronic Signature Law which promotes the use of a specific type of technology for authentication.

These works involve P.R.C. legislation based on model laws developed by United Nations Commission on International Trade Law (UNCITRAL) developed to assist legislators in trading nations to harmonize their national commercial laws in order to eliminate barriers to international trade.①

在这样的国际背景下,大量的商务合同通过网络订立,而其中也必然包括大量与两个或两个以上国家具有某种联系的合同。此时,当电子商务活动发生纠纷时,由于网络的特殊性,使得电子商务活动法律适用所产生的法律问题冲击了传统的商务活动的法律适用制度,从而为我们提出了国际私法领域内的电子商务法律适用这一新问题。

一、电子商务及法律特征

电子商务(electronic commerce)是指以互联网为依托,通过计算机与计算机之间信息的交流与互动而发生的商事活动。②电子商务的中文有多种表述,如电子商务、电子交易、电子商业、电子贸易、网上商务、网上交易以及网上贸易等,在我国香港地区使用得比较多的是电子商贸。相应的英文名称也有多种不同的表述,如electronic commerce (e-commerce, EC), electronic trade (e-trade), electronic business (e-business, EB), cybershopping 等。③

电子商务主要有以下两个法律特征:

第一,电子商务关系的主体主要是网络经营者和网络终端用户。当然也不排除少部分其他电子商务关系的主体,如出版商等。电子商务关系主要发生在网络经营者和网络终端用户之间,另外一部分发生在依靠网络平台进行交易的终端用户之间。

第二,电子商务关系的产生、变更、终止是通过应用电子管理和数据交换系统完成的。有些学者认为电子商务只规范在线交易,不应包括线下交易。而恰恰相反,考虑到目前无论是国外还是国内的电子商务的实际情况,都应当把离线交易纳入电子商务法的规范内。④

---

① Jane K. Winn, Song Yuping, Can China Promote Electronic Commerce Through Law Reform? Some Preliminary Case Study Evidence, 20 *Colum. J. Asian L.* 415,416 (2007).
② 何其生著:《电子商务的国际私法问题》,法律出版社 2004 年版,第 8 页。
③ 李双元、王海浪:《电子商务法若干问题研究》,北京大学出版社 2003 年版,第 3 页。
④ 魏士廪:《电子合同理法论与实务》,北京邮电大学出版社 2001 年版,第 4 页。

二、电子商务领域的立法现状

国际电子商务的法律适用,主要有两个:一是实体法调整方法,即制定国际统一实体规范,直接规定当事人的权利与义务;二是冲突法调整方法,即通过冲突规范来选择特定国家实体法作为准据法。统一实体法是有关国家通过双边或多边国际条约制定的,以避免或消除法律冲突。有关电子商务的实体法主要有:

(一)联合国贸易委员会《电子商务示范法》

位于奥地利维也纳的联合国国际贸易法委员会(**The United Nations Commission on International Trade Law,UNCITRAL**)①是一个为推动国际商业交易而发展示范法和标准文本的组织。

【释义】 The United Nations Commission on International Trade Law

The United Nations Commission on International Trade Law (UNCITRAL) is a subsidiary body of the General Assembly. It plays an important role in improving the legal framework for international trade by preparing international legislative texts for use by States in modernizing the law of international trade and non-legislative texts for use by commercial parties in negotiating transactions. UNCITRAL legislative texts address international sale of goods; international commercial dispute resolution, including both arbitration and conciliation; electronic commerce; insolvency, including cross-border insolvency; international transport of goods; international payments; procurement and infrastructure development; and security interests. Non-legislative texts include rules for conduct of arbitration and conciliation proceedings; notes on organizing and conducting arbitral proceedings; and legal guides on industrial construction contracts and countertrade.②

联合国国际贸易法委员会于 1996 年 6 月完成了《电子商务示范法》(Model Law on Electronic Commerce, or The UNCITRAL E-Commerce Model Law),并于 1996 年 12 月以非投票决议的方式得到联合国大会的批准。该法分为两部分,共 17 条。第一部分涉及电子商务总的方面,主要就适用范围和定义,数据电文的留存、归属、确认收讫,发出和收到数据电文的时间和地点等作了详细规定。第二部分涉及特定领域的电子商务,也就是货物运输中使用的电子商务。《电子商务示范法》是国

---

① 联合国国际贸易法委员会,属于政府间公共机构。
② See http://www.uncitral.org/pdf/english/texts/electcom/06-57452_Ebook.pdf,2008 年 8 月 30 日访问。

际上第一个关于电子数据交换(Electric Data Interchange, EDI)①的示范法,它的出台,向各国立法者提供了一套国际公认的示范法(**model for domestic legislation**),使有关电子数据交换的一些主要法律问题得以解决,为电子商务创造了一个可靠的法律环境。

【释义】   model for domestic legislation

The UNCITRAL E-Commerce Model Law was designed as a model for domestic legislation. Legislation based on the UNCITRAL E-Commerce Model Law has been adopted in: Australia, Bermuda, Colombia, France, Hong Kong, Special Administrative Region of China, Ireland, Philippines, Republic of Korea, Singapore, Slovenia, the States of Jersey (Crown Dependency of the United Kingdom of Great Britain and Northern Ireland) and, within the United States, Illinois. Uniform legislation influenced by the UNCITRAL E-Commerce Model Law and the principles on which it is based has been prepared in Canada as the Uniform Electronic Commerce Act, adopted in 1999 by the Uniform Law Conference of Canada, and in the United States as the Uniform Electronic Transactions Act (UETA), adopted in 1999 by the National Conference of Commissioners on Uniform State Law and the Electronic Commerce Act.②

(二)《统一计算机信息交易法》

美国统一州法全国委员会(National Conference of Commissioners on Uniform State Law)和美国法学会(American Law Institute)于 1999 年 7 月在丹佛举行的第 108 届年会上通过了《统一计算机信息交易法》(The Uniform Computer Information Transactions Act,简称 UCITA)。《统一计算机信息交易法》在立法理由中指出,关于法律适用问题的规定是该法对于电子商务最重要的贡献之一。③

(三)《关于内部市场中与电子商务有关的若干法律问题的指令》(草案)

2000 年 6 月 8 日,欧洲议会及欧盟理事会最终通过并颁布了《关于共同体内部

---

① EDI(Electric Data Interchange,电子数据交换)是一种利用计算机进行商务处理的新方法,它是将贸易、运输、保险、银行和海关等行业的信息,用一种国际公认的标准格式,通过计算机通信网络,在各有关部门、公司和企业之间进行数据交换和处理,并完成以贸易为中心的全部业务过程。由于 EDI 的使用可以完全取代传统的纸张文件的交换,因此也有人称它为"无纸贸易"或"电子贸易"。

② Henry D. Gabriel, United Nations Convention on the Use of Electronic Communications in International Contracts and Compatibility with the American Domestic Law of Electronic Commerce, 7 *Loy. Law & Tech. Ann.* 9—10 (2007).

③ 《统一计算机信息交易法》明文承认当事人选择准据法的效力,是调整软件和计算机信息许可中广泛问题的主要立法,包括在全新的电子商务环境中对这些合同的订立、解释、履行和执行的有关问题进行规定。See Section 2B-107, Reporter's Note: 2. Purpose of Rules.

市场的信息社会服务,尤其是电子商务的若干法律方面的第 2000/31/EC 号指令》(Directive 2000/31/EC of the European Parliament and of the Council of 8 June 2000 on certain legal aspects of information society services, in particular electronic commerce, in the Internal Market),即《电子商务指令》(Directive on Electronic Commerce)。[1]该指令并不旨在建立新的国际私法规则,它规定由成员国负责制定在其领土内设立的信息服务供应商所应适用的规则,以解决目前法律适用的不确定性。

欧盟制定的与电子商务有关的法律文件还有 1997 年 4 月 15 日的《欧洲电子商务提案》(European Initiative on Electronic Commerce)、《欧盟关于数据库法律保护的指令》(The European Directive on the Legal Protection of Database)等。

(四) 联合国《国际合同使用电子通信公约》

联合国《国际合同使用电子通信公约》(United Nations Convention on the Use of Electronic Communication in International Contracts)于 2005 年 11 月在联合国大会上决议通过,它是有关电子商务的第一个专门性公约,也是近年来国际商事立法最重要的成果。公约在第一条对其适用范围(**scope of application**)作出了限定。公约的目的是采用统一规则消除对国际合同使用电子通信的障碍,公约确立了媒介和技术选择自由等原则。

【释义】 scope of application

1. This Convention applies to the use of electronic communications in connection with the formation or performance of a contract between parties whose places of business are in different States.

2. The fact that the parties have their places of business in different States is to be disregarded whenever this fact does not appear either from the contract or from any dealings between the parties or from information disclosed by the parties at any time before or at the conclusion of the contract.

3. Neither the nationality of the parties nor the civil or commercial character of the parties or of the contract is to be taken into consideration in determining the application of this Convention.

三、电子商务的法律适用原则

由于电子商务存在上述的一些特点,使其有别于在实际空间中进行的商业交

---

[1] 该指令对信息服务、服务供应商、服务获取者、消费者等内容进行了详细定义,对电子商务、行业自律、争议的非诉讼解决、司法管辖、电子网络联系等问题进行了规范。See *Official Journal*, L. 178, 7 July 2000, pp. 1—16.

易。上述这些电子商务适用的统一实体法并不具体针电子商务法律适用而制定，这些实体法只能提供原则上的指导，因此仍然必须要依靠冲突规范。因此，在实际生活中，当事人还必须借助冲突规范来选择特定国家实体法作为准据法。

电子商务的法律适用原则的主流做法是：以意思自治原则作为电子商务法律适用的首要原则，以最密切联系原则作为电子商务适用的辅助原则，确保适用保护电子商务中处于消费者一方的强制性规则。

（一）以意思自治原则为首要原则

电子商务是一种自由的商务，互联网具有极高的自治性，然而电子商务冲突法规范尚处于探索阶段，这方面的立法也不完善，所以当事人可以按照他们的意志决定适用于他们之间的法律。美国《统一计算机信息交易法》第 109 条（**UCITA，§109**）不仅允许当事人协议选择法律，而且不要求当事人的法律选择一定要和在线交易有合理联系。

【规则】　　　　　　　　　　**UCITA，§109**

UCITA, §109 (a) The parties in their agreement may choose the applicable law. However, the choice is not enforceable in a consumer contract to the extent it would vary a rule that may not be varied by agreement under the law of the jurisdiction whose law would apply under subsections (b) and (c) in the absence of the agreement.

2000 年欧盟《关于内部市场中与信息社会的服务特别是电子商务有关的若干法律问题的指令》和 2000 年海牙国际私法会议关于消费合同的共识也有类似规定。这就否定了与合同行为有联系的标准，放宽了对意思自治原则的限制，有利于保护当事人的行为预期，稳定电子商务法律关系，降低当事人在线交易的成本和风险，迅速合理地解决电子商务纠纷，促进电子商务的进一步发展。

国际电子商务中，当事人按照意思自治原则选择电子商务适用的法律体现了当事人选择的自主性。但是，为了防止当事人利用意思自治规避内国法，也为了维护法律适用结果的公平正义，需要对当事人的意思自治作出一些限制，即这种协议确定准据法的原则，不能违反国内法禁止性或强行性的规定。例如美国《统一计算机信息交易法》第 109（A）条同时还规定："如果在一项消费合同中作出的法律选择改变了根据有管辖权地区的法律不得以协议加以改变的规则，则此种选择无效。"又如《统一计算机信息交易法》第 104 条（**UCITA，§104**）也规定了一些限制性规则：当事人的协议不能改变不得以约定加以变更的任何规则或程序的适用，即:"在一宗大众市场交易中,协议不能改变下列规则的适用性:(A)消费者保护法(或行政法规);(B)适用于以打印格式存在的信息拷贝的法律;(C)欺诈、因电子错误而引起的消费者抗辩、显失公平原则或基本公共政策或善意义务的可适用性;以及某些法律中的直接适用的条款等。"《统一计算机信息交易法》第105(b)条(UCITA,§105(b))也规定了涉及电子商务条款与公共政策条款冲突时一些限制性的条款[1],即:"如果某一合同违反了某一基本公共政策,则法院可以拒绝执行该合同,而执行该合同中不包含被禁止条款的剩余部分,或限制被禁止条款的适用以避免违反公共政策的结果,在上述情况下,当事人的执行利益应服从禁止该条款执行的公共政策。"

【规则】 UCITA,§104

UCITA,§104 (1) An agreement that this Act governs a transaction does not alter the applicability of any rule or procedure that may not be varied by agreement of the parties or that may be varied only in a manner specified by the rule or procedure, including a consumer protection statute or administrative rule. In addition, in a mass-market transaction, the agreement does not alter the applicability of a law applicable to a copy of information in printed form.[2]

【规则】 UCITA,§10 5(b)

UCITA,§105(b) If a term of a contract violates a fundamental public policy, the court may refuse to enforce the contract, enforce the remainder of the contract without the impermissible term, or limit the application of the impermissible term so as to avoid a result contrary to public policy, in each case to the extent that the interest in enforcement is clearly outweighed by a public policy against enforcement of the term.[3]

类似的规定也体现在修订后的美国《统一商法典》(Uniform Commercial Code, UCC)中,§1-301规定消费者合同允许当事人根据意思自治原则选择所适用的法律,但要考虑公共政策和合理联系。[4]

---

[1] Jerry T. Myers, An Overview of the Uniform Computer Information Transactions Act, 106 *Com. L. J.* 282 (2001).
[2] UCITA, available at http://www.law.upenn.edu/bll/archives/ulc/ucita/ucita200.htm.
[3] Ibid.
[4] UCC, available at http://www.law.cornell.edu/ucc/1/article1.htm#s1-301.

意思自治原则,理论上有明示和默示两种方式。电子商务是通过网络进行的在线交易,双方当事人可能从未谋面,网络的虚拟性容易引发人们的安全性考虑,所以不宜采用默示的方式进行意思自治的表达,应当采用明示的方式来进行。因为一旦允许默示选择,通过计算机网络进行交易的电子商务将难以认定默示选择的标准。

(二) 以最密切联系原则作为辅助原则

在当事人没有进行法律选择时,最密切联系原则将是支配电子商务法律适用的主要原则,作为意思自治原则的补充。[1]最密切联系原则通过赋予法官自由裁量权,由法官根据客观的案件事实,相对合理地确定电子商务的法律适用。尤其是在传统的冲突规则难以适用的情况下,最密切联系原则通过对连接点的软化处理,可以增强电子商务法律选择的灵活性。

电子商务中,互联网服务提供商(Internet service provider, ISP)所在地、服务器所在地、网上广告或特殊要约的内容与实质、电子服务提供地、当事人联网的计算机地址等是重要的连接点或者连接因素,是根据最密切联系地确定电子商务法律适用的重要依据,而其中互联网服务提供商所在地在确定电子商务准据法方面具有特殊意义。按照互联网的特点,网址可以经常变换,但互联网服务提供商的地址却维持相对的稳定性,而用户可以自主地选择互联网服务提供商的地址。这就是说用户选择了互联网服务提供商地址就意味着接受了互联网服务提供商所在地的法律,这个最初选择权完全在电子商务用户自身。[2]针对具体的电子商务案件,与当事人具有最重要关系或最密切联系的,就是双方的互联网服务提供商,通过互联网服务提供商,进而可以指向互联网服务提供商所在地法,以及它所选择适用的法律。各个互联网服务提供商之间用明示方式互相表明自己的所在地和适用的法律,从而使用户在传递信息的过程中,能辨别自己进入了哪种法律区域,应遵循什么样的法律标准。

(三) 确保适用保护电子商务中处于消费者一方的强制性规则

各国在国际民商事法律关系中都规定了一些当事人不能规避的旨在保护消费者利益的强制性规则。电子商务作为国际商务的一种,其法律适用必须遵守这些强制性规则。如美国《统一计算机信息交易法》第 105 条规定,如果本法与消费者保护法发生冲突,则应适用消费者保护法。[3]

---

[1] 郭鹏:《网络消费合同的法律适用》,载《广西社会科学》2006 年第 3 期。
[2] 于志宏、吕国民:《电子商务中的法律适用问题探析》,载《广东商学院学报》2003 年第 1 期。
[3] 参见李双元、王海浪:《电子商务法若干问题研究》,北京大学出版社 2003 年版,第 35 页。

第三节 国际破产关系的法律适用

一、国际破产关系法律冲突与法律适用

（一）国际破产及其法律冲突

破产（insolvency）一词源于拉丁语的 fallitux,其意为失败,是指债务人不能清偿到期债务,法院根据债务人或债权人的申请,将债务人的财产依法分配给债权人的一种制度。其实质是相关经济单位的非正常终结,它既涉及实体问题,又涉及程序问题。[1]

国际破产（international insolvency）,也称为跨国破产（transnational insolvency）、跨界破产（cross-border insolvency）、涉外破产（insolvency involving foreign elements）,是指含有涉外因素或国际因素的破产,即破产程序中的债权人、债务人或破产财产位于两个或两个以上的国家。[2]在国际破产案件中,可能债权人和债务人分属不同的国家,也可能破产财团中的财产分散于不同的国家,或者破产债权是因受外国法支配的一项交易而产生的。[3]在这种情况下,处理该破产案件会涉及不同法律,因而产生诸多问题。近年来,随着贸易和投资在全球范围内的不断发展,国际破产案件的发生与日俱增。但由于各国的破产立法经常与其不同的政治目标及法律文化背景有密切联系,因此对破产的国际协调一直存在诸多困难。[4]

（二）各国破产法律制度的区别

随着国际民商事交往的不断扩大,国际破产问题已经受到国际社会的普遍关注。各国破产法律制度差异较大,法律冲突不断发生。国际破产方面的法律冲突主要体现在破产要件、破产财团、破产债权以及破产管理等方面。例如,各国破产法对破产财团的范围、性质以及与破产财团有关的权利作了不同的规定。德国和

---

[1] 韩德培:《国际私法新论》,武汉大学出版社 1997 年版,第 387 页。
[2] 石静遐:《跨国破产的法律问题研究》,武汉大学出版社 1999 年版,第 6 页。
[3] 黄进主编:《国际私法》（第二版）,法律出版社 2005 年版,第 275 页。
[4] See Jay Lawrence Westbrook, Developments in Transnational Bankruptcy, 39 *St. Louis U. L. J.* 745, 745 (1995).

第十二章 国际商事关系的法律适用

日本等国家采用固定立法体例,以破产宣告时属于破产人的全部财产为破产财团的构成范围;而法国、奥地利、英国、美国和瑞士等国家采用膨胀立法体例,破产财团的范围很宽泛,不仅包括破产宣告时破产人的全部财产,还包括破产宣告后破产程序终结前破产人新取得的财产。在处理国际破产的问题时,法律冲突在所难免。

(三)破产关系法律适用的一般原则

1. 国际公约优先原则

虽然在国际上对于国际破产的问题进行了长时期的讨论,也形成了《关于破产的公约草案》以及《关于国际破产关系的一般规则》,但是没有形成具有正式效力的全球性的国际公约。

1977年12月15日联合国国际贸易法委员会第72次全体会议通过了《联合国国际贸易法委员会跨国界破产示范法》(**UNCITRAL Model Law on Cross-border Insolvency**)(以下简称《跨国界破产示范法》)。①《跨国界破产示范法》的目的,在于为处理跨国界破产案件提供有效机制,以促进达到下述目标:(1)本国法院及其他主管机构与外国法院及其他主管机构之间涉及跨国界破产案件的合作;(2)加强贸易和投资方面的法律确定性;(3)公平而有效率地实施跨国界破产管理,保护所有债权人和其他有关当事人的利益;(4)保护并尽量增大债务人资产的价值;(5)挽救陷入经济困境的企业,从而保护投资和维持就业。

【背景】 **UNCITRAL Model Law on Cross-border Insolvency**

An intergovernmental working group negotiated the Model Law between 1995—1997 over four two-week sessions. The working group consisted of the 36 member states of the Commission, together with interested non-member states. Relevant international organizations, both intergovernmental and nongovernmental, also participated, such as the Hague Conference on Private International Law, the European Insolvency Practitioners Association (EIPA), Instituto Iberoamericano de Derecho Internacional Economico, INSOL International, International Bar Association (IBA) and the International Chamber of Commerce. Two weeks of final negotiations followed the deliberations of the working group during the thirtieth session of UNCITRAL (Vienna, Austria, 12—30 May 1997). The Model Law was adopted by consensus on May 30, 1997.②

---

① 《跨国界破产示范法》共5章32条。主要内容是:序言;第一章,总则(第1—8条);第二章,外国代表和债权人对本国法院的介入(第9—14条);第三章,对外国程序的承认和补救(第15—24条);第四章,与外国法院和外国代表之间的合作(第25—27条);第五章,同时进行的程序(第28—32条)。

② Scott K. Brown, Punching Your Ticket to the High-Speed International Insolvency Train, 26—28 American Bankruptcy Institute Journal 26 (2007).

一些区域性的国际公约对于统一国际破产法也起到了积极的促进作用。例如,1933年《北欧破产法公约》(Nordic Insolvency Convention)①、1995年《欧盟关于破产程序的国际公约》(The UE Convention on Insolvency Proceedings)和《欧盟理事会第1346号关于破产程序的规则》(Council Regulation (EU) No 1346/2000 of 29 May 2000 on Insolvency Proceedings)②等。本着条约必须信守的原则,缔约国应该依照国际公约的规定,解决缔约国之间的国际破产的法律冲突问题。

2. 破产法院地法原则

破产法院地法(lex fori consursus)就是国际破产宣告法院所在国的法律。法院地法在国际破产的法律适用问题上起着重要的作用。因为法院地法对于法官来说,显然更为熟悉,也更为明确。

(四) 破产关系的法律适用

1. 破产程序的法律适用

整个破产程序可分为三个阶段,即破产申请、破产宣告和破产清算。一般来说,法院审理国际破产案件遇到程序方面的问题时,都倾向于适用破产法院地法。③破产法院地法支配破产程序中的所有程序问题,包括破产案件的国内管辖权、破产申请的提出方式、破产管理人的任命范围和程序、债权申报规则、债权人会议的组成和召集、债权人投票的权利分配方式和行使方式、决议的通知等事项。④

2. 破产债权的法律适用

破产债权是指在破产宣告前成立的、对破产人发生的、经依法申报确认、并在破产财产中获得公平清偿的可强制执行的财产请求权。⑤对于国际破产债权的法律冲突,一般主张适用法院地法。戴赛和莫里斯认为,尽管对于某项债权是否存在需要适用原债权本身的准据法,如权利的获得是依受外国法支配的合同产生的,则与该权利有关的问题应适用合同准据法,但关于债权人之间对破产财产的分配及债权间的清偿顺序,如果在英国进行破产宣告,均应适用英国法的有关规定。⑥在英国,债权人之间的财产分配、债权人之间的优先顺序、诉讼的抵消和限制,所有这

---

① 《北欧破产法公约》是由丹麦、芬兰、冰岛、挪威和瑞典在1933年缔结的跨国破产公约,它被认为是世界上最权威的国际破产公约,并在实践中得到不断完善。
② Council Regulation (EU) No 1346/2000 of 29 May 2000 on Insolvency Proceedings, *Official Journal Law* 160, June 30, 2000.
③ 石静遐:《跨国破产的法律问题研究》,武汉大学出版社1999年版,89页。
④ 杜涛、陈力:《国际私法》,复旦出版社2004年版,第549页。
⑤ 王欣新:《破产法专题研究》,法律出版社1999年版,第165页。
⑥ See Dicey & Morris: *Conflict of Law*, 10th., ed., London: Stevens & Sons Limited, 1980, p.709.

些都按照作为法院地法的英国法确定。① 1995 年《欧盟关于破产程序的国际公约》也作了同样的规定。关于跨国破产中破产债权的法律适用,荷兰也主张适用破产法院地法。②

在 Ex Parte Melboura(1870 年)一案中,法院确定当地和国外债权人顺序或优先权的问题应由法院地法支配。

【案例】   Ex Parte Melboura③

    破产人与其妻子结婚时的婚姻住所地在荷兰东印第斯。结婚以前,他们订立了一个协议,旨在排除通常适用于居住在该殖民地的欧洲人的共有财产体制。该协议还划定 7.5 万荷兰盾归妻子单独使用。但是,这项契据未经登记。根据荷兰东印第斯法律,该项契据所起的作用只能使协议在双方当事人之间发生效力,涉及第三方当事人时,配偶双方仍受共有财产法的约束。丈夫在英国取得住所后破产,妻子出示了 7.5 万荷兰盾折合英镑数目的证据。上诉法院支持她的请求。认为她与丈夫之间的合同是有效的,争议问题应依荷兰东印第斯法律决定这一点是公认的。可是,一旦根据该法确定合同成立,涉及其丈夫的其他债权人时,妻子对丈夫要求的合同权利应当给予何种优先权的问题,则是由审判地法解决的问题。这样,妻子被允许对其丈夫在英国的受托人提出权利要求。法院认为在当地破产诉讼中,只要根据产生时所依据的法律,他们的权利要求是有效的,确定当地和国外债权人顺序或优先权的问题就应由法院地法律支配。④

关于确定破产债权存在与否的法律适用,在我国广东国际信托投资公司破产案中所涉及的**中芝兴业财务有限公司诉广信案**适用了破产开始地法(即法院地法)。⑤

【案例】   **中芝兴业财务有限公司诉广信案**

    此案的原告是中芝兴业财务有限公司(CCIC Finance Limited),一家在香港注册和营业的中、美、日合资金融机构,同时它也是判决债权人(judgment creditor)。被告是广

---

① 有关英国破产法中债权人之间的财产分配、债权人之间的优先顺序、诉讼的抵消和限制等问题,参见《英国破产法》,丁昌业译,法律出版社 2003 年版。
② 参见袁泉:《荷兰国际私法研究》,法律出版社 2000 年版,第 261—262 页。
③ Ex Parte Melboura (1870) L R 6 Ch App 64.
④ 案例资料出处参见董丽萍:《澳大利亚国际私法研究》,法律出版社 1999 年版,第 249—250 页。
⑤ 参见石静遐:《我国破产程序的域外效力的实例分析》,载《政法论坛》2002 年第 3 期。

东国际信托投资公司,同时它也是判决债务人(judgment debtor)。因为广东国际信托投资公司在进行破产清算,本案是由清算组进行应诉的。此外,本案中还有一个第三人债务人(garnishee),即广东国际信托投资公司100%持股的子公司。

本案涉及的一个问题是广东国际信托投资公司为中芝兴业财务有限公司与广东国际信托投资公司香港子公司的贷款协议出具的支持函(letter of support)是否构成具有法律效力的合约承诺,而使广东国际信托投资公司在广东国际信托投资公司香港子公司违约时成为中芝兴业财务有限公司的债务人。依大陆法律,该支持函不构成使广东国际信托投资公司承担债务的依据;但依据香港法,该函则构成广东国际信托投资公司承担债务的依据,而且香港高等法院也发出了扣押令,扣押所有广东国际信托投资公司香港子公司对广东国际信托投资公司的到期债务和利息,以偿付判决债务。但基于广东国际信托投资公司已在大陆作出破产宣告的事实,香港高等法院 Gill 法官行使自由裁量权之后作出了拒绝使扣押令成为绝对的判决,使得中芝兴业财务有限公司不能向广东国际信托投资公司申请债权。可以推断此案中如果广东国际信托投资公司不破产,则中芝兴业财务有限公司完全可以按照香港法律依扣押令圆满实现其债权。依此可见,跨国或跨地区破产使普通的法律关系复杂化。此案适用大陆法律完全是执行地法院法官基于礼让原则依据自由裁量权放弃管辖的结果。①

3. 破产财团的法律适用

破产财产也称破产财团,是指在破产程序中,未清偿债权人的需要由破产管理人组织起来的破产人的全部财产。破产财产的范围,有"固定主义"的立法例与"膨胀主义"的立法例之分。

所谓"固定主义",是指破产宣告时,破产人基于破产宣告以前的原因所拥有的财产为破产财团,包括破产宣告前已存在的将来行使请求权的财产,其特点在于破产财产在破产宣告时已经确定。固定主义将破产财产的范围仅限于破产宣告(或受理)时债务人所有的财产。日本、美国、德国采用此立法原则。

所谓"膨胀主义",是指破产财产不仅包括债务人被宣告破产时所有的财产,而且包括其在破产程序终结前新取得的财产。破产宣告后破产程序终结前取得的财产,一般是指在破产宣告后,通过劳动所得到的报酬、收益,他人赠与破产者的财产以及破产宣告后破产者作为继承人所得到的遗产以及遗赠等。英国、法国、意大利、瑞士及我国台湾地区采用此种立法模式。

对于破产财团的法律冲突,一般认为应依破产宣告国法,即法院地国法来解

---

① 参见赵相林:《国际私法教学案例评析》,中信出版社 2006 年版,第 148—149 页。

决。① 1995 年《欧盟关于破产程序的国际公约》规定,构成破产财团的财产,以及对在破产程序开始后债务人获得或接受移交的财产的处置,适用程序开始国法。

对于债权人对破产财团的物权,各国认为应适用物之所地法。但是,对于债务人对抗债权人的抵消权和否认权,则一般认为应适用破产宣告国的法律。1995 年《欧盟关于破产程序的国际公约》规定,对于不动产、船舶、航空器及应进行公共登记的债券等适用其所在地法或保存该登记的机关所在地的法律。

4. 破产管理的法律适用

破产管理包括管理人的任命或指定,债权的申报,债权人会议的成立、召开及其权力,对破产财产的占有、清理、登记、估价、变卖和分配,参与有关破产财产的诉讼、和解或者仲裁,以及办理破产企业的注销登记等方面。② 破产管理既有程序法的问题,也有实体法的问题。对此类问题,一般主张适用管理地法,即破产宣告国法,或法院地法。如 1933 年《北欧破产法公约》规定,国际破产管理人有权收集处于缔约国内的破产人的财产,并得依宣告国法律关于分配顺序和程序的规定进行分配。同时又规定,如果破产财产所在地法要求对财产的变价等应依一定的手续,则必须适用该财产所在地的法律。1995 年《欧盟关于破产程序的国际公约》规定,管理人可依程序开始国法授予的权力而行事,但是行使其权力时,破产管理人应遵守他意欲采取行为所在地的缔约国的法律,尤其是关于变卖财产的程序问题。

二、破产宣告的域外效力

跨国破产的核心关键问题是取得域外效力,得到域外承认与执行,一味地强调法院地法并不见得能取得预期的效果。

(一)破产程序的法律效力

无论是破产和解,还是破产清偿都涉及法律程序。程序主体行为的实施必然随之产生法律所规定的各种法律效果,并在特定的主体之间发生拘束力,这就是破产程序的效力。一般而言,一国法院所作的破产宣告在本国领域内具有当然的法律效力,但内国破产宣告在域外是否有效或外国破产宣告在内国是否有效,则在理论上有很大分歧。自破产制度建立后,只要存在国际经济交往,就会存在债权人、债务人分别位于两个以上国家或债务人在国外有财产的情况,也就有使破产案件存在各法域冲突的可能。

由于破产程序是在债务人不能清偿债务时进行的一种概括性清偿程序,其目

---

① 参见徐文超:《国际破产的法律适用》,载《江淮论坛》2004 年第 4 期。
② 刘仁山主编:《国际私法》,中国法制出版社 1999 年版,第 331 页。

的在于使全体债权人有序、公平地受偿。因此,在跨国破产案件中,最理想的做法是将债务人的所有财产集中到一个程序中,该程序由所有债权人参加,并按所有债权人或大部分债权人都接受的程序性和实体性规则对债务人的财产予以分配。

但各国的法律冲突使得问题变得复杂:各国对同一债权债务关系在适用法律上的冲突会产生有的破产程序承认破产人某些债务的存在,而有的破产程序则否认其存在的情况。个别债权人会利用一个国家不承认外国破产判决的规定,扣押债务人在国外的财产,从而获得比其他债权人更多的偿付。

正因为破产的域外效力与实现公平对待所有债权人这一破产目标紧密联系,域外效力问题就成为跨国破产的核心问题,是进行跨国破产国际合作的基础。同时,跨国破产的域外效力是法律选择和管辖权等其他跨国破产法律问题的理论基础和原动力,它关系到这一领域内所有法律问题的最终解决。如果没有域外效力理论的支持,各国便没有必要考虑外国法的适用,也不可能进行跨国破产领域的国际合作,从而导致内国法独揽天下,跨国破产的法律问题成为法院地法的"专利"的局面。

(二) 破产域外效力的理论基础

1. 普遍破产主义原则

普遍破产主义原则(universality),又称单一破产制(unity)。根据普遍破产主义原则,在跨国破产中,只应该有一个破产宣告,由一个破产程序来解决世界范围内的针对债务人财产的所有求偿要求。该程序一般在债务人的住所地或主要营业地进行,它应当包括债务人的所有财产,无论它们位于何处。①

普遍破产主义原则主张通过一次破产宣告,以债务人的所有财产对所有的债权人进行偿付,程序比较简单、迅捷,也有利于实现债权人的平等待遇。但是,在实践中会遇到一些问题,一国的破产宣告有时难以得到有关国家的承认与协助,其原因在于财产所在地国不愿放弃对当地财产的控制权。

值得一提的是,对于外国破产判决,英国法本身并不承认普遍破产主义(**The doctrine of unity is certainly no part of English law**)。但如果外国破产程序是由债务人住所地法院开始的,并且不损害英国债权人的利益,英国法院很可能会予以承认。可是,仍有一个重要的前提,即该外国是英国《破产法》第426节第(11)项所指定的"有关国家或地区"(relevant country or territory)。②

---

① 石静遐:《跨国破产的法律问题研究》,武汉大学出版社1999年版,第20页。
② 这些国家和地区多是英国的前附属国(如澳大利亚、加拿大)和现在的附属地区(如百慕大)。

【释义】 The doctrine of unity is certainly no part of English law

The doctrine of unity is certainly no part of English law. Though the theoretical convenience of submitting to the forum of the domicile has judicially admitted, there is not a single case in which the court has stayed bankruptcy proceedings in England on that ground alone. There is, no doubt, jurisdiction to do so, but it is a jurisdiction that will not be exercised unless there is some other weighty reason, such as the absence of assets in England, for taking so drastic a step.[①]

2. 属地破产主义原则

属地破产主义原则(territoriality),又称复合破产制(pluralism),强调每个国家对位于本国境内的财产有固有的管辖权。根据该原则,一国法院所作的破产宣告,其效力仅及于破产人在该国领域内的财产,每个国家的法院根据本国破产法,将债务人位于本国境内的财产分配给债权人,法院任命破产管理人的权限也仅限于搜集破产人在本国的财产。破产人位于其他国家的财产不受本国程序的影响,仍继续保留在破产人手中,除非被财产所在国的债权人扣押或在财产所在国开始又一次破产程序。

主张属地破产主义原则的学者认为,该原则的理论基础在于:第一,债权人在同债务人进行交易活动时,其内心仅以债务人在国内的财产作为信用基础,因此破产宣告的法律效力仅应及于债务人的国内财产。第二,如果一国破产宣告的效力及于本国以外,则债权人在同债务人进行交易时会因无法预测在债务人破产时应当适用何种法律而心存疑虑,影响交易的进行。[②]第三,从破产案件的执行来看,它是一种全国的强制执行程序,即利用国家权力进行的一种特殊的债务清偿。国家权力的行使只能在一国有效的管辖范围之内进行,跨越国界便有侵犯其他国家主权之嫌。因此破产的效力不能及于位于他国的财产。这是国际法上国家主权原则在破产领域的具体解释,反映了属地破产主义原则的主导思想和内在精神。[③]

英国承认属地破产主义原则(**separate independent bankruptcies**)。

【释义】 separate independent bankruptcies

Separate independent bankruptcies in each jurisdiction.—This is the principle to which

---

① P. M. North, *Cheshire and North's Private International Law*, 10th ed., London: Butterworths, 1979, p.561.
② 杜中超:《破产的域外效力与我国涉外破产法的完善》,载《河南师范大学学报》(社会科学版)1997年第4期。
③ 参见石静遐:《跨国破产的法律问题研究》,武汉大学出版社1999年版,第23—24页。

English law is committed. The court, if once put in motion, administers such assets as are situated in England according to the rules set out in the Bankruptcy Act 1914, without regard to administrations that may be in process in other countries, though it recognizes the claims of all creditors, foreign as well as English. This does not mean, however, that the status of a foreign trustee in bankruptcy is disregarded. Though English law neglects the doctrine of unity it recognizes the doctrine of universality, that is, it admits that the title of a foreign trustee extends to such movables of the debtor as are found in England, provided that no bankruptcy proceedings have been begun within the jurisdiction.①

在属地破产主义原则方面,值得一提的是 **Solomons v. Ross.** 案。

【案例】 Solomons v. Ross

X & co., Dutch merchants, were declared bankrupt on January 2 and Y was appointed curator of their property by the Chamber of Desolate Estates in Amsterdam. Previously, on December 20, Z, an English creditor of X & Co., had attached £1200 in the hands of A which was due from A to X & Co. In March Z obtained judgment by default on the attachment, whereupon a writ of execution was issued against A. Being unable to pay, A gave Z a promissory note for the amount of the judgment. In proceedings brought by the curator, Y, it was held that A must pay the £1200 to Y, and that the execution creditor, Z, must surrender the promissory note to A.②

3. 折中破产主义原则

由于属地破产主义原则和普遍破产主义原则各有其无法克服的一些弊端,因而理论上遂有关于破产宣告域外效力的折中破产主义原则,期望能在二者之间走一条中间道路,扬长避短。实践之中有两种做法:第一,主张本国的破产宣告具有普及效力,而外国的破产宣告的效力则不能及于本国的财产。也就是说,本国法院作出的破产宣告,其效力及于债务人的所有财产,不论其位于国内还是国外,针对债务人财产的个别执行和扣押必须中止,国内外的债权人都只能向本国的破产管理人申报债权,参加本国的破产程序,依本国的法律得到清偿。但是,外国法院的破产宣告在本国则不具有效力,针对债务人在本国财产的个别执行和扣押无须中止,债务人仍然享有对本国财产的控制权和处分权。第二,对一国破产宣告的域外

---

① P. M. North, *Cheshire and North's Private International Law*, 10th ed., London: Butterworths, 1979, p. 562.
② Ibid., p. 569.

第十二章 国际商事关系的法律适用

效力依财产的性质而有所不同。即一国的破产宣告对债务人位于国外的动产具有普及效力,但对债务人位于外国的不动产则没有效力。主张破产宣告效力及于动产,是因为动产易于转移,应防止债务人利用破产案件的国际管辖权冲突问题非法转移资产,逃避债务,侵害债权人利益。①主张破产宣告效力不及于不动产,则是为尊重不动产所在国的司法管辖权,不动产一般与一国的公共利益和安全关系重大,不允许外国人任意取得。

三、我国的立法与司法实践

（一）我国处理国际破产案的立法现状

随着我国在经济全球化进程中的影响力不断深化,我国法院将不可避免地遇到日益增多的国际破产案件。我国立法机关立足于本国国情,大量参照国际立法,包括联合国国际贸易法委员会制定的《跨国破产示范法》(Model Law on Cross-Border Insolvency)②、《欧盟理事会第1346号关于破产程序的规则》、《美国联邦破产法》、日本《外国倒产程序承认和协助法》以及中国国际私法学会草拟的学术性的《中华人民共和国国际私法示范法》,耗费十年时间,终于制定出了《中华人民共和国企业破产法》(以下简称《企业破产法》),于2006年8月27日通过并于2007年6月1日起施行。

《企业破产法》把破产主体扩大到所有的企业法人,并且创造性地引入了国际破产问题的解决办法,规定了破产程序的域外效力以及对外国法院作出的破产案件的判决、裁定的承认和执行,这为中国法院审理国际破产案件提供了明确的司法依据。

（二）我国有关国际破产案的管辖权问题

国际破产案面临的首要问题就是应由哪一国法院管辖该案的问题,对此各国理论上和实践中存在不同主张。③在我国,根据《企业破产法》第3条的规定,破产案件由债务人住所地的人民法院管辖。《民法通则》第39条规定,法人的住所地应为其主要办事机构所在地。最高人民法院《关于审理企业破产案件若干问题的规定》中也有相关规定,并补充说:"债务人无办事机构的,由其注册地人民法院管辖。"

由此可见,我国对于国际破产案件的管辖适用主要办事机构所在地,或注册地人民法院管辖。这与目前大陆法系的一些国家和少数英美法系国家的做法相似。

---

① 王欣新主编:《破产法》,中国人民大学出版社2002年版,第122页。
② Model Law on Cross-Border Insolvency, Annex I—of the Report of the 30th session of UNCITRAL A/52/17May30.1997.
③ 这些主张主要有:(1)由破产债务人住所地国家法院管辖;(2)由破产债务人的管理中心所在地国家法院管辖;(3)由破产债务人财产所在地国家法院管辖。

(三) 我国有关国际破产的法律适用

1. 破产程序的法律适用

一般来说,法院审理国际破产案件遇到程序方面的问题时,都倾向于适用破产法院地法,我国同样适用了法院地法原则。《企业破产法》第4条规定:"破产案件审理程序,本法没有规定的,适用民事诉讼法的有关规定。"也即《企业破产法》有规定的应当依照该法的规定执行,没有规定的,则适用《民事诉讼法》的一般规定。因为破产程序是民事诉讼程序的一个特别程序,《民事诉讼法》是基本法,它的一般规定也适用于破产程序。

2. 破产债权的法律适用

我国《企业破产法》规定,破产宣告前成立的无财产担保的债权和放弃优先受偿权利的有财产担保的债权为破产债权。有财产担保的债权因其对担保物享有不依破产程序优先受偿的权利,故不属于破产债权,但其债额超过担保物价款未受清偿的部分为破产债权。另外,债权人参加破产程序的费用不得作为破产债权。

关于破产债权的清偿顺序,我国《企业破产法》第113条规定,破产财产在优先清偿破产费用和共益债务后,依照下列顺序清偿:(1)破产人所欠职工的工资和医疗、伤残补助、抚恤费用,所欠的应当划入职工个人账户的基本养老保险、基本医疗保险费用,以及法律、行政法规规定应当支付给职工的补偿金;(2)破产人欠缴的除前项规定以外的社会保险费用和破产人所欠税款;(3)普通破产债权。破产财产不足以清偿同一顺序的清偿要求的,按照比例分配。

3. 破产财产的法律适用

我国《企业破产法》第30条规定:"破产申请受理时属于债务人的全部财产,以及破产申请受理后至破产程序终结前债务人取得的财产,为债务人财产。"由此可见,我国破产法对破产财产范围采用的是"膨胀主义"。

总的来说,我国处理国际破产案时遵循法院地法原则,适用《企业破产法》和《民事诉讼法》,这样能够使法院迅速有效地处理破产案件。

(四) 我国处理国际破产案的司法实践

最近十几年来,跨国破产案涉及的范围越来越广,在20世纪90年代颇具影响的**国际商业信贷银行国际破产案**,涉及中国的债权人和中国的法院。中国银行深圳分行,作为国际商业信贷银行深圳分行的最大债权人,向深圳中院提起宣告国际商业信贷银行破产,并进入破产还债程序的请求。

【案例】   **国际商业信贷银行国际破产案**

国际商业信贷银行(Bank of Commerce and Credit International, BCCI)是一家总部设在卢森堡的跨国银行集团,曾在世界各国设有许多子公司和分支机构,在中国深圳也设有一家分行。1990年之后,先后被六七十个国家的法院宣告破产。中国银行深圳分行作为国际商业信贷银行深圳分行的最大债权人,也向深圳市中级人民法院提起宣告国际商业信贷银行破产并进入破产还债程序的请求。深圳市中级人民法院在1992年受理了该案。根据中国债权人的申请,深圳市中级人民法院迅速冻结了国际商业信贷银行深圳分行位于中国的财产。根据《民事诉讼法》第243条的规定,深圳市中级人民法院任命了清算组,负责国际商业信贷银行深圳分行的清算。清算组的报告表明,深圳分行在中国的财产大约有2000万美元,而其负债达到8000万美元。中国债权人在深圳市中级人民法院开始的破产程序中得到了相应的分配。[①]尽管在该案中存在全球清算程序,但中国债权人没有参加国际商业信贷银行的全球清算。[②]

本案涉及的主要法律问题是中国是否承认外国破产宣告的效力。从本案可以看出,中国法院坚持的是破产属地主义,坚持适用法院地法处理破产中的程序问题和实体问题,这与中国当时缺乏明确的立法有关。特别是当外国当事人持外国法院的破产判决直接请求中国法院予以承认与执行时,法院对于应该考虑何种因素,是否给予承认与执行等问题缺乏应有的了解。但是就目前来看,《企业破产法》对破产程序的域外效力进行了明确的规定,该法第5条规定:"依照本法开始的破产程序,对债务人在中华人民共和国领域外的财产发生效力。对外国法院作出的发生法律效力的破产案件的判决、裁定,涉及债务人在中华人民共和国领域内的财产,申请或者请求人民法院承认和执行的,人民法院依照中华人民共和国缔结或者参加的国际条约,或者按照互惠原则进行审查,认为不违反中华人民共和国法律的基本原则,不损害国家主权、安全和社会公共利益,不损害中华人民共和国领域内债权人的合法权益的,裁定承认和执行。"如果按照本条规定进行裁判,有可能结果会截然不同。

由此可见,《企业破产法》第5条规定的破产的域外效力原则既不是绝对的属地破产主义,也不是绝对的普遍破产主义,而是有限普遍破产主义,即本国开始的破产程序,效力及于债务人在国外的财产;在国外开始的破产程序,经人民法院裁定,对债务人在国内的财产发生效力。这种做法既符合现代破产法的发展趋势,也有利于保护中国债权人的利益及开展跨国破产合作,是一种有限的、有弹性的、有张力的跨国破产原则。

[①] 石静遐:《跨国破产的法律问题研究》,武汉大学出版社1999年版,第70页。
[②] 有关BCCI全球清算的情况,See Christopher K. Grieson, Shareholder Liability, Consolidation and Pooling, in *Current Issues in Cross-Border Insolvency and Reorganization*, E. Bruce Leonard and Christopher W. Besant (edited), 220—225 (1994); See also Christopher K. Grieson, Insolvency of Financial Institutions, 5 *Int'l Bus. Lawyer*, 213 (1996).

【思考题】

- 什么是商人法？商人法的适用有什么特点？
- 国际上第一个关于电子数据交换的国际示范法是哪个？
- 试述电子商务法律适用规则。
- 简述国际破产关系法律适用的一般原则。
- 什么是破产宣告的域外效力？
- 阐述单一破产制和复合破产制的区别。

【重要术语提示与中英文对照】

中文术语	英文对照
商人法	law merchant, *jus mercatorum*
商人的法律	*lex mercatoria*
现代商人法	modern *lex mercatoria*
新商人法	new law merchant
电子商务	electronic commerce (E-commerce, EC)
电子交易	electronic trade (E-trade)
电子商业	electronic business (E-business, EB)
联合国国际贸易法委员会	The United Nations Commission on International Trade Law, UNCITRAL
电子商务示范法	Model Law on Electronic Commerce, The UNCITRAL E-Commerce Model Law
联合国国际合同使用电子通信公约	United Nations Convention on the Use of Electronic Communication in International Contracts
电子数据交换	Electric Data Interchange, EDI
统一计算机信息交易法	The Uniform Computer Information Transactions Act, UCITA
美国法学会	American Law Institute
统一商法典	Uniform Commercial Code, UCC
互联网服务提供商	internet service provider, ISP
破产	insolvency, bankruptcy
1933年北欧破产法公约	Nordic Insolvency Convention
1995年欧盟关于破产程序的国际公约	The UE Convention on Insolvency Proceedings

欧盟理事会第 1346 号关于破产程序的规则	Council Regulation (EU) No 1346/2000 of 29 May 2000 on Insolvency Proceedings
破产法院地法	*lex fori consursus*
破产财团	bankrupt's property
破产管理	administration of bankruptcy
破产清算	liquidation of bankruptcy
破产程序	bankruptcy proceedings
破产宣告	adjudication of bankruptcy
普遍破产主义原则	universality
单一破产制	unity
属地破产主义原则	territoriality
合破产制	pluralism
中芝兴业财务有限公司	Bank of Commerce and Credit International, BCCI

【推荐阅读文献】

- 徐国建:《现代商人法论》,载《中国社会科学》1993 年第 2 期。
- 石静遐:《跨国破产的法律问题研究》,武汉大学出版社 1999 年版。
- 何其生:《电子商务的国际私法问题》,法律出版社 2004 年版。
- 赵相林:《国际商事关系法律适用论》,中国政法大学出版 2005 年版。
- 解正山:《论 COMI 在跨国破产国际管辖中的适用——欧盟及美国的视角》,载《环球法律评论》2009 年第 6 期。
- 贾树学、王从荣:《欧美跨国破产中"主要利益中心"适用的差异性分析》,载《人民司法》2012 年第 23 期。
- Richard E. Coulson, Choice of Law in United States Cross-Border Insolvencies, 59 *Consumer Fin. L. Q. Rep.* 67 (2005).
- Matthew D. Stein, Rethinking UCITA: Lessons From the Open Source Movement, 58 *Me. L. Rev.* 157 (2006).
- JH Dalhuisen, Legal Orders and Their Manifestation: The Operation of the International Commercial and Financial Legal Order and Its Lex Mercatoria, 24 *Berkeley J. Int'l L.* 129 (2006).
- Fabrizio Marrella, Christopher S. Yoo, Is Open Source Software the New Lex Mercatoria? 47 *Va. J. Int'l L.* 807 (2007).
- Henry D. Gabriel, United Nations Convention on the Use of Electronic Communications in International Contracts and Compatibility with the American Domestic Law of

Electronic Commerce, 7 *Loy. Law & Tech. Ann.* 9—10 (2007).
* Bashayreh (M.), Lex Mercatoria and Arbitration Agreements: Perspectives from Greek and Jordanian Law, 62 Rev. *Hellénique Dr. Int'l* 157 (2009).
* Muñoz-López (J.), Internet Conflict of Laws: A Space of Opportunities for ODR, 14 *Rev. Colomb. Der. Int'l* 163 (2009).
* Leibner (J.), An Executory Approach to Cross-Border Insolvencies, 64 *U. Miami L. Rev.* 1171 (2010).
* Stephen Mason, Revising the EU e-Signature Directive, 7 *Comms. L.* 56 (2012).

【扩展阅读资料】

Scope of Uniform Computer Information Transaction Act(UCITA)[①]

A. The Challenges to Defining Scope

Defining the scope of UCITA proved to be one of the most difficult tasks for the drafting committee. The convergence of the software, computer hardware, publishing, entertainment and other industries makes defining the limits of scope a very tricky business. Rules that work well for software licensing may not work well for the sale of a book on a compact disk. Having different rules apply to the sale of a book, depending on whether the book is in print or on a compact disk, is hard to reconcile. Some in industries, such as motion picture, with a long history of successful licensing practices, have found the emerging transactional formats and rules associated with software licensing difficult to reconcile with the rules and practices they have traditionally employed. Industries already subject to pervasive federal regulation may not be eager to embrace a state law that addresses some of their transactional concerns but not others.

B. Included Transactions

UCITA will apply to computer information transactions. n1 A computer information transaction is defined as an agreement to create, modify, transfer or license computer information. "Computer information" means information in an electronic form that is obtained from or through the use of a computer or that is capable of being processed by a computer. "Information" is defined as including "data, text, images, sounds, mask works, or computer programs, including collections and compilations of them."

---

① Jerry T. Myers, An Overview of the Uniform Computer Information Transactions Act, 106 *Com. L. J.* 275, 276—279 (2001).

Determining whether a transaction falls within the scope of UCITA requires a careful examination of the subject matter of the transaction. For example, an agreement for the use of a software program, commonly written in the form of a limited-use license agreement, is a computer information transaction. The subject matter of the transaction is the software program. Not all transactions involving computerized information, however, will come within the scope of the act. For example, the purchase of a book is not a computer information transaction, even though the text of the book may be delivered in an electronic form over the Internet or on a diskette. Nor does it matter that the book was purchased electronically from an Internet bookstore. The subject matter of the transaction is the book, not the media on which it is delivered or the means by which it is purchased.

C. Mixed Transactions

It is common for computer information, such as a computer program, to be delivered to the end user as part of a package of products and services that includes both hardware and software. A primary motivation for creating UCITA was the recognition that there are fundamental differences between a computer information transaction and the sale of goods. In a mixed transaction, it is important to match each component of the transaction with an appropriate set of rules. The parties involved in a computer hardware transaction expect an exchange of property rights normally associated with a sale of goods. When the transaction is completed, the purchaser expects to be the owner of the computer, and the seller expects little more than payment and an obligation to see that any warranties are properly honored. In short, the parties expect UCC Article 2 rules to apply.

The expectations of the parties with regard to the software aspects of the transaction are quite different. The parties do not anticipate a transfer of ownership of the software. Rather, the acquiring party anticipates receiving a contractual right to use the software, while the vendor expects to retain both ownership of the intellectual property rights in the software and associated obligations, such as the burden of defending the acquiring party against claims of infringement by third parties. The parties expect UCITA's rules to apply to the software aspect of the transaction.

In mixed transactions, the body of law which will apply depends on the subject matter under consideration. Section 103(b)(1) provides that UCITA will apply to the computer information aspects of a transaction, leaving the other aspects of the transaction subject to other law. In transactions involving software which is embedded in goods, the same general approach is followed. Where the software program is an inseparable and indistinguishable part of a good, UCITA will not apply. n6 For example, a consumer who suffers a brake failure in an automobile would look to Article 2 rather than UCITA even though the braking system featured an integrated computer chip.

Parties to a mixed transaction may avoid confusion regarding whether and to what degree UCITA applies by agreeing to either opt-in or opt-out of UCITA under section 104. An agreement that UCITA will apply to a transaction does not alter the applicability of other statutes or regulations if their application can not be waived. Similarly, an agreement that UCITA does not apply to a transaction involving computer information will not work to waive the consumer protection aspects of UCITA sections 209, 214 or 816.

D. Excluded Transactions

Persons in the software industry who recognized the need for a uniform body of law actively sought the creation of UCITA. Representatives from other industries whose products and services could be seen arguably within the scope of UCITA, however, were not as quick to embrace the act. In particular, representations from the entertainment, financial services, insurance, and telecommunications industries each sought specific exclusions for their core products and services. For a variety of reasons, members of these industries sought to exclude certain types of transactions from coverage within UCITA. For example, those in the entertainment industry believed the introduction of UCITA's default rules would upset long established licensing models. Likewise, members of the financial services industry, already subject to many state and federal regulations, expressed concern about potential conflicts that might arise with the introduction of yet another layer of statutory law being applied to their core products and services.

As a result of various industry concerns, several specific exemptions are stated in section 103. UCITA does not apply to the following:

- Sales or leases of goods
- Contracts for personal services (except computer information development and support agreements)
- Casual exchanges of information
- Contracts where computer information is not required by the agreement
- Employment contracts
- Contracts where computer information is insignificant
- Computers, televisions, VCR's, DVD players, or similar goods
- Financial services transactions
- Insurance services transactions
- Contracts for print books, magazines, or newspapers
- Contracts for sound recordings and musical works
- Contracts for regulated telecommunications services and products
- Contracts for motion pictures, broadcast or cable programming (except as in Section 103(b)(d).)

第十三章

国际支付关系的法律适用

本 章 导 读

※ 票据是依法可以流通、转让的无条件支付票面金额的一种有价凭证。国际票据关系是基于票据行为而在当事人之间产生的跨国债权债务关系。

※ 根据大陆法系国家的法律规定，票据专指汇票和本票；而英美法系国家的票据除了汇票和本票之外，还包括支票。

※ 票据行为能力适用当事人的属人法，票据权利取得的方式和效力依物之所在地法，票据行为适用行为地法，票据的形式有效性和票据追索权的行使期限适用出票地法。

※ 我国《票据法》有关票据的法律冲突规则为：优先适用国际条约；票据行为能力适用以当事人的本国法为主，辅之以行为地法；票据出票时记载的事项和追索权的行使期限适用出票地的法律；票据的背书、承兑、付款和保证行为，适用行为地法律。

※ 信用证是国际支付中最普遍使用的一种方式，具有自身的独立性。信用证是开证银行根据开证申请人的请求和指示，向受益人签发的规定在符合一定条件时保证付款的书面承诺文件。信用证法律关系表现为信用证开证行与受益人之间的关系。

※ 国际商会 2007 年 7 月 1 日起开始实施的《跟单信用证统一惯例 600 号》是调整信用证法律关系的国际惯例。

※ 根据国际私法中当事人意思自治原则，信用证的当事人可以选择《跟单信用证统一惯例 600 号》(UCP600) 或者相关国家的国内实体法作为信用证的准据法。如果当事人未作选择的，法院应适用与信用证有最密切联系地国家的法律。

※ 确定与信用证有最密切联系地的核心是界定信用证的履行地。英美国家的判例表明，法院对信用证履行地的界定经历了从付款地到信用证开证地的发展历程，而美国《统一商法典（信用证篇）》第 5-116 (b) 条将信用证履行地界定为信用证开证行所在地，并规定适用信用证开证行所在地国家的法律，则是信用证法律适用的新趋势。

※ 在我国的司法实践中承认信用证条款中对《跟单信用证统一惯例 600 号》选择的有效性。

※ 托收，是指卖方以买方为付款人开立汇票，委托银行代向买方收取货款的一种结算方式。

【本章主题词】 票据、信用证、UCP600、UCC、国际托收

第一节 国际票据的法律适用

一、国际票据法律冲突存在的必然性

（一）票据的概念

票据（bills）是依法可以流通、转让的无条件支付票面金额的一种有价凭证。票据具有要式性、文义性、无因性和流通性。票据所具有的特性，使其在一定程度上可代替货币的一些职能，同时也具有一些货币所没有的功能。正是由于票据在社会经济生活中所具有的重要作用，各国在其法律制度中都格外地重视票据法律制度的建设。

在大陆法系国家的票据法中，票据专指汇票（**draft or bill of exchange**）和本票（promissory notes）。

【释义】　　　　　　　　draft or bill of exchange

Draft or bill of exchange is a negotiable instrument that is payable to the seller and drawn on the issuing bank and/or the buyer. Drafts can be either "sight drafts" where the bank pays the full amount of the draft upon the seller's presentation, or "time drafts" where the bank's obligation at the time of presentation is merely to accept the draft for payment at a later date (e.g. 60 days after the seller's presentation).

在英美法系国家的票据法中，尤其是美国的《统一商法典》（Uniform Commercial Code，简称 UCC）中，其票据（**negotiable instruments**）概念与大陆法系有很大的差异。

【释义】　　　　　　　　　negotiable instruments

The UCC defines a negotiable instrument as an unconditioned writing that promises or orders the payment of a fixed amount of money. Drafts and notes are the two categories of instruments. To be considered negotiable an instrument must meet the requirements stated in Article 3 of the Uniform Commercial Code (UCC). Negotiable instruments do not include money, payment orders governed by article 4A (fund transfers) or to securities governed by Article 8 (investment securities).

(二) 票据的法律冲突

从性质上看,大陆法系把票据限于支付凭证,英美法系国家则把票据从支付凭证扩大到了流通证券。[①]从内容上,大陆法系国家的票据法仅仅将票据限于汇票和本票。1988 年《联合国国际汇票和国际本票公约》(United Nations Convention on International Bills of Exchange and International Promissory Notes)第 1 条第 3 款也明确规定该公约不适用于支票。而英美法系国家的票据除了包括汇票和本票之外,还包括支票。[②]从以上分析可以看出,有的国家有票据这个概念,有的国家则没有,在有票据这一概念的国家中还有的不包括支票。[③]因而我们可以说,在世界各国不存在一个统一的"票据"概念,这也是票据法律冲突的一个方面。

二、国际票据法律适用的一般原则

随着票据的广泛使用,在国际私法中解决票据法律适用问题,已经形成了以下较为一致的原则:

(一) 票据行为能力适用当事人的属人法

在票据行为能力法律冲突的解决问题上,大陆法系采取行为能力依本国法为主、行为地法为补充的原则。英国采取住所地法与合同自体法选择适用的原则,美国采取住所地法与合同自体法兼采主义的原则。[④]一些国家的国内法有保护不熟悉商业交易的债务人的特别规则,故民事行为能力的人不一定就当然地具有票据行为能力。[⑤]

(二) 票据权利取得的方式和效力适用物之所在地法

票据权利指持票人因占有票据,根据票据文义行使的权利。债权的发生,必须

[①] 姚梅镇主编:《国际经济法概论》,武汉大学出版社 1989 年版,第 488 页。
[②] 参见顾海波:《国际票据的法律适用规则问题探讨》,载中国国际私法学会主办:《国际私法与比较法年刊》(第二卷),法律出版社 1999 年版,第 108 页。
[③] 参见李红海:《涉外票据的法律适用》,载《广西政法管理干部学院学报》2004 年第 3 期。
[④] 顾益民:《论票据行为能力的法律适用——以实证比较与价值为视角》,载《政法学刊》2007 年第 1 期。
[⑤] 肖永平:《肖永平论冲突法》,武汉大学出版社 2002 年版,第 127 页。

第十三章 国际支付关系的法律适用

做成证券;票据权利的转移,必须交付证券;票据权利的行使,则必须提示证券。所以,票据权利和票据本身不可分离。各国立法和学说在票据权利取得上一般将票据视同有形动产,对票据权利取得的方式和效力依"物之所在地法原则"决定其准据法,如美国诉纽约担保信托公司案(**United States v. Guaranty Trust Co. of New York**)。①

【案例】　　**United States V. Guaranty Trust Co. Of New York**②

The defendant presented to the Federal Reserve Bank at New York a check drawn on the Treasurer of the United States on October 29, 1921, and payable to the order of Louis Macakanja, 37 Sasava Kot Glina, Z. P. Maja, Jugo-Slavia, and received credit for it. The check then was indorsed in the name of the payee. The Federal Reserve Bank of New York presented the check to the Treasurer of the United States, who paid it by giving the Federal Reserve Bank credit for it in December, 1921.

About April 27, 1926, the plaintiff learned that the payee's indorsement on the check was forged, and thereupon demanded reimbursement from the defendant of the money it paid upon presentment of the check. Upon denial by the defendant of liability, this suit was brought.

The essential facts were stipulated, and are that the indorsement of the payee was forged in Jugo-Slavia where the check was then transferred and delivered to the Merkur Bank which took it without notice of the forgery and for a valuable consideration on or about November 30, 1921. This bank acted in good faith and without negligence. It indorsed and transferred the check to the Slavenska Bank D. D. Zagreb, in Jugo-Slavia, for a valuable consideration. The Slavenska Bank acted in good faith without notice of the forgery and without negligence. This bank indorsed the check in Jugo-Slavia to the order of the defendant on or about December 3, 1921, and forwarded it to the defendant in New York. The defendant received it on or about December 21, 1921, and took it for value in good faith without notice of the forgery and without negligence.

---

① ［案情］美国退伍军人管理局于1921年10月29日开具了一张以美国财政部为付款人的、凭住在南斯拉夫梅雅市(Maja)的路易斯·麦卡卡尼亚的指示付款的支票(Check),并将它寄给了在南斯拉夫的受款人。1921年11月30日前后,有人持这么一张支票向银行作付款指示。但该提示的支票是虚假的。该票据的背书经两名证人作证,还附有一张梅雅市政管理机构出具的证明,证明显示"该支票的持有者与其受益人是同一个人"。此后,该支票在南斯拉夫通过另一家南斯拉夫银行转让给了担保信托公司。在这一过程中,每一家银行均支付了对价,并在不知道有关该支票瑕疵的情况下善意地接受了该支票。1921年12月,美国财政部兑现了这张支票。1926年,美国第一次知道了这一伪造背书的情况。此后,它对担保信托公司起诉,要求返还支票项下的款项。参见王军主编:《国际私法案例教程》,中国政法大学出版社1999年版,第120页。

② United States v. Guaranty Trust Co. of New Yorl, No.117, Circuit Court of Appeals, Second Circuit, 69 F.2d 799; 1934 U.S. App. LEXIS 3670, March 12, 1934.

本案法院判决认为：支票的出票及付款均在哥伦比亚特区，根据该特区的法律，伪造受款人签名的背书是完全无效的，对该伪造支付了对价的后手善意持票人，既不能获得对票据的所有权，也无权强制执行该票据。如果他在对伪造不知情的情况下付了款，也无权追回已付的款项。但南斯拉夫的法律规定，尽管存在伪造的情况，票据的正当受让人仍然能获得"对该票据的完好的所有权"，同时，还拥有"索要和保留其收益的权利"。由于美国退伍军人管理局把这张支票寄往南斯拉夫，该伪造的背书和它的转让也发生在那里，南斯拉夫的法律支配该转让的有效性，因而这些银行至少获得了对这张支票的完好的所有权。

在美国诉纽约担保信托公司案中，原、被告之间存在物权关系：被告因受让该支票和支付价金而主张有权保有从原告处兑现的价金，原告以该支票的背书是伪造的为由而主张有权要求被告返还支票项下的价金。既然双方之间的关系是物权关系，解决双方之间争议的法律应是物之所在地法，即权利发生争议的受让人在受让财产时财产所在地的法律。在本案中，被告是在南斯拉夫受让该支票的，因而该国的法律应得到适用。

（三）票据行为适用行为地法

这一原则出自于"场所支配行为"法则。对于同一票据所包含的票据关系，应该依据票据行为，采取分割制，分别制定冲突规则，但所有这些冲突规则的连接点基本上可以统一概括为"票据行为地"。不仅票据行为的方式适用行为地法，而且因票据行为而产生的当事人的权利和义务都可适用行为地法。[①]票据的出票、背书、承兑和保证等行为的形式有效性完全取决于其是否遵守了行为地法。

（四）票据的形式有效性适用出票地法

由于票据法具有强行性，对票据的格式、必须记载的事项等票据的形式有效性应适用出票地法律。

（五）票据追索权的行使期限适用出票地法

这一原则确立的根据在于：追索权的行使最终将集中在出票地，出票地是系列追索行为的"重心"所在地，票据追索权的行使期限适用出票地法。

三、票据法律适用的特点

（一）普遍采用硬性冲突规范

票据具有流通性和无因性，可以依背书或交付方式自由转让和流通，票据关系

---

① 谢怀栻：《评新公布的我国票据法》，载《法学研究》2005 年第 6 期。

与发行、转让票据的原因关系相互分离和独立。票据的上述特征决定了这样一个基本事实:几乎所有国家的票据立法和有关票据的国际公约都立足于保护正当持票人的权利。而要实现上述目的,就必须保证票据的受让人在受让票据时,能够预见自己享有的票据权利和应承担的票据义务,否则,他就不轻易接受票据,从而导致票据流通的阻滞。硬性的冲突规则可以充分保障法律适用的确定性,正好能够满足票据流通性和安全性的需要。正基于此,在解决票据法律适用问题时,无论是大陆法系国家还是英美法系国家,都支持运用硬性的冲突规则来选择票据法律冲突所适用的法律,即使在对传统的硬性的冲突规则进行软化处理已成为国际私法发展趋势的今天也依然如此。一个直接的例证就是各国设计票据法律适用法时都排斥"最密切原则"的运用。①

(二) 排除适用意思自治

票据是严格的要式证券,票据法为保证票据的流通性和安全性,发挥票据商业作用和适应统一性的需要而具有严格的强制性特征,在一定程度上带有公法色彩。票据法的上述特征反映在票据法律适用上就是:两大票据法系国家在解决票据法律冲突时,都不适用当事人意识自治原则,而"票据行为适用行为地法"成为票据法律适用的主要原则。

(三) 普遍运用分割制

票据要求流通,同一票据在流通过程中包含着一系列各自相对独立的票据关系。根据票据行为的单方法律行为说,同一票据所体现的票据关系实质是发票、背书、承兑、付款等各种票据行为的组合;而根据票据行为的合同说,同一票据所体现的票据关系实质是数个性质不同的票据合同关系的组合。票据所承载的票据法律关系的复杂性决定了不宜由单一的准据法来解决同一票据的法律适用问题,而应对同一票据所承载的各种票据法律关系按照票据行为的种类进行分割,根据"票据行为适用行为地法"这一基本原则分别确定不同票据关系的连接点。②同时,对于同一票据行为关系还应分割成票据行为方式和效力,分别适用不同的准据法。分割制的普遍运用构成了票据法律适用的又一特点。

(四) 不同性质的票据行为适用不同的法律

票据是有形动产的一种,因票据的流通而发生的法律关系可能是动产物权关系,也可能是合同关系。而对于出票人将支票背书给银行,让银行办理托收,出票

---

① 孙南申、杜涛主编:《当代国际私法研究——21世纪的中国与国际私法》,上海人民出版社2006年版,第86页。
② 宋航、肖永平:《论涉外票据的法律适用》,载《现代法学》2003年第6期。

人再指示银行将收到的款项存入其指定的账户这样一种行为,应适用什么法律呢? 如果银行收到这张支票是背书人与被背书人之间的动产转让关系,则应适用动产转让时的所在地法;如果出票人与银行之间是托收关系,则属于委托人与付款银行之间的合同关系,应该适用支付地法。这一法律适用规则在**韦斯曼诉布鲁塞尔银行案**(Wessman v. Banque de Bruxelles)①中得到体现。

【案例】　　　　　　　　韦斯曼诉布鲁塞尔银行案

案由:原告是一家纽约州公司的破产财产的受让人,被告是一家位于比利时并在那里从事经营活动的银行。1923年5月14日,美国财政部为返还一笔不合法征收的所得税款,开具了一张凭该纽约州公司的指示付款、面值为9278.40美元的支票,并在华盛顿特区将该支票汇给了该公司。该公司的总裁小本萨德以该公司的名义将该支票背书,接着又背书道:凭布鲁塞尔银行的指示付款,里斯本,1923年6月1日,乔斯·小本萨德(Pay to the order of Banque de Bruxelles, Lisbon, June 1st, 1923, Jose Bensande, Jr.)。之后,将该支票寄给了布鲁塞尔银行,委托该银行收到该支票后办理托收,再将该支票款记入小本萨德的个人账户。布鲁塞尔银行在该支票上背书道:凭华盛顿国家大都会银行的指示付款(Pay to the order of the National Metropolitan Bank of Washington),然后将该支票转给该华盛顿的银行,让它在华盛顿通过与之有关的银行办理托收。在收到支票项下的款项之后,布鲁塞尔银行将其记入了小本萨德的个人账户,并扣留了托收手续费。此后,小本萨德将这笔钱从该银行取出,为其自己所用。在这种情况下,该公司对布鲁塞尔银行提起诉讼。

判决意见:纽约州上诉法院庞德(Pound)法官指出,由于支票是以托收方式交付给布鲁塞尔银行的,银行是背书人的代理人。银行以代理人的身份向美国财政部托收这笔钱,财政部在华盛顿特区,因此,本案应适用华盛顿特区的法律。②

在本案中,依照比利时的法律,被告在依支票收款人的总裁的指示办理托收,再依其指示把托收到的支票款存入其个人账户时,没有义务对总裁的行为是否得到了支票收款人的授权进行调查。而根据本案法院推定的与纽约州的判例一致的华盛顿特区的法律,被告有这样的调查义务,未调查即构成过失,因而须对原告承担责任。上述两种相互冲突的法律哪一种应适用于本案争议,取决于被告收到这张支票时发生了什么性质的法律关系:如果发生的是收款人(背书人)与被告(被

---

① 254 N.Y. 488, 173 N.E. 835 (1930).
② 参见王军主编:《国际私法案例教程》,中国政法大学出版社1999年版,第125—126页。

背书人)之间的动产转让关系,则比利时法律——动产转让时的所在地法应得到适用;反之,如果发生的是小本萨德与被告之间的托收关系,则华盛顿特区的法律应被适用。对于托收关系适用华盛顿特区法律的理由是:在托收关系项下,被告是托收代理人。它进一步委托华盛顿的银行在华盛顿办理托收,这相当于托收委托人亲自在华盛顿办理托收。故托收关系——委托人与付款银行之间的合同关系,发生在华盛顿。因此,该托收关系受华盛顿特区的法律支配。尽管小本萨德对该支票进行了背书,但该支票的转让并没有发生:被告只同意办理托收,不同意受让和立即兑现该支票。因此,本案发生的是托收关系。这导致了华盛顿特区法律的适用和被告的败诉。

在本案中,没有证据表明,小本萨德将支票款据为己有已得到该纽约州公司的同意。假如真的存在这种情况,则该公司不能再对被告主张票据上的权利;该公司的受让人(原告)也就不能再主张这样的权利。

四、我国国际票据的法律适用制度

1996年1月1日起施行的《票据法》对我国国际票据关系的法律适用问题作了明确的规定。① 我国《票据法》有关票据法律冲突及其法律适用的基本规则与世界上多数国家的规定具有相似性,其原因主要是票据的流通在很大程度上具有国际性。

(一)优先适用国际条约

我国《票据法》第95条规定:中华人民共和国缔结或者参加的国际条约同本法有不同规定的,适用国际条约的规定。但是,中华人民共和国声明保留的条款除外。本法和中华人民共和国缔结或者参加的国际条约没有规定的,可以适用国际惯例。

(二)票据行为能力以当事人的本国法为主,辅之以行为地法

我国《票据法》第96条规定:"票据债务人的民事行为能力,适用其本国法律。票据债务人的民事行为能力,依照其本国法律为无民事行为能力或者为限制民事行为能力而依照行为地法律为完全民事行为能力的,适用行为地法律。"上述条文采用了折中主义的立法原则,即当事人的行为能力以本国法为主,以行为地法为补充。我国《票据法》第97条的规定,既符合当前各国国际私法立法实践的普遍趋向,也与我国《民法通则》及其司法解释的规定基本保持一致。

(三)票据出票时记载的事项和追索权的行使期限适用出票地法律

我国《票据法》第97条规定:汇票、本票出票时的记载事项,适用出票地法律。

---

① 郭锋、常风主编:《中外票据法选》,北京理工大学出版社2000年版,第305页。

支票出票时的记载事项,适用出票地法律,经当事人协议,可以适用付款地法律。第100条规定:票据追索权的行使期限,适用出票地法律。

(四)票据的背书、承兑、付款和保证行为,适用行为地法律

我国《票据法》规定涉外票据的背书、承兑、付款和保证行为,适用行为地法律。

第二节 信用证的法律适用

一、信用证的概念及其法律关系

(一)信用证的概念

信用证,在英文中称为跟单信用证(**documentary credits**)或信用证(Letters of Credits,简称 L/C)或商业信用证(Commercial Credits)。从2007年7月1日起开始实施的《跟单信用证统一惯例600号》(Uniform Customs and Practice for Documentary Credits, Publication No 600, UCP600)则更为简单,直接称其为 Credits。

【释义】　　　　　　　　　documentary credits

——Documentary credit refers to a document of undertaking issued by a bank at the request of an applicant (a buyer) to pay to the beneficiary (a seller) a sum of money under specified conditions.[1]

——The engagement is a letter of credit if the issuer has a primary obligation that is dependent solely upon presentation of conforming documents and not upon the factual performance or nonperformance by the parties to the underlying transaction.[2]

——A letter of credit is an instrument whereby the issuer makes an independent commitment, at its customer's request, to honor a third-party's demand for payment, as long as the demand complies with the specified conditions the issuer expressed in the letter of credit.[3]

——Traditionally, commercial letters of credit were used to finance contracts for the sale of

---

[1] John Mo, *International Commercial Law*, 2nd ed., Butterworths, 2000, p.385.
[2] Keith A. Rowley, Inticipatory Repudiation of Letters of Credit, 56 *SMU L. Rev.* 2235, 2235 (2003), note 1.
[3] See *Black's Law Dictionary*, 7th ed., 1999.

goods over long distances between unfamiliar buyers and sellers.①

通常,信用证被视为是开证行向受益人签发的有条件付款的凭证。对于信用证的定义,有各种不同的表述。②《跟单信用证统一惯例 600 号》第 2 条也对信用证的含义(**meaning of credit**)作出了界定。

【释义】   meaning of credit

For the purposes of these Articles, the expressions "Documentary Credit (s)" and "Standby Letter(s) of Credit" (hereinafter referred to as "Credit (s)"), mean any arrangement, however named or described, whereby a bank (the "Issuing Bank") acting at the request and on the instructions of a customer (the "Applicant") or on its own behalf,

I is to make a payment to or to the order of a third party (the "Beneficiary"), or is to accept and pay bills of exchange (Draft(s)) drawn by the Beneficiary, or

II authorizes another bank to effect such payment, or to accept and pay such bills of exchange (Draft(s)), or

III authorizes another bank to negotiate, against stipulated document(s), provided that the terms and conditions of the Credit are complied with. For the purposes of these Articles, branches of a bank in different countries are considered another bank.

尽管信用证的定义存在各种不同的表述,但我们认为,从法律角度看,信用证是开证银行根据开证申请人的请求和指示,向受益人签发的规定在符合一定条件时保证付款的书面承诺文件。③

(二) 信用证开证行与受益人之间的法律关系

信用证支付方式步骤繁复④,涉及的主体众多,法律关系纷繁复杂,但是其中核心的法律关系是信用证开证行与受益人之间的法律关系。这种法律关系的具体依据是信用证。当受益人接受开证行开来的信用证时,就获得了一项开证行提供的在一定条件下保证付款的权利。只要受益人按照信用证条款交运货物、提交单

---

① Henry D. Gabriel, Standby Letters of Credit: Does The Risk Outweigh The Benefits?, 1988 *Colum. Bus. L. Rev* 705, 707 (1988).

② 参见左晓东:《信用证法律研究与实务》,警官教育出版社 1993 年版,第 1 页;杨良宜:《信用证》,中国政法大学出版社 1998 年版,第 1 页;王佩:《信用证下开证银行的审单义务》,载沈四宝主编:《国际商法论丛》(第 1 卷),法律出版社 1999 年版,第 293 页。

③ 徐冬根:《信用证法律与实务研究》,北京大学出版社 2005 年版,第 3 页。

④ For a thorough step-by-step account of the commercial credit transaction, see John F. Dolan, *Fundamentals of Commercial activity* §5.3, at 61—65 (1991).

据,则其开具的汇票将获得银行的付款、承兑或议付。受益人的这种权利是绝对的。开证行与开证申请人之间的关系是以信用证为基础的法律关系,是开证银行向受益人作出的在符合一定条件时保证付款的书面承诺。因此,信用证法律关系表现为信用证开证行与受益人之间的关系。

二、当事人可以根据意思自治原则选择信用证所适用的法律

无论将商业银行信用证①交易视为商业银行的国际单证业务,还是视作贸易公司的国际贸易支付方式,信用证法律关系均属于国际民商事法律关系。

根据国际私法中当事人意思自治原则,信用证的当事人,即信用证开证行②和信用证受益人③,有权通过各种合法的方式,对调整信用证纠纷所适用的法律作出选择。

国际商会《跟单信用证统一惯例600号》和美国统一州法全国委员会(National Conference of Commissioners on Uniform State Laws)与美国法学会(American Law Institute)1995年共同修订的美国《统一商法典》④第五篇(信用证篇)(The Uniform Commercial Code, Revised Article 5, Letter of Credit, 下称"美国《统一商法典(信用证篇)》")⑤,是目前调整信用证关系的两个主要的法律渊源。前者为国际惯例,后者为国内示范法。

《跟单信用证统一惯例600号》承认当事人的意思自治原则,认可当事人在信用证中对自己的选择。它在第1条规定:"跟单信用证统一惯例,2007年修订本,国际商会第600号出版物,适用于所有在正文中标明按本惯例办理的跟单信用证(包括本惯例适用范围内的备用信用证)。除非信用证中另有规定,本惯例对一切有关

---

① For cases providing general definitions of a commercial letter of credit see, e. g., East Girard Sav. Ass'n v. Citizens Nat'l Bank & Trust Co., 593 F.2d 598, 601—602 (5th Cir. 1979); Venizelos, S. A. v. Chase Manhattan Bank, 425 F.2d 461, 464—465 (2d. Cir. 1970); Voest-Alpine Int'l Corp. v. Chase Manhattan Bank, N. A., 545 F. Supp. 301, 303—304 (S. D. N. Y. 1982); Consolidated Aluminum Corp. v. Bank of Va., 544 F. Supp 386, 393—395 (D. Md. 1982).

② "Issuer" is defined as "a bank or other person that issues a letter of credit." U. C. C. §5-102(a)(9) (1995). In other words, provided the beneficiary-seller complies with the terms of the letter of credit, the issuer is the party committed to honoring the beneficiary-seller's demands for payment under the letter of credit.

③ "Beneficiary" is defined as "a[ny] person who under the terms of a letter of credit is entitled to have its complying presentation honored." U. C. C. §5-102(a)(3) (1995).

④ 美国《统一商法典》不是由专门的立法机关组织编纂的,它只是一个"标准法典"或"标本法典",是向各州的立法机关推荐的一个建议性法律文件;它对各州的商法典并没有支配和统领关系,非经各州批准,不对该州产生法律效力。但是,美国《统一商法典》又是一部受到人们广泛推崇的法典,在美国法律制度中具有特殊的法律地位。

⑤ The current version of Article 5 of the U. C. C. was adopted in August, 1995 after four years of revisions.

当事人均具有约束力。"这其中明确规定"适用于所有在信用证文本中标明按本惯例办理的跟单信用证"。就《跟单信用证统一惯例600号》作为国际惯例本身来说,它树立了"当事人选择"的法律选择规则,①也就是说,在当事人在信用证文本中标明适用该惯例的情况下,该惯例对有关当事人具有法律约束力。

美国《统一商法典(信用证篇)》也承认当事人的意思自治原则,确认当事人有权通过明示选择的方式确定信用证所适用的法律。②美国《统一商法典(信用证篇)》有关法律选择的条文是第5-116条。根据美国《统一商法典(信用证篇)》第5-116(a)条的规定,信用证当事人有权自由选择解决信用证争议所适用的法律。根据美国《统一商法典(信用证篇)》的规定,当事人可以就信用证法律适用的选择问题专门订立特别协议,也可以在信用证、保兑书或其他承诺性法律文件中专门设置一个法律选择条款。

(一) 当事人选择《跟单信用证统一惯例600号》作为信用证准据法的法律效力

在信用证支付实务中,对于信用证开证行与受益人之间的法律适用,当事人在大多数情况下均选择《跟单信用证统一惯例600号》。当信用证的当事人选择适用《跟单信用证统一惯例600号》时,它的法律效力如何?这需要从几个方面来考虑:第一,《跟单信用证统一惯例600号》本身如何对待当事人的意思自治?第二,各国国内立法如何对待当事人选择《跟单信用证统一惯例600号》?对于《跟单信用证统一惯例600号》本身如何对待当事人的意思自治这个问题,该惯例第1条的规定,本身已经作出了正面的回答。第二个问题,各国国内立法对当事人选择《跟单信用证统一惯例600号》的态度如何,目前,各国有关国际私法的立法均支持当事人意思自治原则。美国是世界上唯一少数制定有信用证法以及信用证法律适用条款的国家。美国《统一商法典(信用证篇)》明确规定允许当事人选择《跟单信用证统一惯例600号》。如果信用证当事人明示选择适用该惯例,该惯例就成为信用证当事人的准据法。③美国《统一商法典(信用证篇)》不但认可当事人的这种法律适用的选择权,而且还确认了《跟单信用证统一惯例600号》等国际惯例具有优先于美国国内法适用的效力。美国《统一商法典(信用证篇)》第5-116条第3款明确规定,信用证、保兑书或其他承诺性法律文件中如果明确选择了适用《跟单信用证统一惯例600号》,而该信用证、保兑书或其他承诺性法律文件依据冲突规范的指引又适用美国《统一商法典(信用证篇)》关于信用证的规定,且《跟单信用证统一惯

---

① 参见徐冬根:《信用证法律与实务研究》,北京大学出版社2005年版,第42页。
② 参见刘琼瑶:《试析美国〈统一商法典〉中信用证的法律适用》,载《长沙大学学报》2003年第1期。
③ See U.C.P. 600 art. 1 (2007).

例 600 号》的条文与美国《统一商法典(信用证篇)》条文的规定发生冲突,除了不得违背美国法律的强制性规范外①,优先适用《跟单信用证统一惯例 600 号》。

(二) 当事人选择内国实体法作为信用证准据法的法律效力

当然,根据意思自治原则,当事人也可以选择适用除《跟单信用证统一惯例 600 号》之外的其他内国法律作为信用证法律关系的准据法。美国《统一商法典(信用证篇)》允许当事人作出这样的选择,但是当事人所选择的适用于信用证法律关系的法律,不得违背所选法律所属国家的强制性规范和公共秩序。美国《统一商法典(信用证篇)》第 5-116 条规定,当事方虽然选择某一内国法律作为信用证的准据法,但如果当事人所选择的法律违背了当地的公共政策或直接与联邦法相冲突,该选择将无效。②

三、法院对信用证所适用法律的认定

根据国际私法的一般原则,如果信用证交易当事人没有对信用证纠纷所适用的法律作出选择,或者虽然当事人选择了《跟单信用证统一惯例 600 号》作为信用证的准据法,但是信用证纠纷的争议问题超出了《跟单信用证统一惯例 600 号》能够规范的范围,则法院应适用与信用证法律关系有最密切联系地或最大利益地国家的法律为其准据法。

但是究竟什么是最密切联系和最大利益?实践中存在着两种不同的观点和做法,这两种观点和做法最大的分歧就是对信用证履行地(Place of performance)的界定。

(一) 以付款地为履行地

一种意见认为,信用证的履行地为应为议付行或者付款银行的所在地暨信用证的议付地或者付款地(place of payment as place of performance)。英美法系的学者普遍主张适用议付行向受益人付款地的法律,即主张信用证的履行地就是信用证的议付地或者结算地,因此信用证支付纠纷应适用信用证议付地或者结算地的

---

① 这些强制性规范是指美国《统一商法典》第 1-102(3)条中的"禁止合同当事人排除诚实信用(good faith)、尽职(diligence)、合理(reasonableness)和谨慎(care)等法律义务"。See U.C.C. §1-102(3)(1995).

② 纽约州法律修改委员会建议该州采纳新修订的美国《统一商法典》第五章时曾指出:法院将不会强制执行当事人所选择的与公共政策相违背的法律。See Franck Chantayan: Choice of Law Under Revised Article 5 of The Uniform Commercial Code 5-116, 14 *St. John's J. L. Comm.* 199 (1999).

法律。①这种观点认为,信用证是一种独立的合同,其独立性表现在它为受益人和银行之间创设了一种单据买卖关系。这种单据买卖交易的经济价值和功能在于实现向受益人付款。②卖方在交付货物后获得价款的保证,这是信用证制度的核心。因此,调整信用证纠纷的准据法,就是受益人将信用证规定的单据提交给议付行或者通知行并要求议付行或者通知行承兑或付款的地方的法律。

早期,英美法院的司法实践也主要持这种观点。1975 年美国法院所处理的 **J. Zeevi & Sons, Ltd. v. Grindlays Bank（Uganda）Ltd**. 案中③,美国法院认为信用证的履行地是信用证的议付地或者议付行的付款地。这些法院主张,外国的信用证开证行不能援引开证行所在地国家（开证行本国）的法律来免除其信用证项下的付款义务。

【案例】　　J. Zeevi & Sons, Ltd. v. Grindlays Bank（Uganda）Ltd.④

In J. Zeevi & Sons, Ltd. v. Grindlays Bank (Uganda) Ltd., J. Zeevi & Sons, Ltd., an Israeli corporation, received from Grindlays Bank (Uganda) Ltd., an irrevocable letter of credit in the amount of $406846.80. Grindlays allowed negotiating banks in the United States to claim reimbursements via debit of Grindlays' account at First National City Bank (Citibank) in New York City. Following the issuance of the letter of credit, the Ugandan government ordered Uganda's banks not to make foreign exchange payments in favor of Israeli companies or nationals. When Citibank refused to reimburse Chemical Bank, who had negotiated J. Zeevi & Sons' drafts, J. Zeevi & Sons sued Grindlays in New York state court.

Grindlays, claiming that Ugandan law applied, moved to have the court dismiss J. Zeevi & Sons' complaint. The court stated that "the law of the jurisdiction having the greatest interest in the litigation will be applied[.]" The court held the applicable law to be that of New York law because of New York's overwhelming interest in protecting its status as a financial capital, and because the parties agreed to have the funds paid out in U.S. dollars. As a result, the court refused to relieve Grindlays of its $406846.80 obligation to J. Zeevi & Sons.

在本案中,以色列 J. Zeevi & Sons 公司（下称"以色列公司"）因与乌干达公司

---

①　See Franck Chantayan: Choice of Law Under Revised Article 5 of The Uniform Commercial Code 5-116, 14 *St. John's J. L. Comm.* 199, 199 (1999). See also George P. Graham, International Commercial Letters of Credit and Choice of Law: So Whose Law Should Apply Anyway? 47 *Wayne L. Rev.* 201, 201 (2001). 前者主张纽约州统一商法典立法不要采纳美国《统一商法典》之第 5-116 的条款;后者强烈反对《统一商法典（信用证篇）》之第 5-116(b)对信用证法律适用作出相反规定。
②　参见黄亚英、李薇薇:《论国际信用证交易中准据法的确定》,载《中国法学》2002 年第 3 期。
③　333 N. E. 2d 168 (N. Y. 1975).
④　Ibid.

交易而收到乌干达的 Grindlays Bank (Uganda) Ltd.(下称"乌干达银行")一张金额为 406846.80 美元的不可撤销的信用证。乌干达银行指定以它在纽约的第一花旗银行(First National City Bank)账户内的款项来偿还议付行议付信用证的款项。在乌干达银行开出了信用证之后,乌干达政府命令乌干达银行不得向以色列公司或国民支付外汇。

此前,美国纽约化学银行(Chemical New York Corp.)已经根据以色列公司所提交的信用证和全套单证,向以色列公司议付了乌干达银行信用证项下的全部货款。第一花旗银行接到乌干达银行所传递的乌干达政府命令后,拒绝向议付行纽约化学银行偿付信用证项下的已议付款项。

为此,以色列公司在美国纽约州法院起诉乌干达银行,要求支付信用证项下货款。乌干达银行主张本案应当适用乌干达法律,请求法院驳回以色列公司的诉讼请求。纽约州法院认为:信用证诉讼应"适用与信用证有最大利益(the greatest interest)的法律"。本案中,纽约作为国际金融中心,在保护其全球金融中心地位方面具有绝对的重大利益,而且当事人同意用美元作为支付货币。上述各种因素均表明本案与美国以及纽约有最大利益,因此本案应适用信用证的付款地(纽约州)的法律。①最后,纽约法院拒绝适用信用证开证行所在地(乌干达)的法律,而是适用了信用证付款地(纽约州)的法律,拒绝被告乌干达银行提出的根据乌干达政府的命令免除乌干达银行对以色列公司支付信用证项下 $406846.80 的付款义务的要求。

在英国上诉法院 1981 年所处理的 **Power Curber Int'l Ltd. v. Nat'l Bank of Kuwait S. A. K.** 一案中,英国法院以及著名的大法官丹宁勋爵(Lord Denning)就持这种观点,认为信用证应以付款地为履行地。

【案例】 Power Curber Int'l Ltd. v. Nat'l Bank of Kuwait S. A. K. ②

In Power Curber International Ltd. v. National Bank of Kuwait S.A.K., a North Carolina beneficiary sued a Kuwait issuer in England. While Power Curber represents the English position on the place of performance debate, it likewise represents the position taken by the court in J. Zeevi & Sons, Ltd. v. Grindlays Bank (Uganda) Ltd. and the dissent in Chuidian v. Philippine National Bank.

In Power Curber, Power Curber, a North Carolina company, agreed to sell machinery to Hammoudeh & Al Fulaij General Trading & Contracting Co. WLL. (Hammoudeh), a Kuwait company. A portion of the payment, which was to be made a year after shipping, was assured

---

① See 333 N. E. 2d 173 (N. Y. 1975).
② 1 W. L. R. 1233 (C. A. 1981).

by a $75794.46 irrevocable letter of credit issued by Hammoudeh's bank, the National Bank of Kuwait. The bank provided that it would reimburse negotiating banks from its account held with Bank of America in New York. After Power Curber had shipped the goods off to Hammoudeh, Hammoudeh received a Kuwaiti court order prohibiting the National Bank of Kuwait from honoring the letter of credit. After Power Curber failed to receive payment from the National Bank of Kuwait, it filed suit against the bank in England.

In separately announced judgments, the English Court of Appeals unanimously held that the National Bank of Kuwait was required to honor the Power Curber letter of credit. Both Lord Denning and Lord Justice Griffiths expressly rejected the bank's argument that the proper law to apply was that of the issuer's jurisdiction, Kuwait, and not that of the beneficiary's, North Carolina. Lord Denning held that unlike ordinary debts, which a debtor may pay where he resides, a debt incurred under a letter of credit must be paid in "the place where it is in fact payable against documents." Therefore, the National Bank of Kuwait was not relieved of its $75794.46 obligation to Power Curber.

在本案中,一家美国北卡罗来纳州公司 Power Curber Int'l Ltd. (下称"美国公司")同意卖机器给一家科威特公司 Hammoudeh & Al Fulaij General Trading & Contracting Co. WLL. (下称"科威特公司")。买卖合同的部分价款要在机器装船后一年才能支付,并以科威特公司的开户行科威特国家银行签发的、金额为 75794.46 美元的不可撤销信用证为支付方式。科威特国家银行指定以它在纽约的美洲银行(Bank of America)账户内的款项来偿还议付行议付信用证的款项。在美国公司将货物装船运往科威特公司后,科威特公司收到科威特法院的禁令,禁止科威特国家银行兑付信用证。

美国公司未能收到科威特国家银行信用证项下的货款,为此它在英国法院对科威特国家银行提起诉讼。被告科威特国家银行抗辩说,信用证签发地是信用证的履行地,本案应适用信用证的签发地国家的法律,即科威特法律。大法官丹宁勋爵和大法官格里菲斯勋爵不同意被告科威特国家银行的抗辩。丹宁勋爵指出:对于普通债务,债务人可以在他居住的地方支付;但是,在信用证下的支付,必须在"它事实上可以交单付款的地方支付"。①受理本案的英国上诉法院全体法官一致认为,科威特国家银行应当承兑美国公司的信用证。因此,科威特国家银行不应被免除对美国公司支付 75794.46 美元货款的付款义务。

本案的争议焦点之一就是受益人与开证行之间信用证关系的法律适用。如果适用科威特法律,则科威特银行可依科威特法院禁令抗辩并拒绝付款;如果适用北

---

① A letter of credit must be paid in "the place where it is in fact payable against documents." See 1 *W. L. R.* 1240 (C. A. 1981) (Lord Denning).

卡罗来纳州法律,则按科威特法律作出的法院禁令将对本案不适用。英国上诉法院判决该信用证应适用信用证的履行地法,即美国北卡罗来纳州的法律。丹宁勋爵就此指出:信用证的履行地就是银行(包括代理或代表开证行)根据信用证收益人提交的信用证单据进行承兑或付款的地点。雷蒙德·杰克在评析该案时指出:该判决表明,当一份信用证规定,一旦向某一指定银行递交了相符的单据,该银行便应付款时,则该信用证的准据法就应是该付款银行所在地的法律。①

(二)以信用证签发地为履行地

另一种意见认为,信用证的履行地为应为开证行所在地暨信用证的签发地(place of issuance as place of performance),因此信用证应适用信用证开证行的所在地或信用证签发地国家的法律。②主张适用开证行所在地国家的法律的主要理由在于:首先,开证行所在地国家的法律与信用证的成立和履行具有不可替代的重要关系,开证行所在地是申请人与开证行之间代理开证的要约和承诺的完成地,也是信用证关系的产生和最终了结的地方。无论开证行以外的通知行、议付行或保兑行是否向受益人付款,信用证项下的付款义务均源自开证行的开证行为,并因开证行最终承担和履行而终结。其次,信用证一旦开出,开证行所在地这一连接点便是明确和稳定的。因此,适用开证行所在地法律这一冲突规范的优点在于它可以适用于各种不同的信用证交易,而无论其中涉及哪些银行,也无论这些银行位于何处以及是否向受益人实际支付了款项。③反之,如果适用付款地法,由于信用证项下受益人实际取得付款的地点有时无法预先确定,有时仅仅是为了方便向受益人付款才设定的,有时信用证受益人可以向不特定的任何银行议付,或者发生议付之后的整套信用证单证的背书转让等情况,也就是说付款地是不确定的,因此将付款地视为信用证的履行地是不合适的。这方面的代表案例有美国纽约地区上诉法院1981年所处理的 <u>RSB Manufacturing Corp. v. Bank of Baroda</u> 案。

【案例】　　　RSB Manufacturing Corp. v. Bank of Baroda④

In RSB Manufacturing Corp. v. Bank of Baroda, RSB, an American machinery supplier, contracted to sell goods to an Indian business, Elegant Industries Pvt. Ltd. of Bombay. To assure payment of the $54900.00 contract price, RSB insisted Elegant apply for a commercial letter of credit. Elegant subsequently applied for and received an irrevocable letter of credit

---

① Raymond Jack, *Documentary Credits*, 299 (1993).
② 参见刘琼瑶:《试论国际信用证的法律适用》,载《湖南省社会主义学院学报》2004年第1期。
③ 参见黄亚英、李薇薇:《论国际信用证交易中准据法的确定》,载《中国法学》2002年第3期。
④ 9 B. R. 414 (Bankr. S. D. N. Y. 1981), aff'd, 15 B. R. 650 (Bankr. S. D. N. Y. 1981).

from the Bank of Baroda's Bombay branch (Baroda Bombay). Baroda Bombay nominated Chemical Bank in New York as an advising and paying bank.

Subsequent to receiving the RSB letter of credit, Elegant sought and received from Baroda Bombay a second irrevocable commercial letter of credit, this time for the benefit of another American business, P. Romanoff International Ltd., in the amount of $8853.50. For the Romanoff letter of credit, Baroda Bombay nominated its New York branch (Baroda N.Y.) to serve as advising and paying bank.

Subsequent to Baroda Bombay's issuance of the two letters of credit, Elegant, alleging fraud in the underlying sales contracts, obtained from the High Court of Judicature in Bombay a temporary injunction restraining Baroda Bombay from "encashing and/or paying the two letters of credit of U.S. $63500 and U.S. $8853.50 in any manner whatsoever." Without knowledge of the injunction, both beneficiaries (RSB and Romanoff) shipped the contract goods off to Elegant. Following the shipment of the goods, the New York banks (Chemical and Baroda N.Y.), having been advised of the Indian court's injunction, refused to honor drafts submitted by the beneficiaries as required under the terms of the letters of credit. RSB subsequently filed suit against Chemical, Baroda, and Elegant.

Following RSB's filing of its lawsuit, Baroda N.Y., relying on a provision of the New York Banking Law, moved for dismissal of RSB's "complaint for failure to state a claim upon which relief could be granted." The bankruptcy court stated that "the controversy in this proceeding turns on the question of where an irrevocable letter of credit... established in a foreign bank and advised by New York banks is actually 'performed.'" The court held that because only Baroda Bombay assumed the obligations to pay, performance of the letter of credit contracts "take place at the Bombay branch [of Baroda] and not in New York."

On appeal to the district court, RSB argued that because Baroda Bombay had agreed to pay on the letters of credit in New York, the place of performance of the letters of credit was New York, not India. The district court stated that "the fact that Baroda [Bombay] can be sued in New York for breach of contract does not change the parties' substantive agreement regarding the place of performance." The district court held that because the place of performance was Bombay, the Indian court's injunction excused Baroda Bombay's performance of the letters of credit. As a result, Baroda Bombay was relieved of its $72353.50 obligation to RSB.

在本案中,一家美国机械供应商 RSB Manufacturing Corp.(以下简称"美国公司")将货物卖给一家印度工业公司 Elegant Industries Pvt. Ltd. of Bombay(以下简称"印度公司"),双方签订了合同。为了确保收取合同价款,美国公司要求印度公司以商业信用证方式支付。为此,印度巴鲁达银行 Bank of Baroda(以下简称"印度巴鲁达银行")孟买分行应印度公司的要求,开出一张不可撤销信用证,并指定美国纽约化学银行作为通知行和付款行。在印度巴鲁达银行孟买分行开出了信用证后,印度公司提出在信用证的基础合同即双方的货物买卖合同中存在欺诈,为此印度公司从印度孟买高级法院获得了《临时止付令》(temporary injunction),禁止印度

巴鲁达银行孟买分行以任何形式对价款为 63500 美元的信用证付款。而信用证的受益人对禁令并不知情,将当事人之间的货物买卖合同项下的货物装船运送给印度公司。在将货物装船之后,美国纽约化学银行和印度巴鲁达银行纽约分行获悉印度法院的禁令,拒绝受益人根据信用证提交的付款请求。

美国公司在纽约南区破产法院(bankruptcy court)对美国纽约化学银行、印度巴鲁达银行纽约分行、印度公司提起诉讼。美国纽约南区破产法院提出:"本案的争议焦点在于由外国银行签发并由纽约银行通知的不可撤销的信用证,其履行地在哪里。"该法院认为,由于最终承担信用证付款义务的是印度巴鲁达银行孟买分行,因此信用证的履行地"在印度孟买,而不是在纽约"。①美国公司提出上诉。

在纽约地区上诉法院,美国公司提出,由于印度巴鲁达银行孟买分行同意在纽约支付信用证,信用证的履行地点应该是纽约,而不是印度。纽约地区法院则认为:"印度巴鲁达银行孟买分行由于违反信用证约定而在纽约被诉的事实,不能改变信用证当事人对信用证履行地点的实质性选择。"为此,纽约地区法院作出判决:鉴于本案信用证的履行地在孟买,本信用证纠纷案应适用印度的法律;根据印度法院的禁令,应免去印度巴鲁达银行孟买分行基于信用证约定所应该承担的付款义务。为此,印度巴鲁达银行孟买分行被免去了对美国公司的付款义务。

本案中,因发生信用证欺诈,信用证开证行所在地国家法院发出信用证项下款项的止付令,导致信用证开证行不能对外支付。由于处理本案的美国法官认为:信用证履行地就是信用证签发地,本案适用信用证履行地国家的法律,也就是印度法律,美国法院应尊重和承认印度法院的止付令。②最终美国法院认定,信用证的开证行可以因止付令而免于承担对外支付的法律责任。

类似的典型还有美国法院在 1990 年所处理的 **Chuidian v. Philippine Nat'l Bank** 案。③

【案例】　　　　　　　Chuidian v. Philippine Nat'l Bank④

In Chuidian v. Philippine National Bank, as part of the settlement of a lawsuit between Philguarantee, a government agency of the Philippines, and Vincent Chuidian, a Philippine citi-

---

① The bankruptcy court had already correctly held that Chemical and Baroda N. Y., who had both expressly limited their roles to that of advisers and payers, could not be held liable on the letters of credit. See Baroda, 9 B. R. 416 (Bankr. S. D. N. Y. 1981).

② George P. Graham, International Commercial Letters of Credit and Choice of Law: So Whose Law Should Apply Anyway? 47 *Wayne L. Rev.* 201, n157 (2001).

③ 734 F. Supp. 415 (C.D. Cal. 1990), aff'd, 976 F.2d 561 (9th Cir. 1992).

④ 734 F. Supp. 415 (C.D. Cal. 1990).

zen residing in the United States, Philguarantee secured, for the benefit of Chuidian, a $5.3 million dollar irrevocable letter of credit from the Philippine National Bank in Manila (P.N.B. Manila). P.N.B.'s Los Angeles branch (P.N.B. LA.) was nominated as an adviser of the letter of credit, and was authorized to make periodic payments pursuant to the letter of credit.

After Chuidian had received two payments from the counters of P.N.B. LA., the Philippine government issued an order freezing payment on the letter of credit. P.N.B. LA., pursuant to the Philippine government's order, refused to honor Chuidian's demands for further payment under the letter of credit. Chuidian subsequently sued P.N.B.

The district court, relying in part on RSB Manufacturing Corp. v. Bank of Baroda, held that the place of performance on the letter of credit was the Philippines, not Los Angeles. Therefore, since P.N.B. Manila's performance was excused in the Philippines, it was excused in the United States as well.

On appeal, the Ninth Circuit Court of Appeals affirmed the district court. The court held that because P.N.B. LA. was not a confirming bank, the district court had correctly concluded that the place of performance was the Philippines. As a result, PNB was relieved of the balance of its $5.3 million obligation to Chuidian.

在本案中,居住在美国的菲律宾公民 Vincent Chuidian(下称"Chuidian 先生")因交易收到在马尼拉的菲律宾国家银行(Philippine National Bank)开出的金额为 530 万美元的不可撤销信用证。菲律宾国家银行指定其洛杉矶分行为信用证通知行,并授权其根据信用证规定向信用证受益人付款。在 Chuidian 先生从菲律宾国家银行洛杉矶分行柜台收到两次付款之后,菲律宾政府签发了一项冻结该信用证付款的指令。菲律宾国家银行洛杉矶分行依照菲律宾政府的指令,拒绝 Chuidian 先生根据信用证约定付款的后续要求。为此,Chuidian 先生在美国对菲律宾国家银行提起诉讼。

借鉴 RSB Manufacturing Corp. v. Bank of Baroda 案美国法官的观点,美国洛杉矶地区法院主张信用证履行地是信用证的开证地即菲律宾,而不是美国洛杉矶。法院认为,在菲律宾政府签发了冻结该信用证付款的止付禁令后,菲律宾国家银行对外支付信用证项下货款的义务,在菲律宾是被免除的,在美国同样也应该被免除。原告为此提起上诉。

美国第九巡回上诉法院(Ninth Circuit Court of Appeals)维持地区法院的判决。法院认为,地区法院判决履行地在菲律宾是正确的,菲律宾国家银行洛杉矶分行不是信用证的保兑银行。为此,基于美国法院的判决,菲律宾国家银行对 Chuidian 先生的 530 万美元余额的付款义务获得免除。

四、信用证法律适用的新趋势

从上面的案例分析可以看出,早期美国和英国法院判例中将信用证履行地界定为信用证的付款地并适用付款地国家的法律,后期将信用证履行地界定为信用证的签发地,并适用开证行所在地国家的法律。美国法院对信用证法律适用观点的转变,与美国的信用证法典化所采取的立场不谋而合。

根据美国《统一商法典(信用证篇)》第5-116(b)条的规定,如果信用证交易的当事人未选择解决信用证争议所适用的法律,美国法院应适用信用证开证行所在地国家的法律。上述有关信用证的法律适用规则,虽然不是真正意义上的立法条款,但是由于美国《统一商法典》的权威性和统领性,目前美国绝大多数州都已经接受《统一商法典(信用证篇)》的法律适用条款,并将其规定拷贝到各自的州立法中。以美国纽约州为例,由于全世界大多数国际商业银行的信用证都会通过纽约的银行完成支付手续[1],所以美国纽约州的有关信用证法律适用的立法,牵涉到全世界众多国际商业银行的切身利益。尽管一些学者反对美国《统一商法典(信用证篇)》第5-116条的规定,但是纽约州州法修改委员会(New York State Law Revision Commission)认为需要接受《统一商法典(信用证篇)》第5-116条的规定。该委员会认为,如果让纽约州的《统一商法典》与美国《统一商法典》的规定不一致,会对在纽约从事商业活动的个人或者公司带来负面影响。[2]

由于《跟单信用证统一惯例600号》是一个国际惯例,本身没有法律选择条文。这意味着信用证交易中只要一方为美国当事人的,则信用证法律关系除了适用《跟单信用证统一惯例600号》之外,同时还应适用美国《统一商法典(信用证篇)》第5-116(b)条的条文。

由此可见,信用证法律适用的新趋势,是在信用证当事人未对信用证所适用的法律作出选择时,或者虽然当事人选择了《跟单信用证统一惯例600号》作为信用证的准据法但是信用证纠纷的争议问题超出了《跟单信用证统一惯例600号》能够规范的范围时,美国法院必须将信用证的履行地界定为信用证开证行所在地暨信用证的签发地,并适用信用证开证行所在地国家的法律(law of the issuer's jurisdiction)。

美国有些学者不赞同美国《统一商法典(信用证篇)》第5-116(b)条的规定,认

---

[1] See N. Y. U. C. C. 5-102 (McKinney 1991) (stating that most international letter of credit business is handled by New York banks); 29 N. Y. Jur. Cred. Cards 43 (1997) (stating that bulk of international letters of credit in United States are handled by New York banks); Joseph H. Sommer, A Law of Financial Accounts: Modern Payment and Securities Transfer Law, 53 *Bus. Law.* 1181, 1189 (1998) (recognizing that "[a] vast amount of international letter of credit business is customarily handled by certain New York banks); see also Peter Linzer, Non-American Law and the Core Curriculum, 72 *Tul. L. Rev.* 2031, 2040 (1998) (stating that New York is 'the most significant jurisdiction for letter of credit'").

[2] See The New York State Law Revision Commission, *Report on the Proposed Revised Article 5—Letters of Credit—of the Uniform Commercial Code*, 6.

第十三章　国际支付关系的法律适用

为美国《统一商法典(信用证篇)》第5-116条是否适用于国际信用证交易,至少是不清楚的。①其理由是美国《统一商法典(信用证篇)》起草人对第5-116条对国内信用证交易的影响问题进行了分析,但是没有对第5-116条对国际信用证交易的影响问题进行分析。②

我们不同意这样的看法。首先,美国统一州法全国委员会与美国法学会已经对美国《统一商法典(信用证篇)》第5-116(b)条有关信用证法律适用的规则作出规定,这是具有重要导向意义的法典化工作,对法院判案有相当大的影响力。其次,对美国《统一商法典(信用证篇)》第5-116(b)条持反对意见的美国学者,只是看到了问题的表面,即上述规定不利于出口方(信用证受益人)为美国企业的信用证交易。事实上,我们必须透过信用证立法的表面现象,看到问题的本质,即美国不仅仅是一个国际货物买卖的出口大国,也是国际货物买卖的进口大国。因此,理顺信用证交易法律关系,回归信用证交易的履行特征,将信用证的履行地界定为信用证签发地,并没有损害美国的利益。将信用证的履行地界定为信用证签发地,虽然不利于美国的出口企业(信用证的收益人),但是却有利于美国的进口企业(信用证的开证申请人)。因此,总体而言,美国《统一商法典(信用证篇)》第5-116(b)条对信用证法律适用的规则所作出的取舍,其功过不能站在某一侧面的角度来评判,而是应该站在一个全面的综合的视角来审视。

五、我国在适用跟单信用证统一惯例方面的司法实践

在我国的司法实践中,尽管跟单信用证统一惯例作为惯例并不具备法律强制力,但是如果在信用证的申请书里或信用证本身都明确提到该信用证受到跟单信用证统一惯例的约束,法院应尊重当事人在信用证中的约定。

第一,依据当事人在信用证中的约定而适用跟单信用证统一惯例。在瑞士纽科货物有限责任公司诉中国建设银行吉林省珲春市支行一案中③,最高人民法院认为:本案系受益人与开证行之间的信用证项下货款拒付纠纷。双方当事人同意本案的信用证适用《跟单信用证统一惯例500号》,该约定有效,故本案应以该惯例为依据调整当事人的权利义务关系。

北京市高级人民法院在"意大利信贷银行诉哈尔滨经济技术开发区对外经济贸易公司信用证结算纠纷"一案中专门就信用证法律适用和《跟单信用证统一惯

---

① George P. Graham, International Commercial Letters of Credit and Choice of Law: So Whose Law Should Apply Anyway? 47 *Wayne L. Rev.* 201, 212 (2001).
② See U.C.C. §5-116 comment. (1995).
③ (1998)经终字第336号民事判决书,载《最高人民法院公报》1999年第2期。

例 500 号》适用作出判决:"本院认为,信贷银行开出的信用证明确约定适用《跟单信用证统一惯例 500 号》,故对本案的处理应适用该国际惯例。"①

2001 年福建省高级人民法院在"中国北方工业厦门公司诉福建新业银行厦门分行委托开证协议纠纷"一案的判决中②,明确指出:信用证已经约定适用《跟单信用证统一惯例 500 号》,法院认为开证银行厦门新业银行和通知行、保兑行、交单人之间的关系受《跟单信用证统一惯例 500 号》的约束。

在"江都造船厂(以下简称"造船厂")诉中国银行香港分行(以下简称"香港中行")信用证纠纷"一案中③,江苏省高级人民法院 2001 年 4 月 19 日裁定:本院经审查认为:1997 年 5 月 23 日,香港中行开立了以造船厂为受益人的不可撤销跟单信用证,香港中行为该信用证的开证行,造船厂为信用证的受益人,香港中行与造船厂之间形成了信用证法律关系;该信用证约定适用《跟单信用证统一惯例 500 号》。因此,《跟单信用证统一惯例 500 号》是处理本案纠纷的依据。

以上案例表明,一旦当事人选择了跟单信用证统一惯例作为信用证交易的准据法,那么跟单信用证统一惯例的有关规则理所当然地就成为信用证的组成部分,对有关当事人具有约束力,权衡各方当事人是否合理履行义务及能否获得价款也将依据信用证条款而定。

第二,跟单信用证统一惯例作为国际惯例在信用证纠纷案件中得到直接适用。当事人虽然未在信用证申请书或信用证中明确约定适用统一惯例,根据国内法的有关规定,跟单信用证统一惯例作为国际惯例在信用证纠纷案件中也可以得到直接适用。不过,当事人是否选择信用证这一结算方式,对法院在处理信用证案件中是否采用《跟单信用证统一惯例 500 号》来确定各方的权利义务还是具有决定性的影响。如**中国银行新疆分行诉新兴公司信用证交易纠纷案**。

【案例】 中国银行新疆分行诉新兴公司信用证交易纠纷案

案由:1997 年 7 月,原告中国银行新疆维吾尔自治区分行(以下简称"新疆分行")因与被告新疆新兴水利电力实业总公司(以下简称"新兴公司")发生信用证交易纠纷,向新疆维吾尔自治区高级人民法院提起诉讼。本案中,被告新兴公司与乌克兰尼里亚公司签订了一份洋葱种子的进出口合同。随后,原告新疆分行于同年 10 月 17 日收到一份由乌克兰斯拉夫商业银行开出并经德国法兰克福银行加保的不可撤销的信用证。申

---

① 北京市高级人民法院(2000)高经终字第 376 号民事判决书。
② 福建省高级人民法院二审(2000)闽经终字第 058 号民事判决书。
③ 江苏省高级人民法院(2001)苏经初字第 003 号民事裁定书。

请人是乌克兰尼里亚公司,受益人是新兴公司。然而,在该信用证中,当事人并未约定适用《跟单信用证统一惯例500号》。

判决意见:新疆维吾尔自治区高级人民法院认为:本案是因国际贸易中使用信用证结算引起的纠纷。依照《中华人民共和国民法通则》第142条的规定,并根据当事人在信用证中的约定,对本案各当事人在信用证结算中应当承担的责任,可以适用《跟单信用证统一惯例500号》的规定确定。①

根据《中华人民共和国民法通则》的有关规定,国际民商事关系的法律适用应依照我国法律的有关规定,我国法律及我国参加的国际条约没有规定的,可以适用国际惯例。跟单信用证统一惯例规定了在信用证关系中各有关当事人的权利和义务,是信用证业务的统一惯例,故因信用证引起的纠纷及责任认定,除非当事人有相反的约定,否则应当适用该国际惯例。

第三节　国际托收的法律适用

国际托收是国际支付的两大支付方式之一(**one of two types of international payment**),体现为由收款方主动提起的收款请求。

【释义】　　　　**one of two types of international payment**

The first type, called a credit transfer in the terminology of the Uncitral model law. This is the transaction whereby funds are transferred at the initiative of one party (the "Originator") to continue to use the model law's terminology to another party (the "Beneficiary") through one or more banks or other financial intermediaries.

The second type of international payment is a debit transfer, where the payment is made in accordance with an order given by the beneficiary of the payment to the holder of the

---

① 新疆维吾尔自治区高级人民法院1997年7月28日判决,载《最高人民法院公报》1998年第1期。

payor's funds in accordance with a prior authorization by the payor.①

一、国际托收及相关国际惯例

国际托收作为国际支付的一种方式,长期以来已为许多国家所认可与接受。由于各国对托收的规则不尽相同,不可避免地会导致托收的法律冲突。

所谓托收(**collection**),是指卖方以买方为付款人开立汇票,委托银行代向买方收取货款的一种结算方式。国际托收即含有涉外因素的托收。

【释义】　　　　　　　　　　collection

For the purposes of these Articles:

A) "Collection" means the handling by banks of documents as defined in sub-Article 2 (b), in accordance with instructions received, in order to:

1) obtain payment and/or acceptance, or

2) deliver documents against payment and/or against acceptance, or

3) deliver documents on other terms and conditions.

B) "Documents" means financial documents and/or commercial documents:

1) "Financial documents" means bills of exchange, promissory notes, cheques, or other similar instruments used for obtaining the payment of money;

2) "Commercial documents" means invoices, transport documents, documents of title or other similar documents, or any other documents whatsoever, not being financial documents.

C) "Clean collection" means collection of financial documents not accompanied by commercial documents.

D) "Documentary collection" means collection of:

1) Financial documents accompanied by commercial documents;

2) Commercial documents not accompanied by financial documents. ②

托收法律关系比较复杂,涉及的当事人(**parties**)比较多。托收业务中,其基本做法是:卖方/委托人(principal)根据买卖合同先行发运货物,然后开出汇票连同有关货运单据交卖方所在地银行/托收行(remitting bank),委托其通过买方所在地分行或其他银行/代收行(collecting bank/ presenting bank)向买方/付款人(drawee)收取货款,凭买方的付款或承兑向买方交付全套单据(All documents)。

---

① Luca G. Radicati Di Brozolo, International Payments and Conflicts of Laws, 48 *Am. J. Comp. L.* 307, 308 (2000).

② Article 2-Definition of Collection, ICC Uniform Rules for Collections ("URC 522").

【释义】 **parties**

A) For the purposes of these Articles the "parties thereto" are:

1) the "principal" who is the party entrusting the handling of a collection to a bank;

2) the "remitting bank" which is the bank to which the principal has entrusted the handling of a collection;

3) the "collecting bank" which is any bank, other than the remitting bank, involved in processing the collection;

4) the "presenting bank" which is the collecting bank making presentation to the drawee.

B) The "drawee" is the one to whom presentation is to be made according to the collection instruction.①

国际商会于 1967 年拟订了托收统一规则,于 1979 年 1 月 1 日起实施。1995 年公布了新修订本《托收统一规则》(Uniform Rules for Collections, URC 522)。该规则是对国际惯例的总结,具有国际惯例的效力。除这一国际惯例外,许多国家都制定有关于票据、支付和托收的法律,即使当事人选择了《托收统一规则》,亦不得违背有关国家国内法中的强制性规定。

二、国际托收中各方当事人之间的法律关系

对于国际托收中各方当事人之间的法律关系,我国传统观点大多主张,在国际托收中存在着两个独立的委托代理关系,托收行是委托人的代理人,代收行是托收行的代理人,即代理人的代理人,而委托人与代收行之间没有直接的关系。但也有学者主张是复代理关系。②国际托收中,委托人通过向托收行提出托收申请,与托收行之间建立了委托代理关系。托收行以自己的名义向委托人或其自己指定的代收行发出托收委托书,即是其作为代理人为本人选任复代理人的行为。代收行只能依据托收委托书的指示行事。由于根据委托人的指定选择代收行或在委托人未指定的情况下由托收行自行选择代收行是国际托收业务中不可或缺的一个环节,因此,出口商选择托收的结算方式就意味着他已经同意了代理人可以进行转委托。如此,委托人和代收行之间构成复代理关系,代收行是委托人的代理人。实务中,代收行也是以委托人的名义向付款人提示付款或提示承兑的。在这种情况下,托收行并不对代收行的行为负责,而委托人就托收指示的履行对代收行有直接的请求权。

---

① Article 3-Definition of Collection, ICC Uniform Rules for Collections ("URC 522").

② 杜涛:《国际经济贸易中的国际私法问题》,武汉大学出版社 2005 年版,第 272 页。

如果代收行违反托收指示书行事,致使委托人遭受损失的,委托人不能根据委托合同对代收行起诉,而只能通过托收行向代收行起诉。随着国际商会对托收规则的不断修订,特别是在国际贸易实务和法院审判实践中遇到的新情况,如仍以上述观点去理解托收,将无法解决新产生的问题。《托收统一规则》对于委托人与代收行两者的法律关系作了补充,认为委托人与代收行之间存在直接委托代理关系,托收行与代收行是委托人的共同代理人。如果代收行与委托人之间存在法律纠纷,委托人可以直接向代收行提起诉讼。这种改动使得代收行在托收中的定位更趋合理。

三、国际托收的法律适用

国际托收作为一种民商事法律行为,托收当事人可以根据国际私法中的意思自治原则,选择适用调整托收关系的准据法。

国际商会1995年《托收统一规则》是调整国际托收的国际惯例,经托收当事人在相关合同中选择适用,可以作为托收关系的准据法。在**上海兰生公司与华侨银行上海分行、花旗银行国际托收纠纷案**中,我国法院即认可当事人选择的《托收统一规则》作为处理国际托收关系所适用的法律。

【案例】 上海兰生公司与华侨银行上海分行、花旗银行国际托收纠纷案①

案情:上海兰生股份有限公司于1993年4月至10月间向美国L. J. Global公司销售各式鞋类共13批,付款条件为D/P20天或D/P45天。其中第一批货物应于1993年4月23日付款交单,最后一批货物于1993年10月6日付款交单。兰生公司委托华侨银行有限公司上海分行向买方托收货款,将汇票、提单等单证交其签收,并指定花旗银行为代收行。1995年7月6日,兰生公司以华侨银行在指示代收行执行托收业务时未尽职责,致使货款托收未果,违反了两者间的委托代理关系为由,向上海市中级人民法院提起诉讼,要求赔偿托收货款本息。随后申请追加花旗银行为共同被告。

本案的焦点之一就是法律适用问题。在本案应适用的准据法问题上,原告上海兰生公司认为,由于托收指示书明确载明适用《托收统一规则》,故该规则应作为本案的准据法。华侨银行同意上述观点。被告花旗银行则认为,托收指示书只

---

① 参见上海市高级人民法院编:《2002年上海法院案例精选》,上海人民出版社2003年版,第223页。

是华侨银行向其作出的,因而其与兰生公司并无直接的法律关系,故本案不具备适用上述法律的基础。本案应根据《中华人民共和国票据法》的冲突规范,根据《中华人民共和国票据法》冲突规范的指引,最终适用美国《统一商法典》。本案托收指令中所载明的是"在适用的情况下,适用《托收统一规则》",亦即在不适用的情况下可不适用。同时,《托收统一规则》与美国《统一商法典》在过失问题上的规定有冲突,根据国际惯例的效力不得高于当地法律的原则,应适用当地法律。原审法院则认为,根据我国《民法通则》中的冲突法规范,涉外合同的当事人可以选择处理争议所适用的准据法。由于兰生公司和华侨银行就系争法律关系适用《托收统一规则》没有争议,而托收指示中亦明确载明适用该规则,花旗银行接收该指示后并无拒绝办理的意思表示,故本案所适用的准据法应为《托收统一规则》,而不是美国《统一商法典》。

事实上,本案系国际托收纠纷,各方当事人争议的焦点在于托收行和代收行是否违反了托收指令。鉴于托收行为从本质上看属于当事人依合意而产生的特定条件下的委托代理行为,故本案应按债法冲突规范确定准据法,亦即应按我国《民法通则》之规定确定冲突规范。按照我国《民法通则》第150条的规定,准据法可以是内国法,也可以是外国法,还可以是国际条约或国际惯例。鉴于托收指示已经明示选择了适用《托收统一规则》等事实,当事人所选择的国际托收关系的准据法合法有效。故法院就本案适用《托收统一规则》是正确的。

宁波市中级人民法院2005年10月在其受理的**浙江省首起国际托收纠纷案**中,认定本案托收指示中已经明示选择了适用国际商会第522号出版物《托收统一规则》,并确认当事人之间这种法律选择的有效性。

【案例】　　　　　　　　**浙江省首例国际托收纠纷案**①

2003年6月20日,美国Platelite公司向原告宁波保税区三邦工贸有限公司采购了两批发光面板,总金额为16.6万美元,双方约定付款方式为即期D/P(即付款交单。出口商在货物运出后,连同货运单据委托银行办理托收,指示银行在进口商付款后即可领单提货)。按照合同约定,三邦公司在将两批货物装船后把商业发票、装箱单、全套正本提单全部交给了宁波招商银行,委托其办理跟单托收,而美国Frost National Bank作为代收银行负责向Platelite公司收款。同年8月1日,宁波招商银行将两份托收指示函,连同相应的发票、箱单、全套正本提单,邮寄至这家美国银行,后者对上述托收指示函和相

---

① 记者董小军、通讯员陈海滨:《宁波中院判决浙江首例国际托收纠纷案》,载《宁波日报》2005年10月17日。

应的全套单据进行了签收。

但这家美国银行对托收结果一直未作回复。此后,三邦公司获悉美国 Platelite 公司已提走了全部货物,货物承运人也收回了上述货物的全套正本提单,但三邦公司却未收回货款。受到损失的三邦公司在多次交涉无果后将宁波招商银行和这家美国银行告上法庭,要求两被告共同承担赔偿责任。在本案审理过程中,原告向法庭提出,宁波招商银行在托收关系中已履行了应尽的义务,撤回了对其起诉。

法院经审理认为,本案托收指示中已经明示选择了适用国际商会第522号出版物《托收统一规则》,根据《托收统一规则》的规定,这家美国银行在未征得委托人同意的情况下,擅自违反托收指示中的 D/P 付款方式而放单,导致原告未能收到货款,显然未尽到一个代收银行善意和合理的谨慎义务,应当对委托人由此造成的损失承担赔偿责任。

宁波市中级人民法院根据《托收统一规则》的规定,认为被告美国 Frost National Bank 未尽到国际惯例有关托收关系中代收银行善意和合理的谨慎义务,判决其赔偿宁波这家公司的货款损失 16.6 万美元及利息损失 1500 余美元。

【思考题】

- 大陆法系的票据概念与英美法系的票据概念有什么不同?
- 国际票据法律适用的一般原则是什么?
- 你知道《跟单信用证统一惯例600号》和信用证法律适用的规则吗?
- 国际上对信用证履行地有哪些不同的理解?美国《统一商法典(信用证篇)》对此采取什么标准?
- 国际托收的法律适用有什么特点?

【重要术语提示与中英文对照】

中文术语	英文对照
票据	bills, negotiable instruments
汇票	bill of exchange, draft
本票	promissory notes
支票	cheque
联合国国际汇票和国际本票公约	United Nations Convention on International Bills of Exchange and International Promissory Notes

美国诉纽约担保信托公司	United States v. Guaranty Trust Co. of New York
韦斯曼诉布鲁塞尔银行案	Wessman v. Banque de Bruxelles
跟单信用证	documentary cedits
信用证	letters of credits, L/C
商业信用证	commercial credits
跟单信用证统一惯例600号	Uniform Customs and Practice for Documentary Credits, Publication No 600, UCP600
统一商法典第五篇信用证篇	The Uniform Commercial Code, Revised Article 5, Letter of Credit,
美国统一州法全国委员会	National Conference of Commissioners on Uniform State Laws
美国法学会	American Law Institute
信用证履行地	place of performance
付款地即履行地	place of payment as place of performance
签发地即履行地	place of issuance as place of performance
开证行所在地法	law of the issuer's jurisdiction
美国纽约化学银行	Chemical New York Corp.
第一花旗银行	First National City Bank
有最大利益	the greatest interest
丹宁大法官	Lord Denning
美洲银行	Bank of America
印度巴鲁达银行	Bank of Baroda
临时止付令	temporary injunction
破产法院	bankruptcy court
菲律宾国家银行	Philippine National Bank
第九巡回上诉法院	Ninth Circuit Court of Appeals
纽约州州法修改委员会	New York State Law Revision Commission
开证行所在地法	law of the issuer's jurisdiction
托收	collection
当事人	parties
卖方/委托人	principal

卖方所在地银行/托收行	remitting bank,
其他银行/代收行	collecting bank/ presenting bank
买方/付款人	drawee
全套单据	all documents
托收统一规则	Uniform Rules for Collections, URC 522

【推荐阅读文献】

- 肖宏开:《一起票据托收案件引出的法律适用问题》,载《法律适用》1993 年第 3 期。

- 王瀚、黄静:《国际票据法律适用问题比较研究——兼论我国票据法第五章法律适用规范》,载《现代法学》1997 年第 5 期。

- 顾海波:《国际票据的法律适用规则问题探讨》,载《国际私法与比较法年刊》(第二卷),法律出版社 1999 年版。

- 黄亚英、李薇薇:《论国际信用证交易中准据法的确定》,载《中国法学》2002 年第 3 期。

- 徐冬根:《信用证法律与实务研究》,北京大学出版社 2005 年版。

- 赵相林:《国际私法教学案例评析》,中信出版社 2006 年版。

- 徐小薇:《UCP600 规则下信用证贸易融资与风险规避》,载《对外经贸实务》2012 年第 10 期。

- Henry D. Gabriel, Standby Letters of Credit: Does The Risk Outweigh The Benefits?, 1988 *Colum. Bus. L. Rev* 705, 707 (1988).

- James A. Newell, Michael R. Gordon, Electronic Promissory Notes, 31 *Idaho L. Rev.* 830 (1995).

- Franck Chantayan: Choice of Law Under Revised Article 5 of The Uniform Commercial Code 5-116, 14 *St. John's J. L. Comm.* 199 (1999).

- Luca G. Radicati Di Brozolo, International Payments and Conflicts of Laws, 48 *Am. J. Comp. L.* 207 (2000).

- George P. Graham, International Commercial Letters of Credit and Choice of Law: So Whose Law Should Apply Anyway? 47 *Wayne L. Rev.* 212 (2001).

- Keith A. Rowley, Inticipatory Repudiation of Letters of Credit, 56 *SMU L. Rev.* 2235 (2003).

- Eidenmüller (H.), The Transnational Law Market, Regulatory Competition, and Transnational Corporations, 18 *Ind. J. Global Legal Stud.* 707 (2011).

【扩展阅读资料】

The UCC: Various Issues Raised by Electronic Notes. [①]

A. Possession and Writings

In general, if the Uniform Commercial Code were neutral toward electronic notes it would look much as it does now, except current language requiring physical delivery and possession of paper or traditional "writings" would be replaced or supplemented with language permitting their electronic counterparts. Property concepts intertwined with the law of negotiable instruments will need to be examined. Furthermore, the Code will need to recognize that the most important attributes of a promissory note, whether paper-based or electronic-based, are the rights possessed by the holder, i.e., the contract rights and the holder in due course status. For a holder, the continued legal recognition of these rights is far more important than the means by which the rights are set down and preserved. An electronic promissory note, which can be negotiated, notwithstanding the fact that the note is not represented by a paper-based memorial, should be a permissible alternative under the law of commerce.

B. Negotiability

Negotiation, including the conferring of holder in due course status on the transferee, could be accomplished by electronic signature and delivery could be accomplished by electronic transmission to a clearing corporation which would hold the note as custodian for the noteholder. Other than traditional, formal concepts of negotiable instruments, there do not appear to be significant overriding policy considerations that would be violated if electronic notes retain the negotiability afforded their paper-based predecessors. Electronic notes in the secondary market will be negotiated (indorsed) at least once and in many cases several times as mortgages are bought and sold among participants in the secondary mortgage market. Under the current practice of using third-parties in the mortgage loan origination process, there will often be a minimum of two or more noteholders in the chain of ownership before a mortgage is sold into the secondary market.

C. Holder in Due Course

Many mortgages are originated by third-parties who sell the mortgages to mortgage lenders who sell them to other mortgage lenders who eventually sell them into the secondary market. In such cases, the mortgages have been transferred many

---

[①] James A. Newell, Michael R. Gordon, Electronic Promissory Notes, 31 *Idaho L. Rev.* 819, 830—832 (1995).

times before being placed in the secondary market. This means that a large number of notes sold into the secondary market have been negotiated several times. Given the many participants in the mortgage origination process (mortgage brokers, mortgage companies, institutional mortgage lenders) and the speed and volume of mortgage purchases, it is not cost effective for mortgage lenders or secondary market investors such as Freddie Mac to investigate the circumstances surrounding the origination of each and every mortgage loan. It is, therefore, important to most secondary market investors, including Freddie Mac, to be able to rely on the law of negotiability and holder in due course protection as an economic and practical necessity.

Holder in due course protection also affects the cost of doing business with Freddie Mac. Investors who purchase Freddie Mac mortgage-backed securities are guaranteed the return of their principal investment, even if the underlying mortgages go into default. To offset losses resulting from borrower defaults under the mortgage or note and to make a reasonable return for its stockholders, Freddie Mac charges guaranty fees to the mortgage lenders who sell mortgages into the secondary market. For Freddie Mac to be competitive, it must be able to keep its guaranty fees reasonable. Competitive guaranty fees in turn benefit the borrowing public by helping to keep mortgage interest rates at reasonable levels. Freddie Mac closely monitors the risk factors that contribute to losses (e.g. mortgage lender performance and financial condition, real estate market values, national and regional economic conditions, etc.). The guaranty fees charged by Freddie Mac are based on, among other things, the anticipated losses associated with litigation and disposition of real estate owned.

It has been Freddie Mac's general experience that when enforcing it rights under a mortgage contract, defenses to such actions are rarely raised. Furthermore, based on many years of observation, it is believed that if holder in due course protection were not available, more defenses would be raised in an effort to forestall enforcement of the loan contract whether the defenses had merit or not. In the vast majority of cases in which defenses have been raised, the defenses have been found to be without merit and have eventually been dismissed. Prolonged legal action resulting from the filing of additional defenses, otherwise barred by the law of negotiability, would significantly increase the costs associated with enforcing Freddie Mac's rights under the mortgage and note and result in higher guaranty fees and, consequently, higher mortgage interest rates. Thus, holder in due course protection plays a significant role in assisting Freddie Mac in establishing reasonable and competitive guaranty fees and accomplishing its mission of providing a steady flow of funds into the primary mortgage market.

D. Indorsement Liability

It is essential that most of the substantive law governing negotiable instruments be retained. In particular, holder in due course protection is of significant importance to both mortgage lenders and secondary market investors. In most cases, it is far more valuable than indorsement liability which plays a fairly insignificant role in the secondary mortgage market. For instance, mortgage lenders who sell mortgages to Freddie Mac are required by the Guide and, if applicable, other supplemental agreements, to make certain representations and warranties with respect to each mortgage loan. Among other things, the mortgage lenders must represent and warrant that each mortgage was originated in accordance with Freddie Mac's credit and property underwriting requirements. In addition, they must represent and warrant that each note is negotiable. Mortgage lenders are not, however, required to sell mortgages to Freddie Mac "with recourse," unless there are additional risks associated with the mortgages that Freddie Mac is unwilling to assume. Therefore, Freddie Mac seldom relies on indorsement liability when mortgages it purchases go into default or defenses are raised in an enforcement action brought by or on behalf of Freddie Mac.

There are two significant reasons for this approach to purchasing mortgages. First, Freddie Mac assumes the risk of default for mortgages it purchases and manages the risk through applying prudent underwriting standards and charging guaranty fees on its mortgagebacked securities as an offset. If a mortgage loan goes into default after purchase, Freddie Mac absorbs the losses associated with the default, provided the mortgage otherwise complied with the Guide and, if applicable, any supplemental agreement, when the mortgage was sold to Freddie Mac. Second, under FIRREA, most institutional mortgage lenders are required to set aside reserves in most situations in which they have a recourse obligation. This requirement can result in serious financial consequences for institutional mortgage lenders. Accordingly, full recourse sales of mortgages are not favored and are seldom agreed to by mortgage lenders. Therefore, as stated above, holder in due course status is needed to ensure free transferability of an electronic promissory note.

E. Use of Allonges

As suggested above, the method of indorsement of an electronic note could be by separate electronic allonge. The traditional requirement that the allonge be affixed to the instrument would be broadened to permit electronic attachment of an electronic allonge containing the indorser's unique identification and security code. More emphasis on the intention of the parties with respect to indorsements on allonges and less emphasis on formalism is probably appropriate in light of modern commercial practices.

第十四章

国际金融关系的法律适用

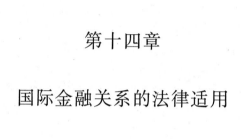

第十四章 国际金融关系的法律适用

本 章 导 读

※ 国际商业贷款是指国际商业银行以收取利息为条件而向借款人提供货币资金融通的一种金融服务方式,具体包括放款、贴现、透支、提供融资担保等。国际贷款合同首先适用当事人所选择的法律。如果当事人没有对准据法作出选择,则适用与贷款合同有最密切联系的国家的法律。

※ 银团贷款,是指由牵头银行牵头,由两家以上的银行依据同样的贷款条件并使用一份共同的贷款合同向借款人发放的由共同代理行管理的贷款。国际银团贷款所适用的准据法一般有以下几个特征:第一,法律制度比较完善;第二,该国政治局势和法律制度相对稳定;第三,该法律能被贷款人所接受。

※ 国际保证属于人的担保。通常各国担保法律规定的保证都是附属性担保,它以基础合同或主合同的履行为基础,只有在被担保人(主债务人)不履行主合同债务的时候,担保人才承担责任。国际保证合同当事人可以选择适用的法律。如果保证当事人没有选择的,则按最密切联系原则适用特征性履行地即担保人的营业所或住所地的法律。

※ 不动产担保物权应适用不动产所在地法,浮动担保适用被担保人所在地法,船舶抵押权适用船旗国法律。

※ 国际独立担保主要有银行担保、见索即付担保和备用信用证担保。国际独立担保的法律适用,首先适用当事人选择的法律;当事人没有选择的,依照最密切联系原则和特征性履行方法,适用担保人营业所所在地国家法律。

※ 独立担保所适用的国际惯例主要有《国际备用信用证惯例》和《国际担保统一规则》。

※ 信托,是指将自己的财产委托给足以信赖的第三者,使其按照自己的愿望和要求进行管理和运作的法律制度。国际信托法律适用遵循独立性原则、分类分割原则和意思自治原则。

※ 海牙国际私法会议于1984年通过的《关于信托的法律适用及其承认的公约》,其法律适用制度包括:广泛适用当事人的意思自治原则、最密切联系原则和优先适用法院地国强行性规则。

※ 国际保险,是指具有国际因素从而涉及不同国家法律适用的保险。国际保险合同法律适用的一般原则为意思自治原则、保护弱方当事人原则和最密切联系原则。

【本章主题词】 国际贷款、国际担保、独立担保、国际信托、国际保险

第一节 国际贷款的法律适用

一、国际商业贷款概述

国际商业贷款(international commercial loan)是指国际商业银行以收取利息为条件而向借款人提供货币资金融通的一种金融服务方式,具体包括放款、贴现、透支、提供融资担保等。国际商业贷款当事人需要订立国际贷款合同来约定当事人之间的权利义务。国际贷款合同(international loan agreement)是指不同国家的当事人之间因贷款而签署的法律文件。[①]

随着我国对外开放的扩大,我国企业参与国际商业贷款数量的增加,在我国境内发生的国际商业贷款纠纷与日俱增,目前我国法院已经审理并判决了大量国际贷款纠纷案件。[②]

在国际贷款中,目前并无国际统一立法,当事人的权利义务主要是依贷款合同约定。贷款合同适用的法律取决于当事人的选择。因此国际贷款中的法律适用绝不是可有可无的。适用哪个国家或者法域的法律将涉及该项国际贷款的合法性、有效性和完整性。国际贷款合同所引起的基本问题,如合同条款的解释、借贷双方权利和义务的确定、合同的履行和解除、司法管辖的确定等,都要由其所适用的法律来确定。

二、国际贷款的法律适用

(一)当事人选择国际贷款合同的准据法

国际贷款合同首先适用当事人根据意思自治原则所选择的法律。当事人可以

---

① 徐冬根:《国际金融法》,高等教育出版社 2006 年版,第 49 页。
② 其中比较典型的涉外商业贷款案有:(1)中国农业银行深圳市分行与香港雄丰企业控股有限公司、雄丰集团(深圳)有限公司借款合同纠纷案;(2)香港中成财务有限公司与香港鸿润(集团)有限公司、广东省江门市财政局借款合同纠纷案;(3)中国银行湛江分行与湛江国际金融大厦(集团)广州公司、香港辉杰企业有限公司等单位借款合同纠纷案;(4)深圳市万山实业股份有限公司与 Plenty International Ltd.、香港永达利企业有限公司借款纠纷案等。参见广东省人民法院编:《涉外商事案例精选精析》,法律出版社 2004 年版。

选择借款人或者贷款人的本国法,也可以选择一些国际金融市场所在地国家或地区的法律,如伦敦金融市场所在地的英国法、纽约金融市场所在地的美国法或者香港金融市场所在地的香港法,作为国际贷款合同的准据法。

在我国江苏省高级人民法院所审理的**荷兰商业银行上海分行诉苏州工业园区壳牌燃气有限公司担保合同偿付纠纷案**中,当事人根据意思自治原则选择了英国法作为贷款担保协议的准据法,江苏省高级人民法院经过审理后,认定当事人在合同中所选择的贷款担保协议准据法合法有效,最终法院依当事人所选择的英国法对案件作出判决。

【案例】 荷兰商业银行上海分行诉苏州工业园区壳牌燃气有限公司担保合同偿付纠纷案①

1997年5月14日,原告荷兰商业银行上海分行(以下简称"上海分行")与苏州工业园区壳牌燃气有限公司(以下简称"苏州壳牌公司")签订了一份融资担保协议,载明由上海分行为苏州壳牌公司开立金额不超过650万美元的备用信用证,以实现苏州壳牌公司因建造厂房、购置设备、营运资本而向国内银行获得人民币融资的目的。在此份融资协议中,明确苏州壳牌公司应向上海分行支付担保融资未使用部分每年0.125%的承诺费,并于接受日期后21日内支付美元价值为本协议额度的0.125%作为安排费;苏州壳牌公司在有效期内可随时向上海分行出具请求函,请求其按本协议的规定出具一份或多份担保书,对于每份担保书,苏州壳牌公司应在担保有效期内每季度后支付年率为担保款额0.75%的佣金(开证费)。上述协议约定,由上海分行发生的与其维护或强制执行其在本协议下的任何权利有关的所有合理的成本和费用(包括律师费和其他费用)应由苏州壳牌公司向上海分行支付,无论本融资的任何部分是否已得到使用。协议还约定:苏州壳牌公司将无条件并不可撤销地补偿因签发任何一份担保书而可能以任何形式发生的一切性质的所有索赔、负债、损失和合理的费用,并在贷款人要求时向贷款人支付贷款人所有款项,该款项是可能由贷款人提出的索赔或贷款人可能支付或成为有责任支付任何一份担保书所规定的或引发的或有关的所有款项,以及支付从贷款人支付或引发相关款项或其他负债那天算起的利息和合理费用。协议又约定了违约事由、违约补偿等款项,并明确本协议经借款人苏州壳牌公司签署后生效,适用法律为英国法律并根据英国法律予以解释,并服从英国法院的非专属管辖;本协议以中英文书写并签署,如两种文本间发生歧义,以英文本为准。苏州壳牌公司、上海分行均在上述协议上签字。嗣后,根据苏州壳牌公司的申请,上海分行开立了受益人为苏州农行、编号

---

① (2000)苏经初字第1号。

为SHSC990039的备用信用证,作为苏州壳牌公司向中资银行获得人民币贷款的担保。1999年11月18日,上海分行收到备用信用证下的受益人的索偿通知,即于次日致函苏州壳牌公司,要求其偿付备用信用证下将支付的所有款项。同年11月26日,上海分行向受益人苏州农业银行苏州工业园区分行(以下简称苏州农行)支付4899669.72美元。然而苏州壳牌公司未清偿其所欠上海分行债务。为此而形成诉讼。上海分行遂于1999年12月22日向江苏省高级人民法院提起诉讼。

本案中,原、被告之间所形成的法律关系属于商业贷款法律关系,原告以备用信用证方式向被告提供的融资担保属于国际商业贷款的组成部分。因此,原告为被告提供担保并承担担保责任之后向被告进行追索,属于国际商业贷款纠纷。本案中,双方当事人约定的"本融资协议应适用英国法律并根据英国法律予以解释",符合《中华人民共和国民法通则》第145条有关涉外合同的当事人可以选择处理合同争议所适用法律的规定,是合法有效的。因此本案双方当事人有权选择英国法律作为适用于该融资担保协议的准据法。江苏省高级人民法院为此根据英国法[①],作出判决,支持原告的诉讼请求。[②]

(二) 当事人未选择准据法时适用最密切联系的法

如果当事人没有对国际贷款合同的准据法作出选择,则根据最密切联系原则,适用与贷款合同有最密切联系的国家的法律。

发生在我国的国际贷款合同,如果国际贷款合同本身没有对合同所适用的法律作出选择,由于贷款合同签订地通常在中国境内,国际贷款合同的借款人通常是中国的企业法人,国际贷款债务需要向中国的外汇管理机构登记,国际贷款合同的履行,即贷款的交付和偿还行为也大部分发生在中国境内,与国际贷款合同有最密切联系的国家是中国,因此国际贷款案件应适用中国法律,如由广东省高级人民法院审理的**深圳市万山实业股份有限公司诉 Plenty International Ltd. 借款纠纷上诉案**。

---

① 在英国法下,对订立合同的主体没有限制性的规定,对使用备用信用证也不存在禁止性的规定。根据英国法,保证人(银行)履行义务后,可以向被保证人求偿。在英国法下,保证人经由债务人的要求提供了担保后,保证人便具有一项默示的合同权利以要求债务人对保证人所承担的所有责任予以补偿,这是一项普遍适用的原则,即合同一方基于另一方的请求或是授权作出给付或者承担了责任的,有权得到偿还或补偿。在本案中,苏州壳牌公司未能向上海分行偿还其支付的款项及相应的利息,应视为壳牌公司违反了双方融资协议的约定,对此苏州壳牌公司应向上海分行偿还信用证项下的款项及相应的利息,并承担相应的违约责任。

② 江苏省高级人民法院(2000)苏经初字第1号《民事判决书》。

第十四章 国际金融关系的法律适用

【案例】 **深圳市万山实业股份有限公司诉**
Plenty International Ltd. 借款纠纷上诉案

1993年8月6日,深圳市万山实业股份有限公司(以下简称"万山公司")、英属维尔京群岛Plenty International Ltd.(普兰提国际有限公司,以下简称"普兰提公司")、香港永达利企业有限公司(以下简称"永达利公司",承包方)签订了一份《协议书》,约定:因万山公司兴建太阳岛大厦项目的需要,由普兰提公司出资港币3,500万元作为投资,但普兰提公司不参与具体的筹建工作,由永达利公司及万山公司负责在两年内向乙方支付3000万元人民币作为投资利润分成,普兰提公司的投资本金也在两年内全部收回。合同签订后,普兰提公司在1993年8月至12月期间共拆借资金港币3500万元给万山公司及永达利公司,永达利公司向普兰提公司开具了收款收据。后因永达利公司及万山公司发生财务困难,未按协议支付约定款项而形成纠纷。

一审法院深圳市中级人民法院认为:本案是借款纠纷。普兰提公司与万山公司、永达利公司约定由普兰提公司出资但不参与具体的筹建工作,而由万山公司及永达利公司在两年内向普兰提公司支付3000万元人民币作为投资回报,并在两年内归还投资本金,这实际上是借贷行为。

二审法院广东省高级人民法院认为:本案原告普兰提公司的商业注册地在英属维尔京群岛,被告之一永达利公司的商业注册地在香港,因此,本案属于涉外民商事纠纷。《中华人民共和国民法通则》第145条规定:"涉外合同的当事人可以选择处理合同争议所适用的法律,法律另有规定的除外。涉外合同的当事人没有选择的,适用与合同有最密切联系的国家的法律。"由于本案当事人没有在有关协议书中约定处理争议所适用的法律,事后也没有达成一致的意见;因本案所涉有关协议书约定的用款人之一万山公司的商业注册地在中华人民共和国境内,本案所涉的款项用于兴建深圳市太阳岛大厦,因此中华人民共和国与本案所涉的有关协议书有最密切的联系。根据上述有关法律的规定,原审法院适用中华人民共和国法律处理本案合同争议,有充分的事实和法律依据,予以支持。①

本案中,广东省高级人民法院在当事人对国际贷款合同准据法未作出选择的情况下,适用了与国际贷款合同有最密切联系的法律作为国际贷款合同的准据法。

三、国际银团贷款的法律适用

(一)国际银团贷款的概念与特点

国际银团贷款(**multi-lender financing**),是指由牵头银行牵头,由两家以上的

---

① 资料来源:广东省高级人民法院网站,网址:http://www.gdcourts.gov.cn/case_all/case_good/MS/t20021214_0939.htm,2008年7月10日访问。

银行依据同样的贷款条件并使用一份共同的贷款合同向借款人发放的由共同代理行管理的跨国商业贷款。①

【释义】 **multi-lender financing**

Typical multi-lender financing is a loan between sophisticated financial institutions. Multi-lender financing is that where a number of financial or commercial institutions combine to finance a borrower. Typically a consortium of banks makes a loan to a borrower; but it is also common for insurance companies, credit unions, pension funds, and trust and loan companies to participate as lenders in such consortia. The borrowers included corporations, banks, public and quasi-public institutions, sovereign and supra-national bodies.

国际银团贷款具有以下特点:第一,国际银团贷款的参与主体众多。国际银团贷款的主体主要是借款人、贷款人和贷款担保人。借款人是银团贷款中的主债务人。贷款人主要是提供贷款的银团银行。银团贷款中的贷款担保人是指以自己的资信向银团贷款人保证对借款人履行还款义务承担责任的法人。第二,国际银团贷款涉及多国法律。国际银团贷款参与的银行多,而且大部分银行并不隶属于同一个国家。国际银团贷款合同是在两个或两个以上不同国家的当事人之间订立,在不同的国家履行的,这就产生了适用哪个国家的法律问题。第三,国际银团贷款所涉及的每个国家的法律对其规定是存在差异的。国际银团贷款当事人所选择的法律只能是根据本国的经验所作出的最好的假设,但这种假设不可避免地会有所冲突。

(二)国际银团贷款中的准据法及其特征

国际银团贷款合同的准据法通常是由当事人根据意思自治原则选择产生的,并在国际银团贷款合同中作出书面约定。

由于国际银团贷款涉及多国当事人和多个国家的法律,而且各个国家的法律对于国际银团贷款的规定又不尽相同,因此并不是每一个国家的法律都可以被选为国际银团贷款合同的准据法。可以成为国际银团贷款合同准据法的法律,一般有以下几个特征:

第一,国际银团贷款所适用的法律,其法律制度比较完善。②贷款合同所适用的法律必须是一种和当前国际金融活动有密切联系的法律,根据这种法律或已有

---

① 参见徐冬根:《国际金融法》,高等教育出版社2006年版,第87页。
② 郭洪俊:《国际银团贷款中的法律问题研究》,法律出版社2001年版,第195页。

的判例能够妥善解决贷款合同执行过程中可能出现的争议。

第二,国际银团贷款所适用的法律,应该是其政治局势和法律相对稳定的国家的法律。银团贷款的期限往往较长,这样就必须保证国际银团贷款所适用的法律具有一定的稳定性和连续性,以防止因所选国际银团贷款所适用的法律的变化而引起不必要的问题。而一国法律的稳定性和连续性在很大程度上取决于该国政治上的稳定程度。一个国家政局稳定,则该国的法律具有合理的延续性和相对的稳定性,同时也为借贷双方预测该国法律在未来的变化提供了可靠的保证。

第三,国际银团贷款所适用的法律能被贷款人所接受。无论适用哪一个国家或地区的准据法,前提是都必须得到贷款人的同意。

第二节 国际担保的法律适用

一、国际担保概述

国际担保是指担保法律关系的主体、客体,或者担保的发生、变更、消灭等法律事实中的任何一方面具有国际因素的担保。国际担保包括人的担保和物的担保两类。人的担保是指自然人或法人以其信誉为他人的债务提供担保,债务人不履行债务时,则由担保人负责清偿。物的担保是指以确保债务清偿为目的,在债务人或第三人的物或权利上设立的一种担保。

国际担保既要受国际民商事法律规范的调整,也要受担保法律规范的调整。我国《境内机构对外担保管理办法》第2条对"**对外担保**"作出了具体的界定。

【释义】　　　　　　　　　对 外 担 保

本办法所称对外担保,是指中国境内机构(境内外资金融机构除外,以下简称担保人)以保函、备用信用证、本票、汇票等形式出具对外保证,以《中华人民共和国担保法》中第34条规定的财产对外抵押或者以《中华人民共和国担保法》第4章第1节规定的动产对外质押和第2节第75条规定的权利对外质押,向中国境外机构或者境内的外资金融机构(债权人或者受益人,以下简称债权人)承诺,当债务人(以下简称被担保人)未按照合同约定偿付债务时,由担保人履行偿付义务。对外担保包括:(一)融资担保;

(二)融资租赁担保;(三)补偿贸易项下的担保;(四)境外工程承包中的担保;(五)其他具有对外债务性质的担保。

担保人不得以留置或者定金形式出具对外担保。

对境内外资金融机构出具的担保视同对外担保。

由此可见,国际担保大致可以分为国际保证合同、国际物权担保和国际独立担保三大类。

二、国际保证合同的法律适用

国际保证属于人的担保。人的担保分为附属性担保(accessory guarantee)和独立性担保(independent guarantee)。通常各国担保法律规定的都是附属性担保,它以基础合同或主合同的履行为基础,只有在被担保人(主债务人)不履行主合同债务的时候,担保人才承担责任。

由于国际保证合同也是合同的一种,因而适用合同法的一般适用原则。当事人意思自治原则是我国国际保证合同法律适用的基本原则。

在国际担保中,我国最高人民法院《关于适用〈中华人民共和国担保法〉若干问题的解释》第6条规定,有下列情形之一的,对外担保合同无效:第一,未经国家有关主管部门批准或者登记对外担保的;第二,未经国家有关主管部门批准或者登记,为境外机构向债权人提供担保的;第三,为外商投资企业注册资本、外商投资企业中的外方投资部分的对外债务提供担保的;无权经营外汇担保业务的金融机构、无外汇收入的非金融性质的企业法人提供外汇担保的;第五,主合同变更或者债权人将对外担保项下的权利转让,未经担保人同意或国家有关主管部门批准的,担保人不再承担任何责任。中国人民银行1996年重新发布的《境内机构对外担保管理办法》第4条第2款规定:除经国务院批准为使用外国政府或者国际经济组织贷款进行转贷外,国家机关和事业不得对外担保;第17条规定:担保人未经批准擅自出具对外担保的,其对外出具的担保合同无效。[①]

由于我国的国际保证合同并不属于法律强制适用的三种合同之一,因此在不违背我国强行性规范和公共秩序的情况下,我国国际保证合同首先适用当事人选择的法律,如果当事人没有对国际保证合同所适用的法律作出选择,则按最密切联系原则适用特征性履行地即担保人的营业所或住所地的法律,如**广东发展银行江门分行与香港新中地产有限公司借款担保纠纷上诉案**。

---

① 杜涛:《国际经济贸易中的国际私法问题》,武汉大学出版社2005年版,第225页。

【案例】 广东发展银行江门分行与香港新中地产有限公司借款担保纠纷上诉案①

1994年5月12日,香港新中公司与香港回丰有限公司(以下简称"回丰公司")签订一份贷款合同。该合同约定:回丰公司向新中公司贷款660万美元用于支付广州市东风路067号地段有关项目的开发,贷款期为两年,年利率25%。回丰公司须于1996年5月12日前将该贷款全部还清。

上述贷款由广东发展银行江门分行(以下简称"江门发展行")为回丰公司提供持续性的担保。为此,1994年4月11日,江门发展行向新中公司出具了一份担保书,同意对上述贷款及其利息提供担保。后因担保履行而涉讼。担保人江门发展行不服一审广东省高级人民法院判决②,而向最高人民法院提起上诉。

最高人民法院经审定认为,本案系涉港经济纠纷案件。根据我国法律规定,涉外案件当事人可以选择处理争议所适用的实体法,但本案当事人未就处理争议所适用的实体法作出选择。本案系担保合同纠纷,根据最密切联系原则,涉外担保应适用担保人所在地国家的法律,即江门发展行所在地国家(即中国)的法律。为此,法院最终以中国法作为涉外担保关系的准据法。

三、国际物权担保的法律适用

物权担保,是指以清偿债务为目的,在债务人或者第三人的财产上设定的一种限度物权,如抵押权、质押权、留置权等。③物的担保,大陆法上称这种权利为担保物权(security interest),英美法则称为担保权益(secured interest)。④英美法中的物权担保(real security)基本可以分为三种类型:一是由债权人取得对担保物的所有权而不依赖于对物的占有的担保,如抵押(mortgage);二是债权人不享有对担保物的所有权但依赖于对物的占有的担保,如质押(pledge)和留置(lien);三是既不依赖于对担保物的所有权,也不依赖于对担保物的占有的担保,如浮动担保。⑤作为担保的财产包括不动产,如土地、建筑物等;有形动产,如货物、机器设备等;无形动产,如股权、专利权等。

(一)不动产物权担保的法律适用

就一般的物权而言,物之所在地法已经成为各国普遍适用的冲突规则。物之

---

① 中华人民共和国最高人民法院《民事裁定书》(2001)民四终字第14号。
② 广东省高级人民法院(1998)粤法经二初字第14号民事判决。
③ 黄进主编:《国际私法》(第二版),法律出版社2005年版,第527页。
④ 参见贺绍奇:《国际金融担保法律理论与实务》,人民法院出版社2001年版,第122页。
⑤ E. L. G, Tyler, *Fisher and Lightwood's Law of Mortgage*, Butterworths, 1977, p.1.

所在地法,是指在解决物权法律关系的冲突时,适用该物之所在地的实体法。

物权担保属于物权的一种,因此应适用关于物权的法律适用原则。不动产物权担保应适用担保物所在地法律。

根据我国《担保法》的规定,国际融资物权担保主要有抵押、质押和留置三大类。①我国《民法通则》第 144 条规定:不动产所有权,适用不动产所在地法律。最高人民法院《关于贯彻执行〈中华人民共和国民法通则〉若干问题的意见(试行)》第 186 条指出:"土地、附着于土地的建筑物及其他定着物、建筑物的固定附属设备为不动产。不动产的所有权、买卖、租赁、抵押、使用等民事关系,均应适用不动产所在地法律。"为此,根据我国的法律和最高人民法院的司法解释,不动产抵押担保应适用不动产所在地的法律。

(二) 浮动担保的法律适用

浮动担保在英文中有两种表达方式:一为 floating charge,多用于英格兰、苏格兰;一为 floating lien,一般用于美国,两种方式中以 floating charge 为常见。②浮动担保是指企业以其现有的和将来取得的全部资产为债权人的利益而设定的一种担保物权。③浮动担保的担保物覆盖面广泛,几乎涵盖了企业经营过程中拥有的所有机器设备、原材料、库存物资、应收账款(trade debt receivable)、合同权利、无形资产(如商誉、商业秘密、商标权、专利权)等。④ 浮动担保所适用的法律,首先是当事人选择的法律,在当事人未选择时,以适用被担保人所在地的法律为宜。

(三) 船舶抵押权的法律适用

对于船舶抵押权的法律适用,各国允许当事人选择船舶抵押的准据法,在当事人未作选择时,一般适用船旗国法律(law of the flag)。船旗国法,实际上就是船舶国籍(the nationality of the vessel)所属国家的法律。⑤

我国《海商法》第 271 条对船舶抵押权的法律适用作了具体的规定:船舶抵押权适用船旗国法律。在"卡帕玛丽"轮(Kappa Mary)抵押合同纠纷案中⑥,我国法院根据我国《海商法》第 271 条的规定,对船舶抵押权适用了船旗国法律。鉴于该轮悬挂塞浦路斯共和国(The Republic of Cyprus)国旗,最后我国法院适用塞浦路斯

---

① 我国《担保法》虽然规定了五种担保方式,但是属于国际融资担保中物权担保的主要有抵押、质押和留置三种方式。
② 参见徐冬根:《浮动担保法律问题比较研究》,上海交通大学出版社 2007 年版,第 2 页。
③ 沈达明、冯大同编:《国际资金融通的法律与实务》,对外经济贸易出版社 1985 年版,第 206 页。
④ 李曙峰:《担保与抵押》,三联书店(香港)有限公司 1993 年版,第 256、258 页。
⑤ See Darrel C. Menthe, Jurisdiction in Cyberspace: A Theory of International Spaces, 4 Mich. Telecomm. Tech. L. Rev. 69, 83 (1997/1998).
⑥ "卡帕玛丽"轮抵押合同纠纷案的案情和法院判决,参见本书第二章第二节。

共和国的法律(即《塞浦路斯共和国海商法(暂行)》)作为处理本案争议的实体法。

四、国际独立担保的法律适用

在国际经济交往中,独立担保近年来得到广泛采用。① 独立担保独立于基础交易合同,担保人的责任不受制于基础合同的实际履行情况,而仅以其自身条款为准。

(一) 国际独立担保概述

1. 银行担保

国际融资担保在大多数情况下,都是由银行充当担保人向债权人提供担保,所以银行担保(**bank guarantee**)是最基本的国际独立担保方式。

【释义】　　　　　　　　bank guarantee

A bank guarantee is an irrevocable undertaking by which the issuing bank holds itself financially liable for the consequences of non-performance of the obligations by a third party towards the beneficiary. Bank guarantees are also referred to as: guarantees, performance guarantees, demand guarantees, first demand guarantees, independent demand guarantees, international demand guarantees, simple demand guarantees, and international bank guarantees. ②

Bank guarantees are consist of following types:

—bid bond: a bid bond guarantee that organizers of the bid will receive a definite sum of money from the bank if the bidders refuse to sign the agreement after they have won the bid

—advance payment guarantee: an advance payment guarantee secures the repayment of the advance by the bank if the payee fails to perform under the agreement.

—performance bond: a performance bond guarantee that the bank will pay a definite sum if the performer fails to perform under the agreement.

—Warrantee guarantee: a warrantee guarantee that the bank will pay a definite sum of money if the performer fails to fulfill his warranty obligations under the contract.

—payment guarantee: a payment guarantee secures that the bank will pay for goods or services if the buyer fails to make the payment for the goods or services.

—loan guarantee: a loan guarantee secures the claim of the lender against the debtor.

---

2. 见索即付担保

见索即付担保(**demand guarantee**)是担保人(通常是银行)应申请人的要求或者指示,对受益人就约定期限内最高不超过约定金额的债务承担担保责任,在担保有效期内,只要受益人要求付款,担保人即应向受益人支付约定金额的一种担保方

---

① 参见张磊:《涉外担保法律与实务》,中国经济出版社 1997 年版,第 41 页。
② David J. Barru, Comparing Surety Bonds with Bank Guarantees and Standby Letters of Credit, 37 Geo. Wash. Int'l L. Rev. n35 (2005).

式。见索即付担保的受益人的付款要求是无条件的,不需要提供任何证明。担保人一旦收到受益人的付款要求,就应当无条件地向受益人付款。

【释义】　　　　　　　　**demand guarantee**

The demand guarantee is independent of the principal obligation or the underlying contract between the customer of the bank (principal obligor) and the beneficiary. In compliance with the terms and conditions of the guarantee the bank is to pay beneficiary against its first demand.

By the Uniform Rules for Demand Guarantees, a demand guarantee means: "any guarantee, bond or other payment undertaking, however named, or described, by a bank, insurance company or other body or person (the Guarantor) given in writing for the payment of money on presentation in conformity with the terms of the undertaking of a written demand for payment and other such documents, as may be specified in the Guarantee, such undertaking being given: at the request, or on the instructions and under liability of a party, i.e. the Principal or, at the request, or on the instructions and under the liability of a bank, insurance company or any other party (the Instructing Party) acting on instructions of the Principal to another party, i.e. the Beneficiary."

见索即付担保的担保人不得以申请人根据基础合同所产生的结果对抗受益人。因此,见索即付担保方式对受益人是十分有利的,因为他可以任意地向担保人提出付款要求,而不管这种要求是否有理,是否符合实际情况。

3. 备用信用证担保

备用信用证(**standby letter of credit**)是应第三人(支付方)的要求,由一方(开证人,一般是银行)开发给另一方的一种证书。它要求受益人出示一定单据或者证件,开证人在单证相符的条件下必须付给受益人一笔规定的款项,或者承兑承诺的票据。①

【释义】　　　　　　　　**standby letter of credit**

Standby letters of credit are used to guarantee the performance of an obligation. If, the parties of the letter of credit intend that the beneficiary will draw under the letter of credit in the event of the non-performance of the applicant in the underlying transaction, the credit is a standby letter of credit. ②

---

① 徐冬根:《国际金融法》,高等教育出版社 2006 年版,第 302 页。
② John F. Dolan, *The Law of Letters of Credit*, 1.01 (rev. ed. 1999). See also Brooke Wunnicke et Al., *Standby and Commercial Letters of Credit*, §2.5, at 17 (2d. ed. 1996 & Supp. 1997).

备用信用证独立于国际贷款债务,因此担保人也就是主债务人,其义务的履行不受国际贷款合同和借款人状态的任何影响,即使借款人的行为在法律上是无效的,备用信用证的开证人仍然要承担担保责任。备用信用证的开证行不负有审查借款人是否真正违约的义务。担保人只根据该证的规定和付款要求付款,而无须对借款人是否真正违约等事实进行审查。

我国《担保法》第 5 条第 1 款规定:"担保合同是主合同的从合同,主合同无效,担保合同无效。担保合同另有约定的,按照约定。"为此,通过约定方式,国际担保可以成为我国《担保法》项下的独立担保。

(二) 国际独立担保的法律适用

对于国际独立担保的法律适用,也应按照一般担保合同的法律适用原则进行确定。在不违背我国强行规范的前提下,首先适用当事人意思自治原则;当事人没有选择时,依照最密切联系原则和特征性履行方法,通常适用担保人营业所所在地国家的法律。

(三) 有关独立担保的国际公约和国际惯例

1.《独立保函和备用信用证公约》

由联合国大会于 1995 年 12 月 11 日通过,并自 2000 年 1 月 1 日起生效的《独立保函和备用信用证公约》(United Nations Convention on Independent Guarantees and Stand-by Letters of Credit),共设 7 章 29 条,主要内容包括适用范围,解释,保函形式与内容,权利、义务及抗辩,临时性法院措施,法律适用,最后条款。公约规定的适用范围是独立保函或备用信用证。

该公约反映了国际贸易实践中独立保函和备用信用证运作的基本法律原则,是解释现在的国际担保和备用信用证的重要工具。尽管公约的法律效力要高于国际商会制定的有关规则,但由于公约的适用是任意性的,不具有强制性,因此当事人可以排除或改变公约规则的适用,而选用其他的惯例规则。

2.《国际备用信用证惯例》

目前,国际上调整备用信用证的国际惯例,除了《跟单信用证统一惯例 600 号》之外,主要是《国际备用信用证惯例》(<u>International Standby Practices, ISP 98</u>)

【释义】　　　　International Standby Practices, ISP 98

The ISP 98 means the International Standby Practices, ICC Publication No.590, effective since January 1, 1999. It was drafted by the Institute of International Banking Law and Practice and the International Financial Services association (IFSA) in 1998, and can be applied to all kinds of standby letters of credit. The great advantage of rules is that they provide well-trodden paths that limit the amount of thought and work otherwise required for any given transaction. Being known, they can either be accepted or rejected or modified. As a result, they make transactions simpler, less expensive, and less troublesome. In three years of use, the ISP has attracted the support and attention of major corporate users and governmental agencies. Major banks report between 35% and 60% of new standbys being issued subject to the ISP in its major markets. Moreover, the degree of use is increasing as time passes. As translations increase and educational opportunities abound, its use throughout the world is increasing as well. Because it was drafted with a view to the purpose of the standby—an undertaking with integrity, the ISP is well on its way to becoming the world standard for standby L/Cs.①

《国际备用信用证惯例》从1999年1月1日开始实施,自该惯例生效以来,我国的国内银行和许多在华的外资银行、跨国公司均按照该惯例所确立的规则,开展备用信用证的业务。②

3.《合同担保统一规则》

现行《合同担保统一规则》(**Uniform Rules for Contract Guarantee,URCG 325**)由国际商会于1978年6月正式通过。《合同担保统一规则》的适用范围比较广泛,它可以适用于一切担保、保证或者类似的义务承担。不论当事人使用什么名称,只要他们在合同中约定适用《合同担保统一规则》,该规则就可以适用于他们之间的担保合同、保证合同或者类似的合同。

【释义】　Uniform Rules for Contract Guarantee,URCG 325

　　Under the Uniform Rules for Contract Guarantee (URCG 325), there are three major types of contract guarantees: tender bonds, performance guarantees and repayment guarantees, and each of the parties involved has a different interest. The ICC Uniform Rules for Contract Guarantees aim to achieve a fair balance between the legitimate interests of all parties.

---

① 参见赵威编著:《国际结算——国际贸易融资支付方法》,东南大学出版社2003年版,第262—263页。
② 参见周辉斌:《银行保函与备用信用证法律实务》,中信出版社2003年版,第378页。

第三节　国际信托的法律适用

英国著名的法律史学家梅特兰(F. A. Maitland)曾指出:信托法是英国人对法学领域作出的最大贡献,是普通法皇冠上的宝石。①这并非是因为信托体现了基本的道德原则,而是由于它的灵活性,它是一种具有弹性和普遍性的制度。近现代的信托制度发源于英国,并在世界各国广泛传播。但是,无论是既有信托制度的英美法系国家,还是继受信托制度的大陆法系国家,其法律规定并非完全一致。此外,有些国家甚至没有信托或类似制度。如此一来,信托法律冲突就成为必然,从而需要确定国际信托的准据法。

一、信托的概念和法律特征

信托(trust),是指将自己的财产委托给足以信赖的第三者,使其按照自己的希望和要求进行管理和运用的法律制度。② 1984年《海牙信托公约》③给信托下了广泛的定义,其第2条第1项规定:"依据本公约的宗旨,信托关系是指由委托人所创立,为了受益人的利益或其他特定目的,以生前转移或遗嘱指定的方式将财产置于受托人控制下的一种法律关系。"

信托具有以下特点:第一,独立性,即信托财产是受托人财产之外的独立财产④;第二,以受托人名义或以代表受托人的另一个人的名义持有信托财产;第三,受托人有根据信托的条件和法律所加于他的特殊职责管理、使用或处分财产的权利和应尽的义务。

1984年《海牙公约》对信托的法律特征(**characteristics of trust**)作出了界定。

---

① 参见徐学鹿主编:《信托法》,人民法院出版社1999年版,第2页。
② 李双元主编:《国际私法学》,北京大学出版社2000年版,第292—293页。
③ 1984年10月,包括中国在内的36个国家参加的海牙国际私法会议第15次会议通过了《关于信托的法律适用及其承认公约》(简称1984年《海牙信托公约》)。
④ 有关信托财产的独立性,参见郭策:《信托财产独立性研究》,载沈四宝主编:《国际商法论丛》(第四卷),法律出版社2002年版,第502页。

> **【释义】** **Characteristics of Trust**
>
> A trust has the following characteristics—
>
> a) the assets constitute a separate fund and are not a part of the trustee's own estate;
>
> b) title to the trust assets stands in the name of the trustee or in the name of another person on behalf of the trustee;
>
> c) the trustee has the power and the duty, in respect of which he is accountable, to manage, employ or dispose of the assets in accordance with the terms of the trust and the special duties imposed upon him by law.
>
> The reservation by the settlor of certain rights and powers, and the fact that the trustee may himself have rights as a beneficiary, are not necessarily inconsistent with the existence of a trust.

二、国际信托法律适用的原则

（一）独立性原则

信托是一种独立形态的权利组合，这种组合既具有物权关系的内容，又具有债权关系的内容，还具有物权关系和债权关系所不能涵盖的内容。信托只有限地转移财产，而且持续时间长，它是一种有关受托人、受益人和财产管理人相互之间的持续的法律关系。因而，将有关财产转移的冲突法规则直接适用于信托并不总是合适的。英美法中的信托合同只要委托人一方同意即可有效，信托的成立以信托财产转移于受托人为标志，信托受益人对受托人不但有债权请求权，对信托财产还有物权请求权。因而，将有关合同之债的法律冲突规则直接适用于信托也是不合适的。信托法律关系的复杂性和特殊性决定了信托准据法（governing law of a trust）的决定应是一套独立的冲突法规则，既不能等同于物权的法律冲突规则，也不能等同于债权的法律冲突规则，也不能是二者的简单糅合。

（二）分类分割原则

信托种类繁多，设立方式多样。信托财产可能是动产或不动产，也可能二者兼有。受益人可能是他人、不特定的社会公众或委托人自己。这些不同类型的信托，有时甚至需要完全不同的法律选择规则来支配。同时，信托法律关系又极为复杂，同一信托所确立的权利义务关系又牵涉到信托财产的有效转移、信托收益权的有效设立、信托文件的解释、信托财产的管理、受托人的权利与义务及其违反信托的责任、收益的分配等问题。这些不同性质的问题应适用不同的法律选择规则。

（三）意思自治原则

在国际信托的法律选择上，当事人意思自治原则发挥着重要的作用。在信托方面,最重要的政策或者目标就是保证委托人处理信托财产的合法期待得以实现。所以,信托法律冲突的法律选择规则应着力体现这一目标和政策,优先考虑信托设立人的意思,只有在该意愿与当地公共政策或强行法规相抵触时才让位于后者。①

三、国际信托的法律适用

目前,解决国际信托法律冲突问题的主要途径仍然是采用传统的冲突法方法,对不同性质的信托加以分类,对同一信托的不同方面加以分割,分别适用不同的法律选择规则,从而以不同的实体法为准据法。

(一)信托有效性的法律适用

信托的有效性(validity of trusts),可分为形式有效性(指支配信托文件的有效性,例如约束遗嘱信托的法律)和实质有效性(指有效的信托文件中指定的支配信托有效性的法律)两个方面。

决定信托形式有效性的准据法为信托自体法、合同履行地法或立遗嘱人最后居住地法,信托的形式效力只要符合其中之一的规定,均为有效。一般情况下,决定信托形式有效性的准据法同样可以用来支配由此而产生的信托的实质有效性问题。

在缺乏当事人对准据法的选择时,信托的自体法将支配它的有效性,而且遗嘱信托的自体法应是立遗嘱人最后住所地法,生前信托的自体法应是与信托有最密切联系的法律。

设定信托的当事人的能力,对信托效力也有至关重要的影响。信托当事人的行为能力由其各自的属人法支配,或由信托自体法支配。②

(二)信托管理的法律适用

信托管理(**administration of trust**)的法律选择规则是信托法律适用的重要内容。

【释义】　　　　　　　　　**Administration of trust**

　　Once it is determined that the trust is valid, many legal questions concerning the administration of the trust may arise. The administration by the trustee is the action of the trustee in carrying out the duties of the trust. In what securities can he invest? What interest should he received on investment? To whom shall he pay the income? To whom should he render an ac-

---

① 参见齐湘泉主编:《涉外民事关系法律适用法》,人民出版社 2003 年版,第 181 页。
② 张茂、湘子:《国际信托法律适用问题初探》,载《法学评论》1996 年第 6 期。

count? There are question of administration of trust. A testamentary trust of movables is administered by the trustee according to the law of the state of the testator's domicile at the time of his death unless the will shows an intention that the trust should be administered in another state.

有关信托管理准据法,多数学者认为应适用信托财产管理地法。英国法院审理的**威尔克斯案**(Re Wilks)即持这一观点。

【案例】 威尔克斯案①

本案中,遗嘱人在加拿大安大略有住所,并死于该地。受托人受托管理死者位于英国的财产。对该信托管理,英国法院认为受托人符合英国法的管理行为是正当的,而没有适用遗嘱及信托有效性的准据法即安大略法。

对于采用信托管理地法作为信托管理的准据法也并非毫无争议。信托管理地法作为准据法主要存在两个问题:首先,当信托的效力由信托自体法支配时,管理地可能并没有信托制度。其次,关于如何确定信托管理地的问题,在管理地很容易确定时,我们可以直接适用信托管理地法。但是,当死亡人在两个以上的国家都有财产,并分别加以管理时,遗嘱信托的受托人可能会发现他的投资权利根据两个不同的管理地的法律是不同的。在数个受托人分别居住在不同的国家或受托人为一家信托公司,并在世界各地设有分支机构时,或对于特定信托的管理,虽然主要由一家分支机构来承担,但这一机构同时需要其他机构的协助时,管理地也难以确定。

对于信托管理事项的范围,英国国际私法学家戴西和莫里斯认为,应包括下列事项:(1) 受托人的权利义务;(2) 受托人违约的责任;(3) 何为收益,何为资本;(4) 如何确定受托人的投资为正当投资;(5) 谁可以任命一个新的受托人;(6) 谁不能被任命为受托人;(7) 法院对于信托的权力,给予忠告的权力;等等。②

(三) 信托文件的理解与解释的法律适用

信托构成的基本要素一般包括确定的信托财产、确定的受益人、确定的信托意图、确定的受托人。其中,既有客观要素,如确定的信托财产、受益人和受托人,也

---

① (1935) Ch.645, Ch. D.
② See Diecy & Morris, *Conflict of Laws*, 11th. ed., 1987, p.1075.

有主观要素,如信托意图。对于信托的客观要素,当事人一般较少发生争议,而对信托的主观要素进行解释时,往往会发生很大的争议。信托意图具有确定受托财产权具体范围和限制受托人财产权行使方式的法律效用。在全部信托条款中,信托意图条款具有核心地位。

关于信托解释可分为对生前动产信托和遗嘱动产信托文件的解释,对生前不动产信托和遗嘱不动产信托文件的解释。在前种情况下,如果委托人或立遗嘱人选择据以解释信托文件的法律,则按其办理;如未选择,对于有关管理事项的内容的解释,应依调整信托管理的法域的解释规则。对其他内容的解释应依信托自体法,在生前信托情况下,就是与信托有最密切联系的法律,在遗嘱信托的情况下,就是立遗嘱时的住所地法。在后种情况下,若委托人或立遗嘱人选择了解释信托文件或遗嘱的法律,则按其办理;如未选择,那么,该信托文件或遗嘱的解释应依信托财产所在地法院选择适用的法律。

(四) 信托变更的法律适用

英国 1958 年《信托变更法》(Variation of Trust Act) 第 1 条规定:若法院承认根据任何遗嘱或其他行为设立的信托,同样法院应当承认信托内容的变更或全部及部分撤销。在 1987 年《海牙公约》生效之前,英国法院认为其对信托变更问题的管辖权没有限制。Cross 法官在 **Re Paget's Settlement** 案中遵循了这一原则,变更了纽约法设立的信托。

【案例】　　　　　　　　　　Re Paget's Settlement[①]

Cross J., while accepting that he had jurisdiction to vary a settlement assumed to be governed by the law of New York, said: "Where there are substantial foreign elements in the case, the court must consider carefully whether it is proper for it to exercise the jurisdiction. If, for example, the court were asked to vary a settlement which was plainly a Scottish settlement, it might well hesitate to exercise its jurisdiction to vary the trusts, simply because some of, or even all, the trustees and beneficiaries were in this country. It may well be that the judge would say that the Court of Session was the appropriate tribunal to deal with the case".[②]

在公益信托的场合,法院可以命令按照捐赠人的意愿或尽可能地按该意愿使

---

① 1867 LR 4 Eq 655.
② Cross 法官在前述判例中提出"在那些有实在的涉外因素的案件中,应当慎重考虑行使管辖权是否适当。如果法院仅仅因为所有或某些受托人和受益人都在英国,就被请求变更一个纯粹的苏格兰信托,那么就很值得考虑了"。

用信托财产。如果在英国法院提出的申请所涉及的信托与外国有密切联系,这时英国法院也可以根据信托的本来目的或近似的目的发出变更信托的命令。在信托管理地在英国以外时,英国法院就不再拥有这种权力了。在这种情况下判例有两种解决办法:一是要求为指定的外国受托人在英国设立支付基金,这是在信托管理地法不存在信托概念时的通常做法。二是在存在信托概念的国家,英国法院可以要求受托人遵循实施管理地法院制定的信托计划。

(五) 我国有关信托法律适用的规定

我国自 2011 年 4 月 1 日起施行的《涉外民事关系法律适用法》第 17 条规定,当事人可以协议选择信托适用的法律。当事人没有选择的,适用信托财产所在地法律或者信托关系发生地法律。

四、《关于信托的法律适用及其承认的海牙公约》

(一)《海牙信托公约》概述

为解决国际信托法律冲突问题,第 15 届海牙国际私法会议于 1984 年 10 月通过了《关于信托的法律适用及其承认的公约》(Convention on the Law Applicable to Trusts and on Their Recognition),即《海牙信托公约》。《海牙信托公约》是国际社会在统一信托冲突法方面取得的主要成果之一,是迄今世界上唯一一部解决国际信托法律适用的统一冲突法公约。普通法系的英国、澳大利亚、加拿大、美国和大陆法系的法国、意大利、比利时、荷兰、卢森堡、塞浦路斯等已批准或签署了该公约,公约已于 1999 年 1 月 1 日开始生效。信托作为一种法律制度,并不像合同制度那样为各国普遍采用,它主要存在于普通法系国家。《海牙信托公约》正是试图解决在一些国家存在,而在另一些国家却不存在的信托法律制度,随着国际法律交往实践所产生的问题,按照瑞士国际私法学者冯欧弗贝克(von Overbeck)教授的说法,该公约正是寻求给民法法系的法官、公证员、律师提供一种理解和处理涉外信托的工具。[①]

《公约》第 1 条规定,该公约用于信托准据法的确定。《公约》第 2 条对信托关系进行了描述,通过对信托关系的特征界定来限制公约适用的范围(**scope of the application**)。

---

① See Generally the *Explanatory Report* of Alfred E. von Overbeck, Published by the Permanent Bureau of the Hague Conference (1986).

第十四章 国际金融关系的法律适用

【释义】　　　　　scope of the application

(Article 2) For the purposes of this Convention, the term "trust" refers to the legal relationships created—*inter vivos* or on death—by a person, the settlor, when assets have been placed under the control of a trustee for the benefit of a beneficiary or for a specified purpose.

《公约》第 3 条在第 1 条和第 2 条的基础上通过信托设立的方式对适用范围进行了限制。《公约》第 8 条（**Article 8 of the Convention**）对"信托的有效性、解释、效力以及管理"的准据法范围问题列出了 10 项具体规定，其意义虽然在于说明根据《公约》第 6 条和第 7 条确定的准据法的适用范围，但也从另一方面界定了公约的适用范围。①

【释义】　　　　　Article 8 of the Convention

The law specified by Article 6 or 7 shall govern the validity of the trust, its construction, its effects, and the administration of the trust.

In particular that law shall govern—

a) the appointment, resignation and removal of trustees, the capacity to act as a trustee, and the devolution of the office of trustee;

b) the rights and duties of trustees among themselves;

c) the right of trustees to delegate in whole or in part the discharge of their duties or the exercise of their powers;

d) the power of trustees to administer or to dispose of trust assets, to create security interests in the trust assets, or to acquire new assets;

e) the powers of investment of trustees;

f) restrictions upon the duration of the trust, and upon the power to accumulate the income of the trust;

g) the relationships between the trustees and the beneficiaries including the personal liability of the trustees to the beneficiaries;

h) the variation or termination of the trust;

i) the distribution of the trust assets;

j) the duty of trustees to account for their administration.

（二）《海牙信托公约》的法律适用制度

《海牙信托公约》第 6 条至第 9 条是规定国际信托关系法律适用（**applicable**

---

①　周玉华：《论国际信托公约中的几个问题》，载《武汉大学学报》（哲学社会科学版）1999 年第 1 期。

law of trust)的条款。《公约》设计的法律选择规则是用来取代信托国家现有规则的,这也就决定了《公约》的规定不可能离开普通法的实践太远,同时这些规则要融入大陆法系国家的国际私法规则中,因此它又不得不和大陆法系国家的法律选择原则相适应,并且需要使用大陆法系国家的法律工作者可以理解和运用的法律概念。①

【释义】　　　　　　　applicable law of trust

(Article 6) A trust shall be governed by the law chosen by the settlor. The choice must be express or be implied in the terms of the instrument creating or the writing evidencing the trust, interpreted, if necessary, in the light of the circumstances of the case.

Where the law chosen under the previous paragraph does not provide for trusts or the category of trust involved, the choice shall not be effective and the law specified in Article 7 shall apply.

(Article 7) Where no applicable law has been chosen, a trust shall be governed by the law with which it is most closely connected.

In ascertaining the law with which a trust is most closely connected reference shall be made in particular to (a) the place of administration of the trust designated by the settlor; (b) the situs of the assets of the trust; (c) the place of residence or business of the trustee; (d) the objects of the trust and the places where they are to be fulfilled.

(Article 9) In applying this Chapter a severable aspect of the trust, particularly matters of administration, may be governed by a different law.

---

1. 广泛适用当事人的意思自治原则

依据《海牙信托公约》第 6 条的规定,国际信托关系准据法可依当事人意思自治原则来确定。动产信托的设立人可以自由决定信托准据法,即承认当事人的意思自治原则。选择方式既包括明示选择也包括默示选择。明示选择是指在信托行为中,如信托合同或者有效遗嘱中,把意欲适用的法律以书面文字的形式明白表示出来。而默示选择是在信托文件中虽没有用文字明白表示出来所欲适用的法律为何国法律,但是从信托行为的内容和信托行为发生的状况来看,可以显示出或推定出所要选择的是何国的法律。

不论是明示,还是默示,都是当事人主观的意思表示。根据《公约》的规定,信托设立人选择法律的范围相当广泛:第一,不区分生前信托(*inter vivos* trusts)和遗

---

① 邹志洪:《论信托关系的法律适用》,载中国国际私法学会主办:《中国国际私法与比较法年刊》(第三卷),法律出版社 2000 年版,第 218 页。

嘱信托(testamentary trust, trust under will),也不界定动产信托和不动产信托,信托设立人都可以选择适用于信托的法律。第二,从《公约》的相关规定看,信托设立人有权选择任何法律,即使选择的法律与信托没有任何实际联系,只要选择的法律是信托国家的法律,并且不违反《公约》第13、15、16条关于不合理选择的限制性规则以及法院地强制性规则。第三,信托设立人可以选择不同的法律适用于信托的不同问题。不仅是在当事人意思自治的场合,在没有选择法律时也是如此。第四,信托设立人选择的法律是可以依情况而变更的。譬如,在某些紧急或者其他允许变化的场合,信托设立人可以改变信托管理地或适用于信托管理地的法律,并且法院也可以享有这种变更的权力。

2. 最密切联系原则

如果信托设立人未在信托行为中明确表示出愿意适用的法律为何国法律,并且信托行为的内容和信托行为发生的状况,都不能足以显示出或者暗示出所愿适用哪一国法律时,或者虽已选择了准据法,但因准据法的选择存在瑕疵,不能被法院地法认可时,则可依《海牙信托公约》第7条的规定适用与之有最密切联系的法律。为此,公约列举了四个与信托有最密切联系的连接点,即财产设立人指定的信托管理地、信托财产所在地、受托人的住所地或营业地,以及信托目的的履行地。在最终确定具有最密切联系的法律时,以上四个因素具有特别重要参考意义,当信托文书中找不到当事人明示或默式选择的法律时,它们应该作为一种事实因素纳入其考虑的范围之内。

3. 优先适用法院地国强制性规则

强制性规则也常被称为公共秩序,《海牙信托公约》对法院地国强制性规则的优先适用作出了明确的规定。《海牙信托公约》第15条旨在保证依法院地的冲突规则所选择的准据法中的强制性规则优先得到适用,不仅不能为其他法律所取代,也不能为《海牙信托公约》所排除。而且,《海牙信托公约》还列举出了一些具体的不能被排除适用的情形:本公约不阻碍法院地冲突规则指引的法律条款的适用,如果这些条款,特别是下列条项,不能以任意行为排除其适用:(1)对未成年人和无行为能力人的保护;(2)婚姻及于身份和财产的效力;(3)遗嘱继承和无遗嘱继承中的继承权,特别是配偶和亲属的不得取消的份额;(4)财产所有权和设定在财产上的担保权益的转移;(5)在破产事件中对债权人的保护;(6)在其他方面对善意第三人的保护。

第四节 国际保险的法律适用

一、国际保险的概念

国际保险(international insurance)是指具有国际因素从而涉及不同国家法律适用的保险。①国际保险对分担国际商事交易的风险具有重要的作用(**the role of insurance in international trade**)。

【释义】 　　　　the role of insurance in international trade

Under the common law, there is no general compulsion for a merchant to insure his goods while they are being shipped. However, commercial considerations often compel him to arrange insurance because, without insurance, it would be necessary for the merchant to set aside a large sum of money to cover possible losses. It would be pointless to hold such large sums in reserve against possible losses when, for a relatively small outlay (i.e., the premium), he could protect himself through insurance. Indeed, it is common sense for the merchant to insure his goods whilst in transit, especially when those goods have been financed on credit.

Insurance is, therefore, an essential element of commerce. While this is true for both domestic and international commerce. Insurance is most crucial in the international context, where there are greater risks involved. Because of the risks inherent in shipping goods across great distances, without insurance, export merchants would likely find it nearly impossible to obtain financing for their ventures. And without financing, the pool of merchants with enough capital to engage in international commerce would be small indeed. For these reasons the insurance policy has been, and remains, an essential part of any international sale of goods. ②

以国际保险活动的不同形式为基础,国际保险法律关系可以分为以下几类③:
第一,跨境销售保险合同法律关系。

---

① 参见龚柏华:《国际金融法新论》,上海人民出版社 2002 年版,第 128 页。
② Ademuni-Odeke, Insurance of F. O. B. Contracts in Anglo-American and Common Law Jurisdictions Revisited, 31 *Tul. Mar. L. J.* 425, 426—427 (2007).
③ 参见刘玮:《国际保险法释义与国际保险法学研究》,载《南开学报》2007 年第 4 期。

跨境销售保险合同方式是指一国(本国)的保险人不需要在另一国注册任何保险经营机构就可以把其在本国销售的保险产品通过网上销售或保险中介人的跨境服务等形式销售到另一国(东道国),该保险合同的投保方则是东道国的跨境保险销售产品的消费者。

第二,跨境经营方式下的保险合同法律关系。

如果一国的保险人在他国(东道国)注册保险经营机构,在他国销售保险产品,则在购买该保险产品的投保方和该保险人之间建立的保险合同法律关系也是一种国际保险合同法律关系。跨境经营方式下签订的保险合同中的保险人的经营地点与销售地点、消费地点、该保险合同的履行地点都在同一个地方——投保方和保障对象所在地(东道国)。

第三,境外消费方式下的保险合同法律关系。

境外消费方式下的国际保险活动是投保方(外国法人或自然人)因工作或其他社会活动需要到另一国家从事某种经济活动或社会活动的过程中,对其会遇到的各种各样的风险向其临时工作或生活地的保险人购买相关保险产品的行为。这种方式产生的保险合同法律关系中的保险人与投保方虽不属于同一国籍,但是保险人的经营地点、投保方的居住地、承保风险所在地、保险合同的履行地等都在保险人的经营所在地。

二、国际保险合同法律适用的一般原则

(一) 意思自治原则

意思自治原则意味着保险合同当事人可以自由选择调整其保险合同权利义务的准据法(**freedom of choice of law**)。

【说理】　　　　　　　　　freedom of choice of law

　　The freedom of choice of law in the field of consumer insurance is not a prerequisite, but rather an obstacle to the effective implementation of the freedom to provide services since consumers would not buy policies subject to foreign law through a choice of law clause. Therefore, the target of allowing the free choice of the applicable law could hardly be regarded as a sufficient justification for the harmonization of the substantive law of insurance contracts.[1]

---

[1] Juergen Basedow, The European Insurance Market, Harmonization of Insurance Contract Law, and Consumer Policy, 7 *Conn. Ins. L. J.* 495, 498(2000/2001).

如果当事人在订立合同时就订立了法律选择条款，一般不会产生疑问。但在保险实践中，当事人有时候在合同生效后再作出法律选择，对这种"浮动选法条款"的效力就有着很大的争议。英国法院不承认"浮动选法条款"。但在其他国家或地区，"浮动选法条款"的效力得到承认。《罗马公约》第3条第2款规定"双方当事人得在任何时候都约定使该合同适用一个并非原先适用于它的法律"，可见《罗马公约》对于国际保险合同法律选择的时间问题，没有对当事人加以限制。中国也允许当事人在保险合同成立时或成立后的任何时候选择其准据法。

当事人虽然可以明示或默示地选择保险合同的准据法，但这种选择必须满足一定条件才会被法院承认。当事人选择准据法首先受到一般的限制，即强制性规则和公共政策的限制，两者的适用实际上将减损当事人选择适用的法律的效力。

（二）保护弱方当事人原则

在国际保险合同中，保险人大多是资金雄厚，拥有众多专业人才的保险公司，被保险人或投保人却没有经验、财力又单薄，双方的议价能力、经济地位一般而言相差较大。投保人、被保险人面对保险公司事先印好的保单、面对保险公司指定的准据法要么全面接受，要么不接受，没有讨价还价的余地，因此常导致保险人所在地的法律（<u>law of the insurer</u>）被适用。

【说理】　　　　　　　　law of the insurer

The conflict of law rules relating to transportation and large risks, are based on the principle of free choice of law. Consequently, insurance companies would likely insert choice of law clauses into their policies declaring their own national law applicable. Therefore, transnational risk pools would in fact be governed by one single law of contract, the law of the insurer.

For insurance involving transportation and large risks, the Commission of the European Community focused on a conflict of laws solution dispensing with the harmonization of substantive law. In its 1979 draft directive, the Commission suggested guaranteeing the freedom to contract for the choice of law, in the first place, and to apply the law of the company's state of origin where no choice was agreed to by the parties.[①]

面对这样的情况，立法者或法官或者基于社会公共利益，或者基于对正义的追求，而倾向于限制意思自治原则在保险合同的法律适用中的显要地位。如美国《第二次冲突法重述》第192节下的"评论五"写道：即使（人身保险中）当事人之间存

---

① Juergen Basedow, The European Insurance Market, Harmonization of Insurance Contract Law, and Consumer Policy, 7 *Conn. Ins. L. J.* 495, 497 (2000/2001).

在法律选择的条款,如果这样的条款所指定的州的法律给予被保险人利益的保护低于依第 192 节本应适用的法律(这样的法律往往是投保时被保险人住所地所在州的法律)给予的保护,则法院是不会承认这样的法律选择条款的。但是如果当事人选择了被保险人住所地的法律,或保险人提供的格式合同中的法律选择条款提供了数个法律选择的可能,其中又包括了被保险人住所地的法律或该保险是团体人身保险或可以判断出当事人的议价实力相等,则当事人的法律选择仍是有效的。

这样,在保险合同的法律适用中运用保护弱势当事人基本权益(**protection of the basic rights of the insured**)的原则成为值得瞩目的趋势,它在某些场合下甚至可以超越意思自治原则。

【说理】　　protection of the basic rights of the insured

In relation to consumer insurance, a different solution was advocated. According to the Commission of European Community, contractual choice of law would be excluded and the applicable law would be the law of the company's state of origin. At the same time, the harmonization of insurance contract law should guarantee that basic rights of the insured are protected once the insured agrees upon a policy governed by foreign law.①

(三) 最密切联系原则

如果保险合同中既没有明示的法律选择条款,法院又找不到当事人默示选择的准据法,法院就将依照最密切联系原则来确定国际保险合同的准据法。各国保险合同冲突法的立法有的仅规定最密切联系原则,有的用特征履行方法来辅助确定,有的则在冲突法规则中根据最密切联系原则对准据法作出明确规定,并允许有所变通。在国际保险合同的法律适用中,美国《第二次冲突法重述》第 192 节和第 193 节规定之外的保险合同允许法院直接依最密切联系原则决定合同的准据法;针对其他的保险合同则规定先依具体的冲突规则,若其他州有与其更密切联系的法律则适用之。与美国不同的是,欧共体指令对于欧共体内部的国际保险合同,仅就非人身保险合同允许法院适用有限制的最密切联系原则,对于人身保险合同则基本直接规定了准据法。后者的规定更多的是依据"保护弱方当事人原则"而排除了最密切联系原则在具体案件中的适用可能。②

---

① Juergen Basedow, The European Insurance Market, Harmonization of Insurance Contract Law, and Consumer Policy, 7 *Conn. Ins. L. J.* 495, 498 (2000/2001).

② 刘玮:《欧盟保险市场一体化研究》,中国金融出版社 2004 年版,第 262 页。

【思考题】

- 什么是国际商业贷款？国际商业贷款通常适用什么法律？
- 国际银团贷款中的准据法有哪些特征？
- 国际贷款担保有哪些方式？国际贷款担保通常适用什么法律？
- 什么是国际独立担保？调整国际独立担保的国际惯例有哪些？
- 什么是信托？信托有哪些特点？
- 信托有效性、信托管理、信托构成及解释和信托变更分别适用什么法律？
- 试述海牙信托公约的法律框架及所构建的信托法律适用制度。
- 国际保险的法律适用有哪些特点？

【重要术语提示与中英文对照】

中文术语	英文对照
国际商业贷款	international commercial loan
国际贷款合同	international loan agreement
普兰提国际有限公司	Plenty International Ltd.
银团贷款	multi-lender financing
附属性担保	accessory guarantee
独立性担保	independent guarantee
担保物权	security interest
担保权益	secured interest
浮动担保	floating charge, floating lien
船旗国法律	law of the flag
船舶国籍	the nationality of the vessel
应收账款	trade debt receivable
"卡帕玛丽"轮	Kappa Mary
塞浦路斯共和国	The Republic of Cyprus
银行担保	bank guarantee
见索即付担保	demand guarantee
备用信用证	standby Letter of credit
独立保函和备用信用证公约	United Nations Convention on Independent Guarantees and Standby Letters of Credit
国际备用信用证惯例	International Standby Practices, ISP 98
合同担保统一规则	Uniform Rules for Contract Guarantee, URCG 325
信托	trust
信托的法律特征	characteristics of trust

信托的准据法	governing law of a trust
信托的有效性	validity of trusts
信托的管理	administration of trust
威尔克斯案	Re Wilks
信托变更法	Variation of Trust Act
关于信托的法律适用及其承认的公约	Convention on the Law Applicable to Trusts and on their Recognition
公约适用的范围	scope of the application
公约的第 8 条	Article 8 of the Convention
信托关系法律适用	applicable law of trust
生前信托	*inter vivos* trusts
遗嘱信托	testamentary trust, trust under will
国际保险	international insurance

【推荐阅读文献】

- 邹志洪:《英国关于信托的法律适用》,载《法学评论》1998 年第 1 期。
- 赵相林、耿勇:《国际信托关系的法律适用》,载《河南省政法管理干部学院学报》1999 年第 5 期。
- 郭洪俊:《国际银团贷款中的法律问题研究》,法律出版社 2001 年版。
- 杜涛:《国际经济贸易中的国际私法问题》,武汉大学出版社 2005 年版。
- 徐冬根:《国际金融法》,高等教育出版社 2006 年版。
- 徐冬根:《浮动担保法律问题比较研究》,上海交通大学出版社 2007 年版。
- 刘胜题:《国际商法:贸易与投融资》,商务印书馆 2007 年版。
- David J. Barru, Comparing Surety Bonds with Bank Guarantees and Standby Letters of Credit, 37 *Geo. Wash. Int'l L. Rev.* 51 (2005).
- K. T. Grozinger, Conflict of Laws and Trusts of Movables in Canada: An Update, 24 *Est., Tr. & Pensions J.* 285 (2005).
- T. M. Buckwold, The Conflict in Conflicts: Choice of Law in Canada-U. S. Secured Financing Transactions, 21 *Bank. & Fin. L. Rev.* 407 (2006).
- Ademuni-Odeke, Insurance of F. O. B. Contracts in Anglo-American and Common Law Jurisdictions Revisited, 31 *Tul. Mar. L. J.* 425 (2007).
- Eaton (M. M.), Feldman, (L. J.) & Chiang (J. C.), The Continuous Ownership Requirement in Shareholder Derivative Litigation: Endorsing a Common Sense Application of Standing and Choice-of-Law Principles, 47 *Willamette L. Rev.* 1 (2010).
- McClanahan (R. D.), Assignment, Delegation, and Choice of Law Provisions in Commercial Agreements, 57 *Prac. Law.* 15 (2011).

【扩展阅读资料】

Bank Guarantees and Standby Letters of Credit[①]

Performance bonds are less common outside of the United States. On international projects, contractor performance is usually guaranteed through the use of a bank guarantee or a standby letter of credit. These two instruments are functionally equivalent. Their primary difference pertains to nomenclature: Standby letters of credit are instruments issued by banks in the United States, whereas bank guarantees are instruments issued by banks throughout the rest of the world. In simplest terms, bank guarantees and standby letters of credit are undertakings or engagements whereby a bank, as opposed to a surety, promises to make payment to a third party—the beneficiary—on the presentation of documents that conform to the requirements set forth in the instrument itself. With these instruments, unlike U. S. -style performance bonds, the issuing bank merely makes payment to the beneficiary in the amount of the credit. The issuing bank will not be of further assistance in completing the project; rather, the beneficiary must determine independently how best to finish the job. Finally, after being required to pay on the beneficiary's demand, the issuing bank will then look to its customer, the credit applicant, for full reimbursement. In construction, the credit applicant is typically the contractor, and the beneficiary is the project owner. Guarantees or standby credits, however, are often used to guarantee subcontracts. In such a situation, the applicant is the subcontractor and the beneficiary is the contractor.

Bank guarantees and standby letters of credit have a long and well-established history. The precursors of these instruments first appeared in commerce nearly three thousand years ago, and use of these instruments has flourished in the intervening years "because of their inherent reliability, convenience, economy and flexibility." The U. S. Court of Appeals for the First Circuit has commented, "The very object of a letter of credit is to provide a near foolproof method of placing money in the beneficiary's hands when he complies with the terms contained in the letter [of credit] itself." On construction projects, these instruments provide the owner with powerful risk management tools. The owner may draw money without having to demonstrate or prove to the bank that the contractor is in default. At most, the owner will have to furnish a certificate or other documents asserting that the contractor is in default. For this reason, these instruments are inherently dangerous to the contractor who furnishes them.

[①] David J. Barru, Comparing Surety Bonds with Bank Guarantees and Standby Letters of Credit, 37 Geo. Wash. Int'l L. Rev. 51, 61—65 (2005).

Bank guarantees and standby letters of credit are "functionally equivalent." Both are credit instruments. The issuing bank merely has an obligation to pay the beneficiary the value of the instrument upon proper demand. The bank is not concerned with whether the parties have properly performed on the underlying contract. "As long as the international bank guarantee represents a primary obligation and depends on the submission of documents and not on compliance with any underlying obligation, the guarantee is essentially the same as the standby letter of credit." This separation of the credit transaction from the underlying transaction is referred to as the "independence principle," or sometimes the "autonomy principle." The one exception to the independence principle is the doctrine of fraud in the transaction.

Courts and commentators generally agree that the law of letters of credit applies to bank guarantees. Moreover, courts have generally regarded both letters of credit and bank guarantees as contracts and routinely use contract principles in their interpretation. There are, however, some formalistic differences between these instruments and traditional contracts. For example, contracts require consideration, whereas these instruments do not. Nonetheless, these differences are largely semantic and have little practical effect.

The most important characteristics of the bank guarantee or standby letter of credit are the ease and speed with which the beneficiary can obtain payment. These characteristics contrast sharply with those of the U. S.-style performance bond, which may require the bond obligee—the project owner—to convince the surety of the contractor's default before the surety will take action on the bond. To receive payment on a letter of credit or bank guarantee, the beneficiary need only make a presentment to the issuing bank that conforms to the requirements of the credit. These requirements can vary. In some cases a bare demand for payment from the beneficiary, usually by presentation of a site draft, is sufficient. No documentation of the applicant's default or non-performance on the underlying transaction is required. These instruments are known as "clean" or "suicide" credit. Clean guarantees are the most dangerous form of credit for the contractor in that they are the most susceptible to abusive calls by the beneficiary. To avoid the inherent risks associated with "clean" credits, "many standby credits require the beneficiary to present, along with his draft or demand, a certification reciting that... the applicant has failed to perform the underlying contract." This requirement is often satisfied with a simple written statement from the owner asserting that the contractor is in default. The beneficiary must make such certification with caution. False certification has been grounds for court-ordered injunctive relief preventing payment of the letter of credit based on fraud, and has been the basis

> for breach of warranty claims. Guarantees or standby letters of credit can be structured to afford the contractor more protection by requiring that the beneficiary submit a certification from an independent third party attesting to the contractor's nonperformance.

第十五章

国际民商事司法管辖权概论

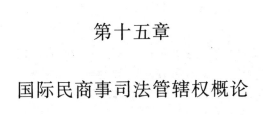

本章导读

※ 国际民商事司法管辖问题所涉及和解决的是某一特定的国际民商事案件究竟应由哪一个国家的法院管辖的问题。

※ 属地管辖权,是各国行使国际民商事诉讼案件管辖的最基本的管辖权。属地管辖原则,是以地域因素作为确定案件管辖权的标准。只要涉外案件的当事人、诉讼标的物或被告的财产位于一国或地区领域之内,或者法律事实发生在一国或地区领域之内的,该国法院即对该案件有管辖权。

※ 1945 年,美国联邦最高法院在国际鞋业公司诉华盛顿一案中,修正了对司法管辖权的严格属地限制,确立了"最低限度联系"标准。

※ 属人管辖权,是以当事人的国籍作为依据而行使的管辖权。凡涉案当事人,无论原告或被告,只要具有某国国籍,即构成了该国行使管辖权的根据。它侧重于诉讼当事人的国籍,强调一国法院对于涉及本国国民的国际民商事案件都具有受理、审判的权利。

※ 协议管辖权,又称合意管辖权,是指当事人达成书面或口头协议,指定将可能发生的纠纷交由某国法院审理而形成的管辖权。

※ 专属管辖权,也称为独占管辖权或排他管辖权,是指一国法院对某些特定的案件所享有的排他管辖权,即国家对特定范围内的民商事案件无条件地保留其受理诉讼和作出裁决的权利,从而排除其他国家法院对这类民商事案件的管辖权。

※ 有时与案例有关的各种连接因素分布在不同的国家,各国均可以根据其中一个或者多个连接因素对案件行使管辖权。这是就是国际民商事诉讼法中的共同管辖权。

※ 挑选法院,又称为择地行诉,是原告为了获得司法上的利益而选择一个可能会对自己作出最有利判决的法院提起诉讼,从而避免在对自己不利的法院进行诉讼的行为。

※ 不方便法院原则,是英美普通法项下法院拒绝行使管辖权的一种重要制度。当法院认为某个案件在另一个法院审理对当事人更方便、更符合正义的要求时,以法官自由裁量权拒绝行使管辖权。民商事诉讼案被告有时也可能以"不方便法院"为理由,拒绝接受立案法院的管辖或者要求更换其他具有管辖权的法院管辖。

【本章主题词】 属地管辖权、对人管辖权、对物管辖、最低限度联系、长臂管辖权、属人管辖权、挑选法院、不方便法院

第一节 国际民商事管辖权概述

一、国际民商事管辖权的概念

韩德培教授认为,国际民商事案件管辖权(**jurisdiction**)是指一国法院或具有审判权的其他司法机关受理、审判具有国际因素或涉外因素的民商事案件的权限。国际民商事案件管辖问题所涉及和解决的是某一特定的国际民商事案件究竟应由哪一个国家的法院管辖的问题。① 李双元教授认为国际民商事管辖权是指一国法院根据本国缔结的或参加的国际条约和国内法对特定的涉外民商事案件行使审判权的资格。② 站在一国法院的角度上,国际民商事管辖权亦称为涉外民商事管辖权。

【释义】   Jurisdiction

Jurisdiction is a word susceptible of several different meanings, but the sense in which it is used in the present account is the power of a court to hear and determine an issue upon which its decision is sought.③

二、国际民商事管辖权的意义

管辖权不仅是国家审理有关国际民商事案件的前提条件(**preliminary issue**),而且影响案件的判决结果,从而影响当事人的合法权益。由于各国实体法、程序法和冲突法各不相同,在不同国家进行诉讼要适用不同的程序规则,根据不同国家的冲突规范可能导致适用不同的实体法,从而导致不同的判决结果。

---

① 参见韩德培主编:《国际私法新论》,武汉大学出版社1998年版,第617页。
② 参见李双元、金彭年、张茂、欧福勇:《中国国际私法通论》,法律出版社2003年版,第513页。
③ P. M. North, *Cheshire and North: Private International Law*, 10th ed., London: Butterworths, 1979, p.77.

【说理】   preliminary issue

The question of which law is applicable in any given case will therefore very much depend on the perspective from which it is raised. In practice this amounts to saying that it depends on where the action will be brought. This in turn means that there is an issue that is preliminary even to that of conflicts law, i.e., the one of jurisdiction. ①

所以,国际民商事案件管辖权问题不仅为各国立法者和司法者所关注,也为当事人高度重视。②当今世界各国都很重视并争夺国际民商事管辖权,不但规定对与本国有某种联系的涉外民商事案件具有管辖权,而且还往往规定,即使案件跟本国没有联系,但如果争议双方当事人合意选择本国法院管辖的,本国法院也可以行使管辖权。③因此,争取合法地解决并合理获取国际民商事管辖权,对保护本国公民、法人和国家的民商事利益有着重要意义。④在国际民商事诉讼中,国际民商事管辖权具有十分重要的意义,具体表现在以下几个方面:首先,正确解决国际民商事管辖权,关系到维护国家的主权。⑤其次,正确解决国际民商事管辖权,是进行国际民商事诉讼程序的前提。只有先确定一国法院具有对某一涉外民商事案件的管辖权之后,才能开始国际民商事诉讼的其他程序,如诉讼文书的域外送达、域外调查取证,以及判决的域外承认与执行等。最后,正确解决国际民商事管辖权,不但有利于诉讼当事人双方进行诉讼活动和法院的审判活动,也有利于判决的域外承认与执行。

第二节 属地管辖权

属地管辖权(territorial jurisdiction)是各国行使国际民商事诉讼案件管辖的最基本的管辖权。属地管辖原则,也称为地域管辖原则,是以地域因素作为确定案件管辖权的标准。只要涉外案件的当事人、诉讼标的物或被告的财产位于一国或地

---

① See Luca G. Radicati Di Brozolo, International Payments and Conflicts of Laws, 48 *Am. J. Comp. L.* 307, 310 (2000).
② 参见肖永平:《国际私法原理》,法律出版社 2003 年版,第 336 页。
③ 参见李双元、金彭年、张茂、欧福勇:《中国国际私法通论》,法律出版社 2003 年版,第 514 页。
④ 参见李双元主编:《国际私法》,北京大学出版社 2000 年版,第 347 页。
⑤ 参见张仲伯:《国际私法》(修订本),中国政法大学出版社 1999 年版,第 409 页。

区领域之内,或者法律事实发生在一国或地区领域之内的,该国法院即对该案件有管辖权。

一、对人管辖权与对物管辖权

在英美法系,根据行使管辖权的依据不同,法院的属地管辖权形成不同的属地管辖权类别,一般可以分为对人管辖权和对物管辖权两大类。

（一）对人管辖权

对人管辖权(**personam jurisdiction**)是指可以对诉讼当事人作出判决的管辖权。在英美法中,凡是涉及钱财的判决,或命令诉讼当事人采取特定行为的判决,法院均以此为依据行使管辖权。

【释义】　　　　　　　　personam jurisdiction

If the defendant has personal contacts with the state, the court may exercise in personam jurisdiction over the defendant. A court with that sort of jurisdiction may render a personal judgment against the defendant that can be satisfied out of any property of hers with the state. A personal judgment creates a judgment debt against her that may be enforced in other states.①

对人管辖权,按照普通法的规定,只有在本国或本州境内向被告直接送达传票或被告本人服从管辖时才开始生效。但成文法把该规则大为放宽,只要被告的住所、居所、国籍、侵权行为地、营业地等在本国或本州境内或与法院所在地国(州)有某种合理的最低限度的联系时,也可对外国或外州的被告发出拟制的传票行使管辖权。②

（二）对物管辖权

有时,法院对当事人并无管辖权,但是由于与案件有关的财产位于法院所在地,法院便以此作为管辖的依据,这类管辖称为对物管辖权(**jurisdiction in rem**)

【释义】　　　　　　　　jurisdiction in rem

"Rem" is a Latin word which means the power against the thing. Originally, the notion

---

① See William Richman & William Reynolds, *Understanding Conflict of Laws*, 3d ed., 2002, pp. 121—122.

② 参见邹喻、顾明主编:《法学辞典》,中国政法大学出版社1991年版,第398页。

of *in rem* jurisdiction arose in situations in which property was identified but the owner was unknown. Courts fell into the practice of styling a case usually followed by a notice by publication seeking claimants to title to the property. This last style is awkward because in law, only a person may be a party to a judicial proceeding, and a non-person would at least have to have a guardian appointed to represent its interests, or the interests of the unknown owner.

Within the US federal court system, jurisdiction in rem typically refers to the power a federal court may exercise over large items of moveable property, or real property, located within the court's jurisdiction. Within the US state court system, jurisdiction in rem may refer to the power the state court may exercise over real property or personal property or a person's marital status. State courts have the power to determine legal ownership of any real or personal property within the state's boundaries.

有关对物的管辖的典型案例是**United States v. Forty Barrels and Twenty Kegs of Coca-Cola**案。

【案例】　United States v. Forty Barrels and Twenty Kegs of Coca-Cola[①]

It was a case under the 1906 Pure Food and Drug Act. At issue was whether the Coca-Cola company had adulterated the product by adding artificial caffeine, and whether Coca-Cola was misbranded because both coca and cola, originally the two main "medicinal" ingredients, had been all but removed from the product at that time.

二、基于被告住所地的管辖权

以住所地尤其以被告住所地为确定管辖权的依据，即由原告向被告住所地国家的法院提起诉讼。这一制度起源于罗马法的"原告就被告法院"(*Actor sequiter forum rei*)原则。由于被告的住所地是被告生活活动的中心，理应与案件有较为密切的联系。这是属地管辖原则中最常用的一种制度。

属地管辖权所涉及的法律关系总是与一国的管辖权具有某种空间上的联系，这种空间上的联系就是所谓的地域基础。它侧重于有关法律事实或法律行为的地域性质或属地性质，强调一国法院对其领域内的一切人和物以及法律事件和行为都具有管辖权，包括以被告的住所地和惯常居所地为标志、以物之所在地为标志与以法律事实发生地为标志作为其管辖权的基础。

这一制度不仅被大陆法系国家所采用，也为许多普通法系国家所采纳。在一

---

① 241 U.S. 265 (1916).

般情况下,除了纯属人身关系的案件外,其他涉及金钱与财产纠纷的案件,被告住所地往往就是其主要的财产所在地。这样,法院就可以比较方便地对涉讼财产采取诉讼保全措施,以利于判决的执行。所以,这一管辖制度为世界上大多数国家所接受。①

三、基于财产所在地的管辖权

基于财产所在地的管辖权,即以诉讼标的物所在地或被告财产所在地作为标志确定管辖权。自13、14世纪由意大利著名法学家、冲突法的鼻祖巴托鲁斯创立法则说时就得到冲突法学者的支持与肯定,并在各国的立法中得以体现。诉讼标的物位于一国领域之内,就意味着与该国有着客观的、空间上的联系,这也是一国行使管辖权的重要依据。由于诉讼标的物通常是诉讼当事人间诉争的财产,而被告的财产是保障判决得以执行的基础,以财产所在地作为法院行使管辖权的依据,不仅有利于法院强制执行,而且有利于保障当事人的合法权益。基于这一优点,世界各国普遍承认这一管辖制度。

第三节 最低限度联系与长臂管辖权

一、国际鞋业公司案

1945年,美国联邦最高法院在国际鞋业公司诉华盛顿(**International Shoe Co. v. Washington**)一案中,修正了对司法管辖权的严格属地限制,确立了"最低限度联系"标准。联邦最高法院认为:"被告须与一州有某种'最低限度联系',使该州法院能够行使管辖权并不违反传统的公平与实质正义观念"②。

【案例】 **International Shoe Co. v. Washington**③

Facts: International Shoe is a Delaware company based in St. Louis. They have some

---

① 参见丁伟主编:《冲突法论》,法律出版社1996年版,第271页。
② 参见郭玉军、甘勇:《美国法院的长臂管辖权——兼论确立国际民事案件管辖权的合理性原则》,载《比较法研究》2000年第3期。
③ International Shoe Co. v. Washington, 326 U.S. 310 (1945).

salesmen on commission in the state of Washington but don't have any offices there. Washington is trying to get the company to ante up for its unemployment fund. Washington served Shoe notice of assessment by personally delivering it to one of their salesmen in Washington as well as sending registered mail to their home office in St. Louis.

Procedural Posture: Shoe made a special appearance in Washington to argue that the service of process on the salesman was not proper and that Shoe wasn't doing business in Washington according to the statute. The courts in Washington found that Shoe was amenable to personal jurisdiction in that state. Shoe appealed up to the U.S. Supreme Court.

Issue: Under what conditions is a corporation subject to personal jurisdiction in a particular state?

Rule: A corporation that is protected by the laws of a state shall be subject to personal jurisdiction in that state.

Analysis: The court interprets the due process clause and the Fourteenth Amendment to mean that if a company has "sufficient contacts" in a state, they may be subject to being sued in that state.

Chief Justice Stone relies upon the concept of "fair play", whereas Justice Black takes a harder line and says that under more or less no circumstances should a state's law be found not to apply simply because it doesn't meet the court's standard of "fair play".

Conclusion: The Supreme Court upheld the lower court's ruling for the state of Washington.

本案中,原告国际鞋业公司成立于特拉华州,其主要营业地在密苏里州,1937年至1940年间,国际鞋业公司在华盛顿州雇用了十几名华盛顿的居民为其公司的推销员。该公司在华盛顿州没有办公室,除了让这些推销员在华盛顿州为其征集订单外,公司在华盛顿没有其他的商业活动,推销员有时在该州租用房间作为公司产品的展厅,租金由公司报销,推销员没有被授权签订合同,推销员的佣金总额为3.1万美元,华盛顿州政府依其法律提起诉讼,试图基于该公司付给居住在本州的推销员的佣金而向公司征收失业救济金。国际鞋业公司在一审败诉后向联邦最高法院提起上诉。① 国际鞋业公司辩称其不是华盛顿州的公司,在华盛顿州也没有"营业活动",因而公司没有"出现"在华盛顿州。该公司认为,华盛顿州法院对其不具有管辖权,其行使管辖权违反了宪法的"正当程序"的规定。

美国联邦最高法院 Stone 大法官认为,如果法院要对被告行使对人的管辖权,而被告没有出现在法院地州,正当程序要求被告与法院地存在着最低限度的联系,以便使法院行使管辖权不会违反传统的公平和实质正义。② 虽然国际鞋业公司不

---

① 参见李智:《美国最低联系标准评析》,载《福建政法管理干部学院学报》2005年第1期。
② Int'l Shoe, 326 U.S. at 311.

第十五章　国际民商事司法管辖权概论

是在华盛顿州成立的,其主要营业地也不在华盛顿州,但由于涉及本案的缴纳义务直接产生于被告在华盛顿州的活动,因此华盛顿州法院对该案行使管辖权是合宪的。①

国际鞋业公司诉华盛顿案允许一个州在适当的情况下对无法在州内送达的被告行使管辖权,而这个适当情况则是指被告与法院地存有最低限度联系且行使管辖权不会违反传统的公平和实质正义的观念。在该案所确立的最低限度联系标准中,在州内送达已不再作为行使管辖权的限制,州的管辖权被扩大,法院的送达也可以跨出本州。对州法院行使管辖权的判断实际上被分成两个部分,即是否存有最低限度联系,以及依在存在最低限度联系的前提下行使管辖权是否合理。

在该案中,最高法院对宪法"正当程序条款"限制下的属人管辖权作出了全新的发展:在历史上,法院在属人诉讼中的管辖权产生于其对被告人身的实际支配能力,因此被告出现在法院所管辖的地域内是被告受法院判决拘束的前提条件。正当法律程序所要求的仅是,如果被告没有出现在法院的辖区,法院要想使其服从于属人诉讼的判决,则被告与法院之间应有某种最低限度联系。最高法院认为,符合法律的最低限度联系的数量和种类取决于诉讼的起因是否产生于该联系。如果诉讼的起因产生于该联系,则即使是单一的独立的联系也足以使被告隶属于该州法院的对人管辖。如果诉讼的起因不产生于该联系,则需要确定该联系是否是连续的、系统的和实质性的,以至于能够使被告在法院应诉是公正合理的。国际鞋业公司诉华盛顿案是美国司法管辖权中对人管辖权确立"最低限度联系"的标志性案件。②该案是美国民商事管辖权理论与实践的一个重要里程碑。

二、最低限度联系原则

最低限度联系(minimum contacts),也称为最低限度接触。什么是最低限度联系?③美国最高法院从来没有下过定义。它在1958年的一个判决中指出,最低限度联系是被告以某种行为有目的地在法院地州从事活动并接受该州法律赋予的利益和保护,由此可见,这一概念具有相当的灵活性。

---

① See Daniel E. Wanat, Copyright Infringement Litigation and the Exercise of Personal Jurisdiction Within Due Process Limits: Judicial Application of Purposeful Availment, Purposeful Direction, or Purposeful Effects Requirements to Finding that a Plaintiff Has Established a Defendant's Minimum Contacts Within the Forum State, 59 *Mercer L. Rev.* 553, 560 (2008).

② Susan Nauss Exon, A New Shoe Is Needed to Walk Through Cyberspace Jurisdiction, 11 *Alb. L. J. Sci. & Tech.* 1, n1 (2000).

③ 一般认为,最低限度联系原则,是指案件被告在法院辖区内有没有交易行为和民事侵权行为,法院要对案件行使管辖权,则被告和该法院间应存在某种最低限度的接触,这种才能满足适当程序条款和公平原则的要求。

法院在确定是否存在最低限度联系时,需要考虑两个因素:第一,当事人与法院之间是否存在最低限度联系;第二,法院的分析是否符合"公平与实质正义"。①

最低限度联系原则对法院涉外案件管辖权的确定具有重要意义。这一原则使法院管辖权的行使不再拘泥于被告的住所、居所等硬性因素而代之以更灵活的管辖权依据。"最低限度联系"原则开始取代传统的"权力支配"理论,成为新的管辖依据。

当前美国司法实践普遍承认,只要不违反基本的正当程序原则,如果被告与某州法院地有着最低限度的联系,则该州法院对其有对人管辖权。但是,美国法院运用"最低限度联系"标准行使管辖权并不是没有限度的,它要符合"正当程序"的标准。

三、正当程序

正当程序条款(due process clause)源于美国《宪法修正案》第14条(U. S. Constitution Amendment XIV)。该条款主要内容是"各州不得制定或执行剥夺美国公民特权或豁免权的法律,也不得未经正当法律程序剥夺人民的生命、自由或财产"②。在法院的对人管辖案件中,如果一个非居民被告没有在法院地"出现"(physical presence),则必须符合正当程序条款,即案件必须与法院地有最低限度的联系(have minimum contacts with a forum state),以满足传统管辖理论中的公正原则和实质正义。③

在进行正当程序分析时,法官引入了三个标准,即相关性标准(relatedness)、有意利用标准(purposeful availment)和合理性标准(reasonableness)。相关性标准要求被告的活动要与原告的诉讼原因有一定的联系。对相关性作出要求有两大意义:一是把特殊管辖权和一般管辖权区分开;二是因果关系是正当程序分析的一个要求。有意利用标准是指作为非法院地居民的被告有意地利用法院地州的法律所提供的保护和利益。合理性标准要求行使管辖权要符合传统的实质正义和公平原则。对合理性标准可以从以下几个因素进行认定:被告出庭的经济问题、法院对于该案是否有利益、是否方便法院以及公正性,等等。正当程序条款要求法院在确定涉外案件管辖权时又必须审查是否符合最低限度联系的要件,因而表现为对管辖权无限扩张的一种理性制约。

---

① World-Wide Volkswagen Corp. v. Woodson, 444 U. S. 286, 291 (1980).
② 该条款原文是:No State shall make or enforce any law which shall abridge the privileges or immunities of citizens of the United States; nor shall any State deprive any person of life, liberty, or property, without due process of law.
③ International Shoe, 326 U. S. at 316.

四、长臂管辖权

最低限度联系标准使得美国的管辖权大为扩张,因此一些学者把美国这种行使管辖权的特点称为"长臂管辖权"(long arm jurisdiction)。①美国伊利诺伊州是第一个制定长臂管辖权法的州。紧随其后,美国的其他州也相继制定了长臂管辖权法。

美国法院对个人司法管辖权的根据有:出现、住所、居所、国籍、同意、作为被告出庭、作为原告出庭、在该州执业、在州内完成的行为和在他处完成但对州内造成影响的行为。②一般来说,法院行使管辖权要遵循两个步骤:首先要分析法院行使管辖权是否满足法院地州的长臂法规;其次,要分析法院行使管辖权是否满足联邦宪法第14修正案的"正当程序条款"。③美国法院在诉讼法实践中也是遵循这两个步骤来行使长臂管辖权的。马萨诸塞州的长臂法规规定,要对被告行使管辖权需要满足:(1)被告在马州有营业活动;(2)被告在州内从事侵权行为;(3)在州外从事侵权行为并在州内造成损害。

在 Digital Equipment Corporation v. Altavista Technology 一案中,法官认为被告的网络行为以及通过网站在马萨诸塞州进行销售和宣传的行为构成了"在马州从事营业活动"。

【案例】 Digital Equipment Corporation v. Altavista Technology④

原告的搜索引擎公司位于马萨诸塞州,该搜索引擎的网站名字为 Altavista。原告与被告(即加利福尼亚州的 Altavista Technology 公司)签订了一份商标权使用许可协议。原告许可被告使用该商标作为其企业的名称和网站域名,但不得作为产品和服务的名称使用。许可协议签订后的两个月,一名网站浏览者发现被告的网站已经开始使用该商标进行产品的宣传和销售活动。并且也开通了以"Digital's Alta Vista"为命名的搜索引擎服务。原告以被告违反商标权使用许可协议和侵权商标权为由向马萨诸塞州地区法院提起上诉。该法院认为被告的网络行为以及在马萨诸塞州的销售和广告行为构成了"在马州从事营业活动"。

在用马萨诸塞州的长臂法规和正当程序分析该案的管辖权前,主审法官表达了这

---

① 参见徐伟功、柳絮:《电子合同管辖权问题探讨——基于欧美和海牙国际私法会议的立法与实践》,载《东方论坛》2005年第6期。
② 李双元、谢石松:《国际民事诉讼法概论》,武汉大学出版社2001年版,第235—237页。
③ 郭玉军、向在胜:《网络案件中美国法院的长臂管辖权》,载《中国法学》2002年第6期。
④ 960 F. Supp. 456.

样一种观点。他认为,本案与马萨诸塞州的"最低联系"不是传统意义上的联系。在经济逐渐全球化的浪潮中,法官应重新评价传统对人管辖权及一些相关的概念。相比以前,对因特网的商业性利用更加检验出传统的以地域为基础的管辖权基础的局限性。因特网打破了传统地域管辖权的界限。当买方和卖方通过因特网进行商业交易时,没有必要通过确定一个物理性质的连接点来决定双方当事人是否要服从对人管辖权。同时该法官也认为,现在就对有广泛争议的网络管辖权问题制定一个宽泛的标准是不必要的,也是不合时宜的。①

马萨诸塞州法官在上述 Digital Equipment Corporation 案中,通过对相关性标准、有意利用标准和合理性标准三个指标的分析后,认为该州法院对被告行使管辖权是符合正当程序标准的。

长臂管辖权理论表明,即使一个非居民被告没有在法院地出现,只要他与法院地有某种联系或有意地与法院地建立了某种联系,法院就倾向于对被告行使一种特别管辖权,这就为扩大州法院的管辖权开辟了一条道路。

五、国际大众公司案与"有意利用"标准

到了 20 世纪 80 年代,"最低限度联系"说又得到了进一步发展。在 1980 年的"国际大众公司诉伍德森"(**World-Wide Volkswagen Corp. v. Woodson**)一案中,美国最高法院将"有意利用"作为判定"最低限度联系"的一个基本标准:即如果被告为自己利益有意地利用法院地的商业或其他条件,以取得在法院地州从事某种活动的权利,进而得到该州法律上的利益与保护,则该州法院可以行使管辖权。这种标准实际上是强调行为的目的性和可预见性。美国最高法院在以后的案件中将这一标准限定在三个方面:(1) 被告是否有意地利用法院地州的有利条件;(2) 原告的诉因是否产生于被告在法院地州的行为;(3) 管辖权的行使是否公正合理。

【案例】　**World-Wide Volkswagen Corp. v. Woodson**②
New York residents Harry and Kay Robinson purchased a new Audi automobile from petitioner Seaway Volkswagen, Inc. (Seaway), in New York, in 1976. The following year the Robinson family, who resided in New York, left that State for a new home in Arizona. As they

---

① 参见徐伟功、柳絮:《电子合同管辖权问题探讨——基于欧美和海牙国际私法会议的立法与实践》,载《东方论坛》2005 年第 6 期。
② 444 U.S. 286; 100 S. Ct. 559; 62 L. Ed. 2d 490; 1980 U.S. LEXIS 65.

passed through the State of Oklahoma, another car struck their Audi in the rear, causing a fire which severely burned Kay Robinson and her two children. The Robinsons subsequently brought a products-liability action in the District Court for Creek County, Okla., claiming that their injuries resulted from defective design and placement of the Audi's gas tank and fuel system.

Petitioners, which were incorporated in New York and did business there, entered special appearances, claiming that, because they had no minimal contacts with the state, Oklahoma's exercise of jurisdiction over them would violate their rights under the Due Process Clause of U.S. Const. amend. XIV. The Oklahoma trial court rejected petitioners' claim, and petitioners sought a writ of prohibition in the Oklahoma supreme court to restrain respondent, a state trial judge, from exercising in *personam* jurisdiction over them. The state supreme court denied the writ, holding that personal jurisdiction was authorized by Oklahoma's long-arm statute, Okla. Stat. tit. 12, §1701.03(a)(4) (1971).

On certiorari, the U.S. Supreme Court reversed on due process grounds, finding that petitioners had no contacts, ties, or relations with the State of Oklahoma. The Court reversed the state supreme court's denial of a writ of prohibition.

本案中，根据上述"最低限度联系"标准，美国最高法院否决了俄克拉荷马州的管辖权，法院指出，被告在俄克拉荷马州没有任何的商业活动，没有销售和服务行为，没有通过销售人员招揽生意，也没有在该州做广告。因此，被告并没有使自己置于俄克拉荷马州的法律所赋予的权利和利益之下。①所以，法院提出了根据最低联系行使管辖权的标准是某一商品被置于商业流程之中并且到达法院地的事实是可以合理预见的，因此，被告能否合理预见到其行为与法院地的联系是法院能否行使管辖权的关键。②

第四节 其他管辖权

一、属人管辖权

属人管辖权（personal jurisdiction），是以当事人的国籍作为依据而行使的管辖

---

① 参见李智：《美国最低联系标准评析》，载《福建政法管理干部学院学报》2005 年第 1 期。
② Daniel E. Wanat, Copyright Infringement Litigation and the Exercise of Personal Jurisdiction Within Due Process Limits: Judicial Application of Purposeful Availment, Purposeful Direction, or Purposeful Effects Requirements to Finding that a Plaintiff Has Established a Defendant's Minimum Contacts Within the Forum State, 59 *Mercer L. Rev.* 553, 560 (2008).

权。凡涉案当事人,无论原告或被告,只要具有某国国籍,即构成了该国行使管辖权的根据。它侧重于诉讼当事人的国籍,强调一国法院对于涉及本国国民的国际民商事案件都具有受理、审判的权利。以法国为代表的拉丁法系国家,包括意大利、荷兰、卢森堡和希腊等欧洲大陆国家,除了以被告住所地为依据外,很大程度上采取属人管辖原则。①这些国家立法的目的是为了保护本国当事人的利益,但是过于保护本国当事人的利益就必然会置外国当事人于不利地位,因此,这一原则未能在国际社会得到普遍的承认。

二、协议管辖权

协议管辖权(consensual jurisdiction),又称合意管辖权,或当事人意思自治原则,是指当事人达成书面或口头协议,指定将可能发生的纠纷交由某国法院审理而形成的管辖权。协议管辖是当事人意思自治这一法律适用原则在管辖权原则上的延伸和体现,是对属人管辖和属地管辖原则的变更和补充。

协议管辖原则自法国法学家杜摩兰首先提出以来,陆续被法国、意大利、英国、美国等国采用,成为目前国际社会普遍承认和采用的一项原则。各国的立法和司法实践都对该原则的具体适用作出了一定的限制,如当事人不能选择与案件没有任何联系的法院。我国2008年施行的《民事诉讼法》第242条规定,有关当事人只能用"书面形式"选择与争议有"实际联系"的法院作管辖法院。②

目前国际上的一般趋势是有条件地承认协议管辖的效力,这些条件是:第一,仅限于财产权请求的诉讼,当事人可以协议指定管辖权法院,而对婚姻等影响国内公共利益的案件,不在此列。第二,即使是财产请求权的诉讼,若涉及一国的专属管辖,当事人不得以任何方式加以排斥。例如作为通例,不动产诉讼由不动产所在地法院专属管辖。第三,一些国家以当事人选择与案件存在某种联系的地点作为允许其协议管辖的前提,如涉及合同纠纷,应以合同订立地、履行地等连接因素为条件;另一些国家则允许当事人将案件提交与此不存在任何联系的第三国法院审理。③

三、专属管辖权

专属管辖权(**exclusive jurisdiction**),也称为独占管辖权或排他管辖权,是指一国法院对某些特定的案件所享有的排他的管辖权,即国家对特定范围内的民商事

---

① 参见黄进主编:《国际私法》(第二版),法律出版社2005年版,第893页。
② 肖永平:《国际私法原理》,法律出版社2003年版,第339页。
③ 丁伟主编:《冲突法论》,法律出版社1996年版,第274页。

案件无条件地保留其受理诉讼和作出裁决的权利,从而排除其他国家法院对这类民商事案件的管辖权。

【释义】 **exclusive jurisdiction**

Courts may also have jurisdiction that is exclusive. Where a court has exclusive jurisdiction over a territory or subject matter, it is the only court that is authorized to address that matter.

根据一国的法律或其所缔结的国际条约的规定,某些涉外案件只能由该国法院管辖,其他国家法院均无权管辖,当事人也不能通过协议来变更专属管辖。由于某些特定案件的特殊性,只有专属于某一国家的法院管辖,才能确保查清案情,便于执行,当今世界上大多数法律体系中都包含有专属管辖这种制度。①它强调一国法院对于那些与其国家国民的根本利益密切相关的案件,如涉及国家公共政策或重要的政治和经济问题的民商事案件无条件地享有管辖权,从而排除其他国家法院对该类民商事案件的管辖。②如各国普遍接受因不动产权利提起的诉讼由不动产所在地法院专属管辖。

从上可见,当事人的住所、合同签订地与履行地、国籍和意思表示均可成为某国法院对涉外案件的管辖依据。而且,特定法院的管辖区域是确定的,有明确的物理空间。

四、共同管辖权

有时与案例有关的各种连接因素分布在不同的国家,各国均可以根据其中一个或者多个连接因素,对案件行使管辖权。这是就是国际民商事诉讼法中的共同管辖权(**concurrent jurisdiction**)。在这种情况下,原告往往可以选择有利于自己的法院作为管辖法院。

【释义】 **concurrent jurisdiction**

Courts may also have jurisdiction that is **concurrent** or **shared**. Where a court has concurrent or shared jurisdiction, multiple courts in the same area can address the matter. Where con-

---

① 黄川:《民事诉讼管辖研究》,中国法制出版社2001年版,第158—159页。
② 黄进主编:《国际私法》(第二版),法律出版社2005年版,第894页。

current jurisdiction exists in civil cases, the parties may attempt to engage in forum shopping, by bringing or moving the case to the court which they deem most favorable to them.

共同管辖可以分为两种情况：一是因诉讼主体的牵连关系发生的共同管辖，如同一诉讼的几个被告住所地、经常居住地在两个以上法院辖区内，各该法院都有管辖权。二是因诉讼客体的牵连关系发生的共同管辖，如同一案件的标的物分散在两个以上法院辖区或者侵权行为地跨越两个以上法院辖区的，各该法院都有管辖权。

第五节 挑选法院与不方便法院

在涉外民商事纠纷案件的诉讼过程中，当事人的一方为实现自己利益的最大化，往往采取种种手法。其中最为典型的是原告挑选法院和被告以不方便法院为由，对法院的管辖权提出异议和抗辩。

一、挑选法院

（一）挑选法院的概念

挑选法院（**forum shopping**）又称为择地行诉，是原告为了获得司法上的利益而选择一个可能会对自己作出最有利判决的法院提起诉讼，从而避免在对自己不利的法院进行诉讼的行为。[1]

【释义】　　　　　　　　**forum shopping**

Forum shopping is the informal name given to the practice adopted by some litigants to get their legal case heard in the court thought most likely to provide a favorable judgment. Some states have, for example, become notorious as plaintiff-friendly jurisdictions and so have become litigation magnets even though there is little or no connection between the legal issues

---

[1] Markus Koehnen: *Forum Shopping: New Principles and Turning the Other Cheek*, http://www.canadalegal.com, 2008 年 8 月 30 日访问。

and the jurisdiction in which they are to be litigated. Through its expansive acceptance of personal jurisdiction, the United States has also attracted foreign litigants wishing to take advantage of the more generous awards of damages and alimony, extensive discovery rules, and the contingent fee system. In addition, the Foreign Trade Antitrust Improvements Act, the Alien Tort Claims Act, and many state product liability laws create legal rights that often do not exist in other jurisdictions.①

挑选法院,是英美法上的一个专门术语。《布莱克法学词典》对挑选法院的解释是:挑选法院系指当事人将自己的诉讼提交到一个他感到可以获得最有利判决的特定法院或者法域的行为。②我国学术界,对 forum shopping 有"挑选法院"、"选购法院"、"择地行诉"和"竞择法院"等不同译法。

挑选法院最早出现于 1938 年美国法院审理的 **Erie Railroad v. Tompkins** 案件中。

【案例】　　　　　　　Erie Railroad v. Tompkins③

Tompkins, a citizen of Pennsylvania, was injured on a dark night by a passing freight train of the Erie Railroad Company while walking along its right of way at Hughestown in that State. To enforce that claim he brought an action in the federal court for southern New York, which had jurisdiction because the company is a corporation of that State. It denied liability; and the case was tried by a jury.

The Erie Railroad insisted that its liability should be determined in accordance with the Pennsylvania law; that under the law of Pennsylvania, persons who use pathways along the railroad right of way are to be deemed trespassers; and that the railroad is not liable for injuries to undiscovered trespassers resulting from its negligence. Tompkins denied that any such rule had been established by the decisions of the Pennsylvania courts; and contended that, since there was no statute of the State on the subject, the railroad's duty and liability is to be determined in federal courts as a matter of general law. The trial judge refused to rule that the applicable law precluded recovery. The jury brought in a verdict of $30000; and the judgment entered thereon was affirmed by the Circuit Court of Appeals.

Outcome: The judgment was reversed and the case remanded for consideration of applicable state law as to Erie railroad company's liability for Tompkins's injuries, the Supreme Court holding that there was no federal general common law, the law to be applied by the fed-

---

① Forum shopping, Wikipedia, http://en.wikipedia.org/wiki/Forum_shopping,2008 年 8 月 30 日访问。
② Bryan Garner, *Black's Law Dictionary*, The Thomson Corp, 8th ed., 2004, p.681.
③ 304 U.S. 64 (1938).

eral courts in diversity cases was the law of the state.[①]

  本案中,美国宾夕法尼亚州居民 Tompkins 在宾州铁路旁行走时受到 Erie 铁路公司火车的伤害而请求赔偿。由于按照宾州法律,居民在铁路旁行走是违法的,铁路公司不承担赔偿责任。为了获得有利于自己的赔偿,Tompkins 不在侵害行为发生地宾州法院起诉诉讼,而是选择 Erie 铁路公司的注册地纽约作为诉讼地,并希望按照纽约法律来获得损害赔偿。本案由此而成为挑选法院的代表案例。

  挑选法院是因各国实体法、诉讼程序和法律选择原则的不同,在不同国家起诉,判决结果会有很大差异,甚至会完全相反,所以原告自然会选择对自己有利的国家或地区的法院起诉。而大多数民商事案件并不属于各国法定的专属管辖范围,几个国家或地区的法院往往都具有管辖权,这就为原告挑选法院提供了客观条件。如根据欧洲法院(the European Court of Jusitice)在一个著名判例 Shevill v. Press Alliance S. A 中确认的,当存在多个侵权行为实施地和侵权结果发生地时,原告有权在此范围内就管辖法院和适用的法律进行选择。

【案例】   **Shevill v. Press Alliance S. A**[②]

  An article had been published in the French newspaper *France-Soir*, alleging Ms Shevill had been involved in money laundering linked to drug trafficking. This was alleged to have taken place whilst Ms Shevill was in the temporary employment of *Chequepoint SARL*, a French company operating *bureaux de change* in Paris, amongst other places. About 0.1% of the total print run was sold in England.

  The European Court of Justice decided that an English domiciliary was able to sue a French domiciled newspaper either in the place where the defendant is established, in this case France, in relation to the entire circulation of the publication, or in any place where the allegedly defamatory publication is distributed, including England but solely in relation to the damage to reputation caused by the distribution of the publication in that jurisdiction. In doing so the Court gave an autonomous interpretation of the "place of the event giving rise to the damage" for the purpose of a libel by a newspaper article distributed in several Contracting States.

---

  ① Erie Railroad Co. v. Tompkins, No. 367, Supreme Court of the United States, 304 U. S. 64; 58 S. Ct. 817; 82 L. Ed. 1188; 1938 U. S. LEXIS 984; 11 Ohio Op. 246; 114 A. L. R. 1487, January 31, 1938, Argued; April 25, 1938, Decided.

  ② Case 68/93, Shevill v. Press Alliance S. A, E. C. R. 415 (1995), available at 1995 ECJ CELEX LEXIS 4862.

(二) 挑选法院的主观动机和形式

诉讼当事人基于各种动机挑选法院（**reasons for forum shopping**）。挑选法院之所以能够产生和存在，其内在的主观动机在于当事人想趋利避害，用最低的诉讼成本获得最大的诉讼利益，使自己的利益最大化。

【释义】　　　　　　　reasons for forum shopping

The plaintiff might have selected one forum because:

——it is believed that the defendant or key witnesses will not be able to travel to the state selected. There may be problems of cost, physical health or visa/entry permit eligibility. This strategy would enable the plaintiff to win the case by default.

——the court or judge or body of law or rules of evidence are most likely to favour the plaintiff's case.

当事人挑选法院的这一内在主观动机主要体现在以下几个方面：第一，适用什么样的实体法会得到最好的判决结果是当事人挑选法院时考虑的首要因素，如离婚、继承等案件适用什么样的实体法可以使问题得到更好的解决，违约、侵权等案件适用什么样的实体法可以获得最高额的赔偿金等。第二，在适用的实体法相同的情况下，适用什么样的程序法会产生较好的判决结果，比如在违约、侵权案件获得相同赔偿金的情况下，适用哪国的程序法可以使诉讼成本最低，可以减轻自己的举证责任等。第三，哪一国法院作出的判决比较容易获得承认与执行，也是当事人挑选法院时考虑的因素，这是因为并不是所有国家之间都存在司法协助关系。

挑选法院主要有三种形式：一是在国际民商事合同领域内，双方当事人通过订立管辖权条款，约定解决争议的地点，这是双方通过合意对法院进行的选择。这种方式在一定程度上已被大多数国家认可。二是在侵权、婚姻、海商、继承、破产等特定案件中，原告在可以选择的范围内，选择一个对其有利的法院提起诉讼的行为。三是原本应成为被告的一方当事人（潜在被告），在双方争议发生后，为防止本应成为原告（潜在原告）的一方当事人选择对其不利的法院行诉，主动在对其有利的法院提起诉讼的行为。

挑选法院，在大多数的情况下是由于原告（<u>forum shopping by the plaintiff</u>）而发生的。

【释义】　　　　　　　forum shopping by the plaintiff

A plaintiff frequently has a choice of bringing a case in one of several jurisdictions, by picking a federal rather than a local jurisdiction, or a local rather than federal jurisdiction, or one of several geographic localities. The defendant in a civil case can usually be sued where he lives, or where the wrong was committed leading to the suit, or where the injury from that wrong was felt. In the United States, the District Court for the Eastern District of Texas in Marshall, Texas has become a popular forum for patent lawsuits, finding in favor of the plaintiff 78% of the time, compared to a national average of 59%.

但是在某些案件中,挑选法院也可能是由于民商事案件的被告而发生的(**forum shopping by the civil defendant**)。

【释义】　　　　**forum shopping by the civil defendant**

A defendant can use various methods to attempt to have a case removed from the court where the plaintiff originally filed it. These include invoking the removal jurisdiction of a federal court to take a claim out of the state court, requests for a change of venue contending that the case was brought in the wrong court within a system, and motions for forum non conveniens asserting that the case was brought in an inappropriate forum based on the locations of the parties or evidence.

(三) 国际社会对挑选法院的态度

国际社会中,学者对挑选法院的态度存在很大分歧,形成对立的两派:一些学者赞成挑选法院的存在,而另一些学者则持反对态度。

赞成的一方学者认为目前各国的立法和司法已经为当事人挑选法院创造了前提条件,那么当事人挑选法院是理所当然的事,它是当事人的一种诉讼策略。如美国 Rehnquist 法官说过:"挑选法院是原告的一种诉讼策略,是为了寻求一个在实体和程序方面更加优惠的一个法院"[1]。

反对的一方学者则认为挑选法院影响了司法管辖权的合理分配,损害了本应该适用的实体法法院的权威,增加了被挑选法院的负担,造成了多重诉讼,导致了司法的不公平,违背了公共利益,因此应予以禁止或限制。如英国大法官 Kerr 在 First National Bank of Boston v. Union Bank of Switzerland(1990)[2]案中对挑选法院作出的定义:尝试说服一国的法院去霸占一个原来更适合属于其他国家法院的管

---

[1] See Friedrich K. Juenger, Forum Shopping: Domestic and International, 63 *Tul. L. Rev.* 553 (1989).

[2] First National Bank of Boston v. Union Bank of Switzerland, [1990] 1 *Lloyd's Rep.* 32 (C. A.).

辖权。①

虽然学者对挑选法院持有不同的态度,但挑选法院已经成为不可避免的诉讼现象,所以对于挑选法院应该全面看待,既要看到挑选法院的优点,又要看到挑选法院存在的不足。对于优点应给予肯定,对于不足应采取各种措施进行限制,以维护当事人之间的诉讼公平和实体公正。

(四)限制当事人挑选法院的措施

由于挑选法院存在影响司法管辖权的合理分配、造成多重诉讼、导致司法不公正等负面影响,因此必须采取相关措施对当事人挑选法院的行为进行限制。目前世界范围内采取的主要措施有以下几种:

第一,当事人双方在合同中设定管辖权条款,约定将来如果发生争议应由某一法院管辖。

第二,采用不方便法院原则,驳回原告的起诉,阻止原告挑选法院的行为。

第三,美国采取案件移送制度。美国的案件移送制度是为了消除不方便法院原则所带来的不公平,提高联邦法院系统的便利,一个联邦地区法院可以将任何民商事诉讼移送给当事人可能提起诉讼的其他联邦地区法院(**transfers between federal district courts**)。

【释义】　　　　**transfers between federal district courts**

In 1948, Congress enacted section 1404(a) of Title 28 to allow transfers between federal district courts. Congress intended the statute to promote convenience in the federal courts. The statute does not specify which state's law applies following a transfer, but in 1964, in *Van Dusen v. Barrack*, the Supreme Court determined that the state law of the transferor court must apply following defendant-initiated transfers. The *Van Dusen* Court reasoned that application of the statute should promote convenience and uniformity and discourage forum-shopping in the federal courts. In 1990, in *Ferens v. John Deere Co.*, the Supreme Court held that the state law of the transferor court must apply following all section 1404(a) transfers. The *Ferens* Court purported to base its decision on *Van Dusen's* rationale and other considerations. The *Ferens* holding, however, violates these principles.②

第四,加拿大采取统一管辖权和程序转移法令。加拿大的方法是通过提供一

---

① 参见杨良宜、杨大明:《禁令》,中国政法大学出版社2000年版,第604页。
② Michael B. Rodden, Is 28 U.S.C. 1404(a) A Federal Forum Shopping Statute? 66 *Wash. L. Rev.* 851 (1991).

系列转移程序把案件移送到另一法院来拒绝管辖权。

国际上为防止挑选法院和平行诉讼,制定了《布鲁塞尔公约》、《卢加诺公约》、《保护儿童海牙公约》和《伦敦原则》等,这些公约和原则在限制挑选法院这一问题上起到了很大的作用。

(五)挑选法院现象的前景

挑选法院是国际民商事诉讼中的普遍现象,由于各国管辖权范围的扩大、冲突规范存在差异等诸多外部客观条件的影响,再加上当事人为寻求诉讼利益最大化这一内在主观动机的刺激,导致挑选法院的产生并将长期存在。各国学者对挑选法院现象持有不同观点,不同国家、不同法系对挑选法院的限制采取了很多措施,但在国际社会范围内仍然没有统一的合理解决方案。因而,挑选法院仍将是国际私法管辖权领域中一个值得探讨和解决的问题。

二、不方便法院

(一)不方便法院的概念

"不方便法院"(**forum non conveniens**)原则,也称作"非方便法院"原则,主要指受案法院虽然对案件具有管辖权,但如果认为审理此案会给当事人及司法带来某种不便之处,从而无法保证司法公正,不能使争议得到迅速有效的解决,此时如果存在对诉讼同样具有管辖权的可替代法院,则受案法院可以不方便为由而拒绝行使管辖权。①

【释义】　　　　　　　　forum non conveniens

Forum non conveniens, which means "inconvenient forum" or inappropriate forum", is a discretionary power of mostly common law courts to refuse to hear a proceeding that has been brought before it. The courts will refuse to take jurisdiction over matters where there is a more appropriate forum available to the parties.

不方便法院是英美普通法项下法院拒绝行使管辖权或者民商事诉讼被告拒绝被管辖而提出管辖抗辩的一种重要制度。不方便法院原则,可以是因为法院主动直接适用,也可以是因为被告提出导致法院被动适用。②在中化国际公司诉马来西亚国际

---

①　张茂:《美国国际民事诉讼法》,中国政法大学出版社1999年版,第94页。
②　如被告认为他在该国应诉得不到公正对待,可以该国法院为不方便法院为由,要求中止诉讼。而受诉法院根据当事人的申请,综合考虑由其受理该案件或者在其他国家(或者地区)进行诉讼,何者对当事人更为方便和公正,从而运用自由裁量权,决定拒绝当事人的申请或者放弃行使管辖权。

第十五章　国际民商事司法管辖权概论

船运公司(**Sinochem International Co. v. Malaysia International Shipping Corp.**)一案中,美国联邦最高法院的判决,使得不方便法院原则的适用更加宽泛化了。

【案例】　　　　Sinochem International Co. v. Malaysia
　　　　　　　　International Shipping Corp. ①

A contract for the purchase of steel coils between Sinochem International Company Ltd. (Sinochem), a Chinese company, and Triorient Trading, Inc. (Triorient), an American company not party to this case. The contract stipulated that payment would be rendered to Triorient upon production of a bill of lading demonstrating that the coils had been loaded for shipment on or before April 30, 2003. Triorient subsequently subchartered a vessel owned by Malaysia International Shipping Corporation (Malaysia International) to transport the coils from Philadelphia to China. A bill of lading dated April 30, 2003 was then issued and payment was made.

In June 2003, Sinochem petitioned a Chinese admiralty court for preservation of a maritime claim against Malaysia International, alleging that the shipping company had fraudulently backdated the bill of lading to trigger payment from the line of credit. The Chinese court ordered the arrest of the ship on the same day Sinochem's petition was filed. Sinochem then filed a formal complaint with the Guangzhou Admiralty Court, Malaysia International's subsequent jurisdictional objections to the complaint were rejected, and the rejection favoring Sinochem was upheld on appeal.

Two weeks after the Chinese court ordered the arrest of the vessel, Malaysia International filed suit in the United States District Court for the Eastern District of Pennsylvania, claiming that Sinochem's petition before the Chinese admiralty court contained misrepresentations and seeking compensation for the arrest of the vessel. Sinochem responded by "moving for dismissal on several grounds, including lack of subject-matter jurisdiction, lack of personal jurisdiction, and forum non conveniens." The district court found that while it had subject-matter jurisdiction over the claims, limited discovery would be necessary to determine whether personal jurisdiction existed. Rather than ordering limited discovery, the district court found that the appropriate forum for the case was the Chinese court and dismissed on forum non conveniens grounds. On appeal, a panel of the United States Court of Appeals for the Third Circuit reversed, finding that although forum non conveniens was not a merits-based adjudication, prior to dismissing a case on forum non conveniens grounds a court must first confirm both personal and subject-matter jurisdiction.

The United States Supreme Court reversed, holding that a district court may dismiss a case on the basis of forum non conveniens without first establishing personal or subject-matter jurisdiction, or considering any other threshold objections.②

---

① Sinochem International Co. v. Malaysia International Shipping Corp. , 127 S. Ct. 1184, 1190 (2007).
② Nathan Viavant, Sinochem International Co. v. Malaysia International Shipping Corp.; The United States Supreme Court Puts Forum Non Conveniens First, 16 *Tul. J. Int'l & Comp. L.* 557, 557—558 (2008).

本案中，中化国际（控股）股份有限公司（以下简称"中化公司"）与美国一家公司 Triorient（不是本案当事人）签订了一份合同。双方约定，中化公司向 Triorient 公司购买一批卷型钢材，以信用证的方式支付，提单中须载明运往中国的钢材已在 2003 年 4 月 30 日前装运完毕。此后，Triorient 公司承租了马来西亚国际船运公司（以下简称"马来西亚公司"）的船舶运送钢材，并且雇佣了 Stevedoring 公司在美国费城将钢材装船。2003 年 4 月 30 日，提单被签发。

2003 年 6 月 8 日，中化公司在广州海事法院以马来西亚公司倒签提单为由申请保全措施，请求扣押该公司船舶。基于请求，广州海事法院扣押了船舶。2003 年 7 月 2 日，中化公司在广州海事法院提起诉讼，在诉讼请求中再次强调了提单的倒签导致了无担保付款。

2003 年 6 月 23 日，马来西亚公司在美国联邦宾夕法尼亚东区地区法院提起紧急诉讼，认为中化公司在广州海事法院的保全申请忽视了"船舶的装货地点"。由于保全措施，马来西亚公司要求赔偿船舶被扣押期间的损失。中化公司则要求驳回马来西亚公司的诉讼请求，认为该法院对该案缺乏对物管辖权和属人管辖权，根据不方便法院理论和国际礼让原则应拒绝管辖。

基于此案已在中国诉讼，广州海事法院具有管辖权并且是适当的法院，美国联邦地区法院根据不方便法院原则拒绝了该案的管辖。

马来西亚公司在美国提起上诉。美国联邦第三巡回上诉法院认同对物管辖权的存在，而属人管辖的确定必须通过审理中证据的披露才能解决。尽管法庭认为运用不方便法院原则作出拒绝管辖并不需要涉及案件的实质问题，但合议庭的多数成员还是认为联邦地区法院在没有明确其具有管辖权的情况下，以不方便法院原则拒绝该案是错误的。美国联邦第三巡回上诉法院推翻了地区法院的裁定。

美国联邦最高法院最后又推翻了美国联邦第三巡回上诉法院的裁定。美国联邦最高法院的判决认为，以中化公司为原告解决当事人之间纠纷的诉讼正在中国进行，广州海事法院的管辖已被最终确立。因此，并非需要在首先明确管辖权的情况下，才能根据管辖权异议或外国司法环境的限制等因素适用不方便法院原则，因此，拒绝了对该案的管辖。[①]根据美国联邦最高法院的意见，在受诉法院不需考虑是否具有管辖权的前提下，只要具有不方便法院的种种因素，该法院即可依据不方便法院原则拒绝行使管辖权。

在被告提出不方便法院的情况下，法院面对被告的管辖权异议请求，会权衡利弊（**balance by the court**），然后根据具体情况作出是否接受被告抗辩的裁定。

[①] 参见宋建立：《不方便法院原则的新发展》，载《人民法院报》2007 年 8 月 30 日。

【释义】 balance by the court

The defendant may move to dismiss an action on the ground of *forum non conveniens*. Invoking this doctrine usually means that the plaintiff properly invoked the jurisdiction of the court, but it is inconvenient for the court and the defendant to have a trial in the original jurisdiction. The court must balance conveniences, but extra weight must be given to the plaintiff's choice of forum. In other words, if the plaintiff's choice of forum was legitimate and reasonable, the defendant must show compelling arguments to convince a court to refuse jurisdiction. If a transfer would simply shift the inconvenience from one party to the other, the plaintiff's choice of forum should not be disturbed.

（二）不方便法院理论的产生与发展

从各国的立法以及司法实践来看，对于不方便法院理论的产生，有关文献并没有确切的记载。一般认为，不方便法院原则起源于苏格兰，早在18世纪，苏格兰法院就已开始采用这一原则。①但是，一直到20世纪中叶，不方便法院理论才开始逐步得到推广。对不方便法院理论发展和进化起着重要作用的则是美国法院和英国法院。

作为典型的判例法国家，美国的不方便法院原则主要是通过判例来体现的。美国的"不方便法院"原则首先在州际民商事诉讼中确立。1947年，美国联邦法院在 **Gulf Oil Corp. v. Gilbert** 一案中采用了"不方便法院"原则。该原则后来为美国许多州法院所遵循。20世纪后半期，不方便法院原则在英国及其他英美法系国家基本得到承认。

【案例】 Gulf Oil Corp. v. Gilbert ②

In Gulf Oil, a Virginia plaintiff sued a Pennsylvania defendant in the United States District Court for the Southern District of New York. The plaintiff claimed that the defendant's negligence in transporting gasoline caused a fire that destroyed his warehouse in Lynchburg. Although jurisdiction and venue were proper, the district court nonetheless dismissed the suit.

In affirming the district court's decision, the Supreme Court held that federal courts may apply forum non conveniens where venue and jurisdiction are proper, but another court is far more convenient and appropriate. The Court was concerned that requiring courts to rely solely on the "open door" of the broadly constructed rules of venue and jurisdiction "may admit

---

① Paul R. Beaumont, A United Kingdom Perspective on the Proposed Hague Judgments Convention, 24 *Brook. J. Int'l L.* 75, 76 (1998).

② Gulf Oil Corp. v. Gilbert, 330 U.S. 501, 505 (1947).

those who seek not simply justice but perhaps justice blended with some harassment. A plaintiff sometimes is under temptation to resort to a strategy of forcing the trial at a most inconvenient place for an adversary, even at some inconvenience to himself." The Court listed multiple factors to be considered when applying the doctrine-namely, interests of the private litigant, such as the "relative ease of access to sources of proof; availability of compulsory process for attendance of unwilling, and the cost of obtaining attendance of willing, witnesses"; and interests of the public sector, such as congestion of the docket and tortuous conflict-of-laws problems. Weighing these factors, the balance must tilt decisively in favor of the defendant if forum non conveniens dismissal is to be exercised. ①

第一次在国际民商事诉讼中采用不方便法院原则的案例,是美国联邦最高法院在1981年所处理的 **Piper Aircraft Co. v. Reyno** 案。

【案例】　　　　　　　　**Piper Aircraft Co. v. Reyno**②

在该案中,一架飞机在苏格兰发生空难,造成6名苏格兰人死亡,事故原因主要是飞机及其部件的质量问题。作为死者遗产管理人的原告在美国法院以美国的飞机及部件制造商为被告提起诉讼,美国法院以不方便法院原则为由拒绝管辖。

在本案中,美国对不方便法院原则的运用主要表现在其强调不方便法院的分析不能着重放在任何一个因素上,包括住所和居所,而是要综合进行评价。

(三) 不方便法院原则在各国法院的实践

一些法院,如美国纽约州法院,对不方便法院的认定,标准非常严格,被告必须对不方便法院承担举证责任(burden of proof)。法院在认定被告所提出的不方便法院方面,设定了非常严格的标准。如美国联邦第二巡回法院2006年在纽约州所处理的著名的彼基诉可口可乐公司(**Bigio v. Coca Cola Company**)案件,就是一个典型的例子。

【案例】　　　　　　　　**Bigio v. Coca Cola Company**③

Coca Cola took over assets of Jews expelled from Egypt in the 1950s and was sued in

---

① Christopher Tate, American Forum Non Conveniens in Light of the Hague Convention on Choice-of-court Agreements, 69 *U. Pitt. L. Rev.* 165, 169 (2007).
② Piper Aircraft Co. v. Reyno, 454 U.S (1981), pp.238—240.
③ 448 F.3d 176 (2d Cir. 2006).

New York. In that case, the plaintiffs were Canadians and non—residents of New York. The court denied Coca Cola's *forum non conveniens* motion and this decision was later affirmed by the U.S. Supreme Court, which denied *certiorari*. The 2nd Circuit stated that the fact that the New York court would need to apply "modest application" of Egyptian law was not a problem because "courts of this Circuit are regularly called upon to interpret foreign law without thereby offending the principles of international comity". Also, the fact that there were witnesses abroad is not a problem either. They can be flown into the U.S. or Letters Rogatory can be issued to the Egyptian courts to collect their testimony. Further, it was held that in a *forum non conveniens* scenario, a court applies the balance of conveniences, but preference (and weight) must be given to the fact that plaintiffs chose this particular forum for "legitimate reasons". The fact that plaintiffs can sue in Canada is not relevant because Coca Cola is a U.S. company and it is "perfectly reasonable to sue in the US".

英国在 **Spiliada Maritime Corp v. Cansulex Ltd** 一案中确立了不方便法院原则,对不方便法院的判断从"程序滥用"标准发展到"更适当法院"标准,适用的前提是有其他更适当的法院,并且偏重私人利益的分析。由此产生了在双方当事人之间分配举证责任的做法:原告负有证明支持其选择该法院的义务,而被告则有举证证明反对被选择法院的义务。除此之外,英国还明确了诉讼中止适用的两步分析(two-step analysis),即存在另一个明显更加适当的法院和存在中止诉讼的正义的需要。

【案例】   **Spiliada Maritime Corp v. Cansulex Ltd**①

Wet sulfur was loaded onto two ships docked in British Columbia causing damage to them. An action was brought in England by the Liberian owners of the "Spiliada" for the damage to the ship against the sulfur exporter. The owners of the second ship, the "Cambridgeshire" also brought an action in England. Both ships were insured by English insurers.

The plaintiffs applied for leave to serve the defendants *ex juris*. The trial judge granted leave. The defendant successfully appealed. The Court of Appeal held that the expenses alone and the existence of a B.C. limitation period was enough to allow the claim to come to England.

Lord Goff, writing for the House of Lords, granted the appeal.

In the leading British case Spiliada Maritime Corp. v. Cansulex Ltd., the House of Lords established a two-step analysis. First, the defendant must show the availability of another clearly more appropriate forum, i.e., one "in which the case could be tried more suitably for the interests of all the parties and for the ends of justice." Second, if the defendant has made a prima facie case for a forum non conveniens dismissal, the plaintiff can show that there are circumstances by reason of which justice requires that the British court exercise its jurisdiction. This is a much

---

① Spiliada Maritime Corpn v. Cansulex Ltd., (1987) A.C 460.

broader test than the initial "oppressive or vexatious" test and requires that all factors relevant to the interests of the parties and to the ends of justice are taken into consideration.①

英联邦国家的新西兰法院和新加坡均毫无保留地接受了英国的做法。②

但是,澳大利亚没有完全接受英国的做法,而是采取了比美国和英国更加严格的标准,如澳大利亚高等法院在 1990 年所受理的 **Voth v. Manildra Flour Mills Pty. Ltd**.案。澳大利亚高等法院在考虑是否以不方便法院为由放弃管辖权的时候,只对诉讼在本地法院进行的有利方面与不利方面进行权衡,而不对本地法院与外国法院作比较分析,在本地法院被证明适合审理的情况下不中止诉讼,法院不太愿意依据不方便法院说拒绝行使管辖权。

【案例】　　　　**Voth v. Manildra Flour Mills Pty. Ltd.**③

Voth was based on a dispute involving two Australian corporations that brought professional negligence claims against a U.S. accountant residing in Missouri, who had given advice to the companies' Missouri subsidiary. The injury was caused to its parent company in New South Wales. Despite the fact that the defendant had done all of the relevant work in Missouri, the plaintiffs filed suit in New South Wales. The defendant requested a stay, arguing that the only proper forum would be a Missouri court, as the damages were allegedly brought about by actions taken in that state. Both the lower court and the court of appeals denied the defendant's request, holding that "the respondents had reasonable justification for resorting to the local jurisdiction."

Voth was appealed to the High Court of Australia. The Court then applied the "clearly inappropriate" test. The Court determined that despite the greater advantage given the plaintiffs under the new test, the proper forum for the case was in Missouri. The Australian Court briefly considered the advantages that existed for the plaintiffs in their chosen jurisdiction, but the plaintiffs' preference, and any benefits that would have come from allowing them to choose the forum, were not granted much weight. In the end, the Court suggested that there was little difference between the final outcome in the "more appropriate" and "inappropriate" forum tests, and the case was stayed in light of the more suitable Missouri forum.④

---

① Martine Stuckelberg, Lis Pendens and Forum Non Conveniens at the Hague Conference, 26 *Brooklyn J. Int'l L.* 949, 955—956 (2001).

② 参见徐卉:《涉外民商事诉讼管辖权冲突研究》,中国政法大学出版社 2001 年版,第 137 页。

③ Voth v. Manildra Flour Mills Pty Ltd., (1990) 171 C. L. R. 538, 565 (adopting "connecting factors" stated by Lord Goff in Spiliada, despite rejecting Spiliada test for burden of persuasion). *Voth* was discussed in detail in Dutson "Product Liability and Private International Law: Jurisdiction in International Product Liability Litigation", 9 *Bond Law Review* 81 (1997).

④ Mary Elliott Rolle, Unraveling Accountability: Contesting Legal and Procedural Barriers in International Toxic Tort Cases, 15 *Geo. Int'l Envtl. L. Rev.* 135, 179 (2003).

第十五章　国际民商事司法管辖权概论

在上述案例中,澳大利亚高等法院采用了"非明显不适当法院"(**clearly inappropriate forum**)标准,即仅需证明本地法院不是明显不适当的法院,非明显不适当法院这一事实不足以让法院拒绝行使管辖权;存在另外一个更适合的审判地,也不足以让法院这样做。

【释义】　　　　　clearly inappropriate forum

The Australian doctrine of forum non conveniens is interesting because it is more restrictive than the U.S. and British doctrines and, therefore, probably more acceptable for civil law countries. In 1988, the Australian High Court, in Oceanic Sun Line Special Shipping Co. v. Fay, refused to follow the evolution of the British doctrine of forum non conveniens reflected in Spiliada. Taking as its departure point the traditional "vexatious or oppressive" test, the Australian High Court adopted a "clearly inappropriate forum" test. Instead of looking—as do the modern British and American doctrines—to whether there is a "clearly more appropriate forum" abroad, the Australian doctrine focuses on whether the Australian forum is "clearly inappropriate," i.e., seriously and unfairly burdensome, prejudicial, or damaging to the defendant. Justice Deane's opinion for the court explained that "it is a basic tenet of our jurisprudence that, where jurisdiction exists, access to the courts is a right. It is not a privilege which can be withdrawn otherwise than in clearly defined circumstances."①

加拿大的法院在依据不方便法院原则分析和决定最恰当法院(the most appropriate venue)时,受到英国 Spiliada 案判决的一定影响。② 尽管如此,加拿大的分析方法总体而言有自己的特色。加拿大采用了有一个"比本法院明显更合适的法院"(**another forum clearly more appropriate than the domestic forum**)的标准。加拿大法院比较注重对当事人利益的分析,特别表现出对原告的尊重,并且对不同国籍的原告相当的公平。③

【释义】　　another forum clearly more appropriate than the domestic forum

In Canada, the doctrine of forum non conveniens in Canada was considered in Amchem Products Inc. v. British Columbia Worker's Compensation Board④. The Court held that the

---

① Martine Stuckelberg, Lis Pendens and Forum Non Conveniens at the Hague Conference, 26 *Brooklyn J. Int'l L.* 949, 957 (2001).
② Donald J. Carney. Forum Non Conveniens in the United States and Canada, 3 *Buff. Jour. Int'l L.* 117, 131 (1996).
③ Ibid., 128.
④ [1993] 1 S.C.R. 897.

test for striking out a claim for forum non conveniens is where "there is another forum that is clearly more appropriate than the domestic forum." If the forums are both found to be equally convenient, the domestic forum will always win out. Convenience is weighed, using a multi-factored test that includes elements such as: the connection between the plaintiff's claim and the forum, the connection between the defendant and the forum, unfairness to the defendant by choosing the forum, unfairness to the plaintiff in not choosing the forum, involvement of other parties to the suit (i.e. location of witnesses), and issues of comity such as reciprocity and standard of adjudication. The Supreme Court has underlined that forum non conveniens inquiries are very similar but distinct from "real and substantial connection" test used in challenges to jurisdiction. The most important difference is that applying forum non conveniens is a discretionary choice between two forums, each of which could legally hear the issue.①

加拿大最高法院所处理的有关不方便法院原则的最典型案例是 **Antares Shipping Corp. v. The Ship Capricorn**。

【案例】　　**Antares Shipping Corp. v. The Ship Capricorn**②

The case arose when one Liberian company seized the Capricorn while pursuing a claim against the Liberian owners of the vessel. The plaintiff sought to serve the foreign owner of the vessel ex juris. The trial and appellate courts held that the Canadian forum was forum non conveniens, therefore, the case should be dismissed. The Canadian Supreme Court reversed, holding that Canada was forum conveniens and that the service should proceed. The majority based its decision on the fact that no other jurisdiction was more appropriate than Canada, and therefore, Canada was "forum conveniens." This analysis was significant because it foreshadowed the emerging trend in Canadian forum analysis to select a trial's forum based on which forum was the most objectively appropriate forum, and rejected the dissent's approach which focused more narrowly on whether the defendant has sufficient ties to Canada.

目前我国在立法上还没有对"不方便法院"原则作出明确规定。但是,在我国法院的司法实践中,已有了这方面的案例。例如日本公民大仓大雄要求在中国起诉离婚案。中国法院实际适用了"不方便法院原则"认定自己为"不方便法院",没有受理此案。③

目前学者对不方便法院原则的评价褒贬不一,观点并不一致。不方便法院原

---

①　forum non conveniens, Wikipedia, http://en.wikipedia.org/wiki/Forum_non_conveniens#An_example.

②　Antares Shipping Corp. v. The Ship Capricorn, 65 D. L. R. 3d 105 (1976).

③　参见郭树理:《不方便法院原则在中国的适用》,载《法学杂志》1999年第3期。

则有助于减少国际民商事诉讼管辖权的积极冲突,使另一更适合的法院审理案件有利于判决的承认,有利于减轻法院负担从而节省司法资源,也有利于平衡原告、被告及法院的利益,从而有利于实现司法公正,采纳该原则符合当今国际民商事诉讼的发展趋势等。但是不方便法院原则含糊不清,错综复杂,难以有统一的操作标准;该原则赋予受案法院过大的自由裁量权,增加了国际民商事诉讼案件管辖权的随意性。

第六节　我国涉外民商事司法管辖权

一、我国有关涉外民商事管辖权的立法

我国国际民商事案件管辖权的法律渊源有两类,一类是国内立法,如《中华人民共和国民事诉讼法》及最高人民法院《关于适用〈中华人民共和国民事诉讼法〉若干问题的意见》、最高人民法院《关于涉外民事案件诉讼管辖若干问题的规定》、《中华人民共和国海事诉讼特别程序法》及最高人民法院《关于适用〈中华人民共和国海事诉讼特别程序法〉若干问题的解释》等;另一类是国际条约,我国缔结或参加的有关国际民商事诉讼管辖权的国际条约主要有:1953 年参加的 1951 年《国际铁路货物联运协定》、1958 年参加的 1929 年《统一国际航空运输某些规则的公约》、1980 年参加的 1969 年《国际油污损害民事责任公约》、1987 年中法《关于民事、商事司法协助的协定》、1980 年《中华人民共和国和美利坚合众国领事条约》等。

我国 1991 年颁布的《中华人民共和国民事诉讼法》除在第 2 章就民事案件管辖权问题作了一般规定外,还特别在第 4 编第 25 章就涉外民事诉讼程序中的管辖权问题作了一些特别规定。①

二、我国有关涉外民商事管辖权的法律制度

综观我国现行的有关立法及最高人民法院所作的司法解释,我国有关涉外国

---

① 黄进主编:《国际私法》(第二版),法律出版社 2005 年版,第 646 页。

际民商事管辖权的规定可大致归纳为以下几个方面:

(一) 普通管辖的规定

我国普通管辖以地域管辖为原则,而且,一般以被告住所地作为管辖权确定的根据。① 另外,除体现"原告就被告"的原则之外,我国立法也有由原告住所地管辖的例外。②

(二) 特别管辖的规定

我国还规定了特别管辖的规则。在合同纠纷上,由合同特征履行地和成立地法院管辖;在侵权纠纷上,由侵权行为地法院管辖;在涉外民商事诉讼中,体现了最密切联系与便利原则,如可以由合同签订地、诉讼标的物所在地、可供扣押财产所在地管辖。应该说,我国特别管辖的规定一方面力图解决被告住所地不在国内,而当事人或行为本身与国内存有联系的情形;另一方面,通过对行为性质、物之所在地的分析,确定与行为有密切联系的国家或地区的法院具有管辖权,其目的是便于诉讼以及保障本国司法管辖权的行使。

(三) 专属管辖的规定

我国还明确规定了人民法院专属管辖的情形:(1) 因不动产纠纷提起的诉讼,由不动产所地的人民法院专属管辖;(2) 因港口作业发生纠纷提起的诉讼,由港口所在地法院专属管辖;(3) 因继承遗产纠纷提起的诉讼,由被继承人死亡时住所地或主要遗产所在地法院专属管辖;(4) 因在我国履行中外合资经营企业合同、中外合作经营企业合同、中外合作勘探开发自然资源合同发生纠纷提起的诉讼,由人民法院专属管辖。③

(四) 协议管辖的规定

我国《民事诉讼法》第 25 条对协议管辖作了明确规定,有关协议管辖的规定一方面肯定了协议管辖的效力,另一方面又对协议管辖作了一定的限制,如对协议范围、选择法院不能违反有关专属管辖与级别管辖的规定以及必须以书面形式进行的限制等。

---

① 《中华人民共和国民事诉讼法》第 21 条规定:对公民提起的民事诉讼,由被告住所地人民法院管辖;被告住所地与经常居住地不一致的,由经常居住地人民法院管辖。对法人或其他组织提起的民事诉讼,由被告住所地人民法院管辖。同一诉讼的几个被告住所地、经常居住地在两个以上人民法院辖区的,各该人民法院都有管辖权。

② 《中华人民共和国民事诉讼法》第 22 条规定了一种例外情况:对不在我国领域内居住的人提起的有关身份关系的诉讼,由原告住所地人民法院管辖;原告住所地与经常居住地不一致的,由原告经常居住地人民法院管辖。

③ 《中华人民共和国民事诉讼法》第 33 条、第 266 条。

第十五章 国际民商事司法管辖权概论

综上所述，我国有关管辖权的立法涵盖了普通管辖、特别管辖、专属管辖和协议管辖等多种管辖形式，并就涉外民商事诉讼管辖权的确定制定了特别规则，基本上形成了一个完整的管辖权确定体系，对于传统民商事案件诉讼管辖权的确定，具有较强的确定性和可操作性。

【思考题】

- 什么是国际民商事管辖权？
- 属地管辖权包括哪些内容？
- 国际鞋业公司诉华盛顿案对司法管辖权的变化有什么影响？
- 什么是最低限度联系原则？它与长臂管辖权是什么关系？
- 你知道国际大众公司诉伍德森案吗？
- 什么是挑选法院？发生挑选法院的原因是什么？
- 什么是不方便法院？
- 试述我国涉外民商事管辖权制度。

【重要术语提示与中英文对照】

中文术语	英文对照
管辖权	jurisdiction
属地管辖权	territorial jurisdiction
对人管辖权	*personam* jurisdiction
对物管辖权	Jurisdiction in *rem*
原告就被告法院	Actor sequiter forum rei
国际鞋业公司诉华盛顿	International Shoe Co. v. Washington
最低限度联系	minimum contacts
正当程序条款	the Due Process Clause
美国宪法修正案第14条	U.S. Constitution Amendment XIV
长臂管辖权	long arm jurisdiction
国际大众公司诉伍德森	World-Wide Volkswagen Corp. v. Woodson
相关性标准	relatedness
有意利用标准	purposeful availment
合理性标准	reasonableness

属人管辖权	personal jurisdiction
协议管辖权	consensual jurisdiction
专属管辖权	exclusive jurisdiction
共同管辖权	concurrent jurisdiction
挑选法院	forum shopping
挑选法院的动机	reasons for forum shopping
不方便法院	forum non conveniens
由法院权衡利弊	balance by the court
彼基诉可口可乐公司	Bigio v. Coca Cola Company
举证责任	burden of proof
最恰当法院	the most appropriate venue
中化国际公司诉马来西亚国际船运公司案	Sinochem International Co. v. Malaysia International Shipping Corp.
非明显不适当法院	clearly inappropriate forum
比本法院明显更合适的法院	another forum clearly more appropriate than the domestic forum

【推荐阅读文献】

- 胡振杰:《不方便法院说比较研究》,载《法学研究》2002 年第 4 期。
- 奚晓明:《不方便法院制度的几点思考》,载《法学研究》2002 年第 1 期。
- 李智:《美国最低联系标准评析》,载《福建政法管理干部学院学报》2005 年第 1 期。
- 乔雄兵:《美国民事诉讼中的挑选法院问题研究》,载《比较法研究》2007 年第 2 期。
- 刘宁元:《自我约束的单边方法和国际协调——以美国反垄断法域外管辖实践为视角》,载《政治与法律》2011 年第 11 期。
- Heiser (W. W.), Forum Non Conveniens and Choice of Law: The Impact of Applying Foreign Law in Transnational Tort Actions, 51 *Wayne L. Rev.* 1161 (2005).
- Doprovich (J.), Dismissal under Forum non Conveniens: Should the Availability Requirement Be a Threshold Issue When Applied to Nonessential Defendants, 12 *Widener L. Rev.* 561 (2006).
- Christopher Tate, American Forum Non Conveniens in Light of the Hague Convention on Choice-of-court Agreements, 69 *U. Pitt. L. Rev.* 165 (2007).
- Tu Guangjian, The Hague Choice of Court Convention: A Chinese Perspective, 55

Am. J. Comp. L. 347 (2007).

- Daniel E. Wanat, Copyright Infringement Litigation and the Exercise of Personal Jurisdiction Within Due Process Limits: Judicial Application of Purposeful Availment, Purposeful Direction, or Purposeful Effects Requirements to Finding that a Plaintiff Has Established a Defendant's Minimum Contacts Within the Forum State, 59 *Mercer L. Rev.* 553 (2008).
- Nathan Viavant, Sinochem International Co. v. Malaysia International Shipping Corp.: The United States Supreme Court Puts Forum Non Conveniens First, 16 *Tul. J. Int'l & Comp. L.* 557 (2008).
- Smerek (S.) & Hamilton (J.), Extraterritorial Application of United States Law After Morrison v National Australia Bank, 5 *Disp. Resolution Int'l* 21 (2011).

【扩展阅读资料】

448 F.3d 176

Raphael BIGIO, Bahia Bigio, Ferial Salma Bigio, and B. Bigio & Co., Plaintiffs-Appellants, v. The COCA-COLA COMPANY and The Coca-Cola Export Corporation, Defendants-Appellees.

United States Court of Appeals, Second Circuit.

Argued: March 16, 2006.

Decided: May 9, 2006.

Nathan Lewin, Lewin & Lewin, LLP, Washington, DC (Alyza D. Lewin, Washington, DC, on the brief), for Plaintiffs-Appellants.

William M. Dreyer, Atlanta, GA (Paul A. Straus, King & Spalding, LLP, New York, NY, on the brief), for Defendants-Appellees.

Before: JACOBS and LEVAL, Circuit Judges, and RAKOFF, District Judge.

RAKOFF, District Judge.

Plaintiffs—three members of the Bigio family and a company they control (collectively, the "Bigios")—appeal from the dismissal of their suit against the Coca-Cola Company and its wholly owned subsidiary (collectively, "Coca-Cola"). When this case was previously before this Court, *see Bigio v. Coca-Cola Co.*, 239 F.3d 440 (2d Cir. 2000), the pertinent allegations were stated in some detail, so here they may be stated briefly. The Bigios had large commercial holdings in Egypt that were wrongfully seized during the Nasser regime because the Bigio family was Jewish. The Bigio family then fled to Canada, but, after Nasser died, the Egyptian Government ordered the property returned to the Bigios. However, the state-owned entity then holding the property refused to comply and, instead, sold or, according to defendants, leased the bottling plant here in issue to a joint venture in which a substantial interest was purchased by the Bigios' former tenant, Coca-Cola, which rejected the Bigios' claims to ownership. Unable to obtain relief in the Egyptian courts, the Bigios brought suit in the United States against Coca-Cola for violation of the Alien Tort Claims Act and for common law claims such as conversion.

In our previous decision, we affirmed the district court's dismissal of the claim under the Alien Tort Claims Act but reversed its dismissal of the common law claims pursuant to the "Act-of-State" doctrine. We found the Act-of-State doctrine inapplicable because "the resolution of this case by United States courts will not likely impact on international relations or embarrass or hinder the executive in the realm of foreign relations." *Bigio*, 239 F.3d at 452 (internal quotation marks omitted). On remand, the district court again dismissed the remaining claims, this time on the ground of international comity or, in the alternative, on the ground of *forum non conveniens*. *Bigio v. Coca-Cola Co.*, No. 97 Civ. 2858, 2005 WL 287397, 2005 U.S. Dist. LEXIS 1587 (S.D.N.Y. Feb. 3, 2005). Plaintiffs appeal from that decision.

As to international comity, while application of this doctrine ordinarily lies within the discretion of the district court, in this instance no such deference is appropriate because the district court applied the wrong legal standard. Specifically, the district court applied the seven-factor test articulated in *Timberlane Lumber Co. v. Bank of Am. Nat'l Trust & Savings Ass'n*, 749 F.2d 1378 (9th Cir. 1984). That test is used to determine whether a court should apply United States law extraterritorially, see *O.N.E. Shipping, Ltd. v. Flota Mercante Grancolombiana, S.A.*, 830 F.2d 449 (2d Cir. 1987), but that is not in issue here. Rather, the only issue of international comity properly raised here is whether adjudication of this case by a United States court would offend "amicable working relationships" with Egypt. *JP Morgan Chase Bank v. Altos Hornos de Mex., S.A. de C.V.*, 412 F.3d 418, 423 (2d Cir. 2005). Cf. *In re Maxwell Comm. Corp.*, 93 F.3d 1036, 1047 (2d Cir. 1996) ("We realize that 'international comity' may describe two distinct doctrines: as a canon of construction, it might shorten the reach of a statute; second, it may be viewed as a discretionary act of deference by a national court to decline to exercise jurisdiction in a case properly adjudicated in a foreign state, the so-called comity among courts."). *See generally Hilton v. Guyot*, 159 U.S. 113, 163—164, 16 S. Ct. 139, 40 L. Ed. 95 (1895)

Throughout the long pendency of this lawsuit, the Government of Egypt has never raised the slightest objection to adjudication of the instant controversy by United States courts. *Cf. Jota v. Texaco Inc.*, 157 F. 3d 153, 157 (2d Cir. 1998). Moreover, this Court has already determined that resolution of this case by United States courts will "not likely impact on international relations" with Egypt. *Bigio*, 239 F. 3d at 452 (internal quotation marks omitted). In its present posture, this is a common law suit for damages primarily between Canadian citizens and a United States company, 1 which may likely focus on what Coca-Cola knew about the Bigios' ownership rights before it acquired its present interest in the Egyptian bottling plant. While adjudication of plaintiffs' common law claims may also require some modest application of Egyptian law, *see Bigio*, 239 F. 3d at 454, the courts of this Circuit are regularly called upon to interpret foreign law without thereby offending principles of international comity. See, e. g., *United States v. Schultz*, 333 F. 3d 393 (2d Cir. 2003) (Egyptian law); *Karaha Bodas Co. v. Perusahaan Pertambangan Minyak Dan Gas Bumi Negara ("Pertamina")*, 313 F. 3d 70 (2d Cir. 2002) (Indonesian law); *cf. First Am. Corp. v. Price Waterhouse LLP*, 154 F. 3d 16, 22 (2d Cir. 1998).

As for *forum non conveniens*, the issue, once again, is not whether the district court abused its broad discretion, but whether it misapprehended or misapplied the relevant legal standards. *See Iragorri v. United Techs. Corp.*, 274 F. 3d 65, 72 (2d Cir. 2001) (*en banc*) ("In our recent cases, we vacated dismissals for *forum non conveniens* because we believed that the district courts had misapplied the basic rules...."). Here, the district court, while reciting the principle that even a foreign plaintiff's decision to sue in a U. S. forum is entitled to some weight, *Bigio*, 2005 WL 287397 at * 4—5, 2005 U. S. Dist. LEXIS 1587, at * 12, appears, so far as its discussion of the balance of conveniences is concerned, to have given the plaintiffs' choice of forum no weight whatsoever, *id.* 2005 WL 287397 at * 5—6, at * 14—17. But as we emphasized in our *en banc* decision in *Iragorri*, the more that a plaintiff, even a foreign plaintiff, chooses to sue in a United States court for "legitimate reasons," the more deference must be given to that choice. *Iragorri*, 274 F. 3d at 73. Furthermore, even where the degree of deference is reduced, "[t]he action should be dismissed only if the chosen forum is shown to be genuinely inconvenient and the selected forum significantly preferable." *Id.* at 74—75.

Here, the district court appears to have overlooked the legitimate and substantial reasons for plaintiffs choosing to bring this suit in defendants' own country, the United States, rather than in Egypt, after plaintiffs' efforts to seek relief from the Egyptian authorities proved abortive. It was perfectly reasonable under these circumstances for the plaintiffs to bring their action against Coca-Cola, the only U. S. company involved, in the United States. While conceivably they might have brought it in Canada (their home base) or in a different district of the United States, those possibilities are not determinative here, for the motion that the district court granted was a motion to dismiss in favor of the courts of Egypt and the only comparison it made was between the U. S. forum and the Egyptian forum. Given the history outlined above, the plaintiffs' choice of the U. S. forum over an Egyptian forum was eminently reasonable and entitled to considerable deference, which the district court failed to give.

Furthermore, counsel suggest that a major focus of the litigation may be whether Coca-Cola knew before it purchased its interest in the joint venture that owns or (defendants say) leases the bottling plant that the plant had been ordered to be returned to the Bigios. The key witnesses to this issue either reside in the United States or Canada or are readily producible here; and to the extent there are witnesses abroad who are beyond the court's subpoena power, their testimony can be provided by depositions taken pursuant to letters rogatory. *See, e. g., Overseas Programming Companies v. Cinematographische Commerz-Anstalt*, 684 F. 2d 232, 235 (2d Cir. 1982). Likewise, the parties and their attorneys are all located in the United States or Canada. More generally, it cannot be said that there are private inconveniences present here that outweigh the deference that the district court should have accorded plaintiffs' choice of forum.

Likewise, in evaluating the "public interest" factors of inconvenience, *Gulf Oil Corp. v. Gilbert*, 330 U. S. 501, 508—509, 67 S. Ct. 839, 91 L. Ed. 1055 (1947), the district court again failed to take account of the deference due the plaintiffs' legitimate choice of forum. Relatedly, the district court stated that "Egypt's interest in deciding this controversy is significant," *Bigio*, 2005 WL 287397 at * 5—6, 2005 U. S. Dist. LEXIS 1587, at *17, whereas the suit is primarily over whether a United States company should be liable in damages. And, as noted, Egypt has never raised any objection to the U. S. court deciding this case.

Upon careful review of the record, we are convinced that none of the alleged private or public inconveniences referenced by the district court overcomes the preference reasonably here accorded plaintiffs in their choice of a U. S. forum and that the dismissal of this case on grounds of international comity and *forum non conveniens* was therefore erroneous as a matter of law. *See generally Wiwa v. Royal Dutch Petroleum Co.*, 226 F. 3d 88 (2d Cir. 2000). Accordingly, we reverse and remand to the district court for further proceedings consistent with this opinion.

Upon careful review of the record, we are convinced that none of the alleged private or public inconveniences referenced by the district court overcomes the preference reasonably here accorded plaintiffs in their choice of a U.S. forum and that the dismissal of this case on grounds of international comity and *forum non conveniens* was therefore erroneous as a matter of law. *See generally Wiwa v. Royal Dutch Petroleum Co.*, 226 F. 3d 88 (2d Cir. 2000). Accordingly, we reverse and remand to the district court for further proceedings consistent with this opinion.

第十六章

国际互联网纠纷的管辖权[①]

[①] 上海交通大学法学院国际法专业博士生时慧媛参与了本章部分内容的研究工作。

第十六章　国际互联网纠纷的管辖权

本章导读

※ 互联网法律关系特征表现为主体的分散性、当事人与法院之间关系的不确定性和网络空间的扩张性。

※ 互联网对管辖权法律制度的影响具体表现在以下方面：第一，网络空间的全球一体化使司法管辖的地理界限变得模糊；第二，互联网的无界性使地域管辖权陷入困境；第三，以国籍等为基础的管辖权根据不能确定。

※ "网络空间自治论"是以美国的约翰逊和波斯特为代表的一种网络理论。该理论的主要观点为：对于网络争议，应该摆脱传统的地域管辖的观念，承认网络虚拟空间就是一个特殊的地域，并承认在网络世界与现实世界中存在一个法律上十分重要的边界，若要进入网络的地域，必须通过屏幕或密码，一旦进入网络的虚拟世界，则应适用网络世界的网络法，而不再适用现实中各国不同的法律，也就是所谓的网络空间自治。

※ 管辖权相对论又称为管辖权独立论。该理论的内容可以概括为：第一，网络空间应该作为一个新的管辖区域而存在，应在此领域内建立不同于传统规则的新管辖权原则。第二，任何国家都可以管辖并将其法律适用于网络空间内的任何活动，其程度与方式与该人或该活动进入该主权国家可以控制的网络空间的程度和方式相适应。第三，网络空间内争端当事人可以通过网络的联系在相关法院"出庭"，法院的判决也可以通过网络手段来加以执行。

※ 最低限度接触原则，是指案件被告在法院辖区内有没有交易行为和民商事侵权行为，法院要对案件行使管辖权，则被告和该法院间应存在某种最低限度的接触，这样才能满足适当程序条款和公平原则的要求。

※ 滑动标尺法，是指根据被告通过互联网所从事的行为与法院地的密切程度来决定法院是否有管辖权的方法，是美国将长臂管辖权应用到互联网的国际民商事案件中确定管辖权的方法。

※ 设想中的虚拟法院是与一套自愿注册系统相连接，专门处理互联网上所发生争端的平台。虚拟法院可以成立一个独立的机关来处理注册系统。当某一当事人在国际虚拟法院中心注册后，一个特别的注册确认通知将会发送到他的网站或电子邮件信箱里，这就意味着该当事人同意由国际虚拟法庭来解决可能发生的争端。

【本章主题词】　互联网、网络服务器所在地、网址、网络空间自治论、互联网管辖权相对论、虚拟法院、长臂管辖权、最低限度联系

第一节　互联网的特点及其对传统管辖权的冲击

一、互联网及其法律特征

(一) 国际私法视野下的互联网

当事人的国籍、住所地、物之所在地、行为发生地,以及合意之所以能够成为确定管辖的根据,主要在于他们与法院辖区保持着某种物理空间上的联系。①然而互联网(internet)的出现使这些关联出现模糊性和不确定性。在国际私法视野下,互联网表现出以下特征:

(1) 互联网是不同于传统物理空间的全球性的客观存在。互联网为虚拟的空间,但却是对我们的生活产生重大影响的客观存在。在此环境中没有领土的概念,也没有任何国界和地区的界限,它使得全球的网民能够紧密地联系在一起,彻底地打破物理意义上的有形世界的限制,这也是产生大量跨国法律问题的根源。②

(2) 互联网的不确定性。现实世界是由各个不同的民族国家构成的,各个国家都依据其享有的属地、属人管辖权,达到对其领域内的人、物、事件、行为的管理,以及对本国人的保护。而互联网环境是一个没有中心、没有集权、大家彼此平等的虚拟世界。③

(3) 互联网动摇了以"地域"为基础的管辖权标准。在互联网环境下,网络交易的双方当事人极可能位于不同的国家,而接收或传送双方信息的服务器则可能在另一个国家,从而使所发生的争议往往涉及不同的国家及其居民。④

(4) 互联网具有随意性和隐蔽性。互联网的访问具有很大的随意性,通过互联网从事某项交易的双方的身份具有隐蔽性,脱离了传统的地域、国籍限制。

---

① 蒋敏:《论网络侵权案件中司法管辖权的确认》,载《重庆邮电大学学报》2007 年第 2 期。
② 徐卉:《涉外民商事诉讼管辖权冲突研究》,中国政法大学出版社 2001 年版,第 57 页。
③ 罗艺方、赖紫宁:《网络空间司法管辖权理论的比较研究》,载《政治与法律》2003 年第 6 期。
④ 余筱兰、金学凌:《国际私法管辖权在网络空间面临的挑战与对策》,载《内蒙古农业大学学报》2006 年第 3 期。

(二) 互联网所涉法律关系的特征

1. 主体的分散性

访问网址的随意性,使得在网络上一个法律纠纷往往涉及众多的当事人,甚至可以达到成千上万。主体的分散性会导致当事人选择起诉法院的分散性,传统属地和属人管辖理论追求的便利诉讼和公平诉讼的目的变得难以操作。诉讼各方的诉讼利益因时空的距离和虚拟性而难以在任何一个法院获得协调。同时,一个被告也极有可能面临着被众多处于不同地区和不同语言的原告起诉的处境。人们对自己的预期能力大大降低。

2. 当事人与法院之间关系的不确定性

传统的属地和属人管辖规则是基于当事人与法院之间具有的现实的、物理上的联系而得以确立的。但网络空间的自由性、虚拟性以及与现实空间巨大的异质性,使得当事人与法院之间的联系处于变化不定之中,当事人与法院之间的关系具有不确定性。

3. 网络空间的扩张性

一些新的网络理论主张网络空间的独立性,试图从根本上否定国家的司法管辖权。有学者指出,无形的虚拟空间是排斥主权的。①虽然网络环境的虚拟性和无国界性促进了经济自由化,加速了经济全球化,并创造了一个信息资源开放共享的时代,但也正是由于网络空间的自由性与主权存在巨大的排异反应,才会使主权不顾一切地寻找扩张的空间。为此,导致互联网法律关系具有网络空间的扩张性特征。

二、互联网对管辖权连接点的影响

(一) 连接点是指引管辖权的路标

连接点既是冲突规范借以确定涉外民商事法律关系应当适用什么法律的依据,也是法院借以确定涉外民商事案件管辖权的依据。连接点具有分配管辖权的功能。②连接点的法律意义表现为把某一法律案件与一定地域的法院联系起来的纽带或媒介作用。从实质上看,这种纽带或媒介又反映了该法律案件与一定地域的法院之间存在着内在的实质联系或隶属关系。正因为如此,连接点的存在和认定不是任意的,更不是虚构的。对法院管辖权的选择,实际上也是对连接点的一种确定,确定了连接点也就确定了管辖案件法院。

---

① 朱萍:《虚拟空间管辖权的确定——美国和欧盟实践的启示》,载《法商研究》2002年第4期。
② 肖永平:《肖永平论冲突法》,武汉大学出版社2002年版,第418页。

经过几百年的发展,国际私法中形成了一系列约定俗成的连接点。这些连接点主要分为体现属地优越权的连接点和体现属人优越权的连接点两大类,前者如合同履行地、合同缔结地、侵权行为地、物之所在地、婚姻缔结地等,后者如国籍、船旗国法等。现有连接点的选择,深深地打上了"地理定位"的烙印。

(二) 互联网对连接点的挑战

传统国际私法连接点以地域性为其主要特征,即以固定的、可触及的物理空间为标志,如供应地、履行地、行为地、住所等。然而,网络空间作为一个全球化的整体,具有无形性的特点,不可能像物理空间那样划分出一个个地理区域。同样,网络行为的不确定性使具体的网络行为无法指向确定的连接因素。当一个终端用户进行远程登录的时候,登录行为涉及的对象、地点,是否侵犯他人的权利等,司法机关很难查明,有时连网络用户本人也无从知道。因此,互联网所依托的全球性、虚拟性的网络空间,对传统国际私法连接点的选择和确定,提出了新的挑战。

1. 互联网对属地连接点的挑战

互联网商务活动与传统的民商事活动有着很大的不同,它是在一种与地理空间完全不一样的网络空间中进行的。任何一笔通过互联网方式进行的交易,其过程和大多数环节都是在网络空间上自动完成的,而网络空间是一个虚拟的世界,地理因素在其中并无太大的实际意义,很难从地域的角度对这些过程和环节予以确定或场所化。有些时候要在网上确定一个地点或是不可能,或是相当困难,如在网上缔结合同就难以确定合同缔结地位于何处。如果网上交易不涉及实物或有形的交付,而是网上定购、支付和交付无形货物和服务,如计算机软件、娱乐信息服务,合同履行地同样很难确定。在网络环境下确定行为地,要比在现实物理空间中复杂得多,因为现有的技术并不能有效地确定网络活动主体的所处位置,尤其是在公共网吧或图书馆公共机房等地实施的行为,由于上网者大多采用匿名或假名,即使查出联网的计算机位置所在,也难以确定具体的行为人。而且行为地有可能是多个,这样的话法院便会无所适从,因为法院不可能根据这么多个连接点去确定管辖法院。因此,在传统国际私法中扮演着十分重要角色的属地连接点,面对互联网,必然会受到很大的冲击和挑战。

2. 互联网对属人连接点的挑战

属人连接点表明当事人与特定国家或地方具有内在联系,如国籍、住所等。互联网是面向任何国家、任何人开放的一种独立自主的系统,用户可以任意到一台联网的计算机上从事网上活动,而且上网时不要求确认身份,因此国家与当事人之间的联系是相当弱的。随着人员跨国流动的日益频繁,国籍、住所作为连接点的作用

第十六章 国际互联网纠纷的管辖权

大不如前,在互联网中以国籍、住所为连接点的意义不大。① 下面我们通过雅虎公司涉嫌拍卖纳粹物品案②(**Yahoo!, Inc. v. La Ligue Contre Le Racisme et L'antisemitisme**),对连接点在互联网商务领域面临的挑战,做出进一步分析。

【释义】　Yahoo!, Inc. v. La Ligue Contre Le
　　　　　Racisme et L'antisemitisme③

　　Defendants *La Ligue Contre Le Racisme Et l'Antisemitisme* ("LICRA") and *L'Union Des Etudiants Juifs De France*, are organizations dedicated to eliminating anti-Semitism. Plaintiff Yahoo!, Inc. ("Yahoo!") is a corporation organized under the laws of Delaware with its principal place of business in Santa Clara, California.

　　LICRA filed a civil complaint against Yahoo! in the Tribunal de Grande Instance de Paris (the "French Court"). The French Court found that approximately 1000 Nazi and Third Reich related objects, were being offered for sale on Yahoo.com's auction site. Because any French citizen is able to access these materials on Yahoo.com directly or through a link on Yahoo.fr, the French Court concluded that the Yahoo.com auction site violates Section R645-1 of the French Criminal Code, which prohibits exhibition of Nazi propaganda and artifacts for sale. On May 20, 2000, the French Court entered an order requiring Yahoo! to (1) eliminate French citizens' access to any material on the Yahoo.com auction site that offers for sale any Nazi objects, relics, insignia, emblems, and flags; (2) eliminate French citizens' access to web pages on Yahoo.com displaying text, extracts; (3) post a warning to French citizens on Yahoo.fr that any search through Yahoo.com may lead to sites containing material prohibited by Section R645-1 of the French Criminal Code, and that such viewing of the prohibited material may result in legal action against the Internet user; (4) remove from all browser directories accessible in the French Republic index headings. The order subjects Yahoo! to a penalty of 100000 Euros for each day that it fails to comply with the order.

---

① 李臣:《略论 Internet 对传统冲突法的挑战》,载《法学》1999 年第 11 期。
② 2000 年 4 月原告全法犹太学生联合会(简称 L'Uejf)和国际反种族歧视及排犹协会(简称 La Licra)在法国巴黎大审法院对美国雅虎公司(Yahoo! Inc.)和法国雅虎公司(Yahoo.fr)提起诉讼。理由是:认为雅虎公司的一个网站 www.yahoo.com(雅虎美国站)收录了一个拍卖纳粹物品的站点,法国用户可以通过雅虎进入到这个拍卖网站,这严重地伤害了他们的感情,侵犯了他们的权利。雅虎公司辩解说,这个拍卖网站不属于雅虎,雅虎只是提供网站地址的分类、查找、链接服务;并且这个拍卖网站只有通过雅虎美国站才可以进入,却不能通过雅虎法国站进入。而雅虎美国站的服务器位于美国,根据美国宪法的有关规定,美国宪法不仅保护言论出版自由,而且亦不禁止展示或出售纳粹物品。法国受诉法院的 Gomez 法官于 2000 年 11 月 20 日对本案作出了裁决。法国法院认为,雅虎公司违反了法国不允许展示或出售纳粹物品的有关规定,要求雅虎公司必须在 3 个月内采取必要的技术措施,以阻止法国用户通过雅虎美国站进入到该拍卖网站。但是,由于雅虎公司在法国没有分公司或任何资产,故该项裁决最终得由美国法院予以承认与执行。2001 年 5 月,雅虎公司在美国加利福尼亚州法院提起上诉,要求该法院裁定法国法院的判决无效。其上诉的主要理由是:法国法院对本案不享有管辖权,而且法国法院适用了不应该适用的法国法。See L'Uejf & La Licra v. Yahoo! Inc. & Yahoo France.
③ 169 F. Supp. 2d 1181; 2001 U.S. Dist LEXIS 18378; 30 Media L. Rep. 1001.

Yahoo! seeks a declaration from this Court that the First Amendment precludes enforcement within the United States of a French order intended to regulate the content of its speech over the Internet. Yahoo! also has shown that an actual controversy exists and that the threat to its constitutional rights is real and immediate. Defendants have failed to show the existence of a genuine issue of material fact or to identify any such issue the existence of which could be shown through further discovery. Accordingly, the motion for summary judgment will be granted.

应该说,雅虎公司涉嫌拍卖纳粹物品案非常典型地反映了互联网对传统国际私法连接点的挑战。归纳起来,它主要表现在对当事人国籍与住所的挑战。在传统国际私法中,涉外民商事法律关系的主体是否具有民商事行为能力、法院管辖权的确定、准据法的选择及外国判决的承认与执行问题,都取决于国际私法主体即当事人的国籍或住所这样一些连接点。他们是冲突规范借以确定涉外民商事法律关系应该适用哪一国法律的根据。可见,当事人的国籍与住所在国际私法中占有重要的地位。现有的国际私法上连接点的选择,不可避免地打上了"地理位置"的烙印。但是,网络案件中涉外民商事法律关系主体的国籍或住所与一般国际民商事案件主体的国籍和住所有什么不同呢?在本案中,雅虎主要是通过其位于美国的服务器与互联网相连来从事活动①,其公司的办公活动场所也位于美国。但由于网络的互联性,法国用户在使用美国雅虎站时,必须通过法国的网络服务提供商(ISP)联入互联网,还必须通过位于法国的网络线路和位于大西洋公海海底的光缆传输信息,这些地点是否也可以看做是雅虎从事经营活动的场所呢?如果把这些必要的路径都看做营业场所,那么这样的营业场所实际上遍及全球,以哪一个作为营业中心呢?另外,雅虎公司在互联网上提供的各种服务都是免费的,它是通过在其网站上发布广告来盈利。广告可以被世界各地的用户看到,雅虎的经营活动也就发生在世界各地。这使得人们很难从它的营业活动地判断它的住所。事实上,由于网络的互联性,传统意义上的住所具有的明显的地域特征变得十分模糊。自然人的住所也一样,以个人的名义从事活动的人虽然也是现实世界中活动的自然人,但一个自然人在网络中可以登记虚假的名字、性别、年龄、国籍,而别人也很难识别其资料的真伪。虽然个人所使用的电脑在联网后便会有一个互联网地址②,从互联网地址可以看出该部电脑所处的地区,但也无法据此来判断该电脑用户的国籍和住所。

---

① 服务器(server)是网络资源存放的地方,通常由若干台电脑(也可以只是一台电脑)组成。服务器既与互联网相连接,又与用户电脑相连接,起到一种中介作用。

② 互联网中的每个电脑都有一个编号,由4组数字组成,这便是互联网地址(Internet Point),经网络服务提供商入网的用户IP又有静态和动态之分,动态的IP每次上网都不同。

3. 互联网对当事人意思自治的挑战

互联网商务合同的订立者极少面对面接触，较少对法律适用问题进行充分协商。对于这种交易，一旦发生争议，很难通过确定连接点指引准据法的适用。有学者认为，当事人就每笔网上交易都达成协议是不现实的，供货商通常都预先在网上制定好格式合同，利用其较为有利的经济地位制定利于己而不利于对方的条款，如免责条款、法律选择条款等，对合同的风险作不合理分配。如，在"点击合同"（click-wrap contract）中①，消费者只要点击"接受"或"拒绝"键，就决定了该合同是否成立。而消费者只有表示全部同意或全部不同意的选择，没有协商的余地。②点击合同是互联网格式合同中最具代表性的一种。另外，在商家对消费者的合同中，各国关于消费者权利保护的规定往往是强制性的，一般不能通过法律选择条款加以排除。

因特网是一个虚拟的世界，许多客观的连接因素难以有效地运用于网络中，人们不得不转而借助主观的连接因素，以让当事人的主观选择发挥更大的作用。因特网本身的构造也为主观连接因素的运用埋下了伏笔。我们知道，因特网是由无数个局域网连接起来的"网络的网络"。较小的网络如果要加入较大的网络，就必须接受其预先设定的条件。由于因特网是一个高度自治的网络空间，用户的自主选择是开展网上活动的前提，因此，主观连接因素，特别是当事人意思自治日益突显其重要性。

主观性连接点以其弹性强、无边界的特点，与网络的主要特征相符。因此，在推崇自由、便捷、高效的无纸贸易的今天，对主观性连接点的限制应逐渐减少，以适合互联网商务不断发展的需要。对于互联网商务争议，在新的连接点尚未得到各国立法认可以前，要选择一个能较好地适用于互联网合同的法律，既不能通过机械的立法一蹴而就，也不能由法院自作主张地实现，而允许当事人就他们之间的互联网商务争议的法律适用达成协议，无疑是解决问题的最好办法。在海牙国际私法会议的讨论中，人们唯一达成一致的就是法院选择条款和法律选择条款。③欧盟通过修订《布鲁塞尔条约》的方式，将其改为《布鲁塞尔一号法案》（**Brussels I Regulation**），以逐步建立互联网的管辖权问题。

---

① 许多网络商店会将交易双方的权利义务制定在网页上，欲进行交易的，必须触按鼠标点击"同意"，表示接受该合同条款的内容，然后才能继续完成交易的后续程序。一旦完成一定程序，即视为接受该合同条款的内容。1998 年美国加州北区联邦地方法院在 Corporation v. Van Money Pie Inc. 一案中作出了首例确认点击合同效力之判决，但该合同的效力仍然受到人们的广泛置疑。

② 何其生：《电子商务的国际私法问题》，法律出版社 2004 年版，第 107 页。

③ 黄进、何其生：《电子商务与冲突法的变革》，载《中国法学》2003 年第 1 期。

【释义】 Brussels I Regulation

In March 2002, the European Council ("EC") revised the Brussels Convention on Jurisdiction and the Enforcement of Judgments in Civil and Commercial Matters ("Brussels Convention") in the form of the Brussels Regulation (Council Regulation 44/2001 of 22 December 2000 on Jurisdiction and the Recognition and Enforcement of Judgments in Civil and Commercial Matters, "Brussels I") which attempted to create a uniform approach to internet jurisdiction within the EU. The legislation that focused on business-to-consumers ("B2C") transactions adopted a country-of-destination approach that is heavily protective of consumers by giving the consumer the choice of litigating in their local jurisdiction. In addition to Brussels I, the EC is also contemplating a proposed revision to the Convention on the Law Applicable to Contractual Obligations (Rome Convention), which dictates the substantive law the Court should apply in a case, known as Rome II.①

在互联网商务领域，当事人既然有权按照自己的意志来协商各自所享有的权利和承担的义务，也应有权决定适用的法律。在美国，《统一互联网计算机信息交易法》(Uniform Computer Information Transactions Act, UCITA)不仅允许当事人协议选择法律，而且起草者认为，在全球进入信息社会的背景下，要求当事人所选择的法律和在线交易有"合理联系(reasonable relation)"是十分不合适和武断的，并将增加互联网商务的成本和不确定性。修订后的美国《统一商法典》的§1-301(f)规定，除了在消费者合同中要考虑公共政策和合理联系的规定外，将无条件地允许当事人意思自治(**parties' power to choose applicable law**)。

【释义】 parties' power to choose applicable law

§1-301(f). Territorial Applicability

Parties' power to choose applicable law, (f) an agreement otherwise effective under subsection (c) is not effective to the extent that application of the law of the State or country designated would be contrary to a fundamental policy of the State or country whose law would govern in the absence of agreement under subsection (d).

三、互联网对管辖权法律制度的影响

无国界的网络交易，对传统管辖权提出了新的挑战，传统的管辖权原则已经不

---

① See Green Paper on the Conversion of the Rome Convention of 1980 on the Law Applicable to Contractual Obligations into a Community Instrument and its Modernisation, COM (02) 654 final (setting out the general text of the legal questions of Rome II), available at http://register.consilium.eu.int/pdf/en/03/st05/st05516en03.pdf (visited Jan. 21, 2008).

能继续在新兴的电子商务诉讼中得以适用,具体表现在以下方面:

(一)网络空间的全球一体化使司法管辖的地理界限变得模糊

在传统管辖权的确定原则中,地域因素是一个非常重要的确定管辖权的基础。由于网络空间的全球性,上网后无论谁点击任何地区或国家的网站都可进入,这种行为彻底打破了这种空间上的有形界限。网上活动可能是多方的,活动者分别处于不同的国家和管辖区域之内,这使法院原来非常明确的管辖区域变得模糊甚至无法划清了。如果在传统规则下确定网上活动的管辖权,可能会产生世界上所有国家的法院对某一网上行为都有管辖权的结果。判断网上活动发生的具体地点和确切范围是很难的,将其对应到某一特定的管辖区域之内就更难了。

(二)互联网的无界性使地域管辖权陷入困境

传统的国际私法的管辖权标准取决于人的住所、居所、国籍,被告的出现,诉讼原因发生地,诉讼标的所在地,被告的财产所在地或者财产扣押的所在地等连接因素,这些管辖权的标准都有较强的地域性,地域是法院在选择管辖时的一个具有决定性意义的连接点。[1]然而网络空间活动的范围与影响具有全球性,难以有针对性地限定它的确切范围。互联网环境是一个开放的全球系统,没有明确的国家界限的划分,人们在网络上的交往往往借助于数字传输,数字传输可以在瞬息间往返于千里之外,甚至是跨越数国,而其本人却无须发生任何空间上的位移变化。而根据属地原则,一国只可以对本国境内的网上行为进行管辖,而不能直接对外国的相关活动实施管辖,否则是有违属地原则的立法本意。在网络空间,我们不可能找到网络活动者的住所、财产等客观因素,也不可能确定活动者的国籍和其登录的确定地点,也难以认定登陆者的身份,所以网络空间活动者的住所、国籍、财产等原来与物理空间密切联系的因素,在进入网络空间后已经失去其本身的意义。于是在这个虚拟的空间中,如何划分各国的相对管辖权以及某一特定法院对于数字传输的管辖究竟是涉及其全过程还是仅仅涉及其中一个或数个环节,就使得以地域为基础的管辖权陷入了困境。

(三)以国籍等为基础的管辖权根据不能确定

传统理论依据属人原则、属地原则以及当事人意思自治原则,通常以住所、国籍、行为地、财产等连接点作为确定管辖权的依据。但在互联网中这些依据相对弱化,并具有多样性,比如在网络中当事人可以在一个地点游历世界上各个国家的网站。以住所、国籍、行为地、财产等连接点为基础的管辖权是指只要所涉及的人、

---

[1] 侯捷:《网络侵权案件管辖权探析》,载《当代法学》2002年第8期。

事与法院地有合理的或有意义的联系,行为地法院就有管辖权。在以网络为基础的联系中,何种程度的联系足以使法院具有管辖权很难确定。

(四) 互联网对管辖权其他方面同样有所冲击

在互联网时代下的虚拟空间中产生的法律纠纷,该由哪个国家行使管辖权是一个非常棘手的问题。网络正以惊人的发展速度影响着我们生活的方方面面,它在给予我们方便与快捷的同时,也带来了一系列的法律问题:网上的著作权如何保护,网络的信息安全以及隐私权的保护等,这些法律问题的解决同样有赖于管辖权的确定。而在虚拟空间中,管辖权的定义本身就受到了质疑。例如,如何来确定网络中的涉外因素,传统观念中,如果民商事法律中主体、客体或是内容之一具有涉外联系的,就可以被认为具有涉外因素;然而"网络无国界"是互联网的最大特点,从传统的观念来看,涉外联系几乎时时刻刻都在发生,而且很多时候,很难预料将会和谁在何处发生怎样的联系,如果将所有这些情况都作为涉外因素加以考虑,势必使民商事关系处于一种十分不稳定的状态,根本就无法确定管辖权,还会大大阻碍互联网的发展。网络的国界隐蔽性特点使得当事人的住所、国籍、行为等面临不确定状况,在管辖权方面,也使传统的管辖基础产生了动摇。①

四、网络服务器所在地成为新的管辖权连接因素

网络服务器(internet server)所在地的法律地位问题对于网络管辖权的确定是一个非常重要的方面。与当事人有关的任何因素如果能够成为法院行使管辖权的依据,必须具备两个条件:一是该因素自身有时间和空间上的相对稳定性,至少是可以确定的;二是该因素自身与管辖区域之间存在一定的关联度。

网络服务器自身所具有的特性能够满足这种要求,服务器所在地应该成为新的管辖依据。网络服务器,或称为服务器,是网络环境下为客户提供各种网络服务的专用计算机。服务器所在地是这种为客户提供各种网络服务的专用计算机的所在地点。网络服务器能够成为新的法院管辖权的连接因素,理由如下:

第一,服务器网址所在地的相对稳定性。服务器所在地并非存在于网络空间,而是真实存在的地理地址。它的变更一般与网络服务提供商(internet service provider, ISP)的变更以及周围环境的变化相关联,如随网络服务提供商一同迁址或放置服务器地点本身不适合继续放置等,但这些情况一般很少发生,所以在特定的时间段内,它是可以确定的。另外服务器是网络环境下为客户提供某种服务的专用计算机,因为服务器是在网络中连续不断工作的,且网络数据流在这里形成了一个

---

① 参见刘力主编:《国际民事诉讼管辖权研究》,中国法制出版社2004年版,第80页。

第十六章 国际互联网纠纷的管辖权

瓶颈,所以服务器的数据处理速度和可靠性比普通计算机高得多,且有更高的技术含量,所以服务器主机所在地要比普通的家用、商务计算机所在地具有更强的相对稳定性。

第二,服务器所在地与管辖区域之间的关联度。既然考虑从网址入手确定网络上各种纠纷的管辖权①,而网址却是网络空间中为确定信息传送起点和终点的虚拟地址,并非法院管辖地域内的地理地址,那么就需要找出与网址相关联的地理地址,才能由此决定管辖该地理地址的法院。一个网址所指向的地理地址实际上就是拥有该网址的主机服务器的所在地,那么依据上面提出的网址关联性分析,服务器所在地更应该成为确定网络管辖权的标准之一。因此,英国在 2000 年海牙国际私法会议上提出在电子商务合同中,拥有管辖权的法院应该是信息传送地,英国对于信息传送的解释是接收信息方提供接收电子信息的服务器所在地。

由此可见,网络服务器的所在地可以被视为网络活动主体的所在地。当一个主体改变其现实住所所在的地区时,其所使用的服务器所在地也必然会发生改变;而主体在某一地区固定居住时,其服务器的所在地也是不变的。可见,服务器所在地具有稳定性,而且在技术上也易于确认。

当然,将服务器所在地作为网络管辖权根据和其他的网络管辖权根据一样,受到诸多因素的限制。有的学者指出行为人如果使用的是带内置的 Medom 和网卡的便携式笔记本电脑,他可以走到哪里就在哪里上网,那么网址所指向的服务器所在地即呈现出不断移动和变化的状态。②即使能够获取电脑的物理空间存放地址,其所指引的仅仅是一台电脑,电脑本身并不能实施任何行为,而只能由操作电脑的人来实施,如果这台电脑属于某个网吧或位于其他公共场所,则未必能查实实施某一行为的具体个人。在这种情况下,该原则的适用是受到限制的。③

---

① 网址与管辖区域有一定的联系,特别是与提供网址的 ISP 所在地区有密切的联系,同时网址活动涉及其他网络参加者时,与其他参加者所在地的管辖区域也产生联系。参见罗艺方、赖紫宁:《网络空间司法管辖权理论的比较研究》,载《政治与法律》2003 年第 6 期。

② 因为互联网是一种面向任何国家、任何人开放的一种独立自主的系统,用户可以任意到一台联网的计算机上从事网上活动,而且上网时并不要求确认其真实身份,随着人员跨国流动的日益频繁,网址所指向的服务器所在地也可能处于移动状态。参见齐爱民、刘颖:《网络法研究》,法律出版社 2003 年版,第 388 页。

③ 曹雪明:《网络侵权的特点及其管辖权确定》,载《人民法院公报》2001 年第 12 期。

第二节 互联网管辖权理论

针对互联网的特性,西方学者们对网络案件的管辖问题提出了各种不同的理论,其中比较有影响的就是网络空间自治论和网络管辖权相对论。

一、网络空间自治论

(一)网络空间自治论概述

网络空间自治论(cyberspace self-governance),以美国的约翰逊(David R. Johnson)和波斯特(David G. Post)为代表。①该理论的主要观点为:对于网络争议,应该摆脱传统的地域管辖的观念,承认网络虚拟空间就是一个特殊的地域,并承认在网络世界与现实世界中存在一个法律上十分重要的边界,若要进入网络的地域,必须通过屏幕或密码,一旦进入网络的虚拟世界,则应适用网络世界的网络法,而不再适用现实中各国不同的法律,也就是所谓的网络空间自治。

早在1996年,美国电子商务领域的先驱人物John Perry Barlow就宣布了《网络独立宣言》(Declaration of the Independence of Cyberspace)②,提出了"网络空间自治论"。③网络空间自治论认为,在网络空间中正在形成一个新的"全球性的市民社会"(global civil society),这一社会有自己的组织形式、价值判断标准和自我规范与裁定功能。它完全脱离政府的管辖,自由地行使自治的权力,从而建立促进自由发展的"网络大同世界"。④在网络空间中没有国家的暴力机关、没有法律、没有警察、没有监狱,每个Internet用户只服从于他的网络服务提供商,而网络服务提供商之间以协议的方式来协调和统一各自的规则,就像协调纯粹的技术标准一样。网络成员之间的冲突由网络服务提供商以仲裁者的身份来解决,裁决也由网络服务提

---

① David G. Post, David R. Johnson, Chaos Prevailing on Every Continent: Towards A New Theory of Decentralized Decision-Making in Complex Systems, 73 *Chi.-Kent. L. Rev.* 1055, 1055 (1998).

② See John Perry Barlow, A Declaration of the Independence of Cyberspace, Electronic Frontier Foundation, Available ate http://www.eff.org/barlow (feb.9.1996).

③ See Neil Weinstock Netanel, Cyberspace Self-Governance: A Skeptical View from Liberal Democratic Theory, 88 *Calif. L. Rev.* 395, 395 (2000).

④ 参见王德全:《试论Internet案件的司法管辖权》,载《中外法学》1998年第2期。

供商来执行。他们认为,网络空间应适用独立于实际空间的法律制度,对网络案件应建立一种独立的管辖体制,新的电子网络应该是一个独立的法律管辖权区域(a separate legal jurisdiction)。网络空间自治论首先是将网络空间作为游离于国家与政府之外的一块自治飞地;其次,该理论试图以自律性管理来代替传统的国家管辖。由于网络空间是无主权之地,各国都可以肆意扩张其网络主权,因而这种名义上自治的主张实际上给发达国家对"主权飞地"进行管辖扩张提供了理论前提。① 后来,被 Netanel 教授称为"网络空间自治论者"(cyberians)②的"网络空间自治论"追随者(supporters)又提出了支持这一理论的几点论据③:首先,网络空间独立的特性可以最大限度地增加财富。这是由于网络脱离了管理集权化与官僚政治化的影响,因此使得交易更灵活、更高效并且更有选择余地。其次,政府所制定的适用于现实空间的规则,对于网络来说,根本是琐碎无用的,因此,政府应该放弃这种尝试。由于网络的非中心化及全球化的特性,任何国家试图给网络烙上自己国家烙印的行为都是惘然的。另外,只有网络空间自治才能完全地实现被许多国家信奉的自由民主思想。④

(二) 对网络空间自治论的解读

网络空间自治论支持者的观点充满想象力。一方面,他们完全忽视了互联网的存在主要是依靠显示空间为依托的,电子商务中货物的收发和货币的支付都是在现实生活中真实存在的。另一方面,这一理论同时也混淆了两种不同的权力和权利,即网络服务提供商之间制定道德与技术标准的权利和国家制定法律进行管辖的权力。公力救济是永远也无法被自我管理和约束的规则所代替的。网络空间现有的技术标准和道德底线也是在国家法律规制的基础上才完好地被遵守和发挥作用的,这是网上自我约束的基石。因此,网络空间自治论的观点是在违背了主权国家管辖权和法律规范作用基础上产生的理论。

首先,网络空间自治论将网络空间作为游离于国家与政府之外的一块自治之地。网络空间自治论者认为国家出手干预网络的管理是很困难的,往往也是徒劳无功的,因为网络是没有国界的,每个国家的历史背景、民族文化、生活习惯等都不尽相同,要形成一个统一的规范是很困难的。另外,网络与其他行业的结合能产生新的行业,由此产生的交叉行业和新兴行业在界定和管理上将出现更大的空隙,导

---

① 王德全:《试论 Internet 案件的司法管辖权》,载《中外法学》1998 年第 2 期。
② Neil Weinstock Netanel, Cyberspace Self-Governance: A Skeptical View from Liberal Democratic Theory, 88 *Calif. L. Rev.* 395, 401 (2000).
③ 参见李增辉:《电子商务国际管辖权制度探析》,载《理论界》2005 年第 8 期。
④ See Llewellyn Joseph Gibbons, No Regulation, Government Regulation, or Self-Regulation: Social Enforcement or Social Contracting for Governance in Cyberspace, 6 *Cornell J. L. &Pub. Pol'y* 475, 475 (1997).

致传统的行政管理的困难。但是,管理困难并不等于无法管理和可以完全放任不管。更为重要的是网络是客观真实存在的,它不能脱离于社会而独立存在。网络管理的非中心化不能否定传统的价值标准和规则,网络空间不能游离于国家、政府之外而不受约束。①

其次,网络空间自治论者忽视了互联网的存在是以客观现实为基础的,它的产生也是从客观存在中发明的,网络空间并非是一个独立的、虚无的空间。"网络社会"的建立不可能绝对摆脱国家对网络的管理和控制,即使"网络社会"存在,也只能是各国利益妥协的产物。随着电子商务的发展,国家会更加频繁地制定相关的法律法规,每个国家都不会放弃对网络空间的管辖,因为这是一个国家主权在网络空间上的体现

最后,网络空间自治论者认为,网络空间可以形成特有的、行之有效的"网络法"。因为互联网是通过自治系统来实施的,人们可以通过建立一个系统来管束自己。但是,所谓的"网络法"只是行业道德和技术标准的混淆物,它完全混淆了两种不同的权力,即网络服务提供商之间制定行业道德与技术标准的权利和主权国家制定法律进行管辖的权力,过分强调了技术标准和行业道德的约束作用。与具有强制力的法律相比,它们对当事人的约束作用实则要弱得多。技术标准和行业道德对法律的形式能够起到一定的促进作用,有时也可能上升为法律,但永远不可能取代法律。同样自律管理也无法替代公力救济。

网络客观性的特点告诉我们,网络是真实存在的,它不能脱离于社会而独立存在。网络管理的非中心化不能否定传统的价值标准和规则,网络不能游离于国家、政府之外而不受约束。任何哲学家在论述市民社会时都未排斥政治国家,只是要求市民社会与政治国家之间二元良性互动,保持一定的理想距离,单独地提及市民社会或者政治国家,都只是一种专制的形式而已。网络空间的发展,关键的问题在于如何使二者相协调,而最大限度地保护网络的发展。因此,网络空间自治论实际上是一种不切实际的空想,当然不能成立。由此推出的否定法院管辖的观点当然也不能成立

(三) 对网络空间自治论的反思

网络空间自治论是关于互联网管辖权问题的争议。对于互联网管辖权的讨论,最重要的是如何看待网络空间这个问题。是将其视为一种通讯交流的工具,还是一种地域。在互联网中的每一台计算机都是属于个人、企业、政府或者其他组织所有的,但是互联网本身却不属于上述主体所有,虽然每一台计算机或者某个区域

---

① See Amy Lynne Bomse, The Dependence of Cyberspace, 50 *Duke L. J.* 1717, 1717 (2001).

的网络受到国家或其他组织的法律约束,但是互联网整体是没有地理位置的,互联网不受任何国家或组织的约束,我们不应该把互联网整体看成是诉讼法意义上的一个"地域"。

虽然互联网不是诉讼法意义上的"地域",但是,在互联网中活动的人是存在于现实世界中的,也一定是在某个特定的地理位置。作为行使管辖权客体之一的"行为或事件",在网络上虽然没有固定的地点,但是,事物都是互相联系的一个整体,网络和现实世界有着紧密的联系。无论网络上的具体行为发生在何处,他们总是会对现实生活中的人或者物产生影响,一旦这种影响达到了法律所要求的结果,这些联系就构成了一个国家法院行使管辖权的基础。

当然,法院行使管辖权,也不应该把"手"伸得过长,对于一些可以通过网络争议解决机制解决的网络问题,就应该鼓励通过网络争议解决机制来解决,如在线调解、在线仲裁、在线和解等,都可以采纳和加以发展。如果当事人愿意将纠纷交给这些机构解决,法院应当尊重当事人的选择。

二、网络管辖权相对论

(一) 网络管辖权相对论的内容

管辖权相对论又称为管辖权独立论。该理论的内容是这样的:

第一,网络空间应该作为一个新的管辖区域而存在,就像公海、国际海底区域和南极洲一样,应在此领域内建立不同于传统规则的新的管辖权原则。从长远的观点看,这才是解决问题的根本办法。一旦进入网络的虚拟世界,则应适用网络空间的网络法,而不再适用现实世界中各国不同的法律。如此一来,就可以不必为行为或交易发生地为何地而争论不休。

第二,任何国家都可以管辖并将其法律适用于网络空间内的任何活动,其程度与方式与该人或该活动进入该主权国家可以控制的网络空间的程度和方式相适应。

第三,网络空间内争端的当事人可以通过网络的联系在相关法院"出庭",法院的判决也可以通过网络手段来加以执行。[①]由于考虑到让一个身居亚洲的人到美国的某地方法院出庭有违合理性原则,法院可以通过电子邮件召开听证会来行使管辖权,而后运用网络过滤器或清除器来执行判决,这个过滤器或清除器可以追踪和阻碍该人以后发送的同类信息。

这一理论旨在通过技术自身的力量来解决技术带来的司法困境,各国对作为

---

① 参见郑成思:《知识产权研究》,中国政法大学出版社1999年版,第266页。

整体的网络空间的管辖权的大小取决于该国接触和控制网络的范围和能力。应摆脱传统地域管辖的观念,而承认网络虚无空间就是一个特殊的地域,并承认在网络世界与现实世界中存在有一个法律上十分重要的边界。若要进入网络的地域,必须通过屏幕或密码,一旦进入网络的虚无世界,则应适用网络世界的网络法,而不再适用现实世界中各国不同的法律。

(二) 对网络管辖权相对论的评价

该理论意欲通过技术自身的力量来解决技术所带来的法律问题。但是它忽视了网络空间与物理空间千丝万缕的联系,单纯的技术力量并不能解决技术造成的管辖权适用上的困难,无法保护网络纠纷中当事人的利益。因此,如果这种相对的理论不能与物理空间中某一主权国家的管辖权相结合,它就不具有真正的可操作性;它如果没有直接的国家强制力加以保障,就没有任何的实际价值。

网络管辖权相对论无论是在目前,还是在我们可以看到的将来都是不现实的。将网络空间看做一个自成一体的社会,完全脱离现实的物理空间是不切实际的,就比如网络侵权行为是在网络空间中发生的,但是受影响的人并不生活在网络中。我们更该考虑如何在传统规则的框架内解决新问题。当然,针对网络空间中的一些特点制定与其相适应的、以一定技术基础为依托的法律规则也是必不可少的。

网络管辖权相对论过分地强调了网络空间的新颖性和独立性,并否定网络以外的法院及其他国家权力对于网络的管辖,割裂了网络空间与物理空间存在着的现实联系,实际已脱离了网络本身就是由现实中的人作为主体、以人的活动为最终客体而形成的"虚拟空间"的理论基础。管辖权相对论试图摒弃传统的国际私法原则和规则,这些都对传统的国际私法理论提出了尖锐的挑战。

第三节 互联网的管辖依据

一、以网址为依据的管辖

(一) Zippo Dot Com 案

网址(websites)具有相对稳定性,它在网络空间中的地位类似于住所地在地理位置上的地址。网址与管辖区域有一定的关联度,特别是与提供网址的 ISP 所在的地理区域有密切而充分的联系。美国法院一系列的司法实践,已经使得该理论的规则逐渐成熟起来。在 **Zippo Manufacturing Corporation v. Zippo Dot Com, Inc**. 一案中,美国联邦宾夕法尼亚西部地区法院(United States District Court for the Western District of Pennsylvania)根据"最低限度联系"原则,判定对美国加州的网络公司的商标侵权行为具有管辖权。

【案例】 Zippo Manufacturing Corporation v. Zippo Dot Com, Inc[①]

〔facts〕This is an Internet domain name dispute. Plaintiff Zippo Manufacturing Corporation ("Manufacturing") has filed a five count complaint against Zippo Dot Com, Inc. ("Dot Com") alleging trademark dilution, infringement, and false designation under the Federal Trademark Act Dot Com has moved to dismiss for lack of personal jurisdiction and improper venue, to transfer the case pursuant to 28 U.S.C. §1406(a).

Manufacturing is a Pennsylvania corporation with its principal place of business in Bradford, Pennsylvania. Manufacturing makes, among other things, well known "Zippo" tobacco lighters. Dot Com is a California corporation with its principal place of business in Sunnyvale, California. Dot Com operates an Internet Web site and an Internet news service and has obtained the exclusive right to use the domain names "zippo.com", "zippo.net" and "zipponews.com" on the Internet. The application is then processed and the subscriber is assigned a password which permits the subscriber to view and/or download Internet newsgroup messages that are stored on the Defendant's server in California.

Dot Com's advertising for its service to Pennsylvania residents involves posting information about its service on its Web page, which is accessible to Pennsylvania residents via the Internet. Defendant has approximately 140000 paying subscribers worldwide. Approximately two percent (3000) of those subscribers are Pennsylvania residents. These subscribers have contracted to receive Dot Com's service by visiting its Web site and filling out the application. Additionally, Dot Com has entered into agreements with seven Internet access providers in Pennsylvania to permit their subscribers to access Dot Com's news service. Two of these providers are located in the Western District of Pennsylvania.

The basis of the trademark claims is Dot Com's use of the word "Zippo" in the domain names it holds, in numerous locations in its Web site and in the heading of Internet newsgroup messages that have been posted by Dot Com subscribers.

本案中,法院认为,被告与宾州居民和服务提供商之间存在着合同关系,允许宾州用户下载网站上的信息,与宾州的商户签订商务代理合同等,这些"最低限度联系"的因素符合行使"长臂管辖权"的要求,因此认定宾州法院对案有管辖权。

---

① 952 F. Supp. 1119; 1997 U.S. Dist. LEXIS 1701; 42 U.S.P.Q.2D (BNA) 1062.

(二) Zippo Cybersell, Inc. 案

但是值得强调的是,如果仅有网址存在这个事实,并不足以构成法院管辖权的充分根据。在美国泽普网络销售公司诉网络销售公司①(**Zippo Cybersell, Inc. v. Cybersell, Inc.**)案中,美国亚利桑那州地区法院和美国联邦上诉法院第九巡回法院均认为仅依靠被动性网址(passive websites)不能确定管辖权。②

【案例】　　**Zippo Cybersell, Inc. v. Cybersell, Inc.**③

Cybersell, Inc. is an Arizona corporation, which we will refer to as Cybersell AZ. It was incorporated in May 1994 to provide Internet and web advertising and marketing services, including consulting. On August 8, 1994, Cybersell AZ filed an application to register the name "Cybersell" as a service mark. The application was approved and the grant was published on October 30, 1995. Cybersell AZ operated a web site using the mark.

Cybersell FL was a Florida corporation (Cybersell FL), with its principal place of business in Orlando. As part of their marketing effort, the Cybersell FL created a web page at http://www.cybsell.com/cybsell/index.htm. The home page has a logo at the top with "CyberSell" over a depiction of the planet earth, with the caption underneath "Professional Services for the World Wide Web" and a local (area code 407) phone number. It proclaims in large letters "Welcome to CyberSell!" A hypertext link allows the browser to introduce himself, and invites a company not on the web—but interested in getting on the web—to "Email us to find out how!"

Cybersell AZ filed the complaint in this action January 9, 1996 in the District of Arizona, alleging trademark infringement, unfair competition, fraud, and RICO violations. On the same day Cybersell FL filed suit for declaratory relief with regard to use of the name "Cybersell" in

---

① 原告泽普网络销售公司(Zippo Cybersell, Inc.)是亚利桑那州的一家公司,被告网络销售公司(Cybersell, Inc.)是佛罗里达州的一家公司,两公司的名称中都有"网络销售"(Cybersell)的字样。被告创建了一个网页,其中包含"网络销售"(Cybersell)的标识,一个本地的电话号码,一个发送电子邮件的邀请函以及一个超文本链接(用户能通过此链接介绍自己的情况)。原告向亚利桑那州地区法院起诉被告侵犯其商标权。地区法院以管辖权不充分为由驳回此案,联邦上诉法院第九巡回法庭维持了该裁决。法院认为,被告在亚利桑那州通过网络并没有任何的商业行为,被告在亚利桑那州没有"有意图地"谋求该州的利益和希望受该州法律的保护。法院最后总结说:"简单地将别人的商标作为域名并放置在网络上,就判定该人的居住地法院有管辖权,这种说法是缺乏依据的"。原告需要证明被告有意图地将他的行为指向诉讼管辖地。

② At one end of the sliding scale are situations in which a defendant uses a Web site to post information, making it accessible to all computer users; these are passive Websites, and generally courts refuse to find jurisdiction based on these Websites alone. The court is finding a lack of jurisdiction based on a passive Web site that allowed customers to sign up and indicate interest in defendant's service and where defendant did not conduct business in the forum state, consummate sales or contracts with forum residents, or otherwise encourage forum residents to access its Web site. See Susan Nauss Exon, The Internet Meets Obi-Wan Kenobi in the Court of Next Resort, 8 B. U. J. Sci. & Tech. L., 1, n6 (2002).

③ 130 F. 3d 414 (9th Cir. 1997).

the United States District Court for the Middle District of Florida, but that action was transferred to the District of Arizona and consolidated with the Cybersell AZ action. Cybersell FL moved to dismiss for lack of personal jurisdiction. The district court denied Cybersell AZ's request for a preliminary injunction, then granted Cybersell FL's motion to dismiss for lack of personal jurisdiction. Cybersell AZ timely appealed.

We conclude that the essentially passive nature of Cybersell FL's activity in posting a home page on the World Wide Web that allegedly used the service mark of Cybersell AZ does not qualify as purposeful activity invoking the benefits and protections of Arizona. As it engaged in no commercial activity and had no other contacts via the Internet or otherwise in Arizona, Cybersell FL lacks sufficient minimum contacts with Arizona for personal jurisdiction to be asserted over it there. Accordingly, its motion to dismiss for lack of personal jurisdiction was properly granted.

AFFIRMED.

考虑网址能否构成新的管辖根据的一个重要因素①,是对"主动性网址"(active websites)、"被动性网址"(passive websites)和"互动性网址"(interactive websites)②的区分。被动性网址只是起到一种发布广告和传播消息的作用,因而不包括在美国"长臂管辖权"的范围之内。因此还要通过网址以外的其他证据和因素的证明,才能行使法院地管辖权,如证明被告通过网址以外的途径和法院地有信件、会议、谈判或其他往来,试图在法院地从事营业活动,或者被告与法院地居民签订电子合同。而在网址上提供了能与用户交换信息的手段,可以推测出被告有意识地将自己置于法院地的司法管辖之下。本案中,被告的网址是被动性网址,法院无法仅依被动性网址判定享有管辖权。泽普网络销售公司诉网络销售公司一案的判决表明,在被告没有从事网络商业活动的情况下,仅依靠被动性网址不能确定管辖权。

(三) 滑动标尺法

滑动标尺法(sliding scale approach)是指根据被告通过互联网所从事的行为与法院地的密切程度来决定法院是否有管辖权的方法,是美国将长臂管辖权应用到涉及互联网的国际民商事案件中确定管辖权的方法③,在上述 Zippo Dot Com 案中,法官首次运用滑动标尺法,认定对案件有管辖权④,因此滑动标尺法又称泽普

---

① 参见刘颖、李静:《网环境下的国际民事管辖权》,载《中国法学》2006 年第 1 期。
② "互动性网址"又称"交互式网址",相关定义参见韦燕:《"最低限度联系"与网络管辖权——美国有关网络管辖权的判例及其发展》,载《河北法学》2001 年第 1 期。
③ Christopher McWhinney, et. al., The "Sliding Scale" of Personal Jurisdiction Via the Internet, 2000 Stan. Tech. L. Rev. 1, 1 (2000).
④ Zippo Mfg. Co. v. Zippo Dot Com, Inc., 952 F. Supp. 1124, 1125—1126 (W. D. Pa. 1997).

标尺法(Zippo sliding scale)①。

二、由虚拟法院进行管辖

在各种理论和适用原则层出不穷的趋势下,越来越多的学者倾向于虚拟法院(Cybercourt, Cybertribunal)管辖原则。②该理论由美国学者 Susan Nauss Exon 提出③,并在世界上引起了广泛关注。该学者认为,设立"国际虚拟法院中心"可以提供诸多便利(**advantages of the international Cybercourt Central**)。

【说理】　　advantages of the international cybercourt central

Proponents of Cybercourt Central have an easy task in persuading others of its convenience and absolute necessity. Although this article concentrates on the use of Cybercourt Central with regard to Internet disputes, Cybercourt Central could function to handle non-Internet disputes as well. The most obvious benefit of Cybercourt Central would be its technological capabilities. Indeed, Cybercourt Central is technology. All parties to legal controversies could enjoy its advantages, including court personnel, jurors, witnesses, attorneys, and disputing parties.

First, the use of technology would bring efficiency to the court system. The management of court pleadings and other documents would be streamlined. With several clicks on a computer mouse, a court clerk could receive, file, and catalog documents into a cybercase file. A judge could then view the court pleadings and documents directly from his or her personal computer, alleviating the necessity for the court staff to manually look for and retrieve paper files. Boxes upon boxes of court files and the need for space to store them could be eliminated almost completely. Cybercase files for concluded cases could be stored on zip disks, CD-ROM, or on the latest electronic storage medium.

Second, the use of technology would assist jurors in performing their duties. Evidence presentation equipment such as the DEPS <tm> could enable jurors to experience physical evidence in much the same manner as the disputing parties did at the time of the dispute. Computers and the Internet are being used already. Jurors could, therefore, visualize exactly what a party had seen on the Internet and how information had been downloaded from it. Through the use of holography, the jurors could perceive the appearances and reactions of all

---

① Susan Nauss Exon, A New Shoe Is Needed to Walk Through Cyberspace Jurisdiction, 11 *Alb. L. J. Sci. & Tech.* 1, 18 (2000).

② 设想中的虚拟法院是与一套自愿注册系统相连接,专门处理互联网上所发生争端的平台。从事电子商务活动的当事人,无论是个人还是公司,都得在中央国际虚拟法院注册。法院可以成立一个独立的机关来处理注册系统。当某一当事人在国际虚拟法院中心注册后,一个特别的注册确认通知将会发送到他的网站或电子邮件信箱里,这就意味着该当事人同意由国际虚拟法庭来解决可能发生的争端。

③ See Susan Nauss Exon, A New Shoe is Needed to Walk Through Cyberspace Jurisdiction, 11 *Alb. L. J. Sci. & Tech.* 1, 54 (2000).

attorneys, parties, and witnesses, enabling them to determine issues of credibility. The juror benefits would apply equally to judges, attorneys and parties. Evidence presentation equipment already enables judges to turn off monitors in front of jurors with just the flick of a switch. Attorneys could streamline the time necessary to present evidence by using such equipment. Since time is money, clients would benefit from shortened trials.

Finally, the use of technology would assist attorneys, their respective clients, and witnesses. Cybercourt Central would be accessible twenty-four hours a day, enabling attorneys to review information in the cybercase file at any convenient time. Attorneys would not have to travel long distances to appear at motion hearings and other pretrial matters because the use of holography as a component of a Cybercourt Central trial would enable disputants to have their day in court without physically going to court. Likewise, witnesses could testify without actually going to a physical courtroom. The relief from long-distance travel would eliminate enormous expenses and save valuable time. Parties, especially small companies, would benefit further by the ability to continue business operations without major interruption. When the trial is not in session, a time period that could amount to several hours each day, parties could maintain a presence in the day-to-day operations of their businesses.①

当事人采用虚拟法庭这种方式解决在电子商务中引起的诉讼案件,不仅节约了当事人的诉讼成本,避免了长途旅行花费的时间和支出,而且极大减轻了当事人的经济负担。从另一角度考虑,虚拟法院的实施具有可行性。当然现在的理论还处于萌芽阶段,必须经过不断的实践加以完善。首先,应该在世界范围内建立起一个相当于国际法庭的虚拟法庭,法庭的构成必须具有国际化性质而不是被几个强国或大国所垄断和控制;其次,要使这种做法成为国际上认可的电子商务民商事管辖权方法,还有赖于世界各国的相关立法的配合和各国国内法的协调。

第四节 国外互联网管辖权的实践

一、美国网络管辖权立法

网络的发展势头正在不断挑战着以物理世界为基础的传统法律制度,为了规

---

① Susan Nauss Exon, The Internet Meets Obi-wan Kenobi in the Court of Next Resort, 8 B. U. J. Sci. & Tech. 1, 18—19 (2002).

范这一空间中的混乱问题,各国都纷纷制定了调整网络法律行为的法律,管辖权这一部分也不例外,许多国家都制定了调整网络民商事案件管辖权的法律,其中以美国的最为丰富。

近几年来,美国制定了几部成文法对电子商务加以系统化、规范化,其中关于网络管辖权方面的有 1999 年 7 月的《统一计算机信息交易法》(The Uniform Computer Information Transactions Act,简称 UCITA)。该法第 110 条规定:"(a)双方可以协议选择一个排他性的管辖法院,除非此种选择不合理且不公平。(b)除非双方协议明确规定,双方协议选择的管辖法院不具有排他性。"该条认可了在线交易当事人可以通过协议的方式选择管辖法院,但在当事人没有有效的商业目的,并且对其他当事人有严重的和不公平的损害时,则协议无效。在当事人没有协议选择管辖法院时,《统一计算机信息交易法》并未对管辖法院的确定作出具体的规定。

二、美国以网址为依据的互联网长臂管辖权实践

长臂管辖权是美国民商事诉讼中的一个重要概念。当被告的住所不在法院地州,但和该州有某种最低限度联系,而且原告所提权利要求的产生和这种联系有关时,就该项权利要求而言,该州对于该被告具有对人管辖权,可以在州外对被告发出传票。以最低限度联系原则为基础的长臂管辖权不但适用于普通的民商事案件,也同样适用于互联网案件,如美国法院所受理的马力斯公司诉网金公司(**Maritz Inc. v. Cybergold Inc.**)案。

【案例】 **Maritz Inc. v. Cybergold Inc.**[①]

CyberGold, Inc. (hereinafter CyberGold) maintains an Internet site on the World Wide Web. The site can be accessed by any Internet user. CyberGold's website provides information about its upcoming service. The website explains that CyberGold's upcoming service will maintain a mailing list of its customers, provide each of these customers with an electronic mailbox, and forward to each customer selected advertisements which match the individual customer's selected interests.

Maritz, Inc. (hereinafter Maritz) filed suit against CyberGold in the United States District Court for the Eastern District of Missouri, seeking preliminary and permanent injunctive relief, as well as damages. Maritz asserted that CyberGold had violated Section 43(a) of the Lanham Act, 15 U.S.C. § 1125(a), by unfairly competing and infringing on Maritz's trademark. CyberGold moved to dismiss for lack of personal jurisdiction, asserting that its only contact with Missouri—operation of a website accessible by Missouri citizens—did not establish the mini-

---

① 947 F. supp. 1328 (E. D. MO. 1996).

第十六章　国际互联网纠纷的管辖权

mum contacts necessary to confer personal jurisdiction over CyberGold in Missouri. [* 847]

In response to CyberGold's motion to dismiss for lack of personal jurisdiction, Maritz asserted two theories which supported the position that the court had personal jurisdiction over CyberGold. First, Maritz contended that CyberGold's website invited Missourians to sign on to CyberGold's mailing list and learn more about CyberGold's upcoming service, and that CyberGold was "actively soliciting advertising customers from Missouri." Maritz asserted that this solicitation was also demonstrated by CyberGold's 131 individual contacts with Missouri customers. Second, Maritz contended that CyberGold's alleged Lanham Act violation caused economic harm to Maritz in Missouri.

The Court held that CyberGold's contact with Missouri satisfied both the statutory and constitutional requirements necessary to establish personal jurisdiction in Missouri, and denied CyberGold's motion to dismiss for lack of personal jurisdiction. The court subsequently denied a motion for reconsideration of the personal jurisdiction issue.①

本案中,原告马力斯公司(Maritz Inc.)是密苏里州的一家公司,被告网金公司(Cybergold Inc.)是加利福尼亚州的公司。被告在加州拥有一个网址,并在其网址上创建了一个邮递列表②,使访问该网址的用户可以通过该邮递列表收到公司服务的信息。原告马力斯公司于1996年4月向密苏里州东区法院起诉,控告被告网金公司侵犯其商标权及进行不正当竞争。网金公司提出了管辖异议,认为密苏里州东区法院无权管辖,但密苏里州东区法院裁决对此案有管辖权。法院认为,被告网址的特性并非是被动的,因为用户可以通过邮递列表收到来自被告公司的信息。这种情况符合美国关于被告和法院所在州间"最低限度联系"的原则,密州法院有权管辖。

在本案中,被告的行为实质上是通过其网址侵犯原告的商标权及进行不正当竞争,因此网址互动性的认定是关键。在网络中,一些网址可以通过用户的登录作出相应的回复,这种网址相对于那些只能被动地被访问的被动性网址来说,称为"互动性网址"。网址的互动通常可通过邮递列表、订阅网上杂志、登记注册等形式表现出来。在本案中,被告依靠邮递列表满足了网址互动的条件,使该网址成为互动性网址。这也是一个典型的运用"最低限度联系"理论所处理的互联网管辖权案例,法院仅依靠被告互动性网址确定了管辖权。法院认为,网络不同于传统的电话,它传递的信息可被所有想看到的人所共享,应当据此拓宽管辖权的行使范围。

---

① Sean M. Flower, When Does Internet Activity Establish the Minimum Contact Necessary to Confer Personal Jurisdiction? 62 *Mo. L. Rev.* 845, 846—847(1997).

② 邮递列表(mailinglist),又称讨论组,其组内的任何成员都可通过电子邮件的形式就某一专题互相发表意见、讨论问题、共享信息等,这个由所有成员组成的集合就称为"邮递列表"。

互动性网址满足了"最低限度联系"的条件,构成对原告所在地的"最低限度"的联系,因此原告所在地法院有管辖权。

对于互联网管辖权案,美国法院将决定管辖依据的重点放在网络交易的卖方的行为(actions of the seller)之上或者网址拥有人(websites owner)之上,而不是消费者。①美国法院通过大量的判例就网络空间的对人管辖权问题初步形成了一些规则,即将网络"对人管辖权"案件大致分为被告在法院管辖地有实际营业活动和无实际营业活动两种类型。对前一类案件,法院对被告有管辖权并没有异议;而对后一类案件,则视具体的情形由法院决定可否对被告行使"长臂管辖"。

美国的法官将长臂管辖理论应用于解决网络民商事案件的管辖的探索是十分有价值的。但是由于长臂管辖权理论的弹性太大,很容易成为管辖权扩张的工具,从而引发国与国之间的管辖权冲突。美国的长臂管辖权是域外管辖权,由于在使用的过程中严重威胁到他国的管辖主权,一直受到其他国家的猛烈抨击。长臂管辖理论的运用可能会使全球所有法域都对网络民商事案件有管辖权,导致国际民商事管辖冲突的泛滥。此外,这一理论尚未被世界多数国家所接受,根据该理论所审理的案件能否得到外国法院的承认和执行也存在很大疑问。作为美国自己的单方面立法,长臂管辖理论对美国本土的网络民商事案权问题的解决起到了决定性作用,它的灵活性也是各国可以借鉴的,但是对这一理论还要仔细考量,寻找并吸收其有益的部分。②

三、欧盟各国互联网诉讼管辖的实践

"欧盟各国法院已在利用基于效果的理论来解决互联网管辖权方面积极行动起来。"③欧盟各国从维护社会公共秩序和保护互联网消费者利益的角度强化了对互联网诉讼的司法管辖,在欧洲形成了1968年《布鲁塞尔公约》、1989年《洛加诺公约》。对消费者实行"原地管辖权"(home jurisdiction),允许不满意的网络购物者在他们居住地的法院对互联网公司起诉,而不管这些公司是否曾在法院地销售商品。④这种管辖权虽然最大限度地保护了消费者的权利,却可能阻碍国际互联网的发展。

---

① Cindy Chen, United States and European Union Approaches to Internet Jurisdiction and Their Impact on E-Commerce, 25 U. Pa. J. Int'l Econ. L. 423, 433 (2004).
② 王永强:《从美国判例看网络纠纷管辖的演变》,载《河北法学》2001年第3期。
③ 参见罗伯特·L.霍格:《因特网与其管辖权》,何乃刚译,载《环球法律评论》2001年春季刊(第23期)。
④ 参见汪金兰:《互联网管辖权规制的探讨》,载《武汉大学学报》(社会科学版)2002年第1期。

第十六章 国际互联网纠纷的管辖权

第五节 网络侵权的管辖权

一、网络侵权的管辖权概述

网上侵权客体和侵权行为的复杂性决定了管辖权确定因素的多样性,网上侵权案件的技术性决定了需要借助技术手段来解决管辖权的问题。在确定何地可作为侵权行为地时,必须考察其是否具有物理位置的关联性、易确定性及损害相关性。因此,网络侵权案件管辖权的确定面临诸多困难(**difficulties of determining jurisdiction in internet cases**)。

【释义】 **difficulties of determining jurisdiction in internet cases**

There are several ways that the infrastructure of the internet has made it difficult to establish the geographic location of the internet user. (1) The internet is insensitive to geographic location and is designed to ignore rather than document geographic location. (2) Addresses on the internet are digital and not geographic addresses. (3) The internet cannot feasibly be closed to users from another state as it is, by nature, an instrument of interstate commerce. (4) The user name and e-mail address are often the only indicators of a user's identity. As a result, a consumer buying goods through a web site may not be sure where the seller is located geographically. (5) Information travels through many different paths through the internet which makes tracing difficult. (6) There is no way to avoid an internet user's message from reaching residents of any particular state.[①]

二、美国网络侵权管辖权问题

美国法院的网络管辖权也有对人管辖权、对物管辖权之分。

(一)对人管辖权

在美国的管辖权中,长臂管辖是一种最主要的对人管辖方式。在美国联邦宪

[①] Cindy Chen, United States and European Union Approaches to Internet Jurisdiction and Their Impact on E-Commerce, 25 *U. Pa. J. Int'l Econ. L.* 423, 432 (2004).

法正当程序条款的限制下,拥有长臂管辖条款的各个州用它界定本州法院对于包括外国人在内的非本州被告的管辖权。它极大地扩大了各个州的管辖范围。

(二) 对物管辖权

美国的对物管辖在网络侵权领域主要应用于域名案件,如因为域名抢注引起的域名纠纷。从历史上看,对物管辖权是在海事或不动产纠纷中使用的。在这种情况下,法院被要求裁决标的物的归属。根据美国联邦最高法院的解释,只有在宪法正当程序允许对标的物的所有人有对人管辖权时才可确定对物管辖权。在美国,根据"网络方案解决公司"(Network Solutions Inc., NSI)①的域名争议政策声明或"互联网名称与数字地址分配机构"(The Internet Corporation for Assigned Names and Numbers, ICANN)②的统一域名争议解决政策寻求救济时,域名注册人的真实身份可以是不相关的。如果一个注册人使用了虚假的联系信息,它就可能永远收不到注册代理机构的通知,其域名就可能因此被冻结。但"网络方案解决公司"政策声明下的诉讼外救济,只适用于与注册标识相同或与域名相同的案件(该类案件对转移客户访问量的域名抢注,不能提供有效救济);互联网名称与数字地址分配机构争议解决办法下的诉讼外救济,只适用于恶意注册、使用域名的行为(不能制裁注册人收藏但不实际使用域名行为),并且要求标识所有人排除任何潜在合理使用的抗辩。

三、我国关于网络侵权管辖权的规定

(一) 我国有关网络侵权的相关规定

根据我国最高人民法院《关于审理涉及计算机网络著作权纠纷案件适用法律若干问题的解释》(以下简称《解释》)来看,我国在网络纠纷管辖的问题上仍然坚持传统的管辖原则,即以被告住所地和侵权行为实施地管辖为一般标准,而以侵权结果地管辖为例外。《解释》中将被告实施侵权行为的网络服务器和终端设备所

---

① 美国 NSI 是国际域名注册的权威机构,该公司的网址是:http://www.networksolutions.com/。
② ICANN 成立于 1998 年 10 月,是一个集合了全球网络界商业、技术及学术各领域专家的非营利性国际组织,负责互联网协议(IP)地址的空间分配、协议标识符的指派、通用顶级域名(gTLD)及国家和地区顶级域名(ccTLD)系统的管理,以及根服务器系统的管理。这些服务最初是在美国政府合同下由互联网号码分配当局(Internet Assigned Numbers Authority, IANA)以及其他一些组织提供的。现在,ICANN 行使 IANA 的职能。作为一个公私结合的组织,ICANN 致力于维护互联网运行的稳定性、促进竞争、广泛代表全球互联网组织以及通过自下而上和基于一致意见的程序制定与其使命相一致的政策。ICANN 负责协调管理 DNS 各技术要素以确保普遍可解析性,使所有的互联网用户都能够找到有效的地址。它通过监督互联网运作当中独特的技术标识符的分配以及顶级域名(如".com"、".info"等)的授权来做到这一点。至于其他互联网用户所关心的问题,如金融交易规则、互联网内容控制、自发的商业电子邮件(垃圾邮件)以及数据保护等,则不在 ICAN 技术协调任务的范围之内。

在地作为确定侵权行为实施地的管辖连接因素,是对传统的侵权管辖依据在网络环境下的改进。

(二) 我国网络侵权案件的司法实践

在我国的司法实践中,尚未出现涉外网络侵权纠纷,但是在国内已经出现了多起网络侵权案件,在被称为"中国第一网页侵权案"的**瑞得(集团)公司诉宜宾市东方信息服务有限公司网页著作权侵权案**(以下简称"瑞得集团诉东方公司案")中,尽管案件本身是一起网页著作权侵权纠纷,但其中管辖权争议的提出,使得本案颇具网络侵权案件的代表性。

【释义】 瑞得(集团)公司诉宜宾市东方信息服务
有限公司网页著作权侵权案

原告、被告均在互联网上拥有自己的站点。1998年底,本案原告瑞得集团(住所地:北京市海淀区车道沟1号)发现被告东方公司(住所地:四川省宜宾市刘臣街14号2楼)的主页在整体版式、色彩、图案、栏目设置、栏目标题、方案、下拉菜单的运用等方面都几乎是照搬原告的主页,原告以被告侵犯其著作权和商业秘密为由向北京市海淀区人民法院起诉。后被告提出管辖异议。被告指出,由于"其住所地在四川省宜宾市,非北京市海淀区,而瑞得集团也未能向东方公司提供可证明其诉称的侵权行为地(包括侵权行为实施地和侵权结果发生地)位于北京市海淀区内的证据",因此认为北京市海淀区人民法院对本案无管辖权,请求裁定将本案移送四川省宜宾市中级人民法院审理。尤其是被告进一步指出,"本案是因互联网网页著作权而提起的诉讼,而互联网不同于传统的传播媒体并具有其本身的特点,我国以往有关侵权诉讼案件管辖的法律规定是否适用于此类案件,目前尚无明确的法律规定"。被告的这一质疑显然是适当的,从而使法院不得不面对网络侵权案件管辖这个问题。

北京市海淀区人民法院作出了裁定书,驳回了被告的管辖权异议,理由主要有三点:第一,瑞得集团的主页在制作完成后,是储存在其特定的硬盘上并通过自有的www服务器向外界发布的,任何人在任何时间、任何地点通过主机接触(包括浏览、复制)该主页内容,必须经过设置在瑞得集团住所地的服务器及硬盘。鉴于瑞得集团以主页著作权侵权为由提起诉讼,是基于其主页被复制侵权这一理由,因此本区应视为侵权行为实施地。第二,瑞得集团不但诉称东方公司复制其主页这一特定的行为,而且还诉称该行为的直接后果是东方公司的主页为访问者所接触。鉴于我国目前的联网主机和用户集中分布于本区等一些特定的地区,因此本区亦应视为侵权结果发生地。第三,东方公司在提出管辖异议的同时,并未举证证明瑞得集团的主页内容是瞬间存在的或处于不稳定状态。

被告不服上诉,向北京市第一中级人民法院提起上诉,北京市第一中级人民法院经审理认为海淀区人民法院有管辖权,故驳回了被告的上诉。

北京市海淀区人民法院的裁定体现了一种有利管辖的思想。在上述案件中,法院实际上通过扩大解释"侵权行为地"与"侵权结果地",使得"侵权之诉由被告住所地或侵权行为地法院管辖"这条传统冲突规则得以适用。尽管从探究立法原意的角度来说,这样的解释在判决当时是无法找到充分的依据的。然而,在美国法院的判例中,法院也使用相同或近似的方法将其"长臂管辖权"延伸到了网络空间之中。这样,在该案件里,其实体现了另一种思想,即无规则之下的扩大解释。这也是我国网络案件管辖权发展的趋势所在。

【思考题】

- 在国际私法视野下,互联网所涉及的法律关系有哪些特征?它对属人连接点和属地连接点有哪些影响?
- 雅虎公司涉嫌拍卖纳粹物品案在国际私法管辖权的发展上有何特殊的意义?
- "网络服务器所在地"作为新的连接因素,对管辖权的确定有怎样的意义?
- 请评析"网络空间自治论"和"网络管辖权相对论"。
- Zippo Dot Com 和 Zippo Cybersell 这两个案件在互联网管辖权理论发展上有什么特殊意义?
- "国际虚拟法院中心"能提供哪些便利?其发展前景如何?
- Maritz Inc. v. Cybergold Inc. 案对"最低限度联系"理论的发展有哪些贡献?

【重要术语提示与中英文对照】

中文术语	英文对照
互联网案件	internet cases
网络服务提供商	internet service provider, ISP
网址	websites
商家对消费者	business-to-consumers, B2C
布鲁塞尔一号法案	Brussels I Regulation
雅虎公司涉嫌拍卖亲纳粹物品案	Yahoo!, Inc. v. *La Ligue Contre Le Racisme et L'antisemitisme*
统一互联网计算机信息交易法	Uniform Computer Information Transactions Act, UCITA
合理联系	reasonable relation

网络服务器	internet server
网络独立宣言	Declaration of the Independence of Cyberspace
网络空间自治论	cyberspace self-governance
独立的法律管辖权区域	a separate legal jurisdiction
全球性的市民社会	global civil society
网络空间自治论者	cyberians
泽普网络销售公司诉网络销售公司	Zippo Cybersell, Inc. v. Cybersell, Inc.
滑动标尺法	sliding scale approach, Zippo sliding scale
虚拟法院	Cybercourt, Cybertribunal
长臂管辖权	long arm jurisdiction
最低限度联系	minimum contacts
马力斯公司诉网金公司	Maritz Inc. v. Cybergold Inc.
主动性网址	active websites
被动性网址	passive websites
互动性网址	interactive websites
网络方案解决公司	Network Solutions Inc., NSI
互联网名称与数字地址分配机构	Internet Corporation for Assigned Names and Numbers, ICANN
原地管辖权	home jurisdiction

【推荐阅读文献】

- 朱萍:《虚拟空间管辖权的确定——美国和欧盟实践的启示》,载《法商研究》2002年第4期。
- 何其生:《电子商务的国际私法问题》,法律出版社2004年版。
- 鞠海亭:《网络环境下的国际民事诉讼法律问题》,法律出版社2006年版。
- 刘颖、李静:《网环境下的国际民事管辖权》,载《中国法学》2006年第1期。
- 李智:《国际私法中互联网管辖权制度研究》,厦门大学出版社2009年版。
- 袁泉等:《互联网环境下国籍民商事法律关系适用》,中国法制出版社2010年版。
- Susan Nauss Exon, The Internet Meets Obi-wan Kenobi in the Court of Next Resort, 8 *B. U. J. Sci. & Tech.* 18—19 (2002).
- Cindy Chen, United States and European Union Approaches to Internet Jurisdiction and Their Impact on E-Commerce, 25 *U. Pa. J. Int'l Econ. L.* 433 (2004).
- Danielle Keats Citron, Minimum Contacts in a Borderless World: Voice over Internet Protocol and the Coming Implosion of Personal Jurisdiction Theory, 39 *U. C. Davis L. Rev.* 1481 (2006).
- Richard K. Greenstein, The Action Bias in American Law: Internet Jurisdiction and

the Triumph of Zippo Dot Com, 80 *Temp. L. Rev.* 21 (2007).
- Kuner (C.), Data Protection Law and International Jurisdiction on the Internet (Part 2), 18 *Int'l J. Law & Inf. Tech.* 227 (2010).
- Svantesson (D.), Recent Developments in Private International Law Applicable to the Internet, 15 *J. Internet L.* 26 (2011).
- Norris (E.), Why the Internet Isn't Special: Restoring Predictability to Personal Jurisdiction, 53 *Ariz. L. Rev.* 1013 (2011).

【扩展阅读资料】

Difficulty of a Hybrid Approach to Internet Jurisdiction [①]

While the United States and EU have adopted different approaches in determining jurisdiction over consumer internet transactions, the largest obstacle concerns trans-Atlantic, or global transactions. If a French consumer purchases a product from an American web site or vice versa, where should a dispute be heard? The obvious solution is for the United States and the EU to cooperate and develop an international framework to follow. The first issue is whether disparate substantive laws between the United States and the EU can be forged into an international framework. The second issue is whether two fundamentally different approaches towards governing the internet and e-commerce development can be reconciled to reach consensus.

1. Risk of an International Regime

Three cases involving Yahoo! Incorporated ("Yahoo!"), a search engine and auction web site, Dow Jones, a publisher, and Kazaa, a music-sharing company, demonstrate the risks posed by the creation of an international framework.

In 2000, a French court required Yahoo!, a U.S. company, to remove Nazi memorabilia from its auction web site because it violated French criminal law which barred the public display of Nazi-related materials in France. This decision ignored Yahoo! 's claim that the French court had no jurisdiction because Yahoo! 's servers housing its web site were located in the United States. Yahoo! subsequently counter-sued in the United States, claiming that the French judgment was unenforceable because obeying the French order would violate free speech guaranteed by the First Amendment. The Northern District of California granted a motion for summary judgment in favor of Yahoo!. However, civil liability was not the only penalty for Yahoo!. Yahoo! 's former executive, Timothy Koogle, was prosecuted

---

① Cindy Chen, United States and European Union Approaches to Internet Jurisdiction and Their Impact on E-Commerce, 25 *U. Pa. J. Int'l Econ. L.* 423, 447—451 (2004).

for criminal violations in France, as well. If found guilty, France would ask the United States to extradite Koogle, which the U.S. State Department would allow only if Koogle was found to have broken a similar U.S. law, which is not the case. The U.S. protection of free speech guaranteed by the First Amendment is much more liberal than many European nations allow within their own countries. If an international framework adopts the substantive law of a nation like France, U.S. companies could be subject to similar foreign liabilities, whereas if an international framework adopts American law, companies could directly contravene European laws.

While an international framework is easy to pontificate, the reality of creating laws that both the United States and EU can live by is much more difficult. There is evidence of resentment in foreign courts about American hegemony and dominance and adherence to U.S. law which ought to worry U.S. companies with an internet presence. Last December in Dow Jones v. Gutnick, the High Court of Australia ruled that an Australian plaintiff could bring suit in Australia against Dow Jones, a U.S.-based publisher who allegedly posted defamatory statements on the web. The Court held that an internet article is "published" wherever it is read, instead of adopting the United States "single publication" rule that says an internet article is published only once at a particular time and place. This case signals the willingness of foreign courts to apply local standards to cases involving American parties when it is believed that the harm suffered in the dispute is local. Given that U.S. companies dominate the e-commerce canvas, the trend to ignore American law and principles can negatively impact e-commerce's growth should these companies deign to go offline.

However, U.S. companies are not the only ones that have reason to be concerned with the risks of an international legal system. In a recent decision, U.S. District Judge Stephen Wilson held that a lawsuit could proceed against Sharman Networks, the parent company of Kazaa, despite Sharman being headquartered in Australia and incorporated in the Pacific Island nation of Vanuatu. While Sharman expanded its commercial activities and advertising within the Kazaa program, it backed away from a plan to offer a paid subscription service as many of the potential subscribers would have been U.S. residents. That move failed to protect it from liability in the United States since the Court found that the number of Kazaa users in the United States satisfied minimum contact to justify the Court's exercise of personal jurisdiction against Sharman. The risk accompanying the creation of an international legal framework to determine jurisdiction is that the law adopted in that framework may be less advantageous than a company's current forum state. While predictability may be of some comfort to companies, one could also argue that the lack of uniformity currently protects companies from exploding global liability.

2. Different Ideological Stances between the United States and EU

Assuming that a common legal framework is desired, it is still extremely difficult for the United States and the EU to come to an agreement as to how that framework should be and what that framework should look like. An example of this predicament is the proposal to revise the Hague Convention. The proposed Hague Convention on Jurisdiction and Foreign Judgments was first proposed in 1992 and, if passed, would be significant because there are potentially fifty signatory countries ranging from China to the United States and the EU. The private sector has raised several concerns that the Draft Proposal of the Hague Convention would impede the growth of e-commerce. While the U.S. delegation originally initiated the impetus for a revision of the Hague Convention in order to allow individuals who won judgments in American courts to enforce them in Europe, as the global impact of e-commerce has expanded, it has quickly backpedaled and tried to limit the scope of the revision. Currently, the delegations have scaled back the scope of the Hague Convention by limiting it to B2B transactions, but there is no guarantee that any final revision will pass.

第十七章

外国法院民商事判决的承认与执行

本章导读

※ 外国法院是指非本法域的法院。外国法院判决是指非本法域的享有审判权的司法机关在民商事诉讼程序中就双方当事人的权利义务关系所作的司法裁决。国际私法中的外国法院的判决包括三层含义:其他主权国家法院所作出的判决;其他法域法院所作出的判决;联合国、欧洲联盟等国际组织所属法院作出的判决。

※ 承认与执行外国法院判决,是指一国根据本国立法或有关国际条约,承认外国法院的民商事判决在本国的效力,并依法予以强制执行。

※ 承认与执行外国法院判决的理论主要有:国际礼让说、既得权说、债务说、一事不再理说和互惠说。

※ 外国法院判决承认与执行的条件:作出判决的法院必须具有管辖权,外国法院的判决应该是具有法律效力的判决,外国法院的判决必须是通过合法手段取得的,且不得违反被申请国的公共政策。

※ 外国法院判决承认与执行的方式主要有:执行令方式、重新审理方式和登记方式。

※ 我国人民法院作出的发生法律效力的判决、裁定,如果被执行人或者其财产不在中华人民共和国领域内,当事人请求执行的,可以由当事人直接向有管辖权的外国法院申请承认和执行,也可以由人民法院依照中华人民共和国缔结或者参加的国际条约的规定,或者按照互惠原则,请求外国法院承认和执行。

※ 外国法院作出的发生法律效力的判决、裁定,需要中华人民共和国人民法院承认和执行的,可以由当事人直接向中华人民共和国有管辖权的中级人民法院申请承认和执行,也可以由外国法院依照该国与中华人民共和国缔结或者参加的国际条约的规定,或者按照互惠原则,请求人民法院承认和执行。

※ 内地人民法院和香港特别行政区法院在具有书面管辖协议的民商事案件中作出的须支付款项的具有执行力的终审判决,当事人可以向内地人民法院或者香港特别行政区法院申请认可和执行。

※ 香港的终审法院、高等法院上诉法庭以及原诉法庭和区域法院作出的判决书、命令和诉讼费评定证明书可以在内地申请承认和执行。其他法院和其他形式的判决目前还无法在内地得到承认和执行。

【本章主题词】 外国法院判决、民商事判决、一事不再理说、终局性判决

第十七章 外国法院民商事判决的承认与执行

第一节 外国法院民商事判决承认与执行概述

一、外国法院判决的概念解析

(一) 外国法院判决的含义

外国法院是指非本法域的法院。[①]外国法院判决(**foreign judgments**)是指非本法域的享有审判权的司法机关在民商事诉讼程序中就双方当事人的权利义务关系所作的司法裁决。国际私法中的外国法院判决有其特殊的含义。

【释义】   **foreign judgments**

Although the term "foreign" applies to both sister state judgments and to foreign nation judgments, the Full Faith and Credit Clause speaks only to sister state judgments. The Clause does not extend to federal judgments, however, the full faith and credit mandate requires that the principles of finality under the law of the state that rendered judgment shall be recognized and enforced in proceedings in other states. The recognition and enforcement of foreign nation judgments are not covered by the Full Faith and Credit Clause, but are governed by the principle of comity, which have developed a matter of international law.[②]

外国法院判决包括以下三层含义:

首先,外国法院判决可以指其他主权国家法院所作出的判决。

其次,外国法院判决可以指其他法域法院所作出的判决。冲突法上的"国家"可以指具有独特法律制度的领土单位。美国冲突法通常将其他国家法院作出的判决称为"外国国家法院判决"(foreign nation judgments),而把美国联邦内其他州作出的判决称为"姊妹州判决"(sister state judgments),两者总称为外国法院判决(foreign judgments)。在中国,内地法院同样把香港、澳门特别行政区法院的判决当

[①] 肖永平:《国际私法原理》,法律出版社 2003 年版,第 418 页。
[②] Luther L. McDougal III, Robert L. Felix, Ralph U. Whitten, *American Conflicts Law: Cases and Materials*, 4th ed., LexisNexis, 2004, p.3.

作外国法院的判决来对待。

最后,外国法院判决也可以指一些如联合国、欧洲联盟等国际组织所属法院作出的判决。①

(二)"法院"的外延

在外国法院的判决中,对法院也要作广义的理解。外国法院不仅应该包括在名称上以"法院"冠名的机构,而且应该包括可行使司法权的其他机构。《现代汉语词典》中关于"法院"的解释是:独立行使审判权的国家机关。在国际民商事诉讼领域,"法院"是指具有民商事管辖权的国家机关,具有广义的性质。国际民商事诉讼中的"法院"既包括普通法院、劳动法院、行政法院等,也包括具有一定审判权的其他机构,只要有关国家承认这些机构的审判管辖权即可。

(三)"判决"的外延

从法院判决承认与执行的意义上说,国际上对法院"判决"一词持宽泛的解释。一般来说,判决是指法院就诉讼各方的权利义务或他们所提出的诉讼请求作出的最后决定。但由于各国法律制度不同,在司法实践中,"判决"往往以不同的名称出现,如裁定、调解书、命令等。只要它是具有审判权的司法机关通过特定民商事诉讼程序作出的,并赋予当事人诉讼权利和实体权利,都是"判决",如1971年海牙《民商事案件外国判决的承认和执行公约》(Convention on the Recognition and Enforcement of Foreign Judgements in Civil and Commercial Matters)(以下简称1971年《海牙公约》)对判决(**decisions**)的规定。

【释义】 decisions

This Convention shall apply to all decisions given by the courts of a Contracting State, irrespective of the name given by that State to the proceedings which gave rise to the decision or of the name given to the decision itself such as judgment, order or writ of execution.②

1971年《海牙公约》第2条规定:本公约适用于缔约国法院作出的全部裁决,不论该国在作出裁决的诉讼中或对该裁决本身如何表述,例如称作判决、命令或执行令等。

---

① 参见李双元、金彭年、张茂、欧福勇:《中国国际私法通论》,法律出版社2003年版,第572页。
② Article 2 of the Convention on the Recognition and Enforcement of Foreign Judgements in Civil and Commercial Matters.

(四) 承认与执行外国法院的判决

承认与执行外国法院的判决(recognition and enforcement of foreign judgments),是指"一国法院依据其国内立法或有关的国际条约,承认外国法院的民商事判决在内国的域外效力,并在必要时依法予以强制执行"①。

二、"民商事范围"的界定

本章所涉及的外国法院判决只限于外国法院所作出的民商事判决(**civil judgments**),刑罚性判决和行政性判决具有惩罚性或较强的公法性质,不能在其他法域内生效。因此,判决的民商事性质是承认与执行的前提。一国法院承认和执行的是外国法院所作出的民商事方面的判决,包括审理刑事案件时就附带民商事诉讼所作出的判决,英国法院即持这一态度。

【释义】　　　　　　　civil judgments

English courts will not enforce foreign penal or revenue laws either directly or through the recognition of a foreign judgment. However, the foreign judgment will be denied recognition only if it falls directly within the area of penal or revenue laws, strictly construed. A civil judgment, though combined with a penal judgment, may be actionable in England as creating a separate and independent cause of action, despite the general principle that penalties imposed abroad are disregarded.②

但是,究竟民商事包括哪些范围?由于各国在法律部门的划分方面存在差异,始终莫衷一是,迄今未能统一。在制定国际公约时,各国多次尝试消除分歧,但收效甚微。在海牙国际私法会议1989年召开的特别委员会(special commission)会议上,与会代表对"民商事"的范围再次进行了讨论,未能作出具体的划分,但形成了以下几点共识:(1)以各国自主的方式解释民商事或商事一词,而不是绝对地指向适用请求国法律或被请求国法律,或合并适用两国法律;(2)对于公法和私法之间的"灰色区域",发展趋势是对民商事和商事一词给予更为灵活的解释,尤其是破产、保险和雇佣关系等案件均应被视为属于这一概念范围之内;(3)相反,这一趋势并不导致将大多数国家都视为属于公法范畴的其他案件,例如税收案件等,解释

---

① 黄进主编:《国际私法》(第二版),法律出版社2005年版,第951页。
② P. M. North, *Cheshire and North's Private International Law*, 10th ed., London: Butterworths, 1979, p. 662.

为属于民商事范围内;(4)然而,缔约国仍可不受妨碍地在其相互关系中将公约(指《海牙送达公约》和《海牙取证公约》)适用于公法案件,且不必对两公约均以同一方式加以适用。上述结论虽不能从根本上解决各国的分歧,但在一定程度上促进了各国在此问题上的合作。

第二节 外国法院民商事判决承认与执行的理论依据

承认与执行外国法院判决,是指一国根据本国立法或有关国际条约,承认外国法院的民商事判决在本国的域外效力,并在必要时依法予以强制执行。

外国法院的判决原则上只具有域内效力。但是,从对外交往的实际需要出发,各国都会在一定条件下通过本国法院来承认与执行外国法院的判决。

承认与执行外国法院的判决是两个法律行为。承认外国法院的判决是执行外国法院判决的前提条件。但是,承认外国法院的判决并不等于一定要执行外国法院的判决。有些外国法院的判决,虽经承认,但是并不能得到执行。当然,如果要执行外国法院的判决,就一定要先承认,然后才能得到执行。从理论上讲,承认与执行外国法院的判决主要有以下几种依据。

一、基于善意的国际礼让说

国际礼让说由17世纪荷兰著名学者胡伯创立,后来,美国国际私法的奠基人斯托雷接受了这一理论并对之作了进一步发展。该学说认为,承认与执行外国法院的判决是基于内国对外国的礼让。早期,美国法院像英国法院一样,对承认和执行外国法院判决不要求对等,而是按胡伯所倡导的国际礼让原则承认和执行(**U.S. courts honored foreign judgments on the basis of Huber's notion of comity**)。

【释义】 **U.S. courts honored foreign judgments on the basis of Huber's notion of comity**

Early U.S. courts, like early English courts, did not condition foreign judgment recognition and enforcement on reciprocity. Instead, U.S. courts honored foreign judgments on the basis of Huber's notion of comity. This approach was well described by Chief Judge Kent in an

1808 New York case:①

  Foreign judgments are never reexamined unless the aid of our courts is asked to carry them into effect by a direct suit upon the judgment. The foreign judgment is then held to be only *prima facie* evidence of the demand; but when it comes in collaterally, or the defendant relies upon it under the *exceptio rei judicatae*, it is then received as conclusive.②

  国际礼让学说一经问世,便被许多学者所接受,并被许多法院视为承认与执行外国法院判决的依据,在普通法系国家得到了普遍的运用。英国法院从17世纪起就承认外国判决,执行的理论被认为是来源于礼让理论。英国法官相信,国际法要求一国法院协助其他国家的法院。他们担心,如果外国判决在英国得不到执行,那么英国的判决在外国也得不到执行。

  美国对国际礼让原则的贯彻在1895年发生了变化。美国联邦最高法院在 *Hilton v. Guyot*③ 案中确定了国际礼让是承认外国法院判决的理论基础,但不应该成为一项义务,并且认为在国际礼让基础上承认和执行外国法院判决,也需要按互惠原则处理。在该案的判决中,美国联邦最高法院对"礼让"(**comity**)的法律含义作出了界定,认为礼让的法律意义,并非是指一项绝对的义务,也非仅仅是一种礼貌或善意,而是指一国通常考虑的国际责任与便利,并在适当考虑本国公民或其他受本国法保护的人的权利后,在其领域内承认他国的立法、行政或司法行为的一种活动。

【释义】   comity

  "Comity", in the general sense, is neither a matter of absolute obligation, on the other hand, nor of mere courtesy and good will, upon the other. But it is the recognition which one nation allows within its territory to the legislative, executive or judicial acts of another nation, having due regard both to international duty and convenience, and to the rights of its own citizens or of other persons who are under the protection of its laws...④

二、基于权利本位的债务说

  债务说(**theory of obligation**)首先是由英国法官帕克(Parker)在1842年的

---

① Smith v. Lewis, 3 Johns. 157, 169, 3 Am. Dec. 469 (N.Y. 1808).
② Eugene F. Scoles et al., *Conflict of Laws*, 3rd ed., 2000, p.1188.
③ Hilton v. Guyot, 159 U.S. 113, 16 S. Ct. 139, 40 L Ed. 95.
④ Peter Hay, Russell J. Weintraub, Patrick J. Borchers, *Conflict of Laws: Cases and Materials*, 12th ed., Foundation Press, 2004, p.215.

Russell v. Smyth①和 1846 年的 Williams v. Jones②两个案件中提出的。

【释义】　　　　　　theory of obligation

It is unnecessary, however, to consider the theory of comity further, for it has been supplanted by a far more defensible principle that has been called "the doctrine of obligation". This doctrine, which was laid down in 1842, is that where a foreign court of competent jurisdiction has adjudicated a certain sum to be due from one person to another, the liability to pay that sum becomes a legal debt. Once the judgment is proved the burden lies upon the defendant to show why he should not perform the obligation.... In other words, a new right has been vested in the creditor and a new obligation imposed upon the debtor the instance of the foreign court.③

后来布莱克本法官(Blackburn J)在 1870 年的 Godard v. Gray④和 Schibsby v. Westenholz⑤两个案件中又对被执行人偿还金钱债务的责任(**a duty or obligation on the defendant to pay the sum**)作了进一步理论阐述。

【释义】　　a duty or obligation on the defendant to pay the sum

Blackburn J. asserted:

We think that... the true principle on which the judgements of foreign tribunals are enforced in England is... that the judgement of a court of competent jurisdiction over the defendant imposes a duty or obligation on the defendant to pay the sum for which judgement is given which the courts in this country are bound to enforce; and consequently that anything which negatives that duty, or forms a legal excuse for not performing it, is a defence to the action.⑥

债务说的核心是当有合法管辖权的外国法院已判决一方当事人支付另一方当事人一笔金钱后,支付该笔金钱就成为一种法律上的债务,可以通过债务诉讼(**debt actions**)在内国履行。这一理论自确立以来,一自为英国法院所采用。

---

① Russell v. Smyth, 152 Eng. Rep. 323 (Exch. 1842).
② Williams v. Jones, 13 M & W 628, 633 (1845).
③ P. M. North, *Cheshire and North's Private International Law*, 10th ed., London: Butterworths, 1979, pp. 630—631.
④ Godard v. Gray, L. R. 6 Q. B. 139 (1870).
⑤ Schibsby v. Westenholz, L. R. 6 QB. 155, 159 (1870).
⑥ Alan Reed, A New Model of Jurisdictional Propriety for Anglo-American Foreign Judgement Recognition and Enforcement: Something Old, Something Borrowed, Something New? 25 *Loy. L. A. Int'l & Comp. L. Rev.* 243, n107 (2003).

第十七章　外国法院民商事判决的承认与执行

【释义】　　　　　　　　　debt actions

English courts recognized foreign judgments through debt actions, wherein foreign judgments were considered analogous to foreign law. The foreign judgment placed a legal obligation on the judgment debtor to pay unless there was "proof that the court rendering the judgment lacked jurisdiction of the person of the defendant or of the subject matter, or that the judgment had been obtained by fraud." At English common law, judgment creditors needed only file a new action in an English court where the foreign judgment was conclusive.[①]

在英国,判决规定债务人偿还债务的法律义务,债务人必须履行,除非有证据证明判决法院对被告没有属人管辖权,或者判决通过欺诈获得。只要判决是终局的,判决债权人就可以在英国法院提起新的诉讼。

三、基于判决效力的一事不再理说

一事不再理说（**theory of *res judicata***）是指有关有管辖权的法院所作的终局判决,具有确定当事人及利害关系人的权利义务关系的效力,并具有绝对禁止一事两诉的效力。因此,针对同一案件的外国法院判决理应得到其他有关国家的承认和执行。也就是说,当有关案件经过具有管辖权的外国法院审理并作出确定性的判决后,内国法院基于当事人的请求,不再另行审理而径自承认与执行该外国法院的判决。

【释义】　　　　　　　　theory of *res judicata*

A foreign judgment does not create a valid cause of action in England unless it is *res judicata* by the law of the country where was given. It must bee final and conclusive in the sense that it must have determined all controversies between the parties. If it may be altered in later proceedings between the same parties in the same court, it is not enforceable by action in England. Thus, a provisional judgment is not *res judicata* if it contemplates that a fuller investigation leading to a final decision may later be held by the leading case of Nouvion v. Freeman.[②]

美国各州彼此承认与执行法院判决的法律基础源自于美国联邦宪法"完全信

---

① Susan L. Stevens, Commanding International Judicial Respect: Reciprocity and the Recognition and Enforcement of Foreign Judgments, 26 *Hastings Int'l & Comp. L. Rev.* 115, 122—123 (2002).

② P. M. North, *Cheshire and North's Private International Law*, 10th ed., London: Butterworths, 1979, p.649.

任与尊重"条款(**The Full Faith and Credit Clause**)。

【释义】　　　　　**The Full Faith and Credit Clause**

The Full Faith and Credit Clause of the United States Constitution provides: "Full Faith and Credit shall be given to each State, to the Public Acts, Records, and Judicial Proceedings of every other States. And the Congress may by general laws prescribe the Manner in which such Acts, Records and Proceedings shall be proved, and the Effect thereof."①

该条款规定:各州对于他州的法令、记录与司法程序,应有完全的诚意与信任。国会得以一般法律规定该项法令、记录与司法程序的证明方法及其效果。但是,如何承认与执行外国法院的判决,从该条款中找不出法律依据,故而发展了一事不再理学说。而且随着理论和实践的发展,逐渐成为美国法院承认与执行外国法院判决的一个理论基础。

四、基于国家利益的互惠说

互惠说(theory of reciprocity)成为外国法院判决承认与执行的理论基础始于19世纪末期,该学说立足于国家主权,从保护本国当事人的利益出发,提出若外国法院承认和执行内国法院判决,则内国法院也承认与执行该外国法院的判决。也就是说,一国法律规定内国法院承认与执行外国法院判决的前提是该外国法院也承认和执行内国法院的判决。如在 **Ritchie v. McMullen** 案中,美国联邦最高法院1895年基于互惠原则,同意承认和执行加拿大的一个判决。

【案例】　　　　　**Ritchie v. McMulle**②

In Ritchie v. McMullen, Supreme Court of the United States held that an Ontario judgment should be enforced without an examination of its merits, as Canada would give conclusive effect to a judgment rendered by a court in the United States. ③

反之,若该外国法院不承认和执行内国法院的判决,则内国法院也不承认和执

---

① U. S. Constitution Art. IV, §1.
② Supreme Court of the United States, Ritchie v. McMullen, 159 U. S. 235 (1895).
③ Peter Hay, Russell J. Weintraub, Patrick J. Borchers, *Conflict of Laws: Cases and Materials*, 12th ed., Foundation Press, 2004, p. 219.

第十七章 外国法院民商事判决的承认与执行

行该外国法院的判决,如美国联邦最高法院1895年所受理 **Hilton v. Guyot** 案。

【案例】　　　　　　　　Hilton v. Guyot[①]

　　Action in a circuit of the United States upon a judgment of a French court against citizens of the United States, and in favor of a French firm, the plaintiffs in the French proceeding. The Answer, setting forth the original dealings between the parties, alleged that the defendants were not indebted to the plaintiffs. The defendants also contended that the French judgment should not be enforced without an examination of the merits of the case, since the courts of French would examine anew the merits of a controversy if an American judgment against a French national were sued on in France. The circuit court entered a judgment and a decree for the French firm without examining the merits.

　　The judgment and the decree were reversed by the Supreme Court of the United States.

　　在该案中,一位法国公民要求美国法院执行法国法院针对一位美国人在法国的业务作出的判决,美国联邦最高法院考察了执行该项法国法院判决的理论基础,认为在承认外国法院判决方面,既没有美国宪法或成文法上的依据,也没有相应的国际法原则,其基础是国际礼让。但是同时美国联邦最高法院强调,礼让必须以互惠和对等为前提。由于法国法院不能对等地执行美国法院在类似情况下作出的判决,美国和法国两国之间缺乏互惠。因此,美国联邦最高法院拒绝执行该法国法院的判决。Hilton v. Guyot案开创了美国联邦普通法上承认和执行外国法院判决以互惠为基础的礼让规则,但是这一规则仅仅对联邦法院有约束力,而对州法院没有约束力。[②]

　　美国许多州,尤其是纽约州,并不坚持以互惠原则为前提。纽约州在 Johnston v. *Compagnie Générale Transatlantique*[③]案的判决中明确抛弃了互惠要求。[④] 目前,美国的《第二次冲突法重述》和《第三次外国关系重述》(Restatement (Third) of Foreign Relations)在承认和执行外国法院判决问题上,原则上均不以互惠为前提。[⑤]

　　互惠(**reciprocity**)说是在礼让说的基础上发展而来的。与其他学说相比,它更接近外国法院判决承认与执行的真正依据和动因。它不是外国法院判决承认与

[①] Supreme Court of the United States, 1895. Hilton v. Guyot, 159 U.S.113, 16 S. Ct. 139, 40 L Ed. 95.

[②] Eugene F. Scoles et al., *Conflict of Laws*, 3rd ed., 2000, p.1190.

[③] Court of Appeals of New York, 242 N.Y. 381; 152 N.E. 121; 1926 N.Y. LEXIS 995; 46 A.L.R. 435, March 30, 1926, Argued, May 4, 1926, Decided.

[④] *Restatement (Second) of Conflict of Laws* 98 at Reporter's Note cmt. e (1995).

[⑤] William S. Dodge, Breaking the Public Law Taboo, 43 *Harv. Int'l L. J.* 161, 227—228 (2002)

执行之"高尚"理由,但它是利益博弈的外化和必然结果。

【释义】　　　　　　　　　　reciprocity

To induce foreign courts to recognize sovereign judgments on the basis of comity, most continental European countries conditioned treaties for the mutual enforcement of foreign judgments on reciprocity.①

During the 19th century, it was common to condition foreign judgments recognition on reciprocity as a unilateral policy in continental European countries such as Germany, where reciprocity remains a condition of foreign judgments recognition today.②

大陆法系国家,通过签订双边条约(**bilateral agreements**)的方法,来落实相互承认和执行法院判决。互惠学说在有关国家制定相互承认与执行外国法院民商事判决的双边条约时被广泛使用,并且通过双边条约,由理论基础上升为法律基础。

【释义】　　　　　　　　　bilateral agreements

Many continental European countries that require reciprocity have entered into bilateral agreements to circumvent the time and expense associated with these procedures. Indeed, the effort to protect litigants and international commerce from overly stringent sovereigns has created a large increase in the number of international treaties between civil-law countries. The Netherlands, for example, conditions all foreign recognition and enforcement on the existence of international treaties.③

而在没有双边条约的国家,互惠也在国内立法上产生了影响,不少国家的立法,在不同程度上规定了法院可以基于互惠原则承认与执行外国法院的判决,也可以基于互惠原则拒绝承认与执行外国法院的判决。如普通法系的英国在1933年制定了《外国判决(相互执行)法》(**Foreign Judgments (Reciprocal Enforcement) Act**),以适应日益增长的司法实践的需要。

---

① Friedrich Juenger, The Recognition of Money Judgments In Civil and Commercial Matters, 36 *Am. J. Comp. L.* 1, 8 (1988).
② see *Restatement (Third) of Foreign Relations Law* 481 & introductory note (1987).
③ Susan L. Stevens, Commanding International Judicial Respect: Reciprocity and the Recognition and Enforcement of Foreign Judgments, 26 *Hastings Int'l & Comp. L. Rev.* 115, 122 (2002).

【释义】 Foreign Judgments (Reciprocal Enforcement) Act

England responded in 1933 when Parliament passed the Foreign Judgments (Reciprocal Enforcement) Act in an effort to increase the recognition and enforcement of English judgments abroad by using a foreign judgment recognition and enforcement procedure similar to exequatur. Although the Foreign Judgments (Reciprocal Enforcement) Act only applies to those countries that grant "substantial reciprocity of treatment" to English judgments, judgment creditors retain the option at common law to file an action on the judgment to enforce those judgments not covered by the Foreign Judgments (Reciprocal Enforcement) Act, an option that does not require reciprocity. ①

第三节 外国法院民商事判决承认与执行的条件

各国通过立法和签订国际公约的方式,对承认与执行外国法院判决的制度作出规定。如英国至今已经制定了三个有关承认和执行外国法院判决的立法(**three statutory avenues for the recognition and enforcement of foreign judgments**)。这些立法和国际公约大多规定了承认与执行外国法院判决应当遵循的条件。

【立法】 three statutory avenues for the recognition
and enforcement of foreign judgments

Today the English legal system provides three statutory avenues for the recognition and enforcement of foreign judgments, in addition to the common-law method of filing an action on the judgment. These are the Administration of Justice Act of 1920, the Foreign Judgments (Reciprocal Enforcement) Act of 1933, and the Civil Jurisdiction and Judgments Act of 1982.②

一般而言,各国立法和国际公约所确立的这些条件是内国法院承认与执行外国法院判决的前提和基础。对于不符合本国有关承认与执行外国法院判决的条件

---

① William S. Dodge, Breaking the Public Law Taboo, 43 *Harv. Int'l L. J.* 161, 194—195 (2002).
② Eugene F. Scoles et al., *Conflict of Laws*, 3rd ed., 2000, pp.1194—1195.

的,不予承认与执行。有关承认和执行外国法院判决的条件,一般规定在国内法和国际公约中,主要有以下几个方面:

一、管辖权基础

在外国法院判决承认与执行的诸多条件或标准中,最基本的要求是作出判决的法院必须具有管辖权。原判决国法院必须拥有管辖权,没有管辖权就谈不上判决的承认与执行。这是承认与执行外国法院判决的公认的条件。

二、外国法院的判决的终局性

外国法院的判决要在内国获得承认和执行,其所确定的权利必须是确定的、具体的和可执行的,也就是说,一国法院需要承认和执行的外国法院的判决应该是具有法律效力的判决,即最终判决。

各国的立法都将外国法院判决的确定性和终局性作为该判决在内国获得承认和执行的最基本的条件。如英国法院处理的 **Nouvion v. Freeman** 案就是这方面比较典型的案例。

【案例】　　　　　　　　　**Nouvion v. Freeman**

X, who had sold certain land in Seville to Y, brought an "executive" action in Spain against Y and obtained a "remate" judgment for a large sum of money. There are two kinds of proceedings under Spanish law: executive or summary proceedings, and "plenary" or ordinary proceedings. In an executive action, upon proof of a prima facie case, the judge without notice to the defendant makes an order for the attachment of his property. Notice of the attachment is given to the defendant and he is at liberty to appear and defend the action. But the defenses open to him are limited in number, and in particular he cannot set up any defense that denies the validity of the transaction upon which he is sued. Either party who fails in executive proceedings may institute plenary proceedings before the same judge, and in these may set up every defense that is known to law.

It was held by the House of Lords, affirming the Court of Appeal, that no action lay on the remate judgment. Since it was liable to be abrogated by the adjudicating court, it was not *res jdicata* with regard to either party, neither did it extinguish the original cause of action.

尽管判决的终局性是判决得以承认与执行的重要条件,但对于怎样的判决具有终局性,各国却有各自的理解。在多数国家看来,当某一判决不能再被提起司法救济时,才是一个终局的判决。因此,非终审法院的判决并不当然具有终局性,只

有当事人放弃了上诉权,在上诉期内没有提起上诉,或者当事人上诉后又撤回了上诉,非终审法院的判决才具有终局的效力。

三、外国法院的判决的合法性

请求承认与执行的外国法院的判决必须是通过合法手段取得的,才能得到承认与执行。反之,如果是通过欺诈等手段得到的,则不能在内国法院得到承认与执行。

英国1933年《外国判决(相互执行)法》(Foreign Judgments (Reciprocal Enforcement) Act of 1933)第1条、第2条、第4条规定,如果能向登记法院证明,判决是以欺诈方法取得的,那么对判决的登记就应撤销。根据该法,外国判决不论是否已经登记以及是否可以登记,如果是用欺诈获得的,那么就不应被承认为是合法的。英国判例也表明,只要能证明判决是通过欺诈获得的,判决债务人就能抵制判决的执行,典型的案例如 **Ochsenbein v. Papelier** 案。本案中,英国对于以欺诈手段取得的外国法院的判决,即不予承认和执行。

【案例】　　　　　　　**Ochsenbein v. Papelier**①

A French seller, in the course of a dispute in Paris with an English buyer, produced a writ showing that he had begun an action to recover the price of the goods. When remonstrated with, however, he burnt the writ then and there and agreed to refer the dispute to arbitration in London. He nevertheless proceeded with the action behind the buyer's back and obtained judgment by default. The seller brought an action in the Court of Queen's Bench upon this judgment, and the court of chancery, when asked by the buyer to restrain the action, refused an injunction as being unnecessary. It was unnecessary, because the above facts, if proved, would afford a good defense to the common law action.

It is clear from this that, as in domestic law, a judgment will be denied recognition if the court had been imposed upon a trick not apparent at the time of the trial, but discovered later.②

四、公共政策标准

公共政策是现代各国判决承认与执行中的一项重要制度,各国均以不得违反被申请国的公共政策作为承认和执行外国法院判决的先决条件。这是承认与执行

---

① (1873) L. R. 8 Ch. 695.

② P. M. North, *Cheshire and North's Private International Law*, 10th ed., London: Butterworths, 1979, p.659.

外国法院判决的前提条件。

公共政策在有关国际条约和各国法律中均被规定为拒绝承认和执行外国判决的理由,但又是最不确定的一个理由。各国在使用公共政策时,均普遍持谨慎的态度,将它保持在一个适当的限度之内,甚至在实践中悬而不用,如美国法院所处理的 **Somportex** 案。

【案例】　　　　　　　　　Somportex[①]

The District Court for the Third Circuit upheld a decision enforcing a British court default judgment against an American corporation. There, the plaintiff, a British corporation, had entered into a contract whereby the American defendant corporation would distribute the defendant's gum in Great Britain. When the transaction failed, the plaintiff filed suit in a British court for breach of contract. The British court entered a default judgment against the defendant, and the plaintiff subsequently sought enforcement of the judgment in a U.S. court. The defendant raised the public policy defense because the British court awarded attorney's fees, which would not have been "recoverable under Pennsylvania law." The defendant argued that enforcement of the attorney's fees was contrary to Pennsylvania public policy. Nevertheless, the court dismissed the defendant's argument and agreed with the district court's decision that the "variance with Pennsylvania law is not such that the enforcement 'tends clearly to injure the public health, the public morals, the public confidence in the purity of the administration of the law, or to undermine that sense of security for individual rights, whether of personal liberty or of private property, which any citizen ought to feel, is against public policy.'" The court concluded that the difference between British and Pennsylvania law was not enough to refuse enforcement on the basis of public policy.[②]

第四节　外国法院民商事判决承认与执行的程序与方式

承认与执行外国法院民商事判决的程序与方式是指内国法院以何种程序、何

---

① Somportex, 453 F. 2d at 444.
② Keri Bruce, The Hague Convention on Choice-of-court Agreements, Is the Public Policy Exception Helping Click-away the Security of Non-Negotiated Agreements? 32 *Brooklyn J. Int'l L.* 1103, 1117—1118 (2007).

种方式承认和执行外国法院的判决。在这方面,大陆法系国家和普通法系国家的规定不尽相同,同一法系不同国家的做法也各异。

一、外国法院民商事判决承认与执行的程序

(一) 承认与执行的请求

任何外国法院的判决,要在内国法院得到承认和执行,必须首先向内国有管辖权的法院提出申请,并经该法院审查后才有可能予以承认和执行。

1. 承认与执行的申请人

承认和执行外国法院判决的申请,由谁提出,各国的规定大致有三种情况:一是规定只能由当事人提出;二是规定只能由原判决法院提出;三是规定既可以由当事人提出,也可以由原判决法院提出。中国属于第三种情况,《中华人民共和国民事诉讼法》第 280 条第 1 款规定:"人民法院作出的发生法律效力的判决、裁定,如果被执行人或者其财产不在中华人民共和国领域内,当事人请求执行的,可以由当事人直接向有管辖权的外国法院申请承认和执行,也可以由人民法院依照中华人民共和国缔结或者参加的国际条约的规定,或者按照互惠原则,请求外国法院承认和执行。"第 281 条规定:"外国法院作出的发生法律效力的判决、裁定,需要中华人民共和国人民法院承认和执行的,可以由当事人直接向中华人民共和国有管辖权的中级人民法院申请承认和执行,也可以由外国法院依照该国与中华人民共和国缔结或者参加的国际条约的规定,或者按照互惠原则,请求人民法院承认和执行。"

2. 承认与执行的管辖法院

关于受理承认与执行外国法院判决的管辖法院,大部分国家都在级别上作了一定的限制。如上所述,在中国,受理这类申请的法院为"有管辖权的中级人民法院"。这里的"有管辖权"指的是对承认与执行事项有管辖权,而不是指对国内案件有管辖权。因此,"有管辖权的中级人民法院"一般是指当事人的住所或惯常居住地的中级人民法院或被执行财产所在地的中级人民法院。在法国,执行令之诉一律由被申请执行人的住所或居所所在地或财产所在地的大审判法院(以合议庭形式)受理。在英国,此类申请一般由高等法院受理。

(二) 承认与执行请求的审查

对请求承认与执行的外国法院判决的审查,各国的做法也不一样,主要有两种情况:实质审查和形式审查。实质审查是指对申请承认和执行的判决,被请求国法院根据本国法律,从法律和事实两个部分进行审查,只要认为该判决在认定事实或适用法律方面不适当,就不予承认和执行。形式审查是指被请求国法院不对请求承认与执行的判决进行认定事实和适用法律方面的审查,而仅就该判决是否符合本国法律规定的承认和执行外国法院判决的条件进行审查。

目前,各国普遍的做法是不对外国法院判决作实质审查,而只进行形式审查,只要外国法院判决在形式上符合承认与执行的条件,便予以承认,并按被请求国法所规定的执行程序交付执行。如英国的许多判决认为,只要外国法院根据英国的冲突法规则有管辖权,就不能对外国法院的判决进行实质审查。

（三）承认与执行外国判决的效力

外国法院判决一旦得到内国法院承认,就可以产生与内国法院判决同等的效力,该外国法院判决在内国境内可以对抗其他人,且若被执行人拒绝履行外国法院判决所确定的义务,另一方当事人就有权请求内国法院强制执行。

二、外国法院民商事判决承认与执行的方式

（一）执行令：大陆法系的传统

大陆法系的法国对外国法院的判决与执行,实行执行令制度（**exequatur procedure**）①。

【释义】　　　　　　　**exequatur procedure**

Modern continental European countries enforce foreign judgments using the exequatur procedure, which is simpler than the common-law Anglo-American enforcement procedure of requiring an action on the foreign judgment. In an exequatur proceeding, the judgment debtor may resist foreign judgment enforcement on the basis of several acceptable circumstances, such as by asserting that the foreign country lacks reciprocity.②

以法国为代表的大陆法系国家法律规定,被请求国法院对申请承认和执行的外国法院的判决进行审查,认为符合本国法律或有关国际公约的规定的,发给执行令（exequatur）,并按被请求国法律规定的程序予以执行。

（二）重新审理：普通法系的惯例

被请求国法院在收到承认和执行外国法院判决的申请后,并不直接承认与执行,而是要求申请人以该外国判决为根据,在被请求国重新提起诉讼,由被请求国进行审查,被申请人提出异议的则进行审理。被请求国法院如果认为判决与本国法律并不

---

① See William S. Dodge, Breaking the Public Law Taboo, 43 *Harv. Int'l L. J.* 1, 194 (defining "exequatur" as a system where "a foreign judgment registered with the High Court would have the same force and effect as if the judgment had been originally given by the registering court").

② Eugene F. Scoles et al., *Conflict of Laws*, 3rd ed., 2000, p.1196.

冲突,则作出一个与外国法院判决内容相同的判决,并按执行本国法院判决的程序予以执行。这样,法院所执行的就是本国法院的判决,而不是外国法院的判决了。

(三) 登记:基于国际条约和双边协定的做法

所谓登记(**registration**),是指被请求国法院在收到当事人的执行申请后,只要查明外国法院判决符合被请求国法律规定的条件,就予以登记,经过登记的外国法院判决就可以得到执行。

【释义】　　　　　　　　registration

The effect of registration is that such Community judgments and decisions shall, for all purposes of execution, have the same force and effect as if they were judgments of the High Court.①

这项制度是普通法国家的外国法院判决承认与执行的一般程序,起源于1801年的《英国王室债务法》(The Crown Debts Act),该法规定对英格兰及爱尔兰高等法院的财务法庭命令(Exchequer Orders)和衡平法院的判决(Chancery Decrees)准许以互惠方式登记并执行。1982年,根据加入的《布鲁塞尔公约》,英国国会制定了《民事管辖和判决法》,对本土法域间及英联邦成员间判决的承认与执行作了重新规范。按照该法规定,在英国境内任一法域的任一法院所作的金钱判决,如该判决的证明书在任一法域的法院依法登记的,该判决即具有如同该法院本身判决相同的效力和执行力,相应的执行程序也将开始。对非金钱判决而言,也适用这一规定,不同之处仅在于此时需以经公证过的判决书副本取代证明书。

第五节　我国关于判决域外承认执行的规定

一、我国关于判决域外承认执行的法律制度

我国人民法院和外国法院相互承认和执行判决的制度规定在2012年修订的

---

① P. M. North, *Cheshire and North's Private International Law*, 10th ed., London: Butterworths, 1979, p.675.

我国《民事诉讼法》第280条、第281条和第282条中。

我国人民法院作出的发生法律效力的判决、裁定,如果被执行人或者其财产不在中华人民共和国领域内,当事人请求执行的,可以由当事人直接向有管辖权的外国法院申请承认和执行,也可以由人民法院依照中华人民共和国缔结或者参加的国际条约的规定,或者按照互惠原则,请求外国法院承认和执行。

外国法院作出的发生法律效力的判决、裁定,需要中华人民共和国人民法院承认和执行的,可以由当事人直接向中华人民共和国有管辖权的中级人民法院申请承认和执行,也可以由外国法院依照该国与中华人民共和国缔结或者参加的国际条约的规定,或者按照互惠原则,请求人民法院承认和执行。

人民法院对申请或者请求承认和执行的外国法院作出的发生法律效力的判决、裁定,依照中华人民共和国缔结或者参加的国际条约,或者按照互惠原则进行审查后,认为不违反中华人民共和国法律的基本原则或者国家主权、安全、社会公共利益的,裁定承认其效力,需要执行的,发出执行令,依照本法的有关规定执行。违反中华人民共和国法律的基本原则或者国家主权、安全、社会公共利益的,不予承认和执行。

二、我国法院判决到国外执行的条件

根据上述《民事诉讼法》的规定,我国法院作出的民商事判决、裁定需要到外国执行的,必须符合以下条件:(1)该判决或裁定在我国已发生法律效力;(2)需要执行的人或物在我国境外;(3)由申请人提出执行的请求,该请求可以由当事人也可以由法院向对方有管辖权的法院提出,但由法院提出的话,必须以有共同受约束的条约或存在互惠为依据;(4)我国与被申请执行国之间有条约的规定或互惠关系。

外国法院作出的民商事判决、裁定需要在我国执行的条件是:(1)该外国法院判决、裁定不违背我国法律的基本原则,不危害我国的国家主权、安全和社会公共利益;(2)我国与委托国之间有司法协助条约或存在着互惠关系;(3)外国法院的判决、裁定可以由当事人申请,也可以由外国法院依照两国缔结或者参加的国际条约的规定申请;(4)被委托执行的外国法院判决必须是在该外国已经发生法律效力的终局判决。符合上述条件的,由我国人民法院作出裁定承认其效力并发出执行令,由执行机关依照我国《民事诉讼法》规定的程序予以执行。我国法院在接受委托协助执行外国法院判决时,不需要进行实质性审查,也不需要申请人就原判决的执行重新提起诉讼,只要进行形式性审查,就可以作出裁定,承认外国法院判决的效力,发出执行令,依照我国《民事诉讼法》执行程序规定交付执行。

第六节　内地与香港法院民商事判决的相互承认与执行

自1997年香港回归祖国十多年来,内地与香港特别行政区在区际司法协助领域先后达成了三项重要协议。1998年双方签署了《关于内地与香港特别行政区法院相互委托送达民商事司法文书的安排》;1999年双方签署了《关于内地与香港特别行政区法院相互执行仲裁裁决的安排》;2006年双方签署了《关于内地与香港特别行政区法院相互认可和执行当事人协议管辖的民商事案件判决的安排》(以下简称《安排》)。这也标志着内地与香港之间的区际司法协助取得了突破性进展。

一、内地与香港相互承认和执行法院民商事判决

内地与香港对于法院民商事判决的相互承认与执行问题,实际上是国际私法中的对于外国法院民商事判决的承认与执行问题。如前所述,在国际私法中,"外国法院的判决"不仅包括其他国家的判决,还包括其他法域和其他国际组织所作出的判决。香港与内地虽然同属于中华人民共和国,但因历史的原因造成了内地与香港的法律分别属于大陆法系和英美法系,事实上是两个不同的法域(**different legal systems**),因而也就产生了对于法院民商事判决的相互承认和执行问题。

【释义】　　　　　　　　　**different legal systems**

The different legal systems adopted in the Mainland, Hong Kong, Macao, and Taiwan, will inevitably create questions as to which regional law should be applied and whether courts in different regions will recognize and enforce the judgments of the courts of other regions. At their core, these inter-regional conflicts of laws may be similar to the interstate conflicts that so frequently arise in the United States.①

---

① Jin Huang, Andrew Xuefeng Qian, One country, Two systems, Three Law Families, and Four Legal Regions: the Emerging Inter-regional Conflicts of Law in China, 5 *Duke J. Comp. & Int'l L.* 289, 292—293 (1995).

二、内地与香港相互承认和执行法院民商事判决的依据

从法律规定上来看,内地与香港之间的相互承认和执行对方法院判决在不同的时期有着不同的规定。

1997年香港回归前,内地方面对于香港法院民商事判决的承认与执行,没有具体的法律规定,只能依据《民事诉讼法》的有关规定。1997年香港回归后到2006年《安排》签订之前,这段时间内虽然香港已经由中国政府收回主权,但是它和内地仍然分属两个不同的法域,双方之间又没有签订关于互相承认双方法院民商事判决的文件,因此内地方面对于香港法院的判决事实上仍然是按照《民事诉讼法》和《香港特别行政区基本法》(以下简称《基本法》)的有关规定操作的。《民事诉讼法》和《基本法》的法律条文都只是原则性的规定,缺乏可操作性,因而在实践中遇到了很多困难。如**远侨投资有限公司申请承认香港法院民事判决法律效力案**就是一个例子。

【释义】 远侨投资有限公司申请承认香港法院民事判决法律效力案

2001年2月23日,申请人远侨投资有限公司向法院提出申请,要求承认香港特别行政区高等法院(以下简称"香港高等法院")原诉法庭对原诉人(即本案申请人)远侨投资有限公司与被告王建全诉讼一案于1999年6月29日作出的高院民事诉讼1999年第1801号判决。福建省泉州市中级人民法院经审查认为:香港特别行政区高等法院原诉法庭1999年1801号判决,不符合我国法律规定的承认外国法院判决效力的条件,据此,申请人提出的申请不予支持。依照《中华人民共和国民事诉讼法》第268条之规定,裁定对香港特别行政区高等法院原诉法庭1999年1801号判决的法律效力不予承认。

从该案可以看出,由于法律只规定了对于外国法院民商事判决的承认与执行的法律原则而没有具体的操作规则,导致了法官在判案时没有明确的法律依据,只能根据自己对法律的理解进行裁判。

2006年《安排》签订之后,内地与香港之间对于双方法院民商事判决的承认与执行终于有了一个基本的协议。它结束了内地与香港之间长期存在的对于双方法院民商事判决的承认与执行无法可依的尴尬局面,在双方的区际司法协助领域具有里程碑式的意义,是内地与香港特区之间的司法协助不断向前推进的标志。①

---

① 中国新闻网:《内地与香港签署相互认可和执行民商事判决的安排》,http://www.chinanews.com.cn/huaren/zgxw/news/2006/07-15/758416.shtml,最后访问时间2008年6月19日。

第十七章 外国法院民商事判决的承认与执行

三、内地与香港相互承认和执行法院民商事判决的条件

（一）积极条件

《安排》第1条规定，内地人民法院和香港特别行政区法院在具有书面管辖协议的民商事案件中作出的须支付款项的具有执行力的终审判决，当事人可以根据本安排向内地人民法院或者香港特别行政区法院申请认可和执行。随后第2条又对该"具有执行力的终审判决"进行了解释和限制，明确了法院的范围和判决书的形式等。据此，香港的终审法院、高等法院上诉法庭以及原诉法庭和区域法院作出的判决书、命令和诉讼费评定证明书可以在内地申请承认和执行。其他法院和其他形式的判决目前还无法在内地得到承认和执行。

（二）消极条件

这里的消极条件是指，内地与香港在某些条件下不承认对方法院的判决的情况。根据《安排》第9条的规定，对申请认可和执行的判决，原审判决中的债务人提供证据证明有下列情形之一的，受理申请的法院经审查核实，应当裁定不予认可和执行：根据当事人协议选择的原审法院地的法律，管辖协议属于无效的，但选择法院已经判定该管辖协议为有效的除外；判决已获完全履行；根据执行地的法律，执行地法院对该案享有专属管辖权；根据原审法院地的法律，未曾出庭的败诉一方当事人未经合法传唤或者虽经合法传唤但未获依法律规定的答辩时间，但原审法院根据其法律或者有关规定公告送达的，不属于上述情形；判决是以欺诈方法取得的；执行地法院就相同诉讼请求作出判决，或者外国、境外地区法院就相同诉讼请求作出判决，或者有关仲裁机构作出仲裁裁决，已经为执行地法院所认可或者执行的。

另外，内地人民法院认为在内地执行香港特别行政区法院民商事判决违反内地社会公共利益，或者香港特别行政区法院认为在香港特别行政区执行内地人民法院民商事判决违反香港特别行政区公共政策的，不予认可和执行。

四、内地与香港相互承认和执行法院民商事判决的程序

在程序方面，概括来说，包括申请的提出、申请的审查和申请的执行三个方面。具体来说，根据《安排》第4条的规定，申请认可和执行符合本安排规定的民商事判决，在内地向被申请人住所地、经常居住地或者财产所在地的中级人民法院提出，在香港特别行政区向香港特别行政区高等法院提出。该《安排》第5条又规定，被申请人住所地、经常居住地或者财产所在地在内地不同的中级人民法院辖区的，申请人应当选择向其中一个人民法院提出认可和执行的申请，不得分别向两个或者

两个以上人民法院提出申请。被申请人的住所地、经常居住地或者财产所在地,既在内地又在香港特别行政区的,申请人可以同时分别向两地法院提出申请,两地法院分别执行判决的总额,不得超过判决确定的数额。已经部分或者全部执行判决的法院应当根据对方法院的要求提供已执行判决的情况。《安排》第7条规定了申请人需要提交的文件。第8条还特别提到,申请人申请认可和执行内地人民法院或者香港特别行政区法院民商事判决的程序,依据执行地法律的规定,但是另有规定的除外。该条的第2款和第3款还分别规定了申请人申请认可和执行的期限(双方有一方或者都是自然人时,该期限为1年;双方都是法人或者其他组织的,该期限为6个月)以及该期限的起算时间等。第13条特别规定了对于申请的审查,实行"一事不再理"原则,即在法院受理当事人申请认可和执行判决期间,当事人依相同事实再行提起诉讼的,法院不予受理。已获认可和执行的判决,当事人依相同事实再行提起诉讼的,法院不予受理。第14条提到了申请的执行,即法院可以根据申请人的申请,对被申请人的财产采取保全或强制措施。

【思考题】

- 什么是外国法院民商事判决?
- 外国法院民商事判决包括哪三层含义?
- 试述"法院"的外延和"判决"的外延。
- 什么是承认与执行外国法院的判决?
- 你知道哪些有关外国法院民商事判决的承认与执行的理论?
- 外国法院民商事判决的承认与执行要符合哪些条件?
- 外国法院民商事判决的承认与执行有哪些不同的方式?
- 你知道我国有关外国法院民商事判决的承认与执行有哪些规定?
- 你知道香港和内地之间的法院民商事判决承认与执行规则吗?

【重要术语提示与中英文对照】

中文术语	英文对照
外国法院判决	foreign judgments
外国国家法院判决	foreign nation judgments
姊妹州判决	sister state judgments
承认与执行外国法院的判决	recognition and enforcement of foreign judgment

民商事判决	civil judgments
海牙民商事案件外国判决的承认和执行公约	Convention on the Recognition and Enforcement of Foreign Judgements in Civil and Commercial Matters
礼让	comity
债务说	theory of obligation
债务诉讼	debt actions
一事不再理说	theory of res judicata
完全信任与尊重条款	The Full Faith and Credit Clause
管辖权	jurisdiction
互惠说	theory of reciprocity
第三次外国关系重述	Restatement (Third) of Foreign Relations
外国判决(相互执行)法	Foreign Judgments (Reciprocal Enforcement) Act
终局性	finality
登记	registration
执行令	Exequatur writ of execution
不同的法域	different legal systems

【推荐阅读文献】

- 张宪初:《内地与香港民商事案件管辖权冲突刍议》,载《法律适用》2004年第9期。
- 贺晓翎:《英国的外国法院判决承认与执行制度研究》,法律出版社2008年版。
- 李广辉、王瀚:《我国区际法院判决承认与执行制度之比较》,载《法律科学》2009年第2期。
- 马永梅:《外国法院判决承认与执行中的公共秩序》,载《政法论坛》2010年第5期。
- 朱志晟:《美国州际法院判决承认与执行制度研究》,载《求索》2011年第1期。
- 钟丽:《如何完善外国法院判决的承认与执行》,载《法制日报》2012年1月17日。
- Susan L. Stevens, Commanding International Judicial Respect: Reciprocity and the Recognition and Enforcement of Foreign Judgments, 26 *Hastings Int'l & Comp. L. Rev.* 115, 122—123 (2002).
- Peter Hay, Russell J. Weintraub, Patrick J. Borchers, *Conflict of Laws: Cases and*

- *Materials*, 12th ed. Foundation Press, 2004.
- William C. Duncan, Survey of Interstate Recognition of Quasi-marital Statuses, 3 *Ave Maria L. Rev.* 617 (2005).
- Xianchu Zhang, Philip Smart: Development of Regional Conflict of Laws: On the Arrangement of Mutual Recognition and Enforcement of Judgments in Civil and Commercial Matters between Mainland China and Hong Kong SAR, 3 *Hong Kong Law Journal* (2006).
- Matthew B. Berlin, The Hague Convention on Choice of Court Agreements: Creating an International Framework for Recognizing Foreign Judgments, *B. Y. U. Int'l L. & Mgmt. Rev.* 43 (2006).
- Keri Bruce, The Hague Convention on Choice-of-court Agreements, Is the Public Policy Exception Helping Click-away the Security of Non-Negotiated Agreements? 32 *Brooklyn J. Int'l L.* 1103 (2007).
- Stewart (D. P.), Recognition and Enforcement of Foreign Judgments in the United States, 12 *Ybk. Priv. Int'l L.* 179 (2010).
- Steinle (J.) & Vasiliades (E.), The Enforcement of Jurisdiction Agreements under the Brussels I Regulation: Reconsidering the Principle of Party Autonomy, 6 *J. Priv. Int'l L.* 565 (2010).

【扩展阅读资料】

Recognition of the Public Policy Exception[①]

> The survey of case law shows that the public policy exception is a very narrow exception and is usually only recognized in instances where there is a violation of a larger state or national public policy, such as a constitutional violation or when the court feels there was a purposeful evasion of U. S. laws. Even in cases where there are differences of procedural or substantive laws, courts have not been willing to recognize the public policy exception.
>
> In most cases in which courts find public policy violations, there is at stake some interest of the forum greater than protecting the litigant, such as a violation of the U. S. Constitution or the desire to prevent individuals from circumventing federal or state laws.

---

① Keri Bruce, The Hague Convention on Choice-of-court Agreements, Is the Public Policy Exception Helping Click-away the Security of Non-Negotiated Agreements? 32 *Brooklyn J. Int'l L.* 1103, 1120—1123 (2007).

In Matusevitch v. Telnikoff, the District Court for the D. C. Circuit refused to enforce a British court libel judgment on grounds that it violated U. S. and Virginia public policy. A British public figure obtained a libel judgment against an American writer. Subsequently, the writer challenged the action in the district court seeking summary judgment on the grounds that the foreign judgment was unenforceable. The court distinguished this case from other cases that had rejected the public policy defense because those cases "concerned minor differences in statutory law and in rules of civil procedure or corporate or commercial law." The court described the United Kingdom libel standards, which place the burden of proving the truth of the statements on the defendant, as contrary to the U. S. libel standards, which require the plaintiff to prove that the statements were false and that the defendant had the necessary intent to commit libel. Based on the evidence, the court concluded that because the defendant's statements were not made with actual malice, enforcement of the British judgment would be "repugnant" to both state and U. S. public policy.

In *Laker Airways*, the plaintiff, British airline Laker Airways, filed an antitrust action in the United States against a group of foreign and domestic airlines, claiming that the defendants' price fixing forced them out of business. Several months later, some of the defendants filed their own suit in the High Court of Justice in the United Kingdom seeking an injunction forbidding the plaintiff from prosecuting them. The British court ultimately issued the injunction, ordering the plaintiff to dismiss its action against the British airlines. In the meantime, Laker Airways sought an anti-suit injunction from the United States Court for the District of Columbia to prevent the remaining defendant airlines from requesting an injunction from the British courts as well. The court granted the anti-suit injunction and held that anti-suit injunctions were justified to prevent litigants' evasion of a forum's public policies.

Although the case did not involve enforcement of a foreign judgment, the court in *Laker Airways* analogized the issuance of an anti-suit injunction to prevent a foreign court judgment with that of non-recognition of a foreign judgment. The court concluded that in both instances, states are "not required to give effect to foreign judicial proceedings" based on "policies which do violence to its own fundamental interest." Here, the court found that the anti-trust laws were of "admitted economic importance to the United States," and thus, public policy mandated that the anti-suit injunction be issued to prevent the defendants from "evading culpability under the statutes."

In *Ackermann v. Levine*, the plaintiff, a member of a German law firm, sought recognition and enforcement of a German default judgment to recover legal fees against the defendant, an American citizen." The defendant had hired the plaintiff to help him negotiate a New Jersey real estate investment deal with some German banks. The defendant had specifically authorized the attorney to represent him in negotiations, but no fees were ever discussed. The plaintiff eventually sent the defendant a bill for his services which were computed in accordance with a German legal fee statute. Three months later, the plaintiff won a default judgment in a West German court against the defendant. The District Court for the Southern District of New York found the German judgment to be unenforceable because it was up to the attorney, not the client, to ensure that the client understood the compensation agreement, and because the parties had never discussed the fees, the judgment violated U.S. public policy.

The Court of Appeals for the Second Circuit reversed the district court's decision in part, holding that the "narrow public policy exception to enforcement [was] not met" just because the defendant was not informed of the German legal fee statute. Furthermore, the court noted that the exception would not be met even if the attorney's fees were more than American attorneys might have charged. However, the court did find a public policy violation on a narrower basis.

The court found that in order to recover attorney's fees, New York public policy requires there be evidence of client authorization for the alleged work performed by the attorney and evidence the attorney actually performed the work for which he charged. The court held that the part of the German judgment that included fees for the "study of project files" and "discussion with client and his counsel" were unenforceable because there was no evidence of authorization for the work or proof of actual work product. The court felt that recognizing this portion of the judgment could cause "American courts [to] become the means of enforcing unconscionable attorney fee awards" which could lead to the endangerment of "'public confidence' in the administration of the law." Furthermore, the court noted, recognizing the foreign judgment would "impose upon American citizens doing business abroad an undue risk in dealing with foreign counsel," which could undermine transnational legal relations. Thus, in a sense, both New York and Germany had a substantial interest in not enforcing unconscionable attorney's fees.

In sum, the public policy exception has been construed very narrowly throughout U.S. jurisprudence regardless of whether the differences in the U.S. federal or state laws are substantive or procedural in nature and whether the outcome would have been different in U.S. courts. In the rare instances when courts have refused recognition or enforcement of a foreign judgment because of public policy, it has been to protect a higher federal or state interest, rather than out of fairness to the litigant.

国际私法文献与资料扩展网络资源

- American Society of Comparative Law

http://www.comparativelaw.org/

- ASIL Guide to Electronic Resources for International Law

http://www.asil.org/resource/pil1.htm

- Hague Conference on Private International Law official website

http://www.hcch.net/index_en.php?act=home.splash

- Max Planck Institute for Comparative and International Private Law

http://www.mpipriv.de

- British Institute of International and Comparative Law (BIICL)

http://www.biicl.org/private_international_law_seminar_series/

- International Chamber of Commerce

http://www.iccwbo.org/

- International Court of Arbitration

http://www.iccwbo.org/index_court.asp

- International Institute for the Unification of Private Law (UNIDROIT)

http://www.unidroit.org/

- News and views in private international law—*Conflict of Laws. Net*

- United Nations Commission for International Trade Law (UNCITRAL)

http://www.uncitral.org/

- U.S. State Department Private International Law Database

http://www.state.gov/s/l/c3452.htm

- EEC Rome convention 1980

http://www.rome-convention.org/instruments/i_conv_cons_en.htm

Private International Law site, maintained by the Office of the Assistant Legal Adviser for Private International Law (L/PIL) at the U.S. Department of State

http://www.state.gov/s/l/c3452.htm

附录二

新世纪中国出版的国际私法著作与教材

陈卫佐:《比较国际私法》,法律出版社 2012 年版。
刘晓红主编:《国际私法:案例与图表》,法律出版社 2012 年版。
刘仁山主编:《国际私法》,中国法制出版社 2012 年版。
王思思:《柯里的利益分析理论研究》,武汉大学出版社 2012 年版。
张湘兰、张辉主编:《国际海事法新发展》,武汉大学出版社 2012 年版。
李广辉主编:《国际私法学》,厦门大学出版社 2012 年版。
李双元、欧福永主编:《国际私法教学案例》(第二版),北京大学出版社 2012 年版。
白龙主编:《国际私法学》,厦门大学出版社 2012 年版。
张磊:《涉外保证的国际私法问题研究》,法律出版社 2012 年版。
崔华强:《网络隐私权利保护之国际私法研究》,中国政法大学出版社 2012 年版。
张仲伯:《国际私法学》,中国政法大学出版社 2012 年版。
袁发强:《国际私法学》,北京大学出版社 2012 年版。
刘恩媛:《国际环境损害赔偿的国际私法问题研究》,中国法制出版社 2012 年版。
孙智慧:《国际私法原理与实务》,中国政法大学出版社 2012 年版。
任际:《国际私法专题研究》,法律出版社 2011 年版。
徐国建:《国际统一私法总论》,法律出版社 2011 年版。
霍政欣:《国际私法》(英文版),对外经济贸易大学出版社 2011 年版。
秦瑞亭主编:《国际私法案例精析》,南开大学出版社 2011 年版。
屈广清等:《国际私法之弱者保护》,商务印书馆 2011 年版。
刘想树主编:《国际私法》,法律出版社 2011 年版。
王祥修、裴予峰主编:《国际私法——理论·实务·案例》,中国政法大学出版社 2011 年版。
李建忠:《古代国际私法溯源》,法律出版社 2011 年版。
沈涓主编:《国际私法学的新发展》,中国社会科学出版社 2011 年版。
邹国勇译注:《外国国际私法立法精选》,中国政法大学出版社 2011 年版。
杜新丽主编:《国际私法》,中国人民大学出版社 2010 年版。
马德才:《国际私法中的公共秩序研究》,法律出版社 2010 年版。
叶竹梅主编:《国际私法》,北京大学出版社 2010 年版。

石蕾编著:《国际私法案例教程》,中央广播电视大学出版社2010年版。
李广辉主编:《国际私法》,武汉大学出版社2010年版。
徐国建:《全球化背景下私法的冲突、协调和统一》,法律出版社2010年版。
徐鹏:《冲突规范任意性适用研究》,厦门大学出版社2010年版。
霍政欣:《中国国际私法(英文)》,法律出版社2010年版。
马志强:《国际私法中的最密切联系原则研究》,人民出版社2010年版。
张庆元:《国际私法中的国籍问题研究》,法律出版社2010年版。
赵相林主编:《国际私法》,中国政法大学出版社2010年版。
田晓云主编:《国际私法》,北京大学出版社2010年版。
杨利雅:《冲突中的单边主义研究》,人民出版社2010年版。
徐冬根:《国际私法》,北京大学出版社2009年版。
顾海波:《国际私法学》,东北大学出版社有限公司2009年版。
刘益灯:《电子商务中消费者保护的国际私法问题研究》,中南大学出版社2009年版。
屈广清主编:《国际私法》(第二版),厦门大学出版社2009年版。
韩德培主编:《国际私法新论(全二册)》,武汉大学出版社2009年版。
丁伟:《中国国际私法和谐发展研究》,上海社会科学院出版社有限公司2009年版。
王军主编:《国际私法案例选评》,对外经济贸易大学出版社2009年版。
屈广清等编:《弱势群体权利保护的国际私法方法研究》,知识产权出版社2009年版。
王国华:《海事国际私法:冲突法篇》,北京大学出版社2009年版。
李智:《国际私法中互联网管辖权制度研究》,厦门大学出版社2009年版。
吴用:《儿童监护国际私法问题研究》,对外经济贸易大学出版社2009年版。
曲波:《国际私法本体下弱者利益的保护问题》,法律出版社2009年版。
胡敏飞:《跨国环境侵权的国际私法问题研究》,复旦大学出版社2009年版。
邢钢:《国际私法视野下的外国公司法律规制》,知识产权出版社2009年版。
王立武:《国际民事责任竞合的冲突法研究》,法律出版社2009年版。
蒋新苗主编:《国际私法》,科学出版社2009年版。
孙智慧主编:《国际私法原理与实务》,中国政法大学出版社2008年版。
王利民主编:《国际私法学》,科学出版社2008年版。
邓杰:《国际私学法》,清华大学出版社2008年版。
粟烟涛:《冲突法上的法律规避》,北京大学出版社2008年版。
尹伟民:《国际民事诉讼中证据能力问题研究》,法律出版2008年版。

刘益灯:《跨国消费者保护的法律冲突及其解决对策》,法律出版社 2008 年版。

何丽新、谢美山:《海事赔偿责任限制研究》,厦门大学出版社 2008 年版。

廖诗评:《条约冲突基础问题研究》,法律出版社 2008 年版。

陈小云:《英国国际私法本体研究》,知识产权出版社 2008 年版。

秦瑞亭主编:《国际私法》,南开大学出版社 2008 年版。

高晓力:《国际私法上公政策的运用》,中国民主法制出版社 2008 年版。

湖北省高院民事庭编:《涉外民事诉讼管辖权问题研究》,武汉大学出版社 2008 年版。

尚清:《欧盟保险合同法律适用论》,武汉大学出版社 2008 年版。

肖永平:《国际私法原理》,法律出版社 2007 年版。

金彭年主编:《国际私法》,浙江大学出版社 2008 年版。

谢石松:《国际私法学》,高等教育出版社 2007 年版。

詹礼愿:《中国区际商事仲裁制度研究》,中国社会科学出版社 2007 年版。

孙建:《国际关系视角下的国际私法问题》,人民出版社 2007 年版。

许军珂:《国际私法上的意思自治》,法律出版社 2007 年版。

刘来平:《外国法的查明》,法律出版社 2007 年版。

杜涛:《国际私法的现代化进程:中外国际私法改革比较研究》,上海人民出版社 2007 年版。

李双元、欧福永主编:《国际私法教学案例》,北京大学出版社 2007 年版。

王葆莳:《国际私法中的先决问题研究》,法律出版社 2007 年版。

杜焕芳:《国际民商事司法与行政合作研究》,武汉大学出版社 2007 年版。

〔美〕戈德雷:《私法的基础:财产、侵权、合同和不当得利》,张家勇译,法律出版社 2007 年版。

欧福永:《国际民事诉讼中的禁诉令》,北京大学出版社 2007 年版。

林燕萍主编:《国际私法案例评析》,北京大学出版社 2007 年版。

〔日〕杉原高嶺:《国际司法裁判制度》,中国政法大学出版社 2007 年版。

杨树明主编:《国际私法》,中国政法大学出版社 2007 年版。

邹国勇:《德国国际私法的欧盟化》,法律出版社 2007 年版。

王国华:《海事国际私法原论》,北京大学出版社 2007 年版。

胡晓红、梁琳、王赫:《网络侵权与国际私法》,工人出版社 2006 年版。

霍政欣:《不当得利的国际私法问题》,武汉大学出版社 2006 年版。

王淑敏:《新型贸易融资的国际私法统一法源研究》,水利水电出版社 2006 年版。

杜涛:《德国国际私法:理论、方法和立法的变迁》,法律出版社 2006 年版。

贺连博:《反致问题研究》,水利水电出版社 2006 年版。

赵秀文主编:《国际私法学原理与案例教程》,中国人民大学出版社 2006 年版。

孙南申、杜涛主编:《当代国际私法研究:21 世纪的中国与国际私法》,上海人民出版社 2006 年版。

沈娟主编:《国际私法》,社会科学文献出版社 2006 年版。

赵相林主编:《国际私法论丛——理论前沿、立法探讨与司法实践》,高等教育出版社 2005 年版。

屈广清、陈小云主编:《国际私法发展史》,吉林大学出版社 2005 年版。

徐冬根:《国际私法趋势论》,北京大学出版社 2005 年版。

徐冬根、王国华、萧凯:《国际私法》(21 世纪普通高等学校法学系列教材),清华大学出版社 2005 年版。

黄进主编:《国际私法》(第二版),法律出版社 2005 年版。

黄进、何其生、萧凯:《国际私法:案例与资料》,法律出版社 2005 年版。

屈广清:《国际私法导论》(第二版),法律出版社 2005 年版。

屈广清:《屈氏国际私法讲义(高等院校文科教材)》,法律出版社 2005 年版。

屈广清:《海事国际私法新编》,法律出版社 2005 年版。

蒋新苗:《国际私法本体论》,法律出版社 2005 年版。

杜新丽:《国际私法实务中的法律问题》,中信出版社 2005 年版。

邓杰:《国际私法分论》,知识产权出版社 2005 年版。

杜涛:《国际经济贸易中的国际私法问题》,武汉大学出版社 2005 年版。

赖来焜编:《两岸国际私法研讨会论文集》,伟大出版社 2005 年版。

杜涛、陈力:《国际私法》,复旦大学出版社 2004 年版。

宋晓:《当代国际私法的实体取向(武汉大学国际法博士文库)》,武汉大学出版社 2004 年版。

李双元、蒋新苗:《国际私法学案例教程》(高等教育法学专业案例教材),知识产权出版社 2004 年版。

张潇剑:《国际私法论》(21 世纪法学丛书),北京大学出版社 2004 年版。

韩德培:《国际私法问题专论》(研究生教学用书),武汉大学出版社 2004 年版。

何其生:《电子商务的国际私法问题》,法律出版社 2004 年版。

袁成第:《国际私法原理》(西南政法大学学子学术文库 39),法律出版社 2004 年版。

于飞:《中国国际私法理论与立法》,中国法制出版社 2004 年版。

肖永平:《国际私法原理》(法学新阶梯),法律出版社 2003 年版。

袁成第:《国际私法原理》(西南政法大学学子学术文库39),法律出版社2004年版。

李旺:《国际私法》(高等学校法学教材),法律出版社2003年版。

韩德培:《国际私法新论》(高等学校法学教材),武汉大学出版社2003年版。

赵相林:《国际私法》(高等政法院校法学主干课程教材),中国政法大学出版社2003年(修订版)。

柯泽东:《国际私法》,中国政法大学出版社2003年版。

王慧:《国际私法》(北京大学远程教育法学系列教材),人民法院出版社2003年版。

王军、陈洪武:《合同冲突法》,对外经济贸易大学出版社2003年版。

顾海波:《国际私法引论》,中国检察出版社2003年版。

张仲伯:《国际私法学》(高等政法院校规划教材),中国政法大学出版社2003年(修订版)。

李双元:《中国国际私法通论》(高等学校法学教材),法律出版社2003年版。

吕国民、戴霞、郑远民编著:《国际私法:冲突法与实体法》,中信出版社2002年版。

赵相林:《中国国际私法立法问题研究》,中国政法大学出版社2002年版。

李双元:《国际私法(冲突法篇)》(修订本)武汉大学出版社2002年版。

丁伟、朱榄叶:《当代国际法学理论与实践研究文集——国际私法卷》,中国法制出版2002年版。

赵相林:《国际私法》,中国政法大学出版社2002年版。

肖永平:《欧盟统一国际私法研究》(欧洲问题研究丛书),武汉大学出版社2002年版。

肖永平:《肖永平论冲突法》,武汉大学出版社2002年版。

刘想树:《国际私法基本问题研究》,法律出版社2001年版。

刘卫翔:《欧洲联盟国际私法》(国际民商法专题研究丛书),法律出版社2001年版。

刘仁山:《加拿大国际私法研究》(中国民商法专题研究丛书),法律出版社2001年版。

赵一民:《国际私法案例教程》(新编成人高等法学案例教程),知识产权出版社2001年版。

李旺:《国际私法新论》,人民法院出版社2001年版。

附录三

最新英文国际私法学术文献[①]

[①] 最新英文国际私法学术文献系本书作者根据 Symeon C. Symeonides, Private International Law Bibliography 2011: U.S. and Foreign Source in English, 60 *Am. J. Comp. L.* 369 (2012); Symeon C. Symeonides, Conflict of Laws Bibliography: U.S. Sources, 2006—2007, 56 *Am. J. Comp. L.* 321 (2008) 以及 Symeon C. Symeonides, Conflict of Laws Bibliography: U.S. Sources, 2005—2006, 54 *Am. J. Comp. L.* 789 (2006) 摘选和综合汇编。

I. Books

Symeonides (S.), Recent Codifications of Private International Law, Martinus Nijhoff Publishers, (2013).

Symeonides (S.), Perdue (W.), Conflict of Laws: American, Comparative, International, Thomson-West, American Casebook Series (3 ed. 2012).

Bariatti (S.), Cases and Materials on EU Private International Law (2011).

Diaz (C.), Czepelak (M.), Benot (R.) & Vazquez (R.) (eds.), Latest Developments in EU Private International Law (2011).

Fallon (M.), Kinsch (P.) & Kohler (C.) (eds.), Building European Private International Law: Twenty Years' Work by GEDIP (2011).

Fawcett (J.) & Torremans (P.), Intellectual Property and Private International Law (2011).

Felix (R.) & Whitten (R.), American Conflicts Law (2011).

Leeming (M.), Resolving Conflict of Laws (2011).

Stevens (R.), Restitution in Private International Law (2011).

Svantesson (D.), Private International Law and the Internet (2nd ed. 2011)

Symeonides (S.), Hay (P.), Borchers (P.), Conflict of Laws, Thomson-West Hornbook Series, 5th ed. 2010.

Born (G.) & Rutledge (P.), International Civil Litigation in United States Courts (4th ed. 2006).

Currie (D.), Kay (H.), Kramer (L.) & Roosevelt (K.), Conflict of Laws: Cases-Comments-Questions (7th ed. 2006).

Castro (P.), Treves (T.) & Seatzu (F.) (eds.), Tradition and Innovation in Private International Law at the Beginning of the Third Millennium (2006).

Carbonneau (T.), International Litigation and Arbitration (2005).

Chow (D.) & Schoenbaum (T.), International Business Transactions: Problems, Cases, and Materials (2005).

Symeonides (S.), The American Choice-of-Law Revolution: Past, Present and Future (Hague Academy Monographs 2006).

Weintraub (R.), International Litigation and Arbitration: Practice and Planning (2006).

Weintraub (R.), Commentary on the Conflict of Laws (5th ed. 2006).

Juenger (F.), Choice of Law and Multistate Justice (Special ed. 2005)

Nanda (V.) & Pansius (D.), Litigation of International Disputes in United States Courts (2d ed. 2005).

Siegel (D.) & Borchers (P.), Conflicts in a Nutshell (3d ed. 2005).

Simson (G.), Issues and Perspectives in Conflict of Laws (4th ed. 2005).

Varady (T.), Barcelo (J.) & Von Mehren (A.), International Commercial Arbitration (3rd ed. 2006).

II. Articles or Essays

2012

Byrne (K.), China's New Conflict of Law Code, 2 *Private Client Business* 38 (2012).

Cianitto (C.), Tirabassi (M.), Conflict of Laws: Adoption—Welfare of Child, 1 *O. J. L. R.* 302 (2012).

Dickinson (A.), Sculpture and Mind Tricks in the Conflict of Laws, *L. M. C. L. Q.* 21 (2012 Feb).

Eeckhout (V.), Corporate Human Rights Violations and Private International Law: a Facilitating Role for PIL or PIL as a Complicating Factor? 6 *H. R. & I. L. D.* 192 (2012).

Fan (X.), Analysis of the Intellectual Property Rights Terms in Chinese Private International Law: on the Perspective of the Latest Regulations, 5 *I. J. P. L.* 303 (2012).

Goessl (S.), Preliminary Questions in EU Private International Law, 8 *J. Priv. Int. L.* 63 (2012).

Jansen (N.), Kieninger (E.), The Proposal for a Regulation on a Common European Sales Law: Deficits of the Most Recent Textual Layer of European Contract Law, 16 *Edin. L. R.* 301 (2012).

Laing (J.), Statutory Restrictions on Party Autonomy in China's Private International Law of Contract: How Far Does the 2010 Codification Go? 8 *J. Priv. Int. L.* 77 (2012).

Mason (S.), Revising the EU e-Signature Directive, 7 *Comms. L.* 56 (2012).

Merrett (L.), Employment Contracts in Private International Law, 133 *Employment Law Journal* 21 (2012).

Melcher (M.), Private International Law and Registered Relationships: An EU

Perspective, 20 *E. R. P. L.* 1075 (2012).

Oster (J.), Conceptualising the EU Private International Law of Internet Torts against Personality Rights, 26 *I. R. L. C. T.* 113 (2012).

Pocar (F.), The European Harmonisation of Conflict of Laws Rules on Divorce and Legal Separation: Is Enhanced Co-operation a Correct Approach? *I. F. L.* 24 (2012 Mar).

Shepherd (P.), The Lex Situs Rule and How it Continues to Trap the Unwary, 27 *B. J. I. B. & F. L.* 277 (2012).

Symeonides (S.), Choice of Law in the American Courts in 2011: Twenty-Fifth Annual Survey, 60 *American Journal of Comparative Law* (2012).

Torremans (P.), Reversionary Copyright: A Ghost of the Past or A Current Trap to Assignments of Copyright? 2 *I. P. Q.* 77 (2012).

Virgos (M.), Garcimartin (F.), Conditional Conflict of Laws Rules: A Proposal in the Area of Bank Resolution and Netting in Cross-border Scenarios, 9 *Int. C. R.* 91—95 (2012).

2011

Anderson (H.), Conflict of Laws, Agents, and Maritime Commerce: An Analysis under U. S. and English Law. 23 *U. S. F. Mar. L. J.* 42 (2010—11).

Basedow (J.), Theory of Choice of Law, 75 *RabelsZ* 32 (2011).

Brilmayer (L.), The New Extraterritoriality: Morrison v. National Australia Bank, Legislative Supremacy, and the Presumption Against Extraterritorial Application of American Law, 40 *Sw. L. Rev.* 655 (2011).

Borchers (P.), J. McIntyre Machinery, Goodyear, and the Incoherence of the Minimum Contacts Test, 44 *Creighton L. Rev.* 1245 (2011).

Cooper (S.), Rule (C.) & Del. Duca (L. F.), From Lex Mercatoria to Online Dispute Resolution: Lessons From History in Building Cross-Border Redress Systems, 43 *UCC L. J.* 749 (2011).

Symeonides (S.), Choice of Law in the American Courts in 2010: Twenty-Fourth Annual Survey, 59 *American Journal of Comparative Law* 303—393 (2011).

Neumann (S.), Intellectual Property Rights Infringements in European Private International Law: Meeting the Requirements of Territoriality and Private International Law, 7 *J. Priv. Int. L.* 583 (2011).

2010

Baker (J.) & Parise (A.), Conflicts in International Tort Litigation Between U. S.

and Latin American Courts, 42 U. Miami Inter-Am. L. Rev. 1 (2010).

Borchers (P.), The Real Risk of Forum Shopping: A Dissent from Shady Grove, 44 *Creighton L. Rev.* 29 (2010).

Borrás (A.), Application of the Brussels I Regulation to External Situations, 12 *Ybk. Priv. Int'l L.* 333 (2010).

Chen (W.), Chinese Private International Law Statute of 28 October 2010, 12 *Ybk. Priv. Int'l L.* 27 (2010).

Chen (W.) & Moore (K.), (translation of) Statute on the Application of Laws to Civil Relationships Involving Foreign Elements of the People's Republic of China, 12 *Ybk. Priv. Int'l L.* 669 (2010).

Symeonides (S.), Codifying Choice of Law for Tort Conflicts: The Oregon Experience in Comparative Perspective, 12 *Ybk. Priv. Int'l L.* 201—245 (2010).

2009

Symeonides (S.), Oregon's New Choice-of-Law Codification for Tort Conflicts: An Exegesis, 88 *Oregon Law Review* 963—1052 (2009).

Symeonides (S.), A New Conflicts Restatement: Why Not? 5 *Journal of Private International Law* 383—424 (2009).

Symeonides (S.), Choice of Law in Cross-Border Torts: Why Plaintiffs Win, and Should, 61 *Hastings Law Journal* 337—411 (2009).

Symeonides (S.), Choice of Law in the American Courts in 2008: Twenty-Second Annual Survey, 57 *American Journal of Comparative Law* 269—329 (2009).

Symeonides (S.), The Conflicts Book of the Louisiana Civil Code: Civilian, American, or Original? 83 *Tulane Law Review* 1041—81 (2009).

Symeonides (S.), Result-Selectivism in Conflicts Law, 46 *Willamette Law Review* 1 (2009).

2008

Courson (Z.), A New Federal Standard—Applying Contracting Parties' Choice of Law to the Analysis of Forum Selection Agreements, 85 *Denv. U. L. Rev.* 597 (2008).

Wanat (D.), Copyright Infringement Litigation and the Exercise of Personal Jurisdiction Within Due Process Limits, 59 *Mercer L. Rev.* 560 (2008).

Strasser (M.), The Future of Marriage, 21 *J. Am. Acad. Matrimonial Law* 87 (2008).

Salamon (N.), Choice of Law Disputes in Insurance Litigation, 30 *Los Angeles Lawyer* 17 (2008).

Symeonides (S.), Conflict of Laws Bibliography: U.S. Sources, 2006—2007, 56 Am. J. Comp. L. 321 (2008).

Symeonides (S.), Choice of Law in the American Courts in 2007: Twenty-First Annual Survey, 56 Am. J. Comp. L. 243 (2008).

Viavant (N.), Sinochem International Co. v. Malaysia International Shipping Corp.: The United States Supreme Court Puts Forum Non Conveniens First, 16 Tul. J. Int'l & Comp. L. 557 (2008).

Zhang (M.), Contractual Choice of Law in Contracts of Adhesion and Party Autonomy, 41 Akron L. Rev. 123 (2008).

2007

Barbosa (R.), International Copyright Law and Litigation: A Mechanism for Improvement, 11 Marq. Intell. Prop. L. Rev. 77 (2007).

Camarce (C.), Harmonization of International Copyright Protection in the Internet Age, 19 Pac. McGeorge Bus. & Dev. L. J. 435 (2007).

Chaissan (S. M.), "Minimum Contacts" Abroad: Using the International Shoe Test to Restrict the Extraterritorial Exercise of United States Jurisdiction under the Maritime Drug Law Enforcement Act, 38 U. Miami Inter-Am. L. Rev. 641 (2007).

Cook (E.), Internationalizing Copyright: How Claims of International, Extraterritorial Copyright Infringement May Be Brought in U.S. Courts, 7 U. C. Davis Bus. L. J. 429 (2007).

D'Souza (F.), The Recognition and Enforcement of Commercial Arbitral Awards in the People's Republic of China, 30 Fordham Int'l L. J. 1318 (2007).

Engle (E.), European Law in American Courts: Foreign Law as Evidence of Domestic Law, 33 Ohio N. U. L. Rev. 99 (2007).

Freer (R. D.), Refracting Domestic and Global Choice-of-forum Doctrine Through the Lens of a Single Case, 2007 BYU L. Rev. 959 (2007).

George (J.) & Teller (A.), Conflict of Laws, 60 SMU L. Rev. 817 (2007).

Goldenhersh (R.), Survey of Illinois Law: Forum non Conveniens, 31 S. Ill. U. L. J. 929 (2007).

Goldsmith (J.) & Sykes (A.), Lex Loci Delictus and Global Economic Welfare: Spinozzi v. ITT Sheraton Corp., 120 Harv. L. Rev. 1137 (2007).

Gordley (J.), When Is the Use of Foreign Law Possible? A Hard Case: The Protection of Privacy in Europe and the United States, 67 La. L. Rev. 1073 (2007).

Greenstein (R. K.), The Action Bias in American Law: Internet Jurisdiction and the Triumph of Zippo Dot Com, 80 *Temp. L. Rev.* 21 (2007).

Harris (S.), Choosing the Law Governing Security Interests in International Bankruptcies, 32 *Brook. J. Int'l L.* 905 (2007).

Hylton (K. N.), Torts and Choice of Law: Searching for Principles, 56 *J. Legal Educ.* 551 (2006).

Ketchel (A.), Deriving Lessons for the Alien Tort Claims Act from the Foreign Sovereign Immunities Act, 32 *Yale J. Int'l L.* 191 (2007).

Levin (H.), What Do We Really Know about the American Choice-of-Law Revolution?, 60 *Stan. L. Rev.* 247 (2007)

Morgan (L.), Choice of Law in Interstate Child Support Modification Cases, 21 *Am. J. Fam. L.* 328 (2007).

Moss (G.), Group Insolvency—Choice of Forum and Law: The European Experience under the Influence of English Pragmatism, 32 *Brook. J. Int'l L.* 1005 (2007).

Oppong (R.), Private International Law in Africa: The Past, Present, and Future, 55 *Am. J. Comp. L.* 677 (2007).

Parrish (A. L.), Storm in a Teacup: The U. S. Supreme Court's Use of Foreign Law, 2007 *U. Ill. L. Rev.* 637 (2007).

Symeonides (S.), The First Conflicts Restatement Through the Eyes of Old, 32 *S. Ill. U. L. J.* 39 (2007).

Traynor (M.), The First Restatements and the Vision of the American Law Institute, Then and Now, 32 *S. Ill. U. L. J.* 145 (2007)

Tu (G.), The Hague Choice of Court Convention: A Chinese Perspective, 55 *Am. J. Comp. L.* 347 (2007).

White (K. E.), The Recent Expansion of Extraterritoriality in Patent Infringement Cases, 11 *UCLA J. L. & Tech.* (2007).

2006

Berlin (M.), The Hague Convention on Choice of Court Agreements: Creating an International Framework for Recognizing Foreign Judgments, *B. Y. U. Int'l L. & Mgmt. Rev.* 43 (2006).

Buckwold (T. M.), The Conflict in Conflicts: Choice of Law in Canada-U. S. Secured Financing Transactions, 21 *Bank. & Fin. L. Rev.* 407 (2006).

Burbank (S.), Federalism and Private International Law: Implementing the Hague Choice of Court Convention in the United States, 2 *J. Priv. Int'l L.* 287 (2006).

Citron (D. K.), Minimum Contacts in a Borderless World: Voice over Internet Protocol and the Coming Implosion of Personal Jurisdiction Theory, 39 *U. C. Davis L. Rev.* 1481 (2006).

Cross (P.) & Oxford (H.), "Floating" Forum Selection and Choice of Law Clauses, 48 *S. Tex. L. Rev. 125* (2006).

Dinwoodie (G.), The International Intellectual Property Law System: New Actors, New Institutions, New Sources, 10 *Marq. Intell. Prop. L. Rev.* 205 (2006).

Doprovich (J.), Dismissal under Forum non Conveniens: Should the Availability Requirement Be a Threshold Issue When Applied to Nonessential Defendants, 12 *Widener L. Rev.* 561 (2006).

George (J. P.) & Teller (A.), Conflict of Laws [Texas], 59 *SMU L. Rev.* 1039 (2006).

Gonzaler (C.), Switzerland and Europe: International Contracts and Characteristics Performance, in *Festschrift Juenger* 45 (2006).

McClean (A. R.), The Extraterritorial Implications of the SEC's New Rule Change to Regulate Hedge Funds, 38 *Case W. Res. J. Int'l L.* 105 (2006).

Micallff (R.), Liability Laundering and Denial of Justice: Conflicts Between the Alien Tort Statute and the Government Contractor Defense, 71 *Brook. L. Rev.* 1375 (2006).

Reyhan (P. Y.), Conflict of Laws [New York], 55 Syr. L. Rev. 855 (2005), 56 *Syr. L. Rev.* 625 (2006).

Rhodes (C. W.), The Predictability Principle in Personal Jurisdiction Doctrine: A Case Study on the Effects of a 'Generally' Too Broad, but 'Specifically' Too Narrow Approach to Minimum Contacts, 57 *Baylor L. Rev. 135* (2005).

Rogers (J. S.), Conflict of Laws for Transactions in Securities Held Through Intermediaries, 39 *Cornell Int'l L. J.* 285 (2006).

Ruhl (G.), Methods and Approaches in Choice of Law: An Economic Perspective, 24 *Berkeley J. Int'l L.* 801 (2006).

Seatzu (F.), The Implementation of the EC Choice of Law Rules for Insurance Contracts in Italy: Some Critical Remarks, in *Festschrift Juenger* 223 (2006)

Talpis (J. A.), Equitable Distribution of Matrimonial Property in Private International Law, 26 *Est. Tr. & Pensions J.* 64 (2006).

Westkamp (G.), The Recognition and Status of Traditional Knowledge in the Conflict of Laws, 88 *J. Pat. & Trademark Off. Soc'y* 699 (2006).

Warshaw (A.), Uncertainty from Abroad: Rome II and the Choice of Law for Defamation Claims, 32 *Brook. J. Int'l L.* 269 (2006).

Zhang (M.), Choice of Law in Contracts: A Chinese Approach, 26 *Nw. J. Int'l L. & Bus.* 289 (2006).

Zhang (M.), Party Autonomy and Beyond: An International Perspective of Contractual Choice of Law, 20 *Emory Int'l L. Rev.* 511 (2006).